CAMPING
AND
CARAVANNING
IN BRITAIN

Editor: Penny Hicks
Designer: Ashley Tilleard

Gazetteer: Compiled by the Publications Research Unit of the Automobile Association
Maps: Prepared by the Cartographic Services Unit of the Automobile Association
Cover Picture: Denny Wood Campsite, Lyndhurst Photobank, Peter Baker

Head of Advertisement Sales: Christopher Heard Tel 0256 20123 (ext 2020)
Advertisement Production: Karen Weeks Tel 0256 20123 (ext 3525)
Advertisement Sales Representatives:
London, East Anglia, East Midlands: Melanie Mackenzie-Aird Tel 0494 40208
Central Southern and South East England: Edward May Tel 0256 20123 (ext 3524) or 0256 67568
South West, West, West Midlands: Bryan Thompson Tel 027580 3296
Wales, North of England & Scotland: Arthur Williams Tel 0222 60267

Phototypeset by: Tradespools Limited, Frome, Somerset
Printed and bound by: William Clowes (Beccles) Ltd, Beccles and London

ISBN 0 86145 188 0

Published by the Automobile Association, Fanum House, Basingstoke, Hampshire RG21 2EA

Contents

About the Book

Whether you are a newcomer to camping and caravanning or an old hand, it is most likely that you were attracted by the freedom such a holiday brings. Not just for the main holiday of the year – once you are kitted up you are free to set off on the merest whim for weekends and short breaks. You can roam the countryside, hopping from site to site with the least effort.

That's the theory, anyway. In practice you will find that certain areas get dreadfully overcrowded at peak periods and often you may head for a less popular area only to drive for miles without seeing a site at all! If you do find a site, how will you know its the kind of place you like? They all vary so much. If you've got teenagers, you might like to take them to one of the lively sites where they can disco the night away. On the other hand, you may prefer the quiet life and all you are looking for is a good pitch and your basic requirements. This is where our system of classification will be invaluable to you.

How we Classify

The first basic requirement we ask of a site is that they are keen to comply with our system and so sites are only considered if they ask to be. In this way we ensure their full co-operation should any problems arise. Once a request is received from a site, it is visited by one of our team of Inspectors. He will look it over carefully to make sure it is up to the required standard and will make a note of all the facilities on offer. It is on this basis that a recommendation is made for a pennant rating. These ratings are fully explained on page 6, but it is fair to say that a five-pennant site offers more extensive facilities and equipment than a one-pennant site. At the same time, the one-pennant site is just as good in its own way.

Even after a site is accepted and classified our checks continue so that standards are maintained and, where appropriate, re-classification can be considered.

The AA Sign

All of the sites listed in the book are able to lease a yellow and black sign from the AA showing the pennant rating awarded. Nevertheless, not all sites take up the offer, and some are precluded from displaying them by local authority regulations. If a site doesn't show a sign, it doesn't mean that we don't list it.

Mainly for Tourers

As this book is primarily intended for touring campers and caravanners, we do insist on certain minimum numbers of touring pitches. Small sites must have at least six; sites with a total of between 60 and 600 pitches must reserve at least 10% for tourers; sites with over 600 pitches must reserve at least 60 for tourers. The gazetteer entry will tell you how many you can expect to find.

Qualitative Assessment

Sometimes our pennant ratings are mistakenly taken for quality ratings when in fact they are a guide to the range of facilities and equipment available. Although all of our sites must be of a sufficiently high standard to qualify for the guide, we have also introduced a grading system for quality. In this system a rating of 1 means adequate, 2 means good and 3 means excellent. The categories, and how they are shown, are:

1 **Environment**
❷ **Sanitary Installations**
⚠ **Equipment and Facilities.**

(*Please note that they only cover facilities actually on the site*).

4

BRANCHES EVERYWHERE

And, of course, friendly, personal service at 180 Club Sites and more than 4,000 'Certificated Locations' situated in every part of the country, plus all the peace and quiet you can handle. Read the list of membership benefits to see just how much you need the Caravan Club. Don't forget we're the biggest organisation of our kind in the world, operating the largest network of private sites in the UK. And that trailer and motor caravanners and owners of trailer tents are equally welcome. Then fill in the coupon without delay; we'll be waiting to hear from you!

★ Sites Directory and Handbook listing 180 Club Sites plus some 4,000 'Certificated Locations' (5-van sites, mostly on farms and exclusive to members) and over 900 more ★ Colour magazine, 'En Route' ★ Red Pennant Foreign Touring Service ★ Information service ★ Rescue reimbursement scheme ★ Public relations for touring caravanners ★ Legal aid ★ Rallies and social events ★ Comprehensive '5 C's' and 'Super 5 C's' caravan insurance schemes ★ Members' finance plan ★ Special car and motorcaravan insurance ★ Practical caravanning courses ★ 'Mayday' recovery scheme.

 The Caravan Club

To: THE CARAVAN CLUB · EAST GRINSTEAD HOUSE · EAST GRINSTEAD · WEST SUSSEX RH19 1UA. TEL: (0342) 26944.

Please send me full details of membership.

NAME . . . .

ADDRESS . . . .

. . . . AAB

Criteria for award of pennants are as follows:

▶
* site licence (unless specially exempted)
* site density not more than thirty (reasonably spaced) per acre of land suitable for camping
* at least 10% of pitches allocated to touring units
* separate toilets with 2 WCs (ladies) and 1 WC and 1 urinal (men) for 30 pitches. Chemical closets allowed if provided at double the ratio
* tap water supply of good quality and quantity
* waste water disposal facilities within 50yd of any touring pitch
* adequate collection, storage, and disposal of refuse, so that the site is always clean and tidy
* regular cleaning of ablution block
* fire precautions that meet local authority regulations
* well-drained ground
* entrance and exit roads wide and well-surfaced enough to eliminate possibilities of damage to towed vehicles
* first aid facilities signposted and emergency telephone numbers displayed

▶▶
* all one-pennant facilities *plus*
* flush toilets
* separate washrooms, with 2 washbasins each sex per 30 pitches, each with hot and cold water
* unless the site only caters for tents and motor caravans, a properly designed point for disposing of chemical closet contents (as some local authorities will not allow such contents to mix with cesspools, there are exceptions to this rule)
* warden available at certain times of the day

▶▶▶
* all the aforementioned facilities, *plus*
* one shower or bath each sex per 30 pitches with hot and cold water
* deep sinks for washing clothes
* electric shaver points and mirrors in washrooms
* all-night lighting of toilet blocks; push button time switches acceptable if time duration clearly displayed after dark
* facilities for buying milk, bread, and basic camping requisites available regularly on site or within 200 yds of site entrance (a formal shop is not necessary, and there is no need for the facility to be provided throughout the day)
* If the size warrants it, there should be internal roads with satisfactory and well-maintained surfaces.
* warden in attendance during day; on call at night

▶▶▶▶
* a higher degree of organisation than on lower graded sites
* attention paid to landscaping
* signposted reception office
* signposted late-arrivals enclosure as near to the entrance as possible
* first aid hut
* properly-equipped shop offering a wide range of food and other camping requisites, open at least six days a week
* access routes to essential facilities lit after dark
* children's playground, fenced or in a safe area
* shelter for campers in case of bad weather
* hard standings for touring vans
* warden in attendance all day; on call at night

* a comprehensive range of services and equipment
* careful landscaping especially in relation to individual pitches
* 24hr supervision by warden on site
* automated laundry, including a selection of washing and drying machines, spin dryer, drying cabinets, irons and ironing boards
* public telephone
* indoor recreational facilities for children
* extra facilities for indoor and outdoor recreation
* must achieve a rating of good ❷ in all areas of qualitative assessment

Camping and Caravanning Survey

An important AA survey, carried out in Spring 1983 has revealed some sharp criticisms of certain aspects of Britain's campsites. A group of over 500 people, selected at random, but all of whom had stayed for at least one night on a British camping or caravan site within the last twelve months were asked about a variety of aspects of their holiday. The most significant finding was that over one in four people considered the toilets unsatisfactory or dirty. In addition, 18% considered the washing facilities unsatisfactory, bringing the total proportion of the sample who were dissatisfied with the basic sanitary facilities to almost 50%. This is a most alarming result and one that needs urgent action.

It is essential to be clear, however, that these comments relate to British campsites in general. Those that receive AA awards are specifically assessed for the standard of their sanitary facilities, and they must meet certain minimum requirements. The symbol used to denote the standard of the sanitary facilities is a black circle containing a number, and these numbers signify:

1.   Adequate
2.   Good
3.   Excellent

These ratings will help readers of the book avoid this problem wherever possible, but the fact remains that a great many people have expressed dissatisfaction with this aspect of campsites in general. We are keen to have your comments and reactions also, and to help you keep us informed, we include a report form in the book which we hope you will use. Our inspectors will certainly be especially vigilant when inspecting campsites during the coming year.

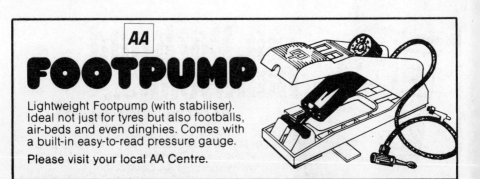

AA Venture Sites

As you will see from the preceding pages, the AA has a comprehensive system of classification for the sites we list in our guide. Nevertheless, for some time we have been increasingly aware that our system is lacking in a certain type of site – that which is designed with the self-contained camper in mind. A large section of the camping and caravanning fraternity set off on their holidays with everything they need – including their own toilet facilities. For them it is not essential to have all the facilities which our pennanted sites are required to offer and they would benefit greatly from a wider range of sites from which to make their choice.

With this in mind, our Inspectors set out this year to find a new category of site and thus broaden the scope of our guide. We call them Venture Sites and they are generally in a quiet, rural environment with a much more informal atmosphere – in fact, a different kind of camping altogether. A kind of camping we think you might like to try. We should stress that they will *not* provide any toilet facilities, so you should only visit them if you take your own. Water will be available within 200 yards of each pitch and there will be suitable disposal points for both waste water and chemical waste. All the sites will have been inspected for well-maintained ground and good access roads and a qualitative assessment (see page 4) will be awarded in the Environment category.

The Venture Sites can be distinguished in the gazetteer by the symbol ▽. To help you find them we list them all below, with the placename under which they appear in the gazetteer.

This is a new venture for us too, and we would certainly appreciate your comments and recommendations, so do give them a try – and Happy Camping!

Acaster Selby	N. Yorks	Hales Hill Farm
Aldingbourne	W. Sussex	Woodland
Alton	Hants	Upper Neatham Mill
Bakewell	Derbys	Haddon Grove Farm
Balmacara	Highland	Balmacara Camp Site
Banbury	Oxon	Bourton Heights Farm
Bardfield (Gt)	Essex	Mandalay Farm
Bishop Monkton	N. Yorks	Church Farm
Bletchington	Oxon	Frogsnest Farm
Bromsgrove	Heref & Worcs	Queens Head
Brockenhurst	Hants	Aldridge Hill
Buckfastleigh	Devon	Beara Farm
Chepstow	Gwent	Howick Farm
Chittering	Cambs	Denny Lodge
Coleford	Glos	Blackthorne Farm
Comberton (Gt)	Heref & Worcs	Shelton Farm
Crockley Hill	N. Yorks	Wigman Hall
Dartmouth	Devon	Bugford Farm
Diddlebury	Salop	Glebe Farm
Dittisham	Devon	Little Coombe Farm
Doverbridge	Derbys	Cavendish Grange
Drayton	Heref & Worcs	Barrow Hill
Drayton Bassett	Staffs	Ashdene Farm
Dunstable	Beds	Balence End Farm
Eavestone	N. Yorks	Hill Top Farm
Elvington	N. Yorks	Lake Cottage
Ely	Cambs	Ely Rugby Club
Gatwick Airport	W. Sussex	Kiln Heath Antlands Lane
Grafton Flyford	Heref & Worcs	Jaspers Farm
Hulme End	Staffs	Endon Cottage
Hargrave	Northants	The Nags Head
Inkberrow	Heref & Worcs	Broad Close Farm
Kingsbury	Warwick	Tame View
Kingsbridge	Devon	Beachcroft
King's Caple	Heref & Worcs	Lower Ruxton Farm
Lyndhurst	Hants	Denny Wood
Lyndhurst	Hants	Holidays Hill
Lyndhurst	Hants	Matley Wood
Matlock	Derbys	Canada Farm
Mersham	Kent	Broad Oak Farm
Middlewich	Cheshire	Briar Pool Farm
Moreton on Swale	N. Yorks	Fairholm
Much Wenlock	Salop	Bourton Westwood Farm
Newton Stewart	Dumf & Gall	Talnotry Caravan Park
Nomansland	Hants	Pipers Wait
Quatt, Bridgnorth	Salop	Coton Hall
Radford	Heref & Worcs	Wheelbarrow Castle
Ripon	N. Yorks	North Sutton Farm
St Lawrence	I. of Wight	The Orchard
Sawley	N. Yorks	Hallgates Farm
Snape	N. Yorks	Castle Arms
Sutton Coldfield	W. Midlands	Uppaland
Sway	Hants	Setthorns
Tiptree	Essex	Villa Farm
Upper Elkstone	Staffs	Mount Pleasant Farm

Freedom Holidays

A series of planned tours for camping and caravanning around Britain

In the following pages we have devised a series of eight tours. Our Inspectors have recommended the sites and our route experts have worked out the best and most scenic way to travel between them if you are towing a caravan or trailer. We also tell you something about places of interest in each area. The only thing we can't do here is direct you from home and back again, but remember that AA members can apply for a specially prepared route from our Routes Processing Centre, Fanum House, Park Row, Bristol, BS1 5LY.

West Country Tour

The Counties of Devon, Cornwall and Somerset are covered here – probably the most visited area in Britain. It does get rather congested at peak holiday times so if you want to take this tour try the spring, or perhaps an 'Indian Summer' holiday.

Bucklegrove Caravan and Camping Park
Rodney Stoke, Somerset

This well sheltered site has a lovely situation on the southern slopes of the Mendip Hills about halfway between Cheddar, with its magnificent gorge and caves, and Wookey Hole. This vast cavern was formed by the River Axe which still flows through it. The adjacent paper mill shows the process of making paper by hand and houses Madame Tussaud's Store Room and the Lady Bangor Fairground Collection. At Wells, England's smallest city, the Cathedral area is particularly attractive and just a short distance to the south is Glastonbury, full of Arthurian atmosphere. Bath is close by with its fine Georgian architecture and Roman Baths and on the outskirts at Claverton is the American Museum. Being so close to Cheddar, it would be a shame not to see its famous cheese in the making – Priory Farm at Chewton Mendip will oblige. For accompaniment, there is a fine vineyard at North Wootton which welcomes visitors. The nearest seaside resort is Weston-super-Mare, and Bristol, to the north is an attractive and interesting city to visit.

Channel View Caravan Park
Lynton, Devon

As its name suggests, this site enjoys magnificent views over the Bristol Channel. It is also situated within the Exmoor National Park which takes in the lovely rolling moorland, lush combes and beautiful rocky coastline. Lynton is perched on the cliff-top high above its sister village of Lynmouth, connected by a water-powered lift. Nearby the Valley of the Rocks is an area of strange rock formations, among which a herd of wild goats roam. Watersmeet is a delightful beauty spot with some lovely riverside walks. Among the Exmoor villages, Exford is a great hunting centre with horses very much in evidence, Brendon is picturesquely sited on the East Lyn River and the tiny hamlet of Oare has Lorna Doone connections. Doone Valley can be explored from Malmsmead, either on foot or horseback. At Dunster there is a fine castle, restored by the National Trust, and a 12th-century Dovecote, complete with revolving ladder. Pretty coastal villages include Porlock Weir, Combe Martin and Woolacombe, while Ilfracombe is a larger resort. From here a passenger ferry operates to the nature reserve island of Lundy.

Leverton Place
Truro, Cornwall

This attractive site is close to the city of Truro, but still in a peaceful setting and is certainly ideally placed for touring this south-western extremity of Britain. Truro is a lovely city which enjoyed a great deal of importance in the 18th century and still retains its air of Georgian elegance. The Cornish coastline hardly needs description. Villages such as Coverack, Cadgwith, and Mevagissey have adorned countless calendars and chocolate boxes and, of course, there is Land's End. Reminders of Cornwall's industrial past can still be seen in the working exhibits at the Poldark Mine at Wendron, the Tolgus Tin Company at Redruth and the Wheal Martyn Museum at St Austell. A delightful place to visit is the Seal Sanctuary at Gweek where sick and injured seals are nursed back to health.

The harbour at St Ives (Cornwall)

River Dart Country Park
Ashburton, Devon

This site lies within the lovely Holne Country Park which occupies some 80 acres on both banks of the River Dart where facilities include adventure playgrounds, a heated swimming pool and fishing. Dartmoor stretches away to the north and west, a mixture of wild moorland and picturesque villages and Dartmeet is a particularly attractive beauty spot. To the south of the site is Buckfastleigh from where the Dart Valley Railway follows the river to Totnes. Dartington has an extensive craft centre by the river, with some delightful signed walks. The Torbay resorts of Torquay, Paignton and Brixham are only a short distance away and at Plympton is the Dartmoor Wild Life Park. Exeter to the north east has a superb Maritime Museum and the city of Plymouth is worth a visit.

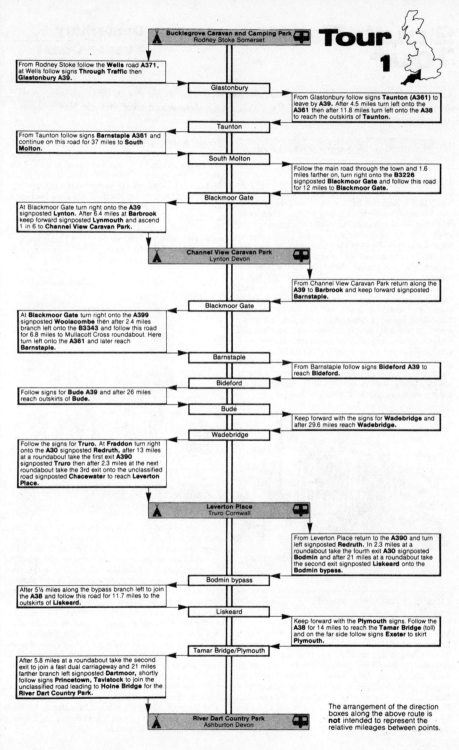

Tour 1

Bucklegrove Caravan and Camping Park
Rodney Stoke Somerset

From Rodney Stoke follow the **Wells** road **A371**, at Wells follow signs **Through Traffic** then **Glastonbury A39.**

Glastonbury

From Glastonbury follow signs **Taunton (A361)** to leave by **A39.** After 4.5 miles turn left onto the **A361** then after 11.8 miles turn left onto the **A38** to reach the outskirts of **Taunton.**

Taunton

From Taunton follow signs **Barnstaple A361** and continue on this road for 37 miles to **South Molton.**

South Molton

Follow the main road through the town and 1.6 miles farther on, turn right onto the **B3226** signposted **Blackmoor Gate** and follow this road for 12 miles to **Blackmoor Gate.**

Blackmoor Gate

At Blackmoor Gate turn right onto the **A39** signposted **Lynton.** After 6.4 miles at **Barbrook** keep forward signposted **Lynmouth** and ascend 1 in 6 to **Channel View Caravan Park.**

Channel View Caravan Park
Lynton Devon

From Channel View Caravan Park return along the **A39** to **Barbrook** and keep forward signposted **Barnstaple.**

Blackmoor Gate

At **Blackmoor Gate** turn right onto the **A399** signposted **Woolacombe** then after 2.4 miles branch left onto the **B3343** and follow this road for 6.8 miles to Mullacott Cross roundabout. Here turn left onto the **A361** and later reach **Barnstaple.**

Barnstaple

From Barnstaple follow signs **Bideford A39** to reach **Bideford.**

Bideford

Follow signs for **Bude A39** and after 26 miles reach outskirts of **Bude.**

Bude

Keep forward with the signs for **Wadebridge** and after 29.6 miles reach **Wadebridge.**

Wadebridge

Follow the signs for **Truro.** At **Fraddon** turn right onto the **A30** signposted **Redruth,** after 13 miles at a roundabout take the first exit **A390** signposted **Truro** then after 2.3 miles at the next roundabout take the 3rd exit onto the unclassified road signposted **Chacewater** to reach **Leverton Place.**

Leverton Place
Truro Cornwall

From Leverton Place return to the **A390** and turn left signposted **Redruth.** In 2.3 miles at a roundabout take the fourth exit **A30** signposted **Bodmin** and after 21 miles at a roundabout take the second exit signposted **Liskeard** onto the **Bodmin bypass.**

Bodmin bypass

After 5½ miles along the bypass branch left to join the **A38** and follow this road for 11.7 miles to the outskirts of **Liskeard.**

Liskeard

Keep forward with the **Plymouth** signs. Follow the **A38** for 14 miles to reach the **Tamar Bridge** (toll) and on the far side follow signs **Exeter** to skirt **Plymouth.**

Tamar Bridge/Plymouth

After 5.8 miles at a roundabout take the second exit to join a fast dual carriageway and 21 miles farther branch left signposted **Dartmoor,** shortly follow signs **Princetown, Tavistock** to join the unclassified road leading to **Holne Bridge** for the **River Dart Country Park.**

River Dart Country Park
Ashburton Devon

The arrangement of the direction boxes along the above route is **not** intended to represent the relative mileages between points.

South East Tour

Canterbury
Sussex Coast
New Forest

The lovely Garden of England and the gateway to the Continent are in Britain's south eastern corner. Farther along the tour are the lovely Sussex downs and coast and the New Forest.

St Martins Touring and Camping Site
Canterbury, Kent

This site is right on the edge of the historic city of Canterbury and within the lovely 'Garden of England'. If you take this trip in the Spring the orchards look wonderful and the best way to enjoy them is by following the signposted orchard tour. Canterbury is a lovely city, its narrow streets dwarfed by the magnificent Cathedral. Parts of the Norman town wall and the castle remain and the many historic buildings include the picturesque Weavers House and the remains of the Grey Friars Monastery. At Bekesbourne the famous Howletts Zoo Park contains a wide variety of wild animals. Kent has many castles, being our most vulnerable coast, but that at Leeds, near Maidstone has been described as the loveliest in the world. It was built on two islands in a large lake and remains intact, with its interior beautifully restored. Chilham Castle is not open to the public, but its grounds are the venue for regular jousting tournaments and falconry displays. On the south coast Dover has interesting Roman remains and a well-preserved castle – or a day trip to France perhaps.

15th-c Old Hospital, Rye

Castle View Caravan Site
Pevensey Bay, East Sussex

The Castle referred to in the site name is that at Pevensey where William the Conqueror disembarked in 1066 and it was he who later built the castle – in case anyone should try to follow in his footsteps no doubt. Nearby is the popular resort of Eastbourne which is over-shadowed by the towering chalk cliffs of Beachy Head. Farther along the coast the resorts of Brighton, Worthing and Bognor Regis are all backed by lovely downland and Alfriston is a delightful downland village, preserving a 14th-century Clergy

House. Nearby is Drusillas Zoo park. At Herstmonceaux, just inland from Pevensey, the Royal Observatory can be visited. Of the many grand houses in this part of the country, Sheffield Park is one of the loveliest. Its gardens (separate entrance) are also superb and from the nearby Sheffield Park Station the restored 'Bluebell Railway' runs. Farther east, Chichester is famous for its Festival Theatre and the nearby Roman Palace which has been extensively excavated, whilst a little way north, at Singleton, is an interesting collection of reconstructed buildings in the Weald and Downland Open Air Museum.

St Leonard's Tower, a fragment of West Malling's Norman castle

Shamba Holiday Park
St Leonards, Dorset

This site is ideally placed for touring the New Forest and the lovely Dorset coast. Bournemouth is just a short distance to the south, a very popular resort which is enhanced by acres of lovely parks and gardens. Stretching away to the east of the site is the New Forest. Although most of its woodland is new planting by the Forestry Commission, there are still some lovely old woods of oak and beech and part of the forest area is heathland with picturesque little streams. In the Forest's most southerly reaches stands Beaulieu, world famous for its magnificent motor museum. The Palace House, and the adjacent Abbey Ruins are also on show. A little way to the south, on the banks of the wide Beaulieu River, is Buckler's Hard. Time seems to have passed by this tiny hamlet which was once an important shipbuilding centre and there is an interesting Maritime Museum. Romsey, is a delightful town with a superb Abbey church and Broadlands, formerly home of Lord and Lady Mountbatten to whom a special exhibition is devoted.

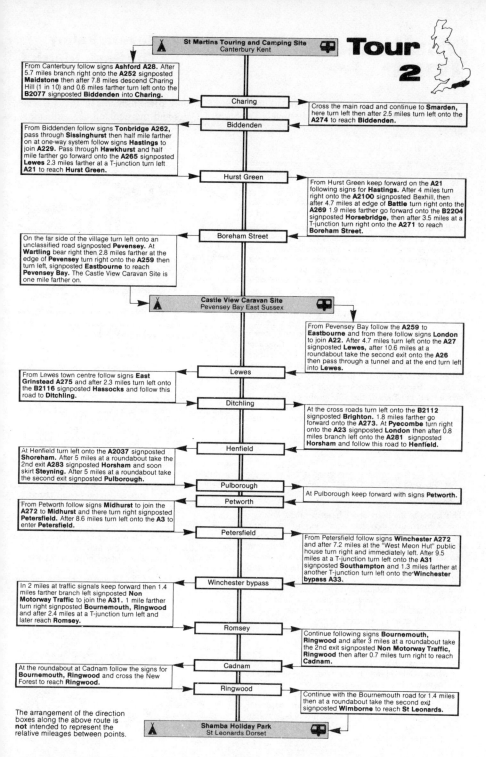

St Martins Touring and Camping Site
Canterbury Kent

Tour 2

From Canterbury follow signs **Ashford A28**. After 5.7 miles branch right onto the **A252** signposted **Maidstone** then after 7.8 miles descend Charing Hill (1 in 10) and 0.6 miles farther turn left onto the **B2077** signposted **Biddenden** into **Charing**.

Charing

Cross the main road and continue to **Smarden**, here turn left then after 2.5 miles turn left onto the **A274** to reach **Biddenden**.

Biddenden

From Biddenden follow signs **Tonbridge A262**, pass through **Sissinghurst** then half mile farther on at one-way system follow signs **Hastings** to join **A229**. Pass through **Hawkhurst** and half mile farther go forward onto the **A265** signposted **Lewes** 2.3 miles farther at a T-junction turn left **A21** to reach **Hurst Green**.

Hurst Green

From Hurst Green keep forward on the **A21** following signs for **Hastings**. After 4 miles turn right onto the **A2100** signposted Bexhill, then after 4.7 miles at edge of **Battle** turn right onto the **A269** 1.9 miles farther go forward onto the **B2204** signposted **Horsebridge**, then after 3.5 miles at a T-junction turn right onto the **A271** to reach **Boreham Street**.

Boreham Street

On the far side of the village turn left onto an unclassified road signposted **Pevensey**. At **Wartling** bear right then 2.8 miles farther at the edge of **Pevensey** turn right onto the **A259** then turn left, signposted **Eastbourne** to reach **Pevensey Bay**. The Castle View Caravan Site is one mile farther on.

Castle View Caravan Site
Pevensey Bay East Sussex

From Pevensey Bay follow the **A259** to **Eastbourne** and from there follow signs **London** to join **A22**. After 4.7 miles turn left onto the **A27** signposted **Lewes**, after 10.6 miles at a roundabout take the second exit onto the **A26** then pass through a tunnel and at the end turn left into **Lewes**.

Lewes

From Lewes town centre follow signs **East Grinstead A275** and after 2.3 miles turn left onto the **B2116** signposted **Hassocks** and follow this road to **Ditchling**.

Ditchling

At the cross roads turn left onto the **B2112** signposted **Brighton**. 1.8 miles farther go forward onto the **A273**. At **Pyecombe** turn right onto the **A23** signposted **London** then after 0.8 miles branch left onto the **A281** signposted **Horsham** and follow this road to **Henfield**.

Henfield

At Henfield turn left onto the **A2037** signposted **Shoreham**. After 5 miles at a roundabout take the 2nd exit **A283** signposted **Horsham** and soon skirt **Steyning**. After 5 miles at a roundabout take the second exit signposted **Pulborough**.

Pulborough

At Pulborough keep forward with signs **Petworth**.

Petworth

From Petworth follow signs **Midhurst** to join the **A272** to **Midhurst** and there turn right signposted **Petersfield**. After 8.6 miles turn left onto the **A3** to enter **Petersfield**.

Petersfield

From Petersfield follow signs **Winchester A272** and after 7.2 miles at the "West Meon Hut" public house turn right and immediately left. After 9.5 miles at a T-junction turn left onto the **A31** signposted **Southampton** and 1.3 miles farther at another T-junction turn left onto the **Winchester bypass A33**.

Winchester bypass

In 2 miles at traffic signals keep forward then 1.4 miles farther branch left signposted **Non Motorway Traffic** to join the **A31**. 1 mile farther turn right signposted **Bournemouth, Ringwood** and after 2.4 miles at a T-junction turn left and later reach **Romsey**.

Romsey

Continue following signs **Bournemouth, Ringwood** and after 3 miles at a roundabout take the 2nd exit signposted **Non Motorway Traffic, Ringwood** then after 0.7 miles turn right to reach **Cadnam**.

Cadnam

At the roundabout at Cadnam follow the signs for **Bournemouth, Ringwood** and cross the New Forest to reach **Ringwood**.

Ringwood

Continue with the Bournemouth road for 1.4 miles then at a roundabout take the second exit signposted **Wimborne** to reach **St Leonards**.

The arrangement of the direction boxes along the above route is **not** intended to represent the relative mileages between points.

Shamba Holiday Park
St Leonards Dorset

Midlands Tour

The Midlands isn't just the industrial connurbation around Birmingham. In this tour we explore agricultural Shropshire, the lovely Derbyshire Dales and the Fenland of Cambridgeshire

Cranberry Moss Caravan and Camping Site
Kinnerley, Shropshire

On the western side of the industrial heart of the Midlands, Shropshire is a peaceful, mainly agricultural area and one of its delights is the lovely Severn Valley. Welshpool is situated upstream just across the Welsh border where Powys Castle is well preserved and surrounded by landscaped grounds. The river makes its way to Shrewsbury, a charming town with many picturesque old timbered buildings, and continues south-eastwards passing under Telford's famous Iron Bridge, which is now at the heart of a complex devoted to our industrial heritage. Then on to Bridgnorth, divided into two parts by a steep ridge down which run twisty roads, flights of steps and a funicular railway. From here the Severn Valley Railway follows its scenic route to Bewdley. Away from the Severn Valley there is still plenty to see and do, including a Working Farm Museum at Acton Scott. Here the agricultural practises of the 19th century are demonstrated, including work by heavy horses. Visitors can participate in some of the work and crafts are also demonstrated at weekends.

Greenhills Caravan Park
Ashford-in-the-Water, Derbyshire

This site is in the heart of the beautiful Peak District, and Ashford-in-the-Water is a delightful village. Nearby Bakewell is an attractive town on the River Wye which is spanned by a 5-arched bridge of medieval origins. Haddon Hall is two miles to the south-east, a fine example of a medieval home, and to the east is Chatsworth. This palatial 17th-century house is home of the Duke and Duchess of Devonshire and contains one of the richest private collections of works of art. There is also a Farming and Forestry Exhibition and lovely landscaped grounds. At Crich is an interesting tram museum with exhibits from all over the world. Castleton is one of Derbyshire's main attractions with its dramatic scenery, its castle and its four caverns. Blue John is Britain's rarest rock formation, only found in this area. Throughout the Derbyshire villages the custom of Well-dressing is celebrated, where thanks are given for the gift of well water. Other places to visit include Eyam, where the Great Plague was contained when the village voluntarily cut itself off from its surroundings to prevent the spread of the disease.

Old Oswestry, an important iron-age hill fort

Old Manor Caravan Park
Grafham, Cambridgeshire

This site, winner of our Campsite of the Year Award in 1981, is small and well run and within a lovely area. Nearby is the vast Grafham Water reservoir with picnic places on its shores and plenty of scope for fishermen. Huntingdon is the nearest town, birthplace of both Oliver Cromwell and Samuel Pepys, and the Cromwell family's former home, Hinchingbroke House, is open. To the south east is the beautiful university town of Cambridge, a mixture of busy streets and tranquil college cloisters. The architecture is quite magnificent, particularly in the famous King's College Chapel and behind the colleges runs the River Cam, with lovely lawns on its banks and attractive bridges crossing over to the 'Backs'. Crossing into the county of Suffolk, the town of Newmarket is well worth a visit. Newmarket *is* horseracing – with its famous racecourse, numerous training establishments and gallops which start as the buildings finish. The Jockey Club, which administers the 'Sport of Kings' has its Headquarters in the main street and it is very fitting, therefore, that this should be the place for the new Museum of Horseracing.

Georgian houses of the North Brink, Wisbech

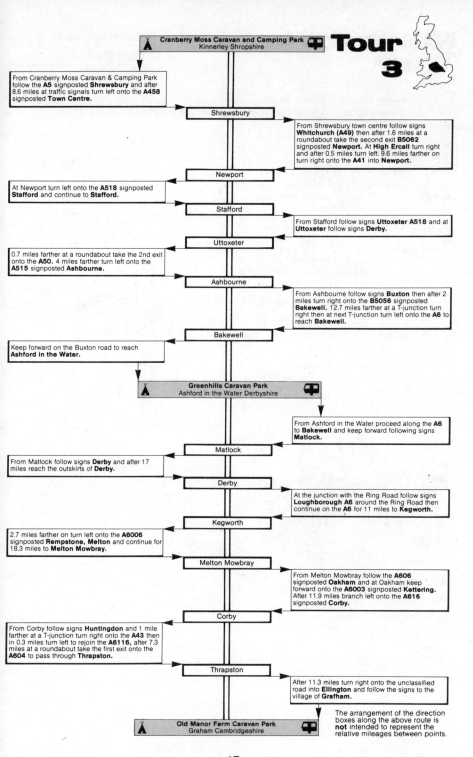

Cranberry Moss Caravan and Camping Park
Kinnerley Shropshire

Tour 3

From Cranberry Moss Caravan & Camping Park follow the **A5** signposted **Shrewsbury** and after 8.6 miles at traffic signals turn left onto the **A458** signposted **Town Centre.**

Shrewsbury

From Shrewsbury town centre follow signs **Whitchurch (A49)** then after 1.6 miles at a roundabout take the second exit **B5062** signposted **Newport.** At **High Ercall** turn right and after 0.5 miles turn left. 9.6 miles farther on turn right onto the **A41** into **Newport.**

Newport

At Newport turn left onto the **A518** signposted **Stafford** and continue to **Stafford.**

Stafford

From Stafford follow signs **Uttoxeter A518** and at **Uttoxeter** follow signs **Derby.**

Uttoxeter

0.7 miles farther at a roundabout take the 2nd exit onto the **A50.** 4 miles farther turn left onto the **A515** signposted **Ashbourne.**

Ashbourne

From Ashbourne follow signs **Buxton** then after 2 miles turn right onto the **B5056** signposted **Bakewell.** 12.7 miles farther at a T-junction turn right then at next T-junction turn left onto the **A6** to reach **Bakewell.**

Bakewell

Keep forward on the Buxton road to reach **Ashford in the Water.**

Greenhills Caravan Park
Ashford in the Water Derbyshire

From Ashford in the Water proceed along the **A6** to **Bakewell** and keep forward following signs **Matlock.**

Matlock

From Matlock follow signs **Derby** and after 17 miles reach the outskirts of **Derby.**

Derby

At the junction with the Ring Road follow signs **Loughborough A6** around the Ring Road then continue on the **A6** for 11 miles to **Kegworth.**

Kegworth

2.7 miles farther on turn left onto the **A6006** signposted **Rempstone, Melton** and continue for 18.3 miles to **Melton Mowbray.**

Melton Mowbray

From Melton Mowbray follow the **A606** signposted **Oakham** and at Oakham keep forward onto the **A6003** signposted **Kettering.** After 11.9 miles branch left onto the **A616** signposted **Corby.**

Corby

From Corby follow signs **Huntingdon** and 1 mile farther at a T-junction turn right onto the **A43** then in 0.3 miles turn left to rejoin the **A6116**, after 7.3 miles at a roundabout take the first exit onto the **A604** to pass through **Thrapston.**

Thrapston

After 11.3 miles turn right onto the unclassified road into **Ellington** and follow the signs to the village of **Grafham.**

The arrangement of the direction boxes along the above route is **not** intended to represent the relative mileages between points.

Old Manor Farm Caravan Park
Graham Cambridgeshire

North Yorkshire Tour

A beautiful and diverse county with its 'James Herriott' country, its wild moorland and its delightful Dales villages – all centred on the magnificent 'capital' city of York.

Rudding Caravan Park
Harrogate, North Yorkshire

This site is just three miles from the centre of Harrogate within the lovely Rudding Park Gardens, and flowers are an important part of this town. It was once a popular spa, and many of the associated buildings of that era remain. Harewood House, to the south, is a magnificent 18th-century mansion surrounded by lovely gardens. Some four acres are given over to a comprehensive bird garden attractively set out beside the lake. Knaresborough is a delightful small town with a castle, a lovely riverside area and the famous Dropping Well where items hung in the flow of water soon become petrified. The magnificent city of York needs plenty of time for exploring its narrow streets, its splendid Minster and its Castle Museum – an outstanding folk museum of Yorkshire life. West of Harrogate, the southern reaches of the Dales include such beauty spots as Malham and Ingleborough Hill whilst to the south Haworth, home of the Brontës, is best reached via the Worth Valley Railway from Keighley. Skipton, too, is interesting, and there is a National Park Information Centre at Grassington.

The picturesque Shambles, York

Brompton-on-Swale Caravan Park
Brompton-on-Swale, North Yorkshire

This site is beautifully situated on the banks of the river Swale just a short distance from the lovely old town of Richmond. A massive Norman Castle is the dominant feature of the town, the rest of which is a maze of narrow, steep alleyways opening out into a huge cobbled market square. Here the Green Howards Regimental Museum can be found. Swaledale extends to the west, surrounded by the high moorlands of the Pennine Chain. At Thwaite, the steep, narrow Buttertubs Pass crosses to the head of Wensleydale, the most famous of all the Dales. At Aysgarth, about half way down the Dale, is a splendid series of waterfalls.

There is a National Park Information Centre here as well as an interesting Museum of Horsedrawn Vehicles in a restored mill building. If you should be in nearby Bainbridge at 9pm, you will be able to witness the ancient custom of blowing the Forest Horn. On the northern side of Wensleydale is Castle Bolton, dating from the late 14th century, which was once a prison of Mary, Queen of Scots. Part has been restored to its original state.

Remains of 13th-c Whitby Abbey

Spiers House Campsite
Cropton, North Yorkshire

Set in a lovely woodland area, this site is right on the edge of the North York Moors National Park. Delightful villages hereabouts include Hutton-le-Hole, at the centre of which is a stream and wide banks of grass. Here, too, is the Ryedale Folk Museum which includes some reconstructed buildings. The wild and remote moorland stretches away to the north and west, the type of land favoured by the 12th and 13th-century religious foundations. Rievaulx Abbey is a particularly fine example, standing beside the River Rye. On the hill above, Rievaulx Terrace is an 18th-century creation of landscaped walks and temples with superb views. Pickering is an ancient market town with some interesting old buildings and coaching inns, and from Pickering Station the steam-hauled trains of the North York Moors Railway run. The line covers some 18 miles following the lovely Newtondale to Grosmant and Newtondale Halt gives access to the forest en route. The popular seaside resort of Scarborough is to the east, centred on the sheltered sandy South Bay. Whitby, to the north is an attractive fishing port and resort with an impressive ruined Abbey.

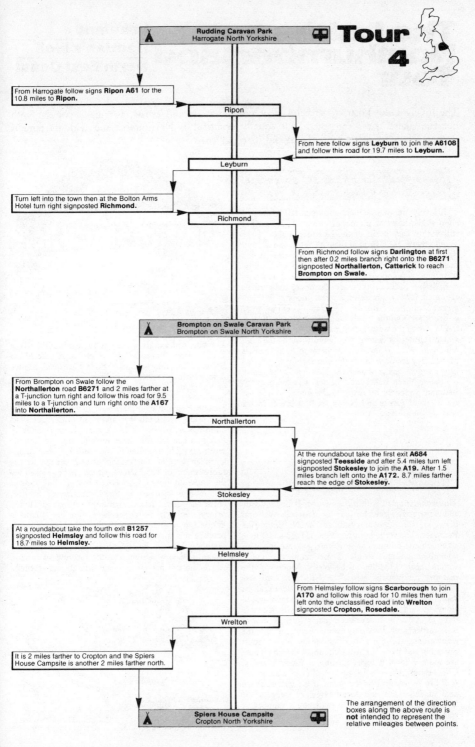

Rudding Caravan Park
Harrogate North Yorkshire

Tour 4

From Harrogate follow signs **Ripon A61** for the 10.8 miles to **Ripon**.

Ripon

From here follow signs **Leyburn** to join the **A6108** and follow this road for 19.7 miles to **Leyburn**.

Leyburn

Turn left into the town then at the Bolton Arms Hotel turn right signposted **Richmond**.

Richmond

From Richmond follow signs **Darlington** at first then after 0.2 miles branch right onto the **B6271** signposted **Northallerton, Catterick** to reach **Brompton on Swale.**

Brompton on Swale Caravan Park
Brompton on Swale North Yorkshire

From Brompton on Swale follow the **Northallerton** road **B6271** and 2 miles farther at a T-junction turn right and follow this road for 9.5 miles to a T-junction and turn right onto the **A167** into **Northallerton.**

Northallerton

At the roundabout take the first exit **A684** signposted **Teesside** and after 5.4 miles turn left signposted **Stokesley** to join the **A19**. After 1.5 miles branch left onto the **A172**. 8.7 miles farther reach the edge of **Stokesley.**

Stokesley

At a roundabout take the fourth exit **B1257** signposted **Helmsley** and follow this road for 18.7 miles to **Helmsley**.

Helmsley

From Helmsley follow signs **Scarborough** to join **A170** and follow this road for 10 miles then turn left onto the unclassified road into **Wrelton** signposted **Cropton, Rosedale.**

Wrelton

It is 2 miles farther to Cropton and the Spiers House Campsite is another 2 miles farther north.

The arrangement of the direction boxes along the above route is **not** intended to represent the relative mileages between points.

Spiers House Campsite
Cropton North Yorkshire

The Lakes and Northumberland Tour

Lakeland
Hadrian's Wall
North East Coast

The lovely Lake District, so beloved of poets, writers and artists, is equally popular with holidaymakers. Less congested, but equally beautiful is Northumberland with its famous Roman Wall, its remote moorlands and its rocky coast.

Neaum Crag Camping and Caravan Site
Skelwith Bridge, Cumbria

This lovely site of woodland and open fell is situated right at the heart of the popular south Lakeland but still within easy reach of the Northern Lakes. Lake Windermere, the largest of them all is the nearest, and by far the best way to see it is from the water. If you don't have your own boat, steamer services operate from several points around the lake, some of which go to Belle Isle in the centre where the house and gardens are open. Other places of interest include Windermere's Steamboat Museum, the National Park Centre at Brockhole and the lovely Stagshaw Gardens. Coniston Water to the west, is best seen via the narrow road which follows its eastern shore. Northwards the high mountain road from Windermere to Ullswater is particularly scenic with superb views of the Cumbrian range and its many waterfalls. Keswick is the centre for the northern Lakeland – wilder, less commercialised and preferred by many to the south. Watch out for lakeland games and hound trailing events in the area – they are fascinating.

Burnfoot Campsite
Haltwhistle, Northumberland

This site is situated within the estate of Bellister Castle and is perfectly placed for touring Hadrian's Wall and the wild, remote countryside of the Northumbrian Pennines. The wall, built between AD122 and 139 is a remarkable monument to Roman engineering with several sections still visible. These include a 110 yard section near Heddon-on-the-Wall. Much of the masonry disappeared when the Military Road was constructed in 1781, but even where no stones can be seen, the bank and ditch earthworks can be traced along the ridges. The defences and the man-power were extensive with seventeen major forts as well as mile-castles and look-out towers between. Of the excavations, the fort at Housesteads is the most revealing and there is also a museum at the site. There are more excavated forts, notably at Chesters and at Chesterholm where a full scale replica of a section of wall has been built. To the north of the wall a remote area of moorland and forest stretches away to the Scottish border whilst to the south are a number of spectacular waterfalls such as Cauldron Snout and High Force.

Gateshead's majestic Tyne Bridge of 1928

Ord House Caravan Park
Berwick upon Tweed, Northumberland

This site is pleasantly situated to the south of the River Tweed near Tweedmouth which is connected to Berwick by three bridges. Beside the Royal Border Bridge, which carries the railway, stands the remains of the castle. Both the town and the castle changed hands with Scotland over the centuries until it finally became England's northernmost town in 1482. The town walls are Elizabethan and many of Berwick's old buildings are protected. If you are in Berwick on May Day you can witness the annual Riding the Bounds ceremony. The coastline to the south has been designated an area of outstanding natural beauty, as has Holy Island, or Lindisfarne, which can be reached via the causeway from Beal (watch out for the tides). Commonly regarded as the birthplace of English christianity, the island, with its castle and ruined priory, is rich in atmosphere. Farther south is Bamburgh, a small resort with an impressive castle perched on a rocky crag which was restored in the 18th century. Also in Bamburgh is the Grace Darling Museum where exhibits include the rowing boat in which she and her father made their daring rescue.

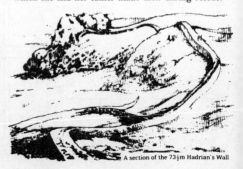

A section of the 73½m Hadrian's Wall

20

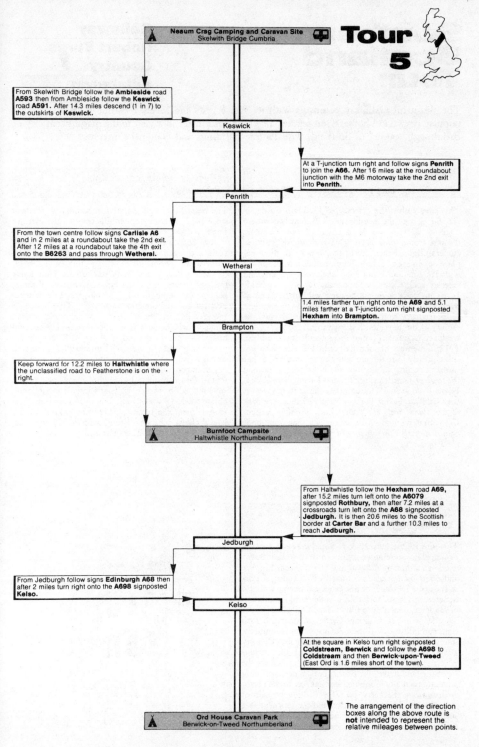

Neaum Crag Camping and Caravan Site
Skelwith Bridge Cumbria

Tour 5

From Skelwith Bridge follow the **Ambleside** road **A593** then from Ambleside follow the **Keswick** road **A591**. After 14.3 miles descend (1 in 7) to the outskirts of **Keswick**.

Keswick

At a T-junction turn right and follow signs **Penrith** to join the **A66**. After 16 miles at the roundabout junction with the M6 motorway take the 2nd exit into **Penrith**.

Penrith

From the town centre follow signs **Carlisle A6** and in 2 miles at a roundabout take the 2nd exit. After 12 miles at a roundabout take the 4th exit onto the **B6263** and pass through **Wetheral.**

Wetheral

1.4 miles farther turn right onto the **A69** and 5.1 miles farther at a T-junction turn right signposted **Hexham** into **Brampton.**

Brampton

Keep forward for 12.2 miles to **Haltwhistle** where the unclassified road to Featherstone is on the right.

Burnfoot Campsite
Haltwhistle Northumberland

From Haltwhistle follow the **Hexham** road **A69**, after 15.2 miles turn left onto the **A6079** signposted **Rothbury**, then after 7.2 miles at a crossroads turn left onto the **A68** signposted **Jedburgh.** It is then 20.6 miles to the Scottish border at **Carter Bar** and a further 10.3 miles to reach **Jedburgh.**

Jedburgh

From Jedburgh follow signs **Edinburgh A68** then after 2 miles turn right onto the **A698** signposted **Kelso.**

Kelso

At the square in Kelso turn right signposted **Coldstream, Berwick** and follow the **A698** to **Coldstream** and then **Berwick-upon-Tweed** (East Ord is 1.6 miles short of the town).

Ord House Caravan Park
Berwick-on-Tweed Northumberland

The arrangement of the direction boxes along the above route is **not** intended to represent the relative mileages between points.

21

Southern Scotland Tour

Galloway
Robert Burns Country
Edinburgh

The Beautiful Galloway peninsula with its vast forests and lovely coastline leads on to Ayr, popular resort and horseracing venue. The tour culminates in a visit to the magnificent city of Edinburgh, capital of Scotland, with its fine buildings and National museums.

Hoddom Castle Caravan Park
Ecclefechan, Dumfries and Galloway

This site, within the grounds of Hoddom Castle, is not far across the border near Ecclefechan where Thomas Carlyle was born in 1795. Just a short distance to the south is Gretna Green where countless elopers plighted their troths in the past. In the area, places of interest include Rammerscales, a fine house with Jacobite and Flora Macdonald connections, and Caerlaverock Castle, a famous medieval stronghold. In its grounds is an outstanding wildfowl refuge of over 1000 acres on the Solway shore with excellent hide facilities and observation points. Across the estuary of the River Nith is Sweetheart Abbey, one of the loveliest monastic ruins in Scotland. It was built in 1273 in memory of John Balliol by his wife, who was subsequently buried there with the 'sweet heart' of her husband resting on her bosom. Northwards, beyond the town of Dumfries, is Ellisland Farm where Robert Burns lived from 1788 to 1791. Away to the west is the Galloway Forest Park, a huge 110,000 acre park of woodland, hills and lochs, Loch Trool is particularly attractive and on its shores is a memorial stone commemorating the victory of Robert the Bruce over the English in 1307.

Moretonhall Caravan Park
Edinburgh, Lothian

The beautiful city of Edinburgh, capital of Scotland since 1437, stands on seven hills between the Firth of Forth and the Pentland Hills. It is a city steeped in history and importance, inhabited for at least 1000 years and location of Scotlands major National museums and galleries. It's crowning glory is, of course, its castle which stands on a massive rock high above the city streets. Here the famous Military Tatoo is held as a highlight of Edinburgh's International Festival in late summer each year. The Palace of Holyroodhouse, the Queen's official residence in Scotland which dates from the 16th and 17th centuries, is open to the public along with many more places of interest in the city. Edinburgh Zoo, is well worth a visit too. Outside the city to the east, Aberlady has an interesting Motor Museum and at East Fortune is the Museum of Flight with many planes and working exhibits on show. East Linton has Scotland's oldest working water mill. South of Edinburgh, at Innerleithen, the beautiful Traquair House is Scotland's oldest inhabited house, with lovely grounds, craft workshops and its own working brewhouse.

Sundrum Castle Holiday Park
Coylton, Strathclyde

This site is just outside Ayr, popular resort and the principal horseracing venue in Scotland. Robert Burns was born at nearby Alloway and was christened in Ayr and many memorials to Scotland's National poet exist in the area. Devotees of his songs and poems will also be interested to see such things as the 'banks and braes' of the River Doon or to follow Tam O'Shanter's ride. To the south is Culzean Castle, a splendid 18th century building by Robert Adam with a magnificent interior. The grounds include Scotland's first Country Park. Between Ayr and the Castle is the curious Electric Brae where an optical illusion caused by the lie of the land makes the road appear to be descending when it is actually climbing. Beyond Ayr to the north, Ardrossan is the ferry port for the lovely 'Isle of Arran'. Vehicles can be carried and the journey takes just under an hour. Glasgow too is within easy reach, a city with many places of interest and lovely parks.

Protestant Reformer John Knox is said to have lived in this house during the 15thc.

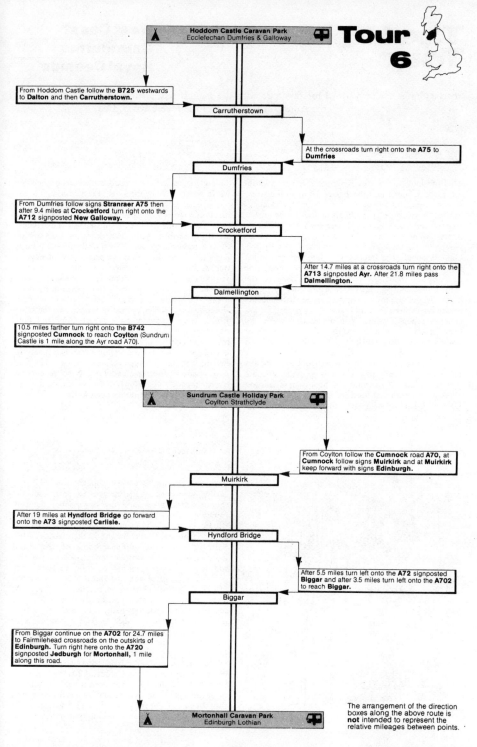

Hoddom Castle Caravan Park
Ecclefechan Dumfries & Galloway

Tour 6

From Hoddom Castle follow the **B725** westwards to **Dalton** and then **Carrutherstown.**

Carrutherstown

At the crossroads turn right onto the **A75** to **Dumfries**

Dumfries

From Dumfries follow signs **Stranraer A75** then after 9.4 miles at **Crocketford** turn right onto the **A712** signposted **New Galloway.**

Crocketford

After 14.7 miles at a crossroads turn right onto the **A713** signposted **Ayr.** After 21.8 miles pass **Dalmellington.**

Dalmellington

10.5 miles farther turn right onto the **B742** signposted **Cumnock** to reach **Coylton** (Sundrum Castle is 1 mile along the Ayr road A70).

Sundrum Castle Holiday Park
Coylton Strathclyde

From Coylton follow the **Cumnock** road **A70**, at **Cumnock** follow signs **Muirkirk** and at **Muirkirk** keep forward with signs **Edinburgh.**

Muirkirk

After 19 miles at **Hyndford Bridge** go forward onto the **A73** signposted **Carlisle.**

Hyndford Bridge

After 5.5 miles turn left onto the **A72** signposted **Biggar** and after 3.5 miles turn left onto the **A702** to reach **Biggar.**

Biggar

From Biggar continue on the **A702** for 24.7 miles to Fairmilehead crossroads on the outskirts of **Edinburgh.** Turn right here onto the **A720** signposted **Jedburgh** for **Mortonhall,** 1 mile along this road.

Mortonhall Caravan Park
Edinburgh Lothian

The arrangement of the direction boxes along the above route is **not** intended to represent the relative mileages between points.

The Highlands Tour

Spectacular is the only word for this tour with the magnificent scenery of the west coast and Glencoe, the winter sports area around Aviemore and the lovely River Dee.

Tralee Bay Caravan Park
Benderloch, Strathclyde

This site looks out across Ardmucknish Bay towards the Firth of Lorn and the Isle of Mull to the west, amidst a beautiful area of mountains, forests and lochs. Scotland's west coast is justifiably famous for its superb scenery and there is hardly any need for places of interest when you have such surroundings as these. Nevertheless, there are plenty of places to visit and Oban is particularly interesting. Here visitors can see Caithness glass in the making, see demonstrations of spinning and weaving at Macdonald's Mill or visit the ruined Dunstaffnage Castle on a promontary to the north. Above the town stands a strange, half-finished edifice resembling the Colosseum – a 19th-century 'job creation scheme' which was abandoned when the benefactor died. Vehicle ferries sail to a number of islands from Oban. Inland, the north end of Loch Awe is the location of the Cruachan Power Station, a spectacular example of hydro-electric power, whilst the nearby Ardanaiseig Gardens provide a more relaxed setting. At Auchindrain there is an interesting open air museum and northwards from the site is the famous Glencoe with its unparalleled mountain scenery.

Glen More
Aviemore, Highland

This site is beautifully situated at the heart of the Glen More Forest Park by the lovely Loch Morlich. Many rare species of birds and animals are protected here including Osprey, Ptarmigan and Blue Hare. The large Capercaille has been re-introduced and reindeer are being farmed in the area. Forestry Commission trails help visitors to see the best of the forest. Nearby Aviemore is best known as our principal winter sports centre, but its facilities are available for summer visitors too. These include skating and curling rinks, a dry ski slope, a go-kart track and a swimming pool. From the station a revived steam railway operates along the Spey Valley to Boat of Garten. To the south Kingussie is the home of the superb Highland Folk Museum with reconstructed buildings, folk life exhibits and craft displays. Nearby the Highland Wild Life Park illustrates the wildlife that has inhabited Britain from the Ice Age to the present day. The road north leads to Inverness and Loch Ness, or alternatively through Grantown-on-Spey and onto the 'Whisky Trail' of distilleries open to the public.

Aboyne Loch Caravan Park
Aboyne, Grampian

Beautiful Deeside is a very popular area and it is hardly surprising, with its famous river and the countless tributaries tumbling down from the surrounding mountain slopes. One such tributary is Clunie Water which flows through Braemar, famous for its Highland Gathering and its picturesque castle. Balmoral, favourite summer home of the Royal Family, lies a little further downstream on the Dee and its grounds are open to the public. Ballater is one of the few towns of any size and it too has a famous Highland Games meeting in August each year. At these colourful events, pipe bands play and kilted contestants compete at many old Scottish sports, including the famous caber tossing. Historic castles abound here, not defences against past invaders, but strongholds of the powerful Clan chieftains. Corgarff, Glenbuchat and Kildrummy are prime examples whilst Craigievar Castle is perhaps the most characteristic example of the Scottish Baronial period. Eastwards, on the coast, Aberdeen is one of Scotland's most important commercial centres, particularly with the advent of North Sea oil, and has for many centuries been a prosperous fishing port, religious and scholastic centre.

Kilcoy Castle at Muir of Ord is considered a good example of 17th-c baronial style.

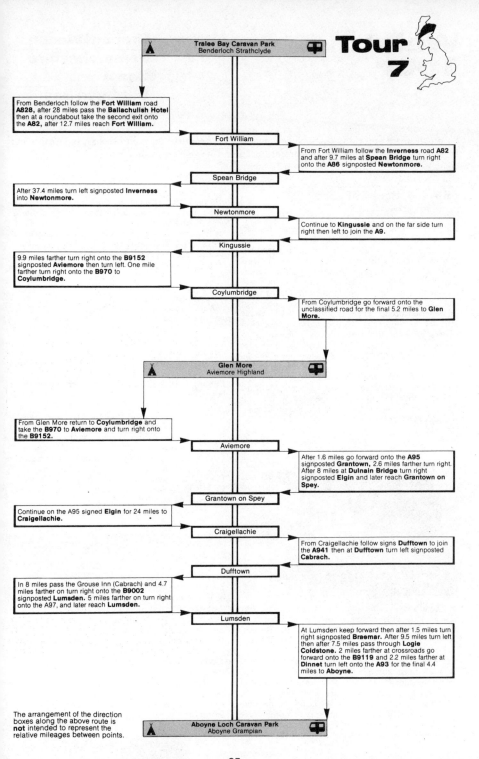

Tralee Bay Caravan Park
Benderloch Strathclyde

Tour 7

From Benderloch follow the **Fort William** road **A828**, after 28 miles pass the **Ballachulish Hotel** then at a roundabout take the second exit onto the **A82**, after 12.7 miles reach **Fort William.**

Fort William

From Fort William follow the **Inverness** road **A82** and after 9.7 miles at **Spean Bridge** turn right onto the **A86** signposted **Newtonmore.**

Spean Bridge

After 37.4 miles turn left signposted **Inverness** into **Newtonmore.**

Newtonmore

Continue to **Kingussie** and on the far side turn right then left to join the **A9.**

Kingussie

9.9 miles farther turn right onto the **B9152** signposted **Aviemore** then turn left. One mile farther turn right onto the **B970** to **Coylumbridge.**

Coylumbridge

From Coylumbridge go forward onto the unclassified road for the final 5.2 miles to **Glen More.**

Glen More
Aviemore Highland

From Glen More return to **Coylumbridge** and take the **B970** to **Aviemore** and turn right onto the **B9152.**

Aviemore

After 1.6 miles go forward onto the **A95** signposted **Grantown,** 2.6 miles farther turn right. After 8 miles at **Dulnain Bridge** turn right signposted **Elgin** and later reach **Grantown on Spey.**

Grantown on Spey

Continue on the A95 signed **Elgin** for 24 miles to **Craigellachie.**

Craigellachie

From Craigellachie follow signs **Dufftown** to join the **A941** then at **Dufftown** turn left signposted **Cabrach.**

Dufftown

In 8 miles pass the Grouse Inn (Cabrach) and 4.7 miles farther on turn right onto the **B9002** signposted **Lumsden.** 5 miles farther on turn right onto the A97, and later reach **Lumsden.**

Lumsden

At Lumsden keep forward then after 1.5 miles turn right signposted **Braemar.** After 9.5 miles turn left then after 7.5 miles pass through **Logie Coldstone.** 2 miles farther at crossroads go forward onto the **B9119** and 2.2 miles farther at **Dinnet** turn left onto the **A93** for the final 4.4 miles to **Aboyne.**

The arrangement of the direction boxes along the above route is **not** intended to represent the relative mileages between points.

Aboyne Loch Caravan Park
Aboyne Grampian

Welsh Tour

So much to see and do in this lovely Principality – beautiful unspoilt beaches, mountains and lakes – it is also famous for its ancient castles and its revived railways.

Riverside Caravan Park
Talgarth, Powys

This site is right on the edge of the Brecon Beacons National Park beneath the Black Mountains, a lovely area of mountains, glacial valleys and waterfalls. Nearby Brecon is the main centre for the National Park, whilst just north of Merthyr Tydfil the Garwnant Forest Centre provides information on the forest areas within the Park. Near Abercraf the Dan yr Ogof and Cathedral Showcaves are the largest of their kind in western Europe. There is also a model Dinosaur Park for the children and Britain's first archaeological showcave. Going underground in a different way is the new Mining Museum – The Big Pit – at Blaenavon where visitors are taken down to the coalface of a recently closed mine and guided round its workings. Farther south Cardiff has a large castle, a particularly interesting Industrial and Maritime Museum and, just outside the city, the Welsh Folk Museum at St Fagans. Centred on St Fagans Castle it includes many reconstructed Welsh buildings.

Magnificent Snowdon from Llyn Llydaw

Caerfai Bay Caravan and Camping Park
St Davids, Dyfed

St David's is Britain's smallest city which would be just a pretty village were it not for its magnificent Cathedral nestling in a hollow beneath the houses. Nearby are the ruins of the once extensive Bishops Palace. This site, too, is within a National Park – the Pembrokeshire Coast Park – which preserves some of Britain's finest unspoilt beaches and cliff tops. The Pembrokeshire Coast Path provides a good way of discovering its delightful little sandy beaches. The only seaside resort of any size is Tenby on the south coast. At Pembroke is the impressive castle where Henry VII was born in 1456. On a smaller scale, Manorbier Castle is very attractive and has a lovely

beach almost beneath its solid walls. Many of the offshore islands around the coast are nature reserves where seals, peregrine falcons and fulmars can be seen. Inland are the Preseli Hills, an area of moorland, heath and bog famous for its prehistoric remains. Near Crymmych is a huge Iron Age hill fort with Bronze Age cairns inside, whilst there is a circle of 16 stones near Mynachlog-ddu.

Woodlands, Caravan Park
Llanon, Dyfed

Llanon lies to the south of Aberystwyth a popular resort about half-way along the wide sweep of Cardigan Bay. Its two beaches are separated by a headland upon which stands the ruin of the castle built by Edward I. It is also a university town, home of the huge National Library of Wales and one of Wales' famous steam railways operates from here. The Vale of Rheidol Light Railway follows the river Rheidol upstream for some 12 miles through lovely scenery to Devil's Bridge. At this famous beauty spot the river Mynach cascades down a 300 foot gorge spanned by three bridges – one on top of the other. Other places of interest include the West Wales Farm Park near Plwmp, the Museum of the Woollen Industry at Dre-Fach-Felindre and the Centre for Alternative Technology at Machynlleth.

Cadnant Valley Camping Park
Caernarfon, Gwynedd

Caernarfon has one of the most impressive castles in Britain, its hourglass shape covering three acres and its outer walls and towers still intact. On the edge of the town are the excavations of the Roman Fort, Segontium, built in AD78, and a museum of finds from the site. Inland is Snowdon and can be climbed from Llanberis – by far the easiest route, unless you take the Snowdon Mountain Railway of course. The scenery in this huge range is quite spectacular and places to see include the lovely Swallow Falls near Betws-y-Coed and the vast slate caverns at Blaenau Ffestiniog. Fort Belan, near Caernarfon, is a Napoleonic fort which is now a leisure centre with a maritime museum, old forge, miniature steam railway, pleasure flights and canon firing displays.

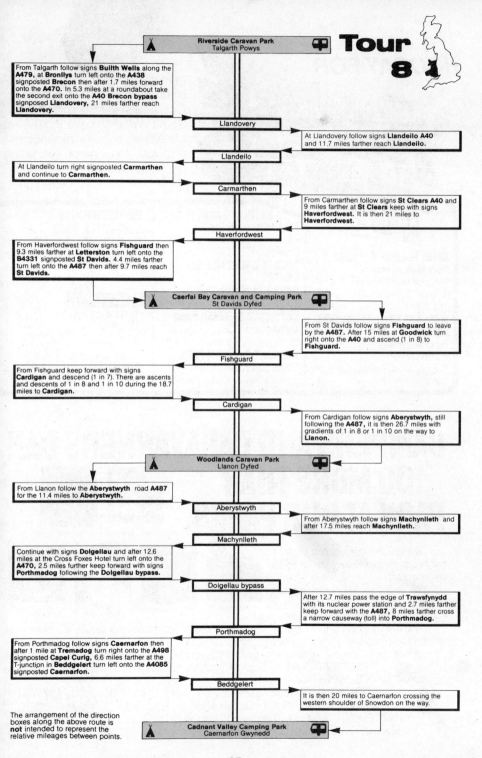

Tour 8

Riverside Caravan Park
Talgarth Powys

From Talgarth follow signs **Builth Wells** along the **A479**, at **Bronllys** turn left onto the **A438** signposted **Brecon** then after 1.7 miles forward onto the **A470**. In 5.3 miles at a roundabout take the second exit onto the **A40 Brecon bypass** signposed **Llandovery**, 21 miles farther reach **Llandovery**.

Llandovery

At Llandovery follow signs **Llandeilo A40** and 11.7 miles farther reach **Llandeilo**.

Llandeilo

At Llandeilo turn right signposted **Carmarthen** and continue to **Carmarthen**.

Carmarthen

From Carmarthen follow signs **St Clears A40** and 9 miles farther at **St Clears** keep with signs **Haverfordwest**. It is then 21 miles to **Haverfordwest**.

Haverfordwest

From Haverfordwest follow signs **Fishguard** then 9.3 miles farther at **Letterston** turn left onto the **B4331** signposted **St Davids**. 4.4 miles farther turn left onto the **A487** then after 9.7 miles reach **St Davids**.

Caerfai Bay Caravan and Camping Park
St Davids Dyfed

From St Davids follow signs **Fishguard** to leave by the **A487**. After 15 miles at **Goodwick** turn right onto the **A40** and ascend (1 in 8) to **Fishguard**.

Fishguard

From Fishguard keep forward with signs **Cardigan** and descend (1 in 7). There are ascents and descents of 1 in 8 and 1 in 10 during the 18.7 miles to **Cardigan**.

Cardigan

From Cardigan follow signs **Aberystwyth**, still following the **A487**, it is then 26.7 miles with gradients of 1 in 8 or 1 in 10 on the way to **Llanon**.

Woodlands Caravan Park
Llanon Dyfed

From Llanon follow the **Aberystwyth** road **A487** for the 11.4 miles to **Aberystwyth**.

Aberystwyth

From Aberystwyth follow signs **Machynlleth** and after 17.5 miles reach **Machynlleth**.

Machynlleth

Continue with signs **Dolgellau** and after 12.6 miles at the Cross Foxes Hotel turn left onto the **A470**, 2.5 miles further keep forward with signs **Porthmadog** following the **Dolgellau bypass**.

Dolgellau bypass

After 12.7 miles pass the edge of **Trawsfynydd** with its nuclear power station and 2.7 miles farther keep forward with the **A487**, 8 miles farther cross a narrow causeway (toll) into **Porthmadog**.

Porthmadog

From Porthmadog follow signs **Caernarfon** then after 1 mile at **Tremadog** turn right onto the **A498** signposted **Capel Curig**, 6.6 miles farther at the T-junction in **Beddgelert** turn left onto the **A4085** signposted **Caernarfon**.

Beddgelert

It is then 20 miles to Caernarfon crossing the western shoulder of Snowdon on the way.

The arrangement of the direction boxes along the above route is **not** intended to represent the relative mileages between points.

Cadnant Valley Camping Park
Caernarfon Gwynedd

27

Tips on Towing

First of all it is important to match the car to the caravan, or vice versa. Whether you have a good car and want to buy a caravan, or you have a good caravan but need a new car, some of the points here might help you to get the best performance from both vehicles.

Basically, the heavier the car the better, but certainly the car's kerbside weight must equal the maximum gross weight of the caravan. Should you have a penchant for long trips over mountainous roads, the car should be at least 25% heavier. The engine must be powerful enough to cope with the extra load too, but maximum brake horse power alone is not enough. A good torque at fairly low revs (something between 2,000 and 3,000 rpm) is what is needed. While high gearing may be conducive to fuel economy and good performance at high speeds, it does mean a lot of gear changing when there is a caravan in tow. Estate cars, which often have lower overall gearing, might be worth consideration. Automatic transmission incorporating a torque converter is ideal for pulling away on a gradient with caravan attached, but check with the manufacturer that it is suitable for towing – the addition of an oil cooler may be necessary.

When choosing a new car remember that cars with more length at the rear, and therefore greater distance between the rear wheels and the towing ball, tend to be more difficult to handle than cars with less overhang. The design and weight distribution of the caravan would, however, tend to have the greatest effect on overall performance.

Towing brackets

Before buying a towing bracket, check with the manufacturer the height of the towing ball from the ground, which should, of course, match up with the caravan coupling. If a perfect match is not possible, adjusters may be necessary to achieve a level ride. (When passengers and luggage are aboard the car and caravan are connected, the ball height will drop, possibly by 50mm (2in) or more.)

There is a vast range of brackets on the market, sometimes with very little to choose between them, and their prices can vary radically. It is best to shop around, but bear in mind that some imported towing brackets have an integral ball which makes height adjustment

impossible. A towing attachment ending in the standard two-holed faceplate is preferable in most cases. The diameter of the ball is defined by a British Standard as 50mm with a tolerance of + nil to − 0.25mm and another British Standard defines the coupling bolt holes as of 15mm (⅝in) clearance at 90mm (3½in) centres and the distance vertically between bolt hole centres and the centre of the ball as 70mm (2¾in). The height of the bolt hole centres above ground is defined as 405mm (16in) + 50mm (2in) with towing vehicle in kerb weight condition.

Fitting

On most cars, towing brackets are fairly easy to fit – all you need are elementary mechanical knowledge, a reasonable tool kit and the use of a pit, ramps or a strong axle stand. However, if you don't feel confident in your ability, don't risk it – the consequences of an incorrectly fitted bracket breaking loose could be very serious indeed. Go instead to a specialist fitter.

Generally it is unlikely that a well-maintained and properly fitted coupling will become detached, but, as an extra precaution, security chains are advised when practicable. Make sure, however, that both the chains and the attachments are strong enough to cope with any sudden impact.

Electrical

An internationally agreed 7-pin plug and socket system, wired in accordance with ISO standards, provides the electrical connections between the car and caravan/trailer. See diagram on page 31.

Since October 1979 it has been a legal requirement that all new cars and caravans (and all but the smallest trailers) are fitted with at least one working rear fog light. Because of this there has been a change in the 7-pin plug and socket wiring necessary when towing a new trailer. Pin 2/52 (blue wire), which was used to supply caravan accessories such as the interior lights, radio, water pump, etc, is now used to supply current for the caravan/trailer rear fog lights. Where a caravan/trailer requires an accessory supply, a separate 12S type plug and socket will be required. The 12S type socket is designed to accept a 7-pin plug which looks similar to the plug providing the trailer's lights but which has a different pin arrangement. The trailer manufacturer or hirer should be able to give advance information on the number and type of sockets which will be required on the towing vehicle.

In order to allow the flashing indicators to operate simultaneously on car and caravan at the legal rate of between 60 and 120 flashes per minute, a heavy-duty flasher unit or relay device is necessary. Wiring of the electrical connections involved in this modification is best left to a garage or auto electrical specialist.

Driving

Having selected a well-matched pair to take out on the road, newcomers to towing might appreciate a few helpful driving hints. First of all, remember that it is illegal for provisional licence holders to drive a car towing a trailer.

Basically, you must remember the three C's – **Care, Courtesy, Consideration** and if you follow the points listed below you won't go far wrong.

1. Know your car and how to drive it well before attempting to tow.

2. Stop before you get tired.

3. Check that car, caravan and towing gear are in top mechanical condition before setting off.

4. Plan the journey in advance, checking that the roads are suitable for towing.

5. Have the right mirrors and use them. Remember Mirror, Signal, Manoeuvre.

6. Keep well to the left of the road so that faster vehicles can overtake. If traffic builds up behind you, pull up in a safe place and let it pass.

7. Keep a safe stopping distance behind the vehicle in front.

8. See and be seen – switch on headlights whenever visibility gets poor.

9. Keep to the speed limit and make good use of the gears, especially on hills.

10. Allow plenty of time when overtaking or pulling across a main road.

11. Never stop on narrow roads, bends, crests of hills, or anywhere that could be dangerous to yourself and other road users.

12. In case of breakdown or accident, use hazard flashers or advance warning triangles.

Problems you may encounter as you drive along are pitching and snaking, which reduce stability and, of course, your control over the vehicle. Pitching and snaking should not occur if the nose weight is correct and if the heavier movable items have been stored as near as possible to the axle of the caravan. Check the nose weight of the laden caravan against the vehicle and caravan manufacturers' recommendations. Failing this, it could be a suspension problem so check that shock absorbers are in good condition and, if necessary, stiffen the rear suspension of the car. Excessive pitching can promote snaking as the vertical movement starts to sway the caravan sideways. The temptation may be to steer against the movement, but this will only make matters worse. The best course is to steer straight and decelerate slowly. If you have taken all the steps to eliminate pitching, you keep to a reasonable speed and snaking still persists, a stabiliser can provide some damping between car and trailer. This can take the form of a special coupling or tow ball mountings, or as a separate linkage.

One final tip – watch out for soft ground which is often encountered within a camp site such as waterlogged ground, sand, stone and shingle. If driving across such difficult terrain is unavoidable, keep moving slowly with a very light throttle. If you stop, do not accelerate hard or the wheels will spin and dig in. Move gently backwards and forwards to get out of the dip. If the driving wheels do dig in, dig out a gradient in front of the wheels and put brushwood or sacks in front of and behind the wheels. To move the trailer manually, pull sideways on the drawbar and work it forwards by chocking alternate wheels.

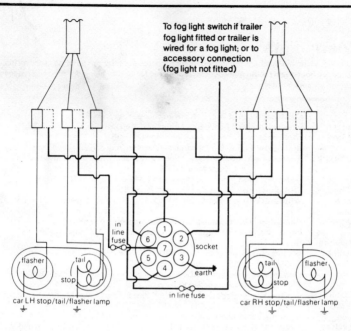

To fog light switch if trailer fog light fitted or trailer is wired for a fog light; or to accessory connection (fog light not fitted)

in line fuse

socket

earth

in line fuse

flasher   tail

stop

car LH stop/tail/flasher lamp

tail   flasher

stop

car RH stop/tail/flasher lamp

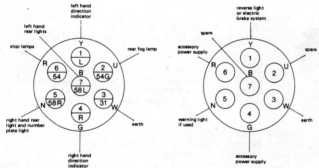

12N trailer lighting socket

left hand direction indicator

left hand rear lights

stop lamps

rear fog lamp

right hand rear light and number plate light

earth

right hand direction indicator

12S accessory socket

reverse light or electric brake system

spare

accessory power supply

spare

warning light if used

earth

accessory power supply

NB: Where the trailer is fitted with rear fog lights Pin 2 in the 12N socket (blue wire) is used for their supply; trailer accessories will require a 12S plug and socket (see diagrams).

Plug and socket Reference	
International Pin Number	Alternative Number
1	L L54
2	54G 52
3	31
4	R R54
5	58R 58S
6	54
7	58L 58C

W	White			R	Red	Y	Yellow
G	Green	N	Brown	B	Black	U	Blue
existing wiring							
additional wiring							
existing single snap connector							
existing single snap connector replaced with double snap connector							

AA Viewpoints

A full list of AA Viewpoints, which provide excellent panoramas of the surrounding countryside, is given below. They are not shown on the atlas but can be roughly located by using the map references given with each Viewpoint's name.

ENGLAND

Avon	Portishead 1 mile W of Portishead village Map 3ST47
Cornwall	Pendennis Head 1 mile SE of Falmouth Map 2SW83
Derbyshire	Highoredish 3 miles E of Matlock Map 84SK35
Dorset	Bulbarrow 5 miles S of Sturminster Newton Map 3ST70
Gloucestershire	Robinswood Hill 2 miles S of Gloucester City Centre in Robinswood Hill Country Park Map 3SO81
	Symonds Yat 3 miles N of Coleford off B4432 Map 3SO51
Hampshire	Portsdown Hill 1 mile N of Cosham Map 4SU60
Hereford & Worcester	Windmill Hill Waseley Country Park 3½ miles S of Halesowen Map 7SO97
Isle of Wight	Bembridge Down 2 miles ENE of Sandown Map 4SZ68
Kent	Farthing Corner on Farthing Corner service area M2 Map 5TQ86
Leicestershire	Beacon Hill 2 miles SW of Loughborough Map 8SK51
Oxfordshire	Wittenham Clumps 1½ miles off A4130 Nr Brightwell Map 4SU59
Shropshire	Clee Hills 6 miles E of Ludlow Map 3SO67
Somerset	Dunkery Beacon between Luccombe and Wheddon Cross Map 3SS84
	Wellington Monument 2½ miles S of Wellington Map 3ST11
Staffordshire	Central Forest Park Stoke-on-Trent. Part of City Centre reclamation scheme. Map 7SJ84
W Sussex	Duncton Hill 5 miles SW of Petworth Map 4SU91
Warwickshire	Magpie Hill in Burton Dassett Hills Country Park between Gaydon and Warmington Map 4SP35
Wiltshire	Barbury Castle in country park 5 miles S of Swindon Map 4SU17
N Yorkshire	Sutton Bank 5 miles E of Thirsk Map 8SE58
W Yorkshire	Holme Moss 1 mile from Holme to East of A6024 Map 7SK00

WALES

Anglesey	South Stack in South Stack reserve (RSPB) 3 miles W of Holyhead Map 6SH28
Dyfed	Foel Eryr 13 miles NE of Haverfordwest ½ mile W of B4329 Map 2SN03
Gwent	Sugar Loaf 3 miles NW of Abergavenny Map 3SO21
Gwynedd	Great Orme's Head on top of Great Orme, Llandudno Map 6SH78

SCOTLAND

Borders	Scott's View 3 miles E of Melrose 12NT53
Central	David Marshall Lodge 1 mile N of Aberfoyle Map 11NN50
	Queen's View Auchineden 6 miles N of Bearsden Map 11NS58
Highland	Bealach Na Ba' *(Pass of the Cattle)* 5 miles SE of Applecross Map 13NG74
	Knockan Cliff 8 miles NE of Ullapool Map 14NC20
	Struie Hill 6 miles SE of Bonar Bridge Map 14NH68
Lothian	Cockleroy Beecraigs Country Park, 2 miles S of Linlithgow Map 11NS97
Tayside	Queen's View 6 miles E of Tummel Bridge on B8019 Map 11NN85

Don't Drink & Drive

CAMPSITE

OF THE YEAR

1984

This year for the first time, the results of our search for the AA Campsite of the Year are being announced here in this guide, rather than in Drive & Trail Magazine. To find the winner we travelled almost the length of Britain, looking at all those sites which have the top qualative assessment in all three categories (see page 4). The nine finalists are all featured in the following pages, beginning with the 1984 winner of the AA Campsite of the Year award.

Winner

Campsite of the Year

Sea View International
Boswinger Cornwall

At Sea View International we found a site that has just about everything going for it — a superb location near the Cornish Coast, a favourable climate, but most of all an enthusiastic and hard-working owner. Donovan Michell and his family run this site on land which was previously farmed by his forbears. 'We started off putting a few campers in with the sheep and it has grown from there' Mrs Michell told us. Grown it certainly has, but not in size, for it is a fairly compact site compared to many. Its growth has rather been in the facilities and services offered to its customers and it is obvious that a great deal of thought has gone before any new development.

The nice thing about Sea View International is that it feels so spacious. Pitches are all numbered to avoid overcrowding in the two paddocks, but there is also plenty of space beyond. There is a four-acre playfield with lots of equipment, including a wooden fort and an aerial cable slide, a large covered barbecue and picnic tables. Beyond this another large area is set aside for campers to exercise their dogs.

The swimming pool area is really something special. The lie of the land enabled the pools to be constructed on a lower level than the rest of the site and they are overlooked by lovely paved terraces and gardens. Lots of sunbeds and patio furniture are set out for guests to use as well as table tennis, giant chess and shuffleboard. There is even a golf driving unit. Even though many campers stay on site during the day to make full use of these facilities, none of the usual shouts and squeals associated with pools and playgrounds penetrates as far as the camping ground. The whole idea is to keep it peaceful — a place for families — and that is why the Michells draw the line at providing a club-house or bar, but they have compromised as far as including an off-licence in their shop.

The single toilet block is ample for the site and is not too far away from any of the pitches. Inside lovely ceramic tiles add a touch of luxury and besides the normal showers there are two baths for small children. There is a well-equipped laundrette too, and at the back of the building a large freezer for campers' use. Here, beneath a delightful covered way, which is brightened by colourful hanging baskets, are two areas fitted out for dishwashing and vegetable preparation. Such buildings as these are so often an eyesore on sites, but here it is hardly visible at all in spite of its central position for it is well camouflaged by lovely flowering shrubs.

Flowers are very much in evidence all around the site, and even the water and waste points and the electricity supply points are disguised with pretty rockeries. Mr Michell is, in fact, a keen gardener, his particular passion being for fuschias which he grows by the hundreds in countless varieties in his nursery at the site. Fellow gardeners can buy cuttings and will no doubt spend a pleasant interlude discussing those delightful blooms with the knowledgable Mr Michell.

Most sites these days provide electric hook ups for caravans, but the Michells are also leading the field here by providing electricity for tents too. A special power pack can be hired which plugs into the normal supply adjacent to the pitch and this provides an electric light and a socket for such accessories as televisions, radios, hair dryers etc.

At the main reception office, where you are guaranteed a friendly welcome, all kinds of useful information is available. Not content with the usual tourist brochures and maps, they have also devised a number of drives to help newcomers to Cornwall to discover the best of the area. There is also a dispenser for free ice cubes which campers can collect whenever the office is open. It is this kind of thoughtfulness and care and attention to every little detail which distinguishes Sea View International and makes it an extremely worthy Campsite of the Year.

RUDA
HOLIDAY PARK

Luxury 6-berth holiday homes, with full facilities (inc. Colour T/V).

Superb camping and caravanning on 33 acres, next to beach and village of Croyde.

Free membership of 'Club Ruda' with top line entertainment - dancing and discos - 3 bars - chef's corner and cluboutique.

Also free entertainment for the younger ones at 'Teans Club' for the under 18s.

Excellent amenities and facilities include Free hot water in showers and wash basins, electric razor points, launderette, self-service shop, boutique, amusement arcade, hairdressing salon, camping equipment shop, burger bar, hair wash and dry and children's playground.

Good base for exploring North Devon and Exmoor.

The whole colourful, happy picture of Ruda, one of the smartest and best rated holiday parks in Britain is shown in our new colour brochure.

RUDA

Write to: **Dept AA,**
RUDA HOLIDAY
PARKS LTD.,
Croyde Bay, Braunton
N. Devon EX33 1NY
Tel: 0271 890671

Winner

South East Region

Bashley Park
New Milton Hampshire

Bashley Park, although very close to the holiday centres of New Milton and Christchurch, enjoys a lovely secluded setting amidst the woodland, gardens and grounds of a large, formerly private house. The approach along a long tree-lined drive is particularly attractive and, although this site includes a large number of static caravans and holiday chalets, the touring pitches are reached without any sight of these. Nice level grass with good roads and hard-standings for all touring caravans are found in the two paddocks which are screened by lovely mature trees and high hedges. Some of the pitches are actually situated amongst the woodland. Each area has its own central block with the usual toilet facilities, wash basins and showers and if you prefer to have a bath there is one available in the main building.

Here the old, red brick house has been converted and considerably extended to house all the reception and club house facilities. The information board just inside the entrance is very comprehensive with tourist leaflets, a large map of the area and lots of useful telephone numbers. The modern extension at the back of the house includes a spacious lounge bar with comfortable seating and an equally large area adjacent which has a dance floor surrounded by tables and chairs. Dances, discos and similar entertainments are a regular feature here throughout the summer season. Children are not allowed into the bar, of course, and so a large family room leads off to one side with a colour television in one corner. During the day this room opens out onto a large patio which surrounds the two heated pools. Lawns and gardens stretch away beyond the pools with open meadowland in the distance. Other facilities include tennis courts, putting, pitch and putt and a large amusement arcade and games room.

There is a very well-stocked supermarket-type shop and a separate shop selling such things as newspapers, books, games and souvenirs, while a useful extra is the hire shop stocking such items as portable televisions, cots and bicycles.

Winner

Midland Region

Moon and Sixpence
Waldringfield Suffolk

Although the site is often used by holidaymakers en route to and from Harwich and Felixstowe for the ferries, it is by no means just a transit site. Yachting enthusiasts also find it perfectly placed for sailing on the wide rivers Deben and Orwell and the surrounding Suffolk countryside is delightful.

The site is attractively laid out on ground which slopes down to its own lake in the centre. With a sandy beach at one end, a lovely wooded island and a family of ducks it is a lovely place to relax and is a natural suntrap. Many of the pitches have lovely views of the lake and some are on a terrace right above its banks. Plenty of mature trees and bushes surround the site and some new planting has been done, whilst here and there a bed of flowers will add a splash of colour.

In the centre of the site the main building, an attractive chalet-style structure contains the reception office, the laundry and toilet facilities. Nearby a low building contains the shop, restaurant and small, attractive clubhouse with rustic seating and doors which open out onto a paved terrace. Chairs and tables are set out here in nice weather to overlook the children's playground and there is a table-tennis table. Take-away meals are available at very reasonable prices and another alternative to cooking in the tent or caravan is the brick-built barbecue and adjacent log cabin which has kitchen facilities.

Additional toilet facilities are provided around the site with very stylish decor — coloured suites, ceramic tiles and vanity units with hand towel rings and liquid soap dispensers. Baths are available as well as showers.

Among the little extras provided on this site is a baby sitting service which operates during the day as well as in the evening for a very moderate cost.

Winner

North Region

Wild Rose Park
Appleby Cumbria

In the season, the hedgerows around the site are ablaze with the colour of the wild roses which give it its name. The surrounding countryside is beautiful too, with the River Eden close by and the dark peaks of the Pennines rising in the distance. The views from the site are far reaching, particularly at its highest point where some of the touring caravans are sited. More pitches are provided on slightly sloping ground lower down the site, where visitors can select their own place to pitch camp.

The toilet facilities are quite outstanding, with attractive ceramic tiles, separate cubicles for washrooms, hot air dryers and plenty of mirrors and shelves. There are also special sinks for washing babies and toilets suitable for wheelchair-bound visitors. The showers are all located at the central block for which keys are issued to all visitors. Behind the toilet blocks, covered areas contain dishwashing and vegetable preparation facilities with stainless steel sinks and drainers.

There is plenty to do on the site with a heated swimming pool, paddling pool and a small but well equipped playground. There is also a badminton court and table tennis tables outdoors. Among the main buildings is a games room with pool tables and a variety of machines and two TV rooms — one for BBC and one for ITV. The latter shows a programme of video films. To help visitors to discover the surrounding area there is a very good information room, its walls lined with posters, leaflets and local newspaper cuttings. In addition to this, each visitor to the park is given a 12-page newspaper packed with local information and useful advertisements.

The laundrette is roomy and well-equipped and has plenty of work surfaces as well as chairs and stacks of magazines to help pass the time. Nearby the Mini Market is crammed full of all kinds of camping requisites as well as groceries, fresh fruit and vegetables and an off-licence.

Wild Rose Park is a perfect choice for exploring the Lake District and the Pennines, or for breaking the long journey to Scotland.

Scottish Region

Craigtoun Meadows
St Andrews Fife

Golfing enthusiasts will be particularly keen to visit this site just a short distance from the lovely old town of St Andrews. The four famous courses are a mecca for golfers the world over, for this is the acknowledged home of the game. If you forget to put your clubs in the car, don't worry, because they can be hired from the site's well-stocked hire shop — and you don't need to belong to any exclusive club to play here.

The site is spacious and well-planned with good tarmac roads and tidily kept grass and is set amidst lovely woodland. The reception area and other facilities are housed in a long, low building right in the centre, with pretty flower borders and a large area for parking in front. Here, not only golf clubs, but also sun loungers, windbreaks and bicycles can be hired and all the usual groceries etc are on sale in the site shop. If you should tire of slaving over a camping stove, there is an attractive little restaurant with meals ranging from pizzas at 95p to T-bone steak at £6.50 and a special children's menu for around £1 (1983 prices). There is also a TV room where a programme of video films are shown with times displayed outside, and a well-equipped laundrette. There are plenty of toilet facilities, both in the touring paddocks and at the central complex.

Pitches are well spaced out with hard-standings and free electricity for all touring caravans, while the tent pitches all have an adjacent supply of water. Mostly the static caravans are separate from the touring pitches and are attractively set out between trees and flower beds. Apart from the lovely mature trees and shrubs, lots of new planting has been done which will continue to enhance the look of this first class site.

Runner Up

Woodland Caravan Park
Trimmingham Norfolk

Essentially a quiet, peaceful site, Woodland Caravan Park is, as its name suggests, beautifully located amidst mature trees not far from the lovely Norfolk coast. In fact, there are good sea views from the site entrance gate, off the coast road from Cromer to Mundesley. The long entrance drive leaves the sea views behind to enter the woodland which protects the site from the sometimes 'bracing' sea breezes. Some of the pitches are among the trees whilst others are on flat grassland and all are numbered to ensure adequate spacing.

Runner Up

Hoburne Farm
Christchurch Dorset

In the same holiday group as the South East Regional Winner, this site is run very much along the same lines, with a great deal of emphasis placed on club house facilities. Here they are contained in a purpose-built complex with a huge lounge bar/dance floor area, family room, restaurant and information area, together with amusement arcade and games room. The heated pools are in an attractive paved area with playground adjacent. There is a modern laundrette. Each of the paddocks for touring caravans has a central toilet block and hard standings with electric hook-ups.

Runner Up

Pentney Park
Narborough Norfolk

This lovely site occupies 17 acres which is a mixture of flat grassland and woodland, with pitches on each. Lovely colourful flower beds enhance the entrance and area around the main buildings which include a games room and a well-stocked shop. Opening times are arranged very much according to popular demand, with times displayed on the door. A children's playground is set out amongst the trees and plans are in hand for another at the other end of the site. A large swimming pool is also due to be ready for the 1984 season and future plans are for more sports facilities.

Runner Up

Leedons Park Broadway
Hereford & Worcester

Situated in the lovely Vale of Evesham, it is hardly surprising that fruit trees should number amongst the foliage around this lovely site. Lots of work has gone into landscaping and providing all the facilities its visitors could wish for. These include luxury toilet facilities with some family bathrooms. There is a kitchen too, which has stainless steel sinks and gas cookers and a fully automatic launderette with irons and ironing boards. For recreation there is a lovely heated swimming pool, two playground areas, games room and two TV rooms.

We've got sites for sore eyes

'No good – TRAIL gives it only three out of five for lack of noise – keep going'

Canny campers and money-conscious motorists never take to the road without *DRIVE&TRAIL* – the AA's monthly magazine. If a site's worth visiting, chances are we've been there before you. And if it's a new tent or tow-car you want, we have the last word in consumer tests by the world's largest motoring organisation. Make sure of your copy with 12 issues by post for £12.95 direct from the AA. Better still, use the special subscription form in *DRIVE&TRAIL* and we'll give you *FREE* the popular *AA Touring Map of Great Britain,* worth £1.50. Or you could qualify for a *FREE Big Road Atlas* worth £3.25. Either way, we'll keep you on the right track in 1984.

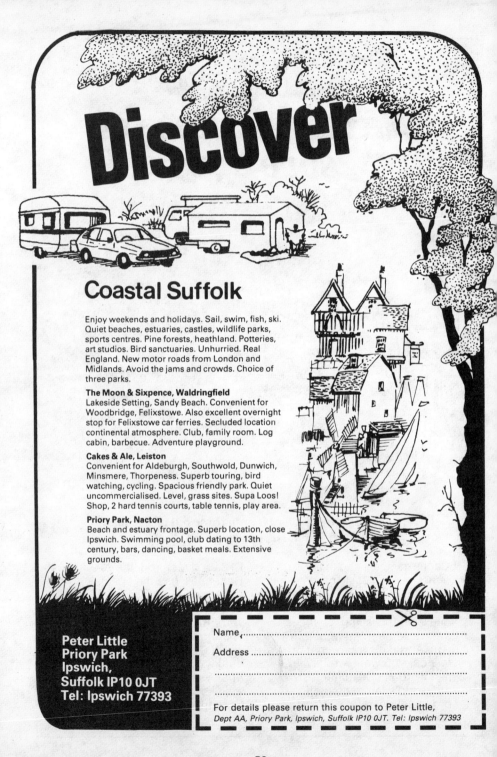

Discover

Coastal Suffolk

Enjoy weekends and holidays. Sail, swim, fish, ski. Quiet beaches, estuaries, castles, wildlife parks, sports centres. Pine forests, heathland. Potteries, art studios. Bird sanctuaries. Unhurried. Real England. New motor roads from London and Midlands. Avoid the jams and crowds. Choice of three parks.

The Moon & Sixpence, Waldringfield
Lakeside Setting, Sandy Beach. Convenient for Woodbridge, Felixstowe. Also excellent overnight stop for Felixstowe car ferries. Secluded location continental atmosphere. Club, family room. Log cabin, barbecue. Adventure playground.

Cakes & Ale, Leiston
Convenient for Aldeburgh, Southwold, Dunwich, Minsmere, Thorpeness. Superb touring, bird watching, cycling. Spacious friendly park. Quiet uncommercialised. Level, grass sites. Supa Loos! Shop, 2 hard tennis courts, table tennis, play area.

Priory Park, Nacton
Beach and estuary frontage. Superb location, close Ipswich. Swimming pool, club dating to 13th century, bars, dancing, basket meals. Extensive grounds.

Peter Little
Priory Park
Ipswich,
Suffolk IP10 0JT
Tel: Ipswich 77393

Name ....

Address ....

....

....

For details please return this coupon to Peter Little,
Dept AA, Priory Park, Ipswich, Suffolk IP10 0JT. Tel: Ipswich 77393

Directory of the Countryside

All over Britain areas of land have been set aside or developed to offer recreational facilities to the public and here we list, in county order, the National Parks, Country Parks and Picnic Sites that you may wish to visit on your travels. The ten National Parks are huge areas in which development is controlled, although much of the land is privately owned. Country Parks, on the other hand, are smaller and operated purely for the visitor. Many come under the management of local or county councils, others are privately owned and sometimes an entrance charge is levied. As for the Picnic Sites, all those that we list have been visited by an AA inspector and recommended as worthy of listing because they are sufficiently attractive and/or provide 'park and walk' access to the countryside. Some bear the name 'Transit Picnic Site' and these, though well-equipped, may be utilitarian in character. We list them for the benefit of those wishing to break a long journey for rest and refreshment.

To help you find the individual categories of places listed we have distinguished them as follows after the name and map reference etc:

CP   Country Park   **PS**   Picnic Site

National Parks are listed first after the county heading

England

AVON

Ashton Park *Map 3 ST57* **CP**
(OS172 ST555725). 1m S of Bristol, entrance from A369 and B3128. A large country house and park in a beautiful setting of grassland, woodland, and flowering shrubs. Deer Park, nature trail, pitch and putt golf. Management: Bristol District Council.

Chew Valley Lake *Map 3 ST56* **(Off B3114)** **PS**
8m S of Bristol centre on NE side of lake, on unclassified road from B3114 (OS172 ST577613). Signposted in advance and at entrance. 4 acres attractively landscaped with grassy mounds, shrubs and trees beside a large lake. Drinking water, furniture, toilet facilities for the disabled, local sailing and fishing. Cafeteria with outdoor seats or takeaway Apr–Oct each day Nov–Mar Sat and Sun only. Toilets. Parking 100.

Doddington House *Map 3 ST77* **CP**
(OS172 ST755795). 200yds from M4 junction 18 A46, near Chipping Sodbury. 365 acres. Landscaped and natural parkland with house, carriage museum and various features of interest. Inclusive admission fee to most amenities. Management: General Manager Doddington Chipping Sodbury.

Tog Hill *Map 3 ST77* **(A420)** **PS**
8m E of Bristol, ½m E of junction with A46 (OS172 ST734728). Signposted in advance and at entrance. Elevated site with grass, trees, shrubs and spectacular views. 2 acres, Drinking water, furniture. Chemical toilets. Parking 80.

BEDFORDSHIRE

Brogborough Hill *Map 4 SP93* **(A5140)** **PS**
On W side of A5140, 3½m NE of Woburn Sands (OS153 SP964386). Hilltop site. Drinking water, furniture. Toilets. Parking 50.

Dunstable Downs *Map 4 TL02* **(B4541)** **PS**
W side of B4541. 2m SW of Dunstable (OS166 TL007200). Signposted in advance and at entrance. Open green heath area. Overlooking the Vale of Aylesbury. Information Centre, refreshments, gliding activities.

Stewartby Lake *Map 4 TL04* **CP**
(OS153 TL008423) 5m SW of Bedford on A5140. 290 acres. Water sports. Management: Bedfordshire County Council.

Stockgrove Country Park, Heath and Reach
Map 4 SP92 **CP/PS**
(OS165 SP918293). 2½m N of Leighton Buzzard. 75 acres of woodland and parkland with lake. Fishing. Management: Bedfordshire County Council. **Picnic Site** on unclassified road, ½m W of A418, 3m NW of Leighton Buzzard (SP917298). Signposted in advance and at entrance. Drinking water, furniture, toilets.

Totternhoe Knolls *Map 4 SP92* **(B489)** **PS**
2m W of Dunstable, on E side of unclassified road off B489 (OS165 SP986216). Signposted in advance and at entrance. In village of Totternhoe. 3 acres. Good views, furniture, access to Norman castle.

Whipsnade Heath and Green *Map 4 TL01*
(Off B4540) **PS**
Adjacent to Whipsnade Zoo (OS166 TL006178). Open grass area. 10 acres. Extensive parking. Toilets.

BERKSHIRE

Alexandra Gardens *Map 4 SU97*
(Off A332 in Windsor) PS
Access via car park in River Street or Barry Avenue on
S side of Thames (OS175 SU962772). Riverside
gardens. 8 acres. Drinking water, furniture. Toilets.
Parking 200.

Bracknell/Bagshot road Transit Picnic Site
Map 4 SU96 **(A332) PS**
(OS175 SU902651). Toilets.

Childe Beale Wildlife Trust Conservation Area
Map 4 SU67 **(A329) PS**
2m NW of Pangbourne on A329 (OS175 SU626772).
Signposted in advance and at entrance. 15 acres.
Panoramic view of Thames, peacock farm, pheasant
aviary, ornamental stonework display, childrens play
area. Toilets. Parking 100 (fee). Open Wednesdays,
Thursdays, Saturdays and Sundays 10am–6pm.

Dinton Pastures *Map 4 SU77* **CP**
(OS175 SU785717). ¾m along B3030 to Twyford from
junction with A329. Entrance on left immediately after
A329M road bridge. Interesting landscape evolved
from gravel workings and containing two rivers and
seven lakes. Preserved wild life habitats, board sailing, fishing, windsurfing, warden service, golf course.

Marlow-Bisham by-pass *Map 4 SU88* **(A404) PS**
East Side: 2½m S of Marlow on A404 (OS175
SU851846); West Side: 3m S of Marlow on A404
(SU842833). Both are signposted in advance and at
entrance. Parking 30 at each.

Marlow, Winter Hill *Map 4 SU88* **PS**
First turn left on S side of Marlow Bridge. After approx
2m on unclassified Marlow/Cookham road, fork left
(OS175 SU875863). Grassy area with beech trees,
high above River Thames. 3 acres. Furniture. Parking
50.

Snelsmore Common *Map 4 SU47* **CP**
(OS174 SU461711). 3m N of Newbury on B4494. 145
acres of woodland and heath. Riding, picnicking.
Management: Newbury District Council.

Windsor Great Park *Map 4 SU97* **(A332) PS**
Ascot Road, 2m S of Windsor (OS175 SU960740).
Signposted in advance and at entrance. Parking.

BUCKINGHAMSHIRE

Black Park *Map 4 TQ08* **CP**
(OS176 TQ005833). Access via Black Park Road
(unclassified) N from A412 3m NE of Slough. 55 acres
of attractive woodland surrounding a lake, fishing,
swimming, pleasant walks, picnicking. Parking 350.
Management: Buckinghamshire County Council.

Burnham Beeches *Map 4 SU98* **(Off A355) PS**
On unclassified road ½m W of A355 at Farnham
Common (OS175 SU951851). Extensive site in forest
setting. Woodland walks, shelters, first aid post, furniture, drinking water. Toilets. Large parking area.

Chilterns Picnic Place (Hodgemoor Wood)
Map 4 SU99 **(Off A355) PS**
¼m E of A355 via Bottrells Lane, Amersham.
Beaconsfield 3m (OS175 SU958942). Woodland setting in Chiltern Hills. Extensive area. Parking 200.

Emberton Country Park *Map 4 SP85* **CP**
(OS152 SP887502) on W side of A509 at Emberton 1m
S of Olney. Signposted in advance and at entrance.

175 acres. Riverside and lakeland setting. Boating,
fishing, children's playground, first-aid post, picnicking. Parking 200. Management: Milton Keynes District
Council.

Langley Country Park *Map 4 TQ08* **CP**
(OS176 TQ009817). Access via Billet Lane (unclassified) S from A412 3m N of Slough. 110 acres. Large
woodland park with secluded gardens. Nature trail,
forest walks, rhododendron gardens, picnicking. Parking 100. Management: Buckinghamshire County
Council.

Wendover Forest *Map 4 SU80* **(Off A4011) PS**
SE of A4011 on unclassified road, signposted St
Leonards, 2m NE of Wendover, 3m SW of Tring
(OS165 SU889090). Signposted at entrance. An ex-
tensive and picturesque woodland site high in the
Chilterns with excellent views from several vantage
points. Walks and nature trails, information board and
map, furniture. Toilets with provision for the disabled.

CAMBRIDGESHIRE

Brandon Creek *Map 5 TL69* **(A10) PS**
2½m N of Littleport Bridge on A10 (OS143 TL608918).
Signposted in advance and at entrance. Landscaped
ground sloping to River Ouse. 4 acres. Drinking water,
furniture, toilet with facilities for the disabled. Parking
100.

Burghley Park *Map 4 TF00* **CP**
(OS141 TF032065). SE of Stamford.

Eaton Ford Picnic Area *Map 4 TL18* **(A45) PS**
Western outskirts of St Neots (OS153 TL180600).
Signposted at entrance. 3 acres, grassy tree-planted
riverside site. Furniture. Toilets. Parking 60.

Elton Park (Private Country Park) *Map 4 TL09* **CP**
(OS142 TL089934) A505 5m NE of Oundle.

Ferry Meadows *Map 4 TL19* **CP**
(OS142 TL145975) 2m W of Peterborough City Centre
on A605 and A57. 500 acres of grassland and lakes.
Within an area which is under development as the
Nene Valley Regional Park. Adjacent to the Nene
Valley footpath and the restored Nene Valley railway.
Own miniature steam railway. Roman remains, picnic
sites, natural history information centre. Facilities for
angling, boating, sailing, wind surfing, model boating,
riding and walking. Parking 100. Management: Peterborough Development Corporation.

Grafham Water (Three Picnic Sites) *Map 4 TL16*
(Off A1) PS
On B661 2½m from Buckden (OS153 TL164667).
Signposted in advance and at entrance. 3 acres. On
B661 3m from Buckden (OS153 TL144672). Sign-
posted in advance and at entrance. 3 acres. ¾m
along unclassified road to Grafham off B661 2m from
Buckden (OS153 TL166652). Signposted in advance
and at entrance, 3 acres. All overlook Grafham Water.
Drinking water, furniture, toilets, total parking 1,100.

Huntingdon *Map 4 TL27* **(A141) PS**
SE side Huntingdon ring road (OS153 TL243717) 2
acres. A strip of grassland with shrubs and trees
beside the Great Ouse River. Furniture, drinking water.
Toilets. Parking 100.

Houghton Mill *Map 4 TL27* **(A1123) PS**
1¼m out of Wyton towards Houghton, in Mill Street
(OS153 TL281720). A field sloping down to the River
Ouse, subject to flooding. 10 acres. Toilets. Parking
(fee).

Thorney *Map 4 TF20* **CP**
(OS142 TF288043) A47 7m NE of Peterborough.

Wandlebury Estate *Map 5 TL45* **CP**
(OS154 TL494536) Cambridge 5m S of City off A604.
Management: Cambridge Preservation Society.

CHESHIRE
Delamere Forest *Map 7 SJ57* **(Off B5152)** **PS**
1m N of Delamere off B5152 (OS117 SJ555700). AA
Viewpoint.

Eastham Country Park *Map 7 SJ38* **CP**
(OS108 SJ363816). Near junction of M53 and A41 S of
Eastham signposted from Eastham town centre. 71
acres. Attractive woodland and grassland beside the
River Mersey and entrance to the Manchester Ship
Canal. Nature trail, playground. Management: Bebing-
ton Metropolitan District Council.

Hartford Transit Picnic Site *Map 7 SJ67* **(A556)**
PS
½m S of Hartford (OS118 SJ691736). Toilets.

Little Budworth Common *Map 7 SJ56* **CP**
(OS117 SJ587657) W of Winsford. 90 acres. Heath,
woodland and moorland. Riding, picnicking. Management: Cheshire County Council.

Lyme Park *Map 7 SJ98* **CP**
(OS109 SJ965820). Near Disley, SE of Stockport.
1,320 acres. Parkland and moorland. Stately home,
children's playground, walking, nature trail, putting,
winter sports, riding. Management: Stockport Metropolitan District Council.

Marbury Park *Map 7 SJ67* **CP**
(OS118 SJ653762) 2m N of Northwich. 190 acres.
Woodland and pasture. Arboretum, lake, waterbus,
picnicking. Management: Cheshire County Council.

Risley Moss *Map 7 SJ69* **CP**
(OS109 SJ663922) Main entrance ¾m SW Junction
11 M62. Ordnance Avenue Birchwood. Visitor Centre,
Ranger Service. Accompanied walk through the
mossland.

Styal Country Park *Map 7 SJ88* **CP**
(OS109 SJ835833). From Wilmslow B5166 to Styal
Village. 80 acres. Wooded river valley. Quarry Bank
Cotton Mill 18th-C and Styal model village with many
unusual buildings. Management: National Trust.

Teggs Nose *Map 7 SJ97* **CP**
(OS118 SJ948724). N of Langley, 2m E of Mac-
clesfield off A537. 135 acres. Foothill of the Pennines
with woodlands, grass and heath. Rugged summit
formerly quarried. Viewpoint, nature trail, picnicking,
riding. Management: Cheshire County Council.

Wirral Countryside Park – see Merseyside

CORNWALL
Mitchell *Map 2 SW85* **(A30)** **PS**
½m E of junction with A30 76 on outskirts of Hamlet of
Mitchell (OS200 SW867548) signposted at entrance.
Separated from A30 by wide grass verge, furniture.
Toilets. Parking 60.

Mount Edgcumbe House and Country Park
Map 2 SX45 **CP**
(OS201 SX455533). Off B3247 to Cremyll. Parkland
and formal gardens under restoration. Tudor mansion
open 1 May–30 Sep, 2pm–6pm (fee). Deer park, play
area, footpaths, bridleways. Warden Service. Management: City of Plymouth and Cornwall County
Council.

Tregadillet Transit Picnic Site *Map 2 SX38* **(A30)**
PS
2m W of Launceston on A30 (OS201 SX305842).
Toilets.

Treliever *Map 2 SW73* **(A394)** **PS**
1½m W of Penryn (OS204 SW767351). Signposted in
advance and at entrance. Tarmac parking area with
grassed picnic section protected by 5ft banks. Drinking water, furniture. Toilets. Parking 25.

Trebarwith Strand *Map 2 SX08* **(B3263)** **PS**
1½W B3263 outskirts of Trebarwith Strand. (OS200
SX052865) signposted at entrance. By a small stream
in a valley leading to a sandy beach. Furniture.
Parking 100.

CUMBRIA
The Lake District National Park (866 square miles)
High mountains, clear blue lakes and woodland.
Correspondence should be sent to Information
Officer, National Park Offices, Busher Walk, Kendal,
Cumbria LA9 4RH *tel* Kendal (0539) 24555.
Information Centres:

Ambleside	Old Court House, Church Street *tel* 3084 summer only
Bowness	Bowness Bay, Glebe Road, *tel* Windermere 2895 closed Jan–Mar
Coniston (caravan)	Village car park *tel* 533 summer only
Glenridding (caravan)	Car Park *tel* 414 summer only
Hawkshead (caravan)	Main car park *tel* 525 summer only
Keswick	Moot Hall *tel* 72883 closed Jan–Mar
Pooley Bridge (caravan)	Car Park *tel* 530 summer only
Seatoller	adjacent to village car park *tel* Borrowdale 294 summer only
Waterhead (caravan)	Car park at head of lake *tel* Ambleside 2729 summer only
Windermere	National Park Centre. Brockhole *tel* 2231 closed Dec–Mar
Caravan Advisory Service	*tel* Windermere 5555/5515
Weather Information Service	*tel* Windermere 5151/2/3/4

Aira Force *Map 11 NY32* **(A5091/A592)** **PS**
6m SW of Pooley Bridge (OS90 NY398201). Signposted at entrance. National Trust property. 50 acres.
View of Ullswater and fells, waterfall and woodland
walks, furniture, no caravans in car park, no camping.
Parking 100.

Allonby & Beckfoot *Map 11 NY04* **(B5300)** **PS**
On B5300, on the coast, within the parish of Allonby
(OS85 NY080430). Signposted in advance and at
entrance. View across Solway Firth. Furniture. Toilets.
Parking 100.

Bardsea Country Park *Map 7 SD27* **CP**
(OS96 SD299740). Morecombe Bay. 2m S of Ulverston on A5087. Woodland and shingle beach. Nature
trail. Management: Cumbria County Council.

Brockhole *Map 7 NY30* **(A591)** PS
2½m N of Windermere, 2½m S of Ambleside (OS90 NY391011) half acre. Parking 20.

Fell Foot *Map 7 SD38* CP
(OS96 SD381869). Near Newby Bridge on E shore of Lake Windermere. 18 acres. Wood and grassland by lake shore, swimming, sailing, canoeing, fishing. Management: National Trust.

Lowther Wildlife Park *Map 12 NY52* CP
(OS90 NY536236). Access near Lowther Village. Off A6 5m S of Penrith.

Ouse Bridge *Map 11 NY23* **(Off B5291)** PS
6m E of Cockermouth (OS90 NY200322). Signposted in advance and at entrance. Half acre. Footpath to Bassenthwaite. Parking 20.

Stock Lane Trànsit Picnic Site *Map 7 NY30* **(B5287)** PS
300yds Grasmere Village. (OS90 NY338074). Toilets.

Talkin Tarn *Map 12 NY55* CP
(OS86 NY545588). 11m S of Brampton E of Carlisle on B6431. 151 acres. Woodland and pasture, lake, rowing, sailing, swimming, fishing, riding. Management: Cumbria County Council.

Waterhead Transit Picnic Site *Map 7 NY30* **(A5075/591)** PS
½m SE of Ambleside. (OS90 NY377032). Toilets.

Whinlatter *Map 11 NY22* **(B5292)** PS
1m from Braithwaite (OS90 NY230237). Signposted in advance and at entrance. Half acre. Extensive view of valley and lake. Parking 20.

DERBYSHIRE
The Peak District National Park (542 square miles)
The Derbyshire Dales, high moorland, caves and stately homes. Correspondence should be sent to Information Officer, Peak District National Park, Aldern House, Baslow Road, Bakewell, Derbyshire DE4 1AE *tel* Bakewell (062981) 4321 (closed weekends).
Information Centres:

Bakewell	Market Hall, Bridge Street *tel* 3227 closed Wed and Thu in winter
Castleton	Castle Street *tel* Hope Valley 20679 closed Mon, Tue, Thu and Fri in winter.
Edale	Field Head *tel* Hope Valley 70207/70216
Goyt Valley	Derbyshire Bridge summer Sundays only
Hartington	Old Station summer Saturdays and Sundays only

Alsop en le Dale Station *Map 7 SK15* **(A515)** PS
On Ashbourne–Buxton road 5½m N of Ashbourne (OS119 SK156549). Signposted at entrance. On former station site lying on the line of the Buxton–Ashbourne Railway, now the Tissington Trail, furniture. Parking 60.

Ashover (Eddlestow) *Map 8 SK36* **(Off A632)** PS
Off A632 (SP Uppertown) 2½m NE of Matlock (OS119 SK324632). Signposted in advance and at entrance. 3 acres. Map of area, furniture. Parking 20.

Black Rocks *Map 8 SK25* **(Off B5036)** PS
E of B5036. 1½m S of Cromford (OS119 SK292557). Signposted in advance and at entrance. 5 acres.

Access to High Peak Trail, drinking water, furniture. Toilets with facilities for the disabled. Parking 25.

Buxton Country Park, Pools Cavern *Map 8 SK07* CP
(OS119 SK048726). Green lane off A515 Buxton, tree-planted limestone quarry. Show cave, woodland walks, nature trail. Management: Buxton and District Civic Association.

Elvaston Castle and Country Park *Map 8 SK43* CP
(OS129 SK406327) 6m SE of Derby off B5010. Can be approached via A52, A6005 or A6. All approaches signposted. 200 acres. Woodland, parkland with gardens and castle, lake, canoeing, fishing, nature trail, children's playground. Car parking charge at weekends. disabled drivers have free access to castle courtyard via Castle Drive and may park in courtyard adjacent to riding school. Management: Elvaston Castle Joint Management Committee (Derbyshire County Council and Derby District Council).

Hardwick Hall *Map 8 SK46* CP
(OS120 SK463638). Doe Lea, 6½m SE of Chesterfield, Hall and parkland, lakes, canoeing, fishing, nature trail within the Peak National Park. Management: National Trust.

Hartington *Map 7 SK16* **(Off B5054)** PS
1½m NE of Hartington (OS119 SK150611). Signposted at entrance. 1½ acres. On the site of old Moneystones Station on the Tissington Trail, drinking water, furniture. Toilets. Parking 60.

Hurdlow *Map 7 SK16* **(Off A515)** PS
¼m W of A515, Monyash–Longnor road (OS119 SK127659). Signposted at entrance. Access to Tissington Trail, furniture. Parking 50.

Longshaw Estate *Map 8 SK27* CP
(OS119 SK260795). 4m NW of Mansfield, 9m SW Sheffield in Peak National Park. Meadows and woodland, nature trail, rock climbing, nature reserve. Management: National Trust.

Middleton Top *Map 8 SK25* **(Off B5023)** PS
S of Rise End, W of B5023 via unclassified road under old railway bridge. 1m NW of Wirksworth (OS119 SK275551). 1 acre. Access to High Peak Trail, Middleton Top Power House, drinking water, furniture. Toilets with facilities for the disabled. Parking 25.

Ogston Reservoir *Map 8 SK36* **(Off B6014)** PS
North: 2m SW of Clay Cross on N side of B6014 on unclassified road at Woolley (OS119 SK368613). Signposted 'car park'. Grass area fenced from water. 5 acres. Drinking water. Toilets.
West: S side of B6014 at N end of reservoir (SK369608). Signposted at entrance. Grass area of ½ acre. Drinking water, toilets, parking 25.

Parsley Hay *Map 7 SK16* **(Off A515)** PS
200yds on W side of A515 8¼m S of Buxton (OS119 SK147636). Signposted in advance and at entrance. 2 acres. Former railway station site on junction between Tissington and High Peak. Trails, Cycles for hire April-October, drinking water, furniture. Toilets. Parking 60.

Shipley *Map 8 SK44* CP
(OS129 SK433440) 8m NE Derby. Off A608 at Heanor. 324 acres. Wood and meadowland, reservoir, zoo, museum, water sports, nature trail, picnicking. Management: Derbyshire County Council.

Staunton Harrold Reservoir *Map 8 SK32*
(Off B587) PS
1m SW of Melbourne. Turn W off B587 along Calke
Lane (OS128 SK379244). Lawns planted with young
trees. 2 acres. Observation tower, drinking water.
Toilets. Parking 70.

Tissington *Map 7 SK15* **(Off A515)** PS
SE corner of Tissington village ½m E of A515. (OS119
SK177521). Signposted at entrance. 2 acres. Situated
on the Tissington Trail, drinking water, furniture.
Toilets. Parking 60.

White Lodge *Map 7 SK17* **(A6)** PS
On W side of A6, 4m W of Bakewell (OS119
SK165709). Signposted in advance and at entrance. 3
acres. Useful access point to Monsal Dale, information
board giving details of local walks, furniture, portaloo.
Parking 40.

DEVON

Dartmoor National Park (365 square miles)
High remote moorland, rocky tors, picturesque vil-
lages and lovely river valleys. Correspondence should
be sent to Information Officer, 'Parke', Haytor Road,
Bovey Tracey, Newton Abbot, Devon TQ13 9JQ, *tel*
Bovey Tracey (0626) 832093.
Information Centres:

Newbridge (caravan)	summer only
Postbridge (caravan)	summer only
Princetown	Town Hall summer only
Steps Bridge (caravan)	summer only
Tavistock	Bedford Square summer only

Exmoor National Park–see under Somerset

Bellever *Map 2 SX67* **(Off B3212)** PS
1¼m S of B3212 at Postbridge (OS191 SX645772).
Moorland. 1 acre. Bridle paths. Toilets. Parking 100.

Berry Head *Map 3 SX95* CP
(OS202 SX941565) E of Brixham. 100 acres. Within
area of outstanding natural beauty. High limestone
headland with lighthouse, Napoleonic fortifications
and linked to a long distance footpath system. Nature
reserve, nature trails, warden, leaflets available, on
site, cafe, car park. Management: Torbay District
Council.

Clyst Honiton Transit Picnic Site *Map 3 SX99*
(A30) PS

½m E of Clyst Honiton (OS192 SX992941). Signposted in advance and at entrance. Adjacent to Exeter
Airport. 1 acre. Furniture. Parking 30.

Eggesford Forest *Map 2 SS61* **(A377)** PS
1m S Eggesford Railway Station (OS191 SS694105).
Signposted at entrance. Close to main road in rural
wooded area, information board. Nature trails. Furniture. Toilets. Parking 20.

Farway Countryside Park *Map 3 SY19* CP
(OS192 SY187932) Holnest Farm 4m S of Honiton. 70
acres. Woodland, heath and pasture, farm animals,
donkeys and ponies. Management: Mrs J M Forbes,
Holnest Farm, Farway, Devon.

Fernworthy Reservoir *Map 2 SW68*
(Unclassified rd) PS
Approach via unclassified rds 3¾m SW of Chagford
(OS191 SW669838). Signposted at entrance. Near
forest and reservoir. 1 acre. Forest trail, signed walks.
Furniture. Toilets including facilities for disabled. Park-
ing 50.

Grand Western Canal Country Park *Map 3 ST91*
CP
(OS181 ST963123). Tiverton Basin car park A373
Tiverton. 11½m of restored canal and towpath with
open views, deep cuttings and wooded banks, running NE from Tiverton and linking a number of quaint
villages. Access parking difficult except at Tiverton
Basin, from which a horsedrawn barge provides
excursions and boats may be hired, non-powered
boats may be licensed by written application to the
County Estates Surveyor. Fishing permits available at
local tackle shops. Toilets at Tiverton Basin. Management: Devon County Council.

Little Haldon *Map 3 SX97* **(B3192)** PS
Exeter–Teignmouth road opposite Teignmouth golf
course (OS192 SX918766). Extensive hill top site with
access to gorseland. No toilets. Parking 100.

Morwellham *Map 2 SX46* **(Off A390)** PS
In Tamar Valley 4m SW of Tavistock, 1m S of A390
(OS201 SX446695). Old iron ore river port of historical
interest. Drinking water, furniture. Toilets. Parking 100.

Newbridge, Holne *Map 3 SX77* **(B3357)** PS
4m W of Ashburton (OS201 SX711709). Signposted in
advance and at entrance. Moorland, woodland walks.
8 acres. Toilets. Parking 100.

River Dart Country Park *Map 3 SX77* CP
(OS202 SX733702) 1m from Ashburton on B3357. 80

acres in South Dartmoor, moorland and riverside walks, boating lake, licensed restaurants, heated swimming pool, adventure playgrounds, nature trail, fishing, picnic site. Entrance fee. Parking 200. Management: The River Dart Country Park Limited.

Tamar Bridge Transit Picnic Site   *Map 2 SX45* **(A38) PS**
At E end of bridge on A38 (OS201 SX438587). Toilets. Parking 50.

Trimstone Cross   *Map 2 SS54* **(Off A361) PS**
1m SW of Mullacott Cross (OS180 SS503430). Signposted at entrance. Old road adjacent to grass area. Attractive site but not easily seen from road. 3½ acres. Furniture. Parking 60.

DORSET

Bishops Lime Kiln   *Map 3 ST58* **(Off B3157) PS**
Off B3157 on narrow steep unclassified road from centre of Abbotsbury to Hardy's monument. ¾ acre. (OS194 ST585857). Signposted at entrance. Remote rural setting with well-preserved remains of lime kiln. Explanatory metal tablet, panoramic views to Chesil Beach. Furniture. Parking 12.

Buckham Down   *Map 3 ST40* **(Off A3066) PS**
1m N Beaminster (OS193 ST476033). Signposted in advance and at entrance. Elevated site with panoramic views (2 acres). Furniture. Parking 20.

Bulbarrow Hill   *Map 3 ST70* **(Off A354) PS**
5m S Sturminster Newton on unclassified road off A354 signposted from Bulbarrow crossroads (OS194 ST775055). Gravelled area on hill top with AA Viewpoint.

Durleston   *Map 3 SZ07* **CP**
(OS195 SZ034773) 1½m S of Swanage on road to Anvil Point Lighthouse. 261 acres of natural coastland within the Dorset Area of Outstanding Natural Beauty and a designated part of the Heritage Coastline forming the SE corner of the Isle of Purbeck. Designated area of scientific interest with geological features and wildlife. Cliffs with seabird colonies, mixed shrubs, trees and grassland. Tilly Whim Caves, 19th-C castle, path to lighthouse, guided walks, picnic areas. Information centre, Warden service, ample centralised car parking. Management: Dorset County Council.

Gallows Hill   *Map 3 SY89* **(Unclassified road) PS**
Adjacent to Army Training Area, from A352 Dorchester–Wareham road on unclassified road N of Wool to Bere Regis road approx 3m on W side (OS194 SY844918). Extensive area of gorse moorland. Signposted walks, furniture. Parking 25.

High Kingston Transit Picnic Site   *Map 3 SY79* **(Off A35) PS**
2¼m E of Dorchester, N side. Wide tarmacadam layby. (OS194 SY724929). Toilets. Parking 40.

Ibberton Hill   *Map 3 ST70* **(Unclassified road) PS**
5m S of Sturminster Newton/Blandford A357 on unclassified road through Okeford Fitzpaine. (OS194 ST784071). Signposted at entrance. Elevated grassy slopes overlooking rural Dorset. 10 acres. Parking 100.

Matchams View   *Map 4 SX10* **(A358) PS**
7m NE Bournemouth on E side of unclassified road (OS195 SX134024). Signposted at entrance. Tarmacadam drive into Avon Pumping Station. Peaceful

wooded area on plateau with winding river, approach through heathland. 30 acres. Parking 40.

Okeford Hill   *Map 3 ST80* **(Unclassified road) PS**
Between Turnworth and Okeford Fitzpaine (OS194 ST813094). Remote isolated site short walk from car park. Furniture.

Steeple Picnic Area   *Map 3 SY98* **(Unclassified road) PS**
Off unclassified roads N of Steeple Village (OS195 SY912818). Level elevated site on ridge with outstanding views. Parking 40.

Thorncombe Wood   *Map 3 SY79* **(Off A35) PS**
2½m E of Dorchester on unclassified road signposted to Higher/Lower Bockhampton (OS194 SY728925). Signposted in advance and at entrance. Attractive woodland. 45 acres. Map display and leaflets. Footpath to Thomas Hardy's cottage. Marked trails, furniture. Parking 30.

Upton Park   *Map 3 SY99* **CP**
(OS195 SY992933) S side of A35. 1m W Fleetbridge intersection entrance off slip road to Upton. Extensive parkland beside Holes Bay, interesting collection of shrubs and trees, nature trail, picnic area, warden service at weekends. Management: Borough of Poole.

DURHAM

Carricks Picnic Area   *Map 12 NZ95* **(B6306) PS**
1½m E of Blanchland, 5m W of Consett, N of B6278, adjacent to Derwent Reservoir and the River Derwent (OS87 NZ976505). Large grassed area, 3 acres.

Collier Wood   *Map 12 NZ13* **(A68) PS**
½m N of junction with A689 midway between Crock and Towlaw (OS92 NZ128364). Signposted in advance and at entrance. Mixed woodland area 8 acres, nature trail, information boards, drinking water, furniture. Toilets. Parking 40.

Cowhill   *Map 12 NZ05* **(B6306) PS**
SE side of Derwent Reservoir on B6306 (OS87 NZ010520).

Crimdon Park   *Map 8 NZ43* **(A1086) PS**
A1086 4m N of Hartlepool (OS88 NZ483370). Signposted in advance 25 acres. Beach bathing, day chalets, first-aid box, furniture. Toilets. Parking 560.

Derwent Walk   *Map 12 NZ1615* **CP**
Access point from B6310 (OS88 NZ104535) Derwent Valley between Swadwell and Consett. 10½m footpath, bridleway and cycle track following an old railway track through a wooded valley, connecting various features converted to picnic sites, including Shotley Bridge, Information Centre at Ebchester Station B6309 (NZ107549). Management: Durham County Council and Tyne & Wear Metropolitan County Council.

Finchale Priory   *Map 12 NZ24* **(A167) PS**
1½m N of Durham. Turn right on to unclassified road at Pity Me and continue for 1¾m (OS88 NZ296472). Wooded priory grounds with river. 10 acres. Drinking water, furniture. Toilets. Unlimited parking.

Hamsterley Forest   *Map 12 NZ03* **(Unclassified road) PS**
Hamsterley is signposted from Witton le Wear off A68 (OS92 NZ073305). Extensive area of wooded hills. Drinking water, furniture, swimming pool. Toilets. Unlimited parking (fee).

Hardwick Hall *Map 12 NZ32* **CP**
(OS93 NZ346289) Sedgefield 10m S of Durham on
A177 40 acres reclaimed from remains of the former
Hardwick Park and Gardens. Serpentine lake partly
restored with the remainder containing a 5-acre fen
traversed by a nature trail raised, upon board walk.
Fishing, picnicking, access from A177. Management:
Durham County Council & Sedgefield DC.

Holmland Park Transit Picnic Site *Map 12 NZ25*
(A167) **PS**
½m from Chester-Le-Street on A167 (OS88
NZ270535).

Middleton-One-Row *Map 8 NX31* **(Off A67)** **PS**
5m SE of Darlington off A67 (OS93 NX350125).
Signposted in advance. River, trees and views of
Cleveland Hills, deep riverbank with paths. Furniture.
Toilets. Parking at roadside.

Park Wall *Map 12 NZ13* **(Off A68)** **PS**
1m S of Tow Law (OS92 NZ131379) 11 acres.

Pow Hill *Map 12 NZ05* **CP**
(OS87 NZ011518). Between Derwent Reservoir and
B6306 Edmundbyers/Blanchland. Laid out with picnic
areas, extensive tree planting, footpaths on upper
slopes overlooking sailing activities. 45 acres. Fishing,
birdwatching. Management: Durham County Council.

Shotley Bridge *Map 12 NZ15* **(B6310)** **PS**
At Shotley Bridge. 1m N of Consett on A694, take
B6310 for ¾m (OS88 NZ104535). Former station yard
with access to Derwent Walk. 3 acres.

Swan House *Map 8 NZ22* **(A68)** **PS**
At junction with A6072 4m NW of Darlington on A68
(OS93 NZ252200) 1½ acres.

Waldridge Fell *Map 12 NZ24* **CP**
1m SW of Chester-le-Street (OS88 NZ250497). Moorland. Management: Durham County Council.

Whorlton *Map 13 NZ11* **(Off A67)** **PS**
3½m SE of Barnard Castle off A67 (OS93 NX350146).
Advance signposting to village only. 10-acre field
beside a river. Drinking water. Toilets. Parking 100
(fee).

Witton le Wear *Map 12 NZ13* **(A68)** **PS**
E of A68 ½m S of Witton le Wear (OS92 NZ147307).
15 acres. Castle, paddling pool, snack bar, drinking
water, furniture. Toilets.

Witton le Wear Lido *Map 12 NZ13* **(A68)** **PS**
½m S of Witton le Wear (OS92 NZ148307). Riverside
area suitable for children. 2 acres. Drinking water.
Toilets. Unlimited parking (fee).

ESSEX

Cudmore Grove *Map 5 TM01* **CP**
(OS168 TM060150) East Mersea, Mersea Island approached from Bromans Lane. 35 acres of coastal
land with access to beach. Warden service. Parking
fee. Management: Essex County Council.

Danbury Park *Map 5 TL70* **CP/PS**
(OS167 TL768048) 5m E of Chelmsford approached
from the A414 on A130 through Sanden Village or Well
Lane, Danbury. Developed from the lakeside gardens
of Danbury Palace and adjoining woodland and parkland. Day permits for fishing available from the water
bailiffs. Management: Essex County Council. **Picnic**

Site adjoining Well Lane on SW side of Danbury
Bridge, off A414 (TL765048). Advance signposting.
Shrubs and grass amidst wooded parkland centred
on well-maintained lake. Furniture, toilets, parking 80.

Hatfield Forest *Map 5 TL52* **CP**
(OS167 TL537201) On A120 4m E of Bishop's Stort-
ford. 1,010 acres of woodland with lake. Boating,
fishing. Management: National Trust.

Langdon Hills West *Map 5 TQ68* **CP**
(OS177 TQ683865) S of Basildon. 200 acres of
woodland and grassland, on one of the highest points
in Essex. Car parks, signposted off Dry Street and
near the Crown Hotel. Management: Essex County
Council.

Naze Point *Map 5 TM22* **(Off A136)** **PS**
N of Walton-on-the-Naze. E side of Old Hall Lane via
Esplanade and Naze Park Road. (OS169 TM264234).
Grassy clifftop area. Nature trail. No caravans or tents.
Toilets. Parking 300.

One Tree Hill *Map 5 TQ68* **(A13/B1420)** **PS**
2m SW of Basildon, N of A13 near junction with B1420
(OS177 TQ695860). Good views of surrounding area.
6 acres. Toilets. Parking 350.

Picnic Site *Map 5 TQ69* **(Off A128)** **PS**
1m SE of Brentwood off 'The Avenue' (OS177
TQ605915). Densely wooded with areas of bracken
and grass. 100 acres.

Thorndon Country Park *Map 5 TQ69* **CP/PS**
(OS177 TQ630900) Brentwood. Off A128 or B186.
Two separate areas approx 2 acres each. Lion Lodge
TQ630900 – area of woodland with wide paths.
Parking off main carriageway through Lion Gates.
Southern Section (TQ615913) off A128 ½m N of
Halfway House roundabout – 50 acres of open grass-
land, 150 acres of woodland with rides and open
glades. Management: Essex County Council. **Picnic
Site** at East Horndon on W side of A128, ½m N of
junction with A127 (TQ631900). Furniture, parking
200.

Upper Mardyke Valley *Map 5 TQ68* **CP**
(OS177 TQ610815) E of S Ockendon between Mol-
lands Lane, Buckles Lane and the Mardyke river. 64
acres under development but open for general use,
sailing, water ski-ing, sub-aqua diving at Grangewater
Water Recreation Centre. Management: Thurrock
Borough Council.

Weald Park *Map 5 TQ59* **CP/PS**
(OS177 TQ570945) 2m NW of Brentwood. 428 acres
of park and woodland. Horse-riding permitted on 56
acres. Parking off Weald Road and Lincolns Lane.
Management: Essex County Council. **Picnic Site** on
unclassified road off A128 at Pilgrims Hatch
(TQ570945). Signposted at entrance. Extensive area.
Drinking water. Parking 200.

Westley Heights *Map 5 TQ68* **CP**
1m S of Basildon off B1007 (OS177 TQ681863) Park,
woodland and nature trails. Management: Essex
County Council.

GLOUCESTERSHIRE

Aust Services Transit Picnic Site *Map 3 ST58*
(M4) **PS**
Off Junction 21 at Severn Bridge (OS162 ST568897).
Motorway sign in advance. 5 acres. Undulating area of

grass overlooking Severn Bridge and estuary. Drinking water, toilets and usual motorway service area facilities. Parking 350.

Beechenhurst *Map 3 SO61* **(B4226)** **PS**
N side of road 2½m E Coleford. ½m W of Speech House. (OS162 SO614119). Forestry Commission sign at entrance. 5 acres in Forest of Dean. Oak Woodland, open lawns, fire hearths, forest trail. Drinking water, furniture. Toilets (closed in winter). Parking 150.

Cannop Ponds *Map 3 SO61* **(B4226)** **PS**
Off B4226 (S side of road) 2m E Coleford 1m W of Speech House (OS162 SO609106). Signposted at entrance. On forest track, around two small lakes in secluded area of Forest of Dean. Fishing (permit required). 2 acres. Signed forest trails. Parking 15.

Coaley Park Picnic Site *Map 3 SO70* **(Off B4066)**
PS
2½m N of Uley (OS162 SO795014). Signposting in advance and at entrance. A superb viewpoint near a gliding centre. Furniture. Toilets. Ample parking.

Edge End *Map 3 SO51* **(A4136)** **PS**
On A4136, 2½m E of Coleford (OS162 SO595135). Signposted in advance and at entrance. Secluded wooded site on the edge of the Forest of Dean. 1 acre. Signed forest walks, drinking water, furniture. Toilets (closed in winter). Parking 50.

Keynes Park (Cotswold Water Park) *Map 4 SU09*
CP
(OS163 SU028957) Ashton Keynes 4m S of Cirencester. Access: off A419 2½m NW of Cricklade or off A417 1m E of Fairford, 3m W of Lechlade. 100 acres. Reclaimed gravel workings forming a series of lagoons which attract a diversity of waterfowl and other wildlife, picnicking areas, fishing by day permit, also sailing subject to evidence of boat insurance, launching facilities, dinghy park, sailing club, warden service. No bathing. Management: Gloucestershire and Wiltshire County Councils and Local Councils through Joint Committee.

Lamsquay *Map 3 SO50* **(B4228)** **PS**
1m S of Coleford (OS162 SO582085). Signposted at entrance, screened parking areas planted with young trees. Play area, pleasant views, furniture, drinking water. Toilets. Parking 120.

Peters Cross Transit Picnic Site *Map 3 ST59*
(A48) **PS**
On the Lydney to Chepstow section of the A48. 1m SW of Alvington (OS162 ST589993). Signposted at entrance. Views over River Severn. Toilets. Parking 15.

Robinswood Hill *Map 3 SO81* **CP/PS**
(OS162 SO835150) 2m S of Gloucester, via Reservoir Road, off the ring road. 97 acres. A conical wooded hill, formerly source of Gloucester's water supply. Well House and Well Cross, footpaths, nature trails, riding, information centre in season. AA Viewpoint. Management: Gloucester District Council. **Picnic Site** (SO836157). Signposted at entrance. 30 acres. Furniture, snack bar, toilets for disabled (closed weekdays). Parking 60.

Speech House *Map 3 SO61* **(B4226)** **PS**
On N side of road 3¼m E of Coleford on outskirts of Speech House village (OS162 SO622125). Forestry Commission sign at entrance. Attractive easily-accessible site in Forest of Dean. 4 acres. Signed forest walks, fire hearths, arboretum, drinking water, refreshment kiosk, furniture. Toilets. Parking 50.

HAMPSHIRE

Abbotstone Down *Map 4 SU53* **(B3046)** **PS**
On the B3046 2m N of Alresford (OS185 SU585362). Signposted at entrance. Extensive area of grass clearings in wood and scrubland. Signed footpaths to Aylesford, Itchen Abbas, Winchester, Micheldever and Preston Candover. Furniture. Toilets May–Sep. Parking 350.

Avington Park *Map 4 SU53* **(Off B3047)** **PS**
1m S of Itchen Abbas next to Avington House (OS185 SU533322). No toilets. Parking 300.

Beacon Hill Transit Picnic Site *Map 4 SU45* **(A34)**
PS
2½m N of Litchfield (OS174 SU460573). Toilets.

The Bench *Map 4 SU30* **(A35)** **PS**
On E side of Lyndhurst (OS196 SU305081). 50 acres area in New Forest. Furniture. Parking 70.

On Bolderwood Ornamental Drive *Map 4 SU20*
(A31) **PS**
3m NW of Emery Down on the Ornamental Drive between the A31 and A35. (OS195 SU242087). Signposted in advance and at entrance. Gravelled clearing in the forest giving access to a number of picnic areas. Marked walks, deer sanctuary, descriptive leaflets, furniture, chemical toilets. Parking 100.

Crab Wood *Map 4 SU42* **(Off A3090)** **PS**
2m W of Winchester on unclassified road off A3090 (OS185 SU432293). Thickly wooded area. 197 acres. Unlimited parking.

Danebury Ring *Map 4 SU33* **(Off A30)** **PS**
2½m NW of Stockbridge on unclassified road (OS185 SU238378). Site of AA tree-planting scheme. Iron-age hill fort. Drinking water. Toilets. Parking 80.

Farley Mount *Map 4 SU42* **CP**
(OS185 SU420294) W of Winchester on unclassified road. 265 acres. Woodland and downland with earthworks and Roman road. Management: Hampshire County Council.

Hawley Common *Map 4 SU85* **(A30)** **PS**
On S side of A30, 4m SW of Camberley (OS175 SU845575). 5 acres. Small lake, drinking water, furniture. Signposted in advance and at entrance. Toilets. Parking 200.

Lepe and Calshot Foreshores *Map 4 SZ49* **CP**
(OS196 SZ461986) 2m S of Fawley on Solent. 122 acres. An open grassed recreational area narrowing to a long strip of grass and woodland beside the foreshore, access to beach, picnicking, barbecue site, fishing, swimming. Management: Hampshire County Council.

Mayflower Park (Southampton) *Map 4 SU41* **PS**
At Royal Pier (OS196 SU416111). Signposted at entrance. Overlooking Southampton Water and new docks. 10 acres.

Old Winchester Hill *Map 4 SU62* **(Off A32)** **PS**
From Warnford or West Meon (OS185 SU648212). Signposted in advance and at entrance. Nature reserve 149 acres. Walks, furniture. Parking 150 (on lay-bys).

Portsdown *Map 4 SU60* **(A333)** **PS**
Near Portsmouth (OS196 SU662063). AA Viewpoint used as picnic site with good view of Portsmouth harbour. 150 acres. Unlimited parking.

Queen Elizabeth Park *Map 4 SU71* **CP**
Butser, Nr Petersfield (Access from A3) 10m N
Portsmouth. Open downland and forest. Within the
boundary Butser Hill is a centre for grass ski-ing,
hang-gliding and flying radio controlled gliders. Picnic
area, bridle paths, waymarked trails, warden service,
forestry demonstrations, information centre with book-
stall and exhibition. Charges for parking. Joint Management: Hampshire County Council, Forestry Commission.

Rhinefield, Putter Bridge, Whitfield Moor *Map 4
SU20* **(A35)** **PS**
2m W of Brockenhurst on unclassified road adjacent
to A35 (OS195 SU272030). Signposted in advance
and at entrance. Leaflets on walks and facilities at
Whitfield House at entrance. Toilets. Parking 500.

Royal Victoria Country Park *Map 4 SU40* **CP**
(OS196 SU464077). 3m S along unclassified road
from A27 at Windhover Roundabout. Site in extensive
parkland of a historic military hospital built shortly after
the Crimean War. Frontage on Southampton Water.
Ranger service, cafe, toilets, parking. Management:
Hampshire County Council.

Southampton Common *Map 4 SU41* **(A33)** **PS**
On A33 London road, 1½m from city centre (OS196
SU415145). Open commonland with some wooded
areas. 328 acres. Paddling pool, model boating lake,
drinking water, furniture. Toilets. Extensive parking on
access roads only.

Stoney Cross *Map 4 SU21* **(A31)** **PS**
In New Forest 2m W of Cadnam off A31 (OS195
SU248128). 2 acres.

Wellington Country Park *Map 4 SU76* **CP**
(OS175 SU724627) Stratfield Saye Estate, Riseley, 5m
from M4 junction 11, 7m from M3 junction 5. 605
acres. Woodland, heath, lake and meadowland. National Dairy Museum, fishing, boating, nature trails,
adventure playground, children, animals, picnicking.
Management: Wellington Enterprises.

Yateley Common *Map 4 SU85* **CP**
(OS175 SU686591) N of A30 to W of Blackwater. 493
acres. Heathland with ponds, riding, fishing. Management: Hampshire County Council.

HEREFORD & WORCESTER
Avoncroft Museum of Buildings Picnic Site
Map 3 SO96 **(Off A4024)** **PS**

Just of the A4024. 2m S of Bromsgrove (OS139
SO955685). Signposted in advance and at entrance.
Close-cropped grass under trees. 3½ acres. Drinking
water, refreshment facilities. Toilets. Parking 160.

Beacon Hill *Map 7 SO97* **(B4096)** **PS**
Monument Lane off B4096 4m NE of Bromsgrove
(OS139 SO995758). Signposted at entrance. 523
acres. Viewpoint with pedestal-mounted map and
telescope on Beacon Hill, drinking water, furniture.
Parking 200.

Broadway Tower *Map SP13* **CP**
(OS150 SP113360) 2m S of Broadway. 35 acres.
Grassland and woodland, nature trail. Management:
Batsford Estate Company.

Bromyard Downs *Map 3 SO65* **(Off A44)** **PS**
Between A44 and B4203 NE of Bromyard (OS149
SO673555). Large area of common land with spectacular views overlooking Bromyard and surrounding
area. Furniture. Parking unlimited, grassed pull-ins off
minor roads.

Castlemorton Common *Map 3 SO73* **(B4208)** **PS**
On Malvern–Gloucester road, 1m S of Welland
(OS150 SO785392). Signposted in advance and at
entrance. 50 acres open common land. Unlimited
parking.

Clent Hills *Map 7 SO97* **CP/PS**
(OS139 SO928798) South of Halesowen. 8m W of
Birmingham off A456. 364 acres. Management:
Hereford & Worcester County Council. **Picnic Site** on
unclassified road off A491 SW of Hagley (SO933795).
Signposted in advance and at entrance. 2,000 acres.
Parking 150.

Dinmore Hill *Map 3 SO55* **(A49)** **PS**
At Queens Wood on Leominster/Hereford road
(OS149 SO507516). 500 acres of woodland. Cafe.
Parking 500.

Evesham, Riverside *Map 4 SP04* **(A435)** **PS**
Abbey Road, Evesham (OS150 035433). 20 acres
meadowland adjacent to tree-lined banks of River
Avon. Drinking water, furniture. Toilets. Parking 250
(fee).

Fish Hill *Map 4 SP13* **(A44)** **PS**
1m S Broadway (OS150 SP117370). Signposted in
advance and at entrance. 2 acres. Summit of Fish Hill
planted with trees and shrubs. Drinking water, furniture. Toilets. Unlimited parking.

Goodrich Castle *Map 3 SO52* **(A40)** **PS**
Ross to Monmouth Road 3½m from Ross (OS162
SO577200). Signposted in advance and at entrance.
3½ acres. Near entrance to a ruined castle in woods
and farmland. Drinking water, furniture. Disabled
toilets. Parking 300.

Hartlebury Castle *Map 7 SO87* **(B4193)** **PS**
Near Hartlebury village (OS138 SO840713). Grass
picnic area 60 yds from car park in castle grounds.
Furniture. Parking 60.

Hartlebury Common *Map 7 SO87* **(A4025)** **PS**
Access from either A4025 or B4193 (OS138
SO825705). Signposted at entrance. 15 acres. Area of
commonland with trees and gorse. Footpaths. Parking
unlimited.

Kingsford *Map 7 SO88* **CP**
(OS138 SO828818) 3m N of Kidderminster, W of
A449. 216 acres. Management: Hereford & Worcester
County Council.

Lickey Hills *Map 7 SO97* **CP**
(OS139 SO998754) B4096 2½m NE of Bromsgrove,
8m SW of Birmingham. 525 acres. Woodland, heath
and meadowland, bird sanctuary, riding, boating.
Management: City of Birmingham.

Lower Malvern Common *Map 3 SO74* **(A449)** **PS**
Situated N' of road entering from Worcester (OS150
SO778470). 4 acres of common land with various
parking areas. Furniture. Parking 60 (fee).

Malvern Hills *Map 3 SO74* **(B4232)** **PS**
On B4232 between A449 and A4105 (OS150
SO769435). Signposted in advance. Extensive open
area piped with spring water. Drinking water. Furniture. Parking 1,000 (fee).

Old Hills *Map 3 SO84* **(B4424)** **PS**
1m S of Callow End on B4424 (OS150 SO829487).
Commonland with views of Malverns. Numerous en-
trances, furniture.

Ravenshill Nature Reserve and Picnic Site *Map 3
SO75* **(Unclassified road)** **PS**
1m N of Alfrick (OS150 SO738537). Signposted in
advance and at entrance. 10 acres in woodland,
natural history museum, drinking water, furniture.
Toilets. Parking 15.

Ross-on-Wye, Riverside *Map 3 SO62* **(Off A49)**
PS
Ross-on-Wye (OS162 SO607246). 10 acres, grassed
area planted with shrubs on bank of the River Wye.
Furniture. Toilets. Parking 100.

**Ross Spur Service Area Eastbound and
Westbound (Transit Picnic Site)** *Map 3 SO62*
(A449) **PS**
Nr junction with M50. 1m from Ross-on-Wye (OS162
SO613235). Signposted in advance and at entrance.
Situated at rear and side of garage. Toilets. Parking 50
per side.

Stourport on Severn, Riverside *Map 7 SO87*
(Off A451) **PS**
Off A451 ¼m W of Stourport town centre (OS138
805713). Signposted in advance, 'Riverside Car Park'.
80 acres tree-planted, grassed and landscaped area.
Steamer trips, motor boat hire, children's playground,
paddling pool, access to riverside fairground, furniture, drinking water. Disabled toilets. Parking extensive (fee).

Symonds Yat Rock (East) *Map 3 SO51* **(Off A40)**
PS
5½m from Ross (OS162 SO564161). Signposted at
entrance 4½ acres. Large woodland area in the Forest
of Dean. Access to extensive walk, cafe, information
bureau, furniture. Toilets. Parking 100.

Symonds Yat (West) Garders Restaurant
Map 3 SO51 **(Off A40)** **PS**
6m from Ross on B4161 off A40 (OS162 SO558158).
Signposted at entrance. 4 acres open grassed area
with footpath to River Wye, hire boats and small
fairground. Drinking water, furniture. Parking 300 (fee).

Walton Hill *Map 7 SO98* **(Off A456)** **PS**
On unclassified road 2m SSW of Halesowen off A456
signposted Kidderminster (OS139 SO944805). Extensive area. Hill adjacent to Clent Country Park.
Panoramic view from summit accessed by steep path
from the car park. Parking 100.

Windmill and Waseley Hills *Map 7 SO97* **CP/PS**
(OS139 SO973778) SW of Birmingham, 1m NW of
Rubery. 131 acres. Elevated grassland. Riding, nature
trails. AA Viewpoint. Management: Hereford and Wor-
cester County Council. **Picnic Site.** 3m S of Haleso-
wen on unclassified road off B4551 (SO937779).
Signposted in advance and at entrance. Furniture.
Parking 100.

Wyche Cutting *Map 3 SO74* **(B4232)** **PS**
3m SW of Great Malvern (OS150 SO768435). Signposted 'The Wyche' in advance. Good views of
Malverns and surrounding countryside. Toilets. Parking 30.

Wyre Forest *Map 7 SO77* **(A456)** **PS**
2½m from Bewdley to Leominster (OS138
SO750740). Signposted at entrance. Extensive area in
coniferous forest, numerous walks, information centre,
furniture, drinking water. Disabled toilets. Parking 50.

HERTFORDSHIRE

Aldenham Reservoir *Map 4 TQ19* **CP/PS**
(OS166 TQ169957). Off A411 NW of Elstree. 185
acres. Meadowland beside Reservoir. Fishing, sailing.
Management: Hertfordshire County Council. **Picnic
Site** on unclassified road off A411 ½m W of Elstree
(TQ172953). Signposted from A5 and A41 and at
entrance. Excellently laid out overlooking reservoir.
Drinking water. Toilets.

Great Wood, Northaw *Map 4 TL20* **CP/PS**
(OS166 TL284042) 4m SE of Hatfield on B157. 247
acres of woodland with marked walks. Riding. Management: Welwyn Hatfield District Council. **Picnic Site**
on N side of B157 1¼m W of Cuffley (TL285038).
Signposted in advance and at entrance. Clearings in
extensive forest area. Furniture, toilets. Parking 50 (fee
at peak periods).

Knebworth *Map 4 TL22* **CP**
(OS166 TQ228210) 1½m SW of Stevenage W of A1
(M) (Access from B197 or B656). 190 acres. Parkland,
house with gardens, riding. Management: Lytton Enterprises Ltd.

Stanborough Park *Map 4 TL21* **(Off A6129)** **PS**
Off A6129 E of junction with A1 at Welwyn Garden City
(OS166 TL225110). Signposted in advance and at
entrance. Lakeside setting. 20 acres. Additional
charges for use of heated open-air swimming pool,
boating and sailing facilities, furniture. Toilets. Parking
250 (fee).

HUMBERSIDE

Burton Constable *Map 8 TA13* **CP**
(OS107 TA184362) Sproatley, 8m NE of Hull. 200 acres. Parkland with stately home. Fishing, boating, swimming, birdwatching, nature trail, museum, animals. Management: Mr Chichester-Constable.

Normanby Hall *Map 8 SE81* **CP**
(OS112 SE892162) 2m N of Scunthorpe. 170 acres. Park and stately home including 40 acres of pleasure grounds. Play area lido, deer park, fishing lake, nature trail, riding school, model railway. Management: Scunthorpe District Council.

Raventhorpe Farm *Map 8 SE90* **(A18)** **PS**
N side of junction with B1398, access for eastbound traffic (OS112 SE937075). Old road screened by hedgerows. 2 acres.

ISLE OF WIGHT

Afton Down *Map 4 SZ38* **(A3055)** **PS**
On A3055, ½m E of Freshwater Bay (OS196 SZ353855). Signposted in advance and at entrance. National Trust land overlooking Freshwater Bay. 1 acre. Parking 30.

Bembridge Down *Map 4 SZ68* **(Off B3395)** **PS**
On unclassified road off B3395. 2½m W of Bembridge (OS196 SZ627859). National Trust property and AA Viewpoint overooking coast. 5 acres. Parking 100.

Blackgang Viewpoint *Map 4 SZ47* **(A3055)** **PS**
1m W of Niton (OS196 SZ488768). Signposted in advance and at entrance. National Trust area overlooking SW coast of island. 1 acre. Furniture. Parking 30.

Brading Down *Map 4 SZ58* **(Off A3055)** **PS**
(OS196 SZ590870). Overlooking Sandown and Shanklin. 10 acres. Parking 100.

Brightstone Forest *Map 4 SZ48* **(Off B3401)** **PS**
On unclassified road between Calbourne and Brightstone (OS196 SZ420847). Signposted at entrance. National Trust. 400 acres. Nature trails to the forest. Parking 60.

Fort Victoria *Map 4 SZ38* **CP**
(OS196 SZ335895) West of Yarmouth. 50 acres. Woodland with access to beach, and fort, picnicking. Management: Isle of Wight County Council.

Parkhurst Forest *Map 8 SZ49* **(A3054)** **PS**
1m W of Newport (OS196 SZ479903). Signposted at entrance. 1,000-acre forest. Nature trails, furniture. Parking 30.

Robin Hill *Map 4 SZ36* **CP**
(OS196 SZ536878) 2m E of Newport. 80 acres. Woodland and farmland. Roman remains, nature trail, animals, playground, picnicking. Management: Dowend Enterprises.

KENT

Bedgebury Pinetum *Map 5 TQ73* **(B2079)** **PS**
E side of B2709, 2m S of Goudhurst (OS188 TQ715336). Signposted in advance and at entrance. Drinking water, furniture. Toilets. Parking 300 (fee).

Camer Park Meopham *Map 5 TQ66* **CP/PS**
(OS177 TQ655670) Between Sole Street and Meopham. 45 acres of wood and grassland within an area of outstanding natural beauty. Management: Gravesham District Council. **Picnic Site** S side of Green Lane (B2009) off A227 ½m N of Meopham (TQ655669). Signposted in advance from both directions, and at entrance for southbound traffic. Headroom 7ft 6in. Drinking water, furniture, toilets. Parking 25.

Dryhill Quarry Transit Picnic Site *Map 5 TQ45* **(Off A25)** **PS**
E side of Dryhill Lane ½m S of A25 (W side A25/A21 interchange) SE of Sundridge. (OS188 TQ497552). Toilets.

Eastcourt Meadows *Map 6 TQ86* **CP**
(OS178 TQ806684) Lower Rainham Road Gillingham. Grassland on bank of River Medway. Fishing, sailing, canoeing. Management: Gillingham Borough Council.

Groveferry, Upstreet *Map 5 TR26* **(Off A28)** **PS**
S side of railway level crossing along Grove Ferry Road, ¼m SE of its junction with A28 (OS179 TR235632). Signposted in advance. Grassed area with shrubs, along River Stour. Boat moorings, fishing by permit. Toilets. Parking 20.

Hothfield Common Transit Picnic Site *Map 5 TQ94* **(A20)** **PS**
Both sides of A20. Ashford 4m. Charing 3½m (OS189 TQ971460). Toilets.

Langdon Cliff *Map 5 TR34* **(Off A258)** **PS**
At bend on unclassified Dover/St Margaret's-at-Cliff road, 1m E of junction with A258 at Dover Castle (OS179 TR335422). Signposted Langdon Cliff, St Margaret's Bay for NE traffic only. Signposted at entrance. Grassed area with shrubs on clifftop overlooking Straits of Dover harbour. Toilets. Parking 150.

Manor Park *Map 5 TQ65* **CP**
(OS188 TQ678573) E of A228 (St Leonards St) S of West Malling, signposted. 52 acres, open parkland with lake fishing, playground. Management: Kent County Council.

Shepherds Gate Transit Picnic Site *Map 5 TQ66* **(A2)** **PS**
At B2009 interchange. 3½m W of Rochester (OS177 TQ680697). Toilets.

Trosley Towers Country Park *Map 5 TQ66* **CP**
(OS188 TQ645611) Off and E of A227 S of Vigo Village N of Wrotham. Signposted. 120 acres. Extensive areas of woodland on top of Downs with scrub and grassland on a steep slope within an area of outstanding natural beauty. Walking, picnicking. Management: Kent County Council.

LANCASHIRE

Beacon Fell *Map 7 SD54* **CP**
(OS102 SD568428) 8m N of Preston, 3m E of M6. 185 acres of conifer woods and moorland in the Forest of Bowland. Picnic area, information centre, nature trail, viewpoint. Management: Lancashire County Council.

Witton Park *Map 7 SD62* **CP**
(OS102 SD56277) On Western outskirts of Blackburn. Woodland and heath. Riding, nature trails, picnicking. Management: Blackburn District Council.

Wycoller *Map 7 SD93* **CP**
(OS103 SD935396) SE of Colne, 363 acres of heath, moor and grassland around the hamlet of Wycoller a designated conservation area. Footpaths and access

to public rights of way, riding, nature trail. Ranger service at weekends. Management: Lancashire County Council.

LEICESTERSHIRE

Beacon Hill *Map 7 SK51* **(B591)** PS
1¼m W of Woodhouse Eaves, N side of B591 (OS129 SK510149). AA Viewpoint. 10 acres. Drinking water. Furniture. Toilets. Parking 50.

Bosworth Park *Map 8 SK40* **(B585)** PS
On B585 ¼m from centre of Market Bosworth (OS140 SK412032). Signposted at entrance. Open area sloping to lake shore. 30 acres. Furniture. Toilets. Parking 50 (fee at peak period).

Bradgate Park and Swithland Woods
Map 8 SK51 CP
(OS129 SK533105) 5m NW of Leicester. 1,223 acres of woods and parkland in Charnwood Forest. Ruins, riding, nature trail. Management: Bradgate Park Management Committee. **Picnic Site** at Old John Tower, 7m NW of Leicester, on B5237 at Newton Linford (SK523117). 6 acres. Drinking water, toilets, parking 400.

Burbage Common *Map 7 SP49* **(A47)** PS
Between A47 and A5070. 1m W of Hinckley. (OS140 SP447953). Signposted at entrance. 3 acres. Access to 29 acres of woodland, controlled section for flying model aircraft. Parking 50.

Nanpantan Outwoods *Map 7 SK51* **(Off B591)** PS
Turn off B591 on to unclassified Woodhouse Eaves/Nanpantan road, 1½m from Woodhouse Eaves (OS129 SK515159). Wooded hillside. 54 acres. Woodland walks. Parking 60.

Tugby Picnic Site *Map 14 SK70* **(A47)** PS
Approx ¼m from Tugby. (OS141 SK764008) Signposted in advance and at entrance. 1½ acres. Landscaped grass area screened by deciduous trees. Drinking water, furniture. Toilets.

Wanlip Park *Map 8 SK61* CP
(OS129 SK606104) 5m NE of Leicester. 49 acres. Farmland with restored gravel pits. Boating, fishing. Management: Wanlip Park Countryside Club Limited.

LINCOLNSHIRE

Cater Plot Transit Picnic Site *Map 8 TF14* **(A17)** PS
1¾m E of Heckington. S side of A17 (OS130 TF168441). Toilets.

Chapel Point *Map 9 TF57* **(Off A52)** PS
1m N of Chapel St Leonards (OS122 TF563732). 10 acres. Drinking water. Toilets. Parking 150.

Hartesholme *Map 8 SK61* CP
(OS121 SK945688) 2m SW of Lincoln. A lake bordered by parkland leading to grassland and woodland. 88 acres. Footpaths, nature trail, fishing, picnic facilities, cafe, warden service. Management: Lincoln City Council.

Hubbard's Hill *Map 8 TF38* **(Off A153)** PS
¼m W of A153, 1½m SW Louth (OS122 TF317861). Signposted in advance. 5 acres. Furniture. Toilets. Parking 30.

Huttoft Bank *Map 9 TF57* **(A52)** PS
E of A52, 3m S of Sutton-on-Sea (OS122 TF547777). Signposted at entrance. On Lincolnshire coast. 10 acres. Toilets. Parking 400.

North Reston *Map 8 TF38* **(A157)** PS
W side of A157, 1m SE of Legbourne (OS122 TF384837). Signposted in advance and at entrance. Open grass area 20ft from road. ½ acre. Furniture. Parking 10.

Seaview Farm *Map 9 TF56* **(A158)** PS
N side of A158, 1½m W of Skegness (OS122 TF545648). Signposted at entrance on W side only. Old road screened by trees. 1 acres. Parking 20.

Tattershall *Map 8 TF25* **(A153)** PS
On NW side of A153 ¾m SW of Tattershall (OS122 TF203572). Signposted in advance and at entrance. Between A153 and Horncastle Canal on line of disused railway. Site of interest in rural area. 4½ acres. Drinking water, furniture, plan of area displayed. Toilets. Parking 100.

Woodhall Spa *Map 8 TF16* **(Off B1191)** PS
½m from centre of Woodhall Spa off Stixwould road (OS122 TF191635). Signposted at entrance. Local authority park. 5 acres. Cricket ground, swimming pool, gardens, furniture. Toilets. Parking 100.

LONDON (GREATER)

Addington Park *Map 4 TQ36* **(A212/B268)** PS
½m W of Addington village (OS177 TQ368638). Signposted at entrance. Pleasant sloping woodland adjacent to Addington Palace, formerly residence of Archbishop of Canterbury. 70 acres. Small children's playground. Parking 100.

Bayhurst Wood *Map 4 TQ08* CP/PS
(OS176 TQ068889) In Colne Valley 2m N of Uxbridge, 1m W of Ruislip Lido. 98 acres of woodland. Barbecue sites. Management: London Borough of Hillingdon. **Picnic site** on unclassified Harefield/Ruislip road, off B455 (TQ068890). Furniture, toilets. Parking 100.

Bushy Park *Map 4 TQ16* **(Off A308)** PS
¼m W of Kingston upon Thames (OS176 TQ155693). Parking 120.

Coulsdon Common *Map 4 TQ35* **(B2030)** PS
1½m NW of Caterham, on North Downs approx 600ft above sea level (OS187 TQ320570). Signposted in advance and at entrance. 130 acres. Nature trail.

Farthing Downs *Map 4 TQ35* **(A23/B2030)** PS
Adjacent to unclassified Coulsdon/Chaldon road 1½m S of junction of A23/B2030 (OS187 TQ300570). Signposted in advance. On North Downs approx 600ft above sea level. 121 acres. Nature trail, furniture. Toilets. Parking 600.

Hainault Forest *Map 5 TQ49* CP/PS
(OS177 TQ474935) E of Chigwell. 960 acres. Well-wooded part of the ancient forest of Essex. Golf course, pleasant walks, riding, fishing, parking. Management: Greater London Council. **Picnic site** E and SE of Chigwell Row (TQ475935). Signposted in advance and at entrance. Drinking water, furniture, toilets. Parking 100.

Mad Bess Wood *Map 4 TQ08* **(B455)** PS
Adjacent to Ruislip/Northwood road. 1½m N of Ruislip (OS176 TQ075895). Signposted at entrance. Pleasant woodland, part of which is a bird sanctuary. 186 acres.

North Cray Transit Picnic Site *Map 5 TQ47* **(A223)** PS
A223 North Cray Road. 1m N of Ruxley Corner (A20). 1½m S of Bexley. (OS177 TQ484718). Toilets.

Richmond Park *Map 4 TQ27* **(A3/A308)** PS
(OS176 TQ200720). Parking 500.

Trent Park *Map 4 TQ29* **CP/PS**
(OS176 TQ282973) West of Enfield. 412 acres. Nature trail, woodland trail for the blind, fishing, riding, parking. Management: Greater London Council. **Picnic site** off A111 ½m N of Cockfosters, 3m S of Potters Bar (TQ280970). Signposted at entrance. Furniture, toilets, parking 200.

MANCHESTER (GREATER)
Chadkirk *Map 7 SJ99* **CP**
(OS109 SJ940900) S of Romily on A627. 70 acres. Wood and farmland. Riding, canoeing, fishing, picnicking. Management: Stockport Metropolitan District Council.

Daisy Nook *Map 7 SD90* **CP**
(OS109 SD923009) 3m S Oldham. Wooded parkland with canal and lake. Management: Oldham MBC/Greater Manchester MBC.

Etherow Park *Map 7 SJ99* **CP**
(OS109 SJ973918) Off B6104 at Compstall. 165 acres, mixed woodland, open countryside, marshland and fishponds next to River Etherow. Nature Reserve, fishing, sailing, rowing, canoeing, nature trail. Management: Stockport Metropolitan District Council.

Haigh Hall *Map 7 SD50* **CP**
(OS108 SD595079) 2m NE Wigan, woods and heathland, lake, fishing, nature trail, arboreta. Management: Wigan Metropolitan Borough Council.

Hollingworth Lake *Map 7 SD91* **CP**
(OS109 SD940154) 3m NE of Rochdale on B6225. Woods and grassland with lake, sailing, boating, fishing, nature reserve. Management: Rochdale Metropolitan Borough Council.

Jumbles Reservoir *Map 7 SD71* **CP**
(OS109 SD734144) 4m N of Bolton. 255 acres. Reservoir with woods and meadows. Riding, boating, fishing. Management: Blackburn District Council.

Tandle Hill *Map 7 SD90* **CP**
(OS109 SD906088) Off A627 at Royton, 110 acres. Management: Oldham District Council.

MERSEYSIDE
Croxteth Park *Map 7 SJ49* **CP**
(OS108 SJ409944) 6m NE of Liverpool, park and woodlands with walled garden. Management: Merseyside County Council.

Eastham Woods *Map 7 SJ38* **CP**
(OS108 SJ363816) Off A41 at Eastham. Woodland and grassland beside River Mersey, nature trail, playground. Management: Wirral Metropolitan Borough Council.

The Wirral *Map 7 SJ28* **CP**
(OS108 SJ238834) Between West Kirby and Parkgate, near Dee estuary. Access from A540 Chester to Hoylake Road at Croft Drive, Caldy; Station Road, Thurstaston; Parkgate Baths, The Parade, Parkgate; Hadlow Road, Willaston. 105 acres developed from 12m length of disused railway line; picnicking, riding, fishing. Information centres at Thurstaston, Caldy and Heswell. Management: Cheshire and Merseyside County Councils.

NORFOLK
Bridgham Lane *Map 5 TL98* **(Off A1066)** PS
On unclassified road 6m E of Thetford (OS144 TL968826). Furniture. Parking.

Emily's Wood *Map 5 TL78* **(A1065)** PS
On the Mundford/Brandon road, 2m S of Mundford (OS144 TL797895). Open area of several hundred yards, backed by forest. 40 acres.

Fritton Lake Country Park *Map 5 TG40* **CP**
(OS134 TG476001) Off A143 Fritton-Great Yarmouth Road. 170 acre lake edged with reeds, gardens and woodland with grassed areas. Fishing, boat hire, picnic areas, gift and tackle shop, children's assault course and play area. Parking free, entrance fee to park. Management: Lord Somerleyton.

Grimes Graves *Map 5 TL89* **(A134)** PS
On the Thetford/Mundford road 6m from Thetford, (OS144 TL815918). Signposted in advance. Access through forest to open grass area surrounded by trees in Thetford Chase. 5 acres. Ancient monument nearby. Grimes Graves and Weeting Castle. Parking 50 (fee).

Hockham *Map 5 TL99* **(A1075)** PS
1m W of Great Hockham (OS144 TL938919). Signposted at entrance. Rough grassland adjacent to pine woods. 2½ acres. Walks. Parking 40.

Life Woods *Map 9 TF63* **(A149)** PS
On A149 1m S of Ingoldsthorpe (OS132 TF686317). Signposted at entrance. 10 acres undulating ground amidst deciduous woods. Numerous walks. Drinking water, furniture. Toilets. Parking 100.

Lynford *Map 5 TL89* **(A314)** PS
1m SE of Mundford (OS144 TL813917). Signposted at entrance. 60 acres. Level grassland in Thetford Forest. Drinking water and nature trails, children's play area. Toilets. Parking.

Punchbowl *Map 5 TL88* **(Unclassified road)** PS
3½m N of Thetford on unclassified road (1m N of Croxton) (OS144 TL877892). Signposted at entrance. 10 acres. Large open area on the edge of Croxton Heath (Thetford Forest). Numerous forest walks. Toilets. Parking 50.

Sandringham *Map 9 TF62* **CP/PS**
(OS132 TF679280) 8m NE of King's Lynn. 720 acres of woodland and heath. Management: Sandringham Estate. **Picnic site** opposite main gates of the Royal Fruit Farm overlooking the gates of Sandringham House (TF696292). Signposted in advance and at entrance. 5 acres set among tall evergreen trees on the edge of forest land. Drinking water furniture, toilets.

Two Mile Bottom *Map 5 TL88* **(A134)** PS
3m NW of Thetford (OS144 TL845878). Signposted in advance and at entrance. 25 acres. Open woodland by roadside, extending back to pine wood walks. Extensive parking.

NORTHAMPTONSHIRE
Barnwell *Map 4 TL08* **CP/PS**
(OS141 TL035873) S of Oundle on Barnwell Road A605. Restored gravel pits on bank of the River Nene. Angling for disabled, riverside walk, warden service. Management: Northamptonshire County Council. **Picnic Site** in 30 acres of landscaped grounds.

Closes 6pm. Drinking water, furniture, toilets with provision for the disabled.

Harlestone Heath *Map 4 SP76* **(A428)** PS
1m SE of Harlestone. A428 Northampton/Rugby road (OS152 SP712637). Large lay-by set in woodland. 100 acres. Walks. Parking 40.

Little Irchester *Map 4 SP96* CP
(OS152 SP913660) S of Wellingborough. 200 acres of forest. Nature trail, picnicking. Management: Northamptonshire County Council.

Pitsford Reservoir *Map 4 SP76* **(Off A508)** PS
On unclassified road, ½m E of A508, 5½m N of Northampton (OS152 SP761686). Signposted in advance and at entrance. Parking 100.

Salcey Forest *Map 4 SP75* **(Off B526)** PS
On unclassified Quinton/Hartwell road, off B526 1m from Hartwell (OS152 SP793518). Signposted in advance. 6 acres Crown Land. Walk through Salcey Forest game reserve. Dogs must be on lead. Toilets.

Wakerley Great Wood *Map 4 SP99* **(Off A43)** PS
Unclassified road off A43. 2½m SW of Duddington. (OS141 SP967984). Wooded area. Toilets with provision for disabled. Parking 100.

NORTHUMBERLAND
Northumberland National Park (398 square miles)
Remote hill pastures, forests, lovely valleys and Hadrian's Wall. Correspondence should be sent to Information Officer, Northumberland National Park, Eastburn, South Park, Hexham, Northumberland NE66 1BS *tel* Hexham (0434) 605555.
Information centres:

Byrness	9 Otterburn Green, *tel* Otterburn 20622 summer only
Harbottle	Forestry Commission Car Park
Ingram	Old School House *tel* Powburn 248 summer only
Once Brewed	Military Road, Hexham *tel* Bardon Mill 396 summer only
Rothbury	Church House, Church Street *tel* 20887 summer only

Blanchland *Map 12 NY95* **(B6306)** PS
In the village (OS87 NY964505). Signposted in advance. Picnic area by river and woods near Derwent Reservoir. Parking 100 (fee).

Bolam Lake *Map 112 NZ08* CP
(OS81 NZ080819) Belsey, nr Morpeth. 90 acres of woodland, fishing, nature trail. Management: Northumberland County Council.

Breamish Valley *Map 12 NU01* **(Off A697)** PS
8½m S of Wooler, following signs to Ingram (OS81 NU020160). Signposted in advance and at entrance. Grass valley following river Breamish into the Cheviot foothills. 50 acres. Toilets. Parking 1,000.

Brocolita *Map 12 NY87* **(B6318)** PS
3m W of Chollerford (OS87 NY860712). 30 acres. Parking 40.

Cragside *Map 12 NU00* CP
12m SW of Alnwick at Rothbury. Entrance off the B6344 Morpeth road. Landscaped grounds of country house with lakes, walks and viewpoints. Management: The National Trust.

Housesteads *Map 12 NY76* **(B6318)** PS
9m E of Greenhead (OS87 NY790687). Signposted in advance. 30 acres. Museum on site. Parking 60.

Plessey Woods *Map 12 NZ27* CP
(OS88 NZ240799) 1½m SW of Beldington on A1068. 100 acres, grass and woodland with lake. Riding, fishing, nature trail, picnicking. Management: Northumberland County Council.

Twice Brewed Car Park Transit Picnic Site *Map 12 NY76* **(B6318)** PS
11m W of Chollerford (OS87 NY761669). Parking.

Wansbeck *Map 12 NZ28* CP
(OS81 NZ266862) ½m S Ashington. Grass and woodland river valley. Boating, picnic site. Management: Wansbeck District Council.

Winshields Crag *Map 12 NY76* **(B6318)** PS
5m E of Greenhead (OS87 NY755618). Signposted in advance. Near Roman wall. 50 acres. Parking 40.

NOTTINGHAMSHIRE
Burnstump *Map 8 SK55* CP
(OS120 SK578507) 3m N of Nottingham off A60. 61 acres. Woods and parkland. Nature trail, picnicking. Management: Geding District Council.

Colwick *Map 8 SK63* CP
(OS129 SK608395) 1½m E Nottingham. Woodlands and water. Fishing, nature trail. Management: Nottingham City Council.

Clumber Park *Map 8 SK67* CP
(OS120 SK630750) 2½m SE of Worksop. 3,784 acres. Woodland, farmland and grassland with lake. Fishing. Management: Clumber Park Management Committee.

Holme Pierrepont *Map 8 SK63* CP
(OS129 SK619394) 2m W of Radcliffe, N of A52. 239 acres. Restored gravel pits by River Trent. Mainly for water sports. Admission fee varies according to events. Management: Nottinghamshire County Council.

Major Oak, Sherwood Forest *Map 8 SK66* CP
(OS120 SK623683) N of Edwinstowe off A614. 84 acres. Forest. Nature reserve. Management: Nottinghamshire County Council.

Newstead Abbey Gardens *Map 7 SK55* **(Off A60)** CP
4½m S of Mansfield. (OS120 SK541537) Cultivated gardens set in abbey grounds. 70 acres.

Rufford Park *Map 8 SK66* CP
(OS120 SK644650) 3m S of Ollerton on A614. 90 acres. Woodland and parkland with lake. riding, fishing, nature trail. Management: Nottinghamshire County Council.

OXFORDSHIRE
Abbey Meadow *Map 4 SU59* **(Off A415)** PS
Adjacent to Abingdon town centre (OS164 SU500970). Signposted 'car park at Abbey Hall'. Alongside River Thames adjacent to Abbey Gardens. 5 acres. Swimming pool, tennis courts, pitch and putt. Toilets.

Cowleaze Wood *Map 4 SU79* **(Off A40)** PS
On unclassified road at Christmas Common off A40, 2m W of Stokenchurch, 4m SE of Watlington (OS165 SU726956). Woodlands on the edge of the Chiltern escarpment. Forest walks, drinking water. Toilets. Parking 100.

Oxford Transit Picnic Site Map 4 SP50 **(A40)** **PS**
1½m SE of ring road (OS164 SP575075). Toilets.

Sinodun Hills (Wittenham Clumps) Map 4 SU59 **(Off A4130)** **PS**
On unclassified road between Brightwell and Little Wittenham, 4m NW of Wallingford (OS164 SU566 928). Wooded hilltop with pleasant views. 5 acres. Parking 30.

White Horse Hill Nr. Uffington Map 4 SU38 **(Off B4507)** **PS**
3m advance of B4507 E of Ashbury (OS174 SU302866). Signposted in advance. Iron-age hill fort. 10 acres. Parking 40.

SHROPSHIRE

Bridgnorth, Severn Park Map 7 SO79 **(A442)** **PS**
Edge of Bridgnorth Low Town, alongside A442 Bridgnorth–Telford road (OS138 SO723934). Signposted at entrance. 30 acres. Riverside park. Pitch and putt, putting. Parking unlimited.

Brown Moss Map 7 SJ53 **(Off A41)** **PS**
1½m SE of Whitchurch (OS126 SJ562395). Signposted in advance and at entrance. 80 acres of commonland crossed by open tracks and footpaths, areas of bracken and open grazing, woodland and a number of pools, fishing, warden. Furniture. Parking 100.

Cardingmill Valley Map 7 SO49 **(Off B4370)** **PS**
On edge of Church Stretton village (OS137 SO445346). Signposted in advance and at entrance. Small attractive river valley, 250 acres. Hill walking, drinking water, furniture. Parking 700 (fee).

Cleehill Map 7 SO57 **(A4417)** **PS**
At Cleehill between Ludlow and Cleobury Mortimer (OS138 SO594754). Signposted in advance. Grass common and numerous quarries adjacent to road. 2,000 acres. Panoramic views. Toilets. Parking 1,000.

Colemere Map 7 SJ43 **(Off A528)** **PS**
Off A528 to Colemere village then follow sign to Lyneal for ½m (OS126 SJ434328). Signposted at entrance. 7 acre grassed area surrounded by trees overlooking mere. Fishing, furniture, drinking water. Toilets. Parking 30.

Corbett Wood Map 7 SJ52 **(Off A49)** **PS**
3m S of Wem (OS126 SJ536238). Signposted in advance and at entrance. 23 acres of mixed woodland on Grinshill, footpaths, good views, drinking water. Parking 30.

Ellesmere, The Mere Map 7 SJ43 **(A495)** **PS**
On A495 SE of town, ½m from town centre (OS126 SJ405347). Signposted in advance. Partly a bird sanctuary. 171 acres. Drinking water, furniture, warden during season. Toilets. Parking (fee).

Ercall Wood Map 7 SJ60 **(Off A5)** **PS**
1m SSW of Wellington off unclassified road from Haygate on A5 to Shrewsbury (OS127 SJ643097). 5 acres. Wooded area on hillside with footpaths to summit. Furniture. Parking 30.

Long Mynd Map 7 SO49 **(Off A49)** **PS**
Unclassified road 2m from Church Stretton (OS137 SO420945). Signposted in advance and at entrance. Extensive area of gorse and grass-covered undulating ground rising to 1,666ft traversed by rough tracks,

hazardous for vehicles in places. Hang-gliding. Parking unlimited.

Market Drayton, Swimming Pool Map 7 SJ63 **(Off A529)** **PS**
Off A529 to Hinstock approximately 400 yards from town centre (OS127 SJ676338). 1½ acres. Pleasant grassed site on bank separated from car park by a small stream, flower borders, shrubs, trees. No dogs, furniture, drinking water. Parking 100.

Oswestry, Old Racecourse Map 7 SJ23 **(B4580)** **PS**
2m NW of Oswestry on B4580 (OS126 SJ258310). Commonland with gorse and trees 50 acres. Panoramic views. Toilets. Parking 40.

Whitcliffe Common Map 7 SO57 **(Off A49)** **PS**
On unclassified road off A49, 2m W of Ludlow (OS137 SO505743). Signposted in advance and at entrance. Small picnic areas surrounded by scrub and gorse on commonland. 20 acres. Parking 50.

Whittington Castle Map 7 SJ33 **(A5)** **PS**
Just N of Whittington (OS126 SJ325312). Signposted at entrance. 20 acres within castle ruins, landscaped area of grass on banks of moat. Furniture, playground. Parking 70.

SOMERSET

Exmoor National Park (265 square miles)
Rolling moorland, combes and a lovely rocky coastline. Correspondence should be sent to Information Officer, Exmoor National Park Department, Exmoor House, Dulverton, Somerset TA22 9HL tel Dulverton (0398) 23665/6.
Information Centres:

Combe Martin (caravan)	Beach Car Park tel 3319 summer only	
County Gate	A39 between Porlock and Lynmouth tel Brendon 321 summer only	
Lynmouth	Parish Hall, Watersmeet Road tel Lynton 2509 summer only	

Brent Knoll (East & West) Transit Picnic Site Map 3 ST35 **(M5)** **PS**
North and southbound carriageways 2m N of junction 22, 5m S of junction 21 25m S of Bristol (OS182 ST357525). Signposted in advance and at entrance. Public telephone, snacks, shop. Toilets. Parking 200 (fee after 2 hours), overnight caravan parking.

County Gate Transit Picnic Site Map 3 SS74 **(A39)** **PS**
7m W of Porlock 4½m E of Lynton (OS180 SS795486). Signposted in advance and at entrance. Natural wooded site. In Exmoor National Park. Views over Exmoor, Doone Valley, Bristol Channel. 1 acre. Furniture. Toilets. Parking 70.

Ham Hill Map 3 ST41 **CP**
(OS193 ST478171) of Stoke-sub-Hamdon, 6m W of Yeovil off A3088. 155 acres. Restored quarry of archaeological interest. Management: Yeovil Borough Council.

Pittcombe Head Map 3 SS84 **(Off A39)** **PS**
3¼m W of Porlock (OS181 SS841463). In Exmoor National Park. At junction with Porlock Hill toll road, access requires caution. Signposted at entrance. 2 acres. Situated in woodland, good access point for Exmoor walks. No toilets. Parking 50. (Parking lanes cut in small woods).

Directory of the Countryside

Sutton Bingham Reservoir *Map 3 ST51* **(Off A37) PS**
S of Yeovil approached by unclassified road signed Sutton Bingham. (OS194 ST547113). Signposted at entrance. 5 acres adjacent to controlled facilities for trout fishing and sailing. Open 8am to dusk April–Sept. Furniture, toilets with facilities for the disabled. Parking 40.

STAFFORDSHIRE

Cannock Chase *Map 4 SJ91* **CP/PS**
(OS127 SJ987174) N of Hednesford. 2,687 acres. Management: Staffordshire County Council. **Picnic Site** 4m ESE of Stafford at Milford Village adjacent to common (SJ974214). Signposted in advance. 3,000 acres. Area for flying model aircraft. German War Cemetery. Toilets.

Central Forest Park *Map 4 SJ84* **PS**
(OS118 SJ886485) Stoke on Trent. Part of reclamation scheme in city centre. AA Viewpoint. 80 acres.

Churnet Picnic Area *Map 7 SK04* **(B5417) PS**
Cheadle Road, Oakamoor 3m E of Cheadle (OS128 SK053446). 16 acres. Signposting at entrance. Village picnic site on the River Churnet. Drinking water, furniture. Toilets.

Froghall *Map 7 SK04* **(Off A52) PS**
On edge of Froghall village (OS128 SK018478). Elevated position adjacent to disused lime kilns.

Greenway Bank *Map 4 SJ85* **CP**
(OS118 SJ893554) Knypersley off A527, 4m N Stoke-on-Trent. 121 acres. Wooded valley with lake and rocky features. Management: Staffordshire County Council.

Hanchurch Hills *Map 7 SJ83* **(Off A519) PS**
3m S of Newcastle-under-Lyme (OS127 SJ840399). Portion of hilltop with fine turf and gorse. 80 acres. No caravans allowed. Parking 200.

Highgate Common *Map 7 SO89* **CP/PS**
(OS138 SO840900) S of Wolverhampton. 327 acres of heath and woodland. Riding. Management: Staffordshire County Council. **Picnic Site** off unclassified roads, adjacent to Enville golf course, 2m N of Enville (SO838896). Signposted in advance. Furniture, toilets, parking 1,000.

Himley Country Park *Map 7 SO89* **CP**
(OS139 SO886913) off B4176 Wombourne to Dudley road. Large undulating area with trees and shrubs. Picnic area, cafe, boating lake, pitch and putt, nature walk. Open 8am–8pm. Parking.

Ilam *Map 7 SK15* **CP**
(OS119 SK135508) 6m NW of Ashbourne. 140 acres of parkland with woodland and river. Nature trail. Management: National Trust.

Parkhall *Map 7 SJ94* **CP**
(OS118 SJ930450) Weston Coyne. E of Stoke. Heath and woodland, nature trail, fishing, model aircraft flying, bridleways, information centre. Management: Stoke District Council/Staffordshire County Council.

SUFFOLK

Brandon Park *Map 5 TL78* **CP**
(OS144 TL785851) 1m S of Brandon on B1106. 32 acres. Landscaped grounds of Brandon House in Thetford Forest, nature trail, picnicking, riding. Management: Suffolk County Council.

Clare Castle and Bailey *Map 5 TL74* **CP**
(OS155 TL772452) Between Clare village and River Stour. 18½ acres. Remains of castle and bailey with old railway station developed as a country park and picnic place by conservation corps volunteers. Management: Suffolk County Council.

Easton Farm Park *Map 5 TM25* **CP**
(OS156 TM275582) W of Easton. 32½ acres. Displays and demonstrations of both early and modern dairy farming, bee keeping, farm animals including rare breeds, pets paddock, early agricultural machinery, nature trail, fishing, craft shop, tea room, facilities for disabled. Admission fee. Management: Mr J M Kerr.

Haughley *Map 5 TL96* **(A45) PS**
4m NW of Stowmarket (OS155 TL995615). Signposted in advance and at entrance. Sharply sloping grassland with young trees. 5 acres. Drinking water. Toilets. Parking 80.

The King's Picnic Place *Map 5 TL87* **(B1106) PS**
E side of B1106. 7m N of Bury St Edmunds (OS144 TL826750). Signposted at entrance. Areas of grass between trees. 7 acres. Furniture. Parking 150.

Knettishall Heath *Map 5 TL87* **CP/PS**
(OS144 TL895780) 4m SE of Thetford, Norfolk (near Euston Park). 240 acres. Claimed to be the first country park developed under the National Parks Act. Wild breckland along the valley of the River Little Ouse. Traversed along the western boundary by the Peddars Way. Management: Suffolk County Council. **Picnic Site** on unclassified road from Euston, 3m from Hopton (TL950805). Signposted in advance and at entrance. 10 acres. Parking 200.

Mildenhall Woods Transit Picnic Site *Map 5 TL77* **(A1065/A11) PS**
Barton Mills roundabout E side of A1065 ¾m N Barton Mills (OS143 TL728744). Signposted in advance and at entrance. 5 acres of grassland backed by pinewoods. Furniture. Toilets. Parking 50.

Rampart Field *Map 5 TL77* **(Off A1101) PS**
1m S of Icklingham on unclassified road to West Stow (OS144 TL790715). Signposted in advance and at entrance. 30 acres undulating shrubland with play area. Furniture. Parking 100.

SURREY

Box Hill *Map 4 TQ15* **CP/PS**
(OS187 TQ181519) 1½m NE of Dorking. 560 acres of commonland with woods and downland. Management: National Trust. **Picnic Site** on unclassified road 1m NE of Dorking 1m E of A24 (TQ173516). Signposted at road and at entrance. 50 acres. Drinking water, furniture, toilets, parking 150.

Epsom Downs *Map 4 TQ25* **(B290) PS**
1½m SE of Epsom (OS187 TQ218575). Extensive area crossed by minor roads.

Frensham Common *Map 4 SU84* **CP/PS**
(OS186 SU849401) 3m S of Farnham on A287. 778 acres of commonland and heath with pond. Boating and fishing. Management: Waverley District Council. **Picnic Site** at Frensham Ponds, 4m S of Farnham (SU849401). Signposted at entrance. Large open area of 3 acres. Toilets, parking 250.

Gibbet Hill, Devil's Punch Bowl *Map 4 SU83* **(A3) PS**
½m N of junction with A287 at Hindhead (OS186

66

SU896358). Signposted at entrance. 2 acres. Nature trail, drinking water, furniture. Toilets. Parking 180.

Horton *Map 4 TQ16* **CP**
(OS187 TQ190628) NW of Epsom. 205 acres. Farm and woodland. Nature trail, fishing. Management: Epsom & Ewell District Councils.

Leith Hill *Map 4 TQ14* **(Off A25)** **PS**
5m SW of Dorking on unclassified road off A25 (OS187 TQ135433). Highest point in Surrey (National Trust Property). Furniture. Parking 60.

Lightwater *Map 4 SU96* **CP**
(OS186 SU913619) W of Lightwater Village Inn S of Bagshot. 125 acres. Woodland and heath. Riding, fishing. Management: Surrey Heath District Council.

Newlands Corner *Map 4 TQ04* **(A25)** **PS**
On A25 at its junction with A247 3m E of Gomshall (OS186 TQ042492). Signposted in advance and at entrance. Furniture. Toilets. Parking 200.

Puttenham Common *Map 4 SU94* **(Off A31)** **PS**
1½m SW of Puttenham (OS186 SU915465). Grassy slopes with wide views of surrounding countryside. Parking 3,000.

Ranmore Common *Map 4 TQ15* **(Off A25)** **PS**
Unclassified road off A25, 2m NW of Dorking (OS187 TQ133504). Signposted at entrance. National Trust Property which gives access to good walking area. Parking 250.

Tilburstow Hill Viewpoint *Map 4 TQ35* **(Off A22) PS**
1½m S of Godstone (OS187 TQ345501). Viewpoint comanding wide areas of surrounding countryside. Parking 65.

Virginia Water *Map 4 SU96* **(A30)** **PS**
On A30, 2m NE of Sunningdale (OS175 SU977687). Large lake surrounded by parkland (part of Windsor Great Park). Toilets.

SUSSEX (EAST)
Ashdown Forest *Map 5 TQ43* **(A22/A275)** **PS**
Brick Kiln Farm: on N side of unclassified Wych Cross/Coleman's Hatch road, 1m E of Wych Cross (OS187 TQ437324). Signposted at entrance for eastbound traffic. Grassy area with trees, gorse and fern, ¾ acre. Furniture. No camping or caravanning. **Wych Cross:** on S side of unclassified Sharpthorne/Wych Cross road, 1m W of Wych Cross (TQ404323). Signposted at entrance for westbound traffic. Parking 300. No camping or caravanning.

Beachy Head *Map 5 TV59* **(Off B2103)** **PS**
3m SW of Eastbourne (OS199 TV595965). Signposted in advance. Clifftop affording excellent views of sea, coastline and lighthouse. Furniture. Toilets. Parking 300.

Ditchling Common *Map 4 TQ31* **CP/PS**
(OS198 TQ334186) E of Burgess Hill, 2m N of Ditchling. Pastures and scrubland with ponds. Fishing, nature trail, riding. Management: East Sussex County Council. **Picnic Site** at Ditchling Beacon off B2112 between Brighton (6m) and Ditchling (2m) (TQ332131). Signposted in advance. Access to South Downs Way. Parking 100.

Forest Way *Map 5 TQ43* **CP**
(OS187 TQ425355) 9 mile linear park along the route of the former railway line from Ashurst Junction to East Grinstead. Car park and main access from A22 at Forest Row, Foresters Arms. Walking, riding, cycling. Management: East Sussex County Council.

Hastings Country Park *Map 5 TQ81* **CP**
(OS199 TQ859119) Located between Hastings and Fairlight, access via entrance close to Fairlight Church, 260 acres. Meadowland with woods and heath. Fishing, boating and swimming. Management: Hastings District Council.

Piltdown Pond *Map 5 TQ42* **(B2102)** **PS**
4m from Uckfield via A22 and B2102 (OS198 TQ444223). Natural site overlooking 4 acre pond. ¼ acre. Parking 45.

Seven Sisters *Map 5 TV59* **CP**
(OS199 TV529984) 5m W of Eastbourne between A259 and the coast. Downland and marshland. Nature trail, fishing. 700 acres. Management: East Sussex County Council.

Vine Hall Forest Trail *Map 5 TQ72* **(B2089)** **PS**
S side of B2089 between A21 and A299, 3m SE of Robertsbridge (OS199 TQ764203). Signposted in advance 'Car-Park' for westbound traffic and at entrance 'Forestry Commission Vine Hall Forest'. Extensive forest area. Access to pleasant walks, furniture. Parking 35.

SUSSEX (WEST)
Cowdray Hill (Benbow Pond) *Map 4 SU92* **(Off A272) PS**
Situated N side of A272 at east end of Cowdray Park, Midhurst 2m, Petworth 4¾m (OS197 SU915223). Signposted in advance. Pleasant woodland with pond 2 acres. Parking 65.

Devil's Dyke *Map 4 TQ21* **(A23/A281)** **PS**
5½m NW of Brighton (OS198 TQ259108). 5 acres. Refreshment facilities, coin-operated telescope viewpoint, furniture. Toilets. Parking 90.

Duncton Hill *Map 4 SU91* **(A285)** **PS**
1m S of Duncton (OS197 SU955162). Signposted at entrance ⅓ acre. Nature trail, AA Viewpoint. Parking 15.

Fairmile Bottom Transit Picnic Site *Map 4 TQ01* **(A29)** **PS**
¼m NE Whiteways Lodge. NW of Arundel. (OS167 TQ002111). Toilets.

Finch's Field *Map 5 TQ33* **(Off B2028)** **PS**
West Hoathly (OS187 TQ365325). 2 acres. Parking 40.

Goodwood Estate *Map 4 SU81* **CP**
(OS197 SU890111) 6m N of Chichester. 60 acres. Within area of outstanding natural beauty, woods and downland, nature trail for the blind. Management: Goodwood Terrana Ltd.

Marden Forest *Map 4 SU81* **(Off B2146)** **PS**
On unclassified road 1m NE of Stoughton (OS197 SU924126). Signposted 'Marden Forest' in advance and at entrance. Forest area. 5 acres. Marked walks. Parking 150.

Weald and Downland Open Air Museum
Map 4 SU81 **CP**
(OS197 SU873126) ¼m SW of Singleton. 35 acres. Lake, woodland and meadows within area of outstanding natural beauty. Museum and historic build-

ings. Management: Weald and Downland Open Air Museum.

Whiteways Lodge *Map 4 TQ01* **(A29)** PS
A29 at its junction with A284 3m N of Arundel (OS197 TQ002108). Signposted in advance and at entrance. 3 acres. Nature trail, drinking water, furniture. Toilets. Parking 80.

WARWICKSHIRE

Burton Dassett Hills *Map 4 SP35* CP/PS
(OS151 SP396520) 4m NE of Kineton. 100 acres. Grassland and farmland. Footpath and bridleways. Management: Warwickshire County Council. **Picnic Sites:** off A41 8m N of Banbury near Avon Dasset (SP398518), 20 acres on high ground, furniture, parking 200; **also** off A41 9¾m N of Banbury (SP398519), signposted in advance and at entrance. 100 acres of open, sheep-grazed grassland. Access by tarmac roads and very safe for children. Toilets, unlimited parking (ticket meter).

Coombe Abbey *Map 4 SP37* CP
(OS140 SP395795) 4m E of Coventry city centre on A427. 290 acres. Gardens and woodland with lake. Boating, fishing, nature trail. Management: Coventry Metropolitan District Council.

Hartshill Hayes *Map 4 SP39* CP
(OS140 SP316947) 4m NW of Nuneaton off B4114 (formerly A47). Wood and grassland. Management: Warwickshire County Council.

Kingsbury *Map 4 SP29* CP
(OS139 SP209959) 12m NE of Birmingham. W of Kingsbury. Approach from A4091 or A4097. 1,050 acres. Lakes within reclaimed gravel pits. Fishing.

Yarningdale Common *Map 4 SP16* **(B4095)** PS
½m NW of Claverdon unclassified road off B4095 5m W Warwick (OS151 SP190660). Signposted in advance. 20 acres grass and gorseland. Parking 50.

WEST MIDLANDS

Cofton Common *Map 7 SP07* **(B4096)** PS
Lowhill Lane, Rednal. 3m NE of Bromsgrove (OS139 SP005764). Signposted at entrance. 130 acres. Public park. Drinking water. Furniture. Parking 60.

Lickey Hills *Map 7 SO97* CP/PS
(OS139 SO998754) 8m S of Birmingham. 530 acres of meadows, woodland and heath. Riding, boating. Management: Coventry County Borough. **Picnic Sites** at: Recreation Park on NW side of B4096, 4½m NE of Bromsgrove (SO996759). Signposted at entrance. 7 acres of picturesque park, pools, gardens, children's playground, furniture, drinking water, toilets, parking 120; Warren Lane on E side of B4096, 4½m NE of Bromsgrove (SO995755). Area bordered by small wall with cafe, children's playground. Parking 200.

Sandwell Valley *Map 7 SP09* **(Off A41)** PS
Park Lane (between A41 and A4041) West Bromwich 1¾m ENE opposite football ground (OS139 SP025923). Signposted at entrance. Open land with picnic site, located on the edge of large lake, sailing, nature trail, play area, miniature golf course. Furniture. Drinking water. Toilets. Parking 100.

Shenstone Woods *Map 7 SO98* **(A458)** PS
¾m NE of Halesowen (OS139 SO975838). 3½ acres. Grassed hill, small lake and woods, children's playground. Furniture. Parking 100.

Sutton Park *Map 7 SP19* **(A453)** PS
1m from centre of Sutton Coldfield (OS139 SP100965). Signposted in advance and at entrance. Large natural park with lake and woodlands, surrounded by urban development. Drinking water, furniture. Toilets. Extensive parking.

WILTSHIRE

Barbury Castle *Map 4 SU17* CP
(OS173 SU157761) 5m S of Swindon access from M4 (Junction 15) and Swindon via A345 or A361 then B4005 from Wroughton. 130 acres of downland incorporating an important iron age fort. Lond Distance Route 'The Ridgeway Path', public paths, walking and picnicking, information display, AA Viewpoint. Vehicles restricted to car park. Management: Wiltshire County Council.

Barton Farm *Map 3 ST86* CP
(OS173 ST823605) Bradford-on-Avon access from A363 in town centre. 36 acres of pastureland fringed by woodland following the River Avon and enclosed to the south by the Kennet and Avon Canal, access to canal towpath, information boards, fishing by day permit from Bradford-on-Avon and District Angling Association. Boats may be launched subject to licence from the Wessex Water Authority. No vehicles. Adjacent parking at town centre car park. Management: Wiltshire County Council.

Highwood and Hazel Wood Woodland Park
Map 3 ST55 CP
(OS183 ST835524) Brokerswood nr Westbury. 120 acres of preserved woodland with a 120-acre lake stocked with waterfowl and fish. The Phillips Countryside Museum of Natural History and Forestry adjoins the lake. Picnicking, woodland walks, fishing charged by the day limited to four rods, moderate entrance fee, up to three children free. Management: Private.

Inglesham/Lechlade *Map 4 SU29* **(Off A361)** PS
¼m S of Lechlade off A361 on W side adjoining Lechlade bridge (OS163 SU212993). Signposted 'Riverside Park' in advance and at entrance. 20 acres. Large fenced meadow adjacent to river and moorings, planted with shrubs and trees. Drinking water, furniture. Toilets. Extensive parking.

King Alfred's Tower *Map 3 ST73* **(Off B3092)** PS
2½m NW of Stourton 2½m SW of Kilmington on unclassified road (OS183 ST745351). Signposted in advance and at entrance. Meadowland in extensive natural woodland surrounding a brick tower circa 1271. Forest walks. Parking 150 (Voluntary fee).

Kingston Langley Transit Picnic Sites East and West *Map 3 ST97* **(A429)** PS
2m N of Chippenham (OS173 ST912763). Signposted in advance and at entrance. Both sides of carriageway screened from traffic. Landscaped grassed areas planted with shrubs and trees. Wooden fencing. Toilets with facilities for the disabled.

Pepperbox Hill *Map 4 SU22* **(A36)** PS
On NE side of A36 SE of Salisbury, ¾m NW of AA Box. Rough single track approach (OS184 SU212248). National Trust site on pleasant hill top with extensive views. Site of ornamental tower which is local landmark, grassland, shrubs and trees, play area.

Postern Hill (Savernake Forest) *Map 4 SU26* **(A346)** PS
1m S Marlborough (OS173 197683) Signposted at entrance. Level clearings with access road extending

into forest. Access point for walking. Drinking water, furniture, toilets. Unlimited parking.

Stourhead *Map 3 ST73* **(Off B3092) CP**
3½m NW of Mere in Stourton village (OS183 ST780345). Signposted in advance and at entrance. In extensive and elaborately landscaped grounds of house of historical interest owned by National Trust. 2 acres. Ideal for children, wooded walks, lakes, follies and miniature architectural reproductions, furniture, drinking water, refreshment facilities near house. Toilets. Parking (voluntary fee), house and landscaped grounds not included.

YORKSHIRE (NORTH)
The North York Moors National Park **(553 square miles)**
Beautiful wild moorland, rugged coast, pretty villages and ruined abbeys. Correspondence should be sent to Information Officer, North York Moors National Park, North Yorkshire County Council, The Old Vicarage, Bondgate, Helmsley, North Yorkshire YO6 5BP *tel* Helmsley (04392) 70657.
Information centres:

Danby	National Park Centre, Danby Lodge, Nr Whitby *tel* Castleton 654 weekends only in winter
Hutton-le-Hole	Ryedale Folk Museum *tel* Lastingham 367 (owned and managed by the museum) summer only
Pickering Station	*tel* 73791 (owned and managed jointly with North York Moors Railway Trust)
Ravenscar	National Trust Information Centre *tel* Scarborough 870138
Sutton Park	top of Sutton Bank, Thirsk *tel* Thirsk 597426

The Yorkshire Dales National Park **(680 square miles)**
High moorland, pretty Dales villages, waterfalls and rushing streams. Correspondence should be sent to Information Officer, Yorkshire Dales National Park, Yorebridge House, Bainbridge, Leyburn, North Yorkshire DL8 5BP *tel* Wensleydale (0969) 50456.
Information Centres:

Aysgarth Falls	Car Park *tel* 424 summer only
Clapham	Reading Room *tel* 419 summer only
Hawes (caravan)	Station Yard *tel* 450 summer only
Malham	Car Park *tel* Airton 363 summer only
Sedbergh	72 Main Street *tel* 20125

Weather Information Service *tel* Horton-in-Ribblesdale 333 normal office hours (except Tuesdays).

Bickley Gate *Map 8 SE99* **(Off A171) PS**
On unclassified road 6m W of A171 at Scalby (OS101 SE913912). Signposted at entrance. Natural site on hilltop above village. ⅓ acre. Furniture. Parking 10.

Bolton Abbey (Cavendish Pavilion) *Map 8 SE05* **(Off B6160) PS**
On unclassified road W of Bolton Abbey (OS104 SE071539). 9 acres.

Brimham Rocks *Map 8 SE26* **CP/PS**
(OS99 SE206650) 3½m NW of Ripley off B6165. Unusual rock forms on elevated moorland. Cafe and information centre under development in old shooting lodge. Parking fee. Management: National Trust.
Picnic Site 3m E of Pateley Bridge, N of B6165 and S of B6265, signposted from both, in advance and at entrance. (SE212650) Drinking water, toilets, parking 150.

Church Cliff *Map 8 TA18* **CP**
(OS101 TA121814) Filey. Management: Scarborough Borough Council.

Clay Bank *Map 8 NZ50* **(B1257) PS**
3m S of Broughton (OS93 NZ572040). 842ft above sea level. Parking 50.

Cockmoor Hill, Troutsdale *Map 8 SE98* **(Off A170) PS**
On unclassified Snainton/Hackness road. Snainton 3m (OS101 SE915868). Signposted at entrance. Commonland surrounded by woods. ½ acre. Parking 15.

Falling Foss *Map 8 NZ80* **(Off B1416) PS**
Off unclassified road to Ruswarp off B1416 (OS94 NZ889038). Signposted in advance and at entrance. ¾ acre. Parking 30.

Hardrow Scaur *Map 7 SD89* **(Off A684) PS**
2m N of A684 from Hawes on unclassified road to Hardrow (OS98 SD870915). Signposted in advance and at entrance. Natural site with a waterfall reputed to be the longest in England. Admission charge with access from Green Dragon Inn. Drinking water, furniture. Toilets. Parking 50.

Ingleby Bank *Map 8 NZ50* **(Off B1257) PS**
½m E of Ingleby Greenhow on unclassified road from Broughton (OS93 NZ580062). Signposted in advance. In Forestry Commission and National Parkland. Parking 30.

Reasty Hill Top *Map 8 SE99* **(Off A171) PS**
On unclassified road to Harwood Dale 4m W of A171 at Scalby (OS101 SE966944). Signposted at entrance. On brow of steep hill with narrow steeply ascending approach for cars. ⅛ acre. Furniture. Parking 10.

River Swale *Map 8 NZ10* **(A6108) PS**
1m W of Richmond (OS92 NZ147005). 135 acres.

Sheep Wash *Map 8 SE48* **(Off A19) PS**
On unclassified road, signposted Osmotherley and Swainby, off A19 11m N of Thirsk (OS100 SE460985). Reservoir and streams set in picturesque surroundings. 2½ acres. Parking 50.

Sil Howe *Map 8 NZ80* **(Off A169) PS**
Off A169 7m S of Whitby (OS94 NZ853028). Elevated moorland area. Parking 6.

Skelder Top *Map 8 NZ80* **(A171) PS**
S side of A171 4m W of Whitby (OS94 NZ841087). On E side of N Yorkshire moors. ½ acre. Parking 100.

Sledgates, Fylingdales *Map 8 NZ90* **(Off A171) PS**
½m along unclassified road off A171). Signposted Fyling Thorpe (OS94 NZ931020). Signposted at entrance. Under brow of steep hill. ⅛ acre. Parking 50.

Staxton Hill *Map 8 TA07* **(A64) PS**
½m from Staxton village (OS101 TA012784). Signposted in advance and at entrance. Sloping tree-planted grass area adjoining separate car park, panoramic views, furniture, drinking water, disabled toilets. Parking 40.

Sutton Bank *Map 8 SE58* **(A170)** PS
A170 6m E of Thirsk (OS100 SE515830). Signposted
at entrance. AA Viewpoint. 4 acres. Parking 220.

YORKSHIRE (SOUTH)

Cannon Hall Park *Map 8 SE20* CP/PS
(OS110 SE274081) 4½m W of Barnsley. 70 acres. Hall
with parkland, gardens and lake. Fishing, footpath.
Management: Barnsley Metropolitan District Council.
Picnic Site off A635, ½m N of Cawthorne (SE272085).
Parking 150.

Cusworth Country Park *Map 8 SE50* CP
(OS111 SE546038) 2m W of Doncaster nr Sprot-
borough. 57 acres of woodland and gardens developed from parkland of Cusworth Hall which is now
a museum. History trail, fishing. Management: Doncaster District Council.

Howell Wood *Map 8 SE40* CP
(OS111 SE437092) 1½m SE of South Kirby. 115 acres
of woodland under development as a country park,
specimen trees, nature trails. Management: North
Yorkshire County Council.

Worsborough Mill *Map 8 SE30* CP
(OS111 SE346033) S of Worsborough off A61. 95
acres of woodland and farmland under development
as a country park around a reservoir, mill pond and
working corn mill restored as an industrial museum
interpretation centre, fishing, sailing, nature trail.

YORKSHIRE (WEST)

Penistone Hill *Map 8 SE03* CP
(OS104 SE022367) Keighley. Haworth near Bronte
Museum. Heathland, old quarry workings, railway,
nature trail. Management: West Yorkshire Metropolitan
County Council.

Wales

CLWYD

Bod Petryal *Map 6 SJ03* **(B5105)** PS
In Clocaenog Forest on B5105, Llanfihangel Glyn Myfr
3½m (OS116 SJ037512). Open area among trees with
small lake. 1½ acres. Furniture. Parking 20.

Erddig Park *Map 7 SJ34* CP
(OS117 SJ335486) 1m SW Wrexham. Parkland and
woodland with river. Picnic site, industrial trail, agricultural museum. Management: National Trust.

Loggerheads *Map 6 SJ16* CP
(OS116 SJ198629) 2m W of Mold on A494, 65 acres.
Woodland in river valley. Information centre, nature
trail. Management: Clwyd County Council.

Moel Arthur *Map 6 SJ16* CP
(OS116 SJ151625) 5m equidistant from Mold, Ruthin,
Denbigh and Holywell. Access road poor. 300 acres.
Moorland, Hill fort, Offa's Dyke. Management: Clwyd
County Council.

Moel Famau *Map 6 SJ16* CP/PS
(OS116 SJ142671) 6m W of Mold, access roads poor.
1,800 acres of moorland with reservoir, hill fort and
part of Offa's Dyke. Management: Clwyd County
Council. **Picnic Site** ¾m N of Llanferres on unclassified road off Mold/Ruthin road (SJ172611). 1 acre.
Parking 30.

DYFED

Pembrokeshire Coast National Park (225 square
miles)
Beautiful, unspoilt sandy beaches, grassy cliff-top
walks, offshore nature reserve islands. Correspondence should be sent to Information Officer, Pembrokeshire Coast National Park, County Offices,
Haverfordwest, Dyfed SA61 1QZ *tel* Haverfordwest
(0437) 3131.
Information Centres:

Broad Haven	Car Park *tel* 412	
Haverfordwest	40 High Street *tel* 66141	
Kilgetty	Kingsmoor Common *tel* Saun-dersfoot 812175	
Newport	Carn Ingli, East Street *tel* 820912	
Pembroke	Castle Terrace *tel* 2148	
St David's	City Hall *tel* 392	
Tenby	The Norton *tel* 3510	

Abergorlech *Map 2 SN53* **(B4310)** PS
At Abergorlech village 12m N of Llandeilo between
Brechfa and Llansawel (OS146 SN587336). Signposted in advance and at entrance. Small attractive
site bordering a small stream, grassy banks and
young trees. 1 acre. Forest walks, furniture. Parking
20.

The Arch *Map 6 SN77* **(B4974)** PS
2m S of Devil's Bridge (OS135 SN765755). Forestry
Commission signpost at entrance. 1½ acres. Furniture, chemical toilets. Parking 30.

Black Mountains *Map 3 SN71* **(A4069)** PS
4m N of Brynamman (OS160 SN732189). A small site
provided as part of the National Park amenities. 1
acre. Furniture. Parking 20.

Bwlch Nant-Yr-Arian (Rheidol Forest) *Map 2 SN24*
(A44) PS
10m E Aberystwyth (OS135 SN718813) 10 acres.
Signposted in advance and at entrance. Undulating
wooded site. Information board. Forest trail, Jubilee
walk. Viewpoint. Visitor centre, drinking water, furniture. Toilets with facilities for disabled.

Carew Mill *Map 2 SN00* **(Off A4075)** PS
On unclassified road 400 yds from A4075 at Carew
(OS158 SN045040). Signposted in advance at entrance. Pleasant, open grass area overlooking estuary
and Carew Mill. 1 acre. Furniture. Parking 25.

Coed-Craig-yr-Ogof *Map 6 SN67* **(Off B4340)** PS
½m E of B4340 on unclassified road from Llanafan
Bridge to Pontrhydygroes (OS135 SN 695717). Signposted in advance and at entrance. On riverside in
wooded area. 1 acre. Forest walk, furniture. Parking
10.

Coed Deufor *Map 2 SN24* **(A474)** PS
S side A474 ¾m W Cenarth (OS145 SN255422).
Signposted at entrance. 1 acre sloping woodland.
Walk, furniture. Parking 20.

Ffynnon Byrgwm, Brechfa *Map 2 SN53* **(B4310)**
PS
Between Brechfa and Abegoroch, 2m NE Brechfa.
(OS146 SN544315). Signposted in advance and at
entrance. Set among mature trees on elevated position with extensive views. 1 acre. Forest walks, furniture, ample parking.

Fishguard Harbour Transit Picnic Site
Map 2 SN93 **(A40)** PS

Between Fishguard and Goodwick 1m from Fishguard town centre (OS157 SN952377). 1 acre. Signposted at entrance. Purpose built terrace overlooking the harbour. Furniture. Toilets. Parking 14.

Llyn Brianne Dam   *Map 2 SN74*
(Unclassified road)   PS
Access N from A40 at Llandovery, via 12 miles of well-signed unclassified roads. (OS146 SN794482) secluded area overlooking reservoir. Portaloo.

Pont Abraham Transit Picnic Site   *Map 2 SN50*
(M4/A48)   PS
At Junction 49 on A48 adjacent to M4 (OS159 SN576074). Designated Rest Area, Cafe, Modern toilets with facilities for disabled. Parking 50.

Pwllpeiran   *Map 6 SN77* **(Off B4574)**   PS
On unclassified road off B4574 2½m SE of Devil's Bridge (OS135 SN774748). 1 acre. Parking 10.

Transit Picnic Site   *Map 2 SN11* **(A40/A478)**   PS
1½m N of Narberth (OS158 SN122167). Signposted in advance and at entrance. Useful level area. Furniture. Facilities for the disabled. Toilets. Parking 50.

GLAMORGAN (MID)
Garwnant Forest Centre   *Map 3 SO01* **(Off A470)**
PS
5m N Merthyr Tydfil ¼m W A470 (OS160 SO003132) Forestry site on wooded high ground with views of Llwyn Reservoir. Visitor Centre & forest walks, furniture. Toilets. Parking 50.

Taf Fechan Reservoir   *Map 3 SO01*
(Unclassified road)   PS
Near Merthyr Tydfil on Talybont road. 1m N of Pontsticill (OS160 SO057122) 2 acres amidst trees overlooking reservoir. Furniture. No Toilets. Parking 30.

GLAMORGAN (SOUTH)
Cefn Onn   *Map 3 ST18*   CP
(OS171 ST175845) 3m N of Cardiff. 135 acres of ponds, arboreta and gardens. Cafe. Management: Cardiff City Council.

Comeston   *Map 3 ST16*   CP
(OS171 ST182689) 1m S of Penarth on B4267 to Barry. 10 acres of reclaimed land. Nature conservation area with observation points, signed walks, sailing, fishing, canoeing, model boating, sub aqua diving, picnic area. Management: Vale of Glamorgan Borough Council.

Porthkerry Park   *Map 3 ST06*   CP
(OS171 ST092672) Between Barry and Rhoose. 225 acres. A wooded valley ending at the seashore, beach, nature reserve, pitch and putt, shop. Management: Vale of Glamorgan District Council.

GLAMORGAN (WEST)
Afan Argoed   *Map 3 SS89*   CP
(OS170 SS817950) 5m NE of Port Talbot on A4107. 140 acres, forested valley with short forest walks and longer forest trails. Countryside Centre, Welsh Miners Museum, disabled facilities including walks, access to Afan Valley scenic route, orienteering course. Management: West Glamorgan County Council and Forestry Commission.

Margam Park   *Map 3 SS88*   CP
(OS170 SS813849) Access 2m NW of Pyle on A48. 800 acres. A leisure park. Park and ride buses,

marked walks, parkland centre. Charge for parking. Management: West Glamorgan County Council.

GWENT
Barnets Wood   *Map 3 ST59* **(B4235)**   PS
2m W of Chepstow (OS162 ST518944). Signposted at entrance. Simple site on the edge of Great Barnets Wood. 1 acre. Horse riding trail, signposted forest walks. Parking 20.

Cadira Beeches   *Map 3 ST49* **(Off A48)**   PS
5m SE of Usk 6½m NW Chepstow on unclassified road between A449 and A48 (OS171 ST423948). Forestry Commission sign at entrance. Natural forest site. 2 acres. Viewpoint, forest walks, furniture. Parking 50.

Caldicot Castle   *Map 3 ST48*   CP
(OS171 ST486884) Near Caldicot town centre. 53 acres. Parkland around castle with wooded slopes and open meadowland. Management: Gwent County Council and Monmouth District Council.

Llandegfedd Reservoir, Eastern, Usk Point, Pettingdale Point and Sor Brook Picnic Areas
Map 3 ST39 **(Off A449/A4042)**   PS
8m N of Newport signed off A449 and A4042. 3m SE of Pontypool 4m W of Usk (OS171 ST329984). Signposted in advance and at entrance. A developed site which has retained its natural beauty. Eastern Picnic Area is a good vantage point. Usk Point Picnic Area, is accessible via footpath from the car park and also by road. Pettingdale Point Picnic and Viewing Area, is accessible via Gluvad Lane and footpath 1½m. Sor Brook Picnic Area, below the dam, is a secluded spot bordered by streams. Footpaths, fishing from the bankside and hired boats, both seasonal and daily fishing permits may be obtained from the Welsh Water Authority, Gluvad Lane, Pontypool, Gwent. Tel. Pontypool 55333, also seasonal sailing permits and daily sailing permits can be obtained on site from a self-service machine. Furniture, drinking water, warden service. Toilets. Extensive parking.

Mitchell Troy Transit Picnic Site   *Map 3 SO41*
(A449)   PS
On dual carriageway linking M4/M50. 1m S of Monmouth on N carriageway. (OS162 SO498110). Signposted in advance and at entrance. Small pleasantly laid-out site. ¼ acre. Toilets. Parking 50.

Nine Wells   *Map 3 ST49* **(Off A48)**   PS
5m SE of Usk on unclassified road between A449 and A48 in Wentwood Forest (OS171 ST426943). Forestry Commission sign at entrance. Attractive sheltered area. 2 acres. Forest walks, furniture. Parking 25.

Pen-y-Fan Pond   *Map 3 SO10*   CP
(OS171 SO196006) Access via new industrial estate road off the B4251. Blackwood to Crumlin road. Area around a canal feeder pond with access to many public paths and providing good walking terrain. Picnic area, rowing boats for hire, fishing by permit, model boating, refreshment kiosk. Warden Service. Management: Gwent County Council.

Prysgau Bach   *Map 3 ST49* **(B4235)**   PS
3m W of Chepstow (OS162 ST494943). Signposted in advance. On edge of forest overlooking valley. ½ acre. Furniture. Parking 20.

Tintern Railway Station Picnic Area   *Map 3 ST50*
(A466)   PS
A seasonal site open 10.30am–6pm. Right-hand side

of road N from Tintern (OS162 ST536005). Signposted in advance and at entrance. Furniture, drinking water, guided walks, railway exhibition, warden, information service, on route of 16m Wye Valley Walk. Toilets. Parking 50 (fee).

Tredegar House (Urban Fringe Country Park)
Map 3 ST28 **CP**
(OS171 ST295854) Off A48 2m W of Newport, on unclassified road. Signposted in advance from A48 and at entrance. 90 acres. The house and grounds of Tredegar House in the process of long term restoration to show decor and gardening styles of various periods. Access at moderate additional charge to the house, boating lake, rare breeds farm with bird garden and aquarium. Donkey rides, fishing, woodland walk, picnic site, play area, cafe. Management: Newport Borough Council.

Wentwood Lodge *Map 3 ST49*
(Unclassified road) **PS**
5½m E Usk. 6½m NW Chepstow. (OS171 ST429937). Quiet site with viewpoint, furniture, toilets. Parking 50.

Wentwood Reservoir *Map 3 ST49*
(Unclassified road) **PS**
6m Usk 9m Chepstow. On unclassified road between A48 and A449 (OS171 ST429939). Signposted 'Wentwood' at entrance. Quiet area with excellent views, on elevated position overlooking reservoir. 10 acres. Drinking water, furniture. Toilet facilities for disabled. Parking 50.

Whitehall Picnic Area Transit Picnic Site
Map 3 ST39 **(A449)** **PS**
Both sides A449 Coldra Usk road 3m N of M4 Junction 24 (OS171 ST389940). Signposted in advance and at entrance. Toilets for disabled.

Whitestone *Map 3 SO50* **(Unclassified road)** **PS**
1½m W Llandogo 1½m SE Trelleck on unclassified road between A466 and B4293 (OS162 524030). Signposted at entrance. Attractive wooded site in elevated position. 2 acres. Signed forest walks, furniture. Portaloos. Parking 40.

GWYNEDD

Snowdonia (838 square miles)
Dramatic mountain scenery, Snowdonia Forest Park, windswept coastline and steam railways. Correspondence should be sent to National Park Officer, Snowdonia National Park, Penrhyndeudraeth, Gwynedd LL48 6LS *tel* Porthmadog (0766) 770274.
Information Centres:

Aberdovey	The Wharf *tel* 321 summer only
Bala	Old British High School, High Street, *tel* 367 summer only
Betws-y-Coed	Royal Oak Stables summer only
Blaenau Ffestiniog	Queens Bridge *tel* 360 summer only
Conwy	Castle Street *tel* 2248 summer only
Dolgellau	Beechwood House *tel* 422888 summer only
Harlech	Gwyddfor House, High Street *tel* 658 summer only
Llanberis	Community Centre *tel* 765 summer only
Plas Tan y Bwlch (caravan)	

Aberhirnant Valley *Map 6 SH72* **(Off A470)** **PS**
Along unclassified road approx 1m S of Ganlwyd (OS124 SH 727232). ¼ acre. Parking 12.

Bala Lake Foreshore *Map 6 SH93* **(B4403)** **PS**
Alongside B4403 approx 3½m W of Bala near Llangower (OS125 SH905327). ½ acre. Access to lake, furniture. Parking 15.

Bont Newydd *Map 6 SH74* **(A 470)** **PS**
1m SE of Ffestiniog (OS124 SH713408). Signposted at entrance. Grassy riverbank with young trees. 2 acres. Parking 6.

Cae'n-y-Coed Arboretum *Map 6 SH75* **(A5)** **CP**
2½m W of Betws-y-Coed (OS115 SH779569). Signposted in advance and at entrance. 2 acres. Attractive area in wooded valley. Forest walks, furniture, aboretum. Toilets with facilities for disabled. Parking 25 (fee).

Crogenan Lakes *Map 6 SH61* **(Off A493)** **PS**
In Snowdonia Forest Park 6m SW of Dolgellau. 5 gates along approach (OS124 SH658146). Unsuitable for large vehicles and caravans. 1 acre. Parking 60.

Dolgyfeilliau Bridge *Map 6 SH72* **(Off A470)** **PS**
Alongside River Eden approx 1½m N of Ganllwyd (OS124 SH722269). Signposted in advance and at entrance ½ acre. Furniture. Chemical Toilets. Parking 18.

Gwydyr Uchaf *Map 6 SH76* **(B5106)** **PS**
1m W Llanrwst almost opposite Gwyder Castle (OS115 796609). Signposted at entrance. ½ acre. Views over Vale of Conway. Visitor centre, furniture. Toilets. Parking 8.

Lyn Padarn *Map 6 SH56* **CP**
(OS115 SH585602) E of Llanberis. 320 acres. Wood and heathland, disused quarry containing lake. Water sports, nature trail, industrial trail, woodland walks, descriptive leaflets on site. Management: Gwynedd County Council.

Pont-Caer Gors *Map 6 SH55* **(A4085)** **PS**
2m N of Beddgelert (OS115 SH576509). Signposted at entrance. 1 acre. Furniture. Toilets. Parking 30.

Tyn-y-Groes Transit Picnic Site *Map 6 SH72* **(Off A470)** **PS**
Alongside River Mawddach off A470 1m S of Ganllwyd (OS124 SH731235). Signposted in advance and at entrance. ¼ acre. Forest trail, furniture. Chemical toilets. Parking 20 (fee).

POWYS

Brecon Beacons National Park (519 square miles)
High mountains, forests, rushing mountain streams and waterfalls. Correspondence should be sent to Information Officer, Brecon Beacons National Park, Glamorgan Street, Brecon, Powys LD3 7DP *tel* Brecon (0874) 4437.
Information Centres:

Aberclydach	near Talybont-on-Usk (owned and managed by Welsh Water Authority) open mainly summer weekends
Abergavenny	Monk Street *tel* 3254 summer only, closed Sunday

72

Craig-y-Nos Country Park — Pen-y-Cae *tel* Abercrave 395. Information staff on duty mainly during summer weekends

Danywenallt Study Centre — near Talybont-on-Usk, Brecon *tel* 677 (admission by arrangement)

Libanus — Mountain Centre *tel* 3366

Llandovery — 8 Broad Street *tel* 20693

Brecon Beacons Mountain Centre *Map 3 SN92* **(Off A4215)** PS
Off A4215 5m SW of Brecon (OS160 SN977262). Signposted in advance and at entrance. Within National Park. Drinking water, furniture, preparation and washing-up facilities, facilities for disabled, cafeteria daily closing 5–8pm

Craig-y-Nos *Map 3 SN81* CP
(OS160 SN845155) 6m N of Ystradgynlais on the A4067. Swansea-Sennybridge Road. 40 acres of woodland and meadow with river and artificial lake, access by footpath to Dan-yr-Ogof caves, tickets and licences available for fishing. Management: Brecon Beacons National Park Authority.

Ffawyddy *Map 3 SO22/SO23* **(Off A40 & A465)** PS
In **Mynydd Ddu Forest**: on unclassified road to Grwyne Fawr Reservoir from Abergavenny via unclassified roads from A40 and A465 (OS161 SO266252). Signposted in advance and at entrance. Flat grassy riverside area bordered by mature trees. 1 acre. Forest walks, furniture, parking 20. **Also** At head of **Grwyne Fawr Valley** approx 11m N of Abergavenny via unclassified roads from A40 and A465. (SO241328). Signposted at entrance. Flat grassy area by river running through forest. 2 acres. Furniture. Parking 20.

Hafren Road *Map 6 SN88* **(Off A470)** PS
7m from Llanidloes off A470 (OS135 SN865868). Signposted in advance and at entrance by Forestry Commission sign. 1 acre. Open ground in wooded valley overlooking stream. Cautious approach advised on narrow road with bends. Furniture. Children's climbing frame.

Llyn Clywedog *Map 6 SN98* **(Off B4518)** PS
Bwlch-y-Gele Dam on B4518 4m NW of Llanidloes (OS136 SN922883). Signposted 'Parking Area' at entrance. Three parking areas beside lake. ¾ acre. Grassy hollow with views. Furniture, toilets, parking 30. **Clywedog Dam** 2m NW of Llanidloes and ½m NW of Stylittle via 'scenic route' (SN915870). Good views over surrounding countryside. Nature trail, Bryntail mine, furniture, toilets. Parking 50 (via single track).

Sugar Loaf *Map 2 SN84* **(A483)** PS
4m SW of Llanwrtyd Wells adjacent AA box 429. (OS147 SN838429). Signposted in advance and at entrance. 26 acres. Attractive site amidst fine wooded hills affording hillside walks and views. Furniture. Parking 30.

Scotland

BORDERS

Cambridge Picnic Site *Map 12 NT54* **(A697)** PS
A697 Lauder 3½m, at junction with unclassified road to Spottiswoode (OS74 NT585482). Signposted in advance and at entrance. Converted lay-by with grassed picnic areas. ½ acre, furniture. 'Portaloo'. Parking 20.

Cardrona Forest Walks *Map 11 NT23* **(B7062)** PS
3m E Peebles (OS73 NT295383). Signposted at entrance. 2 acres. Within Glentress Forest by small burn. Access to various forest walks. Furniture. Parking 20.

At Chirnside *Map 11 NT84* **(Junction B4355/B6437)** PS
Outside village (OS74 NT877567) 1½ acre grassy area with outlook across the Tweed Valley. Furniture. No Toilets. Parking 12.

At Coldstream *Map 12 NT83* **(Off A697)** PS
W side of Coldstream (OS74 NT841396) Signposted at entrance. Tree studded site by small burn. 2 acres. Furniture. Parking 10.

Glenmayne Haugh *Map 12 NT53* **(Off A7T)** PS
2m SE Galashiels on unclassified road between A7 and A6091. (OS73 NT504337) on N bank of River Tweed. 4 acres. Fishing, drinking water, furniture. Toilets. Parking 120.

Glentress Forest *Map 12 NT23* **(A72)** PS
Off A72 2m E Peebles (OS73 NT284396). Signposted in advance and at entrance, area by small burn with access to forest trails. Information centre, furniture. Toilets. Parking 20.

Mayfield Riverside Walk (Kelso) *Map 12 NT73* PS
Abbotsford Grove on river bank by Kelso Abbey (OS74 NT730337). Signposted in advance and at entrance, ¼m of grass and mature tree-studded land along the River Tweed. Fishing by permit. Bathing dangerous. Drinking water, furniture. Parking 50.

Meikle Harelaw Picnic Area *Map 12 NT64* **(A697)** PS
Coldstream Careffraemill Road 3½m W of Greenlaw. (OS74 NT657470). Signposted in advance and at entrance. Area cleared from section of old road. Grass with gorse and trees. Exceptional view. Furniture. Parking 30.

Meldons Picnic Area *Map 11 NT24* **(Unclassified road)** PS
Three separate areas within ½m on unclassified road linking A72 and A703, through Meldon Hills (OS73 NT215435). Signposted in advance and at entrance. Close to Meldon Burn and many archaeological features. Cairn marker on each site with display of interesting items. Drinking water, furniture. Toilets. Parking 200.

Rankleburn *Map 11 NT31* **(Off B709)** PS
¾m SE of Tushielawon B711 off B709. (OS79 NT310169). Parking 100.

St. Mary's Loch *Map 11 NT22* **(A708)** PS
Mid-way between Selkirk and Moffat (OS73 NT238205). Grass on shingle between two lochs. 3 acres. Yacht club. Toilets with facilities for the disabled. Parking 50.

Teviothead *Map 12 NT40* **(A7)** PS
W side of A7 1m S of Teviothead Post Office (OS79 NT401042). Signposted in advance. Grassy riverside site with tarmac parking area. 2 acres. Drinking water, furniture. Toilets. Parking 12.

Thornylee *Map 11 NT43* **(Off A72)** PS
3m E Walkerburn (OS73 NT406364). Signposted in advance. Exposed site high on bracken clad hillside, forest walks, furniture. No Toilets. Parking 6.

CENTRAL

David Marshall Lodge (Carnegie Building)
Map 11 NN50 **(A821)** PS
¾m E of Aberfoyle (OS57 NN520014). Signposted in advance and at entrance. Extensive area of forestry land with parking and adjacent grassed picnic areas, grouped around central lake. Furniture, drinking water, restaurant, information centre, static displays and maps of local features. AA Viewpoint, disabled toilets. Parking 50.

Gallochy *Map 10 NS39* **(Continuation of B837)** PS
On unclassified road approx 2½m S of Rowardennan (OS56 NS390950). Woodland site on shore of Loch Lomond.

Garron Forest B *Map 11 NS68* **(B818)** PS
4.2m E Fintry (OS57 NS681859). Signposted in advance and at entrance. On grass knoll amidst the forest incorporating ruins of Dundaff Castle. Furniture. Parking 80.

Garron Valley Forest *Map 11 NS78* **(B818)** PS
1½m N Garron Bridge. (OS57 NS721838). Signposting in advance and at entrance. Level grassy site by River Garron close to the foot of the reservoir, adjacent to forest. Number of signed walks. Furniture. Toilets. Parking 40.

Kincardine Bridge *Map 11 NS98* **(A88)** PS
Near S access to bridge on A88. (OS65 NS912859). Signposted at entrance. Toilets. Parking 50.

Leanach Car Park and Walks *Map 11 NS50* **(A821)** PS
3.8m E of Aberfoyle (OS57 NS516049). Signposted in advance and at entrance. Elevated grassy site with good views close to the edge of The Achray Forest. Marked Forest Walks. Furniture. Parking 15.

Loch Lubhaia *Map 11 NN42* **(A85)** PS
3m E Crianlarich (OS51 NN427268). A level roadside site with viewpoint and lochside walks sited at the foot of Ben More by Loch Lubhaia. Access restricted to 6'6" high. Furniture. Parking 20.

Mealldhuinne *Map 11 NS39*
(Continuation of B837) PS
On unclassified road approx 1m S of Rowardennan on E side of loch (OS56 NS365984). Signposted in advance and at entrance. Natural woodland site with stream. 3 acres. Parking 70.

Milarrochy *Map 10 NS49* **(B837)** PS
1m N of Balmaha (OS56 NS408928). Natural woodland on loch shore. 2 acres.

Ochil Hills, Woodland Park *Map 11 NS89* **(A91)** PS
E of Alva (OS58 NS893973). Signposted at entrance, 15 acres of woodland on the 'Ochil Fault'. Viewpoints, woodland walks, furniture. Parking 20.

Picnic Site *Map 11 NN52* **(A85)** PS
3½m W of Lochearnhead village. Lochearnhead to Crianlarich road (OS51 NN559283). Signposted in advance and at entrance. Rugged, elevated site. Parking 20.

Queens View *Map 11 NS58* **(A809)** PS
On A809 4m S of Drymen (OS64 NS500830). Signposted at entrance. On the edge of moorland. 1 acre. AA Viewpoint. Access to hill walking. Parking 60.

Rowardennan *Map 10 NS39*
(Continuation of B837) PS
On unclassified road adjacent to village (OS56 NS366985). On hillside adjacent to right of way to Ben Lomond. 3 acres. Access to hill walking. Parking 150.

Strathyre *Map 11 NN51* **(A84)** PS
Outside Strathyre village (OS57 NN562165). Signposted in advance and at entrance. Large grassy area beside river. 10 acres. Toilets. Parking 50.

Wilmirnog *Map 11 NN60* **(A821)** PS
400yds from junction with A84 (OS57 NN607082). Signposted at entrance. Landscaped close to River Leny with access to the former Stirling–Oban railway now a footpath. Furniture. Parking 15.

DUMFRIES & GALLOWAY

Forest of Ae *Map 11 NX99* **(Unclassified road)** PS
½m NW Ae Village access via Forestry Commission road (OS78 NX982911). Signposted in advance and at entrance. 2 acres secluded riverside clearing. Forest walks. Furniture. No Toilets. Parking 10.

Garries Park *Map 11 NX55* **(A75)** PS
200yds from car park and Tourist Information Centre, Gatehouse of Fleet (OS83 NX599561) 2 acres. Furniture. Toilets with facilities for the disabled. Parking 45.

Grey Mare's Tail *Map 11 NT11* **(A708)** PS
Between Moffat and Selkirk (OS79 NT187147). Signposted at entrance. Parking areas and riverside picnic spots in the Valley of the Moffat Water, hill walks to imposing waterfall. Parking 30.

Opposite Glenairlie Bridge *Map 11 NS80* **(A76)** PS
On W side 4½m S of Sanquhar (OS71 NS835056). Signposted in advance and at entrance. Attractive riverside environment fenced from road. Furniture. Drinking water. Toilets with facilities for the disabled. Parking 20.

At Langholm Transit Picnic Site *Map 11 NY34* **(Off A7)** PS
Northern edge of town (OS78 NY364848). 1 acre grass strip on the River Ewes. Drinking water. Furniture. Toilets. Parking 50.

Mabie Forest *Map 11 NX38* **(Off A710)** PS
6m S Dumfries, access via tarred driveway (OS84 NX950712). Signposted at entrance. 2 acres of grassy clearing amidst woodland. Forest Walks, furniture. Parking 15.

Murray Centre *Map 11 NX65* **(Off A75)** PS
E of Gatehouse of Fleet (OS84 NX657486). Signposted in advance and at entrance. 1 acre wooded site close to Forest Information Centre. Drinking water. Furniture. No Toilets. Parking 10.

Port Logan Shore *Map 10 NX14* **(B7065)** PS
At Port Logan (OS82 NX100410). Fishpond. Drinking water, furniture. Toilets.

Portpatrick Harbour *Map 10 NW95* **(A77)** PS
A77, N side of harbour above sea wall (OS82 NW999541). Signposted at entrance. Paddling pool, cliff and rock walks. Toilets. Parking 100.

St Medan, Monreith *Map 10 NX34* **(A747)** PS
1m SE of Monreith village, turn off at Knock School Caravan Site (OS83 NX360407). On shoreline. Rock fishing, safe bathing. Parking 100.

Sandhead Beach *Map 10 NX15* **(A715/A716)** PS
Junction A715/A716 (OS82 NX100510). Overlooking
Luce Bay. Safe bathing, drinking water.

Stranraer *Map 10 NX06* **(A77)** PS
1m N Stranraer (OS82 NX083630). Signposted in
advance and at entrance. Situated on shore with views
over Loch Ryan and the town of Stranraer. 2 acres.
Drinking water, furniture, toilets. Parking 20/30.

Un-named Site *Map 11 NX64* **(B427)** PS
3m Kirkcudbright 2½m Borque (OS84 NX657486).
Signposted at entrance. 3 acres grassy area in rocky
bay on pebble beach. Furniture. Toilets with facilities
for the disabled. Parking 50.

FIFE

Craigmead, Lomond Hills *Map 11 NO20* PS
On unclassified road between Leslie and Falkland
(OS58 NO227064). Signposted at entrance. 2 acres in
sheltered area with access to country walks. Furniture.
Toilets with facilities for the disabled, open during
summer. Parking 30.

Craigtoun Country Park *Map 12 NO41* CP
(OS59 NO477142). 2½m SW of St Andrews. Off
unclassified road from B939 in St Andrews to Pitscot-
tie. 50 acres.

East Common (Tayport) *Map 11 NQ42* PS
NE side (OS NO467284). 10 acres. Landscaped site
on reclaimed ground with outlook across Tay Estuary,
childrens play area, shore walks, furniture. No Toilets.
Parking 15.

Edensmuir *Map 11 NO20* **(B937)** PS
½m W Ladybank (OS59 NO293094). Signposted in
advance and at entrance. 3 acres bordered by Cupar
Forest. Forest walks. Furniture. Toilets with facility for
disabled. Parking 20.

Lochore Meadows Country Park *Map 11 NT19* CP
(OS58 NT176958). At Crosshill on the B290 from
Lochgelly to Ballingry centred in a district wasted by
extensive coal mining and subjected to Britains
largest land reclamation scheme. A loch surrounded
by attractive countryside. Sailing, canoeing, boating,
angling, ranger service, information centre. Management: Fife Regional Council.

GRAMPIAN

Broddie Castle *Map 14 HG95* **(A96)** PS
4½m W Forres (OS27 NH979577). Signposted in
advance and at entrance. 175 acres. Level grassy
area set amidst mature woodland forming heart of
castle grounds. Woodland walks, pictish stone, adventure playground. Furniture. Toilets. Parking 150.

Drumin Picnic Site *Map 15 NJ12* **(B9136)** PS
9½m NE Tomintoul (OS36 NJ182295). Signposted in
advance and at entrance. Level grassy roadside area
in open country overlooking R. Avon. ½ acre. Furniture. Parking 10.

Haddo Country Park *Map 15 NO83* CP
(OS30 NJ867346). 20m N Aberdeen off B9005. 180
acres of mature parkland with lake and mixed woodland supporting a variety of wildlife. Picnic sites,
footpaths, information centre, ranger service. Management: Grampian Regional Council.

Haughton House *Map 15 NJ51* CP
(OS37 NJ583169). Wooded parkland within grounds

of Houghton House. 50 acres. Nature trail, walks,
narrow gauge railway, shop. Parking controlled by
ticket machine. Management: Grampian Regional
Council.

Near Aboyne *Map 15 NO49* **(A93)** PS
2m W of Aboyne (OS44 NO495987). Signposted in
advance. Roadside site with outlook across Deeside.
Furniture. Parking 24.

Near Kildrummy Castle *Map 15 NJ41* **(A97)** PS
1m N Kildrummy Castle (OS37 NJ465175). Signposted at entrance. Simple grassed site planned with
young trees. ½ acre. Furniture. Parking 10.

Near Newburgh *Map 15 NK02* **(A975)** PS
2m N of Newburgh by Ythan Estuary (OS38
NK006284). Signposted at entrance. ½ acre. Outlook
across estuary and bird sanctuary.

Potarch Green *Map 15 NO69* **(B933)** PS
Off B933 near Potarch Bridge 4m W Banchory (OS37
NO607973). Signposted at entrance. 5 acres. Flat
grassy area surrounded by trees, close to River Dee
and various forest walks. Furniture. Toilets. Parking 20.

Roseisle Picnic Site *Map 15 NJ16* **(B9089)** PS
3m SW of Burghead (OS28 NJ1024655). Signposted
in advance and at entrance. 30 acres in Scots Pine
Forest, 150yds from sandy beach. Drinking water,
furniture. Toilets. Parking 60.

Speymouth *Map 15 NJ35* **(A98)** PS
½m E of Fochaber (OS28 SJ358587). Signposted in
advance and at entrance. On forest road in woodland
area. 5 acres. Forest walks, viewpoint, furniture.
Toilets. Parking 30.

Un-named Transit Picnic Site *Map 15 NJ53* **(A97)**
PS
On outskirts of Huntly between town and by-pass
roundabout (OS29 NJ525395). Signposted in ad-
vance from by-pass. Pleasant enclosed grassed area.
Drinking water, furniture. Toilets. Parking 50.

Well of Lecht *Map 15 NJ21* **(A939)** PS
5m SE of Tomintoul (OS36 NJ235153). Signposted in
advance and at entrance. Mountain streams, footpaths to old iron-stone mine. Drinking water. Parking
10.

HIGHLAND

Coldbackie Sands *Map 14 NC66* **(A836)** PS
3m NE of Tongue (OS10 NC612600). 200 yds from
sheltered sandy bay with steep approach. Parking 8.

Dalcraig *Map 14 NH41* **(B852)** PS
1m SW Foyers (OS34 NH493183). Signposted at
entrance. 2 acres. Small level site set among bushes
on S bank of River Foyers. Furniture. Parking 15.

Foulis Ferry *Map 15 NH56* **(A9)** PS
1m SW Evanton (OS21 NH599636). Signposted at
entrance. Landscaped site on the Cromarty Firth.
Restaurant, craft shop, furniture. Toilets. Parking 20.

Glenn Finnan Transit Picnic Site *Map 14 NM98*
(A830) PS
At the head of Loch Shiel between Fort William and
Mallaig (OS40 NM905808).

Gludie *Map 14 NH36* **(A832)** PS
At W end of Loch Luichart 5m W Garve (OS20
NH311625). Signposted at entrance. Riverside site

close to loch, falls and hydro electric development. Furniture. Parking 7.

Landmark Visitors' Centre, Carrbridge
Map 14 NH92 **(Off A9)** PS
Off A9 at Carrbridge (OS36 NH908224). Signposted in advance and at entrance. Tourist complex in heavily wooded area. Nature trail, sculptures, audio visual display. Drinking water, furniture. Toilets. Parking 200.

Little Garve *Map 14 NH36* **(Off A835)** PS
1m NE junction with A832 (OS20 NH396629). Forestry Commission. Signposting at entrance. 1 acre wooded sited by rocky banks of River Blackwater rapids. River walks. Furniture. Parking 10.

Loch Linnhe *Map 14 NN07* **(A82)** PS
3m S Fort William W side A82 (OS41 NN075705). Signposted in advance and at entrance. 1 acre. Small area utilising the natural rocky shore line of Loch Linnhe with fine views across the loch to the mountains of Morven. Furniture. Parking 10.

Loch Maree *Map 14 NH06* **(A832)** PS
2½m NW of Kinlochewe (OS19 NH001649). Signposted at entrance. Sheltered sites on loch shore. Nature reserve, walks, furniture.

Loch Oich *Map 14 NH39* **(A82)** PS
2m S Invergarry (OS34 NH302987). Signposted at entrance on Loch Oich. Drinking water, furniture. Toilets. Parking 20.

North Kessock *Map 14 NH64* **(A9)** PS
Access from N bound lane dual carriageway 200 yds from N side of Kessock Bridge (OS26 NH655481). Signposted in advance and at entrance. Elevated site above North Kessock with views over the Beauly Firth, bounded by shrubs, trees and grass bank. Furniture. Toilets with facilities for the disabled. Parking 40.

Ralia Transit Picnic Site *Map 14 NN79* **(B9150)** PS
At Junction with A9 2m S Newtonmore (OS35 NN707974). Signposted in advance and at entrance. Grassed undulating area with panoramic views. Viewpoint, drinking water, furniture. Toilets. Parking 50.

Redburn *Map 14 NH78* **(A9)** PS
2m SE Eddelton (OS21 NH735840). Signposted at entrance. Wooded roadside site with access to forest walks. Furniture. Parking 12.

Sangomore *Map 14 NC46* **(A838)** PS
At Durness (OS9 NC406675). Sandy bays. Near Smoo Cave. Parking 20.

LOTHIAN

Bilsdean Transit Picnic Site *Map 12 NT77* **(A1)** PS
N of Cockburnspath (OS67 NT766725). Signposted at entrance. Small roadside site with individual parking spaces by furniture and toilets. Parking 10.

Pencraig Picnic Place *Map 12 NT57* **(A1)** PS
N side of A1 4m E Haddington 1m W of East Linton (OS67 NT573765). Signposted at entrance. On high ground within wooded area. 1 acre. Tourist Information Centre, drinking water, furniture. Toilets. Parking 20.

STRATHCLYDE

Burnfoot Picnic Area *Map 10 NS25* **(A78)** PS
S end of Fairlie Village (OS63 NS206546) Signposted in advance and at entrance. Grassy headland planted with young trees with access to foreshore, panoramic views over Firth of Clyde. Tourist Information Board, drinking water, furniture. Toilets. Parking 20.

Cauldshore *Map 10 NX19* **(A77)** PS
At Girvan (OS76 NX181980). Signposted in advance and at entrance. On sandy foreshore. 1½ acres, toilets, furniture.

Duck Bay *Map 10 NS38* **(A811)** PS
1m N of Balloch (OS56 NS380823). Signposted in advance and at entrance. 2 acres grassy area bordered by trees with view of Loch Lomond. Furniture, drinking water. Toilets with facilities for the disabled. Parking by roadside.

Finnarts Bay *Map 11 NX02* **(A77)** PS
3m N of Cairnryan (OS76 NX052725). Signposted at entrance. Parking 100.

Garelochhead *Map 11 NS29* **(A814)** PS
1m N of Garelochhead (OS56 NS236916). Signposted at entrance. Small trees on heather slopes. 10 acres. No overnight parking, drinking water, furniture. Toilets. Parking 20.

Jubilee Picnic Site *Map 10 NS07* **(A8003)** PS
2m N of Tighnabruaich (OS63 NS000760). Signposted in advance and at entrance. Steep hillside with bays carved into thick undergrowth, cooking area in rocks. 2 acres. Pay telescope, drinking water, furniture. Parking 30.

Lendalfoot *Map 10 NX18* **(A77)** PS
Girvan/Stranraer road ½m S Lendalfoot Village (OS76 NX125895). Exposed level grassed area with picnic areas set in gravelled hollows, service road and parking bays. Sea views, access to rocky foreshore. Furniture. Parking 30.

Lunderston Bay Picnic Site *Map 10 NS27* **(A78)** PS
In Clyde Muirshiel Regional Park, Inverkip-Gourock Road 2m N Inverkip (OS63 NS204742). Signposted in advance and at entrance. Grass slope to rock and shingle foreshore, drinking water, furniture. Toilets. Parking 70.

St Columb's Bay *Map 11 NM94* **(A828)** PS
10m NE of Oban (OS49 NM945413). Signposted at entrance. Cleared forest area. 10 acres. Furniture. Parking 100.

TAYSIDE

Allean-Tummel Forest *Map 14 NN86* **(B8019)** PS
7m NW of Pitlochry ¼m W Queens View (OS43 NN856602). Signposted in advance and at entrance. 2 acres. Hillside site with part excavated ring fort, forest walks. Drinking water, furniture. Disabled toilet. Parking 20.

Birks O'Aberfeldy *Map 14 NN85* **(A826)** PS
At Aberfeldy (OS52 NN855485). Furniture.

Un-named Site *Map 11 NO37* **(Off B955)** PS
At Ogilvy Arms Hotel, Clova Village (OS44 327731). Small site surrounded by trees close to a small burn in Glen Clova. Hill walking, drinking water, furniture. Toilets. Parking 10.

Cullow Market, Glen Clova *Map 11 NO36* **(B955)** PS
On E side of road, ¾m N of Dykehead (OS44 NO386612). Signposted at entrance. Small wooded

picnic site amidst hills, trees and farmland N of Dykehead (OS44 NO386612). Signposted at entrance. Small wooded picnic site amidst hills, trees and farmland N of Dyke Head Village. Furniture. Parking 10.

Dalerb *Map 11 NN74* **(A827)** PS
On N shore at east end of Loch Tay, ¾m from Kenmore (OS52 NN761452). Signposted at entrance. Landscaped field with access to rocky shore. Bathing dangerous. Furniture, drinking water, disabled toilets. Parking 50 (fee).

At East Haven Beach *Map 12 NO53* **(Off A93)** PS
1½m SE of Muirdrum 1½m NE of Carnoustie (OS54 NO591362). Access under low bridge and on single, unmetalled track to grass area giving access to sandy beach and coastal walks. Toilets. Parking 20.

Gella Bridge *Map 15 NO36* **(B955)** PS
3½m N Dykehead, on R South Esk (OS44 NO374654). Signposted at entrance. Two areas either side of road. Level grassy on river bank. Furniture. Parking 20.

At Glen Isla *Map 15 NO26* **(Off B951)** PS
(OS44 NO214604). Signposted at entrance. Grassy picnic site in attractive setting by the River Isla. 1½ acres. Furniture. Toilets. Parking 20.

Loch Leven Picnic Area *Map 11 NT19* **(B9097)** PS
In National Nature Reserve 1½m NW of Ballingry and 3m SE Kinross S side of Loch Leven (OS35 NT169992). Signposted at entrance. Roadside car park giving access to Nature Reserve. Vane Farm Nature Centre ½m W. Extensive grass and gorse clad

slopes bordering and overlooking loch. Drinking water. Toilets open during season and suitable for disabled. Parking 175.

By Loch Tay *Map 11 NN62* **(A85)** PS
4.7m E Lochernhead (OS51 NN661245). On N shore of Loch Tay part of old road among pine woods. Furniture. Parking 30.

Montrose Links *Map 12 NO75* **(Off A92)** PS
1m off A92 E of Montrose (OS54 NO726582). Parking 200.

Queens View Tourist Park *Map 14 NN85* **(B8019)** PS
a. On B8019 (OS52 NN859600). Signposted in advance and at entrance. Forest walks, furniture. Parking 40.
b. 400 yds W of above. Signposted in advance and at entrance. Forming part of an extensive tree-studded area. AA Viewpoint, Forestry Commission Tourist Information Centre. Forest Walks. Toilets. Parking 100.

Tummel Forest-Faskally Walk *Map 14 NN95* **(A9)** PS
2m N Pitlochry (OS52 NN923592). Signposted in advance and at entrance. 10 acres. Forest walks, play area, wildlife hide, drinking water, furniture. Toilets. Ample parking (ticket machine).

Victoria Park *Map 12 NO64* **(Off A92)** PS
¾m E of Arbroath (OS54 NO653412). Public park bordering promenade. Drinking water, furniture. Toilets. Parking 200.

Island Camping

Guernsey

Towed caravans are only allowed temporarily on to the island in exceptional circumstances. Apply in advance to the Island Development Committee. Longstore House, St Peter Port, Guernsey. Motorised caravans may be temporarily imported provided the following are complied with:

1 The vehicle is used as a means of transport only and not as sleeping or habitable accommodation.
2 Previous arrangements have been made with a campsite owner for the motorised caravan to be put under cover when not being used as a means of transport.

Jersey

Importation of domestic caravans is not permitted other than for residents, and this is subject to the vehicles not being used for habitation while on the island, and to other conditions. Camping is permitted only at recognised sites. Trailer tents may be imported and used, but only on recognised campsites. With the introduction of roll-on/roll-off ferries, the authorities have banned motor caravans completely.

Isle of Man

Trailer caravans are not permitted on the island, unless they are to be used in connection with trade, at shows and exhibitions, or for demonstration purposes; they must not be used for living accommodation.

Isles of Scilly

No sites on the Isles of Scilly hold AA classifications. Caravans and motor caravans are not allowed on the islands; tents only are permitted. **Note** – Strict control is kept on the landing of animals in the islands. Booking is essential on all sites. For details about the licensed site on St Mary's write: Mr E A F Davison, Garrison, St Mary's. For details about sites on Bryher, St Agnes, and St Martin's write: The Town Hall, St Mary's.

How to use the Gazetteer

Apply to
This wording appears after the campsite name if, for booking purposes, application must be made to a place other than the campsite.

Booking
It is advisable to book in advance during the peak holiday season – from June to August inclusive and at public holidays. Any other recommended booking period specified by the site is noted in the gazetteer. Where individual sites always require advance booking, 'must book' appears in the entry. It is also wise to check whether a reservation entitles you to a particular pitch or not. It does not necessarily follow that an early booking will get you the best pitch on site, you may just have the choice of what is available at the time you check in at the site.

Some sites will not accept overnight bookings unless payment for a full minimum period (eg two or three days) is made. If you are not sure whether your type of equipment will be acceptable at a site, check with the proprietor beforehand.

The AA cannot undertake to find accommodation or make reservations.

Chemical closet disposal point (cdp)
A point is usually a requirement for sites rated above one pennant, except those catering only for tents, or motor caravans. They may consist of a specially constructed unit, or a wc permanently set aside for this purpose with adjacent rinsing and soak-away facilities. However, some local authorities are concerned about the effect of chemicals on bacteria in cesspools etc and the provision of cdp's in these areas may be limited or non existent.

Cold storage
This takes the form of a fridge and/or freezer for the use of the campers and caravanners.

Complaints
Inform the site proprietor or supervisor immediately if you have any complaints, so that the matter can be dealt with promptly. If a personal approach fails, members should inform the AA Regional Office nearest to the establishment concerned.

Electrical hook up
There may be only a few of these available so check when booking.

Gazetteer
The gazetteer includes Great Britain, Channel Islands and Isle of Man, place names being arranged in alphabetical order. Sites on off-shore islands, eg Isle of Wight and the Scottish Islands, are listed under individual place names. You may find it helpful to refer to the location atlas in the first instance (except for the Isles of Scilly for which no maps are included). Sites are listed alphabetically in order of pennant status (starting with five pennants), followed by Venture Sites. Establishment names shown in *Italics* indicate that particulars have not been confirmed by the management.

Individual Pitches
Sites offering this facility have marked out individual pitches for tourists.

Last arrival
Unless otherwise stated, sites will usually accept arrivals at any time of the day or night. Some sites have a special 'late arrivals' enclosure where you can pitch temporarily to avoid disturbing everyone else late at night.

Last departure
At many sites the overnight charge covers a specified period of time, eg noon of one day to noon of the next. If you overstay the departure time you could be charged for an extra day. It is therefore advisable to check this point on arrival at the site.

Maps
Location maps
The location maps at the end of the book make a good first reference point, especially since sites can be situated at places with unfamiliar names. The maps will also show you if there are any other sites in the area you have chosen.

Planning your route
The location map is not a road map and does not show roads suitable for caravans. The *AA Camping & Caravanning Map of Great Britain* on a scale of 10 miles to one inch shows suitable roads, gradients, direction of slopes, sites, etc.

Map reference
If you use the gazetteer to find a site, the place can be identified on the location maps by using the map reference alongside the entry: the first figure is the map page number, then follows the National Grid reference. An explanation of how to use this is given on the National Grid chart preceding the atlas and it is also referred to in the *Explanation of a gazetteer entry* on page 81. In addition six figure references are given after the campsite name. These can be used in conjunction with larger scale Ordnance Survey maps to pinpoint the position.

District maps on a larger scale, covering the more popular areas appear in the campsite gazetteer near the main place in the area they cover. Beneath the maps other place names under which sites are listed in the gazetteer are indicated; these are keyed by numbers to the district map.

Motor caravans

At some sites motor caravans are only accepted if they remain static throughout the stay.

Parking

Some site operators ask that cars be put in a parking area separate from the pitches, others will not allow more than one car on site for each caravan or tent.

Pitches and charges

10⊕£3
10⊕£3
10▲£3

The **number of pitches** available for each type of outfit allowed on a site is indicated immediately before the relevant symbol. If the entry reads 10⊕£3 or 10⊕£3 or 10▲£1.50, it means that the site has a maximum number of 10 pitches that can be used by caravans, motor caravans or tents. The **site charges** given immediately after the appropriate symbol apply to the overnight cost for:

one tent or caravan, one car, two adults, one child over 10yrs, one child under 10yrs, or one motor caravan, two adults, one child over 10yrs, one child under 10yrs.

They are intended to indicate what an average family can expect to pay. If your group contains more or less people than the 'norm' you can expect to pay correspondingly more or less for your pitch. The set figure also makes comparison between site charges easier. It should be noted however that some sites now have a fixed fee per pitch regardless of the number of persons. But remember that some site facilities may have a charge over and above the pitch fee, if so they are bracketed (1→) in the gazetteer entry. **When sites have been unable to furnish us with their proposed 1984 prices, those for 1983 are quoted where known, prefixed by an asterisk.**

Restricted service

Restricted service means that full site services are not available during the period stated. The facilities withdrawn during these periods vary from one site to another, so check with the site before setting off.

Shop

The range of food and equipment in site shops is usually in proportion to the size of the site. As far as our pennant requirements are concerned a general store within 200yds of the site entrance is acceptable for a three-pennant rating, but four- or five-pennant sites should have a site shop. Where a mobile shop calls at least five days a week, this is shown in the text.

Signposted

This does not refer to AA signs but indicates that the site is signposted on the nearest main road by an officially prescribed sign.

Site rules

Most sites display a set of rules and it is worthwhile to read these on your arrival. Sites where all dogs are banned are indicated in the gazetteer by the appropriate symbol. On the other sites, dogs are allowed as long as they are kept on a lead. Some proprietors will not admit larger breeds. Sleeping in cars is not encouraged by most proprietors. Some sites accept neither single sex groups nor groups of unsupervised youngsters. Young people or motorcyclists should ask proprietors in advance whether any conditions govern their acceptance.

Static van pitches

Information on static/residential pitches is limited to the number available in order to give a clearer picture of the nature of the site. Our system is geared to touring campers and caravanners, the inspectors do not vet the fixed types of accommodation. Static van pitches are not included in the pennant rating, and we cannot take responsibility for the condition of the caravans or chalets concerned.

Supervised

If this word appears in a gazetteer entry it means that the site is supervised 24hrs a day. Other sites may have less comprehensive cover

Telephone

Unless otherwise stated the **telephone exchange** is that of the town under which the establishment is listed. Where the exchange for a particular establishment is not that of the town under which it appears, the name of the exchange is given after the telephone symbol ☎ and before the number. During the currency of this guide the telephone authorities are liable to change some telephone numbers. If you have any difficulty in contacting a site, check with the telephone operator.

28-day rule

SA indicates that the site operates an annexe under the '28-day rule' which permits any number of tents and three caravans at a time to occupy a site of five or more acres for up to 28 days in a 12-month period.

WC lit all night
Because the general standard of lighting on sites at night varies so much, we specify only whether the toilet blocks are lit.

Explanation of a gazetteer entry

The example is **fictitious**

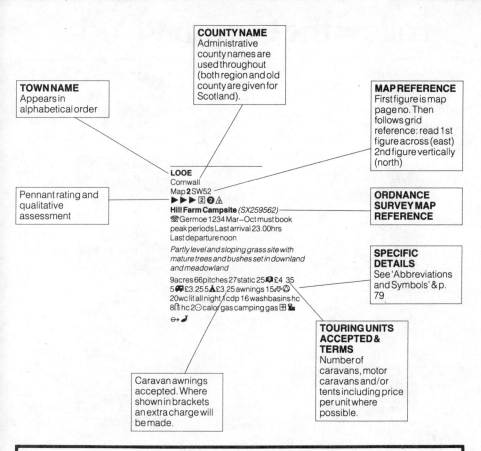

COUNTY NAME
Administrative county names are used throughout (both region and old county are given for Scotland).

TOWN NAME
Appears in alphabetical order

MAP REFERENCE
First figure is map page no. Then follows grid reference: read 1st figure across (east) 2nd figure vertically (north)

Pennant rating and qualitative assessment

LOOE
Cornwall
Map **2** SW52
▶ ▶ ▶ ② ❷ ⚠
Hill Farm Campsite *(SX259562)*
☎ Germoe 1234 Mar–Oct must book peak periods Last arrival 23.00hrs Last departure noon

Partly level and sloping grass site with mature trees and bushes set in downland and meadowland

9 acres 66 pitches 27 static 25 ⚲ £4 35 5 ⚲ £3.25 5 ▲ £3.25 awnings 15 ⚲ ⚲ 20 wc lit all night 1 cdp 16 washbasins hc 8 🚿 hc 2 ⊙ calor gas camping gas ⊞ 🛒 ⊖→ ♪

ORDNANCE SURVEY MAP REFERENCE

SPECIFIC DETAILS
See 'Abbreviations and Symbols' & p. 79

TOURING UNITS ACCEPTED & TERMS
Number of caravans, motor caravans and/or tents including price per unit where possible.

Caravan awnings accepted. Where shown in brackets an extra charge will be made.

Follow the Country Code

Enjoy the countryside and respect its life and work.

Guard against all risk of fire.

Fasten all gates.

Keep your dogs under close control.

Keep to public paths across farmland.

Use gates and stiles to cross fences, hedges and walls.

Leave livestock, crops and machinery alone.

Take your litter home.

Help to keep all water clean.

Protect wildlife, plants and trees.

Take special care on country roads.

Make no unnecessary noise.

Gazetteer

The gazetteer gives locations of sites in England, Wales and Scotland, Channel Islands and Isle of Man, in one list of placenames arranged alphabetically. Details for islands are shown under individual placenames; the gazetteer text also gives appropriate cross-references. A useful first point of reference is to consult the location maps which show where sites are situated. N.B. *There is no map for Isles of Scilly.*

ABBEY WOOD (SE2)
Gt London
Map 5 TQ47
See London for details

ABERCHIRDER
Grampian *Banffshire*
Map 15 NJ65

▶ 1 2
McRobert Park *(NJ624527)* Signposted ☎Macduff (0261) 32861 May–Sep must book Last arrival 21.00hrs Last departure 09.00hrs

A small level grassy site adjacent to playing fields just off the centre of this small town, 9m S of Banff on the A97.

½acre 15pitches 5static 10🚐 or 10🚐 5▲ (awnings)

2🏕 3wc lit all night 4 washbasins hc central hot water 🛁hc calor gas camping gaz paraffin 🛒

↔ ✦ pub

ABERCRAVE (ABERCRAF)
Powys
Map 3 SN81

▶▶ 2 ⚠
Dan-yr-Ogof Abercraf Caves Caravan Park *(SN841160)* Signposted ☎(0639) 730693 Etr–Oct no bookings Last arrival 22.00hrs Last departure noon

A part level grassy site with mature trees. Hardstanding for caravans. Set in mountainous country, within Brecon Beacons National Park, with a river on one side. 3m N of village on A4067 Sennybridge road. Follow signs for 'Dan-yr-Ogof Caves'.

5acres 60pitches SA 30🚐 £3.50 or 30🚐£3.50 30▲£3 awnings

5🏕 ⦿ 9wc lit all night 1cdp 9washbasins hc 6🛁hc ⦿ supervised calor gas cafe mobile shop

↔ stables ✦ pub 🛒

ABERDEEN
Grampian *Aberdeenshire*
Map 15 NJ90

▶▶▶ 2 ⚠
Hazlehead Caravan & Tent Site *(NJ893057)* Groats Rd Apply to: Aberdeen City District Council, St Nicholas House, Aberdeen AB1 1XJ Signposted ☎(0224) 642121 ext489 Apr–Sep must book Jun–Aug

---

A level grass site with mature trees, set in woodland countryside. 3m W of Aberdeen on A944.

6acres 165pitches 35static SA 165🚐£4.40 or 165🚐£4.40 or 165▲fr£2.20 awnings

5🏕 Individual pitches wc lit all night 🛁hc ⦿ (wash) spin dry childrens playground calor gas ☎ 🛒

↔ stables golf cinema launderette

ABERFELDY
Tayside *Perthshire*
Map 14 NN84

▶▶ 1 ⓞ ⚠
Municipal Caravan Site *(NN858495)* Dunkeld Rd, Apply to: Perth & Kinross District Council, Parks & Recreation Dept., Area Office, Bank St, Aberfeldy, Perthshire PH15 2AQ Signposted Apr–Oct no bookings Last departure noon

A level grass site with a perimeter of mature trees, situated at the eastern end of the town and lying between main road and banks of the River Tay. Good views, from site, of surrounding tree-clad Perthshire hills.

5acres 110pitches 40static 60🚐 or 60🚐 50▲ (awnings)

4🏕 Individual pitches ⦿ 20wc lit all night 1cdp washbasins hc central hot water 🛁hc ⦿ childrens playground ☎🛒

↔golf cinema ✦ pub

ABERLOUR (Charlestown of Aberlour)
Grampian *Banffshire*
Map 15 NJ24

▶▶ 3 ⓞ ⚠
Aberlour Gardens Caravan Park *(NJ282434)* Signposted ☎(03405) 586

Aberlour Gardens Caravan Park.

Charlestown of Aberlour on Spey, Moray
Telephone: Aberlour (03405) 586

Stances for touring caravans and tents. Electric points. Laundry and public telephone. Children's play area. Beautiful setting within grounds of the old Aberlour Estate, a 10 foot high wall surrounds the site providing an extremely sheltered position.

Apr–Oct Last arrival 23.00hrs Last departure noon

Site within the beautiful setting of the Old Aberlour Estate with its walled gardens. Off A95.

3acres 58pitches 17static 21🚐£3 or 21🚐£3 37▲£3 (awnings) ltr

4🏕 Individual pitches ⦿ late arrivals enclosure 5wc lit all night 1cdp 🖳 2washbasins hc 2central hot water (2🛁hc) 2⦿ (wash spin) dry iron cold storage childrens playground calor gas toilet fluid ☎ mobile shop

↔ stables golf ✦ launderette pub 🛒

ABERMULE
Powys
Map 6 SO19

▶ 1 ⓞ ⚠
Ye Old Smithy Caravan Park *(SO161947)* ☎(068 686) 657 Apr–Sep must book peak periods

A mainly level grassy site with trees and bushes set in meadowland near river and main road.

2acres 20pitches 50static 20🚐£3 or 20🚐£3 or 20▲£3 awnings ltr

2🏕 9wc lit all night washbasins hc (🛁hc) ⦿ supervised spin (✗) calor gas camping gaz ☎ ⊞ 🛒

↔golf cinema ✦ launderette pub

ABERSOCH
Gwynedd
Map 6 SH32

▶▶▶ 3 ⓞ ⚠
Bryn Cethin Bach Caravan Park *(SH304290)* ☎(075881) 2719 Apr–Oct rs Mar (limited time opening hrs) must book Spring Bank Hol & end Jul–Aug Last arrival 21.00hrs Last departure noon no tents

The site is set in meadowland with trees and open aspects. From harbour turn right at 'Land & Sea' garage. Off A499, ½m uphill on the right.

3acres 15pitches 51static 15🚐 or 15🚐 awnings

1🏕 Individual pitches late arrivals enclosure 9wc lit all night 1cdp 🖳 washbasins hc 🛁hc ⦿ supervised (wash) spin (dry) (cold storage) calor gas camping gaz ☎🛒

↔ stables golf ✦ launderette pub

▶▶▶ 1 ⓞ ⚠
Haulfryn Camping Site *(SH318307)* Signposted ☎(075881) 2045 3 Apr–8 Oct rsMar–2 Apr & 9–30 Oct must book Jul & Aug Last arrival 18.00hrs Last departure 11.30hrs 🎯 no single sex groups no motor cycles

Slightly sloping site backed by wooded hills, overlooking Cardigan Bay. 2m N of Abersoch on A499.

28 pitches SA 28▲£4.50 awnings

Individual pitches 10wc lit all night 1cdp washbasins hc central hot water 11🛁hc ⦿ supervised wash spin cold storage (licensed bar/club) private beach calor →

gas camping gaz paraffin toilet fluid cafe restaurant ☎🖳

� stables golf ⚑ 🖈 launderette pub

▶🗓 ❶
Pant-Gwyn Cottage *(SH305262)* Sarn Bâch Signposted ☎(075881) 2268 Mar–Oct must book Last arrival 23.00hrs Last departure noon

Gently sloping site in quiet elevated position near to Abersoch, on the Lleyn Peninsula. Very sharp turn opposite the telephone kiosk in Sarn Bâch for site 200yds on right.

Dogs must be on lead 5acres 62pitches 4static SA 62🚐fr£3 or 62▲fr£3 awnings 4🏕☯ 12wc lit all night (🛁hc) ☺ supervised iron (cold storage) ☎ (200 yds) camping gaz🖳

↳ stables golf ⚑ 🖈 launderette pub

ABERYSTWYTH
Dyfed
Map 6 SN58

▶🗓 ❶🔺
'U' Tow Caravans Aberystwyth Holiday Village *(SN586809)* Signposted ☎(0970) 4211 All year no single sex groups

Flat grassy site set on a roadside approx 1m from town centre off A487 Aberaeron road.

32acres 152pitches 160static 52🚐£2.90–£4.75🚐£2.90–£4.50 50▲£2.90–£4.75 (awnings) ltr

11🏕 22wc lit all night 4cdp 🔌 washbasins hc central hot water 🛁hc ☺ supervised (wash dry) iron 🍳 games room CTV cold storage licensed club/ bar childrens playground calor gas camping gas toilet fluid cafe restaurant ☎ 🖳 launderette sauna fishing

↳ stables golf ⚑ cinema pub

ABOYNE
Grampian *Aberdeenshire*
Map 15 NO59

▶▶▶ ③ ❸🔺
Aboyne Loch Caravan Park
(NO538998) Signposted ☎(0339) 2244 Apr–Oct no bookings Last arrival 20.00hrs Last departure 14.00hrs no tents

Attractively sited caravan park set amidst woodland beside Aboyne Loch in scenic Deeside.

2acres 45pitches 50static 45🚐£4.70 or 45🚐£4.70 (awnings)

🏕 Individual pitches 18wc lit all night 1cdp 🔌 washbasins hc central hot water 🛁hc ☺ (wash) (iron) childrens playground calor gas camping gaz toilet fluid ☎🖳

↳ stables golf ⚑ 🖈 pub

ACASTER MALBIS
North Yorkshire
Map 8 SE54

▶▶▶ ② ❷🔺
Chestnut Farm Caravans *(SE589456)* Signposted ☎York (0904) 706371 Apr– Oct must book public hols Last arrival 23.00hrs Last departure noon

Level, grassy site with assorted trees and shrubs, adjacent to river.

2acres 30pitches 50static 30🚐 or 30🚐 or 30▲ (awnings) ltr

6🏕 Individual pitches ☯ 14wc lit all night 1cdp washbasins hc (🛁hc) ☺ supervised spin iron cold storage calor gas camping gaz toilet fluid 🖳

↳ stables golf ⚑ cinema 🖈 launderette pub

▶▶▶ ② ❷🔺
Mount Pleasant Caravan Village
(SE583445) Signposted Apr–Oct no bookings Last arrival mdnt no motorcycles

This site is secluded but not remote and is close to the River Ouse, with trees and gardens. Off A64 from Tadcaster.

6acres 120pitches 265static 50🚐 10🚐 60▲ (awnings) ltr

🏕 ☯ late arrivals enclosure 34wc lit all night 4cdp washbasins hc (🛁hc) ☺ supervised (wash spin dry) childrens

playground calor gas camping gaz toilet fluid ☎ 🛄

↔ stables golf ⚓ 🏌 launderette pub

▶▶ 🗆 ❶ ⚠

Moor End Farm *(SE589457)* Signposted ☎York (0904) 706727 Apr–Oct booking advisable peak periods Last arrival 22.00hrs Last departure 14.00hrs no unaccompanied persons under 18yrs

Level, grassy site with hedges. Set in meadowland adjacent to road.

¼acre 10pitches 5static 10🚐£3.30 or 10🚙£3.30 or 10▲£3.30 (awnings) ltr

2🏕 Individual pitches ◐ 4wc lit all night 1cdp 🔌 washbasins hc central hot water (🛆hc) ◑ supervised 🛄

↔ 🏌 launderette pub

ACASTER SELBY
North Yorkshire
Map 8 SE54

▽ 🗆

Hales Hill Farm *(SE584423)*
☎Appleton Roebuck (090484) 317 booking advisable

Level grass paddock on banks of the Ouse.

18pitches 8🚐✳£1.50 or 8🚙£1.50 10▲£1.50

2🏕 cdp

ACTON BRIDGE
Cheshire
Map 7 SJ57

▶ 🗆 ❶ ⚠

Woodbine Cottage *(SJ603755)*
☎Weaverham (0606) 852319 Mar–Oct Last departure 12.30hrs

Part level, part sloping grassy site situated by the banks of the River Weaver in open countryside on the A49.

1½acres 28pitches 30static 10🚐£3 8🚙£3 10▲£3 (awnings) ltr

8🏕 Individual pitches ◐ 8wc lit all night 1cdp 🔌 washbasins hc (🛆hc) ◑ supervised (wash dry) iron (cold storage) childrens playground calor gas cafe ☎ baby sitting 🛄

↔ golf ⚓ 🏌 launderette pub

ALCESTER
Warwickshire
Map 4 SP05

▶ 🗆 ❶ ⚠

Hoo Mill *(SP108579)* ☎(0789) 762515 Mar–Nov rs Dec–Feb must book peak periods Last arrival 22.00hrs Last departure noon

Level grassy site with mature trees.

2acres 40pitches 60static 40🚐£3.20 or 40🚙£3.20 or 40▲£3.20 awnings

5🏕 Individual pitches 10wc 2cdp supervised calor gas

↔ launderette pub 🛄

ALDINGBOURNE
West Sussex
Map 4 SU90

▽ 🗆

Woodland *(SU937045)* Hook Lane ☎Eastergate (024368) 2467 Etr–Oct must book Jul & Aug Last arrival 20.00hrs Last departure noon ✝ nc10 no motorbikes no single sex groups

On grassland and well screened by hedges in the summer. The site is in a quiet lane 2mS of Fontwell at north side of level crossing turn right into Hook Lane.

½acre 4pitches 4🚐£2.75 or 4🚙£2.75 or 4▲£2.75 awnings

1🏕 2wc 1cdp ◑ supervised 🛄

↔ stables cinema 🏌 launderette pub

ALFORD
Grampian *Aberdeenshire*
Map 15 NJ51

▶▶▶▶ 🗆 ❸ ⚠

Haughton House Caravan Site*(NJ583169)* Signposted ☎(0336) 2107 Mar–Sep Last departure noon →

This impressive site with central mansion house dating back to 1800, is part of an estate set amongst woodland and beside the River Don. Approx ½m NW of Alford. Situated within country park.

10acres 135pitches 40static 73☎£4 62☎£4 or 62▲£4 (awnings) ltr 19⚡ Individual pitches ☾ 35wc lit all night 2cdp ⚡ washbasins hc (🚿hc)☺ supervised (wash dry iron) games room CTV childrens playground calor gas toilet fluid ☎ 🛉

⇔ golf ◢ launderette pub

ALLERTON PARK
North Yorkshire
Map 8 SE45

▶▶▶ ①❶⚠
Allerton Park Caravan Site *(SE417576)*
Signposted ☎Green Hammerton (0901) 30569 Apr–Oct booking advisable public hols Last arrival 20.00hrs Last departure 14.00hrs no single sex groups

Gently sloping, grass site with varied types of trees in sylvan surroundings, adjacent to main road.

3acres 44pitches 80static SA 44☎£3.50 or 44☎£3.50 44▲£3 (awnings) ltr
2⚡ wc lit all night 1cdp washbasins hc (🚿hc)☺ iron (cold storage) childrens playground calor gas toilet fluid ☎ 🛉

⇔ ◢ launderette pub

ALTON
Hampshire
Map 4 SU73

▽③
Upper Neatham Mill *(SU734405)* Upper Neatham Mill Ln ☎(0420) 84188 must book

In pleasant wooded grounds a 12 acre camping area beside the River Wey on the site of an old mill.

14pitches 2☎ or 2☎ 10▲
⚡cdp fishing

ALVES
Grampian *Morayshire*
Map 15 NJ16

▶▶▶▶ ③❷⚠
North Alves Caravan Park *(NJ122633)*
Signposted Apr–Oct booking advisable Jul & Aug Last arrival 23.00hrs Last departure noon

A pleasant grassy site with views over farmland. 1m N of Alves village off A96 Elgin and Forres road.

10acres 80pitches 25static 80☎£3–£4 or 80☎£3–£4 or 80▲£3–£4 (awnings)
8⚡☾ 15wc lit all night 1cdp washbasins hc 🚿hc ☺ (wash spin) iron games room TV cold storage childrens playground calor gas camping gaz toilet fluid ☎⊞🛉

⇔ stables golf ⚲ cinema ◢ launderette pub

ALVINGTON
Gloucestershire
Map 3 SO60

▶▶▶ ②❷⚠
Clanna Caravan & Camping Park
(SO023584) signposted ☎Netherend (059452) 214 or 493 All year booking advisable public hols Last arrival 22.30hrs Last departure 12.30hrs

6½acres 45pitches SA 45☎£3.50 or 45☎£3.50 or 45▲£3.50 (awnings) ltr
10⚡ Individual pitches ☾ late arrivals enclosure 12wc lit all night 1cdp washbasins hc central hot water ➡hc (🚿hc) ☺ iron licensed club/bar calor gas camping gaz paraffin toilet fluid ☎ ⊞🛉

⇔ stables golf ⚲ cinema ◢ launderette pub

AMBLESIDE
Cumbria
Map 7 NY30
See Windermere sketch map

▶▶▶ ②❶⚠
Skelwith Fold Caravan Park
(NY355029) Signposted ☎(09663) 2277

Mar–14 Nov booking advisable public hols & Jul–Aug Last departure noon no tents

Situated in 125 acres of natural woodland among flowers and shrubs. On the B5286, 2m from Ambleside.

8acres 125pitches 300static 100☎£3 or 25☎£3 (awnings) ltr

24⚡ late arrivals enclosure 53wc lit all night 3cdp washbasins hc (🚿hc) ☺ (wash) (dry) iron (cold storage) childrens playground calor gas toilet fluid ☎ 🛉

⇔ stables ⚲ cinema ◢ launderette pub

▶▶ ①❶⚠
Low Wray National Trust Campsite
(SD372013) Low Wray ☎Ambleside (09663) 2810 wk before Etr–Oct no bookings Last arrival 23.00hrs no cars by tents

Delightful site on western shore of Lake Windermere. It is divided into three camping fields; one set aside especially for families, with direct access to the lake; one with an open aspect and the third amongst trees and bushes. 3m SW via A583 to Clappersgate then B5286 and unclass road.

200pitches 5static 200▲ ltr
8⚡☾ lit all night 2cdp washbasin hc 🚿hc private beach calor gas camping gaz ☎🛉

⇔ stables ⚲ cinema ◢ launderette pub

AMISFIELD
Dumfries & Galloway *Dumfriesshire*
Map 11 NY08

▶▶ ②❸⚠
The Caravan Park *(NY002831)* Glen Clova Signposted ☎(0387) 710447 Mar–Oct booking advisable Jul & Aug Last arrival 22.00hrs

Adjacent to the busy A701, Moffat-Dumfries road. A level grassy site bordered by trees and on the edge of the village.

2½acres 30pitches 30☎ or 30☎ or 30▲ (awnings)

3⚡8wc lit all night 🔌 washbasins hc
🚿hc ☉ (☎) calor gas mobile shop
↪ golf 🏌 pub

ANDOVER
Hampshire
Map 4 SU34

▶ 🔢 ❷ ⚠
**Wyke Down Touring Caravan &
Camping Park** *(SU403476)* Picket Piece
Signposted ☎(0264) 52048 All year no
bookings Last departure noon
*A level grassy site situated in rural area
with pleasant views.*

7acres 100pitches 100⚑£4 or
100⚑£4 or 100▲£4 (awnings)
9⚡9wc lit all night 1cdp washbasins hc
central hot water (🚿hc) ☉ supervised
(wash) 🚿 games room CTV licensed
club childrens playground calor gas
camping gaz paraffin toilet fluid ☎ 🛒
↪ stables golf cinema 🏌 launderette

ANNAN
Dumfries & Galloway *Dumfriesshire*
Map 11 NY16

▶ 🔢 ❷ ⚠
Galabank Caravan & Camp Site
(NY193673) North St Signposted Etr–
Oct no bookings Last departure noon
*Mainly level, grassy site situated on
B722 off A75 Dumfries-Carlisle road.*

1acre 30pitches SA 30⚑ or 30⚑ or
30▲ (awnings) ltr
1⚡6wc lit all night washbasins hc
(🚿hc) ☉
↪ stables golf cinema 🏌 launderette 🛒

APPLEBY
Cumbria
Map 12 NY62

▶ ▶ ▶ 🔢 ❸ ⚠
Wild Rose Park *(NY698165)* Ormside
Signposted ☎(0930) 51077 All year
must book public hols Last departure
noon no unaccompanied teenagers
*This site is set in peaceful surroundings
on rising ground overlooking the Eden
Valley in the midst of a good touring
area.*

6acres 264pitches 184static SA 184⚑
or 184⚑ 80▲ (awnings) ltr
100⚡Individual pitches ⊘ late arrivals
enclosure 36wc lit all night 3cdp 🔌
washbasins hc 🚿hc ☉ supervised
(wash spin dry) iron 🚿 games room
CTV (cold storage) childrens playground
calor gas camping gaz toilet fluid ☎ ⊞
🛒
↪ golf 🏌 launderette pub

APPLECROSS
Highland *Ross & Cromarty*
Map 13 NG74

▶ 🔢 ❷ ⚠
Applecross Campsite *(NG714443)*
☎(05204) 268 May–Sep rsApr & Oct no
bookings
*Level, grass site with trees and bushes,
set amidst mountains and moorland,
adjacent to sea and beach. Caravans
should approach via Shieldaig.*

6acres 60pitches 6static 60⚑£3.40 or
60⚑£3.40 or 60▲£3.40 awnings
6⚡12wc lit all night 2cdp washbasins
hc (🚿hc) ☉ supervised (wash dry) (cold
storage) childrens playground calor gas
camping gaz 🛒
↪ 🏕 🏌 launderette pub

ARDGARTAN
Strathclyde *Argyllshire*
Map 10 NN20

▶ ▶ ▶ 🔢 ❶ ⚠
Ardgartan Camp Site *(NN275030)*
Apply to: Forestry Commission,
Ardgartan Forest, Arrochar,
Dunbartonshire Signposted ☎Arrochar
(03012) 293 Apr–Sep Last arrival
20.00hrs
*Level, grass and gravel site with trees,
set in hilly woodland country adjacent to
sea, beach, river and Loch Long. 3m SW
of Arrochar on A83.*

10acres 200pitches 200⚑ or 200⚑ or
200▲ awnings
12⚡Individual pitches ⊘ late arrivals
enclosure 22wc lit all night 2cdp

---

washbasins hc central hot water 🚿hc ☉
supervised (dry) games room calor gas
camping gaz ☎ 🛒
↪ 🏕 🏌

ARDMAIR
Highland *Ross & Cromarty*
Map 14 NH19

▶ ▶ ▶ 🔢 ❸ ⚠
Ardmair Point Campsite *(NH108983)*
☎Ullapool (0854) 2054 Etr–Sep
booking advisable Jul & Aug for
caravans Last arrival 22.30hrs Last
departure noon
*Touring site set on small peninsula 3½m
N of Ullapool with superb views of
surrounding mountains and sea lochs.*

3½acres 45pitches 1static SA
45⚑£3.25 or 45⚑£3.25 or 45▲£3.25
(awnings)
4⚡Individual pitches 9wc lit all night
1cdp 🔌 washbasins hc (4🚿hc) 2☉
supervised (spin dry) calor gas camping
gaz paraffin toilet fluid ☎ boat & fishing
tackle for hire 🛒
↪ stables 🏕 🏌 launderette pub

ARDUAINE
Strathclyde *Argyllshire*
Map 10 NM17

▶ ▶ 🔢 ❶ ⚠
Arduaine Caravan Site *(NM101800)*
%Loch Melfort Hotel ☎Kilmelford
(08522) 233 Etr–Oct must book Jul &
Aug Last departure 21.00hrs
*Slightly sloping grassy fields at lochside
by small jetty, offering views of Shuna
and Luing backed by A816.*

45pitches 15⚑£6 or 15⚑£6 30▲£3
3⚡⊘ 5wc lit all night 1cdp washbasins
hc central hot water (🚿hc) ☉ (cold
storage) private beach calor gas
camping gaz 🛒
↪ stables 🏕 🏌 pub

ASHBOURNE
Derbyshire
Map 7 SK14

▶ ▶ ▶ 🔢 ❶ ⚠
Sandybrook Hall Holiday Centre
(SK179481) Signposted ☎(0335)   →

42679 Mar–Oct booking advisable public hols no unaccompanied teenagers

Grassy site with a slight gradient set in downland and meadowland, adjacent to road. 1m N of Ashbourne on A515.

6acres 100pitches 100🚐 or 100🚐 or 100▲ (awnings)

🅰⊘ late arrivals enclosure 11wc lit all night 10washbasins hc central hot water 🛁hc ☉ supervised (wash spin dry) games room TV licensed club/bar childrens playground calor gas camping gaz toilet fluid 🏪

⟷ stables golf launderette

ASHBURTON
Devon
Map 3 SX77

▶▶▶ 🙎 ❶ ⚠

Ashburton Caravan Park *(SX753718)*
Waterleat ☎Moretonhampstead (0647) 40543 All year booking advisable Jul & Aug no caravans

Mainly level grass site with trees and bushes on partly level ground. Set in hilly meadowland with some woodland; adjacent to a rock stream.

2acres 30pitches 40static 30 🚐 £4.50 or 30▲£4.50

3🅰 10wc washbasins hc 🛁hc ☉ supervised (wash dry) cold storage childrens playground calor gas camping gaz 🛁 🏪

⟷ stables ⌀ launderette pub

▶▶▶ 🙎 ❷ ⚠

River Dart Country Park *(SX734700)*
Holne Park ☎(0364) 52511 Etr–Sep Last departure 10.30hrs

Mainly level site in Holne Country Park just off the B3357. Adjacent to river.

8¾acres 120pitches 🚐£9 🚐£9 120▲£9 awnings

🅰 Individual pitches ⊘ 16wc lit all night 1cdp washbasins hc 🛁hc ☉ (wash dry) iron ⊒ ℘ games room CTV (cold storage) licensed bar childrens playground calor gas camping gaz cafe 🛁 🏪

⟷ stables ⌀ launderette pub

ASHFORD IN THE WATER
Derbyshire
Map 7 SK16

▶▶▶ 🙎 ❸ ⚠

Greenhills Caravan Park *(SK202693)*
Crow Hill Ln Signposted ☎Bakewell (062981) 3467 or 3052 Mar–Oct rs early & late season must book public & school hols Last arrival 22.00 Last departure 16.00hrs

Grass site with assorted trees and bushes on partly level ground. Set in hilly meadowland with some woodland.

6acres 55pitches 45static SA 55🚐£4 or 55🚐£3.75 or 55▲£4 (awnings)

8🅰 Individual pitches ⊘ 14wc lit all night 1cdp 🚽 washbasins hc central hot water 🛁hc ☉ (wash spin dry) games room cold storage licensed club/bar calor gas ☎

⟷ launderette pub 🏪

ASHTON
Cornwall
Map 2 SW62
See Praa Sands sketch map

▶▶ 🙎 ❷ ⚠

Boscreage Caravan Park *(SW591303)*
Signposted ☎Germoe (073676) 2231 Apr–Oct must book Jun–Aug Last arrival 21.00hrs ✝

Level, grass site with varied trees and bushes. Set in mixed woodland and meadowland adjacent to sea. Good sandy beach and main road nearby.

1acre 15pitches 24static 15🚐£2.90 or 15🚐£2.90 or 15▲£2.90 (awnings)

3🅰 6wc lit all night 1cdp washbasins hc (🛁hc) ☉ supervised spin iron games room TV childrens playground

⟷ stables golf ⌁ cinema ⌀ launderette pub 🏪

ASHURST
Hampshire
Map 4 SU31

▶▶ 🙎 ❸ ⚠

Ashurst Camp *(SU332102)* Signposted ☎Lyndhurst (042128) 3771 (from early 1984) or 3141 (Forestry Commission Office) 13 Apr–4 Nov must book Spring Bank Hol Last departure noon ✝

Situated just off the A35 Southampton-Bournemouth road, this quiet, secluded Forestry Commission site is set amongst woodlands and heathland on the fringe of the New Forest. See under 'Forestry Commission' for further information.

23acres 280pitches 280🚐 or 280🚐 or 280▲ awnings

7🅰 29wc lit all night 4cdp washbasins hc 🛁hc ☉ supervised calor gas camping gaz ☎ disabled facilities mobile shop

⟷ stables golf pub launderette 🏪

ASTON CANTLOW
Warwickshire
Map 4 SP15

▶ 🙎 ❶ ⚠

Island Meadow Caravan Park *(SP137596)* The Mill House ☎Great Alne (078981) 273 Mar–Oct booking advisable peak periods Last arrival 23.00hrs no tents

Meadowland bordered by the River Alne and its mill stream. Mature willows line the banks. ¼m W of Aston Cantlow on the road to Alcester.

2acres 15pitches 50static 15🚐£3 or 15🚐£3 (awnings)

4🅰 12wc lit all night 1cdp (washbasins hc) (🛁hc) ☉ supervised cold storage calor gas camping gaz toilet fluid 🏪

⟷ stables ⌀ launderette pub

AUCHENBOWIE
Central *Stirlingshire*
Map 11 NS78

▶▶ 🙎 ❶ ⚠

Auchenbowie Caravan & Camping Site *(NS795880)* Signposted ☎Denny (0324) 822141 Apr–Oct booking advisable mid Jul–mid Aug

A partly level and sloping grassy site. ½m S of M80 Snabhead Interchange on A872.

3acres 50pitches 50🚐£3 or 50🚐£3 or 50▲£3 awnings

6🅰 15wc lit all night 1cdp 🚽 washbasins hc (🛁hc) ☉ childrens playground calor gas camping gaz paraffin ☎ mobile shop

⟷ ⌀ launderette 🏪

AUCHENMALG
Dumfries & Galloway *Wigtownshire*
Map 10 NX25

▶▶▶ 🗊 ❷ ⚠

Cock Inn Caravan Park *(NX238518)*
Signposted ☎(05815) 227 25 May–Aug rsMar–24 May & 2 Sep–Oct booking advisable Spring Bank Hol & last wk Jul–1st wk Aug Last arrival 23.00hrs Last departure noon no single sex groups under 21yrs

Part level, part sloping, grass site set in meadowland, close to sea, beach and main road; A747 Glenluce-Port William road. Overlooks Luce Bay.

3acres 70pitches 50static 65🚐£3.50 or 65🚐£3.50 5▲£3.50 (awnings)

4🅰 Individual pitches 19wc lit all night 2cdp 🚽 washbasins hc central hot water (🛁hc) ☉ supervised (wash) (dry iron) (cold storage) licensed club/bar calor gas camping gaz toilet fluid cafe restaurant 🛁

⟷ ⌁ ⌀ launderette pub

AVIEMORE
Highland *Inverness-shire*
Map 14 NH81

▶▶▶ 🙎 ❷ ⚠

Aviemore Centre Caravan Park *(NH894120)* Signposted ☎(0479) 810751 Dec–Oct booking advisable public hols & Jul–Aug Last arrival 18.00hrs Last departure noon no tents no motor cycles

Set amongst pine trees, adjacent to the Aviemore Centre where caravanners can make full use of the facilities.

9acres 90pitches 90🚐£4 or 90🚐£4 (awnings)

8🅰 Individual pitches 18wc lit all night cdp washbasins hc (🛁hc) ☉ (wash spin dry iron ⊡) (cold storage) (licensed bar) childrens playground calor gas camping gaz toilet fluid cafe restaurant ☎ 🏪

↔ stables golf ⅄ cinema ♪ launderette

▶▶▶ ② ⓘ △

Dalraddy Caravan Park (NH859083)
Signposted ☎(0479) 810330 Dec–Oct must book peak periods Last arrival 22.00hrs Last departure 11.30hrs

A well-secluded site situated off the A9, 4m S of Aviemore, set amidst heather and young birch trees, looking towards the Cairngorm mountains.

25acres 205pitches 65static SA 55🚐 £3.50 or 55🚐 £3.50 150▲£3.40 awnings

28⚏ Individual pitches for caravans ⊘ 34wc lit all night 1cdp 🔌 washbasin hc 🛁hc ☉ supervised (wash spin) (iron) (cold storage) childrens playground calor gas camping gaz toilet fluid ☎ 🎣

↔ stables golf ⅄ cinema ♪ launderette pub

▶▶▶ ② ❸ △

Glen More (NH975097) Apply to: The Head Forester, Forestry Commission, Glen More, Aviemore, Inverness-shire PH22 1QU ☎Cairngorm (047986) 271 All year must book wk before–wk after Etr, Spring Bank Hol & Jul–Aug Last arrival 21.00hrs Last departure noon

This site lies close to the eastern end of Loch Morlich at the head of Glenmore, surrounded by conifer woodlands. There are sandy beaches close by.

See previous page for entry.

17acres 220pitches 70🚐 fr£3.25 or 70🚐 fr£3.25 150▲fr£3.25 awnings

6⚏ Individual pitches ⊘ 24wc lit all night 2cdp 36washbasins hc 20🛁hc 6☉ (wash spin dry) calor gas camping gaz toilet fluid cafe ☎ 🎣

↔ ⅄ ♪ launderette

▶▶▶ ① ⓘ △

Speyside Caravan Park (NH895115)
Signposted ☎(0479) 810236 26 Mar–16 Apr & 25 Jun–3 Sep rsmid Dec–25 Mar, 17 Apr–24 Jun & 4 Sep–Oct booking advisable peak periods Last arrival 19.00hrs Last departure 10.00hrs no motorcycles

Level, grass and gravel site with trees and bushes, set in hilly country and woodland, adjacent to River Spey. Immediately S of Aviemore close to junction of A9 and A951.

5acres 51pitches 53static SA 51🚐 or 51🚐 or 51▲ (awnings) ltr

8⚏ Individual pitches late arrivals enclosure 21wc lit all night 1cdp 🔌 ☉ supervised (wash spin dry iron) calor gas toilet fluid ☎ 🎣

↔ cinema ♪ launderette

AYR
Strathclyde *Ayrshire*
Map 10 NS32

▶▶ ② ❷ △

Crofthead Caravan Park (NS365199)
Signposted ☎(0292) 263516 All year Last arrival 21.00hrs no single sex groups

2 miles south west of Ayr in pleasant rural surroundings the converted first World War 1 isolation hospital sheds are surrounded by neatly planned and well maintained site.

2½acres 50pitches 60static 30🚐 fr£3 10🚐 fr£2.50 10▲ fr£3 (awnings) ltr

7⚏ Individual pitches ⊘ late arrivals enclosure 15wc lit all night 1cdp washbasins hc (🛁hc) ☉ supervised (wash dry) iron games room CTV (cold storage) childrens playground calor gas camping gaz toilet fluid ☎ ⊞ 🎣

↔ stables golf ⅄ cinema ♪ launderette

AYSIDE
Cumbria
Map 7 SD38
See Cark-in-Cartmel sketch map

▶ ① ⓘ △

Oak Head Caravan Park (SD389839)
Signposted ☎Newby Bridge (0448) 31475 Mar–Oct must book public hols Last arrival 23.00hrs Last departure noon no single sex groups →

Level and sloping site, set in hilly country with woodland, close to A590.

4acres 60pitches 71static SA 30🚐 £3 or 30 🚐 £3 30▲£3 awnings

10🚐 Individual pitches ⊘ 30wc 1cdp 🚐 washbasins hc (🛁 hc) ⊙ supervised (spin) iron (cold storage) calor gas camping gaz ☎

⊕ stables golf ⭐ ☛ pub ☎

BACTON
Norfolk
Map 9 TG33

►►► ① ❸ △

Cable Gap Caravan Park *(TG342343)*
Coast Rd ☎Walcott (0692) 650667
20 Mar–Oct must book peak periods
Last arrival 23.00hrs Last departure
11.00hrs no tents

Neat low density site on level ground between B1159 and the beach.

2acres 30pitches 59static 30🚐 fr£4 or 30 🚐 fr£4 awnings

2🚐 Individual pitches late arrivals enclosure 9wc lit all night 1cdp 🚐 washbasins hc 🛁 hc ⊙ supervised calor gas camping gaz ☎

⊕ stables golf ☛ pub

BAKEWELL
Derbyshire
Map 8 SK26

▽ ②

Haddon Grove Farm *(SK177662)*
Haddon Grove, Over Haddon (3m W off B5055) ☎(062981) 2343

Level tree bordered field overlooking Larkhill Dale. On the B5055 W of Bakewell turn S in 3m cn unclass road to Haddon Grove farm entrance in ¼m.

15pitches 5🚐 ✳£1.50 15▲£1.50

🚐 cdp

BALA
Gwynedd
Map 6 SH93
See sketch map

►►► ② ❷ △

Pen-y-Garth Farm *(SH938348)* Rhos-y-Gwalia ☎(0678) 520485 Mar–Oct must book public hols Last arrival 22.00hrs Last departure 16.00hrs

A level site with well-laid out pitches for tourers, amidst attractive scenery.

2acres 48pitches 46static SA 20🚐 fr£3.50 or 20 🚐 fr£3.50 28▲ fr£3 (awnings)

6🚐 Individual pitches ⊘ late arrivals enclosure 11wc lit all night 1cdp washbasins hc 🛁 hc ⊙ supervised (spin dry iron) games room childrens

playground calor gas camping gaz ⊞ ☛

⊕ stables golf ⭐ ☛ launderette pub

►► ② ❶ △

Penybont Touring Park *(SH932350)*
Llangynog Rd ☎(0678) 520549 Etr–mid Sep must book peak periods Last arrival 23.00hrs Last departure 14.00hrs
🏕

Part level, part sloping, grass and gravel site with trees and bushes set in mountainous woodland country, adjacent to River Dee and Bala Lake. ½m from Bala on side of B4391.

9acres 75pitches 25🚐 £3.75 or 25 🚐 £3.75 50▲£3 (awnings)

7🚐 Individual pitches ⊘ 9wc lit all night 1cdp washbasins hc (🛁 hc) ⊙ supervised (cold storage) calor gas camping gaz toilet fluid ☛

⊕ stables golf ⭐ cinema ☛ launderette pub

► ② ❶ △

Ty Isaf Caravan & Camping Park *(SH957355)* Signposted ☎(0678) 520574 Apr–Oct must book Last arrival 22.00hrs Last departure noon

A level and grassy attractive farm site.

2acres 30pitches 30🚐 or 25 🚐 or 25▲ awnings

2🚐 ⊘ 6wc lit all night 1cdp 🚐 (washbasins hc 🛁 hc) ⊙ (1dry) (cold

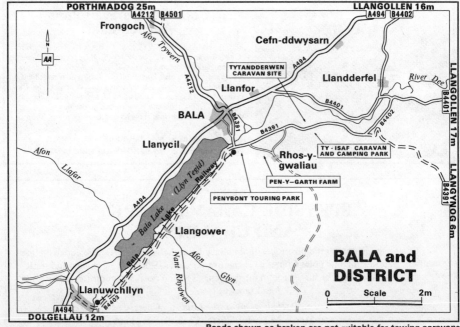

Sites listed under: **1** Bala   **2** Llandderfel   **3** Llanuwchllyn

storage) calor gas camping gaz ⊞

↔ golf ⅄ cinema ♪ launderette pub ⚓

▶ ③ ❷

Tytandderwen Caravan Site
(SH953363) Signposted ☎(0678)
520273 Etr–Oct Last arrival 22.00hrs
Last departure noon

3m SE of Bala on the Bala–Llangynog
road (B4391).

3½acres 10pitches 60static 10♣
fr£2.50 or 10▲£2.40 (awnings)

2♨⊘ 10wc lit all night 1cdp ▣
(washbasins hc) central hot water ⋔hc
cold storage calor gas camping gaz
mobile shop

↔ golf ⅄ cinema ♪ launderette pub ⚓

BALLATER
Grampian Aberdeenshire
Map 15 NO39

▶▶ ①❷⚠

Ballater Caravan & Camping Site
(NO371955) Apply to: Leisure &
Recreation Officer, Kincardine &
Deeside District Council, Viewmount,
Stonehaven, Kincardineshire.
☎Stonehaven (0569) 62001 2 Apr–Oct
Last arrival 20.00hrs Last departure
10.00hrs

A level, grassy site near the river, set in
hilly country with nearby woodland and
moorland.

5acres 38pitches 82static 38♣ or 38♣
or 38▲ ltr

4♨ Individual pitches ⊘ 23wc lit all
night 2cdp washbasins hc (⋔hc) ⊙
(wash spin dry iron) childrens
playground calor gas ⚓

↔ golf ♪ launderette

BALLOCH
Strathclyde Dunbartonshire
Map 10 NS38

▶▶▶ ②❸⚠

Tullichewan Caravan Park (NS383816)
Old Luss Rd Signposted ☎Alexandria
(0389) 59475 Apr–21 Oct booking
advisable Jul & Aug Last departure noon
no single sex groups

A quiet and pleasant rural site near Loch
Lomond, surrounded by woodland and
hills. Close to the A82.

12acres 190pitches 10static 80♣ 80♣
30▲ (awnings) ltr

8♨ Individual pitches ⊘ late arrivals
enclosure wc lit all night ♨ ⋔hc ⊙
supervised (wash) spin (dry iron cold
storage) childrens playground calor gas
camping gaz toilet fluid ☎ ⚓

↔ stables golf ⅄ cinema ♪ pub

BALMACARA
Highland Ross and Cromarty
Map 14 NG82

▶▶ ②❷⚠

Reraig Caravan Site (NG815272)
Signposted ☎(059986) 285 May–Sep

no bookings Last arrival 22.00hrs Last
departure noon

Set on level, grassy ground surrounded
by trees, the site looks south towards
Loch Alsh and Skye.

2acres 40pitches 40♣£3.10 or
40♣£3.10 or 40▲£3.10 (awnings)

3♨ 9wc lit all night 1cdp washbasins hc
(⋔hc) ⊙ supervised ⚓

▽ ②

Balmacara Camp Site (NG802279)
☎Achnashellach (05206) 273

Near the coast on the Kintail Peninsula.
On unclass rd 1½m N of A87 3½m E of
Kyle of Lochalsh.

50pitches 50♣ or 50♣ or 50▲

♨cdp

BALMAHA
Central Stirlingshire
Map 10 NS49

▶▶▶ ②❷⚠

Cashell Caravan & Camping Site
(NS396939) Signposted ☎Drymen
(0360) 60255 Apr–2 Oct booking
advisable peak periods Last arrival
20.00hrs Last departure noon

An attractive and well-wooded site, lying
on the eastern shores of Loch Lomond
within the Queen Elizabeth Forest Park,
offering seclusion to campers and
splendid views over the loch.

12acres 200pitches 200♣ or 200♣ or
200▲ awnings ltr

6♨ Individual pitches late arrivals
enclosure 24wc lit all night 2cdp 31
washbasins hc 10⋔hc 7⊙ supervised
(wash spin) private beach calor gas
camping gaz paraffin toilet fluid cafe ☎
⚓

↔ stables ⅄ ♪ pub

BALMINNOCH
Dumfries & Galloway Wigtownshire
Map 10 NX26

▶▶▶ ③❷⚠

Three Lochs Caravan Park (NX272655)
Signposted ☎Kirkcowan (067183) 304
Etr–Sep

Level, grass and sand site with trees and
bushes set in meadowland and
woodland with access to river and lake.
5m N of Kirkcowan off A75.

15acres 80pitches 120static 80♣£4.25
or 80♣£4.25 or 80▲£4.25 awnings ltr

12♨ 18wc lit all night 2cdp ▣
washbasins hc ⋔hc ⊙ supervised
(wash) (dry iron) games room CTV (cold
storage) childrens playground calor gas
camping gaz toilet fluid ☎ Sailing,
fishing, ⚓

↔ ♪ pub

BAMBURGH
Northumberland
Map 12 NU13

▶▶ ①❶⚠

Glororum Caravan Park (NU166334)
Glororum Farm Signposted ☎(06684)
205 Apr–Oct must book peak periods no
tents

A pleasantly situated site off B1341 1m
W of Bamburgh. The open countryside
setting gives views of Bamburgh Castle
and surrounding farmland.

6acres 100pitches 125static 100♣ or
100♣ (awnings)

7♨ 35wc lit all night 3cdp washbasins
hc central hot water ⋔hc ⊙ (wash) (dry)
iron childrens playground calor gas ☎
⚓

↔ stables golf launderette pub

BANBURY
Oxfordshire
Map 4 SP44

▽ ②

Bourton Heights Farm (SP449464)
Southam Rd Signposted ☎Cropredy
(029572) 8107 All year Last departure
noon

East side of A423 3¾m N of Banbury
within 1m past signpost for Great
Bourton and Cropredy.

10acres ♣£2 ♣£2 ▲£2 (awnings) ltr

2♨⊘ 1wc lit all night 1cdp washbasins
hc central hot water (⋔hc) ⊙ supervised
(iron)

↔ stables ⅄ cinema ♪ launderette
pub ⚓

BANFF
Grampian Banffshire
Map 15 NJ66

▶▶▶ ②❸⚠

Banff Links Caravan Site (NJ672646)
Apply to: Banff & Buchan D. C., Director
of Leisure & Recreation, 1 Church St,
Macduff, Banffshire AB4 1UF
Signposted ☎Macduff (0261) 32861
May–Sep must book Last arrival
21.00hrs Last departure 09.00hrs

Mainly static site set right on sea front,
bordered by fine beach and with golf
links to one side. Situated off A98, 1m W
of Banff on B9139.

5acres 30pitches 100static 25♣ 5▲
(awnings)

5♨ 28wc lit all night 1cdp 20washbasins
hc central hot water 12⋔hc 4⊙
supervised (wash spin dry) (licensed
club/bar) childrens playground calor
gas camping gaz paraffin toilet fluid cafe
restaurant ☎

↔ golf ⅄ ♪ launderette pub

BARCALDINE
Strathclyde Argyllshire
Map 10 NM94

▶▶▶ ②❸⚠

Barcaldine Garden Caravan Park
(NM955415) Signposted ☎Ledaig
(063172) 348 Jun–Oct rsApr & May
booking advisable Jul & Aug Last arrival
20.00hrs Last departure noon no tents→

Mainly level grass site with young trees and bushes. Set in mountainous woodland country with a lake nearby. Off A828.

5acres 75pitches 75🚐 or 75🚙 (awnings)

4🏕 late arrivals enclosure 17wc lit all night 1cdp 🔌 washbasins hc (🚿hc) ☺ supervised spin iron cold storage private beach calor gas camping gaz toilet fluid 🕿 🛒

⊖ stables 🏇 🍴

BARDFIELD, GREAT
Essex
Map 5 TL63

▽ ②

Mandalay Farm (TL705299) 🕿 Great Dunmow (0371) 850443

Gently sloping field in attractive remote surroundings. W off B1053 at Shalford on unclass road to Great Bardfield site in 1½m on right.

4acres 3pitches 3🚐 ✳£1.25 or 3🚙£1.25 or 3🛖£1.25

🏕 cdp

BARMOUTH
Gwynedd
Map 6 SH61

▶ ① ❶ △

Hendre Mynach Caravan Park (SH605170) Signposted 🕿 (0341) 280262 Etr–Oct rsMar must book peak periods Last arrival 23.00hrs Last departure noon

Situated off the A496 on the outskirts of Barmouth and near to railway and beach.

9½acres 250pitches 35🚐£3–£5.50 or 35🚙£3–£4 215🛖£3–£4.50 awnings ltr

10🏕 ☉ 23wc lit all night 1cdp 🔌 washbasins hc (central hot water) (🚿hc) ☺ (wash spin iron cold storage) calor gas camping gaz toilet fluid cafe restaurant 🕿 🛒

⊖ stables 🍴 launderette pub

BARNSTAPLE
Devon
Map 2 SS53

▶▶▶ ② ❷ △

Midland Caravan Park (SS532346) Braunton Rd Signposted 🕿 (0271) 3691 mid May–mid Sep rsApr–mid May & mid Sep–Oct Last arrival 22.00hrs Last departure noon

Level, grassy site with trees and bushes. Set in hilly country near to river about 1¼m W of Barnstaple on A361.

8acres 105pitches 61static SA 35🚐 35🚙 35🛖 (awnings)

14🏕 ☉ 24wc lit all night 1cdp washbasins hc central hot water (🚿hc) ☺ supervised (wash spin dry) iron CTV (cold storage) licensed club/bar childrens playground calor gas camping gaz toilet fluid cafe restaurant 🕿 ⊞ 🛒

⊖ stables golf 🏇 cinema 🍴 launderette pub

BARROW-IN-FURNESS
Cumbria
Map 7 SD16

▶▶▶ ① ❶ △

South End Caravan Site (SD208628) Walney Island Signposted 🕿 (0229) 42823 Mar–Oct must book Jul, Aug & Public Hols Last arrival 22.00hrs Last departure noon no single sex groups

Mainly level grass site adjacent to sea, on Walney Island 1m SE.

5acres 80pitches 100static 60🚐£3.50 10🚙£3.50 10🛖£3.50 (awnings) ltr

2🏕 6wc lit all night washbasins hc 🚿hc ☺ supervised (wash spin dry iron) games room CTV cold storage licensed club/bar childrens playground private beach calor gas camping gaz toilet fluid 🕿 🛒

⊖ golf cinema 🍴 launderette pub

BASSENTHWAITE LAKE
Cumbria
See map 11 for locations of sites in vicinity

BATH
Avon
Map 3 ST76

▶▶▶ ② ❸ △

Newbridge Caravan Park (ST719655) Newbridge Signposted 🕿 (0225) 28778 All year booking advisable peak periods Last arrival 18.00hrs Last departure noon no tents

Situated on the edge of Bath in parklike grounds among maturing trees and shrubs. Hard standings throughout.

2acres 72pitches 72🚐 (awnings)

5🏕 Individual pitches late arrivals enclosure 12wc lit all night 2cdp 🔌 washbasins hc ✦hc (☉) supervised (wash spin) iron childrens playground 🕿 ⊞ 🛒

⊖ stables golf 🏇 cinema 🍴 launderette pub

▶▶▶ ② ❸ △

Newton Mill Touring Centre (ST715649) Newton St Loe (3m NW off A4) Signposted 🕿 (0225) 333909 All year Last arrival 22.00hrs Last departure noon no unaccompanied children under 16

Tranquil site with wooded slopes and trout stream within easy reach of main traffic routes.

4acres 120pitches 90🚐£9 or 90🚙£8 30🛖£8 awnings

6🏕 Individual pitches ☉ 24wc lit all night 1cdp 🔌 16washbasins hc 12🚿hc 3☉ supervised (wash spin dry iron) (games room) (cold storage) childrens playground calor gas camping gaz toilet fluid 🕿 off-licence & fishing 🛒

⊖ stables golf 🏇 cinema 🍴 launderette pub

BEADNELL
Northumberland
Map 12 NU22

▶▶ 🎦 ❶ ⚠
Beadnell Links *(NU233287)* The
Chimes Signposted ☏Chathill
(066589) 241 Apr–Oct booking
advisable public & school hols Last
departure noon no tents

*Level site lying in farmland, with grass,
gravel and sand surface. Beadnell Bay
and beach nearby.*

1acre 10pitches 140static 10🚐£3.50 or
10🚐£3.50 (awnings)
5🏕 32wc lit all night 5cdp washbasins
hc 🚿hc ☺ calor gas ☎ 🛒
↔ stables golf ⛳ ⛵ launderette pub 🛒

▶ 🎦 ❶ ⚠
Annstead Camping Site *(NU233284)*
☏Seahouses(0665) 720586 Apr–Sep
must book Public Hols & Jul–Aug Last
arrival 22.00hrs Last departure noon no
caravans

*Level, grassy site set in coastal area with
access to sea, beach and main road.
From A1 follow B1340 signposted
Seahouses-Bamburgh.*

6⅓acres 150pitches awnings
7🏕 Individual pitches 19wc lit all night
1cdp washbasins hc central hot water
🚿hc ☺ supervised (iron) (cold storage)
camping gaz ☎ 🛒
↔ stables golf ⛵ launderette pub

BEATTOCK
Dumfries & Galloway *Dumfriesshire*
Map 11 NT00

▶▶ 🎦 ❶ ⚠
Beattock House Caravan Park
(NT079027) Signposted ☏(06833) 403
Apr–Oct Last arrival 23.00hrs Last
departure 10.30hrs

*Small, level grass touring site with some
mature trees set in the grounds of a
country house, near main road.*

2¾acres 15 pitches SA 15🚐fr£3 or
15🚐fr£3 or 15🅰fr£3 (awnings) ltr
4🏕 3wc lit all night 1cdp washbasins hc
central hot water 🚿hc ☺ supervised

see previous page for entry

---

licensed club/bar ☎ 🛒
↔ stables golf ⛳ ⛵ launderette pub

BEAULY
Highland *Inverness-shire*
Map 14 NH54

▶▶▶ 🎦 ❷ ⚠
Cruivend Camping & Caravan Site
(NH516446) Signposted ☏(0463)
782367 15 Mar–14 Oct must book Jul &
Aug Last arrival 23.00hrs Last departure
noon

*Level, grassy site situated off A9 and 1m
S of Beauly.*

2acres 30pitches 4static SA 10🚐£3.20
10🚐£3.20 10🅰£3.20 (awnings) ltr
2🏕 Individual pitches 8wc lit all night
1cdp (washbasins hc central hot water
🚿hc) ☺ supervised cold storage
childrens playground calor gas camping
gaz paraffin ☎ 🛒
↔ stables golf ⛵ launderette pub

▶▶▶ 🎦 ❶ ⚠
Lovat Bridge Caravan & Camping Site
(NH517452) Signposted ☏(046371)
2374 16 Mar–16 Oct booking advisable
Last arrival 23.00hrs Last departure
noon

*Set in a wooded clearing on the south
bank of the River Beauly in the shadow
of the Telford Bridge from which the site
takes its name.*

7acres 75pitches 10static 75🚐 or 75🚐
or 75🅰 awnings
6🏕 ☺ late arrivals enclosure 16wc lit all
night 1cdp washbasins hc central hot
water 🚿hc ☺ supervised (cold storage)
childrens playground calor gas toilet
fluid ☎
↔ stables golf ⛳ ⛵ pub 🛒

BEAUMARIS
Gwynedd
Map 6 SH67

▶ 🎦 ❷ ❶ ⚠
Pine's Country Club & Caravan Park
(SH622794) Penmon ☏Bethesda

(0248) 600486 Apr–Oct must book Last
arrival 22.00hrs Last departure 12.00hrs

*The site is situated on the Isle of
Anglesey 3m NE of Beaumaris. It is on
the shores of the Menai Straits which
afford bathing and fishing.*

7acres 30pitches 24static SA 6🚐 or
6🚐 24🅰 awnings
3🏕☺ 4wc lit all night 1cdp
2washbasins hc 🚿hc ☺ supervised
(games room) CTV (licensed club/bar)
private beach calor gas restaurant ☎
slipway, boating, fishing
↔ pub 🛒

BECKFOOT
Cumbria
Map 11 NY04

▶▶ 🎦 ❷ ⚠
Abbey Holme Caravan Park
(NY095498) Signposted ☏Silloth
(0965) 31653 Mar–Oct must book Jul &
Aug Last arrival 22.00hrs

*Level site, with grass and gravel surface
overlooking Solway Firth. Adjacent to
B5300 Silloth-Maryport road. Ideal
position for touring the northern Lake
District.*

2½acres 25pitches 25static 25🚐£4 or
25🚐£4 or 25🅰£4 (awnings)
9🏕 11wc lit all night 1cdp 11washbasins
hc 2central hot water 6🚿hc 2☺
supervised (spin iron) cold storage
childrens playground calor gas ☎ ⊞ 🛒
↔ stables golf ⛳ ⛵ launderete pub

BEDDGELERT
Gwynedd
Map 6 SH54

▶ 🎦 ❷ ⚠
**Snowdonia Forest Park Camping
Ground** *(SH578491)* Signposted
☏(076686) 288 Apr–Oct rsNov–Mar no
bookings Last arrival 22.00hrs Last
departure 14.00hrs

*Part level, part sloping grass and gravel
site amidst trees and bushes. Set in
mountainous woodland country near to
river and road.*

280pitches 140🚐 or 140🚐 140🅰
awnings →

Touring caravan park only five minutes
drive from central Bath.

Run by Bath City Council, this attractively landscaped site overlooks the River Avon only 1½
from the tourist attractions of Britain's top inland resort.
★ Hard standing for 57 vans with electric points for 23. ★ 15 grass sites available for
late arrivals only. ★ Hot and cold showers. ★ Shaver points ★ Drying areas. ★ Flush toilets.
★ Laundry and washing facilities. ★ Children's playground. ★ Dogs allowed
on leash. ★ Open 365 days a year.

The site is situated 1½ miles from City centre on
Upper Bristol Road (A4) at Brassmill Lane, Newbridge,
Bath. For advanced bookings and information, please
write to: Mr. E. Loxton, Warden, Newbridge, Caravan Park,
Brassmill Lane, Bath, Avon, or telephone Bath (0225)
28778. Sorry, no camping.

8⚡ Individual pitches ☾ 28wc lit all night 2cdp washbasins hc ⋔hc ☉ (1wash 2dry) calor gas camping gaz toilet fluid cafe restaurant ☎ 🏬 ⟿ stables ☑ launderette

BELFORD
Northumberland
Map 12 NU13

▶▶▶ ② ❶ ⚠

Waren Caravan Park(NU155343)
Waren Mill Signposted ☎Bamburgh (06684) 366 Apr–Oct booking advisable peak periods Last arrival 22.00hrs Last departure noon

Seaside site within walking distance of beach; surrounded by a slight grassy embankment affording shelter for caravans. All pitches are numbered and situated around a central green. 2m E of town on B1342 Bamburgh road.

4acres 105pitches 277static SA 105🚐£3–£5 or 105🚐£3–£5 or 105▲£3–£5 (awnings) ltr

4⚡ Individual pitches 17wc lit all night 1cdp washbasins hc ⋔hc ☉ supervised (wash) (dry) iron (games room) childrens playground calor gas camping gaz toilet fluid ☎ 🏬 ⟿ stables golf ☑ launderette pub

BELTON
Norfolk
Map 5 TG40
See Yarmouth (Great) sketch map

▶▶▶ ② ❷ ⚠

Wild Duck Caravan & Chalet Park
(TG475028) ☎Great Yarmouth (0493) 780268 Etr–Oct must book Last arrival 23.00hrs no single sex groups

Level grassy site with bushes and mature trees, with access to woodlands and bracken heath.

15acres 150pitches 150static 150🚐£2–£3.50 or 150🚐£2–£3.50 or 150▲£2–£3.50 (awnings)

16⚡ Individual pitches ☾ 44wc lit all night cdp washbasins hc central hot water (⋔hc) supervised iron ⟿ TV childrens playground calor gas camping gaz toilet fluid cafe restaurant ☎ ⊞ 🏬 ⟿ ⟿ 🐾 launderette

BENDERLOCH
Strathclyde *Argyllshire*
Map 10 NM93

▶▶▶ ② ❶ ⚠

Tralee Bay Caravan Park (NM896393)
Signposted ☎Ledaig (063172) 255 Apr–Oct must book Last arrival 18.00hrs Last departure noon no cars by tents

Attractive site on level ground, sloping gently towards the sea. Outstanding views over Ardmuckmish Bay towards Oban. A 16th-C castle lies N of the site on the same peninsula.

3½acres 96pitches SA 28🚐£3.30 28🚐£3 40▲£3.30 (awnings) ltr

9⚡☾ late arrivals enclosure 28wc lit all night 1cdp washbasins hc (central hot water ⋔ hc) ☉ supervised (wash) spin (dry) iron (cold storage) childrens playground private beach calor gas camping gaz toilet fluid ☎ ⊞ 🏬 ⟿ stables 🐾 ☑ pub

BERRYNARBOR
Devon
Map 2 SS54
See Ilfracombe sketch map

▶▶▶▶ ② ❷ ⚠

Watermouth Cove (SS558477)
Signposted ☎Ilfracombe (0271) 62504 Whit–Sep rsEtr–Whit must book peak periods Last arrival 20.00hrs Last departure 11.00hrs no motorcycles no tents

Mainly level, grass site amidst trees and bushes, set in meadowland with access to sea, beach and main road.

2½acres 90pitches 90🚐£4.50–£9.50 or 90🚐£4.50–£9.50 (awnings) ltr

14⚡ Individual pitches late arrivals enclosure 26wc lit all night 🚻 washbasins hc central hot water ⋔ hc ☉ supervised (wash spin) iron ⟿ (games room) CTV (cold storage) licensed club/bar childrens playground private beach calor gas cafe restaurant ☎ ⊞ 🏬 ⟿ stables golf 🐾 cinema ☑ launderette pub

▶▶▶▶ ③ ❷ ⚠

Sandaway Holiday Park (SS568474)
☎Combe Martin (027188) 3155 mid May–Oct rs15 Mar–mid May booking advisable Jul & Aug Last departure 10.00hrs no single sex groups

Well-designed site, carefully screened and well laid out, overlooking the sea. Situated on A399, ¼m from Combe Martin on coast side of road.

1¼acres 61pitches SA 21🚐 fr£3.30 or 21🚐 fr£3.30 40▲fr£3.30 awnings

9⚡ Individual pitches ☾ late arrivals enclosure 28wc lit all night 1cdp 🚻 12washbasins hc (10⋔hc) 4☉ (wash)

(dry iron) ⟿ games room CTV (cold storage) licensed club/bar childrens playground private beach calor gas camping gaz toilet fluid cafe ☎ ⊞ amusement arcade disco/video room 🏬 ⟿ stables golf 🐾 ☑ launderette pub

see advertisement on page 117

▶ ① ❶ ⚠

Napps Camping Site (SS565476) Old Coast Rd Signposted ☎Combe Martin (027188) 2557 Whit–Sep rs Etr–Whit & Oct–Nov Last arrival 22.30hrs Last departure noon

Site is situated on cliff top adjacent to Combe Martin where seclusion is guaranteed. Turn north off A399 W of Combe Martin at bottom of hill.

4½acres 85pitches SA 85🚐£4 or 85🚐£3 or 85▲£2.80 (awnings)

5⚡ Individual pitches 20wc lit all night 1cdp washbasins hc (⋔hc) ☉ (wash spin dry iron) (cold storage) childrens playground calor gas camping gaz toilet fluid ☎ Hair dryers sauna 🏬 ⟿ stables golf 🐾 cinema ☑ launderette pub

BERWICK-UPON-TWEED
Northumberland
Map 12 NT95

▶▶▶ ② ❶ ⚠

Ord House Caravan Park (NT982515) East Ord Signposted ☎(0289) 305288 Apr–Sep rsMar & Oct booking advisable peak periods & Public Hols Last arrival 23.00hrs Last departure noon no tents

Situated on the A698, 1m from Berwick; the site is set in pleasant surroundings with mature trees and bushes.

12acres 60pitches 200static 50🚐£2.20–£5 10🚐£1.70–£4.50

6⚡ Individual pitches 48wc lit all night 3cdp 30washbasins hc (central hot water ⟿hc ⋔hc) ☉ (wash spin dry iron) licensed club/bar childrens playground calor gas camping gaz toilet fluid ☎ 🏬 ⟿ golf 🐾 cinema ☑ launderette pub

BETHESDA
Gwynedd
Map 6 SH66

▶▶▶▶ ② ❶ ⚠

Ogwen Bank Caravan Park & Country Club (SH626656) Signposted ☎(0248) 600486 Spring Bank Hol–Sep rsEtr–Spring Bank Hol & Oct must book Last arrival 22.00hrs Last departure noon no tents

Part level, part sloping, grass and gravel site with mature trees and bushes set in mountainous country adjacent to river. On A5 between Betws-y-Coed and Bangor.

7acres 66pitches 100static 66🚐£2.50–£9 or 66🚐£2.50–£9 awnings

58🏕 Individual pitches late arrivals enclosure 60wc lit all night 1cdp 56🚐 60washbasins hc 60🛁hc 60☺ supervised (wash spin dry iron) games room CTV (cold storage licensed club/bar) childrens playground calor gas camping gaz toilet fluid ☎ ⊞ 🖳

↩ stables cinema ✂ launderette

BETTWS EVAN
Dyfed
Map 2 SN34

▶▶▶ 🖪 🟢 ⚠
Pilbach Caravan Park *(SN306476)*
Signposted 🕾Rhydlewis (023975) 434
Mar–Oct must book Jul–2 Sep Last
arrival 23.00hrs Last departure noon

An exceptionally well-run small site set in secluded countryside. 3m N of Newcastle Emlyn and 7m E of Cardigan.

3acres 70pitches 70static 55🚐£3.50 5🚐£3.50 10▲£3.50 (awnings)

8🏕 Individual pitches ☺ late arrivals enclosure 10wc lit all night 1cdp 🚐 washbasins hc central hot water (🛁hc) ☺ supervised (wash spin dry) iron (♨) (cold storage licensed club/bar) childrens playground calor gas camping gaz toilet fluid ☎ 🖳

↩ stables golf ⚓ ✂ pub

BETWS GARMON
Gwynedd
Map 6 SH55
See Caernarfon sketch map

▶▶▶ 🖪 🟢 ⚠
Bryn Gloch Caravan & Camping Park
(SH535574) Signposted 🕾Waunfawr
(028685) 216 Mar–Oct booking
advisable public & school hols Last
departure 10.30hrs

A well-maintained site with a sloping grassy surface, situated close to the main road; on the fringe of the Snowdonia National Park, with good country views.

6acres 100pitches 14static SA 27🚐£3.60 or 27🚐£3.40 73▲£3.40 (awnings)

6🏕 Individual pitches ☺ late arrivals enclosure 13wc lit all night 1cdp washbasins hc central hot water(🛁hc) ☺ supervised (spin dry iron) (games room) (cold storage) calor gas camping gaz toilet fluid cafe restaurant cot hire 🖳

↩ stables ⚓ ✂ launderette pub

BEWALDETH
Cumbria
Map 11 NY23

▶▶▶ 🖪 🟢 ⚠
North Lakes Caravan & Camping Park
(NY205356) Bassenthwaite Lake

Signposted 🕾Bassenthwaite Lake
(059681) 510 Etr–Sep rsMar–Etr & Oct–
15 Nov booking advisable public hols
Last arrival 21.00hrs Last departure
noon

Tranquil rural site set in wooded hilly countryside. A small beck meanders through the site and small bridges have been placed across it to facilitate short walks in the surrounding wooded area. Adjacent to A591 Keswick-Carlisle road.

25acres 195pitches 51static SA 95🚐 or 95🚐 100▲ (awnings)

15🏕 Individual pitches ☺ late arrivals enclosure 46wc lit all night 3cdp 52 washbasins hc (20🛁hc) 12☺ supervised (wash dry iron) games room (cold storage) licensed club/bar calor gas camping gaz toilet fluid ☎ facilities for wheelchairs 🖳

↩ stables golf ✂

see advertisement on page 161

BICKINGTON *(Near Ashburton)*
Devon
Map 3 SX87

▶▶▶ 🖪 🟢 ⚠
Lemonford Holidays *(SX793723)*
Signposted 🕾(062682) 242 15 Mar–
Oct booking advisable Jul & Aug Last
arrival 22.00hrs

Small secluded and well-maintained site approached on old A38 from Drumbridge or from A383 Newton Abbot road.

3acres 20pitches 17static SA 20 🚐 or 20🚐 or 20▲ (awnings)

4🏕 Individual pitches ☺ wc lit all night 1cdp 🚐 (8washbasins hc) (4♨hc) 2☺ supervised (wash spin dry) iron calor gas camping gaz 🖳

↩ stables golf ✂ launderette pub

BIDDENDEN
Kent
Map 5 TQ83

▶▶▶ 🖪 🟢 ⚠
Woodlands Park *(TQ867372)*
Tenterden Rd Signposted 🕾(0580)
291216 Apr–Oct rsMar Booking
advisable Public Hols Last departure
18.00hrs

Ten-acre site of level grassland with hedges and trees surrounding. 1½m S of Biddenden on northern side of A262. Ideal centre for Kent, Sussex and Channel ports.

9acres 200pitches 205static SA 200🚐£4.50–£5 or 200🚐£4.50–£5 or 200▲£4.50–£5 (awnings) ltr

8🏕 20wc lit all night 1cdp washbasins hc (🛁) ☺ (iron) licensed club/bar childrens playground calor gas camping gaz toilet fluid cafe restaurant ☎ 🖳

↩ stables golf ✂ pub

▶ 🗊 🟏 ⚠
Spilland Farm Holiday Caravan & Tourer Park *(TQ849369)* Benenden Rd
Signposted 🕾(0580) 291379 Apr–Oct
booking advisable peak periods Last
arrival 20.00hrs Last departure noon no
mixed teenage groups

Grassy, sloping site, surrounded by trees and situated on attractive old farm. Ideal for touring the Weald.

4acres 65pitches 65static 65🚐£4.50 or 65🚐£4.50 or 65▲£4.50 (awnings) ltr

10🏕 Individual pitches late arrivals enclosure 9wc lit all night 1cdp 🚐 washbasins hc (🛁hc) ☺ supervised (wash spin iron) cold storage childrens playground calor gas 🖳

↩ stables cinema ✂ pub

BILLINGSHURST
West Sussex
Map 4 TQ02

▶ 🗊 🟏
Limeburner's Arms *(TQ073254)*
Newbridge Signposted 🕾(040381)
2311 Apr–14 Oct booking advisable
public hols & Jul–Aug Last arrival
21.00hrs

Secluded rural site alongside the attractive 'Limeburner's Arms' public house. Located a short distance from the village of Billingshurst on the A272 Midhurst road and the peaceful course of the River Arun.

3acres 42pitches 30🚐 or 42🚐 or 42▲ awnings

2🏕 Individual pitches 4wc lit all night 1cdp ☺ supervised licensed bar calor gas camping gaz

↩ stables ✂ launderette pub 🖳

BIRCHINGTON
Kent
Map 5 TR26

▶▶ ② ❷ ⚠

Quex Caravan & Camping Park
(TR321685) Park Rd Signposted
☎Thanet (0843) 41273 Mar–Oct no
bookings Last arrival 20.00hrs Last
departure noon

*Small site surrounded by tall hedges and
mature trees, with a wooded tent area in
quiet secluded field. From Birchington
(A38) turn SE into Park Road, site in 1m
at junction of B2049.*

6acres 150pitches 80static SA 150🚐£4
or 150🚐£4 or 150▲£4 (awnings)

8🚗 28wc lit all night 3cdp washbasins
hc (central hot water) (🛁hc)☉
supervised (wash) (dry iron) childrens
playground calor gas camping gaz toilet
fluid 🛒

⊖ stables golf ⛳ cinema ♪
launderette pub

BIRNAM
Tayside *Perthshire*
Map 11 NO04

▶▶▶▶ ② ❸ ⚠

Erigmore House Caravan Park
(NO036416) Signposted ☎Dunkeld
(03502) 236 Apr–Oct rsMar must book
Last arrival 22.30hrs Last departure
noon

*A predominantly touring site in the tree-
studded grounds of 18th-C Erigmore
House which offers a wide variety of
unusual trees including Japanese maple
and cherry. Site well-secluded from the
main road and a considerable degree of
privacy can be found. Situated on B898
just off A9 through Birnam village.*

22acres 240pitches 60static 178🚐£5
22🚐£4.50 ▲£3 (awnings)

29🚗 Individual pitches Ⓐ late arrivals
enclosure 39wc lit all night 1cdp
washbasins hc (♨hc 🛁hc)☉
supervised (wash spin dry) iron ♒
games room licensed bar childrens
playground calor gas cafe restaurant ☎
⊞🛒

⊖ stables golf ♪ pub

BISHOP MONKTON
North Yorkshire
Map 8 SE36

▽ ③

Church Farm *(SE328658)*
Knaresborough Rd Signposted
☎Ripon (0765) 87297 & 87405 Apr–Oct
must book Peak periods no motorcycles

*Mainly level tree lined field, adjacent to
farm in picturesque village.*

2acres 5pitches 5🚐£1.50 or 5🚐£1.50
▲£1.50 awnings

2🚗Ⓐ 1cdp supervised (cold storage)
childrens playground calor gas camping
gaz toilet fluid 🛒

⊖ stables golf ⛳ ♪ launderette pub

BLACKFORD
Cumbria
Map 11 NY36

▶▶ ② ❷ ⚠

Dandy Dinmont Caravan Site
(NY399620) Signposted ☎Rockcliffe
(022874) 611 Etr–Oct rsMar must book
Jul & Aug Last departure 16.00hrs

*A level sheltered site, screened on two
sides by hedgerows. Situated alongside
A7 about 1m N of junction 44 of M6.*

3acres 47pitches 15static 27🚐£3.80–
£4 or 27🚐£3.80–£4.20▲£2.40–£2.80
(awnings)

6🚗Ⓐ 14wc lit all night 1cdp 🔌
washbasins hc 🛁hc ☉ cold storage
calor gas

⊖ stables ♪ launderette 🛒

BLACKPOOL
Lancashire
Map 7 SD33

▶▶ ① ❶ ⚠

Cropper Caravan Park *(SD345334)*
Cropper Rd, Marton Signposted
☎(0253) 62051 Mar–Oct must book
Public Hols & Jul–Oct Last arrival
22.00hrs Last departure noon no
motorcycles, no single sex groups

Situated on flat open countryside near to

*M55 terminus. Site is well signposted on
approaches.*

7acres 126pitches 126🚐£3.50 or
116🚐£3.50 10▲£3.50 (awnings)

5🚗 27wc lit all night 3cdp 🔌
17washbasins hc 4central hot water
(14🛁hc) 6☉ supervised (wash spin dry
iron) (games room) (cold storage)
childrens playground calor gas toilet
fluid ☎ Battery charger Bikes for hire 🛒

⊖ stables golf ⛳ cinema ♪
launderette pub

BLACKWATER
Cornwall
Map 2 SW74
See Redruth sketch map

▶▶▶ ① ❶ ⚠

Trevarth Caravan Park *(SW744468)*
☎Truro (0872) 560266 Apr–Oct
booking necessary Jul & Aug Last arrival
21.00hrs Last departure noon

*An established, mainly level grassy farm
site, on high ground. Approx 4½m NE of
Redruth, on N side of the A30 just W of
junc with the B3277.*

4acres 60pitches 61static 30🚐£3.50 or
30🚐£3.50 30▲£3.50 (awnings) ltr

5🚗 late arrivals enclosure 15wc lit all
night 1cdp washbasins hc (🛁hc)☉
supervised (wash spin dry iron) (games
room) (cold storage) childrens
playground calor gas camping gaz toilet
fluid ☎ 🛒

⊖ stables golf ⛳ ♪ launderette pub

see advertisement on page 216

BLAIR ATHOLL
Tayside *Perthshire*
Map 14 NN86
See Pitlochry sketch map

▶▶▶▶ ③ ❸ ⚠

Blair Castle Caravan Park *(NN874656)*
Signposted ☎(079681) 263 Apr–Sep
booking advisable Jul & Aug Last arrival
21.30hrs Last departure noon

*This is a predominantly touring site set in
tree-studded land within the grounds of
Blair Castle and bordered on one side
by the River Tilt. Although situated near
to the main road there is ample
screening by trees to provide seclusion.*

20acres 330pitches 100static
200⚐£4.50 30⚐£4.50 100▲£4.50
(awnings)

25⚏ Individual pitches ⚠ late arrivals
enclosure 108wc lit all night 4cdp 🔌
92washbasins hc 10🚿hc 39☺ (wash dry
iron) (cold storage) childrens
playground calor gas camping gaz toilet
fluid cafe ☎ ⊞ 🛒

↔ stables golf ⚒ cinema ⚓
launderette pub

►►► ①❷⚠
River Tilt Caravan Park *(NN875653)*
Signposted ☎(079681) 467 All year
must book Jul & Aug

*Level, grass site with trees and bushes
set in hilly woodland country with access
to River Garry. 7m N of Pitlochry on A9.*

4acres 50pitches 92static 50⚐£3.25 or
50⚐£3.25 or 50▲£2.50 (awnings)

9⚏ 14wc lit all night 1cdp 🔌
washbasins hc (central hot water 🚿hc)
☺ supervised (wash spin dry iron) (cold
storage) calor gas camping gaz toilet
fluid 🛒

↔ stables golf ⚓ launderette pub

BLAIRLOGIE
Central *Stirlingshire*
Map 11 NS89

►► ②❶⚠
**Witches Craig Farm Caravan &
Camping Park** *(NS823967)*
☎Stirling (0786) 4947 Apr–Oct Last
arrival 21.00hrs Last departure 13.00hrs

*A level grassy site on the main road with
tree-studded hills to the rear. 3m from
town centre on A91.*

5acres 60pitches 8static 30⚐£4
10⚐£3.75 20▲£4 (awnings)

3⚏ 5wc lit all night 1cdp washbasins hc
(🚿hc) ☺ supervised (wash spin dry)
cold storage childrens playground calor
gas camping gaz toilet fluid ☎ 🛒

↔ stables golf ⚒ cinema ⚓
launderette pub

BLAIRMORE
Strathclyde *Argyllshire*
Map 10 NS18

►► ③❷⚠
Gairletter Caravan Park *(NS193844)*
☎Ardentinny (036981) 208 Apr–Oct
must book Last departure noon no tents,
no single sex groups

*On the W shore of Loch Long, south of
Ardentinny, this site gives outstanding
views of mountains and Loch. Off A815
from Glasgow.*

½acre 4pitches 20static 4⚐£3.30 or
4⚐£3.30

2⚏ late arrivals enclosure 7wc 1cdp 🔌
4washbasins hc central hot water
(2🚿hc) 2☺ supervised (wash spin dry
iron) cold storage childrens playground
private beach calor gas paraffin ☎ 🛒

↔ stables cinema launderette

BLETCHINGDON
Oxfordshire
Map 4 SP51

►►► ③❸⚠
**Diamond Farm Caravan & Camping
Park** *(SP513170)* Heathfield Signposted
☎(0869) 50749 Mar–Oct booking
advisable public hols & Jul–Aug Last
arrival 21.30hrs Last departure 15.00hrs

*A level site situated alongside the B4027
– 1m from the A43 and 7m N of Oxford in
the heart of the Thames Valley. Ideal for
touring the Cotswold and Chiltern hills.*

2acres 34pitches 34⚐£4–£5 or
34⚐£4–£5 or 34▲£4–£5 awnings

4⚏ Individual pitches 8wc lit all night
1cdp 🔌 washbasins hc central hot
water 🚿hc ☺ supervised iron ⌱ games
room TV (cold storage) licensed bar
calor gas camping gaz paraffin 🛒

↔ golf ⚓ pub

▽②
Frogsnest Farm *(SP517167)* Islip Rd
☎(0869) 50389 May–Oct Last arrival
21.00hrs Last departure noon

*Peaceful site screened by hedges; off
A43 4m N of Oxford.*

½acre 10pitches 3⚐£1.75 or
3⚐£1.75 7▲£1 awnings

1⚏ 1cdp

↔ pub 🛒

BLUE ANCHOR
Somerset
Map 3 ST04
See Watchet sketch map

►►►► ②❷⚠
Beeches Holiday Site *(ST039433)*
Signposted ☎Washford (0984) 40391
Mar–Oct booking advisable Jun–Aug &
Public Hols Last arrival 21.00hrs Last

RIVER TILT
CARAVAN PARK

**TOURING CARAVANS
MOTOR HOMES, TENTS &
HOLIDAY HIRE CARAVANS**

**Bridge of Tilt
Blair Atholl
Perthshire
Scotland
PH18 5TE**

**Telephone
Blair Atholl
(079 681) 467**

departure noon no single sex groups

*Set amidst trees and bushes with
extensive views of Welsh Coast. ½m E of
village on the Old Cleeve Road.*

3acres 35pitches 130static 35⚐£3.80–
£4.80 or 35⚐£3.80–£4.80 or
35▲£3.80–£4.80 (awnings)

8⚏ Individual pitches ⚠ late arrivals
enclosure wc lit all night 2cdp ☺
washbasins hc central hot water 🚿hc ☺
supervised (wash dry) iron ⌱ cold
storage childrens playground calor gas
camping gaz toilet fluid ☎ ⊞ 🛒

↔ stables golf ⚒ cinema ⚓
launderette pub

►①❶⚠
Blue Anchor Bay Caravan Park
(ST025434) ☎Dunster (064382) 360
Apr–mid Sep rsMar & mid Sep–Oct no
bookings Last arrival 22.30hrs Last
departure noon no tents no single sex
groups

*Large coastal site, partly wooded on
level ground overlooking bay with
individual acres screened. ¼m E of
West Somerset Railway Station on
B3191.*

3acres 75pitches 455static 75⚐£3.25
or 75⚐£3.25 awnings

2⚏ 45wc lit all night 1cdp (central hot
water) (🚿hc) ☺ supervised iron calor
gas camping gaz toilet fluid cafe ☎ 🛒

↔ stables golf cinema ⚓ launderette
pub

BOAT OF GARTEN
Highland *Inverness-shire*
Map 14 NH91

►►► ②❶⚠
Campgrounds of Scotland
(NH939191) Signposted ☎(047983)
652 Closed Nov booking advisable peak
periods

*Level, grass site with young trees and
bushes set in mountainous woodland in
the village itself, near the River Spey and
Loch Garten, off A95.*

3acres 37pitches 60static 37⚐ or 37⚐
or 37▲ awnings ltr

7⚏ Individual pitches ⚠ late arrivals
enclosure 22wc lit all night 1cdp 🔌
24washbasins hc (6🚿hc) 4☺
supervised (wash dry iron) games room
CTV cold storage childrens playground
calor gas camping gaz paraffin toilet
fluid cafe ☎ ⊞ hair dryers, bicycle-hire
ski hire, baby sitting 🛒

↔ stables golf ⚒ ⚓ pub

BODIAM
E. Sussex
Map 5 TQ72

►► ②❶⚠
*Terrace Wood Caravan & Camping
Site* *(TQ769257)* ☎Staplecross
(058083) 658 Apr–Oct must book Jul &
Aug Last arrival 22.00hrs Last departure
16.00hrs

Although situated on the main A229 →

road, the site is surrounded by woodlands giving seclusion. It was originally a Guinness hop pickers camp and the huts are still on the slightly sloping and grassed site.

2acres 40pitches 40🚐 or 40🚐 or 40▲ awnings ltr

1🏕 late arrivals enclosure 10wc lit all night 1cdp washbasins hc 🛁hc ⊙ supervised games room cold storage licensed bar restaurant 🛒

⊖ golf cinema 🍴 launderette pub

▶ 2 ❶ ⚠

Park Camp *(TQ772252)* Park Farm (off A229) ☎Staplecross (058083) 514 Etr–Oct Last arrival 21.00hrs Last departure 18.00hrs

The site is surrounded by trees in a rural setting near the River Rother.

5acres 50pitches SA 50🚐£3 or 50🚐£3 or 50▲£3 awnings ltr

3🏕 6wc lit all night 1cdp 7washbasins hc 5🛁hc 1⊙ fishing

⊖ stables golf 🍴 launderette pub 🛒

BODINNICK
Cornwall
Map 2 SX15

▶▶ 2 ❶ ⚠

Yeate Farm *(SX134526)* ☎Polruan (072687) 256 Etr–Sep booking advisable Jul–Aug Last arrival 22.00hrs Last departure noon

Situated on a level field bordered with shrubs and the Fowey Estuary.

1acre 30pitches 2static 30🚐£3.45–£4.60 or 30🚐£3.45–£4.60 or 30▲£3.45–£4.60 awnings

2🏕 Individual pitches 3wc 1cdp washbasins hc (🛁hc) ⊙ iron (cold storage) calor gas camping gaz slipway

⊖ 🍴 🍴 launderette pub 🛒

BODMIN
Cornwall
Map 2 SX06

▶ 2 ❶ ⚠

Camping Club Site *(SX079675)* Old Callywith Rd Signposted Apr–Sep Last arrival 22.00hrs Last departure noon

Undulating grassy site with trees and bushes set in meadowland within urban area, close to main road and river.

10acres 200pitches 200🚐£3.90–£4.90 or 200 🚐£3.90–£4.90 or 200▲£3.90–£4.90 awnings

20🏕 Individual pitches 18wc lit all night 3cdp (central hot water) 🛁hc ⊙ supervised (spin iron) childrens playground calor gas camping gaz ☎

⊖ stables cinema 🍴 launderette pub 🛒

BOLNEY
West Sussex
Map 4 TQ22

▶▶▶ 2 ❶

Alder House, Tent, Dormobile &

Caravan Site (TQ268238) Broxmead Ln Signposted ☎(044482) 378 All year no bookings Last departure noon

Pleasant, secluded site a short distance from A23 London–Brighton road at Bolney. Attractively terraced layout with good access roads.

4acres 50pitches 50static 50🚐 or 50 🚐 or 50▲ (awnings)

20🏕 ⚙ 13wc lit all night 4cdp washbasins hc central hot water (➡hc) (🛁hc) ⊙ (wash spin dry) licensed bar calor gas camping gaz toilet fluid cafe ☎ ⊞ ▲

BOLTON-LE-SANDS
Lancashire
Map 7 SD46
See Morecambe sketch map

▶▶▶ 2 ❷ ⚠

Sandside Caravan & Camping Site *(SD472681)* St Michaels Lane Signposted ☎Hest Bank (0524) 822311 Mar–Oct must book Public Hols Last arrival 22.00hrs Last departure noon no single sex groups

A well-maintained site pleasantly situated on sloping ground overlooking Morecambe Bay; distant views of the Lake District. Leave junction 35 to M6; A6 through Carnforth turn right at Little Chef in Bolton-le-Sands, over level crossing to site.

8acres 100pitches 35static SA 40🚐£3 10 🚐£2.60 50▲£2.20 (awnings)

⚙ 12wc lit all night 3cdp 🚐 washbasins hc (🛁hc) ⊙ supervised (wash dry iron) (cold storage) childrens playground calor gas camping gaz toilet fluid ☎ battery charger 🛒

⊖ stables golf 🍴 cinema 🍴 launderette pub 🛒

▶▶ 1 ❶ ⚠

Bolton Holmes Farm *(SD481693)* ☎Carnforth (0524) 732854 Etr–Sep booking advisable public hols

A gently sloping site forming part of a farm complex, offering good views across Morecambe Bay and to the hills of the Lake District.

4acres 30pitches 45static 30🚐✱£2 or 30 🚐£2 or 10▲£2 (awnings)

3🏕 16wc lit all night 1cdp (washbasins hc) (🛁hc) ⊙ supervised (cold storage) calor gas 🛒

⊖ stables 🍴 🍴 launderette pub

▶▶ 1 ❶ ⚠

Detron Gate Farm *(SD478683)* ☎Carnforth (0524) 732842 Apr–Oct rsMar must book except for public hols Last arrival 21.00hrs Last departure 13.00hrs no motorcycles no unaccompanied teenagers.

Conveniently positioned to A6. A popular site on sloping ground with a small farm

adjacent. Views across Morecambe Bay.

9acres 192pitches 52static 92🚐 or 92 🚐 100▲ (awnings)

5🏕⚙ wc lit all night 1cdp washbasins hc (🛁hc) ⊙ supervised (wash spin) CTV (cold storage) childrens playground calor gas camping gaz 🛒 🛒

⊖ stables golf 🍴 cinema 🍴 launderette

BOLVENTOR
Cornwall
Map 2 SX17

▶▶▶ 2 ❶ ⚠

Lords Waste Country Club & Caravan & Camping Site *(SX170740)* Signposted ☎Cardinham (020882) 335 Etr–Oct must book Jul & Aug

The site is on Bodmin Moor not far from the A30 at Bolventor and is well situated for moorland walks.

50pitches 50🚐£2.50 or 50 🚐£2.50 or 50▲£2.50 (awnings) ltr

2🏕 Individual pitches late arrivals enclosure 6wc lit all night 1cdp washbasins hc central hot water (🛁hc) ⊙ (wash spin) TV (licensed club/bar) childrens playground calor gas camping gaz cafe restaurant ☎ 🛒

⊖ stables 🍴 launderette pub

BONCHESTER BRIDGE
Borders Roxburghshire
Map 12 NT51

▶▶▶ 2 ❸ ⚠

Bonchester Bridge Caravan Park *(NT586123)* Fernbank Signposted ☎(045086) 676 Etr–mid Oct Last arrival 23.00hrs

Lovely little site by the banks of a small river, in country village.

2½acres 20pitches SA 20🚐 or 20 🚐 or 20▲ awnings

3🏕 Individual pitches for caravans ⚙ 10wc lit all night 1cdp washbasins hc central hot water 🛁hc ⊙ supervised wash spin iron cold storage paraffin toilet fluid

⊖ 🍴 pub 🛒

BOOSBECK
Cleveland
Map 8 NZ61

▶▶▶ 2 ❷ ⚠

Margrove Park *(NZ656159)* Signposted ☎Guisborough (0287) 53616 Apr–Oct Last arrival 21.00hrs Last departure 11.00hrs

A grassy site 500yds from the Moors on northern edge of National Park. Situated in a well wooded and attractive valley.

8acres 130pitches 100🚐 or 100 🚐 30▲ (awnings) ltr

5🏕⚙ late arrivals enclosure 10wc lit all night 1cdp 12washbasins hc 5🛁hc 4⊙ supervised (wash spin) iron games room childrens playground calor gas camping gaz paraffin toilet fluid ☎ ⅄

↔ stables cinema ⌦ launderette pub

BOSWINGER
Cornwall
Map 2 SW94

▶▶▶▶ ③ ❸ ⚠

Sea View International Caravan & Camping Park *(SW990412)* Signposted ☎St. Austell (0726) 843425 19 Apr–Sep booking advisable 16 Jul–20 Aug Last arrival 22.00hrs Last departure 11.00hrs no single sex groups

A picturesque site overlooking Veryan Bay, situated 3½m SW of Mevagissey harbour. It is on level ground with varied trees and shrubs. Access to sea and beach in ½m.

13acres 172pitches 59static 172🚐£5.50–£7.28 or 172🚐£5.50–£7.58 or 172▲£5.50–£7.58 (awnings)

30🏕 Individual pitches ⓐ late arrivals enclosure 35wc lit all night 2cdp 🍴 washbasins hc (🚻hc 🛁hc) ☺ supervised (wash spin dry iron) 🏊 games room cold storage childrens playground calor gas camping gaz toilet fluid ☎ ⊞ ⅄

↔ ✈ ⌦ launderette pub

see advertisement on page 217

BOTHWELL
Strathclyde *Lanarkshire*
Map 11 NS75

▶▶▶ ② ❸ ⚠

Strathclyde Park Caravan Site *(NS717585)* Bothwellhaugh Rd Signposted ☎Motherwell (0698) 66155 All year Last arrival 22.45hrs Last departure noon

A mainly level grass site with saplings and bushes situated amidst woodland and meadowland. Close to the M74 with direct access through the park to junction 5.

20acres 150pitches 100🚐£3.85 or 100🚐£3.85 50▲£3.30 (awnings) ltr

5🏕 Individual pitches ⓐ late arrivals enclosure 25wc lit all night washbasins hc 🛁hc ☺ (wash spin dry) childrens playground ☎ ⊞

↔ golf ⅄ ⌦ launderette pub

BOURNEMOUTH
Dorset
Map 4 SZ09
See Christchurch sketch map

▶▶▶ ② ❷ ⚠

Cara Caravan Park *(SZ138935)* Old Bridge Rd, Iford Signposted ☎Christchurch (0202) 482121 All year must book Last arrival 20.30hrs Last departure 10.00hrs ✗no tents & no single sex groups

Picturesque site on level ground with grass and gravel surface; varied trees and bushes. Direct access to river and A35.

2¾acres 40pitches 75static SA 30🚐 10🚐 (awnings)

8🏕 Individual pitches late arrivals enclosure 22wc lit all night 1cdp 🍴 8washbasins hc (4🛁 hc) 6☺ supervised iron cold storage calor gas ☎ ⊞ fishing ⅄

↔ stables golf ⅄ cinema ⌦ launderette pub

▶▶▶ ② ❷ ⚠

Chesildene Touring Caravan Park *(SZ107951)* 55 Chesildene Av, Throop Signposted ☎(0202) 513238 Apr–Oct booking advisable Spring Bank Hol & Jul–Aug no tents

This well maintained, level site is an oasis in the centre of a quiet residential area. Located very conveniently for the town centres of Bournemouth and Poole with adjacent beaches and woodland. From Ringwood direction; 1m SW leave A31 and take A338 signposted Bournemouth. In 7m at roundabout turn right onto A3060 then in 1m turn right at signpost.

3acres 60pitches 60🚐 or 60🚐 (awnings)

6🏕 Individual pitches wc lit all night 1cdp 10🍴 12washbasins hc 2central hot water (6🛁 hc) 2☺ supervised (wash dry iron) games room (cold storage) childrens playground calor gas toilet fluid ☎ ⅄

↔ stables golf ⅄ cinema ⌦ launderette pub

BOUTH
Cumbria
Map 7 SD38
See Cark-in-Cartmel sketch map

▶ ① ❶ ⚠

Black Beck Caravan Park *(SD335855)* Signposted ☎Greenodd (022986) 274 Mar–Oct Last arrival 20.00hrs Last departure 13.00hrs

A secluded site situated in woodland, with a stream (from which the site's name is derived) running through the middle. N of A590.

2acres 50pitches 35🚐£3 or 35🚐£3 15▲£3 (awnings)

10🏕 Individual pitches ⓐ late arrivals enclosure 48wc lit all night 2cdp (washbasins hc) 🛁hc ☺ supervised (wash spin dry iron) TV childrens playground calor gas camping gaz ☎ ⅄

↔ stables launderette ⌦ pub

BOWNESS-ON-WINDERMERE ●
Cumbria
Map 7 SD49
Sites are listed under Windermere

BRADFIELD
Essex
Map 5 TM13

▶ ① ❶ ⚠

Strangers Home Inn *(TM143308)* The Street ☎Wix (025587) 304 Mar–Oct must book public hols & Jul–Aug Last arrival 23.00hrs

Neat, well drained, level grass site, close to the Stour estuary.

2¼acres 69pitches 25🚐£3.50–£4 or 25🚐£3.50–£4 44▲£3.50–£4 awnings

3🏕 Individual pitches 10wc 1cdp 🛁hc ☺ supervised games room TV (licensed bar) childrens playground calor gas camping gaz restaurant ☎

↔ stables ⌦ launderette pub ⅄

BRADWELL
Norfolk
Map 5 TG50
See Yarmouth (Great) sketch map

▶▶▶▶ ① ❸ ⚠

Blue Sky Caravan Park *(TG501051)* Burgh Rd Signposted ☎Great Yarmouth (0493) 780571 Spring Bank Hol–Sep rsApr–Spring Bank Hol & Oct must book Jul–Aug Last departure noon no single sex groups

Level, grassy site close to Gt Yarmouth, set in mixed woodland.

8acres 240pitches 275static SA 80🚐£3.75 80🚐£3.75 80▲£3.75(awnings) ltr

18🏕 ⓐ late arrivals enclosure 36wc lit all night 3cdp 🍴 washbasins hc central hot water 🛁hc ☺ supervised (wash spin iron) games room CTV (cold storage) licensed club/bar childrens playground calor gas camping gaz toilet fluid ☎ ⅄

↔ stables golf ⅄ cinema ⌦ launderette pub

see advertisement on page 264

BRAINTREE
Essex
Map 5 TL72

▶ ① ❶ ⚠

Sun Lido Caravan Park *(TL742228)* Essex Barn Restaurant, Rayne Rd ☎(0376) 25445 or 25228 Mar–Oct Last arrival 22.00hrs

Small simple level grass site, located behind Essex Barn just off the A120.

24pitches 12🚐 or 12🚐 12▲

6🏕 6wc 🛁hc ☺

BRAITHWAITE
Cumbria
Map 11 NY22

▶ ① ❶ ⚠

Scotgate Caravan Site *(NY235235)* ☎(059682) 343 Mar–Oct no bookings Last arrival 22.00hrs Last departure 11.00hrs

Two large fields in a pleasant rural setting with views of the distant hills. Situated at junction of A66 and B5292.

6acres 135pitches 35static 15🚐£3.75–£4 120🚐£3.40–£3.60 or 120▲£3.70–£4 (awnings)   →

4♨◎ 28wc lit all night 1cdp washbasins (central hot water) (🏠hc) ☉ (wash spin dry iron) (games room) cold storage calor gas camping gaz ☎ 🛒

↔ stables ⚍ cinema ✦ laundrette pub

BRAMPTON
Cumbria
Map 12 NY56

▶▶ ①❶⚠

Irthing Vale Caravan Park (NY522613)
Old Church Ln Signposted ☎(06977) 3600 Mar–Oct must book public hols & Jul–Aug Last arrival 23.30hrs Last departure 11.00hrs no teenage single sex groups

Situated in a rural setting on the fringe of the market town on the A6071.

3¾acres 30pitches 21static 20🚐£3.85 or 20🚐£3.85 10▲£3.85 (awnings)

4♨ Individual pitches 8wc lit all night 1cdp washbasins hc (🏠hc) ☉ supervised (wash spin iron)⟶ calor gas

↔ stables golf ⚍ ✦ pub

BRANSGORE
Hampshire
Map 4 SZ19
See Christchurch sketch map

▶▶▶ ②❷⚠

Heathfield Caravan Park (SZ209985)
Signposted ☎(0425) 72397 5 Mar–Oct must book Last departure 11.00hrs no tents

A well-laid out site situated amongst open countryside, set away from main road and on fringe of New Forest. Within easy reach of the sea.

14acres 200pitches 200🚐 or 200🚐 (awnings)

28♨ Individual pitches late arrivals enclosure 39wc lit all night 2cdp washbasins hc central hot water 🏠hc ☉ calor gas camping gaz toilet fluid 🛒

↔ stables pub

BRAUNTON
Devon
Map 2 SS43
See Ilfracombe sketch map

▶▶ ②❷⚠

Lobb Fields Caravan & Camping Park (SS475378) Staunton Rd Signposted ☎(0271) 812090 Etr–Sep must book Last departure 11.30hrs

Gently sloping grassy site on outskirts of Braunton; good wide entrance.

14acres 180pitches SA 100🚐£2.50–£4.50 or 100🚐£2–£3.50 80▲£2.50–£3.50 awnings ltr

18♨ Individual pitches ◎ late arrivals enclosure 37wc lit all night 2cdp 🚩 washbasins hc 🏠hc ☉ supervised spin iron (cold storage) childrens playground calor gas camping gaz toilet fluid ☎ 🛒

↔ stables golf ✦ launderette pub

BRIDESTOWE
Devon
Map 2 SX58

▶ ①❶⚠

Bridestowe Caravan Park (SX519893)
Signposted ☎(083 786) 261 Etr–Oct booking advisable Jul & Aug Last arrival 22.00hrs Last departure noon

Site enjoys a secluded position in close proximity to the A30. Pitches are level and of grass. Situated ½m SE of Bridestowe; approach road is unclassified and leaves B3278 in Bridestowe village near the inn. Close to Dartmoor National Park.

½acre 13pitches 32static 13🚐£3 or 13🚐£3 or 13▲£3 awnings ltr

2♨ Individual pitches 12wc lit all night 1cdp washbasins hc 🏠hc ☉ supervised (spin) (iron) games room cold storage calor gas camping gaz ☎ 🛒

↔ ✦ pub

BRIDGE OF ALLAN
Central *Stirlingshire*
Map 11 NS79

▶ ②❷⚠

Allanwater Caravan Site (NS787981)
Blairforkie Dr Signposted ☎(0786) 832254 Apr–Sep no bookings Last departure 14.00hrs

Secluded site set on level grass on the banks of the River Allan, surrounded by wooded hills. N of the town with good access.

5acres 51pitches 20static 51🚐£3.50 or 51🚐£3.50 or 51▲£3.50 (awnings)

10♨ 10wc lit all night washbasins hc (🏠hc) ☉ (wash dry iron) ☎ 🛒

↔ stables golf cinema ✦ launderette

BRIDGERULE
Devon
Map 2 SS20

▶▶▶ ②❷⚠

Hedley Wood Caravan Park (SS262013) Signposted ☎(028 881) 404 mid Mar–mid Oct booking advisable Jul & Aug Last arrival 21.00hrs Last departure 21.00hrs no tents

From B3254 take Widemouth road (unclass) at the Devon/Cornwall boundary.

7acres 82pitches 1static 52🚐£3.50 or 52🚐£3 30▲ (awnings) ltr

7♨ late arrivals enclosure 16wc lit all night 2cdp 16washbasins hc 12🏠hc 4☉ supervised (spin iron) (cold storage) childrens playground calor gas camping gaz toilet fluid 🛒

↔ stables ✦ pub

BRIDLINGTON
Humberside
Map 8 TA16

▶ ①❶⚠

Poplars Caravan Site (TA194701)
45 Jewison Ln, Sewerby Signposted ☎(0262) 77251 All year must book peak season & public hols

A part level, part sloping grassy site with mature trees, in an urban area adjacent to a main road. From Bridlington follow the Flamborough road B1255 then turn left into Jewison Lane, signed Bempton, for the site entrance on left.

1¼acres 30pitches 30🚐£3 or 30🚐£3 or 30▲£3 (awnings)

3♨ Individual pitches 8wc 1cdp washbasins hc (🏠hc) ☉ (cold storage) calor gas camping gaz

↔ stables golf cinema ✦ launderette pub ✖

BRIDPORT
Dorset
Map 3 SY49

▶ ①❶⚠

West Bay International Holiday Centre (SX461908) (2m S off B3157) Signposted ☎West Bay (0308) 22424 15 Mar–Oct must book Jul & Aug Last arrival 19.00hrs Last departure 10.30hrs no single sex groups no motorcycles

5acres 150pitches 300static 150🚐£4–£5 or 150🚐£4–£5 or 150▲£4–£5 (awnings)

14♨ Individual pitches ◎ 75wc lit all night 1cdp washbasins hc 🏠hc ☉ (spin dry iron) (games room) cold storage childrens playground calor gas camping gaz ☎ 🛒

↔ stables golf ⚍ cinema ✦ launderette pub

BRIGHOUSE BAY
Dumfries & Galloway *Kirkcudbrightshire*
Map 11 NX64
See Gatehouse of Fleet sketch map

▶▶▶▶ ③❸⚠

Brighouse Bay Holiday Park (NX628453) Signposted ☎Borgue (05577) 267 Apr–Oct booking advisable peak periods Last arrival 21.30hrs Last departure 11.30hrs

Part level, part sloping grass site with mature trees and bushes set in downland, wood and meadow country. Adjacent to sea and wide sandy beach.

12acres 190pitches 120static SA 120🚐 fr£3.75 or 120🚐 fr£3.75 70▲ fr£3.75 (awnings)

10♨ Individual pitches ◎ late arrivals enclosure 24wc lit all night 1cdp 🚩 washbasins hc (➹hc 🏠hc) ☉ supervised (wash spin dry iron) cold storage childrens playground private beach calor gas camping gaz paraffin toilet fluid ☎ ⊞ slipway, water sports school, pony trekking, boats for hire, fishing, solarium 🛒

↔ pub

BRIXHAM
Devon
Map 3 SX95

▶▶ ② ❹ 🄰

Upton Manor Farm Camping Park
(SX925549) St Mary's Rd Signposted
☎(08045) 2384 Spring Bank Hol–Sep
no bookings Last arrival 21.00hrs Last
departure 11.00hrs no groups of young
males no caravans

Gently sloping, grass site with trees and
bushes set in meadowland, about ¼
mile from the sea and beach and close
to the town centre.

7¼acres 175pitches 170🚐 or 175🛆
8🏕 49wc washbasins hc 🗄hc ☉ iron
(cold storage) calor gas camping gaz
mobile shop 🛒
↔ stables golf 🏌 🟊 launderette pub

BRIXTON
Devon
Map 2 SX55

▶ ② ❶ 🄰

Brixton Camping Site *(SX550520)* Venn
Farm Signposted ☎Plymouth (0752)
880378 15 Mar–14 Nov Last departure
noon

3½acres 80pitches 30🚐 fr£2.80 or
30🚐 fr£2.80 50🛆 fr£2.80 awnings

3🏕 ⊘ 8wc 1cdp central hot water (🗄hc)

☉ supervised iron cold storage private
beach camping gaz paraffin 🛒
↔ stables 🟊 launderette pub

BROAD HAVEN
Dyfed
Map 2 SM81

▶▶ ② ❹ 🄰

Rosehill Country Hotel Caravan
Park*(SM892152)* Portfield Gate
☎(043783) 304 Etr–Oct

Small, secluded touring site in sheltered
situation amidst trees.

1¼acres 20pitches 20🚐

2🏕 4wc 1cdp 4washbasins hc 2🗄hc
2☉ supervised CTV licensed bar
restaurant ☎

▶ ② ❶ 🄰

Creampots Farm Caravan and
Camping Park *(SM882130)* (4m W of
Haverfordwest on B4327) Signposted
☎(043783) 359 Mar–Oct booking
advisable mid Jul–Aug

4½acres 45pitches 1static 25🚐 £2.50–
£3.50 or 25🚐 £2–£3 20🛆£2–£3
(awnings)

3🏕 ⊘ late arrivals enclosure 6wc lit all
night 1cdp washbasins hc central hot

---

water 🗄hc ☉ wash spin dry iron (cold
storage) (childrens playground) calor
gas camping gaz toilet fluid
↔ stables 🏌 🟊 pub 🛒

BROADWAY
Hereford & Worcester
Map 4 SP03

▶▶▶ ③ ❹ 🄰

Leedon's Park *(SP080384)*
Childswickham Rd Signposted
☎(0386) 852423 All year booking
advisable peak periods Last arrival
23.00hrs Last departure 11.00hrs

The site is situated on the edge of the
Vale of Evesham, 1m from the historical
village of Broadway; an ideal base from
which to tour the Cotswolds.

15acres 325pitches 40static SA
325🚐£2.50–£4 or 325🚐£2.50–£4 or
325🛆£2.50–£4 (awnings) ltr

50🏕 Individual pitches ⌾ 41wc lit all
night 2cdp ⚡ (washbasins hc) (🚿hc
🗄hc) ☉ supervised (wash dry iron)
⚊ (heated) games room CTV childrens
playground calor gas camping gaz
paraffin toilet fluid ☎ ⊞ 🛒

BROCKENHURST
Hampshire
Map 4 SU30

→

▶▶ ② ❶ ⚠

Hollands Wood Camp Site(SU303038)
Signposted ☎Lyndhurst (042128) 3141
(Forestry Commission Office) or 3771
(from early 1984) 13 Apr–Sep booking
advisable Spring Bank Hol Last
departure noon

*Large secluded site within the New
Forest. See under 'Forestry Commission'
for further information.*

168acres 600pitches 600🚐 ✱£3.20–
£4.20 or 600🚐£3.20–£4.20 or
600▲£3.20–£4.20 awnings

9⇆◉ 48wc lit all night 3cdp
washbasins hc 🛁hc ☉ supervised calor
gas camping gaz ☎ facilities for
disabled mobile shop

↦ stables golf ✦ launderette pub 🛒

▽ ②

Aldridge Hill Camp Site (SU282035)
(2mNW) Signposted ☎Lyndhurst
(042128) 3771 (in early 1984) or 3141
(Forestry Commission Office) 13 Apr–
Sep booking advisable Spring Bank Hol
Last departure noon

Open site on heathland.

200pitches 200🚐 ✱£2–£2.20 or
200▲£2–£2.20 awnings

2⇆ 2cdp calor gas camping gaz mobile
shop

↦ stables golf launderette pub 🛒

BRODIE
Grampian *Morayshire*
Map 14 NH95

▶▶▶ ② ❷ ⚠

Old Mill Inn (NH980570) Signposted
☎(03094) 244 Apr–Oct Last arrival
22.30hrs Last departure noon

*Level, grassy site, bordered by trees
with a small river on the west side. Well-
screened from main road.*

3acres 40pitches 60static 40 🚐 or
40🚐 or 40▲ (awnings)

4⇆ late arrivals enclosure 21wc lit all
night 2cdp washbasins hc 🛁hc ☉
supervised licensed club/bar childrens
playground calor gas camping gaz toilet
fluid cafe restaurant ☎ 🛒

↦ golf ✦ pub

BROMPTON-ON-SWALE
North Yorkshire
Map 8 SE29

▶▶▶ ② ❶ ⚠

Brompton-on-Swale Caravan Site
(NZ199002) Signposted ☎Richmond
(0748) 4629 Apr–Oct booking advisable
peak periods & public hols Last arrival
22.00hrs Last departure 13.00hrs

*A mainly level grass and gravel site set
in meadowland adjacent to main road on
the banks of the River Swale.*

7½acres 150pitches 17static
150🚐£4.50 or 150🚐£4 or 150▲£4
(awnings)

5⇆ late arrivals enclosure 12wc lit all
night 2cdp ⚑ washbasins hc 🛁hc ☉
supervised dry games room CTV cold
storage childrens playground calor gas
camping gaz toilet fluid ☎ 🛒

↦ golf ✦ launderette pub

BROMSGROVE
Hereford & Worcestershire
Map 7 SO97

▽ ❶

Queens Head (SO961679) Sugarbrook
Ln, Stoke Pound (2mSE) ☎(0527)
77777

*Level grassy field adjacent to canal and
inn.*

20pitches

⇆ cdp

BROMYARD
Hereford and Worcester
Map 3 SO65

▶▶▶ ③ ❶ ⚠

Bromyard Caravan Park (SO657544)
Bishell House, Petty Bridge Signposted
☎(0885) 82267 18 Mar–23 Oct Last
arrival 20.00hrs no tents

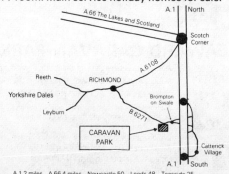

Undulating grassy site with trees and bushes, set in downland and adjacent to main road.

6½acres 15pitches 135static 15♥£2.50 or 15♥£2.25 (awnings)

5⚶ 20wc lit all night 1cdp washbasins hc (🛁hc) ☺ supervised (cold storage) childrens playground calor gas camping gaz toilet fluid 🏪

↔ stables ⚓ pub

▶▶▶ 🛈 ❷ ⚠
Saltmarshe Castle *(SO671579)*
☎(08852) 3207 15 Mar–Oct Last arrival mdnt no tents

Level grassy site in wooded downland, 2½m NE of Bromyard on B4203 Bromyard–Stourport road.

4acres 40pitches SA 40♥ or 40♥ (awnings) ltr

4⚶ late arrivals enclosure 42wc 4cdp (washbasins hc) central hot water (🛁hc) ☺ supervised (cold storage) licensed club/bar childrens playground calor gas toilet fluid ☎ 🎱 🏪

↔ stables launderette

BRONLLYS
Powys
Map 3 SO13

▶▶▶ 🛈 ❷ ⚠
Anchorage Caravan Park *(SO142351)*
Signposted ☎Talgarth (0874) 711246 Etr–Oct rsNov–Etr must book public hols Last arrival 23.00hrs

Touring pitches are on grassy slopes with good mountain views of the Brecon Beacons. 8m NE of Brecon.

7acres 110pitches 101static SA 60♥£4 10♥£4 40▲£4 (awnings)

10⚶☼ 26wc lit all night 1cdp 🔌 washbasins hc (🚿hc🛁hc) ☺ supervised (wash spin dry iron) CTV (cold storage) childrens playground calor gas camping gaz paraffin toilet fluid ☎

wc suitable for disabled persons 🏪

↔ stables ⚓ launderette pub

BRORA
Highland *Sutherland*
Map 14 NC90

▶ 🛈 ❷ ⚠
Riverside Caravan Site *(NC888036)*
Stonehouse Doll Signposted ☎(04082) 353 May–Oct booking advisable Last arrival 22.00hrs Last departure 11.00hrs

Part level, part sloping grass site with meadowland adjacent to River Brora.

Bromyard
—
Brynteg

Turn left at red-roofed cottage on right side of road 4m N of Golspie and 1m S of Brora.

2acres 21pitches 2static 21♥£1.70 or 21♥£1.60 or 21▲£1.50 awnings ltr

2⚶ 4wc lit all night washbasins hc central hot water (🛁hc) ☺ childrens playground calor gas camping gaz

↔ golf ⚓ pub 🏪

BROUGHTON
Humberside
Map 8 SE90

▶▶ 🛈 ❷ ⚠
Briggate Lodge Caravan & Picnic Site
(SE955068) ☎Brigg (0652) 54275 All year

Level, grassy site with gravel paths, trees and bushes. Set in woodland adjacent to main road and junc 4 of M180 (Scunthorpe bypass).

5¾acres 40pitches 25♥£3.50 or 25♥£3.50 or 15▲£2.50 awnings ltr

4⚶ late arrivals enclosure 5wc lit all night 1cdp washbasins hc (🛁hc) ☺ childrens playground ☎

↔ golf ⚓ launderette pub 🏪

BRYNCRUG
Gwynedd
Map 6 SH60

▶▶▶ 🛈 ❶ ⚠
Woodlands Holiday Park *(SH618035)*
(2m NE) Signposted ☎Tywyn (0654) 710471 Etr–Oct must book Last arrival 22.00hrs Last departure 11.30hrs no tents

Attractive, well laid out site, situated on terraced wooded hillside affording lovely country views. 2m from Tywyn on B4405 road to Tal-y-Llyn.

2acres 20pitches 122static 20♥ or 20♥ awnings ltr

2⚶ 6wc lit all night 1cdp washbasins hc 🛁hc ☺ (wash spin dry iron) 🌊 (games room) TV licensed club/bar childrens playground calor gas restaurant ☎ amusement arcade 🏪

↔ stables golf ⛳ cinema ⚓ launderette

BRYNSIENCYN
Gwynedd
Map 6 SH46

▶▶ 🛈 ❷ ⚠
Fron Farm *(SH472669)* Signposted ☎(024873) 310 Apr–Sep booking

---

advisable Spring Bank Hol & Jul–Aug Last arrival 23.00hrs Last departure noon

Small farm site in convenient situation for touring North Wales. Off A4080 Llanfair PG–Newborough road.

5acres 79pitches 1static SA 39♥£3 or 39♥£2.50 40▲£2.50 (awnings)

4⚶ Individual pitches ☼ late arrivals enclosure 8wc lit all night 1cdp (5washbasins hc 5central hot water 10🛁hc) ☺ supervised (cold storage) childrens playground calor gas camping gaz paraffin toilet fluid ☎ 🏪

↔ stables ⚓ pub

BRYNTEG
Gwynedd
Map 6 SH48

▶▶▶ 🛈 ❸ ⚠
Glan Gors Caravan Park *(SH499819)*
Signposted ☎Tynygongl (0248) 852334 Mar–Oct booking advisable peak periods Last departure noon 🎯 no motorcycles no single sex groups

Secluded country site within easy reach of the coast. From Benllech take B5108 for 1½m.

6acres 55pitches 95static 55♥£2.50–£4 or 55♥£2.50–£4 or 55▲£2.50–£4 awnings

4⚶ Individual pitches 23wc 1cdp 🔌 23washbasins hc 6🛁hc 2☺ supervised (wash spin dry) iron 🌊 games room childrens playground calor gas camping gaz ☎ 🏪

↔ stables ⛳ ⚓ launderette pub

▶▶▶ 🛈 ❷ ⚠
Nant Newydd Caravan Park
(SH485814) ☎Tynygongl (0248) 852842 Mar–Oct must book Jul–Aug

Gently sloping grass site with mature trees and bushes set in meadowland adjacent to main road, 1m from Brynteg on B5110 towards Llangefni.

3acres 45pitches SA 35♥£2.75 15♥£2.25 or 15▲£2.25 (awnings) ltr

5⚶ ☼ late arrivals enclosure 9wc lit all night 2cdp 🔌 washbasins hc (🛁hc) ☺ supervised (wash spin dry) iron games room cold storage childrens playground calor gas camping gaz toilet fluid ☎ 🏪

↔ stables golf ⛳ cinema ⚓ launderette pub

𝔑𝔞𝔫𝔱 𝔑𝔢𝔴𝔶𝔡𝔡 𝔓𝔞𝔯𝔨

Brynteg, Benllech, Isle of Anglesey.
Tel. Tynygongl (0248) 852842 or 852266

Proprietors: Mr & Mrs B W Jones

The perfect setting for a healthy, carefree and economical family holiday – totally uncommercialised. Located within a small valley and sheltered by trees and gorse bushes, a peaceful country atmosphere. Superb toilet facilities, hot showers and laundry rooms with washer and dryer all in hygenic condition. Cars may be parked by the side of caravans. The land is slightly sloping and well drained. Tourers and campers are especially welcome but advance booking is advisable. Pets are welcome but are to be kept under strict supervision.

▶ ① ❶ ⚠
Garnedd Touring Site (SH495818)
Garnedd Signposted ☎Tynygongl
(0248) 853240 14 Mar–Oct booking
advisable public & schools hols Last
arrival 23.00hrs

Mainly level grass site set in
meadowland close to sea, beach and
main road. Off A5025 Menai Bridge–
Amlwch road.

5acres 50pitches 1static 15🚐 35🚐 or
35▲ (awnings) ltr

3🏕 Individual pitches ⚪ late arrivals
enclosure 6wc lit all night 2cdp (central
hot water) (🚿hc) ☺ supervised cold
storage calor gas camping gaz ⊞ 🗲
↔ stables golf ⚒ cinema ↙
launderette pub

BUCKFASTLEIGH
Devon
Map 3 SX76

▶▶ ② ❷ ⚠
Buckfast Caravan Park (SX742670)
Signposted ☎(03644) 2479 Apr–28
Oct booking advisable peak periods
Last arrival 21.00hrs Last departure
noon no tents

Level, grassy site with numbered
pitches, well screened by young
saplings and within walking distance of
the Abbey. River Dart borders eastern
side of site and entrance is by Municipal
Car Park on the Abbey Road, just NW of
A38.

2½acres 99pitches SA 99🚐 or 99🚐
(awnings) ltr

3🏕 Individual pitches late arrivals
enclosure 20wc lit all night 1cdp

---

washbasins hc (8🚿hc) ☺ supervised
(wash dry) iron (cold storage) childrens
playground calor gas camping gaz toilet
fluid ☎ 🗲
↔ stables ↙ launderette pub

▽ ③
Beara Farm (SO751645) Colston Rd
☎(0364) 42234 All year must book for
caravans no motorcycles

Level site, close to the River Dart and the
Dart Valley steam railway line. Easy
reach of sea and moors.

3½acres 30pitches 5🚐 £3 5 🚐 £3
20▲£3 (awnings)

1🏕 2wc 1cdp
↔ ↙ pub 🗲

BUCKIE
Grampian Banffshire
Map 15 NJ46

▶ ① ❶ ⚠
Strathlene Caravan Site (NJ446668)
Apply to: Moray District Council, Dept. of
Recreation, 30–33 High St, Elgin,
IV30 1EX ☎Elgin (0343) 45121 Etr–20
Sep must book peak periods Last arrival
20.00hrs Last departure noon

Level, stony and grassy site situated 2m
from town on A942.

1acre 16pitches 16static 8🚐 £3.20 or
8 🚐 £3.20 8▲£2.55–£3.20 (awnings) ltr

4🏕 Individual pitches 16wc lit all night
washbasins hc (🚿hc) (wash dry) (▭)
↔ golf ⚒ ↙ launderette pub 🗲

BUDE
Cornwall
Map 2 SS20

▶▶▶ ② ❷ ⚠
Bude Holiday Park (SS205082) Maer Ln
☎(0288) 2472 Spring Bank Hol–Sep
rsEtr no bookings Last arrival 23.00hrs
Last departure 14.00hrs

Site situated on gently sloping land, with
cliffs and the Atlantic Ocean nearby. 1m
from the town; approach is by way of
town centre.

11acres 300pitches 150static SA 100🚐
100🚐 100▲ awnings ltr

20🏕 50wc lit all night 1cdp washbasins
hc central hot water (🚿hc) ☺ (wash spin
dry) iron (🚿 CTV (licensed club/bar)
childrens playground calor gas camping
gaz ☎ 🗲
↔ stables golf ⚒ cinema ↙
launderette pub

▶▶▶ ② ❷ ⚠
**Wooda Farm Camping & Caravanning
Park** (SS229080) Poughill (2m E)
☎(0288) 2069 Spring Bank Hol–Sep
rsApr–Spring Bank Hol & Oct booking
advisable Jul & Aug Last arrival 21.00hrs
Last departure noon no single sex
groups

There are sea views from this site as it
stands on raised ground overlooking
Bude Bay. From the A39 at the edge of
Stratton follow the unclassified Coombe
Valley road.

9acres 200pitches 50static
200🚐£2.50–£4.30 or 200🚐 £2.20–£4
or 200▲£2.50–£4.30 (awnings)

16[icon] late arrivals enclosure 32wc lit all night [icon] washbasins hc ([icon]hc) ☺ (wash dry iron) (cold storage) childrens playground calor gas camping gaz toilet fluid [icons]

↔ stables golf [icon] cinema [icon] launderette pub

BUNGAY
Suffolk
Map 5 TM38

►►► 1 2 ⚠

Outney Meadow Caravan Park
(TM333905) Broad St Signposted ☎(0986) 2338 All year booking advisable public hols

10acres 30pitches 16static 30[icon]£4 or 30[icon]£4 or 30▲£1.50–£4 (awnings)
4[icon]wc lit all night 2cdp [icon] washbasins hc [icon]hc ☺ supervised (wash spin dry iron) (cold storage) calor gas camping gaz toilet fluid ☎ fishing boats [icon]
↔ stables golf cinema [icon] launderette pub

BURGH CASTLE
Norfolk
Map 5 TG40
See Yarmouth (Great) sketch map

►►► 1 0 ⚠

Cherry Tree Holiday Park (TG490044)
Mill Rd Signposted ☎Great Yarmouth (0493) 780229 Spring Bank Hol–mid Sep rsEtr–Spring Bank Hol & mid–end Sep must book Jul & Aug Last departure 11.00hrs no single sex groups

Flat, grassed site, with many fruit trees situated in rural surroundings 4m from sea; off A143 Beccles–Yarmouth road.

6acres 125pitches 212static 35[icon]£1.95–£3.95 90[icon]£1.95–£3.95 or 90▲£1.95–£3.95 (awnings) ltr
22[icon] 42wc lit all night 2cdp washbasins hc [icon]hc ☺ supervised (wash dry iron) ([icon]) (games room) licensed club/bar childrens playground calor gas camping gaz toilet fluid cafe ☎ putting [icon]
↔ stables golf [icon] cinema [icon] launderette pub

see advertisement on page 264

BURNHAM-ON-SEA
Somerset
Map 3 ST34

►►► 2 3 ⚠

Home Farm Touring Park (ST328492)
Edith Mead Signposted ☎(0278) 783632 Etr–Oct rs Nov–Mar must book Whit & Jul–Aug no single sex groups no groups of motorcyclists

30acres 270pitches SA 210[icon] ✳£3.50 or 210[icon]£3.50 60▲£3.50 (awnings)
19[icon] late arrivals enclosure 30wc lit all night 2cdp [icon] 30washbasins hc

(14[icon]hc) 8☺ (wash spin iron) games room TV (cold storage) (licensed club/bar) childrens playground calor gas camping gaz toilet fluid cafe ☎ wc disabled, bicycle hire, fishing & pony riding, barbeque facilities [icon]

↔ stables golf cinema [icon] launderette pub

BURNISTON
North Yorkshire
Map 8 TA09

►► 1 0 ⚠

Whitby Road Garage & Caravan Park
(NZ009933) High St ☎Scarborough (0723) 870326 Etr–Oct rs Mar & Oct booking advisable school holidays Last departure 10.00hrs no tents

Small site behind the village filling station, well maintained pitches. Located 4½m N of Scarborough on A171 Whitby–Scarborough coastal road.

1acre 22pitches 22[icon] fr£2.50 or 22[icon] fr£2.50 (awnings) ltr
2[icon] Individual pitches 6wc lit all night 1cdp [icon] washbasins hc ([icon]hc) ☺ ([icon]) cold storage childrens playground calor gas camping gaz paraffin toilet fluid bowls [icon]
↔ stables golf cinema [icon] launderette pub

BUTLEY
Suffolk
Map 5 TM35

►► 2 2 ⚠

Tangham Campsite (TM355485)
Signposted ☎Orford (03945) 707 Apr–Oct booking advisable Spring & Aug Bank Hols

Good quiet level grass site, situated on the edge of a deep forest with attractive walks.

7acres 90pitches SA 90[icon]£3.50–£4 or 90[icon]£3.50–£4 or 90▲£3.50–£4 awnings
3[icon] late arrivals enclosure 12wc lit all night 3cdp washbasins hc (central hot water) ([icon]hc) ☺ supervised (iron) (cold storage) childrens playground calor gas camping gaz ☎ ⊞ mobile shop
↔ stables [icon]

BUXTON
Derbyshire
Map 7 SK07

► 1 0 ⚠

Dukes Drive Caravan Site (SK068725)
Signposted ☎(0298) 2777 Mar–Oct must book public hols Last arrival 22.00hrs Last departure noon

Simple site situated in a long valley on gently sloping ground with some trees and bushes. An impressive railway viaduct lies at one end of the valley. Located 1m from town centre.

25pitches 25static SA 25[icon]£3 or 25[icon]£2.50 or 25▲£2.50 (awnings) ltr
6[icon] late arrivals enclosure 9wc lit all night 1cdp washbasins hc central hot water [icon] ☺ iron ☎
↔ stables golf [icon] cinema [icon] launderette pub

CABUS
Lancashire
Map 7 SD44

►►► 1 0 ⚠

Robinsons Caravans Claylands Farm
(SD496485) Signposted ☎Forton (0524) 791242 Mar–Oct rsNov–Feb Last arrival 23.00hrs Last departure 14.00hrs

A pleasant site set in a valley between the M6 and A6.

5acres 64pitches 22static 64[icon]£3 or 64[icon]£3 or 64▲£3 (awnings) Individual pitches ◎
5[icon] 11wc lit all night [icon] washbasins hc ([icon]hc) ☺ (wash dry) games room (cold storage) childrens playground calor gas camping gaz toilet fluid ⊞ [icon]
↔ launderette

CAERNARFON
Gwynedd
Map 6 SH46
See sketch map on page 106

►►► 2 2 ⚠

Cadnant Valley Camping Park
(SH487628) Llanberis Rd ☎(0286) 3196 Etr–Oct booking advisable school hols Last arrival 22.30hrs Last departure noon no single sex groups

Situated close to the main Caernarfon–Llanberis road and conveniently near the town. These level, terraced pitches are set in a secluded, landscaped, wooded valley with some camping pitches near a stream.

4acres 62pitches 32[icon]£3.50 or 32[icon]£3 30▲£2.70 (awnings) ltr
4[icon] Individual pitches ◎ 17wc lit all night 1cdp [icon] (washbasins hc [icon]hc) ☺ supervised (iron) (cold storage) childrens playground calor gas camping gaz paraffin toilet fluid [icon]
↔ stables golf [icon] cinema [icon] launderette pub

CAIRNRYAN
Dumfries & Galloway *Wigtownshire*
Map 10 NX06

►►► 1 2 ⚠

Cairnryan Caravan & Chalet Park
(NX075673) Signposted ☎(05812) 231 Apr–Oct must book Jul & Aug Last arrival 23.00hrs Last departure 10.00hrs no tents

Neatly laid-out site, standing on sloping ground exposed to Loch Ryan. Adjacent to ferry terminal for Northern Ireland.

22pitches 100static 22[icon]£4–£5 or 22[icon]£4–£5 awnings ltr →

4👥 Individual pitches 32wc lit all night 1cdp washbasins hc 🚿hc ☉ (wash spin iron) ♨ games room CTV cold storage licensed bar childrens playground calor gas cafe ☎ snooker 🎱

↤ stables ⚓

CAISTER-ON-SEA
Norfolk
Map 9 TG51
See Yarmouth (Great) sketch map

▶▶▶ ① ③ ⚠
Grasmere Caravan Park *(TG521115)*
7 Bultitude's Loke, Yarmouth Rd Signposted ☎Great Yarmouth (0493) 720382 Apr–mid Oct booking advisable school hols Last arrival 22.00hrs Last departure 10.00hrs 🍴 no groups of teenagers no tents

Mainly level grass and gravel site with mature trees. Set in meadowland in an urban area with access to A149.

2acres 49pitches 74static 50🏠 £2.75–£3.25 or 50🚗 £2.75–£3.25 (awnings)

6👥 Individual pitches 24wc lit all night 1cdp washbasins hc (🚿hc) ☉ (wash dry) childrens playground calor gas ☎ 🎱

↤ stables golf ⛳ cinema ⚓ launderette pub

▶▶ ① ❷ ⚠
Old Hall Caravan Park *(TG521122)*
High St ☎Great Yarmouth (0493)

720400 Whit–Sep rsEtr–Whit must book Last arrival 23.30hrs Last departure 10.00hrs 🍴 no single sex groups no tents

A comparatively small park named after the Georgian house around which the site is located.

2acres 38pitches 29static 38🏠 £2.50–£5 or 38🚗 £2.50–£5 (awnings)

6👥 Individual pitches 9wc lit all night 1cdp 🚿 washbasins hc central hot water 🚿hc ☉ supervised (wash spin dry iron) ♨ (games room) (cold storage) licensed club/bar childrens playground calor gas cafe restaurant ☎ solarium jacuzzi 🎱

↤ stables golf ⛳ cinema ⚓ launderette pub

CALLANDER
Central *Perthshire*
Map 11 NN60

▶▶▶ ③ ❷ ⚠
Callander Holiday Park *(NN615073)*
Invertrossachs Rd Signposted ☎(0877) 30265 15 Mar–Oct must book Last arrival 22.00hrs Last departure 10.30hrs (high season) no tents

This is an attractive terraced site situated in a tree-studded estate to the NW of

Callander with splendid views over the surrounding countryside.

5acres 54pitches 110static 54🏠 fr£3.60 or 54🚗 fr£3.60 awnings

10👥 Individual pitches late arrivals enclosure 18wc lit all night 1cdp washbasins hc (🚿hc) ☉ supervised (wash spin) iron childrens playground calor gas mobile shop

↤ golf ⛳ ⚓ launderette pub 🎱

▶▶▶ ② ❷ ⚠
Gart Caravan Park *(NN643070)* The Gart Signposted ☎(0877) 30002 Apr–14 Oct Last arrival 22.00hrs Last departure 10.30hrs (high season) no tents

A well-developed mainly level grass site lying back from main road and screened by shrubs and trees. 1m E of Callander on A84.

15acres 120pitches 61static 120🏠 fr£3.65 or 120🚗 fr£3.65 (awnings)

24👥 Individual pitches late arrivals enclosure 20wc lit all night 3cdp washbasins hc 🚿hc ☉ supervised (wash spin) childrens playground calor gas ☎ 🎱

↤ golf ⛳ ⚓ launderette pub

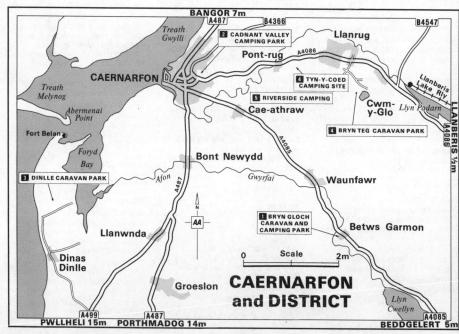

Sites listed under: **1** Betws Garmon **2** Caernarfon **3** Dinas Dinlle **4** Llanrug **5** Pont-Rug

CAMBORNE
Cornwall
Map 2 SW64

▶▶ 🅩❶⚠

Magor Farm Caravan Site (SW633427)
Tehidy Signposted ☎(0209) 713367
Mar–Oct must book

*This site is surrounded by trees and very
sheltered with easy access. A short drive
from beaches, Leisure centre and town.*

7½acres 45pitches 45🚐fr£2.25 or
45 🚐fr£2.25 or 45▲fr£2.25 (awnings)

4🚐 18wc lit all night washbasins hc
(central hot water) 🏠hc ☺ supervised
(iron) cold storage childrens playground
calor gas camping gaz

↔ stables golf ✦ leisure centre pub

CAMELFORD
Cornwall
Map 2 SX18

▶▶▶ 🅩❷⚠

Juliot's Well Holiday Park (SX095829)
Signposted ☎(0840) 213302 Mar–Oct
must book Jun–Aug Last arrival
19.00hrs Last departure 10.00hrs no
cars by caravans

*Sloping, grassy site with woodlands, 1m
SW of Camelford off the A39.*

8acres 60pitches 30static 60🚐£4–
£5.50 or 60 🚐£4–£5.50 or 60▲£4–
£5.50 awnings

3🚐 Individual pitches wc lit all night
1cdp 🚻 washbasins hc 🏠hc ☺ (wash
dry iron) ♪ (♪ games room) TV
licensed bar childrens playground calor
gas camping gaz ☎ 🛒

↔ stables ✦ launderette pub

▶▶▶ 🅩❸⚠

Valley Truckle Touring Caravan Park
(SX098829) Signposted ☎(0840)
212206 Etr–Oct must book Aug Last
departure noon

*Part level, part sloping grass site, set in
typical Cornish downland.*

5acres 78pitches 3static 78🚐 or 78🚐
or 78▲ (awnings) ltr

6🚐 Individual pitches ◎ late arrivals
enclosure 12wc lit all night 1cdp 🚻
washbasins🏠hc hc central hot water 🏠hc ☺
supervised (wash spin dry iron) ♪ (cold
storage) childrens playground calor gas
camping gaz toilet fluid ☎ ⊞ 🛒

↔ stables ✦ launderette pub

CAMUSTIANAVAIG
Isle of Skye, Highland *Inverness-shire*
Map 13 NG53

▶ 🅟❶⚠

Braes Caravan Site (NG501390)
20 Jun–Aug no bookings Last arrival
23.00hrs Last departure noon no tents

*Part level, part sloping, grass and gravel
site with mature trees, set in
mountainous, hilly country with access to
sea, beach and loch. 4½m SE of Portree
on B883.*

2acres 12pitches 6static 12🚐£2.45 or
12 🚐£2.45 awnings

3🚐 4wc lit all night washbasins hc
(🏠hc) ☺

↔ golf ✦ cinema ✦ launderette pub

CANEWDON
Essex
Map 5 TQ99

▶▶ 🅩❷⚠

Riverside Trailer Park Ltd (TR929951)
Creeksea Ferry Rd, Wallasea Island
Signposted ☎(03706) 297 Mar–Oct
booking advisable public hols

*Level, grassy site with many trees, in
rural setting. Sea wall and River Crouch
on two sides.*

5acres 30pitches 150static SA 30🚐£4
or 30 🚐£4 or 30▲£4 (awnings) ltr

5🚐 Individual pitches 15wc lit all night
2cdp washbasins hc 🏠hc ☺ (wash spin
dry) iron childrens playground calor gas
☎ mobile 🛒

↔ stables golf ✦ ✦ pub 🛒

CANTERBURY
Kent
Map 5 TR15

▶▶▶ 🅟❷⚠

St Martins Touring & Camping Site
(TR173575) Bekesbourne Ln
Signposted ☎(0227) 51755 Apr–Sep
no bookings Last departure noon

*An attractive tree-screened site in
pleasant rural surroundings. Off A257
Canterbury–Sandwich road.*

200pitches 160🚐 ✳£3.50 or
160 🚐£3.50 140▲£1.25 (awnings)

♨ ☺ 24wc lit all night 1cdp washbasins
hc 🏠hc ☺ supervised (wash spin) calor
gas camping gaz toilet fluid ☎ 🛒

↔ stables golf ✦ cinema ✦
launderette pub

CARGILL
Tayside *Perthshire*
Map 11 NO13

▶▶▶ 🅩❷⚠

Beech Hedge Restaurant & Caravan
Park (NO165374) Signposted
☎Meikleour (025083) 249 Apr–Oct Last
arrival 22.00hrs Last departure 11.30hrs

*Part level, part sloping grass and gravel
site, set in hilly woodland area close to
River Tay and A93 Perth–Blairgowrie
road.*

¼acre 12pitches 8static 8🚐 fr£2.50
2 🚐 fr£2.50 2▲ fr£2 (awnings)

2🚐 Individual pitches 6wc lit all night 🚻
washbasins hc (🏠hc) ☺ supervised
(wash spin dry iron) childrens
playground calor gas camping gaz
restaurant ☎ 🛒

↔ ✦

CARK-IN-CARTMEL
Cumbria
Map 7 SD37
See sketch map on page 108.

▶▶ 🅩❶⚠

Old Park Wood Caravan Site
(SD335785) Apply to: Holker Estates Co,
Cark-in-Cartmel, Grange-over-Sands,
Cumbria Signposted ☎Flookburgh
(044 853) 266 Mar–Oct must book
public hol wknds Last arrival 23.00hrs
Last departure 11.00hrs no tents

*A delightful secluded site surrounded by
woodland and overlooking part of
Ulverston Sands. Hill and mountain
views form the background. The
spacious grass fields are divided by
neatly constructed stone walls. 4½m W
of Grange-over-Sands off B5277.*

5acres 87pitches 292static 87🚐 or
87 🚐 awnings

6🚐 Individual pitches 22wc lit all night
5cdp washbasins 🏠hc ☺ (wash dry iron)
supervised (wash dry iron) (cold
storage) calor gas toilet fluid ☎ 🛒

↔ launderette pub

CARLEEN
Cornwall
Map 2 SW63
See Praa Sands sketch map

▶▶▶ 🅩❷⚠

Lower Polladras Camping (SW617308)
Signposted ☎Germoe (073676) 2220
Apr–Oct booking advisable Jul & Aug
Last arrival 22.00hrs Last departure
noon

*Situated in secluded valley at Polladras
on A394, this site provides an ideal base
from which to tour the Land's End
peninsula.*

4acres 60pitches 60🚐 £5.45 or
60 🚐£5.45 or 60▲£5.45 awnings

6🚐 12wc lit all night 1cdp washbasins
hc central hot water 🏠hc ☺ supervised
(wash) spin (dry iron) (cold storage)
childrens playground calor gas camping
gaz toilet fluid (hairdryers) 🛒

↔ stables golf ✦ cinema ✦
launderette pub

see advertisement on page 149

▶ 🅟❶⚠

Poldown Caravan Park (SW629298)
Poldown Signposted ☎Helston (03265)
4560 Apr–Oct must book Jul & Aug Last
arrival 22.30hrs Last departure noon

*A small, quiet site set in attractive
countryside. From A394 turn off onto the
B3302 Hayle road at Hilltop Garage,
then take second left to Carleen for site
which is ¾m on right.*

1acre 10pitches 5static 10🚐£4 or
10 🚐£4 or 10▲£4 (awnings)

1🚐 Individual pitches ◎ 4wc lit all night
1cdp (2central hot water) (🏠hc) ☺
supervised (cold storage) childrens
playground calor gas camping gaz

↔ stables golf ✦ cinema ✦
launderette pub 🛒

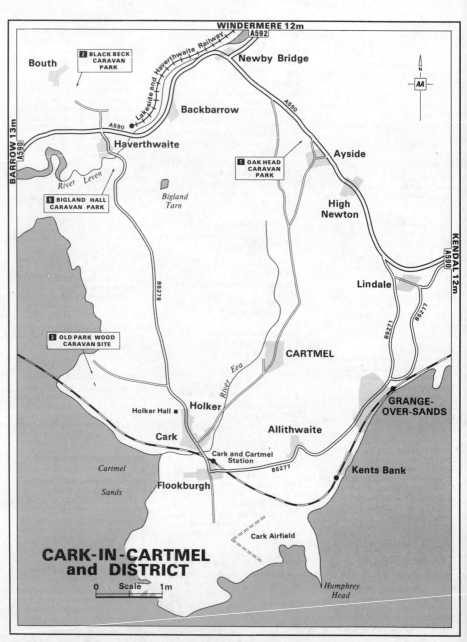

CARK-IN-CARTMEL and DISTRICT

0   Scale   1m

Sites listed under: **1** Ayside   **2** Bouth   **3** Cark-in-Cartmel   **4** Haverthwaite

CARLISLE
Cumbria
Map 12 NY45

▶▶▶ ①❶⚠

Orton Grange Caravan Park
(NY355519) Orton Grange, Wigton Rd
Signposted ☎(0228) 710252 All year
booking advisable peak periods Last
arrival 22.00hrs Last departure noon

*Small quiet wooded site. Situated on the
A595, four miles SW from the city centre.*

3acres 50pitches 21static 30❐£4.10–
£5.30 or 30❐£4.10–£5.30 20▲£4.10–
£5.30 (awnings) ltr

7⅋ Individual pitches ◎ 11wc lit all
night 1cdp ❷ 14washbasins hc
(2central hot) (ffhc) ☺ supervised
(wash dry iron) ⌲ CTV (cold storage)
childrens playground calor gas camping
gaz ☎ off-licence ┺

↔ stables golf cinema ♪ pub

CARLYON BAY
Cornwall
Map 2 SX05
See St Austell sketch map

▶▶▶ ②❶⚠

**Bethesda Farm Caravan & Camping
Park** *(SX052526)* Cypress Av
Signposted ☎Par (072681) 2735 Apr–
Sep booking advisable Jul & Aug Last
departure 14.00hrs

*Situated in urban area, this sloping,
grass site with trees and bushes is set in
meadowland, with access to sea, beach
and A390.*

12acres 180pitches 50❐£4.50
130❐£4.50 or 130▲£4.50 (awnings)

6⅋◎ late arrivals enclosure 30wc lit all
night 2cdp ❷ 26washbasins hc (ffhc)
☺ supervised (spin iron) games room
CTV (cold storage) childrens playground
calor gas camping gaz toilet fluid ☎ ┺

↔ stables golf cinema ♪
launderette pub

see advertisement on page 218

CARNFORTH
Lancashire
Map 7 SD47
See Morecambe and district sketch map

▶▶ ①❶⚠

Netherbeck Caravan Site *(SD509711)*
North Rd, Netherbeck ☎(0524) 733218
Mar–Oct booking advisable public hols

*A sloping site with mature trees and
bushes. Situated 1m NE of town on an
unclassified road.*

12pitches 32static 12❐£2.50'or
12❐£2.50 or 12▲£2.50 (awnings) ltr

2⅋ Individual pitches wc lit all night
washbasins hc (ffhc) ☺ supervised
cold storage childrens playground calor
gas ☎

↔ stables golf ♪ launderette pub ┺

CARNON DOWNS
(near Truro) Cornwall
Map 2 SW84

▶▶ ②❶⚠

**Carnon Downs Caravan & Camping
Park** *(SW805406)* Signposted ☎Truro
(0872) 862283 Apr–14 Oct must book
Jul & Aug

*A level, grassy site with mature trees, set
in meadowland and woodland just
outside the urban area, adjacent to A39
Falmouth–Truro road.*

14acres 100pitches 50❐££4 10❐£4
40▲£4 awnings ltr

9⅋ 18wc lit all night 2cdp ❷
19washbasins hc (8ffhc) 2☺
supervised (wash spin dry) games room
CTV (cold storage) calor gas camping
gaz toilet fluid ┺

↔ stables golf cinema ♪
launderette pub

▶▶ ②❷⚠

Ringwell Holiday Park *(SW792408)*
Bissoe Rd Signposted ☎Truro (0872)
862194 Etr–Oct booking advisable Jul &
Aug Last arrival 23.00hrs Last departure
16.00hrs

*A level grassy site with mature trees, set
in hilly country and woodland just
outside the urban area, adjacent to A39
Falmouth–Truro road.*

3acres 45pitches 30static SA
45❐£1.50–£5 or 45❐£1.50–£5 or
45▲£1.50–£5 (awnings)

7⅋ Individual pitches ◎ late arrivals
enclosure 14wc lit all night 1cdp ❷
washbasins hc (central hot water) ffhc
☺ (wash spin dry) ⌲ games room CTV
cold storage licensed club/bar childrens
playground calor gas camping gaz toilet
fluid cafe ☎ ┺

↔ stables golf ┶ cinema ♪
launderette pub

CARNOUSTIE
Tayside *Angus*
Map 12 NO53

▶▶▶ ②❷⚠

Woodlands Caravan Park *(NO560350)*
Newton Rd Signposted ☎(0241) 52258
& 54430 Apr–mid Oct must book no
tents

*A mainly touring site set in 4 acres. Level
grass with mature trees, in pleasant and
relatively secluded location near
town in rural area.*

4½acres 116pitches 4static
116❐£3.70 or 116❐£3.70 (awnings)

5⅋ Individual pitches 24wc lit all night
2cdp central hot water ffhc ☺ wash spin
dry games room childrens playground
☎ ┺

↔ stables golf ♪ launderette pub

CARRADALE
Strathclyde *Argyllshire* ¹
Map 10 NR83

▶▶ ②❷⚠

Carradale Bay Caravan Site
(NR815385) The Steading ☎(05833)
665 Whit–Sep rsEtr booking advisable
peak periods

*Rolling grass site near beach with views
over Kilbrannan Sound to Isle of Arran.
Approach from north is via Tarbert,
leaving by A83 Campbeltown road;
within 5m turn onto B8001, then B842
Carradale road. This is a 20-mile single
track road with passing places. In
Carradale take road to the pier, site is in
½m.*

9acres 60pitches 50❐ fr£3.90 or 50❐
fr£3.90 10▲ fr£3.90 (awnings) ltr →

5🐾 Individual pitches Ⓐ late arrivals enclosure 12wc lit all night 2cdp washbasins hc 🛁hc ☺ supervised spin dry iron childrens playground private beach calor gas camping gaz ✦

↪ golf ⚒ pub 🛍

CASSINGTON
Oxfordshire
Map 4 SP41

▶▶ 🛂 ❷

Cassington Mill Caravan Park
(SP449099) Eynsham Rd Signposted ☎Oxford (0865) 881081 Apr–Oct booking advisable Jul & Aug public hols & wknds Last arrival 21.00hrs Last departure 14.00hrs

Secluded site situated on the banks of the River Evenlode. Left onto the B4449, 5m W of Oxford.

4acres 83pitches 50static 83🏕 ✳£3.90 or 83 🚐£3.90 or 83▲£3.90 (awnings)

14🐾 15wc lit all night 1cdp central hot water 🛁hc ☺ calor gas camping gaz toilet fluid ☎

↪ ✦ launderette pub 🛍

see advertisement on page 197

CASTERTON (GREAT)
Leicestershire
Map 4 TF00

▶▶▶ 🛂❶🅰

Casterton Filling Station & Motel
(TF007083) Old North Rd ☎Stamford (0780) 52441 All year must book Jul & Aug Last arrival mdnt Last departure 14.00hrs

A level grass site with mixed vegetation set in downland and meadowland, just outside the urban area, adjacent to main road.

1½acres 45pitches 18static 45🏕 or 45 🚐 or 45▲ (awnings)

🐾 late arrivals enclosure 8wc lit all night 1cdp 🚰 washbasins hc (➼hc 🛁hc) ☺ supervised (wash spin dry iron) (cold storage) licensed club/bar calor gas camping gaz paraffin toilet fluid cafe restaurant ☎ ⊞ 🛍

↪ stables golf ⚒ cinema ✦ pub

CASTLE DOUGLAS
Dumfries & Galloway *Kirkcudbrightshire*
Map 11 NX76

▶▶▶ 🛂❷🅰

Lochside Park *(NX765618)* Apply to: Stewartry District Council, Environmental Health Dept, Dunmuir Rd, Castle Douglas, Kirkcudbrightshire Signposted ☎(0556) 2949 Etr–mid Oct Last departure noon

Municipal touring site incorporating park with recreational facilities, situated on southern edge of town in attractive setting adjacent to Carlingwark Loch. The site has two types of standings, asphalted area with marked pitches and more informal grassed areas. Site is located SW of the town, 150yds off main A75 from Dumfries–Castle Douglas.

5¾acres 161pitches 108🏕 fr£3.50 or 108 🚐 fr£3.50 53▲ fr£3.50 awnings ltr (Apr–Jun)

7🐾 Individual pitches Ⓐ 26wc lit all night 3cdp washbasins hc 🛁hc ☺ (wash iron) (cold storage) childrens playground ☎ boats for hire, putting green

↪ stables golf ⚒ cinema ✦ pub 🛍

CASTLESIDE
Co Durham
Map 12 NZ04

▶▶▶ 🛂❶🅰

Allensford Park Caravan Site
(NZ083505) Apply to: Derwentside District Council, Council Offices, Consett, Co. Durham DH8 5JA Signposted ☎Consett (0207) 509522 Apr–Oct Last arrival 22.00hrs Last departure noon

Gently sloping parkland with mature trees. Set in hilly moorland and woodland country near the urban area adjacent to River Derwent and A68. Situated approx 2m SW of Consett, N on A68 for 1m then right at Allensford Bridge.

14acres 52pitches 50static 26🏕£4 6 🚐£4 20▲£2.80–£3 (awnings) ltr

3🐾14wc litallnight 2cdpwashbasinshc 🛁hc ☺ supervised (wash) spin (dry) iron cold storage childrens playground calor gas camping gaz cafe ☎ 🛍

↪ stables golf cinema ✦ launderette

CASTLE SWEEN
Strathclyde *Argyllshire*
Map 10 NR77

▶ 🛂❶🅰

Castle Sween Bay Holidays
(NR712788) Signposted Apr–Sep rs Mar & Oct

Predominantly static site, laid out in terraces on a hillside above Loch Sween. The ruins of a 13th-C castle are in the centre of this site.

20acres 25pitches 230static 20🏕£4 or 20 🚐£3 5▲£4 awnings ltr

3🐾 14wc lit all night 1cdp (🛁hc) ☺ supervised (wash spin dry) iron licensed club/bar childrens playground private beach calor gas camping gaz toilet fluid restaurant bicycles & windsurf boards for hire putting green 🛍

↪ stables ✦ launderette pub

CÂTEL (FAUXQUETS VALLEY)
Guernsey, Channel Islands
Map 16

▶ 🛂❸🅰

Fauxquets Valley Farm Campsite
Fauxquets Valley Farm ☎Guernsey (0481) 55460 Etr–Sep must book 15 Jul–Aug no all male groups no caravans or motorvans

Level grass site with bushes in hilly woodland; access to sea and beach at Cobo and Vazon Bays.

3acres 90pitches 90▲£5.40 awnings

3🐾 7wc lit all night washbasins hc 🛁hc ☺ supervised dry iron games room CTV (cold storage) childrens playground calor gas camping gaz paraffin ☎ bicycles & tents for hire 🛍

↪ stables cinema ✦ launderette pub

CATON
Lancashire
Map 7 SD56
See Morecambe sketch map

▶▶ 🛂❷🅰

Crook O'Lune Caravan Park
(SD519643) ☎(0524) 770216 Mar–Oct booking advisable peak periods Last arrival 21.00hrs Last departure 13.00hrs no cars by caravans

Set in hilly woodland, adjacent to river, main road and exit 34 of M6.

1acre 20pitches 139static SA 15🏕 5🚐 or 5▲ (awnings) ltr

1🐾 Individual pitches Ⓐ 4wc lit all night 1cdp 🚰 4washbasins hc (2🛁hc) 1☺ (wash dry iron) games room childrens playground calor gas camping gaz ☎ 🛍

↪ stables cinema ✦ launderette

CATSFIELD
East Sussex
Map 5 TQ71

▶ 🛂❶🅰

Tellis Coppice Touring Caravan Park
(TQ712148) ☎Battle (04246) 3969 Mar–Oct must book public & school hols Last arrival 20.00hrs Last departure noon

Site located in a woodland setting in close proximity to Battle Abbey, off A269.

5acres 32pitches 32🏕£3 or 32 🚐£3 or 32▲£3 (awnings)

4🐾 Individual pitches 6wc lit all night 1cdp (🛁hc) ☺ supervised cold storage calor gas camping gaz 🛍

↪ stables ✦ pub

CAWSTON
Norfolk
Map 9 TG12

▶ 🛃❶🅰

Haveringland Hall Caravan Park
(TG153213) Haveringland Hall Farm Signposted ☎Norwich (0603) 871302 Apr–Oct booking advisable public hols & Jul–Aug Last arrival 20.00hrs Last departure noon

A level, grassy site with mature trees set in woodland and meadowland with direct access to lake. 10m N of Norwich on Cawston road, turn right at Stump Cross.

12acres 40pitches 117static 40🏕£3.80 or 40 🚐£3.80 50▲£3.80 (awnings) ltr

8[tap] ⊘ late arrivals enclosure 9wc lit all night 1cdp 12washbasins hc [shower]hc ⊙ supervised iron (cold storage) calor gas camping gaz toilet fluid ☎ [shop]

⇴ stables [fishing] launderette pub

CENARTH
Dyfed
Map 2 SN24

▶▶ ③ ❸ ⚠
Aberdwylan Caravan Park *(SN271415)* Abercych Signposted ☎Boncath (023974) 476 Apr–Oct booking advisable peak periods no tents

On banks of River Cych, 1¾m SW of Cenarth on B4332. After Penlan take second lane on the left.

1acre 10pitches 60static 10[caravan]£2.50 or 10[motorvan]£2.50 awnings

1[tap] 8wc lit all night 1cdp 8washbasins hc (1central hot water) (4[shower]hc) 2⊙ supervised (wash spin) iron cold storage childrens playground calor gas ⊞

⇴ [fishing] launderette pub [shop]

CERNE ABBAS
Dorset
Map 3 ST60

▶ ① ❶ ⚠
Giant's Head Caravan & Camping Park *(ST675029)* Giant's Head Farm, Old Sherborne Rd ☎(03003) 242 Etr–Oct Last arrival mdnt Last departure 13.00hrs

Part level, part sloping, grassy site set in Dorset downland near Cerne Giant (a figure cut into the chalk). Adjacent to main road, 2m NE from Cerne Abbas.

3acres 60pitches 60[caravan]£2.50–£3.50 or 60[motorvan]£2.25–£3 or 60[tent]£2.50–£3.50 (awnings)

2[tap] ⊘ 6wc lit all night 1cdp (washbasins hc) [shower]hc ⊙ TV (cold storage licensed bar) calor gas camping gaz [shop]

⇴ stables pub

▶ ① ❶ ⚠
Lyons Gate Caravan Park *(ST 663064)* Lyons Gate ☎Buckland Newton (03005) 260 16 Mar–Oct booking advisable peak periods & public hols

A flat, grassy site, surrounded by woodland and lying well back off the A352 and approached by a driveway.

8acres 60pitches 40[caravan]£3 10[motorvan]£3 10[tent]£3 (awnings)

3[tap] ⊘ 6wc lit all night 1cdp ([shower]hc) ⊙ [swimming] (cold storage) [shop]

⇴ stables [fishing] pub

CERRIGCEINWEN
Gwynedd
Map 6 SH47

▶▶▶ ② ❶ ⚠
Tregof Caravan Park *(SH413745)* Llangefni Signposted ☎(0407) 720315 Apr–Oct no bookings

From A5 junc B4422 Cerrigceinwen–Llangefni road; take A5 westwards for 1½ miles and turn left (unclass) or from Holyhead direction take A5 through Gwalchmai and in 2 miles turn right (unclass). Set amidst trees and bushes within easy reach of the sea and golf course.

6acres 88pitches 48[caravan]£2.50 or 48[motorvan]£2.50 40[tent]£2.50 (awnings)

4[tap] 16wc lit all night 2cdp washbasins hc central hot water ([shower]hc) ⊙ (cold storage) childrens playground calor gas camping gaz toilet fluid [shop]

⇴ stables golf [fishing] pub

CHACEWATER
Cornwall
Map 2 SW74
See Redruth sketch map

▶▶▶ ① ❷ ⚠
Chacewater Caravan & Camping Park *(SW740438)* Coxhill Signposted ☎St Day (0209) 820762 Etr–Oct must book Jul & Aug

A level grassy site with young trees set in meadowland.

5acres 90 pitches 10 static SA 90[caravan]£3–£4.20 or 90[motorvan]£3–£4.20 or 90[tent]£3–£4.20 awnings

4[tap] ⊘ 16wc lit all night 1cdp [caravan] washbasins hc [shower]hc ⊙ supervised (dry iron) games room CTV (cold storage) childrens playground calor gas camping gaz [shop]

⇴ stables golf cinema launderette pub

see advertisement on page 247

CHANNEL ISLANDS
Map 16
Sites are listed under individual placenames.
See under Guernsey or Jersey for details

CHAPEL HILL
Lincolnshire
Map 8 TF25

▶▶▶ ① ❷ ⚠
Orchards Caravans *(TF208543)* Signposted ☎Coningsby (0526) 42414 Mar–Oct rs Dec & Feb must book Last arrival 22.45hrs Last departure noon

Level, grassy site with assorted trees and bushes set in meadowland with direct access to River Witham and near to A153. The site is signposted from Tattershall.

1½acres 35pitches 48static 3[caravan]£3 (awnings)

5[tap] 12wc lit all night 2cdp washbasins hc ([bath]hc [shower]hc) ⊙ supervised (wash spin iron) [swimming] CTV cold storage licensed club/bar childrens playground calor gas camping gaz toilet fluid ☎ [shop]

⇴ stables golf [airport] cinema [fishing] launderette pub

CHAPEL PORTH
Cornwall
Map 2 SW64
See Perranporth sketch map

▶▶▶ ② ❷ ⚠
Chapel Porth Caravan Park *(SW705495)* Signposted ☎St Agnes (087 255) 2824 Etr–Sep must book public hols & Jul–Aug Last departure noon

Undulating, grassy site with young trees and bushes, situated in hilly moorland country and adjacent to the sea and beach. 1m SW of St Agnes off B3277.

½acre 10pitches 16static 10[caravan] or 10[motorvan] or 10[tent] (awnings)

2[tap] Individual pitches 6wc lit all night 1cdp 4washbasins hc (1central hot water) (2[shower]hc) 1⊙ iron cold storage childrens playground calor gas ☎ [shop]

⇴ stables [fishing] launderette pub

CHAPMANS WELL
Cornwall
Map 2 SX39

▶▶▶ ② ❷ ⚠
Chapmanswell Caravan Park *(SX355932)* Signposted ☎Ashwater (040921) 382 Mar–Oct must book Jul & Aug

This site is situated on A388 in open country with panoramic views across Dartmoor. From Launceston take the A388 towards Holsworthy, site is just off the main road, 2m N of St Giles.

4acres 40pitches 40static SA 40[caravan] or 40[motorvan] or 40[tent] (awnings) ltr

5[tap] ⊘ late arrivals enclosure 15wc lit all night 1cdp 15washbasins hc 2central hot water (4[shower]hc) 2⊙ wash spin dry iron TV cold storage childrens playground calor gas camping gaz paraffin toilet fluid ☎ [shop]

⇴ [fishing] pub

CHARMOUTH
Dorset
Map 3 SY39

▶▶▶ ② ❷ ⚠
Newlands Caravan & Camping Park *(SY374935)* 2 Camping Site Signposted ☎(0297) 60259 24 May–Sep rs Mar–Etr must book school & Jul–Aug hols Last arrival 21.00hrs Last departure 10.30hrs no motorcycles

Gently sloping, grass and gravel site in hilly country near the sea. 4m W of Bridport on A35.

12acres 240pitches 81static SA 120[caravan]£5 20[motorvan]£4 100[tent]£4 awnings

25[tap] Individual pitches ⊘ late arrivals enclosure 35wc lit all night 1cdp [caravan] washbasins hc [shower]hc ⊙ wash spin dry [swimming] games room TV cold storage licensed club/bar childrens playground calor gas camping gaz toilet fluid ☎ [shop]

⇴ stables golf [airport] cinema [fishing] launderette pub

► ① ❶ ⚠
**Manor Farm Caravan & Camping
Parks** *(SY368937)* ☎(0297) 60226 All
year (for tents) 16 Mar–Oct (caravans &
motorvans) must book Jul & Aug Last
arrival mdnt Last departure noon

*Pleasant sloping meadowland with open
rolling views of the Dorset countryside.
On the A35 Charmouth–Bridport road.*

15acres 254pitches 15static SA

54🚐 fr£3.50 or 54 🚐 fr£3 200▲fr£3
(awnings)
8⚄⚆ late arrivals enclosure 53wc lit all
night 1cdp 🚿 (washbasins hc) (🚿hc) ☺
supervised (wash dry iron) ⚄ games
room (cold storage) licensed bar
childrens playground calor gas camping
gaz cafe ☎ 🦮

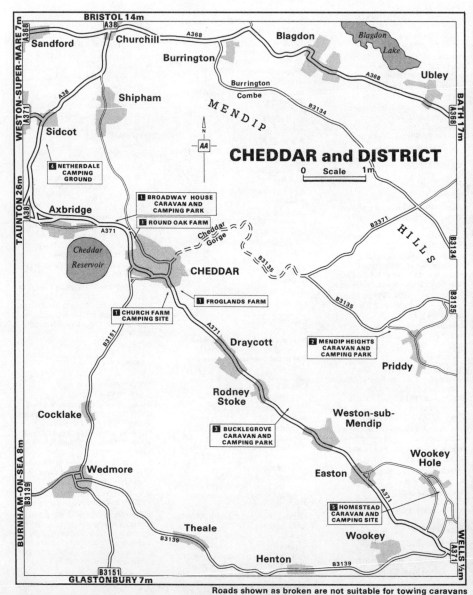

BRISTOL 14m
A38
Sandford
Churchill
A368
Blagdon
Blagdon Lake
Burrington
Ubley
A368
Burrington Combe
Shipham
B3134
MENDIP
Sidcot
N
AA
CHEDDAR and DISTRICT
0 Scale 1m
4 NETHERDALE CAMPING GROUND
Axbridge
A371
1 BROADWAY HOUSE CARAVAN AND CAMPING PARK
1 ROUND OAK FARM
Cheddar Gorge
B3371
HILLS
B3134
B3135
Cheddar Reservoir
CHEDDAR
1 FROGLANDS FARM
B3135
1 CHURCH FARM CAMPING SITE
B3151
A371
Draycott
2 MENDIP HEIGHTS CARAVAN AND CAMPING PARK
Priddy
Rodney Stoke
Cocklake
3 BUCKLEGROVE CARAVAN AND CAMPING PARK
Weston-sub-Mendip
Wookey Hole
Wedmore
B3139
Easton
A371
5 HOMESTEAD CARAVAN AND CAMPING SITE
WELLS ½m
A371
Theale
B3139
Wookey
Henton
B3139
B3151
GLASTONBURY 7m

WESTON-SUPER-MARE 7m
A368
A371
A38
TAUNTON 26m
A38
BURNHAM-ON-SEA 8m
B3139
BATH 17m
A368

Roads shown as broken are not suitable for towing caravans

Sites listed under: **1** Cheddar **2** Priddy **3** Rodney Stoke **4** Sidcot **5** Wookey Hole

↔ stables golf ⅄ cinema ✦ launderette pub

CHEADLE
Staffordshire
Map 7 SK04

▶▶ ② ❷ ⚠

Hales Hall Caravan & Camping Park
(SK021441) Oakmoor Rd ☎(0538)
753305 All year must book public hols

Set in 20 acres of gardens and parklands in the grounds of a country house.

2½acres 30pitches 30☔£2.50 or 30☔£2.50 or 30▲£2.50 (awnings) ltr

6↝ Individual pitches late arrivals enclosure 10wc lit all night 1cdp washbasins hc ♨hc ☺ supervised (wash) games room CTV (cold storage) licensed bar childrens playground calor gas camping gaz toilet fluid cafe donkey rides ▨

↔ ✦ launderette

CHEDDAR
Somerset
Map 3 ST45
See sketch map

▶▶▶ ② ❸ ⚠

Broadway House Caravan & Camping Park *(ST448547)* Signposted ☎(0934) 742610 Mar–Oct rs Mar–May & Oct

Level, grassy site with varied trees and bushes, set in hilly woodland country with direct access to main road. Midway between Cheddar and Axbridge on A371.

15acres 200pitches 35static SA 200☔ ✳£6 or 200 ☔ £6 or 200▲£6 (awnings) ltr

6↝ late arrivals enclosure wc lit all night 2cdp ☔ washbasins hc (✦hc ♨hc) ☺ supervised (wash spin dry iron) ☌ games room CTV cold storage licensed club/bar childrens playground calor gas camping gaz toilet fluid cafe ☎ ⊞ video films hairdryers ▨

↔ stables golf ✦ launderette pub

▶▶▶ ② ❸ ⚠

Froglands Farm *(ST462529)*
Signposted ☎(0934) 742058 or 743304 Etr–Oct booking advisable school hols Last arrival 23.00hrs Last departure noon no motorcycles no single sex groups

Farmland site set on undulating ground with trees and shrubs. It is located on A371 Weston-super-Mare–Wells road on SE outskirts of Cheddar.

4½acres 60pitches 18☔ fr£3.30 or 18☔ fr£3 42▲ fr£3 (awnings)

6↝ Individual pitches ◍ late arrivals enclosure 12wc lit all night 1cdp 10washbasins hc (6♨hc) 2☺ supervised (wash dry iron) (cold storage) calor gas camping gaz toilet fluid battery charging ▨

↔ stables ✦ launderette pub

▶▶ ① ❶

Church Farm Camping Site
(ST460529) Church St Signposted ☎(0934) 743048 Etr–Oct booking advisable public hols Last arrival 21.00hrs no motorcycles groups

Field behind farmyard, for both camping and touring vans; has flat surface and hedge screening.

5acres 42pitches 3static SA 42☔ ✳£3 or 42☔ £3 or 42▲£2.50–£3 (awnings)

6↝ 12wc lit all night 1cdp washbasins hc (central hot water) (♨hc) ☺ supervised (dry iron) (cold storage) calor gas camping gaz hair dryers ▨

↔ stables ⅄ ✦ launderette pub

▶ ② ❷ ⚠

Round Oak Farm *(ST452542)*
Signposted ☎(0934) 742561 Etr–Sep booking advisable public hols Last arrival 22.00hrs Last departure noon

Camping field behind farmyard with trees and hedge screening. Adjacent to B3151 Wells–Bristol road.

3acres 60pitches 12☔ ✳£2.50 48 ☔ £2.50 or 48▲£2 (awnings)

3↝ ◍ 12wc lit all night 1cdp washbasins hc (central hot water ♨hc) ☺ supervised (cold storage) calor gas camping gaz ▨

↔ stables ✦ launderette pub

CHEPSTOW
Gwent
Map 3 ST59

▽ ①

Howick Farm *(SO502956)* Itton (2½m NW on B4293) ☎(02912) 2590

Mainly level field on slightly elevated ground.

30 pitches ☔ ✳£1 ▲£1

↝ cdp

CHESTER
Cheshire
Map 7 SJ46

▶▶ ① ❷ ⚠

Chester Southerly Caravan Park
(SJ385624) Balderton Ln, Marlston-cum-Lache Signposted ☎Farndon (0829) 270791 Mar–Nov no bookings Last departure noon

6 acres 90pitches 70☔£2.50–£3 or 70☔£2.50–£3 20▲£2.50–£3 (awnings)

3↝ ◍ 13wc lit all night 1cdp ☔ washbasins hc (♨hc) ☺ (dry) childrens playground calor gas camping gaz ☎

↔ golf ⅄ cinema ✦ launderette pub

▶▶ ① ❷ ⚠

Racecourse Caravan Park *(SJ399662)*
Signposted ☎(0244) 23170 & 23211 Etr & Whit–Sep no bookings (the site is not available in the wk prior to each race meeting) Last arrival 20.00hrs Last departure noon no tents

Well-equipped site adjacent to Roodee (Chester Racecourse) and close to city centre.

1½acres 33pitches SA 33☔£3.50 or 33☔£3.50

3↝ Individual pitches late arrivals enclosure 6wc lit all night 1cdp washbasins hc ♨hc ☺ supervised (dry iron) cold storage licensed bar calor gas camping gaz restaurant ☎ ▨ →

⊖ stables golf ⤚ cinema ♪ launderette pub

CHICHESTER
West Sussex
Map 4 SU80

▶▶▶ 2 ❷ ▲
Southern Leisure Centre (SU876032)
Vinnetrow Ln ☎(0243) 787715 Mar–Oct no tents

Well constructed Leisure Park close to Chichester and the Goodwood Estate, within easy reach of the sea. The park is surrounded by twelve lakes which provide good coarse and trout fishing.

7acres 141🛖 or 141🚐

4⚡ late arrivals enclosure 20wc lit all night 1cdp 16washbasins hc ⇔hc 16🛁hc 8☺ supervised ⊞ 🥾

⊖ golf ⤚ ♪

CHICKERELL
(near Weymouth) Dorset
Map 3 SY68

▶▶▶ 2 ❷ ▲
Bagwell Farm Camping & Caravanning Site (SY627816)
Signposted ☎Weymouth (0305) 782575 Etr–Oct rs16 Mar–Etr booking advisable school hols Last arrival mdnt Last departure noon

Mainly level site with some terraced and gently sloping areas. Situated 4m W of Weymouth on the B3157 Abbotsbury–Bridport road, 500yds past the 'Victoria Inn' public house.

14acres 320pitches 150🚐£3.50–£4.25 or 150🚐£3–£4 170▲£2–£3.25 (awnings)

10⚡ Individual pitches for caravans ☺ late arrivals enclosure 34wc lit all night 1cdp ⇔ washbasins hc central hot water (🛁hc) ☺ (wash spin iron) (cold storage) childrens playground calor gas camping gaz toilet fluid ☎ 🥾

⊖ stables golf ♪ launderette pub

▶▶▶ 1 ❶ ▲
Gloucester Farm Caravan Park (SY648795) Apply to: Kestrel Homes Ltd, Beechwood, 57 Church St, Epsom, Surrey KT17 4PX ☎Epsom (03727) 40071 15 Mar–7 Nov must book Jul & Aug for motorvans Last arrival 20.00hrs Last departure 10.00hrs no tents

Level grass site with trees and bushes in urban area. 2½m W of Weymouth on B3157.

1acre 30pitches 44static 30🚐£3–£5.50 or 30🚐£3–£5.50 (awnings)

5⚡ Individual pitches 3wc lit all night 1cdp washbasins hc (central hot water 🛁hc) ☺ supervised (1wash 1spin 1dry 2iron) childrens playground calor gas ☎ 🥾

⊖ stables golf ⤚ cinema ♪ launderette pub

see advertisement on page 255

CHIDEOCK
Dorset
Map 3 SY49

▶▶▶ 3 ❸ ▲
Golden Cap Caravan Park (SY422919)
Seatown (1m S of village at Seatown) ☎(029789) 341 Apr–Sep must book Last arrival 22.00hrs Last departure noon

The site is situated overlooking the sea and surrounded by National Trust parkland.

50pitches 63static 17🚐 or 17🚐 33▲ (awnings)

13⚡ Individual pitches wc lit all night 2cdp ⇔ 13washbasins hc 1⇔hc 7🛁hc 5☺ supervised (spin) iron cold storage calor gas camping gaz ☎ 🥾

⊖ stables golf ⤚ cinema ♪ launderette pub

CHILLINGTON
Devon
Map 3 SX74

▶▶ 2 ❷ ▲
Union Inn Caravan Site (SX793427)
☎Kingsbridge (0548) 580241 15 Mar–Oct booking advisable Jul & Aug Last arrival 22.30hrs Last departure 11.00hrs no tents

Level, grass and gravel site with mature trees, saplings and bushes. Set in woodland and meadowland adjacent to beach and A379 Kingsbridge road.

10pitches 4static 10🚐 or 10🚐 (awnings)

2⚡ Individual pitches 2wc lit all night 1cdp washbasins hc (🛁hc) ☺ supervised (spin) iron licensed club/bar childrens playground calor gas camping gaz restaurant ☎ 🥾

⊖ stables ♪ pub

CHINGFORD (E.4)
Gt London
Map 4 TQ39
See under London for details

CHITTERING
Cambridgeshire
Map 5 TL47

▽ 1
Denny Lodge (TL495695) Signposted ☎Cambridge (0223) 860223 no bookings

Small level sheltered paddock adjacent to farm building in open country.

2acres 5🚐£1 or 5🚐£1 ▲£1 (awnings)

1⚡ 1wc lit all night 1cdp ☺ supervised
⊖ ⤚ ♪ pub

CHIVENOR
Devon
Map 2 SS53
See Ilfracombe sketch map

▶ 1 ❷ ▲
Chivenor Holiday Centre (SS508350)
☎Barnstaple (0271) 812217 15 Mar–15 Nov must book Last arrival 23.00hrs Last departure 10.00hrs

Well laid out and maintained level site with good facilities. Adjacent to A361 and RAF Chivenor.

1½acres 30pitches 30🚐£1.50–£4 or 30🚐£1.50–£4 or 30▲£1.50–£4 awnings ltr

2⚡ Individual pitches 6wc lit all night (washbasins hc central hot water) 🛁hc ☺ supervised (wash spin dry iron) (🛁) games room licensed club/bar childrens playground calor gas camping gaz ☎ 🥾

⊖ golf cinema ♪ launderette pub

CHRISTCHURCH
Dorset
Map 4 SZ19
See sketch map

▶▶▶▶ 3 ❸ ▲
Hoburne Farm Caravan Park (SZ194937) Highcliffe Rd Signposted ☎Highcliffe (04252) 3379 or 71064 Mar–Oct rsNov–Feb (except Xmas) must book May–Sep Last arrival 21.00hrs Last departure 10.00hrs 🐕on touring pitches no tents & no single sex groups

Level, grassy site with gravel paths, mature trees, saplings and bushes, set in meadowland and adjacent to sea, beach and main road.

20acres 285pitches 301static 285🚐£3.60–£7.35 or 285🚐£3.60–£7.35 awnings

100⚡ Individual pitches late arrivals enclosure 40wc lit all night 4cdp ⇔ washbasins hc ⇔hc🛁hc (☺) supervised (wash spin dry iron) 🛁 (👨) (games room) CTV (cold storage) (licensed club) childrens playground calor gas toilet fluid cafe restaurant ☎ 🥾

⊖ stables golf ⤚ ♪ launderette pub

▶▶▶ 2 ❸ ▲
Grove Farm Meadow Holiday Caravan Park (SZ136640) Stour Way Signposted ☎(0202) 483597 Mar–Oct must book peak periods Last arrival 22.00hrs Last departure noon no children no teenage groups no tents

A level, grassy site with mature trees; near the River Stour.

2acres 47pitches 193static 47🚐£3–£5 47🚐£3–£5 (awnings)

20⚡ Individual pitches late arrivals enclosure 33wc lit all night 1cdp ⇔ washbasins hc (central hot water) (⇔hc) (🛁hc) ☺ supervised (wash spin dry iron) childrens playground calor gas camping gaz toilet fluid ☎ ⊞ fishing on site 🥾

⊖ stables golf ⤚ cinema ♪ launderette pub

▶▶ 2 ❷ ▲
Haven Caravan Park (SZ180923) Bure Ln, Mudeford Signposted ☎Highcliffe (04252) 4662 or 5353 Mar–Oct

no bookings Last departure 10.00hrs
no single sex groups no tents

*Level, grassy site with varied trees and
bushes. Set in woodland within the
urban area with direct access to sea,
beach and main road.*

26pitches 132static 26⚡ £5–£6 or
26 🚐 £5–£6 awnings

🚐 Individual pitches 25wc lit all night
2cdp washbasins hc ♨ hc ☉ supervised
wash spin iron childrens playground
calor gas camping gaz ☎ 🛒
⟿ stables golf ⛳ cinema ♪
launderette pub

CHUDLEIGH KNIGHTON
Devon
Map 3 SX87

▶ ▶ ② ❶ ⚠
Ford Farm *(SX847775)* ☎Chudleigh
(0626) 853253 Mar–Oct must book for
caravans

*Small grassy secluded site with varied
trees and bushes. From A38 Exeter–
Plymouth road take B3344 for Chudleigh
Knighton.*

2acres 30pitches SA 12⚡ or 12 🚐 18🅰
(awnings)

2🚐 6wc lit all night 1cdp (central hot
water ♨ hc) ☉ supervised (wash spin
dry iron) calor gas camping gaz 🛒
⟿ stables golf ♪ launderette pub

CHURCH STOKE
Powys
Map 7 SO29

Christchurch
—
Clifford Bridge

▶ ▶ ▶ ② ❷ ⚠
Mellington Hall Caravan Park
(SO258920) Signposted ☎(05885) 456
Mar–Oct must book public hols Last
arrival 22.30hrs Last departure 18.00hrs
no tents

*Well-maintained site with level pitches, in
the grounds of a gracious country house
hotel. Magnificent views of the Welsh
Border Counties. 4m SE of Montgomery
on B4385.*

22acres 20pitches 140static 10⚡ 10 🚐
awnings ltr

13🚐 14wc lit all night 1cdp 🚿
8washbasins hc (6♨ hc) ☉ (wash dry)
iron TV cold storage licensed club/bar
childrens playground calor gas toilet
fluid restaurant ☎ 🛒
⟿ stables launderette pub

CHURT
Surrey
Map 4 SU83

▶ ① ❶
Symondstone Farm *(SU845381)* Apr–
Oct booking advisable public hols

*Secluded site surrounded by woodlands
on the Surrey/Hampshire border, close
to the village of Churt; once the home of
Lloyd George. For sailing enthusiasts,
close by are the famous Frensham
Ponds.*

8acres 70pitches 70static 70⚡ or 70 🚐
or 70🅰 awnings

4🚐 5wc 1cdp ☉ calor gas ☎
⟿ stables

CLACTON-ON-SEA
Essex
Map 5 TM11
**See St Osyth for details of sites in the
vicinity**

CLIFFORD BRIDGE
Devon
Map 3 SX78

▶ ▶ ▶ ③ ❸ ⚠
Clifford Bridge Caravan Park
(SX780897) ☎Cheriton Bishop
(064724) 226 15 Mar–14 Nov must book
public hols & Jul–Aug Last arrival
23.00hrs Last departure 11.00hrs

*A level, grassy site with mature trees and
bushes. Situated in moorland and
woodland country but not too far from
the River Teign, 2m W of Dunsford off
B3212.*

5acres 15pitches 15static SA 15⚡ £4.60
or 15 🚐 £3.90 or 15 🅰£3.90 (awnings)

4🚐 Individual pitches ⌚ late arrivals
enclosure 8wc lit all night 1cdp
(4♨ hc) 4☉ supervised (wash) spin (dry)
iron ⊿ games room cold storage
licensed bar childrens playground calor
gas camping gaz toilet fluid restaurant
⊞ ☎ take away food battery charging
🛒

⟿ stables golf fishing pub

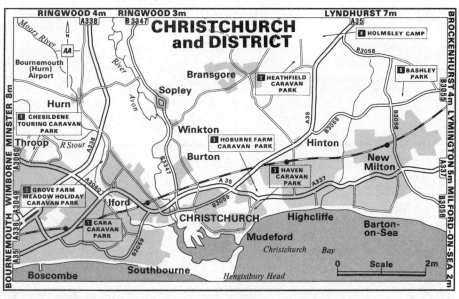

RINGWOOD 4m   RINGWOOD 3m   LYNDHURST 7m

CHRISTCHURCH
and DISTRICT

Moors River   A338   B3347

Bournemouth
(Hurn)
Airport

Branscore

Sopley

2 HEATHFIELD
CARAVAN
PARK

4 HOLMSLEY CAMP

B3058

5 BASHLEY
PARK

Hurn

1 CHESILDENE
TOURING CARAVAN
PARK

Winkton

Throop   R Stour

3 HOBURNE FARM
CARAVAN PARK

Hinton

Burton

New
Milton

3 HAVEN
CARAVAN
PARK

3 GROVE FARM
MEADOW HOLIDAY
CARAVAN PARK

Iford

1 CARA
CARAVAN
PARK

CHRISTCHURCH   Highcliffe

Barton-
on-Sea

Mudeford

Christchurch   Bay

Boscombe   Southbourne   Hengistbury Head

BROCKENHURST   LYMINGTON 5m MILFORD-ON-SEA 2m

BOURNEMOUTH WIMBORNE MINSTER 8m

0   Scale   2m

Sites listed under: **1** Bournemouth   **2** Branscore   **3** Christchurch   **4** Holmsley   **5** New Milton

115

CLIPPESBY

Norfolk
Map 9 TG41

▶▶▶ ③ ❷ ⚠
Clippesby Holiday Caravan Park
(TG423147) Signposted ☎Fleggburgh
(049377) 367 Spring Bank Hol–Sep
must book school hols Last arrival
18.00hrs Last departure 10.00hrs

*A mainly level site with slight gradients
and grass surface with trees and
bushes, situated amidst woodland.*

60pitches SA 60🛋 or 60🚐 or 60▲
(awnings) ltr

🏕 Individual pitches Ⓛ late arrivals
enclosure 15wc lit all night 2cdp
washbasins hc (central hot water) (🛁hc)
☺supervised (wash dry iron) ➘ ✐
games room CTV licensed club/bar
childrens playground calor gas camping
gaz toilet fluid cafe ☎ garden centre 🏪
↔ stables 🐴 ✦ launderette pub

CLYNDERWEN

Dyfed
Map 2 SN11

▶ ① ❶ ⚠
Derwenlas Caravan Park (SN122207)
Derwenlas Signposted ☎(09912) 324
Mar–13 Nov must book Aug Last arrival
23.00hrs Last departure noon no
motorcycles

*A small touring site on level grassy field.
N of village on A478 Tenby–Cardigan
road 2m N of A40.*

½acre 20pitches 10static 10🛋 5🚐 5▲
(awnings) ltr

4🏕 5wc lit all night 1cdp washbasins hc
central hot water (🛁hc)☺(iron) cold
storage childrens playground calor gas
↔ ✦ pub 🏪

COCKBURNSPATH

Borders *Berwickshire*
Map 12 NT77

▶▶ ② ❸ ⚠
Chesterfield Caravan Site (NT772701)
Neuk Farm Signposted ☎(03683) 226
Apr–Sep Last arrival 17.00hrs Last
departure noon

*Secluded grass site set in Border
country, screened by gorse-covered
hills. Situated approx ½m from the
village and within 3m of the sea.*

5acres 44pitches 84static 44🛋£3 or
44🚐£3 or 44▲£3 (awnings)

4🏕 Individual pitches Ⓛ late arrivals
enclosure 17wc lit all night 1cdp
washbasins hc 🛁hc ☺supervised iron
cold storage childrens playground calor
gas ☎

COCKERMOUTH

Cumbria
Map 11 NY13

▶▶ ② ❶ ⚠
Violet Bank Caravan Site (NY126295)
Off Lorton Rd ☎(0900) 822169 Mar–
Oct must book Last departure noon

*Well-maintained, mainly level, some
slight gradient, grassy site in pleasant
rural setting affording excellent views of
Buttermere Hills. Approach by way of
A5292 Lorton Rd, via town centre.*

2acres 60pitches 40static SA 60🛋 or
60🚐 or 60▲(awnings)

5🏕 Individual pitches Ⓛ 10wc 1cdp 🔥
washbasins hc central hot water (🛁hc)
☺supervised (wash spin dry iron)
(games room) (cold storage) childrens
playground calor gas camping gaz ☎
🏪
↔ stables golf 🐴 ✦

COLCHESTER

Essex
Map 5 TM02

▶▶▶ ② ❷ ⚠
**Colchester Camping, Touring
Caravan & Camping Park** (TL971252)
Cymbeline Way, Lexden Signposted
☎(0206) 45551 Etr–15 Oct booking
advisable public hols Last arrival mdnt

*A well designed campsite on level
grassland, lying on west side of
Colchester near town centre. Close to
main routes to London (A12) and East
Coast.*

12acres 185pitches 185🛋 ✳£5 or
185🚐£5 or 185▲£5 (awnings)

8🏕 Individual pitches Ⓛ late arrivals
enclosure 26wc lit all night 3cdp 🔥
(washbasins hc central hot water) (🛁hc)
☺ supervised games room TV (cold
storage) childrens playground calor gas
camping gaz toilet fluid ☎ 🎯 🏪
↔ stables golf 🐴 cinema ✦
launderette pub

COLEFORD

Gloucestershire
Map 3 SO51

▶▶ ① ❸ ⚠
*Woodlands View Caravan & Camping
Site* (SO582087) Sling (2m S B4228)
☎Dean (0594) 35127 Mar–Oct must
book public hols

Small, friendly site in peaceful situation.

1½acres 20pitches SA 20🛋 or 20🚐 or
20▲ awnings

5🏕 6wc lit all night 1cdp 6washbasins
hc (4🛁hc) 2☺ cold storage calor gas 🏪
↔ golf cinema ✦ launderette pub

▽ ①
Blackthorne Farm (SO572139)
Hillersland ☎Dean (0594) 32062
booking advisable

*Mainly level small meadow close to farm
yard and adjacent to B4432.*

25pitches 5🛋 ✳£1.50 or 5🚐£1.50
20▲£1.50

🏕 cdp

COLL SANDS

Lewis, Western Isles *Ross and Cromarty*
Map 13 NB43

▶ ① ❷ ⚠
Broad Bay Caravan Site (NB462383)
Signposted ☎Stornoway (0851) 2053
Apr–Oct must book

*A sandy site near the beach and sea,
situated on the coast road between Tong
and Upper Coll.*

½acre 20pitches 12static 10🛋 or 10🚐
10▲ awnings ltr

2🏕️⏾ wc lit all night 1cdp washbasins hc (🚿hc) ⊙ private beach calor gas ☎ ⊞ 🛁

⊶ golf ⌇

COMBE MARTIN
Devon
Map 22 SS54
See also Berrynarbor.

▶▶▶ ②❸⚠
Stowford Farm Meadows *(SS560427)*
Signposted ☎(027188) 2476 Whit–Oct rs Etr booking advisable Jul & Aug Last arrival & departure 20.00hrs no single sex groups

Very gently sloping grassy, sheltered and south facing site approached down a wide well kept ¾ mile driveway.

20acres 416pitches 300🚐£2.85–£4 66🚐£2.85–£4 50🛖£2.85–£4 (awnings)

25🏕️ late arrivals enclosure 84wc lit all night 4cdp 40🚰 washbasins hc central hot water (🚿hc) ⊙ (spin dry iron)

Coll Sands
▬
Comberton, Great

(games room) licensed bar childrens playground calor gas camping gaz toilet fluid cafe ☎ ⊞ 🛁

⊶ stables golf ⌖ ⌇ launderette pub

COMBERTON
Cambridgeshire
Map 5 TL35

▶▶▶ ②❷⚠
Highfield Farm Camping Site *(TL388573)* Long Rd Signposted ☎(022 026) 2308 Apr–Oct booking advisable peak periods & public hols Last arrival 22.00hrs Last departure 14.00hrs

A level, grassy site set in farmland and screened by conifers and hedges. 3m W of Cambridge between A45 and A603.

4acres 80pitches 40🚐£3.55 or 40🚐£3.40 40🛖£3.55 (awnings)

6🏕️ Individual pitches ⊘ late arrivals enclosure 13wc lit all night 2cdp 🚰 12washbasins hc (2central hot water) (4🚿hc) 2⊙ supervised (dry iron) (cold storage) childrens playground calor gas camping gaz paraffin toilet fluid ☎ ⊞ 🛁

⊶ ⌇ launderette pub

COMBERTON, GREAT
Hereford & Worcestershire
Map 3 SO94

▽②
Shelton Farm *(SO956424)* ☎Elmley Castle (038674) 243 Mar–Oct must book Last arrival 21.00hrs Last departure 17.00hrs

Level grass meadowland close to the River Avon at the foot of Bredon Hill.

15acres 8🚐£1.50 8🚐£1.50 🛖£1.50 awnings

2🏕️ mobile shop

⊶ stables ⌖ ⌇ launderette pub 🛁

COMRIE
Tayside *Perthshire*
Map 11 NN72

▶▶▶ 🏕 ❷ ⚠
Twenty Shilling Wood Caravan Park
(NN763221) Signposted ☎(0764)
70411 30 Mar–2 Oct Last arrival
22.00hrs Last departure 15.00hrs no
tents

*This secluded site of level pitches on
gravel bases is set in tree-studded hill
country lying to west of picturesque
village. Off A85.*

2½acres 30pitches 30static 30🚐£4 or
30🚐£4 awnings

8⚕ late arrivals enclosure 14wc lit all
night 1cdp washbasins hc (🛁hc) ☺
supervised (wash spin dry iron) (cold
storage) calor gas toilet fluid ☎ 🏪

↔ golf ✦ pub

▶▶ 🏕 ❷ ⚠
West Lodge Caravan Site *(NN785225)*
Lawers Signposted ☎(0764) 70354
Apr–Oct must book wknds & Jul–Aug
Last arrival 19.00hrs Last departure
noon 🍴

*A sloping, grass site set amidst wooded
hillside adjacent to A85 and screened by
wall and hedge.*

½acre 20pitches 40static 20🚐£3 or
20🚐£2.50 or 20🏕£2.50 (awnings)

6⚕ late arrivals enclosure 13wc lit all
night 2cdp 🚿 washbasins hc (🛁hc) ☺
supervised (wash spin) calor gas
camping gaz

↔ golf ✦ 🏪

CONEYSTHORPE
(near Malton), North Yorkshire
Map 8 SE77

▶▶▶ 🏕 ❷ ⚠
**Castle Howard Caravan & Camping
Site** *(SE705710)* Apply to: Castle
Howard Estate Ltd, Estate Offices,
Castle Howard, York YO6 7DA
Signposted ☎(065384) 366 Mar–Oct
must book peak periods Last arrival
19.00hrs Last departure 10.30hrs

*An attractive rural site adjacent to lake
on Castle Howard Estate. It is ideally
positioned for visiting Castle Howard,
York and the North York Moors National
Park. Off A64.*

9acres 70pitches 80static 40🚐 fr£4 or
40🚐 fr£4 30🏕 fr£3.68 (awnings) ltr

6⚕ late arrivals enclosure Ⓐ 23wc lit all
night 3cdp washbasins hc 🛁hc ☺
supervised spin iron calor gas camping
gaz ☎ 🏪

↔ stables ✦ pub

CONINGSBY
Lincolnshire
Map 8 TF25

▶▶▶▶ 🏕 ❷ ⚠
Castle Leisure Park *(TF207573)*
Tattershall (1m SW A153) Signposted
☎(0526) 43193 Mar–Oct Last arrival &
departure 22.30hrs

*An extensive complex with lakes and
woods catering for numerous indoor and
outdoor leisure pursuits. Situated on the
main A153.*

10acres 127pitches 29static SA
127🚐£3.50 40🏕£3.50 awnings ltr

9⚕ Ⓐ late arrivals enclosure 24wc lit all
night 2cdp 🚿 washbasins hc 🛁hc ☺
supervised games room CTV cold
storage (licensed club/bar) childrens
playground private beach calor gas
camping gaz toilet fluid cafe restaurant
☎ ⊞ 🏪 stables boats fishing

↔ golf cinema launderette

CONSTABLE BURTON
North Yorkshire
Map 7 SE19

▶▶ 🏕 ❷ ⚠
Constable Burton Hall Caravan Park
(SE158907) Signposted ☎Bedale
(0677) 50428 Etr–Oct must book public
hols Last arrival 22.00hrs no tents

*A part level, part sloping site situated
within parkland of Constable Burton Hall
in unspoilt farmland at entrance to
Wensleydale. Located off A684 but
screened behind old deer park wall.*

10acres 100pitches 100🚐 fr£3.50 or
100🚐 fr£3.50 (awnings)

6⚕ Individual pitches late arrivals
enclosure 14wc lit all night 3cdp
washbasins hc 🛁hc ☺ supervised
(wash spin dry iron) (cold storage)
licensed bar calor gas camping gaz
restaurant ☎ hair dryers

↔ ✦ pub 🏪

CONWY
Gwynedd
Map 6 SH77

▶▶▶ 🏕 ❶ ⚠
Bwlch Mawr Farm *(SH779772)* Gyffin
(1½m S on B5106) Signposted
☎(049263) 2856 Etr–Sep booking
advisable public hols & Jul–Aug Last
arrival 23.00hrs Last departure noon no
single sex groups no motorcycles

15acres 60pitches SA 60🚐£3
(awnings)

12⚕ Individual pitches late arrivals
enclosure 20wc lit all night 2cdp 🚿
washbasins hc 🛁hc ☺ supervised
(wash spin dry) iron (games room) cold
storage childrens playground calor gas
camping gaz toilet fluid ☎ 🏪

↔ stables golf 🛩 cinema ✦
launderette pub

CORFE CASTLE
Dorset
Map 3 SY98

▶▶ 🏕 ❶ 🆔
Woodland Camping Park *(SY953818)*
Glebe Farm, Bucknowle Signposted
☎(0929) 480280 May–Sep no bookings

Last arrival 21.00hrs Last departure
11.00hrs no caravans

*Undulating grass site with trees and
bushes. Set in woodland adjacent to
main A351 road to Swanage.*

7acres 60pitches 60🚐£3.50 or
60🏕£4.50 (awnings)

3⚕ Ⓐ 10wc 8washbasins hc 🛁hc ☺
supervised (cold storage) camping gaz
stables 🏪

↔ pub

CORPACH
Highland *Inverness-shire*
Map 14 NN07

▶▶▶▶ 🏕 ❷ ⚠
Linnhe Caravan Park *(NN074771)*
Signposted ☎(03977) 376 Etr–Sep
Last departure noon no tents

*Situated 1m W of Corpach on A830 on
shores of Loch Eil with Ben Nevis to E
and mountains of Sunart to W. Although
site is predominantly static, caravans are
accommodated on landscaped
terracing with uninterrupted views of
surrounding countryside.*

8acres 100pitches 90static 100🚐£3–£4
or 100🚐£3–£4 (awnings)

10⚕ 30wc lit all night 🚿 (washbasins
hc) (🛁hc) ☺ supervised (spin dry) iron
childrens playground private beach
calor gas ☎ 🏪

↔ stables golf 🛩 ✦ launderette

COVE
Devon
Map 3 SS91

▶▶ 🏕 ❶ ⚠
Orchard Caravan Park Signposted
☎Bampton (0398) 31563 Etr–Oct must
book peak periods

*This site overlooks the River Exe and is
adjacent to A396 Tiverton–Bampton
road. Its pitches are well spaced
between apple trees.*

¾acre 15pitches 2static 15🚐 or 15🚐
or 15🏕 (awnings)

2⚕ late arrivals enclosure 4wc
washbasins hc (2🛁hc) ☺ calor gas
camping gaz 🏪

↔ ✦

COWES
Isle of Wight
Map 4 SZ49

▶▶▶ 🏕 ❷ ⚠
Gurnard Pines Holiday Village
(SZ476947) Gurnard (1m W) ☎(0983)
292395 Jun–Sep rsMar–May booking
advisable Jul & Aug Last departure
14.00hrs (Aug only) 🍴 no caravans no
motorcycles no single sex groups no
open fires

*Slightly sloping grass site in quiet rural
surroundings.*

2½acres 60pitches 38static 8🚐 52🏕
awnings

6⚘ Individual pitches late arrivals enclosure 10wc lit all night 2cdp washbasins hc central hot water (🚿hc) ☺ supervised (wash) (dry iron) ⌔ games room (cold storage) licensed club/bar childrens playground calor gas cafe restaurant ☎ 🛒

↔ stables golf ⛳ ♫ launderette pub

COYLTON
Strathclyde *Ayrshire*
Map 10 NS41

▶▶▶▶ ☑ ❷ ⚠

Sundrum Castle Holiday Park
(NS405208) Signposted ☎Ayr (0292) 61464 Apr–Sep rsOct–Mar (wknds only & Xmas eve–New Years Day) must book Jul & Aug Last arrival 23.59hrs Last departure 14.00hrs no single sex groups

Set in beautiful 'Burns Country' just a 10 minute drive from the centre of the county town of Ayr. Off A70.

4acres 52pitches 200static 52🚐£5 or 52🚘£4.25 or 52▲£5 (awnings) ltr

8⚘ Individual pitches late arrivals enclosure wc lit all night 1cdp ⊟ washbasins hc 🚿hc ☺ supervised (wash spin dry) iron 🗕 ♇ games room CTV cold storage licensed club/bar childrens playground calor gas camping gaz toilet fluid cafe ☎ ⊞ night club junior disco take-away food 🛒

↔ stables golf ♫ launderette pub

CRACKINGTON HAVEN
Cornwall
Map 2 SX19

▶▶▶ ☑ ❶ ⚠

Hentervene Caravan & Camping Park
(SX153940) Signposted ☎St Gennys (08403) 365 Apr–Oct booking advisable Jul & Aug Last arrival 23.00hrs Last departure 10.00hrs

Gently sloping grass site with trees and bushes set in hilly meadow country 2m from the sea and beach on A39.

2acres 35pitches 9static SA 35🚐£4.55 or 35🚘£4.55 or 35▲£4.55 (awnings)

5⚘ Individual pitches late arrivals enclosure 7wc lit all night 2cdp washbasins hc (central hot water) (🚿hc ☺) supervised (spin iron) cold storage

childrens playground calor gas camping gaz ☎ 🛒

↔ stables ♫ launderette pub

CRAIL
Fife
Map 12 NO60

▶▶▶ ☑ ❷ ⚠

Sauchope Caravan Site *(NO623078)*
Apply to: North East Fife District Council, Dept of Recreation, Cairngreen, Cupar, Fife ☎(03335) 460 or Cupar (0334) 53722 late Mar–early Oct must book Last arrival 20.00hrs Last departure 20.00hrs

This is a sloping grassy site comprising a large stretch of land bordering rocky foreshore on Fife coast. Secluded but somewhat exposed to sea breezes with panoramic views over Fife estuary to island of May, Bass Rock and Berwick Law.

1acre 15pitches 135static 15🚐£3.20 or 15🚘£3.20 or 15▲£1.70–£3.20 (awnings)

14⚘ Individual pitches 30wc lit all night 1cdp 29washbasins hc 16🚿hc 4☺ (wash dry) ☎ 🛒

↔ golf ⛳ ♫ launderette pub

▶ ☐ ❶ ❷ ⚠

Balcomie Links Caravan Park
(NO612079) 8 Balcomie Rd ☎(03335) 383 Jun–Aug rsApr–May & Sep–Oct Last arrival 22.00hrs Last departure 14.00hrs no tents

Slightly sloping, grass site with young trees and bushes, set in downland and meadowland adjacent to sea and sandy beach – within the urban area. Junction of A917 and A918.

3acres 7pitches 68static 7🚐 or 7🚘 awnings

4⚘ Individual pitches wc lit all night ⊟ washbasins hc (🚿hc ☺) (wash) spin iron calor gas camping gaz 🛒

↔ golf ⛳ ♫ launderette pub

CRANTOCK
(near Newquay), Cornwall
Map 2 SW75
See Newquay sketch map

▶▶▶▶▶ ☐ ❸ ⚠

Trevella Caravan Park *(SW801599)*
Signposted ☎(0637) 830308 Etr–Oct must book peak periods

A pleasant touring caravan and camping site, surrounded by trees and hedgerows, situated in rural area close to Newquay between Crantock and A3075.

15acres 295pitches 33static 295🚐 or 295🚘 or 295▲ awnings

18⚘ Individual pitches ☺ late arrivals enclosure 53wc lit all night 2cdp ⊟ washbasins hc central hot water (🚿hc) ☺ supervised (wash) spin (dry) iron ⌔ games room CTV cold storage childrens playground calor gas camping gaz toilet fluid cafe restaurant ☎ ⊞ crazy golf, fly fishing 🛒

↔ stables golf ⛳ cinema ♫ launderette pub

see advertisement on page 189

▶▶▶ ☑ ❷ ⚠

Treago Farm Caravan Site *(SW782601)*
Signposted ☎(0637) 830277 May–Oct rsApr Last arrival 22.00hrs Last departure 22.00hrs

Grass site set in open farmland in a south-facing sheltered valley: direct access to Crantock and Polly Joke beaches, National Trust Land and many natural beauty spots.

4acres 93pitches 7static 20🚐 or 20🚘 73▲ awnings

9⚘ Individual pitches ☺ late arrivals enclosure 10wc lit all night 1cdp ⊟ 22washbasins hc (10🚿hc) 5☺ supervised (wash) (dry) iron games room CTV cold storage childrens playground calor gas camping gaz toilet fluid ☎ hair dryers 🛒

↔ stables golf ⛳ cinema ♫ launderette pub

CREETOWN
Dumfries & Galloway *Kirkcudbrightshire*
Map 11 NX45

▶▶▶ ② ❷ ⚠
Cassencarie Holiday Park *(NX475576)*
Signposted ☎(067182) 264 Whit–mid
Sep rs mid Sep–Oct & Mar–Whit must
book Jul & Aug Last arrival 20.00hrs Last
departure noon no single sex groups

*A mainly level, grassy site with trees and
bushes set in meadowland and
woodland just off A75, ½m from
Creetown.*

5acres 50pitches 9static 50🚐£3.50–£4
or 50🚐£3.50–£4 or 50▲£3.50–£4
(awnings)

4🚐 late arrivals enclosure 12wc lit all
night 1cdp 16washbasins hc (4🚿hc) 2☺
(wash spin iron) ♨ (games room) TV
childrens playground calor gas camping
gaz toilet fluid 🛒

↔ 🍴 launderette

CRICCIETH
Gwynedd
Map 6 SH43
See sketch map

▶▶ ② ❷ ⚠
Cae-Canol Caravan & Camping Site
(SH488402) ☎(076671) 2351 Apr–Oct
booking advisable 20 Jul–20 Aug

*A level grassy site with trees set in
meadowland 2m from Criccieth on the
B4411.*

2½acres 28pitches 20static 8🚐£3 or
8🚐£3 20▲£2.50 (awnings)

3🚐 6wc lit all night 1cdp (washbasins
hc) (🚿hc) ☺ supervised (cold storage)
calor gas camping gaz

↔ stables golf ⚑ cinema launderette
pub 🛒

▶▶ ① ❶ ⚠
Eisteddfa Campsite *(SH524398)*
Pentrefelin Signposted ☎(076671)
2104 Etr–Oct no bookings Last arrival
mdnt no single sex groups no caravans

*Part level, part sloping site in hilly
countryside. At Pentrefelin 1½m NE on
A497.*

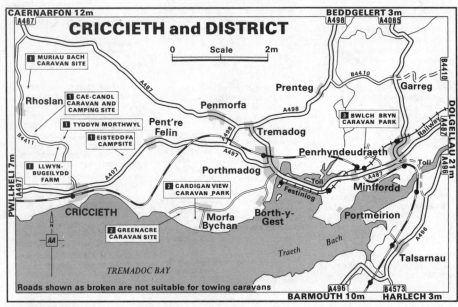

Sites listed under: **1** Criccieth   **2** Morfa Bychan   **3** Penrhyndeudraeth

15acres 150pitches 6static SA 150 🚐 £3 or 150▲£3 awnings

10♨ 20wc lit all night 2cdp washbasins hc (ⓘhc) ☺ supervised (wash spin dry iron) cold storage childrens playground calor gas camping gaz toilet fluid ☎ 🛁 ↔ stables golf 🦌 cinema ♪ launderette pub

▶ ① ❶ △
Llwyn-Bugeilydd Farm *(SH498398)*
Llwyn Bugeilydd Signposted
☎(076671) 2235 Apr–Oct must book peak periods Last departure 11.00hrs

A level site with sea and mountain views. Situated 1m W of Criccieth on B4411. First site on right.

40pitches 20🚐 £2–£3 or 20 🚐 £2 20▲£1.50–£2.50 (awnings)

5♨ Individual pitches for caravans ⓐ 6wc lit all night 1cdp (washbasins hc central hot water) (ⓘhc) ☺ supervised calor gas camping gaz
↔ stables golf cinema ♪ launderette pub 🛁.

▶ ② ❶ △
Muriau Bach Caravan Site *(SH484418)*
Muriau Bach, Rhoslan ☎Garn Dolbenmaen (076675) 642 Mar–Oct booking advisable peak periods

A small farm site approximately 3m NW of Criccieth on B4411.

1½acres 20pitches 20🚐 fr£1.50 or 20 🚐 fr£1 20▲ awnings

3♨ Individual pitches for caravans ⓐ 5wc lit all night 1cdp (ⓘhc) ☺ supervised battery charger
↔ stables golf 🦌 launderette pub 🛁

▶ ② ❶
Tyddyn Morthwyl *(SH493399)*
☎(076671) 2115 Etr–Oct booking advisable Spring bank hol & Jul–Aug (must book for caravans) Last arrival 23.00hrs Last departure noon

Site has good level grass pitches, sheltered by trees, conveniently situated north of the B4411 1½m from centre of Criccieth.

8acres 50pitches 22static SA 10🚐 £3 or 10 🚐 £3 40▲£3 (awnings) ltr

5♨ 8wc lit all night 1cdp washbasins hc (ⓘhc) ☺ games room (cold storage) calor gas camping gaz
↔ stables golf 🦌 ♪ launderette pub 🛁

CRIEFF
Tayside *Perthshire*
Map 11 NN82

▶▶▶ ③ ❷ △
Crieff Holiday Village *(NN857225)*
Turret Bank Signposted ☎(0764) 3513 All year must book Jul & Aug Last arrival mdnt

Level, gravel site with trees and bushes set in woodland within the urban area and with access to river. 1m W of Crieff on A85.

2½acres 70pitches 40static 60🚐 or 60 🚐 10▲ (awnings)

5♨ Individual pitches ⓐ late arrivals enclosure 13wc lit all night 1cdp 🚐 washbasins hc (ⓘhc ☺ supervised (wash spin dry iron) games room TV (cold storage) childrens playground calor gas camping gaz toilet fluid ☎ ⊞ 🛁
↔ stables golf 🦌 cinema ♪ launderette pub

CROCKETFORD
Dumfries & Galloway *Kirkcudbrightshire*
Map 11 NX87

▶▶▶▶ ③ ❸ △
Brandedleys Cara Farm *(NX830725)*
Signposted ☎(055669) 250 Apr–Oct rsMar must book peak periods Last arrival 22.00hrs Last departure noon

Grass and gravel, part level, part sloping site with trees and bushes, set in hilly meadowland and country adjacent to lake. Off A75.

5acres 60pitches 20static SA 45🚐 £4–£5.50 or 45 🚐 £4–£5.50 15▲£4–£5.50 (awnings)

4♨ ⓐ late arrivals enclosure 12wc lit all night 1cdp 🚐 19washbasins hc 1➔hc

---

4ⓘhc 2☺ supervised (wash spin dry iron) ⌫ ℘ games room CTV (cold storage licensed club/bar) childrens playground calor gas camping gaz toilet fluid cafe restaurant ☎ ⊞ bicycles for hire badminton putting 🛁
↔ 🦌 ♪ launderette pub

CROCKEY HILL
North Yorkshire
Map 8 SE64

▽ ①
Wigman Hall *(SE650456)* (off unclass rd between Crockey Hill and Wheldrake)
☎Wheldrake (090489) 221

Narrow paddock in open farmland adjacent to wood.

15pitches 5🚐 ✳£1.50 or 🚐 £1.50 10▲£1.50

♨cdp

CROESGOCH
Dyfed
Map 2 SM83

▶▶▶ ② ❶ △
Torbant Caravan Park *(SM844308)*
Signposted ☎(03483) 261 Spring Bank Hol–Oct rs Etr–Spring Bank Hol booking advisable Aug Last arrival mdnt Last departure noon 🛉in static vans

Part sloping grass site with separate field for tents, 1m from sea. On A487 St Davids to Fishguard road, ¾m N of Croesgoch village.

8acres 60pitches 60static 30🚐 or 30 🚐 30▲ (awnings)

♨ Individual pitches for caravans 15wc lit all night 1cdp washbasins hc (ⓘhc) ☺ supervised (dry) games room TV childrens playground calor gas camping gaz ☎ 🛁
↔ pub

CROMARTY
Highland *Ross and Cromarty*
Map 14 NH76

▶▶ ② ❷ △
Shore Mill *(NH749656)* ☎Poyntzfield (03818) 216 Apr–Sep must book Jul & Aug Last arrival 22.00 hrs Last departure 11.30hrs →

Part level, part sloping grass site set in meadowland on shore of Cromarty Firth overlooking Invergordon and the North. 3m SW of Cromarty on B9163.

2½acres 15pitches 3static 15🚐£2.25 or 15🚙£2.25 or 15▲£2.25 awnings ltr

4🏕3wc lit all night 1cdp washbasins hc central hot water 🚿hc ☉ supervised cold storage private beach ⊞

↔ golf 🎣 pub 🛒

CROPTON
North Yorkshire
Map 8 SE78

▶▶▶ � 🄞🅐
Spiers House Campsite *(SE756918)*
Etr–Sep no bookings Last arrival 22.00 hrs Last departure noon

Set in woodland area with views over woods and hills. 1m N of Cropton on the road to Hartoft.

10acres 150 pitches 100🚐£3–£4 or 100🚙£3–£4 50▲£3–£4 awnings

6🏕☉ late arrivals enclosure 15wc lit all night 1cdp washbasins hc central hot water 🚿hc ☉ supervised (wash spin iron) childrens playground calor gas camping gaz 🕿 🛒

↔ stables 🎣 pub

CROSSGATES
Powys
Map 3 SO06

▶▶ 🄴🄞🅐
Park Caravan & Camping Site
(SO081651) Rhayader Rd 🕿Penybont (059787) 201 Mar–Oct must book public hols & Aug Last arrival 22.00hrs Last departure 17.00hrs no single sex groups under 25yrs

This quiet rural site, set in beautiful countryside, has flat pitches and is well sheltered by trees. It is an ideal touring centre, situated off A44.

¾acre 20pitches 15static 10🚐£3.80 5🚙£3.80 5▲£3.80 awnings

3🏕4wc lit all night 1cdp 🄴 6washbasins hc 2🚿hc 1☉ supervised ⚱ licensed

---

Cromarty
—
Crowhurst

club/bar childrens playground calor gas camping gaz cafe restaurant 🕿 🛒

↔ golf 🎣 launderette pub

CROSSWAYS
Dorset
Map 3 SY78

▶▶▶▶ 🄴🄸🅐
Heathfield Caravan Site *(SY775884)*
Signposted 🕿Warmwell (0305) 852357 16 Mar–Oct must book public hols & Jul–Aug Last arrival mdnt Last departure 11.00hrs

Gently sloping site with grass, sand and gravel surfaces. Set in meadowland with an abundance of trees and bushes. Very pleasant rural setting with gardens around pool. On B3390 Bere Regis–Weymouth road.

8½acres 160pitches 110🚐£4.50 or 110🚙£4.50 50▲£4.50 (awnings)

13🏕 Individual pitches ☉ late arrivals enclosure 25wc lit all night 1cdp 🄴 washbasins hc central hot water 🚿hc ☉

---

supervised (wash spin dry iron) ⚱ games room TV (cold storage) childrens playground calor gas camping gaz toilet fluid cafe 🕿 ⊞ 🛒

↔ stables golf cinema 🎣 launderette pub

CROSTHWAITE
Cumbria
Map 7 SD49
See Windermere sketch map

▶ 🄴🄞🅐
Lambhowe Caravan Park *(SD422914)*
Signposted 🕿(04488) 483 Mar–Oct must book public hols no tents

An attractive site, on rising ground, set amidst a Lakeland wood. Off A5074.

1acre 14pitches 111static 14🚐£3.50 or 14🚙£3.50

1🏕 15wc lit all night 1cdp central hot water (🚿hc) 1☉ wash dry games room TV licensed club/bar childrens playground calor gas 🕿

↔ stables golf 🎣 pub 🛒

CROSTON
Lancashire
Map 7 41

▶▶▶ 🄴🄞🅐
Royal Umpire Caravan Park
(SD504190) Moor Rd 🕿(0772) 600257 Mar–Oct must book public hols Last arrival 22.30hrs Last departure 16.00hrs

A pleasant newly developed site set in open level countryside.

7acres 74pitches SA 54🚐£2.50 or 54🚙£2.50 20▲£1.50 awnings ltr

4🏕 Individual pitches ☉ late arrivals enclosure 6wc lit all night 1cdp 🄴 washbasins hc (🚿hc) ☉ supervised (wash spin dry iron ⊡) childrens playground calor gas cafe 🕿 ⊞ 🛒

↔ stables 🎣 launderette pub

CROWHURST
East Sussex
Map 5 TQ71

▶▶▶ 🄴🄞🅐
Brakes Coppice Farm Park
(TQ 765134) Brakes Coppice Farm

Signposted ☎(042483) 322 Apr–Oct must book peak periods & for groups of motorcyclists Last arrival 22.00hrs Last departure 16.00hrs

Secluded, farm site in meadow surrounded by woodland with small stream and fishing lake. Off A2100.

3acres 30pitches 30🚐£3.75 or 30🚐£3.75 or 30▲£3.75 (awnings) ltr 6🏕 Individual pitches ⊘ late arrivals enclosure 3wc lit all night 1cdp 5washbasins hc (2🛁hc) 2⊙ ♒ (cold storage) childrens playground calor gas camping gaz toilet fluid 🧺

↔ stables golf 🏊 pub

CROYDE BAY
Devon
Map 2 SS43
See Ilfracombe sketch map

▶▶▶▶ 🔲❸⚠
Ruda Holiday Park (SS438397)
Signposted ☎Croyde (0271) 890671
Spring Bank Hol–Oct rs Etr–Spring

Crowhurst — Croyde Bay

Bank Hol must book peak periods Last arrival 21.00hrs Last departure 10.00hrs 🎯 no single sex groups

Level, part sloping, mainly grass surface with trees and bushes. Close to sandy beach and National Trust beauty spot 'Baggy Point'. Off B3231.

16acres 400pitches 211static 65🚐£3.60–£7.10 335 🚐£3.60–£6.60 or 335▲£3.60–£6.60 (awnings) 17🏕 Individual pitches ⊘ late arrivals . enclosure 109wc lit all night 2cdp 🔲 77washbasins hc 4 central hot water 2🔧 70🛁hc 32 ⊙ (wash spin dry) iron games room (cold storage) licensed club/bar childrens playground calor gas camping gaz toilet fluid cafe restaurant ☎ ⊞ 🧺

↔ stables golf 🏊 launderette pub

▶▶▶ 🔲❶⚠
Croyde Bay Holidays (SS436395)
Signposted ☎(0271) 890351 Etr–15 Nov rs 16 Mar–Etr must book Whit & Jul–Aug Last arrival 21.00hrs Last departure 11.30hrs 🎯

Level grassy site adjacent to the beach and sand dunes.

12acres 112pitches 50static SA 112🚐 or 112 🚐 or 112▲ awnings

30🏕 Individual pitches ⊘ late arrivals enclosure 36wc 4cdp 🔲 washbasins hc central hot water 🛁hc ⊙ supervised (wash spin dry iron) (cold storage) licensed club bar childrens playground calor gas camping gaz toilet fluid cafe restaurant ☎ 🧺

↔ stables golf cinema 🏊 launderette pub

CUBERT
Cornwall Map 2 SW75
See Newquay sketch map

▶▶ ☑ ❶ ⚠
Treworgans Farm (SW782590)
Signposted ☎Crantock (0637) 830200
Apr–Sep booking advisable Jul & Aug
Last arrival 22.00hrs Last departure
noon

*Site has level grassy pitches and is
situated off Cubert–Crantock road, SW
of Newquay.*

¾acre 20pitches 20static 20🚐 or 20🚐
or 20▲ (awnings)

2🏕 wc lit all night 1cdp (washbasins hc)
(📶hc) ☺ supervised 🎣

↔ stables golf 🏌 launderette pub

CULLEN
Grampian *Banffshire*
Map 15 NJ56

▶▶ ☑ ❷ ⚠
Logie Camping & Caravan Site
(NJ516674) Signposted ☎Elgin (0343)
45121 Etr–20 Sep must book peak
periods Last arrival 20.00hrs Last
departure noon

*Part level and sloping grassy site near
sea and beach. ¼m E of A98.*

65pitches 60static 40🚐 £3.20 or
40🚐 £3.20 25▲£2.55–£3.20 (awnings)
ltr

4🏕 Individual pitches 32wc lit all night
1cdp washbasins hc central hot water
(📶hc) (wash dry) childrens playground
☎🎣

↔ golf 🏌 pub

CUMINESTOWN
Grampian *Aberdeenshire*
Map 15 NJ85

▶ ☑ ❶ ⚠
A B Caravans (NJ842516) Signposted
☎(08883) 261 Apr–Oct must book Jul &
Aug Last arrival 20.00hrs Last departure
11.00hrs
*Mainly grass site set in agricultural land.
3m NE with access from New Deer to
New Byth unclass road.*

1acre 20pitches 12static SA 6🚐 2🚐
12▲ awnings ltr

2🏕 ⚪ late arrivals enclosure 6wc lit all
night 1cdp washbasins hc central hot
water (📶hc) ☺ supervised (wash spin)
iron games room TV cold storage
childrens playground calor gas camping
gaz paraffin toilet fluid mobile shop 🎣

↔ stables 🏌 launderette pub

CUMWHITTON
Cumbria
Map 12 NY55

▶ ☑ ❶ ⚠
Cairndale Caravan Park (NY518523)
☎Croglin (076886) 280 Mar–Oct must
book Jul & Aug Last arrival 22.00hrs no
tents

*Mainly level grass site set in tranquil
Eden Valley. Off A69 at Warwick Bridge*

*on unclassified road through Great
Corby to Cumwhitton, turn left at village
sign, then site in 1m.*

¾acre 5pitches 15static 5🚐£2.20–
£2.50 or 5 🚐£2.20–£2.50 (awnings)

7🏕 Individual pitches 5wc lit all night
1cdp 🚿 5washbasins hc central hot
water (2📶hc) 1☺ supervised cold
storage calor gas

↔ golf 🏌 🏊 pub

DALBEATTIE
Dumfries & Galloway *Kirkcudbrightshire*
Map 11 NX86

▶▶ ☑ ❷ ⚠
Islecroft Caravan Site (NX837615)
Colliston Pk, Mill St Signposted
☎Castle Douglas (0556) 3131 31 Mar–
Oct no bookings Last departure noon

*A neat site in two sections tucked away
to rear of town, close to local park.*

3acres 74pitches 46🚐£2.75–£3 or
46 🚐£2.75–£3 39▲£2.75–£3 awnings

2🏕 Individual pitches 10wc lit all night
1cdp washbasins hc central hot water
📶hc ☺ wash spin ☎ 🎣

↔ stables golf 🏌 🏊 pub

DALRYMPLE
Strathclyde *Ayrshire*
Map 10 NS31

▶▶▶ ☑ ❷ ⚠
Doon Valley Caravan Park (NS365145)
☎(029256) 242 mid May–Sep rs Oct–
mid May must book Jul & Aug no tents
no cars by caravans

*Part level, part sloping grass site with
trees and bushes, set in downland and
meadowland, with access to main road.
5m SE of Ayr off B742.*

6acres 10pitches 90static 10🚐 or 10🚐
awnings ltr

6🏕 late arrivals enclosure 9wc lit all
night 1cdp 🚿 12washbasins hc 2central
hot water 6📶hc 2☺ (wash) (dry) iron
games room CTV cold storage childrens
playground calor gas camping gaz toilet
fluid ☎ 🎣

↔ launderette pub

DALSTON
Cumbria
Map 11 NY34

▶▶ ☑ ❷ ⚠
Dalston Hall Caravan Park (NY378519)
Dalston Hall Estate Signposted
☎Carlisle (0228) 710165 & 25014 Mar–
Oct must book public hols & Jul–Aug

*An exceptionally well-maintained site, on
level grassy ground, situated in grounds
of estate located between Carlisle and
Dalston on B5299. Ideal position for
touring northern Lake District, Carlisle
and surrounding country.*

4acres 60pitches 60🚐£3.50 or
60 🚐£3.50 or 60▲£2.50 awnings

6🏕 Individual pitches for caravans 15wc
lit all night 1cdp washbasins hc (📶hc) ☺
(wash dry Iron) (games room) (cold
storage) childrens playground calor gas
camping gaz ☎ fishing 🎣

↔ stables golf 🏌 cinema 🏊
launderette pub

DALWOOD
Devon
Map 3 ST20

▶▶ ☑ ❷ ⚠
Andrewshayes Caravan Park
(SY248988) ☎Wilmington (040483)
225 May–Sep rs 15 Mar–April & Oct
booking advisable Jul & Aug Last arrival
22.00hrs Last departure noon

*Slightly sloping site within easy reach of
Lyme Regis, Seaton, Branscombe and
Sidmouth. Adjacent to A35.*

6acres 60pitches 80static SA 60🚐£4.25
or 60 🚐£3.75 80▲£4.25 (awnings) ltr

6🏕 Individual pitches ⚪ 24wc lit all night
2cdp 🚿 washbasins hc 📶hc ☺
supervised (wash spin dry iron) 🏊
(games room) (cold storage) childrens
playground calor gas camping gaz toilet
fluid ☎ 🎣

↔ stables golf 🏊 launderette pub

DARTMOUTH
Devon
Map 3 SX85

▶▶ ☑ ❷ ⚠
Little Cotton Caravan Park (SX858508)
Little Cotton ☎(08043) 2558 15 Mar–15
Nov must book Aug Last arrival 22.00hrs
Last departure noon

*Slightly sloping meadow site with open
country views located on outskirts of
Dartmouth.*

3½acres 64pitches SA 64🚐£3.60
(awnings)

4🏕 12wc lit all night 4cdp washbasins
hc (📶hc) ☺ (cold storage) calor gas
camping gaz 🎣

↔ stables 🏌 cinema 🏊 launderette
pub

▽ ☑
Bugford Farm (SX834511) Bugford (3m
W off B3207) ☎Blackawton (080421)
464 mid Jun–Oct rs Apr–mid Jun
booking advisable Apr–1st Jun no
single sex groups

Level hedged field in remote rural area.

1acre 5pitches 5🚐£1.75 or 5 🚐£1.75
or 5▲£1.75 awnings

1🏕

↔ stables 🏌 cinema 🏊 launderette
pub 🎣

DAVIOT
Highland *Inverness-shire*
Map 14 NH73

▶▶▶ ☑ ❸ ⚠
Auchnahillin Caravan Park

(NH742386) Signposted ☎(046 385) 223 15 Mar–Oct booking advisable Jul & Aug Last arrival 23.00hrs Last departure noon

Level grassy site surrounded by hills and forest. Situated 7m SE of Inverness on B9154 (Moy road) off A9.

Daviot
—
Dawlish

5acres 65pitches 17static 45⚪£3–£3.50 or 45⚪£3–£3.50 20▲£3–£3.50 (awnings)

9⚪ Individual pitches ⚪ late arrivals enclosure 12wc lit all night 1cdp 🔲 washbasins hc (🚿 hc) ☺ supervised (wash spin dry) iron games room cold storage childrens playground licensed. club licensed bar calor gas camping gaz restaurant ☎ 🛒
↪ 🔱

DAWLISH
Devon
Map 3 SX97

▶▶▶ 🅲 ❸ 🅰
Lady's Mile Farm *(SX968784)*
Signposted ☎(0626) 863 411 15 Mar–Oct must book public hols & Jul–Aug Last arrival 20.00hrs Last departure 11.00hrs

This site is fairly central for the surrounding beaches. The good level pitches are surrounded by hedges and trees. 1m N of Dawlish on A379.

16acres 286pitches SA 286⚪£3.70–£5.10 or 286⚪£3.70–£4.80 or 286▲£3.70–£4.80 (awnings)

14⚪ Individual pitches late arrivals enclosure 68wc lit all night 1cdp 🔲 washbasins hc central hot water 🚿 hc ☺ (wash spin dry iron) ⚐ (games room) CTV (cold storage) childrens playground calor gas camping gaz toilet fluid ☎ take away food 🛒
↪ golf 🏌 🔱 pub

DELABOLE
Cornwall
Map 2 SX08

►►► ② △

Planet Park *(SX072842)* Signposted
☎Camelford (0840) 213361 Etr–Oct
booking advisable late Jul & Aug Last
arrival 22.00hrs Last departure noon ✻

*This site has panoramic views and is
situated off B3314 coast road.*

3acres 60pitches 37static 60☎£3 or
60☎£3 or 60▲£3 (awnings) ltr

5☼ 10wc lit all night 1cdp washbasins
hc (🔥hc) ☺ supervised (wash dry iron)
calor gas camping gaz 🔥

↔ ✔ pub

DENSOLE
Kent
Map 5 TR24
See Folkestone sketch map

► 🔢 ❶ △

Black Horse Farm *(TR211418)* 385
Canterbury Rd Signposted ☎Hawkinge
(030389) 2665 Apr–Oct rs Nov–Mar
booking advisable peak periods Last
departure noon

*Level, grass site with views over
farmland. Adjoining A260 Folkestone to
Canterbury road.*

1¼acres 30pitches SA 30☎£3.20 or
30☎£3.20 or 30▲£3.20 (awnings) ltr
for senior citizens

6☼ Individual pitches late arrivals
enclosure 5wc lit all night 1cdp
washbasins hc central hot water (🔥hc)
☺ supervised calor gas camping gaz ☎

↔ stables golf 🏌 cinema ✔launderette

DERBY
Derbyshire
Map 8 SK33

►►► 🔢 ❷ △

Alvaston Mobile Home Park
(SK381342) Meadow Ln ☎(0332)
72204 All year must book ✻ no tents no
motorcycles

*Mainly level grass site, 3m SW of Derby
off A6.*

5pitches 137static 5☎£2.82 or
5☎£2.82

1☼ 5wc lit all night washbasins hc 🔥 ☺
supervised (wash spin) ☎ 🔥

↔ ✔ landerette pub

DEREHAM (EAST)
Norfolk
Map 9 TF91

►► 🔢 ❷ △

Dereham Touring Caravan Park
(TG005134) Norwich Rd Signposted
☎(0362) 4619 Mar–Nov Last arrival
23.30hrs Last departure 16.00hrs

*Level grass site situated 1m E of
Dereham off A47.*

3acres 45pitches 45☎£3.50 or
45 ☎£3.50 or 45▲ fr£2 (awnings)

2☼ Individual pitches late arrivals
enclosure 5wc lit all night 1cdp 🔥
washbasins hc central hot water 🔥hc ☺
supervised childrens playground

↔ 🔥

DEVIZES
Wiltshire
Map 4 SU06

►►► ② ❷ △

Lakeside *(SU992626)* Rowde (2m NW
A342) ☎(0380) 2767 29 Mar–Oct
booking advisable peak periods Last
arrival 21.00hrs Last departure noon

*Pleasant level site on lakeside with
attractive trees and shrubs within urban
area.*

☎✳£3.40 ☎£3.40 ▲£3.40 (awnings)

2☼ 8wc 1cdp 🔥 (central hot water)
🔥hc (☺) (cold storage) calor gas
camping gaz fishing 🔥

DIDDLEBURY
Shropshire
Map 7 SO58

▽ ③

Glebe Farm *(SD508855)* Signposted
☎Munslow (058 476) 221 May–Oct
must book public hols Last arrival
22.00hrs Last departure noon

*Secluded wooded paddock adjacent to
small stream in farm grounds.*

5acres 5pitches 5☎£1.50 or 5 ☎£1.50
or 5▲£1 awnings

1☼ 1cdp

↔ stables ✔ pub

DINAS CROSS
Dyfed
Map 2 SN03

►►► ② ❶ △

**Fishguard Bay Caravan & Camping
Site** *(SN005395)* Signposted ☎(03486)
415 & 285 Apr–7 Oct booking advisable
Jul & Aug

*Partly level and sloping grass site with
bushes, near the sea. 1m N of A487.*

3acres 30pitches 50static 30☎£3.50 or
30 ☎£3.50 or 30▲£3.50 (awnings) ltr

4☼☀ 18wc lit all night 1cdp 🔥
washbasins hc central hot water (♨hc)
🔥hc ☺ (wash dry) iron TV (cold storage)
private beach calor gas camping gaz
toilet fluid ☎ 🔥

↔ stables 🏌 cinema ✔ launderette
pub

DINAS DINLLE
Gwynedd
Map 6 SH45
See Caernarfon sketch map

►►► 🔢 ❷ △

Dinlle Caravan Park *(SH443568)*
Signposted ☎Llanwnda (0286) 830324
May–Sep rs Mar & Oct booking
advisable peak periods Last arrival
23.00hrs Last departure 11.00hrs

*Well-kept grassy level site, adjacent to
sandy beach; good views to Snowdonia.*

10acres 144pitches 138static SA
84☎✳£3.50 or 84 ☎£3.25 60▲£3.25
(awnings)

12☼ Individual pitches ☀ late arrivals
enclosure 37wc lit all night 2cdp
33washbasins hc 19🔥hc 4☺ supervised
(wash spin dry) iron games room
licensed club/bar childrens playground
calor gas camping gaz toilet fluid ☎ ⊞
take away food video films 🔥

↔ ✔ launderette pub

DINGESTOW
Gwent
Map 3 SO41

▶▶▶ ② ❷ ⚠

Bridge Caravan Park & Camping Site
(SO459104) Bridge Farm Signposted
☎(060083) 241 Etr–Oct booking
advisable public hols Last arrival
22.00hrs Last departure 16.00hrs

In quiet village setting, the site is
signposted from Raglan and located off
the A449, South Wales–Midlands road.

5acres 90pitches 34static SA 30🚐
30🚐 30▲ awnings

3🛖 Individual pitches ⚠ late arrivals
enclosure 10wc lit all night 1cdp
10washbasins hc 1central hot water
(4🛁 hc) 2☉ supervised (wash spin dry
iron) cold storage childrens playground
calor gas camping gaz toilet fluid ☎ ⊞
fishing 🦞

↔ golf launderette pub

DINGWALL
Highland Ross & Cromarty
Map 14 NH55

▶▶ ❷ ❶ ⚠

Camping & Caravanning Club
(NH557588) Jubilee Park Signposted
☎(0349) 62236 Apr–Sep must book Jul
& Aug Last arrival 22.00hrs Last
departure noon

Close to town centre and well-
maintained.

2½acres 60pitches SA 60🚐 or 60🚐
60▲ awnings

3🛖 Individual pitches 13wc lit all night
1cdp wash basins hc 🛁 hc ☉ supervised
☎ ⊞ 🦞

↔ stables golf cinema ♪ launderette

DITTISHAM
Devon
Map 3 SX85

▽ ②

Little Coombe Farm (SX848538)
☎(080422) 240 must book no caravans
or motor vans

Isolated farm site on mainly level ground
in secluded wooded valley. Camping

around a small artificial lake. Approach
is by rather steep decline.

8 pitches 8▲✳£1.50

4🛖 cdp

DOBWALLS
Cornwall
Map 2 SX26

▶▶▶ ② ❸ ⚠

Pine Green Caravan Park (SX198648)
(1m W of Dobwalls S off A38 at first
crossroads signposted) ☎(0579)
20183 Etr–Oct Last arrival 23.00hrs Last
departure noon

Terraced site with scenic views over the
surrounding countryside and Fowey
River Valley. Ideal touring base.

2acres 50pitches 50🚐£2.60–£3.60 or
50🚐£2.60–£3.60 or 50▲£2.60–£3.60
(awnings) ltr

5🛖 Individual pitches 6wc lit all night
1cdp washbasins hc (🛁 hc) ☉
supervised (wash) iron cold storage
calor gas camping gaz toilet fluid ☎ 🦞

↔ stables pub

DORNEY REACH
Buckinghamshire
Map 4 SU97

▶ ① ❶ ⚠

Amerden Caravan Park (SU912798)
Old Marsh Ln ☎Maidenhead (0628)
27461 Apr–Oct Last arrival 21.00hrs
Last departure 16.00hrs

A small, level grass site, situated in an
old orchard, alongside the River
Thames, but beneath the M4 motorway.

1acre 10pitches 16static 10🚐 or 10🚐
or 10▲ (awnings)

3🛖 3wc lit all night 1cdp washbasins hc
central hot water 🛁 hc calor gas

↔ stables golf 🎣 cinema ♪
launderette pub 🦞

DORNOCH
Highland Sutherland
Map 14 NH78

▶▶▶ ② ❷ ⚠

Grannie's Heilan Hame (NH818924)
Signposted ☎(0862) 810260 Jun–Aug
rs Sep–May Last arrival 22.00hrs

This site is in a coastal setting amidst
grass and sand dunes.

50acres 334pitches 66static 234🚐£2–
£4 or 234 🚐£2–£4 100 ▲£2–£4
awnings ltr

20🛖 ⚠ late arrivals enclosure 56wc lit
all night 1cdp 🔌 60washbasins hc
(18🛁 hc) 12☉ supervised (wash spin dry
iron) games room TV cold storage
licensed club/bar childrens playground
private beach calor gas camping gaz
toilet fluid cafe restaurant ☎ ⊞ petrol
station fish & chip shop live
entertainment 🦞

↔ stables golf 🎣 ♪

▶▶▶ ② ❷ ⚠

**Royal Dornoch Links Caravan &
Camping Site** (NH804888) Apply to:
District Amenities Officer, Sutherland
District Council, Golspie, Sutherland
KW10 6RB Signposted ☎(0862)
810423 Apr–23 Oct must book Jul &
Aug Last arrival 22.00hrs Last departure
noon

A level, grass and sand site set in hilly
woodland and moorland. It is near the
sea and beach, 2m E of Dornoch off A9.

10acres 160pitches 40static 160🚐 or
160🚐 or 160▲ (awnings) ltr

15🛖 38wc lit all night 3cdp washbasins
hc (🛁 hc) ☉ (wash spin dry iron) (games
room) CTV childrens playground ☎
putting green

↔ stables golf 🦞

DOVER
Kent
Map 5 TR34
See under Martin Mill

DOVERIDGE
Derbyshire
Map 7 SK13 →

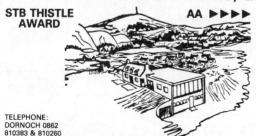

▽ ②
Cavendish Garage *(SK122342)*
☎Uttoxeter (08893) 2092 All year

Level fenced field with some trees at the rear of a service station, on the east side of village.

4acres ⛺£1.30 🚐£1.30 ⛺£1.30 awnings ltr

1🅰 1wc lit all night 1cdp calor gas camping gaz paraffin

↔ golf cinema ⌂ launderette pub 🛉

DRAYTON
Hereford & Worcester
Map 7 SO97

▽ ②
Barrow Hill *(SO909753)*
☎Belbroughton (0562) 730629

Mainly level pastureland on high ground with excellent country views.

10pitches
♨ cdp

DRAYTON BASSETT
Staffordshire
Map 7 SK10

▽ ①
Ashdene Farm *(SP183999)* Portleys Ln
☎Tamworth (0827) 284617 All year
booking advisable Last arrival 22.30hrs

Level open meadow in rural area adjacent to farm buildings.

3acres ⛺£1 🚐£1 ⛺£1 awnings

2♨🅐 1wc 1cdp

↔ stables golf ⚼ cinema launderette pub 🛉

DRINNISHADDER
Harris, Western Isles *Inverness-shire*
Map 13 NG19

▶ ① ❶ ⚠
Laig House Caravan Site *(NG171951)*
Signposted ☎(085981) 207 Apr–15
Oct must book Jul & Aug Last arrival mdnt Last departure noon

Part level, part sloping, sand-surfaced site with mature trees set in mountainous and hilly country with access to sea and beach. 4½m S of Tarbert.

2acres 16pitches 5static 16🚐£2.25 or 16 🚐£2.25 or 16⛺£1.90 (awnings)

2♨🅐 late arrivals enclosure 5wc lit all night 1cdp ⚙ washbasins hc ☺ supervised ℘ cold storage childrens playground private beach calor gas camping gaz toilet fluid ☎ fishing

↔ ⚼

DULAS
Gwynedd
Map 6 SH48

▶▶ ② ❶ ⚠
Tyddyn Isaf Caravan Park *(SH486873)*
Lligwy Bay (½m off A5025 between Benllech and Amlwch) Signposted
☎Moelfre (024 888) 203 Mar–Oct booking advisable peak periods Last arrival 23.00hrs Last departure 11.00hrs families only

Site located on gently rising ground adjacent to sandy beach affording magnificent views.

6acres 92pitches 50static 12🚐 fr£3.50 80 🚐 fr£3 or 80⛺ fr£3 (awnings)

11♨ late arrivals enclosure 12wc lit all night 1cdp washbasins hc central hot water (🚿 hc) ☺ supervised (spin dry iron) CTV (cold storage licensed club/bar) childrens playground calor gas camping gaz ☎ 🛉

↔ stables golf ⚼ ⌂ launderette pub

DUMFRIES
Dumfries & Galloway *Dumfriesshire*
Map 11 NX97

▶▶ ① ❷ ⚠
Newbridge Caravan Park *(NX952787)*
Glasgow Rd Signposted ☎Newbridge (0387) 720249 Mar–Oct must book Last arrival 22.00hrs Last departure noon ⚼ no tents

Level, grassy site on outskirts of busy town. Long and narrow site with central hard core road. 2m N on A76.

30pitches 100static 30🚐£2.50 or 30 🚐£2.50 (awnings)

3♨ Individual pitches late arrivals enclosure 5wc lit all night 1cdp washbasins hc central hot water 🚿 hc ☺ childrens playground calor gas camping gaz toilet fluid 🛉

↔ stables golf ⚼ cinema ⌂ launderette

DUNBAR
Lothian *East Lothian*
Map 12 NT67

▶▶ ① ❶ ⚠
Kirk Park Caravan Site *(NT667789)*
Apply to: East Lothian DC, Leisure and Recreation Dept, Brunton Hall, Ladywell Way, Musselburgh, Midlothian mid Mar–Oct no bookings Last departure 10.30hrs

Part level, part sloping site, in meadowland adjacent to A1 off A1087.

22pitches 100static 22🚐£3.50–£4 or 22 🚐£3.50–£4 or 22⛺£3.50–£4 (awnings) ltr

3♨ Individual pitches 14wc lit all night 2cdp 16washbasins hc calor gas camping gaz 🛉

↔ stables golf ⚼ launderette pub

▶▶ ① ❶ ⚠
Winterfield Caravan Site *(NT673793)*
West Prom Signposted Apply to: East Lothian DC, Leisure and Recreation Dept, Brunton Hall, Ladywell Way, Musselburgh, Midlothian Apr–Sep no bookings Last departure 10.30hrs

Level, grassy site with access to the sea and beach. Situated on the corner of the Back Road and Knockenhair Road.

17pitches 72static 17🚐£3.50–£4 or 17 🚐£3.50–£4 or 17⛺£3.50–£4 (awnings) ltr

3♨ Individual pitches 16wc lit all night 3cdp 12 washbasins hc 2🚿 hc 6☺ childrens playground calor gas camping gaz ☎ 🛉

↔ golf ⚼ launderette pub

DUNBEATH
Highland *Caithness*
Map 15 ND12

▶ ① ❶ ⚠
Inver Caravan Park *(ND167300)* Inver Guesthouse, Inver (½m N on A9)
☎(05933) 252 All year rs winter months

Small grass site surrounded by trees with several hens, ducks and sheep roaming the site.

1acre 15pitches 15🚐 fr£1 or 15 🚐 fr£1 or 15⛺ fr£1 awnings

1♨ 3wc washbasins hc 🚿 hc ☺

↔ stables ⚼ 🛉

DUNDEE
Tayside *Angus*
Map 11 NO33

▶▶ ② ❷
Camperdown Caravan Site
(NO361325) Camperdown Park Apply to: The General Manager of Parks, Parks Department, 353 Clepington Rd, Dundee DD3 8PL Signposted ☎(0382) 23141 (ext. 413) Apr–Sep must book Jul & Aug Last arrival 21.00hrs Last departure 12.30hrs

---

Modern neatly laid out touring site adjacent to municipal park, just off Dundee by-pass at its western end. Degree of seclusion despite close proximity of industrial estate.

8½acres 90pitches 90🚐 or 90🚙 or 90🛖 awnings

4🏕 Individual pitches 20wc lit all night 2 cdp washbasins hc (🚿hc) ☺ (👤) childrens playground cafe restaurant ☎ ⊞ Putting, pitch & putt, horse riding & wildlife centre mobile shop

↔ stables golf cinema ♨ launderette 🛒

DUNKELD
Tayside *Perthshire*
Map 11 NO04

▶ ② ❷ ⚠

Inver Mill Caravan Site *(NO015422)* Signposted Apr–Oct no bookings no motorvans or tents

A level and grassy site with mature trees and bushes set in hilly country with nearby moorland, woodland and river. Turn off A9 onto A822 then immediately right to Inver.

2½acres 50pitches 80static SA 50🚐 (awnings)

15🏕☺ 14wc lit all night washbasins hc 🚿hc ☺ supervised

↔ golf ♨ pub 🛒

DUNKESWELL
Devon
Map 3 ST10

▶▶ ② ❷ ⚠

Fishponds House Campsite *(ST154074)* ☎Luppitt (040 489) 698 Etr–Oct must book Last arrival 22.00hrs Last departure 11.00hrs no caravans or motorvans

Site is set in wildlife sanctuary, surrounded by trees.

1acre 15pitches SA 15🛖£4.50 awnings ltr

2🏕 4wc lit all night 1cdp washbasins hc 🚿hc ☺ supervised 📺 (👤) (games room) cold storage childrens playground

↔ pub

DUNNET
Highland *Caithness*
Map 15 ND27

▶▶ ② ❷ ⚠

Dunnet Bay Caravan Club Site *(ND219703)* Signposted ☎Castletown (084 782) 319 22 May–22 Sept rs 14–21 May must book peak periods Last departure noon

This is a mainly level grassy site with gravel driveways, set alongside 3 miles of white shell sands. Access is directly onto A836 approx 8m E of Thurso, immediately W of the village of Dunnet.

8acres 45 pitches 45🚐 or 45🚙 or 45🛖 (awnings)

9🏕 individual pitches ☺ late arrivals enclosure wc lit all night 1cdp washbasins hc

---

central hot water (🚿hc) ☺ supervised (wash spin dry) calor gas camping gaz toilet fluid 🛒

↔ stables ⚓ ♨ launderette pub

DUNOON
Strathclyde *Argyllshire*
Map 10 NS17

▶▶ ① ❶ ⚠

Cowal Caravan Park *(NS183792)* Victoria Rd, Hunters Quay Signposted ☎(0369) 4259 All year Last arrival 22.30hrs Last departure noon 🍴 no single sex groups or motorcycles no tents

Quiet, walled site in former market-garden, 2m from Dunoon and 75yds from the shore and Clyde–Argyll car-ferry terminal.

6pitches 26static 6🚙£4 or 6🚙£4 ltr

3🏕 Individual pitches 29wc lit all night 1cdp washbasins hc central hot water (🚿hc) ☺ supervised (wash spin dry iron) calor gas

↔ stables golf ⚓ cinema ♨ launderette pub 🛒

DUNSTABLE
Bedfordshire
Map 4 TL02

▽ ①

Valence End Farm *(SP995186)* Dagnall Rd (3m SW B4506)

Take B489 SW for 2½m to B4506 turn SE site in ½m.

5acres 12pitches 12🚙 or 12🚙 or 12🛖

🏕 cdp

DUNVEGAN
Isle of Skye, Highland *Inverness-shire*
Map 13 NG24

▶▶ ① ❷ ⚠

Dunvegan Caravan Park *(NG260477)* Signposted ☎(047022) 362 Etr–Sep rs early & late season booking advisable peak periods no tents

A mainly level site set in hilly moorland.

2acres 33pitches 33🚙£2–£3 or 33🚙£2–£3 awnings

🏕 Individual pitches 18wc lit all night 1cdp washbasins hc 🚿hc ☺ (wash dry)

↔ ⚓ ♨ pub 🛒

DURNESS
Highland *Sutherland*
Map 14 NC36

▶▶ ② ❷ ⚠

Sango Sands Caravan Site *(NC406678)* Sangomore (1m E) Signposted Etr–Sep no bookings Last arrival 18.00hrs Last departure noon

On the outskirts of Durness on A838 this open cliff-top site overlooks Sango Bay,

---

and is mainly grass and sand.

10acres 75pitches 75🚙£3.60 or 75🚙£3.60 or 75🛖£3.60 awnings ltr

8🏕 16wc lit all night 2cdp washbasins hc (🚿hc) ☺ supervised spin games room cold storage licensed club/bar calor gas camping gaz cafe restaurant ☎ bicycles for hire 🛒

↔ stables ♨ pub

EAMONT BRIDGE
Cumbria
Map 12 NY52

▶▶ ② ❷ ⚠

Lowther Caravan Park *(NY517239)* Signposted ☎Penrith (0768) 63631 mid Mar–Oct must book public hol wknds no cats

A partly level and sloping grass site with mature trees and bushes. River and lake nearby. Good centre for touring Lake District, 3m S of Penrith off A6.

12acres 196pitches 375static 146🚙£4–£5 or 146🚙£4–£5 50🛖£4–£5 awnings ltr

40🏕☺ late arrivals enclosure 114wc 5cdp washbasins hc (🚿hc) ☺ supervised (wash dry) childrens playground calor gas camping gaz toilet fluid ☎ fishing, 🛒

↔ stables golf cinema launderette pub

EAST ALLINGTON
Devon
Map 3 SX74

▶ ② ❶ ⚠

Mounts Farm *(SX757488)* The Mounts Signposted ☎(054852) 225 20 Mar–Sep must book Last arrival 23.00hrs Last departure noon no pets no motorcycles

2acres 27pitches 5🚙 22🛖 awnings

4🏕 Individual pitches ☺ 4wc ☺ supervised calor gas camping gaz 🛒

↔ stables ⚓ cinema ♨ launderette pub

EAST ANSTEY
Devon
Map 3 SS82

▶▶▶ ① ❷ ⚠

Zeacombe Caravan & Camping Park *(SS859240)* Blackerton Cross Signposted ☎Anstey Mills (03984) 279 Apr–Oct rs 16–31 Mar & 1–15 Nov

Site has good panoramic views of surrounding countryside and is situated within 100yds of A361 Taunton-Barnstaple road.

3acres 40pitches SA 40🚙£2–£2.50 or 40🚙£2–£2.50 or 40🛖£2–£2.50 awnings

5🏕 9wc lit all night 1cdp 🔌 washbasins hc (🚿hc) ☺ supervised (cold storage) calor gas camping gaz 🛒

↔ stables ♨ pub

EAST BERGHOLT
Suffolk
Map 5 TM03

▶▶▶ ② ❸ △

Grange Caravan Park *(TM098353)* The
Grange Signposted ☎Colchester
(0206) 298567 Apr–Oct rs Nov–Mar no
bookings Last arrival 22.00hrs

*A level, grassy site with mature trees and
bushes situated in hilly woodland with
some moorland nearby. 3m off A12
between Colchester and Ipswich.*

8acres 145pitches 55static 90🏕 £5.80
10🏕 £5 50▲£5.80 (awnings)
40🚐⏱ late arrivals enclosure 40wc lit
all night 3cdp 🔌 washbasins hc central
hot water (🚿hc) ☺ supervised (wash
dry) iron ⟋ games room (cold storage)
licensed club/bar childrens playground
calor gas camping gaz toilet fluid
restaurant ☎ 🏪
↔ stables ⚒ ⟋launderette pub

EASTRIGGS
Dumfries & Galloway *Dumfriesshire*
Map 11 NY26

▶ ① ❶ △

Gemmel Caravan Site *(NY245666)*
Central Rd Signposted ☎(04614) 304
Apr–Sep must book Jul Last arrival
23.00 hrs Last departure 11.30hrs

*Part level, part sloping, grass site set in
meadowland and adjacent to sea and
river. 4m N of Gretna off A75.*

1½acres 30pitches SA 20🏕 £2 or
20🏕 £2 10▲£2 (awnings)
1🚐 4wc lit all night ☺ calor gas 🏪
↔ cinema ⟋ launderette

EAST RUNTON
Norfolk
Map 9 TG14

▶▶▶ ② ❶ △

Woodhill Camping Site *(TG195428)*
Laburnum Farm Signposted ☎West
Runton (026375) 323 or Cromer (0263)
512242 Etr–Sep no bookings no
caravans or motorcycles

*Gently sloping, grass site with bushes
set in meadowland adjacent to sea,
beach and the coast road (A149).*

12acres 300pitches 60🏕 240▲
(awnings)
12🚐⏱ 50wc lit all night (washbasins hc
central hot water) childrens playground
calor gas camping gaz ☎ 🏪
↔ stables golf cinema ⟋ launderette
pub

▶ ② ❷ △

Woodhill Caravan Park Signposted
Etr–Sep no bookings no motorcycle
groups

*Gently sloping grass site set in
meadowland off the main A149 coast
road.*

12acres 321pitches 116static 21🏕
300🏕 or 300▲ (awnings)
12🚐⏱ 65wc lit all night 1cdp
(washbasins hc) central hot water (🚿hc)
☺ childrens playground calor gas
camping gaz ☎ 🏪
↔ stables golf cinema ⟋ launderette
pub

EAST WORLINGTON
Devon
Map 3 SS71

▶▶▶ ② ❸ △

Yeatheridge Farm Caravan Park
(SS768110) ☎Tiverton (0884) 860330
Spring bank hol–Aug rs Etr–Spring bank
hol & 1–17 Sep must book school hols
Last arrival & departure 22.00hrs

*Gently sloping grass site with young
trees set in meadowland in rural Devon.
On B3042 ¼m W of Thelbridge Arms
Inn. Site is **not** in East Worlington village.*

7acres 50pitches 3static 50🏕 £1.73–
£3.80 or 50 🏕 £1.73–£3.80 or
50▲£1.73–£3.80 (awnings)
7🚐 Individual pitches ⏱ late arrivals
enclosure 8wc lit all night 1cdp
washbasins hc (central hot water) (🚿hc)
☺ supervised (wash spin dry iron) ⟋
games room TV (cold storage) calor gas
camping gaz ☎ 🏪
↔ ⟋ pub

EAVESTONE
North Yorkshire
Map 8 SE26

▽ ①

Hill Top Farm *(SE222678)* ☎Sawley
(076586) 662

Mainly level field close to farm.

15pitches 5🏕 ✳£1 or 5🏕 £1 10▲£1
🚐cdp

ECCLEFECHAN
Dumfries & Galloway *Dumfriesshire*
Map 11 NY17

▶▶▶▶ ③ ❷ △

Hoddom Castle Caravan Park
(NY154729) Hoddom Signposted

☎(05763) 251 Apr–Oct must book peak periods Last arrival 21.30hrs Last departure 08.00hrs no motorcycles no single sex groups

Predominantly touring site created within the grounds of Hoddom Castle, the keep and outhouses now incorporate the site amenities. Situated 2m SW of Hoddom Bridge which carries the B725 over the River Annan.

12acres 190 pitches 29static SA 190🚐£3–£4.10 or 190🚐£2.80–£3.60 or 190▲£2.80–£4.10 (awnings)

37🚐 Individual pitches late arrivals enclosure 40wc lit all night 1cdp washbasins hc 🛁hc ☺ supervised (wash spin dry iron) games room CTV (cold storage) licensed bar childrens playground calor gas camping gaz toilet fluid restaurant ☎ fishing battery charging 9 hole golf course 🛒

ECCLESTON (GREAT)
Lancashire
Map 7 SD43

▶ 🚻 ➊ ⚠

Meadowcroft Caravan Park
(SD405403) Garstang Rd Signposted
☎(0995) 70266 Mar–Oct must book Last arrival 22.00hrs no tents

A mainly residential site located on A586 in pleasant open countryside. 6m E of Blackpool on A586.

½acre 5pitches 40static 5🚐 or 5🚐 awnings ltr

2🚐 9wc lit all night washbasins hc (🛁hc) ☺ supervised (spin dry) iron cold storage childrens playground calor gas camping gaz toilet fluid ☎

↔ stables golf ⏳ launderette pub 🛒

EDALE
Derbyshire
Map 7 SK18

▶ ▶ 🚻 ➊ ⚠

Coopers Caravan Site *(SK121859)*
Newfold Farm, Edale Village ☎Hope Valley (0433) 70372 All year must book public hols Last arrival 23.00hrs Last departure noon no groups of motorcyclists

Situated behind a working farm with an entrance through the farm yard from the village with Post Office and shop actually inside the entrance. Grassed rising land divided by a wall into two fields culminating in the 2062ft Edale Moor of the Peak itself. Facilities are converted or additional to the original farm buildings.

6acres 135pitches 11static 15🚐£2.75 120🚐£2.75 or 120▲£2.75 (awnings)

3🚐 16wc lit all night 1cdp washbasins hc (🛁hc) ☺ supervised calor gas camping gaz paraffin ☎ 🛒

↔ stables pub

EDGCUMBE
Cornwall
Map 2 SW73

▶ ▶ ▶ ②➊⚠

Retanna Country Park *(SW720331)*
Signposted ☎Constantine (0326)
40643 Apr–Oct must book peak periods Last arrival 22.00hrs Last departure 22.00hrs

This well-kept site is situated on the A394 4m E of Helston.

5acres 44pitches 26static 44🚐 or 44🚐 or 44▲ (awnings)

6🚐 Individual pitches ⚲ late arrivals enclosure 10wc lit all night 1cdp 12 washbasins hc 2 central hot water 8🛁hc 2spin 2iron cold storage childrens playground calor gas camping gaz toilet fluid ☎ ⊞

↔ stables golf ⚓ cinema ⏳ launderette pub

see advertisement on page 134

EDGERLEY
Shropshire
Map 7 SJ31

▶ 🚻 ➊ ⚠

Royal Hill *(SJ352175)* ☎Nesscliffe (074381) 242 Apr–Oct must book Last arrival 23.00hrs

1½acres 15pitches 5static SA 5🚐£2 or 5🚐£2 or 5▲£2 awnings

1🚐 Individual pitches ⚲ late arrivals enclosure 4wc lit all night 1cdp central hot water (🛁hc) ☺ supervised cold storage licensed club/bar childrens playground calor gas

↔ stables ⏳ pub 🛒

EDINBANE
Isle of Skye, Highland *Inverness-shire*
Map 13 NG35

LOCH GRESHONNISH
CARAVAN AND CAMPING SITE
Borve: Arnisort:
Edinbane: Skye.
Tel: (047082) 230.

12 miles on A850, Portee/ Dunvegan Road.
Flush toilets, H&C showers, washing & drying facilities, shaver points. Fishing, boating.

Proprietor: Joyce MacDonald.

▶ ▶ ②➋⚠

Loch Greshonnish Caravan Site *(NG343524)* ☎(047082) 230 Apr–Oct Last arrival 22.00hrs

12 miles from Edinbane on the A850 Portree/Dunvegan road.

5acres 60pitches 3static 25🚐 5🚐 30▲ awnings

3🚐 9wc lit all night 1cdp 8washbasins hc (4🛁hc) 2☺ (spin dry)

↔ ⚓ 🛒

EDINBURGH
Lothian *Midlothian*
Map 11 NT27

▶ ▶ ▶ ②➌⚠

Mortonhall Caravan Park *(NT265680)* 30 Frogston Road East Signposted ☎031–664 1533 28 Mar–Oct must book Jul–7 Sept Last arrival 22.30hrs Last departure noon

Located on the S side of Edinburgh within 20 minutes' car ride of the city centre, this site is part of a 200-acre estate surrounding the 18th-C Mortonhall mansion designed by Robert Adam.

15acres 250pitches 250🚐 or 250🚐 or 250▲ (awnings)

8🚐 Individual pitches late arrivals enclosure 48wc lit all night 1cdp 🚽 washbasins hc 🛁hc ☺ supervised (wash spin dry) iron games room CTV (cold storage) licensed bar childrens playground calor gas camping gaz toilet fluid cafe restaurant ☎ 🛒

↔ stables golf cinema ⏳ launderette pub

see advertisement on page 132

▶ ▶ ▶ 🚻 ➋ ⚠

Little France Caravan Park *(NT289704)* 219 Old Dalkeith Rd Signposted ☎031–664 4742 Apr–Oct must book Jul & Aug Last arrival 22.30hrs Last departure 14.00hrs

Spacious touring site on southern fringe of city, on A68 3m from city centre.

8acres 287 pitches 287🚐£5 or 287🚐£5 or 287▲£5 awnings ltr

6🚐 44wc lit all night 1cdp washbasin hc 🛁hc ☺ (wash spin) iron (cold storage) calor gas camping gaz toilet fluid ☎ 🛒

↔ stables golf cinema ⏳ launderette pub

see advertisement on page 132

EDMONTON (N.9)
Gt London
Map 4 TQ39
See under London for details

ELGIN
Grampian *Morayshire*
Map 15 NJ26

▶ ▶ ▶ ②➊⚠

Riverside Caravan Park *(NJ197627)*
West Rd ☎(0343) 2813 Apr–Oct →

no bookings Last arrival mdnt Last departure noon

Pleasant grassy site on banks of River Lossie, partly surrounded by trees. Situated ½m W of Elgin on A96.

1½ acres 82 pitches 10 static 52🚐 or 52🚐 30▲ awnings ltr

5🏕️ Individual pitches for caravans Ⓐ 11wc lit all night 1cdp washbasins hc (🚽hc🚿hc)☺ supervised wash spin iron games room childrens playground calor gas camping gaz toilet fluid ☎ 🖳

⌁ golf ⚘cinema ♪ launderette pub
see previous page for entry

▶ ② ❶ ⚠
Spynie Hall Caravan Site *(NJ182641)*
Spynie Signposted Apr–Sep no bookings Last arrival 21.30hrs no single sex groups

A simple site in attractive position on hillside overlooking Moray Firth.

2 acres 12 pitches 6🚐 £23 🚐 £23▲ £2 awnings ltr

1🏕️4wc lit all night 1cdp 4 washbasins hc 1☺ supervised

⌁ stables golf ⚘cinema ♪ launderette pub 🖳

ELVASTON
Derbyshire
Map 8 SK43

▶ ▶ ② ❸ ⚠
Elvaston Castle Park Site *(SK413332)*
Borrowdale Rd Apply to: Assistant Manager Club Sites, The Caravan Club, East Grinstead House, East Grinstead, W. Sussex RH19 1UA Signposted

---

MORTONHALL CARAVAN PARK
IN THE BEAUTIFUL CITY OF EDINBURGH

Regional Winner
TRAIL CAMPSITE
OF THE YEAR
AWARD 1981

The Caravan Park, by repute one of the best in the U.K., is situated within the beautiful parkland of a large private estate only 20 minutes by car from the centre of Edinburgh. The site has every modern amenity including a well-stocked licensed mini-market, top-class bar with meal service, games room, TV lounge and a large well-equipped laundry, and is an ideal base for those wishing to see the historic capital of Scotland, or those on their way north or south.

'Member The Best of Britain Caravan & Camping Parks'

Write now for free colour brochure and 1982 tariffs to: MORTONHALL CARAVAN PARK, Frogston Road East, Edinburgh EH16 6TT. Tel: 031-664 1533.

EDINBURGH

LITTLE FRANCE
CARAVAN PARK
OLD DALKEITH ROAD
031-664 4742

★

Situated on the A68 South of the City. Direct access to City Centre (3 miles) by car or public transport.

★

All of Edinburgh's amenities easily accessible from the caravan site, ie.:

- ★ Royal Commonwealth Pool
- ★ Castle
- ★ Royal Mile
- ★ Meadowbank Sports Centre
- ★ Museum
- ★ Botanic Garden
- ★ Theatres, Cinemas, etc.

★

There is a laundry room and licensed shop on the park.

★

Opposite park is lounge bar which provides bar lunches and evening meals.

☎Derby (0332) 73735 frMar must book peak periods Last departure noon no tents

Situated within country park, the site is run by the Caravan and Camping Club. The thoughtful layout and range of amenities make this a very attractive site. Off B5010, which runs between the A6, 2m W of Shardlow and Borrowash on A6005.

5acres 90pitches 90🚐 or 90🚐 (awnings)

Individual pitches wc ⋔ hc ☺ supervised calor gas ☎

↪ ♪ launderette

ELVINGTON
North Yorkshire
Map 8 SE64

▽ ③

Lake Cottage *(SE684469)* ☎(090485) 255

Level grass paddock with shrubs and trees at lakeside.

13pitches 13🚐 ✳£1.50 or 13🚐 £1.50 or 13▲£1.50

2⚘ cdp game and coarse fishing

ELY
Cambridgeshire
Map 5 TL58

▽ ①

Ely Rugby Club *(TL532815)* Downham Rd ☎(0353) 2156

Level winter playing fields with views of Ely Cathedral.

30 pitches 5🚐 ✳£1.50 or 5🚐£1.50 25▲ fr50p

⚘ cdp

EVERSHOT
Dorset
Map 3 ST50

►►► ② ❷ △

Clay Pigeon Tourist Park *(ST609024)* Wardon Hill (A37) ☎(093583) 492 16 Mar–Oct must book Jul & Aug

A level grassy site overlooking the Blackmore Vale, off A37 adjacent to Clay Pigeon Lodge Cafe.

Elvaston
—
Eype

3½acres 60pitches SA 60🚐£4 or 60 🚐£3.50 or 60▲£3.50 (awnings) ltr

3⚘ 6wc lit all night 1cdp 🚿 washbasins hc (⋔hc) ☺ supervised cold storage licensed club/bar calor gas camping gaz toilet fluid cafe restaurant 🍴

↪ pub

EVESHAM
Hereford & Worcester
Map 4 SP04

►►► ② ❷ △

Weir Meadow Holiday Park *(SP047443)* Lower Leys Signposted ☎(0386) 2417 Apr–Oct must book public hols Last arrival & departure dusk no tents no single sex groups no motorcycles

A town centre caravan site situated on the banks of the River Avon. Turn off Port Street by Workmen's Bridge in Evesham, A44.

4acres 100pitches 70 static 100🚐£3.40 or 100 🚐£3.40 (awnings)

7⚘ 75wc lit all night 1cdp 🚿 washbasins hc ⋔hc ☺ (wash spin dry iron) cold storage private beach calor gas paraffin toilet fluid 🍴

↪ stables golf ⛳ cinema ♪ launderette pub

EWHURST GREEN
East Sussex
Map 5 TQ72

► ② ❶ △

Lordine Court Caravan Park *(TQ802227)* Signposted ☎Staplecross (058083) 209 May–Sep rs Mar–May & Oct Last arrival 22.00 hrs Last departure noon ✗ nc18 no motorcycles

Situated away from villages and main roads in the heart of the Sussex countryside. Off B2165 midway between A28 and A229.

4½ acres 120pitches 150static SA 120🚐£3–£3.50 or 120 🚐£3–£3.50 or 120▲£3–£3.50 (awnings) ltr

4⚘ ⊘ 10wc (central hot water ➡hc ⋔hc ☺) iron 🎣 games room licensed club/bar

---

childrens playground calor gas camping gaz restaurant ☎ bar food 🍴

↪ stables ♪ launderette pub

EXFORD
Somerset
Map 3 SS83

► ② ❶ △

Westermill *(SS824398)* ☎(064383) 238 Spring Bank Hol–Oct rs May–Spring Bank Hol booking advisable peak periods no caravans

Site situated alongside river with partial wooded areas, in sheltered valley in the heart of Exmoor. Four waymarked walks over 500 acre working farm. Leave Exford on the Porlock road, after ¼m fork left. Continue for 2¼m along valley past another campsite until 'Westermill' sign seen on tree, then fork left.

6acres 60pitches 7static SA 60 🚐£4.02 or 60▲£4.02 awnings

3⚘ 12wc (1 central hot water ⋔hc) ☺ supervised (spin) (cold storage) calor gas camping gaz ☎ 🍴

↪ stables ♪

EYPE
Dorset
Map 3 SY49

►►► ② ❸ △

Highlands End Farm Caravan Park *(SY454913)* Signposted ☎Bridport (0308) 22139 Apr–Sep must book Last arrival 22.00hrs Last departure noon

Well kept grass site on high ground adjacent to National Trust land and overlooking Lyme Bay.

8acres 120pitches 160static 20🚐 fr£4.20 or 20 🚐 or 100▲ fr£3.60 (awnings)

7⚘ ⊘ 36wc lit all night 🚿 washbasins (⋔hc) ☺ supervised spin iron 🅿 calor gas camping gaz ☎ 🍴

↪ stables golf ⛳ cinema ♪ launderette pub

EYTON
Clwyd
Map 7 SJ34

▶▶▶▶ ③ ❸ ⚠

Plassey Touring Caravan Park
(SJ452353) Signposted ☎Bangor-on-Dee (0978) 780277 Mar–Oct must book public hols Last arrival 22.00hrs Last departure noon no unaccompanied groups of teenagers.

A mainly level grassy site with trees, woodland and meadowland, off the B5426.

6acres 120pitches SA 120🚐 fr£3 50 or 120🚐 fr£3.50 or 120⚑ fr£3.50 (awnings)

6⚶ Individual pitches late arrivals enclosure 15wc lit all night 2cdp ❷ washbasins hc (🚿hc) ☺ supervised (wash) spin (dry) iron (🔲) games room (cold storage) (licensed club) childrens playground calor gas camping gaz toilet fluid ☎ ⊞ sauna, badminton court, pitch & putt 🏌

↦ stables golf ✦ launderette pub

FAIRWOOD
West Glamorgan
Map 2 SS59

▶ ② ❷ ⚠

Blackhills **Caravan Park** (SS581915)
Blackhills Rd, Fairwood Common
Signposted ☎Swansea (0792) 207065

Apr–Oct must book peak periods Last arrival 21.00hrs Last departure noon

Mainly level grass site set in meadowland. 6m SW of Swansea along A4118 then unclass. road for 1m.

▶▶▶

Quiet, family-run eight acre park with luxury caravans for hire and sale, together with numbered pitches for tourers and tents. Situated midway between Falmouth and Helston, ideal for exploring West Cornwall.

Phone Falmouth (0326) 40643 for brochure or write:
Retanna Country Park, Edgcumbe, Helston, Cornwall TR13 0EJ

12acres 300pitches 120static 100🚐 100🚐 100⚑ (awnings)

8⚶ ⚙ 50wc lit all night 3cdp ❷ washbasins hc central hot water (🚿hc) ☺ (wash spin dry) childrens playground calor gas camping gaz ☎ 🏌

↦ stables golf launderette pub

FAKENHAM
Norfolk
Map 9 TF92

▶▶▶ ② ❷ ⚠

Crossways Caravan Park (TF973328)
Holt Rd, Little Snoring Signposted ☎Thursford (032877) 335 21 Mar–Oct must book Last arrival 21.00hrs Last departure noon no tents

A level site with mature trees and bushes set in woodlands and near the sea. 3m E of Fakenham on A148.

1½acres 25 pitches 25🚐£3 or 25 🚐£3 (awnings)

2⚶ Individual pitches late arrivals enclosure 7wc lit all night 1cdp ❷ (4washbasins hc) (2🚿hc) 1☺ supervised iron (cold storage) calor gas camping gaz ☎ 🏌

↦ ✦ launderette pub

FALMOUTH
Cornwall
Map 2 SW83
See sketch map

▶▶▶ 🅰🔢⚫⚠

Maen Valley Caravan Park *(SW788310)*
Signposted ☎(0326) 312190 Whit–Sep
rs Etr–Whit & Oct must book Jul & Aug
Last arrival 22.00hrs Last departure
noon

*This site is situated in a picturesque
valley with a stream. 1½m SW of
Falmouth but within walking distance of
Swanpool beach.*

6acres 150pitches 138 static SA
150🚐£3.50–£5.00 or 150🚐£3.50–
£5.20 or 150▲£3.50–£5.20 (awnings)
30🚐 late arrivals enclosure 32wc lit all
night 3cdp 🚐 32washbasins hc (🚿hc)
☺supervised (wash spin dry iron)
games room cold storage licensed club/
bar childrens playground calor gas
camping gaz toilet fluid ☎ ⊞ 🧺

↔ stables golf 🛫 cinema 🍴
launderette pub

▶▶▶ 🅰🔢❶⚠

Golden Bank Caravans *(SW794313)*
(No. 1 Site) Swanpool Rd Signposted
☎(0326) 312103 Etr–Oct must book
Jun–Aug Last arrival 22.00hrs Last
departure 10.00hrs no single sex groups
no tents

*Gently sloping, grass site with mature
trees and bushes. Set in meadowland,
the site is adjacent to the main road.*

2acres 6pitches 40static 6🚐£3–£6 or
6🚐£3–£6 awnings ltr
3🐾 Individual pitches 7wc lit all night
1cdp washbasins hc central hot water
(🚿hc) ☺ supervised (wash spin) iron
cold storage calor gas camping gaz
cafe restaurant ☎ 🧺

↔ stables golf 🛫 cinema 🍴
launderette pub

▶▶▶ 🅰🔢❷⚠

Tremorvah *(SW798313)* Swanpool
Signposted ☎(0326) 312103 May–Oct
must book Jul & Aug Last arrival
22.00hrs Last departure 10.00hrs no
caravans no motorvans no single sex
groups

*Pleasant site situated near the
Swanpool; trees and bushes
predominate in this meadowland setting.
Adjacent to sea and beach.*

3acres 72pitches SA 72▲£3–£6 ltr
6🐾 late arrivals enclsoure 13wc lit all
night 1cdp washbasins hc central hot
water (🚿hc) ☺ supervised (wash spin
dry) iron cold storage calor gas camping
gaz cafe restaurant hair dryers 🧺

↔ stables golf 🛫 cinema 🍴
launderette pub

Humberside
Map 8 SE75

▶▶ 🅰🔢⚫⚠

Fangfoss Old Station Caravan Park
(SE747527) Old Station House
Signposted ☎Wilberfoss (07595) 491
Apr–mid Oct Last arrival 23.00hrs Last
departure noon

*The Park is sited on the old railway
station and goods yard in a rural
situation. The railway lines have been
removed and the caravans are pitched
on what was the track and goods yard
alongside the platforms. The station
master's house forms the reception.
Tents are pitched on an adjacent
attractive grasssy area with hedges and
tree screens.*

4½acres 45pitches SA 45🚐✳fr£2.60
or 45🚐 fr£2.60 or 45▲ fr£2.30
(awnings)

6🐾 Individual pitches ⊘ 9wc lit all night
1cdp washbasins hc (🚿hc ☺ supervised
(cold storage) childrens playground
calor gas camping gaz toilet fluid 🧺

↔ stables 🛫cinema 🍴 launderette pub

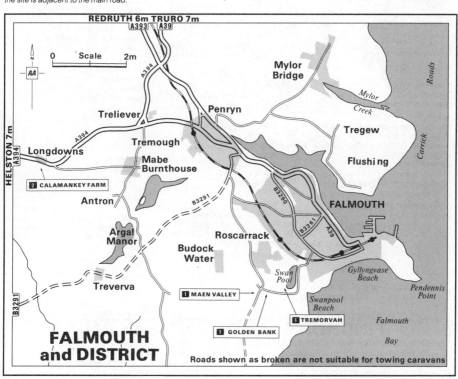

REDRUTH 6m TRURO 7m
A393 A39

N AA
0 Scale 2m

HELSTON 7m
A394

Mylor Bridge

Mylor Creek

Treliever

Penryn

Tregew

A394

Tremough

Longdowns

Mabe Burnthouse

Flushing

Carrick Roads

2 CALAMANKEY FARM

B3291

Antron

B3290

FALMOUTH

Argal Manor

Roscarrack

B3361 A39

Budock Water

Swan Pool

Gyllyngvase Beach

Pendennis Point

B3291

Treverva

1 MAEN VALLEY

Swanpool Beach

1 TREMORVAH

Falmouth

1 GOLDEN BANK

Bay

FALMOUTH and DISTRICT

Roads shown as broken are not suitable for towing caravans

Sites listed under: **1** Falmouth   **2** Long Downs

FAR FOREST
Hereford & Worcester
Map 7 SO77

▶ ☑ ❷ △

Acre Farm Caravan Park *(SO720748)*
Signposted ☏Rock (0299) 266458
Apr–Oct booking advisable mid summer
Last arrival 22.00hrs no cars by
caravans no awnings no tents

*Part level, part sloping, grass site with
varied trees, set in hilly woodland
country. Situated 300yds off the A4117
Ludlow Road.*

8pitches 85static 8🚐£3.45 or 8🚐£3.45
12🚏 Individual pitches wc (🏠hc)
supervised childrens playground calor
gas pony rides

↔ stables ✦ pub 🏠

FAZELEY
Staffordshire
Map 4 SK20

▶ ① ❶ △

Drayton Manor Park *(SK195014)*
Signposted Etr–Oct no bookings Last
departure 10.00hrs no groups of young
people no motorcycles

*Gently sloping, grass site with wooded
parkland and lakes. Within 160 acre
entertainment park with zoo etc.
Adjacent to A5 and A4091.*

4acres 75pitches 75static SA 75🚐£2.80
or 75🚐£2.80 or 75▲£2.80 (awnings)
6🚏 20wc 2cdp 🏠hc ☺ licensed club/
bar childrens playground cafe
restaurant ☏

↔ golf ⚓ cinema launderette pub 🏠

FENNY BENTLEY
Derbyshire
Map 7 SK14

▶ ▶ ▶ ☑ ❶ △

Highfield Caravan Park *(SK168506)*
Highfield Farm Signposted ☏Thorpe
Cloud (033529) 228 Mar–Oct must book
public hols Last arrival 22.00hrs Last
departure 14.00hrs no single sex groups
no motorcycles

55pitches 50static SA 55🚐£2.80 or
55🚐£2.80 55▲£2.80 (awnings)

8🚏 Individual pitches ◎ 21wc 2cdp
washbasins hc central hot water 🏠hc ☺
(cold storage) childrens playground
calor gas camping gaz

↔ stables golf ✦ launderette pub 🏠

Bank Top Farm *(SK181498)* ☏Thorpe
Cloud (033529) 250 Etr–Sep must book
peak periods Last arrival 22.00hrs Last
departure 15.00hrs no unaccompanied
teenagers

*Sloping grass site on working dairy farm,
set in hilly meadowland country just off
B5056.*

36pitches 15static 36🚐£2.80 or
36🚐£2.80 or 36▲£2.80 (awnings) ltr

3🚏 9wc lit all night 1cdp 2washbasins
hc (2 central hot water) (🏠hc) ☺ (cold
storage) 🏠

↔ stables golf ✦ launderette pub

FILEY
North Yorkshire
Map 8 TA18
See Scarborough sketch map

▶ ▶ ▶ ① ❷ △

Filey Brigg Touring Caravan Site
(TA121811) Arndale Apply to:
Department of Tourism & Amenities,
Londesborough Lodge, The Crescent,
Scarborough, N. Yorks. Signposted
☏Scarborough (0723) 66212 25 Mar–
Sep booking advisable Spring Bank &
School Hols, wkly bookings only Jul &
Aug Last arrival 19.00hrs & 21.00hrs Fri
& Sat Last departure noon no tents no
unaccompanied under 18's

*A level, grass site with mature trees near
the sea and beach, located within a
country park.*

9acres 122pitches 122🚐 or 122🚐
(awnings)

5🚏 late arrivals enclosure 16wc lit all
night 1cdp 20washbasins hc 1central
hot water (8🏠hc) 8☺ supervised (wash
dry) calor gas camping gaz toilet fluid
☏ mini golf 🏠

↔ stables golf ⚓ cinema ✦
launderette pub

FINDHORN
Grampian *Morayshire*
Map 14 NJ06

▶ ▶ ▶ ▶ ① ❷ △

Findhorn Bay Caravan Park
(NJ048637) Signposted Jul–Sep rs Oct–
Jun no bookings Last arrival 20.00hrs
Last departure noon

*A level, grass and sand site near sea
and beach.*

10acres 130pitches 175static 130🚐 or
130🚐 or 130▲ (awnings)

4🚏◎ 38wc lit all night 2cdp
45washbasins hc (4central hot water
13🏠hc) 4☺ (2wash 1dry iron) calor gas
camping gaz toilet fluid ☏ ⊞ theatre/
cinema 🏠

↔ stables golf ✦ ✦ launderette

▶ ▶ ☑ ❷ △

Findhorn Sands Caravan Park
(NJ040647) Signposted ☏(03093)
2324 Apr–Oct no bookings Last arrival
19.00hrs Last departure 19.00hrs

*Mainly level site with bushes set in
moorland and facing Moray Firth; 4m N
of Forres on B9011.*

8acres 50pitches 150static 50🚐£3–£4
or 50🚐£3–£4 or 50▲£3–£4 awnings ltr

1🚏 14wc lit all night 1cdp washbasins
hc (🏠hc) ☺ wash spin dry 🏠

↔ golf ⚓ cinema ✦ launderette pub

FINDOCHTY
Grampian *Banffshire*
Map 15 NJ46

▶ ☑ ❷ △

Findochty Caravan Site *(NJ458679)*
Signposted May–20 Sep booking
advisable peak periods Last arrival
20.00hrs Last departure noon

*A neat touring site set on sea front
overlooking rocky bay, on the edge of a
quaint fishing village.*

3acres 27pitches 22🚐£3.19 or
22🚐£3.19 5▲£2.53–£3.19 (awnings)
ltr

2🚏 Individual pitches ◎ 6wc lit all night
1cdp washbasins hc (🏠hc) (wash)
licensed bar/club childrens playground
calor gas camping gaz 🏠

↔ golf ⚓ ✦ 🏠

FISHGUARD
Dyfed
Map 2 SM93

▶ ▶ ☑ ❷

Tregroes Touring Park *(SM942361)*
Tregroes Signposted ☏(0348) 872316
Etr–Oct booking advisable in high
season

*Well-drained elevated grassy site with
views over Fishguard harbour, situated
on a working farm. Located on edge of
National Park. Signposted from A40 and
A487.*

5acres 45 pitches SA 45🚐£4 or
45🚐£4 or 45▲£4 awnings ltr

4☊ Individual pitches ⊘ 9wc lit all night
1cdp 🔌 washbasins hc 🚿hc ☉
childrens playground calor gas camping
gaz

↔ stables ⅄ cinema ✈ launderette
pub 🍴

FLEET
Dorset
Map 3 SY68

▶▶▶ 🔢 ❶ ⚠

Sea Barn Farm Camping Site
(SY626805) Signposted ☎Weymouth
(0305) 782218 Whit–Sep rs 16 Mar–Whit
& Oct booking advisable school hols no
caravans or motorcaravans

*Spacious level site with panoramic views
of sea and country; overlooking Lyme
Bay and the Chesil Bank.*

11acres 250pitches 250▲£1.70–£3.50
ltr

8☊ 26wc lit all night 1cdp (🚿hc) ☉
supervised (wash spin dry) iron games
room CTV (cold storage) childrens
playground calor gas camping gaz ☎

↔ stables golf ✈ launderette pub

▶▶▶ 🔢 ❷ ⚠

West Fleet Holiday Farm (SY627811)
Signposted ☎Weymouth (0305)
786242 Etr–Oct must book mid July–
Aug Last arrival 22.00hrs Last departure
noon no caravans or motorvans

*Part level, part sloping grass site with
young trees and bushes, set in
meadowland, adjacent to lake and sea.
From Weymouth take B3157 Bridport
road for 3½m, turn left at Fleet signs, site
is 1m on right before Moonfleet Manor
hotel.*

12acres 250pitches 250▲£1.90–£3.20

6☊⊘ late arrivals enclosure 26wc lit all
night 2cdp (washbasins hc) (🚿hc) ☉
(wash spin dry iron) ⌖ (games room)
TV cold storage childrens playground
calor gas camping gaz paraffin toilet
fluid ☎ ⊞ 🍴

↔ stables golf launderette pub

FLEET HARGATE
Lincolnshire
Map 9 TF32

▶▶ 🔢 ❸ ⚠

Matopos Caravan & Camp Site
(TF388248) Main St Signposted
☎Holbeach (0406) 22910 Mar–Oct
booking advisable early Jun (Spalding
Flower Show) Last arrival 22.30hrs Last
departure 14.00hrs no ball games

*Level grass site with mature hedges and
trees.*

1½acres 25pitches 25🚐£4.18 or 25
🚐£3.63 or 25▲£3.96 (awnings)

1☊ Individual pitches 5wc lit all night
1cdp 6washbasins hc 4🚿hc 2☉
supervised calor gas 🍴

↔ golf ✈ launderette pub

FLEETWOOD
Lancashire
Map 7 SD34

▶ 🔢 ❶ ⚠

Broadwater Holiday Centre
(SD325455) Fleetwood Rd Signposted
☎(03917) 2796 Spring Bank Hol–Sep rs
Mar–Spring Bank Hol & Oct Last arrival
mdnt Last departure 11.00hrs 🏍 no
single sex groups no tents

*A large, busy commercial site situated
on the main road between Thornton and
Fleetwood, A587.*

45pitches 409static 45🚐£3 or 45 🚐£3
(awnings) ltr

16☊ Individual pitches 42wc lit all night
washbasins hc 🚿hc ☉ supervised
(wash dry) TV cold storage licensed
club/bar calor gas toilet fluid ☎ ⊞
amusement arcade fish & chip shop
video room & hairdressers 🍴

↔ golf ⅄ ✈ laundrette

FLOOKBURGH
Cumbria
Map 7 SD37

▶▶▶ 🔢 ❶ ⚠

Lakeland Caravan Park (SD372743)
Moor Ln Signposted ☎(044 853) 235
25 Jun–Sep rs Mar–25 Jun & Oct
booking advisable public hols Last
arrival 21.00hrs Last departure 11.00hrs
🏍 (mid Jul–mid Aug) no single sex
groups under 18yrs

*Flat, grassy site situated about ½ mile
from Morecambe Bay.*

3½acres 100pitches 510static 100🚐 or
100🚐 30▲ awnings ltr

4☊ Individual pitches ⊘ 20wc lit all
night 2cdp washbasins hc 🚿hc ☉
supervised (wash spin dry iron ▭)
games room) (cold storage) licensed
club childrens playground calor gas
camping gaz toilet fluid cafe ☎ 🍴

↔ stables launderette pub

FOCHABERS
Grampian *Morayshire*
Map 15 NJ35

▶▶▶ 🔢 ❷ ⚠

Burnside Caravan Site (NJ350580)
Keith Rd Signposted ☎(0343) 820362
Apr–Oct Last departure noon
no motorcycles

*This site is on level ground amidst
natural landscaping with a burn flowing
through. ½m E of town off the A96.*

120pitches 120🚐 or 120🚐 or 120▲
awnings

8☊ Individual pitches ⊘ 20wc lit all
night 2cdp 20washbasins hc 2central
hot water 8🚿hc 8☉ wash spin iron ▭ ⅌
games room childrens playground calor
gas ☎ 🍴

↔ golf ✈ pub

FOLKESTONE
Kent
Map 5 TR23
*See sketch map on page 138. See also
Densole*

▶▶▶ 🔢 ❶ ⚠

Camping Club Site (TR247377) The
Warren Signposted ☎(0303) 55093
Apr–Sep must book Whit & Jul–Aug
Last arrival 21.00hrs Last departure
noon

*This site is situated at the foot of the
world famous 'White Cliffs' and
immediately adjacent to a sandy beach.
The pitches are on different levels, some
of which are secluded and sheltered.*

4acres 100pitches awnings

5☊⊘ 16wc lit all night washbasins hc
central hot water (🚿hc) ☉ supervised
(cold storage) camping gaz ☎ 🍴

▶▶ 🔢 ❶ ⚠

**Little Switzerland Camping & Caravan
Site** (TR247377) The Warren Signposted
☎(0303) 52168 Mar–Oct booking
advisable public hols & Jul–Aug Last
departure noon no cars by tents

*Situated on high ground overlooking the
sea, amidst mature trees and well
sheltered from the west winds by steep
hills.*

15pitches 24static 15🚐 or 15🚐 or
15▲ (awnings)

6☊⊘ 13wc lit all night 1cdp
washbasins hc (🚿hc) ☉ supervised
cold storage calor gas licensed
restaurant 🍴

↔ stables golf ⅄ cinema ✈
launderette pub

FORESTRY COMMISSION CARAVAN
AND CAMPSITES
Forestry Commission sites which come
within the scope of the Automobile
Association's Caravan and Campsite
classification scheme are listed in this
guide. In addition there are entries for
sites which are deliberately maintained
as minimum-facility sites and are
suitable for the camper or caravanner
who prefers to be completely self-
sufficient and carries his own chemical
toilet.
The following pamphlets give details of
all recreational facilities in forests:
*See Your Forests–Northern England
See Your Forests–Southern England
See Your Forest–Wales
See Your Forest–Scotland
Forestry Commission Cabins and
Holiday Houses*
Copies will be sent on application to the
Forestry Commission, 231 Corstorphine
Road, Edinburgh EH12 7AT

FORFAR
Tayside *Angus*
Map 15 NO45

▶▶ 🔢 ❶ ⚠

Lochside Caravan Park (NO450505)
Signposted ☎(0307) 62528 Apr–mid →

Oct must book Jul & Aug Last arrival 21.00hrs Last departure noon no tents no motorcycles no single sex groups

Pleasant, well laid-out touring site just off the Ring Road, close to recreation centre.

48pitches SA 48🚐 or 48 🚐 (awnings) ltr

4🏕 Individual pitches 11wc lit all night 1cdp 6washbasins hc 4🛁hc 2☺ (1 wash 1 spin) childrens playground mobile shop 🛒

↔ golf cinema ⚓ launderette pub

FORT WILLIAM
Highland *Inverness-shire*
Map 14 NN17

▶ ▶ ▶ ③ ❶ △
Glen Nevis Caravan & Camping Park
(NN124722) Glen Nevis Signposted

☎(0397) 2191 9 Apr–6 Oct Last arrival 22.30hrs Last departure noon no large groups of motorcyclists

At the foot of Ben Nevis, bordered by ragged pine-covered forests, the site is 2m from Fort William, in this most impressive glen. Off A82.

19acres 380pitches 30static 150🚐£3.10–£4.30 or 150 🚐£2.70–£3.80 230▲£2.80–£4 (awnings)

13🏕 ⊘ 62wc lit all night 1cdp 16🔌 washbasins hc (🛁hc) ☺ supervised (wash spin dry) iron (licensed bar) childrens playground calor gas camping gaz toilet fluid restaurant ☎ freezer packs 🛒

↔ stables ⚓ launderette pub

FOWEY
Cornwall
Map 2 SX15

▶ ① ❶ △
Penhale Camping & Caravanning Park
(SX103527) ☎(072683) 3425 Apr–Oct

Part level, part sloping, mainly grassy site with trees and bushes set in meadowland adjacent to sea and beach. 2m W of Fowey on A3082.

10acres 50pitches 34static SA 50🚐 or 50🚐 or 50▲ (awnings)

12🏕 18wc lit all night 2cdp (washbasins hc 🛁hc) ☺ dry (iron cold storage) calor gas camping gaz toilet fluid ☎ 🛒

↔ stables golf ⚓ cinema ⚓ launderette pub

Sites listed under: **1** Densole   **2** Folkestone

FRASERBURGH
Grampian *Aberdeenshire*
Map 15 NJ96

▶▶ 🔟 ❷ ⚠
Kessock Road Caravan Site
(NJ999661) Esplanade, Kessock Rd
Apply to: Banff & Buchan District
Council, Leisure & Recreation Dept., 1
Church St, Macduff, Banffshire, AB41UF
Signposted ☎Macduff (0261) 32861
Apr–Sep must book Last arrival
21.00hrs Last departure 09.00hrs
*A level and grassy site near the sea and
beach, 100yds off A92 on Kessock
Road.*

70pitches 50static 30🛋 or 30 🚐 40▲
(awnings)
3🅿 12wc lit all night 1cdp 16washbasins
hc 6🚿hc 8☺ (wash spin dry) (ⓧ)
childrens playground calor gas camping
gaz paraffin toilet fluid cafe restaurant
☎ 🛒
↔ stables golf ⅄ ✎ launderette pub

▶ 🔟 ❷ ⚠
Esplanade Caravan Site *(NK000662)*
Harbour Rd Apply to: Banff & Buchan
District Council, Leisure & Recreation
Dept., 1 Church St, Macduff, Banffshire,
AB 1UF Signposted ☎Macduff (0261)
32861 May–Sep must book Last arrival
21.00hrs Last departure 09.00hrs no
tents
*Mainly level, grass and sand site, in
urban area near sea, beach and main
road.*

1¼acres 40pitches 20static 40🛋 or 40
🚐 (awnings)
2🅿 15wc lit all night 1cdp 8 washbasins
hc 🚿hc 4☺ (wash spin dry) (ⓧ)
childrens

see previous page for entries

---

playground calor gas camping gaz
paraffin toilet fluid cafe restaurant ☎ 🛒
↔ stables golf ⅄ ✎ launderette pub

FYLINGDALES ('FLASK' INN)
North Yorkshire
Map 8 NZ90

▶▶▶ ☑ ❷ ⚠
Grouse Hill Caravan Park *(NZ928002)*
Flask Bungalow Farm Signposted
☎Whitby (0947) 880543 30 Etr–Sep
must book public hols no motorcycles
*Situated in the North York Moors
National Park adjacent to A171 Whitby–
Scarborough road. Site overlooks a
wooded valley and heather-clad
moorland.*

14½acres 300pitches 180🛋 £2–£3.50
20 🚐 £2–£3.50 100▲£2–£3.50
(awnings) ltr
10🅿 Individual pitches ⓪ late arrivals
enclosure 45wc lit all night 3cdp
washbasins hc 🚿hc ☺ supervised (spin
dry games room cold storage) childrens
playground calor gas camping gaz toilet
fluid ☎ 🛒
↔ stables golf ⅄ ✎ pub

GAIRLOCH
Highland *Ross and Cromarty*
Map 14 NG87

▶▶▶ ☑ ❷ ⚠
Sands Holiday Centre *(NG758784)*
Signposted ☎(0445) 2152 Whit–mid

Sep rs Apr–Whit & mid Sep–Oct
booking advisable July & Aug Last
arrival 22.30hrs Last departure 13.00hrs
*Part level site set in moorland, 3m W of
Gairloch on B8021.*

50acres 360pitches 11 static
160🛋 £3.80 or 160 🚐 £3.50 200▲£3.80
(awnings)
10🅿 ⓦ wc lit all night 1cdp 🚿
washbasins hc (🚿hc) ☺ (wash spin dry
iron cold storage) private beach calor
gas camping gaz toilet fluid ☎ rowing
boats for hire boat slipway 🛒
↔ ⅄ ✎ launderette pub

GAIRLOCHY
Highland *Inverness-shire*
Map 14 NN18

▶ 🔟 ❷ ⚠
Gairlochy Caravan Park *(NN187835)*
Signposted ☎(039782) 229 Apr–Sep
no bookings Last departure 11.00hrs
*Site near river, loch and canal, 2m NW of
junc A82/B8004, on B8004.*

2acres 10pitches 4static SA 10🛋 or
10🚐 or 10▲ (awnings) ltr
1🅿 4wc lit all night 1cdp washbasins hc
🚿hc ☺ supervised calor gas
↔ golf ⅄ ✎ 🛒

GARTMORE
Central *Perthshire*
Map 11 NS59

▶▶ ☑ ❷ ⚠
Cobeland Campsite *(NS531989)*
Signposted ☎Aberfoyle (08772) 392
Etr–Sep booking advisable Last
departure 10.00hrs no firearms   →

Set within the Queen Elizabeth Forest Park, this grass and tree-studded site offers seclusion, views, forest walks and free fishing on the River Forth which borders the camping area.

8acres 75pitches 15static SA 75🛖 or 75🛖 or 75🛆 awnings

4🛈 14wc lit all night 1cdp washbasins hc 🛁hc ☺ ☎ 🛒
⟿ stables golf 🛥 🏌

GATEHOUSE OF FLEET
Dumfries & Galloway *Kircudbrightshire*
Map 11 NX65
See sketch map

Gartmore
═══
Gatehouse of Fleet

▶ ▶ ▶ ▣ ❷ 🛆
Anwoth Caravan & Camping Site
(NX595563) Signposted ☎Gatehouse (05574) 333 Apr–Oct Last arrival 22.00hrs Last departure noon

Compact touring site situated on southern edge of small holiday town. Although the site lies just off the main road behind garage/filling station, the trees surrounding most sides still manage to create a degree of seclusion.

3½acres 65pitches 14static 45🛖£3.30 or 45🛖£3.30 20🛆£3.30 (awnings)

5🛈 Individual pitches ☺ 13wc lit all night 1cdp 🔲 washbasins hc 🛁hc ☺ supervised (wash spin dry iron) games room (cold storage) calor gas toilet fluid 🛒

⟿ golf 🏌 launderette pub

▶ ▶ ▣ ❷ 🛆
Cardoness Caravan Site *(NX564534)*
Cardoness Estate Signposted ☎Mossyard (055724) 288 Apr–Oct must book Etr & Jul–Aug Last arrival 21.30hrs Last departure noon no tents

Beautifully situated park created out of the woodland and coastline of the Cardoness Estate, 3m SW of Gatehouse of Fleet.

GATEHOUSE OF FLEET and DISTRICT

Roads shown as broken are not suitable for towing caravans

Sites listed under: **1** Brighouse Bay **2** Gatehouse of Fleet **3** Kirkcudbright

3acres 24pitches 188static SA 24🚐£4
or 24🚙£4 (awnings)

7🅿 Individual pitches 8wc lit all night
4cdp 8washbasins hc (2🏠hc) 4☺
supervised (wash dry) (𝒫) childrens
playground private beach calor gas
toilet fluid ☎ sailing putting green 🏊

⟿ stables golf cinema ♪ launderette
pub

GATWICK AIRPORT
West Sussex
Map 4 TQ24

▽ ①

Kiln Heath (TQ312405) Antlands Ln,
Shipley Bridge, Horley (off B2037
Horley–East Grinstead road; ½m E of
Shipley Bridge approached from B2036
or B2028) ☎Horley (02934) 72637
May–Sep wknds & public hols only
booking advisable nc

*Mature woodland provides a choice of
secluded pitches on level ground amidst
the trees or on grass in small fenced
areas of cleared land.*

1acre 3 pitches 3🚐£1.50 or 3🚙£1.50
or 3▲£1.50 awnings

1🅿 1wc 1cdp

⟿ golf launderette pub 🏊

GILCRUX
Cumbria
Map 11 NY13

▶▶▶ ② ❷ ⚠

Beeches Caravan Park (NY114381)
☎Aspatria (0965) 21555 Mar–13 Nov
must book Last arrival 23.00hrs Last
departure 10.30hrs

*Small family site situated in a rural village
between the Lake District National Park
and the Solway Coast.*

⅓acre 10pitches 22static 10🚐 or 10🚙
or 10▲ (awnings) ltr

3🅿 Individual pitches 6wc lit all night
1cdp 🚽 washbasins hc (➔🏠hc) ☺
supervised (wash spin dry) iron games
room cold storage childrens playground
calor gas camping gaz ♪ sauna 🏊

⟿ stables golf cinema ♪ launderette
pub

GISBURN
Lancashire
Map 7 SD84

▶▶▶ ② ❶ ⚠

Todber Caravan Park (SD833466)
☎(02005) 322 Apr–Oct rs Mar booking
advisable public hols Last arrival
21.30hrs Last departure noon

*A rural site on sloping ground with good
views all round. An interesting steam
museum is located on the site. Situated
off A682.*

4½acres 80pitches 254static SA
70🚐£2.50 5🚙£2.50 5▲£2.50 awnings
ltr

4🅿 Individual pitches 15wc lit all night
1cdp washbasins hc 🏠hc ☺ supervised
(wash dry) (games room) (cold storage)

licensed club/bar childrens playground
calor gas camping gaz toilet fluid ☎ 🏊

⟿ pub

GISLEHAM
Suffolk
Map 5 TM58

▶ ② ❷

Chestnut Farm Touring Park
(TM510866) Signposted ☎Lowestoft
(0502) 740227 Etr–Oct booking
advisable peak periods

*Level, grass site with trees and bushes.
Set in meadowland, close to sea, beach,
river and main road. In Kessingland
follow signs for Mutford/Rushmere at S
end of village.*

3acres 30pitches SA 30🚐£2–£2.25 or
30🚙£2–£2.25 or 30▲£2–£2.25
(awnings)

5🅿 4wc lit all night 1cdp (🏠hc) ☺
supervised (cold storage) calor gas
camping gaz private fishing

⟿ stables golf 🎣 ♪ laundrette pub 🏊

▶ ① ❶ ⚠

White House Farm Caravans White
House Farm Signposted ☎Lowestoft
(0502) 740248 Apr–Oct must book
public hols

*An open, level field situated off the A12
in quiet position*

4½acres 50 pitches 50🚐£2.50
50 🚙£2.50 or 50▲£2.50 (awnings)

4🅿 6wc lit all night 1cdp washbasins hc
(🏠hc) ☺ supervised cold storage
childrens playground calor gas camping
gaz toilet fluid 🏊

⟿ stables golf 🎣 cinema ♪
launderette pub

GLAN-YR-AFON (near Corwen)
Clwyd
Map 6 SJ04

▶▶ ① ❶ ⚠

**Llawrbettws Farm Caravan &
Camping Park** (SJ016424) Signposted
☎Maerdy (049081) 224 Mar–Oct must
book Jul & Aug Last arrival 23.00hrs Last
departure 15.00 hrs

*Mainly level site with grass and mature
trees, 3m W of Corwen off A494 Bala
road.*

5acres 65pitches 70static SA 35🚐£3
10 🚙£2 20▲£2.50 (awnings) ltr

11🅿 Individual pitches ⏱ late arrivals
enclosure 14wc lit all night 1cdp 🚽
washbasins hc central hot water (🏠hc)
☺ supervised (wash) spin games room
(cold storage) childrens playground
calor gas camping gaz toilet fluid ☎ ⊞
fishing & pony riding 🏊

⟿ stables golf 🎣 cinema ♪
launderette pub

GLENCOE
Highland *Argyllshire*
Map 14 NN15

▶▶▶ ② ❷ ⚠

Glencoe Campsite (NN111578)
Signposted ☎Ballachulish (08552) 397
no bookings

*Part level, part sloping, grass, gravel
and sand site with young trees and
bushes in mountainous woodland. Direct
access to river and main road (A82).*

11¼acres 200pitches 200🚐 or 200🚙
or 200▲ awnings

5🅿 Individual pitches 16wc lit all night
1cdp 19washbasins hc (🏠hc) ☺ (wash
spin) calor gas camping gaz ☎

⟿ ♪ pub 🏊

▶▶ ② ❷ ⚠

Invercoe Caravan Site (NN098594)
Signposted ☎Ballachulish (08552) 210
Etr–mid Oct Last departure 13.00hrs

*Level, grass site set in mountains with
access to sea, beach and river. On A82
from Fort William, turn left to
Kinlochleven.*

5acres 60pitches 5static 40🚐 fr£3
10 🚙 fr£3 10▲fr£3 (awnings)

6🅿 Individual pitches 12wc lit all night
1cdp 8washbasins hc (2central hot
water) (4🏠hc) 2☺ supervised (wash
dry) iron (cold storage) private beach
calor gas camping gaz toilet fluid ☎ 🏊

⟿ 🎣 ♪ launderette pub

GLENDARUEL
Strathclyde *Argyllshire*
Map 10 NR98

▶▶▶ ③ ❷ ⚠

Glendaruel Caravan Park (NS005865)
Signposted ☎(036982) 267 Apr–Oct
booking advisable July–Aug Last arrival
22.00hrs Last departure noon

*Mainly level grass site in valley adjacent
to river and main road.*

3acres 40pitches 30static 30🚐£3.50 or
30 🚙£3.50 10▲£3.50 (awnings) ltr

3🅿 Individual pitches ⏱ late arrivals
enclosure wc lit all night 1cdp 🚽
washbasins hc 🏠hc ☺ (spin dry iron)
(games room) (cold storage) childrens
playground calor gas camping gaz toilet
fluid cafe ☎ bicycles for hire fishing 🏊

⟿ ♪ pub

see advertisement on page 142

GLENLUCE
Dumfries & Galloway *Wigtownshire*
Map 10 NX25

▶▶▶ ② ❷ ⚠

Glenluce Caravan Site (NX201576)
Signposted ☎Stranraer (0776) 2447
Etr–mid Oct booking advisable mid Jul–
mid Aug Last arrival 21.30hrs Last
departure noon no all male groups of
more than four persons

*Partly level site in sylvan surroundings
off A75 Stranraer road. Concealed
entrance at telephone kiosk in centre of
main street.*   →

2acre 40pitches 30static 25⊞fr£3 25🚐fr£3 20🅰fr£3 (awnings)

5🏕☉ 13wc lit all night washbasins hc (central hot water 🚿hc) ☺ (wash spin dry iron cold storage) childrens playground calor gas camping gaz toilet fluid 🧺

↔ stables golf 🚶 ✦ pub

GLEN TROOL
Dumfries & Galloway *Kirkcudbrightshire*
Map 10 NX47

▶▶▶ ③ ❶ ⚠
Caldons Caravan & Camping Ground
(NX400790) Apply to: Recreation Forester, Forest Office, Glen Trool, Newton Stewart, Wigtownshire DG8 6SZ Signposted ☎Bargrennan (067184) 218 Apr–Sep booking advisable public hols Last arrival 22.00hrs Last departure 13.00hrs

Level, grass site with trees and bushes, set in hilly, wooded, moorland country, with access to river and Loch Trool. 7m N of Newton Stewart off A714.

3acres 150pitches 150🚐£2.50–£3.70 or 150🚐£2.50–£3.70 or 150🅰£2.50–£3.70 awnings

11🏕 28wc lit all night 2cdp washbasins hc central hot water 🚿hc ☺ dry calor gas camping gaz ☎ 🧺

Glenluce
‒
Goonhavern

▶▶ ① ❷
Merrick Caravan Park *(NX354775)*
Signposted ☎Bargrennan (067184) 280 Mar–Oct booking advisable public hols Last arrival mdnt Last departure 11.00hrs no tents

Part level, part sloping, gravel and sand site with trees and bushes, set in mountainous moor and woodland, adjacent to river estuary and lake in the heart of Galloway National Forest Park. Off A714 Girvan–Newton Stewart road.

1acre 16pitches 24static 16⊞£3 or 16🚐£2.80 (awnings)

2🏕 9wc lit all night 1cdp 12washbasins hc (4🚿hc) 2☺ supervised games room cold storage calor gas camping gaz

↔ ✦ pub 🧺

GLYN CEIROG
Clwyd
Map 7 SJ23

▶ ② ❶ ⚠
Glan Llyn Caravan Park *(SJ208379)*
Glan Llyn ☎(069172) 320 Apr–Sep must book Last arrival 22.00hrs

Level, grass and gravel site with trees and bushes, set in hilly wood and

---

meadowland country, adjacent to river. Off B4500.

1¼acres 10pitches 5static SA 7🚐£2.90 or 7🚐£2.90 or 3🅰£2.90 (awnings)

4🏕 4wc 1cdp (🚿hc) ☺ supervised calor gas camping gaz trout fishing

↔ stables pub 🧺

GOONHAVERN
Cornwall
Map 2 SW75
See Perranporth sketch map

▶▶▶ ③ ❸ ⚠
Silverbow Park *(SW782531)* Perranwell
Signposted ☎Perranporth (087 257) 2347 Whit–Oct rs Etr–Whit must book Jul & Aug Last arrival 22.00hrs Last departure noon no single sex groups

Small, spacious and sheltered site with a gently sloping surface. Hard roads and paths serve the grassed area, which is set in meadowland. Site lies adjacent to the A3075 road, ½m S of village.

5½acres 77pitches 15static 77🚐£3.50–£6.50 or 77🚐£3.50–£6.50 or 77🅰£3.50–£6.50 awnings ltr

10🏕 Individual pitches late arrivals enclosure 15wc lit all night 2cdp 🚐 washbasins hc (🚿🚿hc) ☺ supervised (wash spin dry iron) 🎱 games room cold storage childrens playground calor gas

camping gaz toilet fluid ☎ badminton courts ⛆

⊖ stables golf ⅃ ∫ launderette pub

▶▶ ② ❷ ⚠
Rosehill Farm Tourist Park
(SW787540) Signposted ☎Perranporth (087257) 2448 Whit–Oct rs Etr–Whit booking advisable Jul & Aug Last arrival mdnt Last departure noon no motorcycles

Part level, part sloping grass site with young trees and bushes set in hilly meadowland, ½m W of village on B3285.

3acres 65pitches 65🚐£3 or 65 🚐 £3 or 65🅰£3 awnings

4🌦 Individual pitches ⊘ 9wc lit all night 1cdp washbasins hc ⋒hc ☉ supervised (wash spin dry iron) childrens playground calor gas camping gaz ⛆

⊖ stables golf ⅃ ∫ launderette pub

GORRAN
Cornwall
Map 2 SW94

▶▶▶ ② ❷ ⚠
Tregarton Farm Caravan & Camping Park *(SW984437)* ☎Mevagissey (0726) 843666 Apr–Oct must book Jul & Aug Last arrival 22.00hrs Last departure noon

Spacious site set in undulating meadowland with mature trees and bushes. The site lies 2m from the sea and adjacent to a minor road to Gorran Haven.

10acres 150pitches SA 150🚐£3.50–£5.50 or 150 🚐£3.50–£5.50 or 150🅰£3.50–£5.50 (awnings)

6🌦 15wc lit all night 1cdp 🚻 20washbasins hc·10⋒hc 4☉ supervised (spin dry iron) (cold storage) childrens playground calor gas camping gaz paraffin toilet fluid ☎ tent & camping equipment for hire ⛆

⊖ ⅃ ∫ launderette pub

GRAFHAM
Cambridgeshire
Map 4 TL16

▶▶▶ ③ ❸ ⚠
Old Manor Caravan Park *(TL157695)* Church Ln Signposted ☎Huntingdon (0480) 810264 Apr–Oct must book Last arrival 21.00hrs Last departure noon

A well kept site situated in quiet, picturesque countryside.

6acres 52pitches 10static 52🚐✳ fr£3.50 or 52 🚐 fr£3.50 or 52🅰 fr£4 (awnings)

10🌦 Individual pitches 7wc lit all night 2cdp 🚻 washbasins hc (⋒hc) ☉ supervised (wash) iron ⌁ cold storage childrens playground calor gas camping gaz ☎ ⛆

⊖ stables golf ⅃ ∫ launderette

Goonhavern
–
Gristhorpe Bay

GRAFTON FLYFORD
Hereford & Worcester
Map 3 SO95

▽ ②
Jaspers Farm *(SO971574)*
☎Himbleton (090569) 213 must book

Level orchard type paddock with mature trees in rural surroundings in the Vale of Evesham.

15pitches 5🚐✳£1 or 5 🚐 £1 10🅰£1

⛆cdp

GRAMPOUND
Cornwall
Map 2 SW94
See St Austell sketch map

▶▶▶ ② ❷ ⚠
Lynwood Camping & Caravan Park
(SW936487) Mill Lane Signposted ☎St Austell (0726) 882458 Etr–Oct rs 1 Mar–Etr must book Jul & Aug Last arrival 22.00hrs Last departure 11.00hrs

Quiet, level, site in sheltered Fal Valley; grassed surface with trees and bushes, set in highland meadow country.

1¼acres 28pitches 3static SA 14🚐£2.80–£3.50 or 14 🚐 £2.80–£3.50 or 14🅰£2.80–£3.50 (awnings)

5🌦 Individual pitches ⊘ 7wc lit all night 1cdp washbasins central hot water (⋒hc) ☉ supervised (♐) (cold storage) calor gas camping gaz paraffin toilet fluid ⛆

⊖ stables pub

GRANTOWN-ON-SPEY
Highland *Morayshire*
Map 14 NJ02

▶▶▶ ② ❷ ⚠
Grantown on Spey Camping & Caravan Site *(NJ028283)* Seafield Av Signposted ☎Grantown (0479) 2474 Apr–Sep no bookings Last departure noon

Part level and sloping, grass site with mature trees and bushes near river and set amidst hills, mountains, moorland and woodland. ½m from town centre.

15acres 115pitches 70static SA 115🚐£3 or 115 🚐 £3 40🅰£3 awnings ltr

20🌦 Individual pitches ⊘ 24wc lit all night 1cdp washbasins hc central hot water

🛶 ⋒hc ☉ supervised wash spin (dry) iron cold storage chidrens playground calor gas camping gaz toilet fluid ☎ ⊞ ⛆

⊖ stables golf ⅃ cinema ∫ launderette pub

GREAT
Placenames incorporating the word 'Great', such as Gt Malvern and Gt Yarmouth, will be found under the actual placename, *eg* Yarmouth.

GRETNA
Dumfries & Galloway *Dumfriesshire*
Map 11 NY36

▶① ⚠
Braids Caravan Site *(NY314675)* The Braids Signposted ☎(04613) 409 May–Sep rs Oct–Apr booking advisable Jul & Aug Last arrival 23.00hrs Last departure noon

Small, peaceful touring site bordered by fields on N side of B721, 1m W of Gretna Village.

1½acres 30pitches 30🚐£2 or 30 🚐 £2 or 30🅰£2 (awnings) ltr

2🌦 Individual pitches late arrivals enclosure 4wc lit all night 🚻 washbasins hc (⋒hc) ☉ supervised (wash) (cold storage) calor gas camping gaz toilet fluid ⛆

⊖ cinema ∫ pub

GRETNA GREEN
(A74 Service Area, northbound)
Dumfries & Galloway *Dumfriesshire*
Map 11 NY36

▶▶ ① ❸ ⚠
Canny Scots Caravan Park
(NY306688) Northbound Service Area Signposted ☎Gretna (04613) 598 Etr–Oct Last arrival mdnt Last departure noon

Part level, part sloping, mainly grassy site overlooking the Solway Firth. 1m N of the border on A74.

6acres 100pitches 100🚐 or 100 🚐 or 100🅰 (awnings) ltr

2🌦 15wc lit all night 1cdp washbasins hc ⋒hc childrens playground cafe restaurant ☎ petrol station ⛆

⊖ golf cinema ∫ pub

GREWELTHORPE
North Yorkshire
Map 8 SE27

▶▶ ② ❷ ⚠
Newholme Caravan Site *(SE232758)* Signposted ☎Kirkby Malzeard (076583) 225 Apr–Sep must book ✟ no motorcycles no tents

A small, peaceful farm site in rural setting and surrounded by neat hedgerows and stone walls.

3acres 10 pitches 20static SA 10🚐 or 10 🚐 (awnings) ltr

4🌦 Individual pitches 6wc 1cdp washbasins hc ☉ calor gas

⊖ stables golf pub ⛆

GRISTHORPE BAY
North Yorkshire
Map 8 TA08
See Scarborough sketch map

▶▶▶ ① ❷ ⚠
Blue Dolphin Holiday Park *(TA090830)* Signposted ☎Scarborough (0723) 512219 Spring Bank Hol–Sep rs Etr–Spring Bank Hol booking advisable Last arrival 20.00hrs Last departure 10.00hrs no motorcycles no single sex groups →

Undulating grass site set in meadowland, on the coast and lying adjacent to A165 Scarborough road.

30acres 520pitches 307static 400🚐 or 400🚐 120🛆 awnings ltr

12⚡◐ late arrivals enclosure 104wc lit all night 3cdp 70washbasins hc 28🚿hc 16☺ supervised (5 wash) 3spin (5dry 10iron) ⊿ games room cold storage licensed club childrens playground calor gas camping gaz toilet fluid cafe ☎ ⊞ childrens theatre 🎣

↔ golf cinema 🏊 launderette pub

GUARDBRIDGE *(near St Andrews)*
Fife
Map 12 NO41

▶▶▶▶ ⓩ❷⚠
Clayton Caravan Park *(NO432182)*
Signposted ☎Balmullo (0334) 870242 or 870630 Apr–Sep rs Mar & Oct must book Jun–Aug Last departure noon

This is a level tree-studded grassy site adjoining farm, in gently rolling hill land. On south side of A91, midway between Cupar and St. Andrews.

7acres 75pitches 160static 75🚐 £5 or 75🚐£5 or 75🛆£5 awnings ltr

10⚡◐ late arrivals enclosure 15wc lit all night 1cdp 🚽 washbasins hc (central hot water) (🚿hc 🚿hc) ☺ supervised (wash spin iron) games room CTV cold storage (licensed bar) childrens playground calor gas camping gaz cafe restaurant ☎ ⊞ fishing golf practice net crazy putting 🎣

GUERNSEY
Channel Islands
Map 16
See Câtel (Fauxquets Valley)

GUISBOROUGH
Cleveland
Map 8 NZ61

▶▶▶ ⓩ❷⚠
Tockett's Mill Caravan Park
(NZ626182) Skelton Rd Signposted ☎(0287) 35161 Mar–Oct Last arrival 22.00hrs Last departure noon

Situated in a private wooded valley alongside a stream; the site is centered around the Old Grain Mill now being restored to working order.

5acres 100pitches 87static 100🚐£3.60 or 100🚐£3.60 or 100🛆£3.60 (awnings) ltr

10⚡ 23wc lit all night 3cdp 🚽 21washbasins hc 1central hot water (12🚿hc) 3☺ supervised (wash dry iron cold storage) licensed club/bar childrens playground calor gas camping gaz toilet fluid ☎ bar meals take away food 🎣

↔stables 🏊 launderette

GULWORTHY
Devon
Map 2 SX47

▶▶ ⓷❷⚠
Woodovis Caravan Park *(SX432744)*

Apr–14 Nov must book

Level and sloping grass site in secluded surroundings. Take A390 Tavistock–Liskeard road, after 2m at Gulworthy crossroads turn right, for site on left in 1½m.

3acres 60pitches SA 60🚐£3.80 or 60🚐£3.80 or 60🛆£3.80 (awnings)

5⚡ Individual pitches late arrivals enclosure wc lit all night 1cdp washbasins hc central hot water 🚿hc ☺ supervised (spin iron) cold storage childrens playground calor gas camping gaz paraffin toilet-fluid ☎ 🎣

↔ stables golf 🏊 launderette pub

HADDINGTON
Lothian *East Lothian*
Map 12 NT57

▶▶▶ ⓵❶⚠
Monksmuir Caravan Park *(NT559762)*
Signposted ☎East Linton (0620) 860340 Apr–Sep rs Oct–Mar Last departure noon no open fires

Mainly level site with trees and bushes set in meadowland off A1 Edinburgh–Dunbar road, equidistant to Haddington and East Linton.

5½acres 43pitches 7static SA 23🚐 fr£3.70 or 23🚐 fr£3.70 20🛆 fr£3.70 (awnings) ltr

7⚡ 14wc lit all night 2cdp 🚽 14washbasins hc (4central hot water) 6🚿hc 6☺ supervised (wash spin dry) iron (cold storage) calor gas camping gaz cafe ☎ hairdryer 🎣

↔ stables golf 🏊 launderette pub

HALE
Cumbria
Map 7 SD57

▶▶▶ ⓩ❶⚠
Fell End Caravan Park *(SD505780)*
Slackhead Rd Signposted ☎Milnthorpe (04482) 2122 Mar-16 Nov rs 17 Nov–Feb

Pleasantly situated, partly level and sloping gravel site with mature trees, saplings and bushes. Within easy reach of the lakes and south Cumbria. 4¾m from junction 35 of M6.

11acres 70pitches 215static 50🚐 ✱£3 or 50🚐 £2.50 20🛆£3 (awnings)

6⚡◐ late arrivals enclosure wc lit all night cdp washbasins hc central hot water (🚿hc) ☺ iron (games room) CTV (cold storage) childrens playground calor gas camping gaz paraffin toilet fluid ☎ Facilities for disabled 🎣

↔ stables golf 🏊 launderette pub

▶▶ ⓵❶⚠
Hallmore Farm Caravan Park
(SD503786) Signposted ☎Milnthorpe (04482) 2375 Mar–Oct booking

---

advisable public hols Last arrival 22.00 Last departure noon

A mainly level grassy site set in meadowland, adjacent to main road.

5acres 80pitches 56static 40🚐£3 or 40🚐£3 40🛆£3 awnings ltr

5⚡◐ 7wc lit all night 2cdp washbasins hc (central hot water) (🚿hc) ☺ supervised iron cold storage calor gas camping gaz ☎ ⊞ trout lake

↔ stables golf 🏊 launderette pub 🎣

HALKIRK
Highland *Caithness*
Map 15 ND15

▶▶ ⓩ❷⚠
Banniskirk House Camping & Caravan Site *(SJ158576)* (3m SE off A895 & 1½m S Georgemas Junction station) Signposted ☎(084 783) 609 mid Apr–Sep Last departure noon

Level grass site with trees and bushes forming its boundaries; on the A895 approx 2m S of the junc. with the Wick–Thurso road.

2½acres 24pitches 6static ✱24🚐£4 or 24🚐£3.50 or 24🛆£4 (awnings)

7⚡ 6wc lit all night 1cdp washbasins hc 🚿hc ☺ supervised calor gas camping gaz restaurant

↔ stables 🏊 pub 🎣

HALTWHISTLE
Northumberland
Map 12 NY76

▶▶▶ ⓩ❷⚠
Burnfoot Campsite *(NY685622)*
Bellister Estate, Featherstone Signposted ☎(0498) 20106 mid Mar–mid Oct booking advisable public hols & Aug Last arrival 21.00hrs Last departure noon no caravans no cars by tents

An attractive site set on the banks of the River South Tyne, amid mature trees, on the Bellister Castle estate. An ideal location for exploring Hadrians wall and the surrounding Roman remains.

3½acres 60pitches 60🚐£5 or 60🛆£5 awnings

2⚡ late arrivals enclosure 9wc lit all night 1cdp 12washbasins hc 4🚿hc 2☺ supervised camping gaz ☎ 🎣

↔ golf 🏊 pub

▶ ⓵❶⚠
Yont the Cleugh *(NY699588)*
Coanwood Signposted ☎(0498) 20274 Mar–Oct booking advisable Jul & Aug Last arrival 22.00hrs Last departure 15.00hrs

This remote rural site has a small wood with stream adjoining and offers distant views of the Cheviots and Hadrian's Wall. The approach is by a rather narrow and hilly road and is located 4½m S of Haltwhistle. Signposted from the A69; also from the A689 at Lambley.

2acres 25pitches 35static SA 25🚐£4.50 or 25🚐£4.50 10🛆£4.50 (awnings) ltr

2♨ 6wc lit all night washbasins hc 🛁hc ☉ (wash spin) CTV licensed club/bar childrens playground calor gas 🏪
↦ golf 🏌 ⚓

HARDWICK (Near Witney)
Oxfordshire
Map 4 SP30

▶▶▶ ②❸⚠
Hardwick Parks *(SP386048)*
Signposted ☎Standlake (086731) 501 or Witney (0993) 75272 Apr–Oct booking advisable public hols Last arrival 22.00hrs Last departure 17.00hrs
40acres 150pitches 100static 80♥£3.50 20♥£3.50 50▲£3.50 (awnings) ltr
40♨ late arrivals enclosure 40wc lit all night 1cdp 🔌 washbasins hc 🛁hc ☉ (wash dry iron) calor gas camping gaz toilet fluid ☎ fishing windsurfing dinghies 🏪
↦ 🏂 cinema ✦ launderette pub

HARGRAVE
Northamptonshire
Map 4 TL07

▽ ②
Nags Head *(TL037707)*
☎Wellingborough (0933) 622368
Enclosed level tree bordered paddock at rear of 400 year old inn.
20pitches 5♥✳£2 or 5♥£2 15▲fr50p
♨ cdp

HAROME
North Yorkshire
Map 8 SE68

▶▶▶ ❸❸⚠
Foxholme Caravan Park *(SE660830)*
Signposted ☎Helmsley (0439) 70416 & 71696 Etr–Oct booking advisable public hols Last arrival 23.00hrs Last departure noon
1m S of Beadlam, this level site is set in open countryside, within 4m of North York Moors National Park.
6acres 60pitches 60♥£2.50–£3 or 60♥£2.50–£3 6▲£2.50–£3 (awnings)
9♨ Individual pitches late arrivals enclosure 16wc lit all night 2cdp 14🔌 washbasins hc central hot water (🛁hc) ☉ (wash spin dry iron) (cold storage) calor gas camping gaz toilet fluid ☎ 🏪
↦ stables golf ✦ pub
see advertisement on page 148

HARRIS, (ISLE OF)
Western Isles *Inverness-shire*
Map 13 NG
See Drinnishadder

HARROGATE
North Yorkshire
Map 8 SE35

▶▶▶ ②❸⚠
High Moor Farm Park *(SE244566)*
Skipton Rd Signposted ☎(0423) 63637

Apr–Sep rs Oct must book public hols Last arrival 23.30hrs Last departure noon
Situated beside a small wood and surrounded by thorn hedges. On the A59, Harrogate–Skipton road, 4m from Harrogate.
15acres 140pitches 160static SA 130♥£3.75 10♥£3.75 or 150▲£3.75 (awnings) ltr
15♨ Individual pitches ☉ late arrivals enclosure 27wc lit all night 1cdp 🔌 20 washbasins hc (12🛁hc) 5☉ supervised (wash spin dry iron) 🖼 games room (cold storage) licensed club/bar childrens playground calor gas camping gaz toilet fluid cafe ☎ ⊞ 🏪
↦ golf cinema ✦ launderette pub

▶▶▶ ②❷⚠
Rudding Caravan Park *(SE333525)*
Rudding Park, Follifoot Signposted
☎(0423) 870439 23 Mar–3 Nov rs 1–22 Mar must book public hols
Site set amidst gardens of Rudding Park and screened by walls and hedges. Situated 3m SE of Harrogate off A661.
25acres 141pitches 54static SA 141♥£4–£5 or 141♥£4–£5 or 141▲£4–£5 awnings ltr
9♨☉ late arrivals enclosure 35wc lit all night 2cdp 🔌washbasins hc central hot water (🛁hc) ☉ supervised (wash spin) iron (cold storage) childrens playground calor gas camping gaz toilet fluid ☎ 🏪
↦ stables golf 🏂 cinema ✦ launderette pub

▶▶ ①❶⚠
Shaws Trailer Park *(SE325557)*
Knaresborough Rd Signposted
☎(0423) 884432 All year booking launderette public hols & Jul–Aug Last arrival 20.00hrs Last departure 14.00hrs

▶▶▶

Hardwick Parks

Standlake (A415), Nr Witney, Oxfordshire
Caravan & Camping Park

All modern amenities ✶ 40 acre lake for fishing ✶ Swimming, windsurfing etc ✶ Shop ✶ Laundry ✶ Electric hook ups ✶ Picnic area on lakeside ✶ Rally field. Dogs allowed on leads. A very spacious park set in rural countryside and within easy reach of Oxford and the Cotswolds.

Write, enclosing a SAE or telephone:
Una Hunt,
138 Brize Norton Road,
Minster Lovell, nr Witney, Oxon
(086 731) 501 or Witney 75272

A level, grassy site with mature trees. On A59 Harrogate–Knaresborough road.
4acres 65pitches 146static 43♥ 10♥ 12▲ (awnings) ltr
25♨☉ late arrivals enclosure 25wc lit all night 1cdp 🔌 washbasins hc central hot water (➔hc 🛁hc) ☉ supervised calor gas cafe & licensed restaurant ☎ 🏪
↦ stables golf 🏂 cinema ✦ launderette pub

HARTINGTON
Derbyshire
Map 7 SK16

▶ ①❶⚠
Barracks Farm Caravan Site *(SK127585)* Beresford Dale ☎(029884) 261 Etr–Oct
A level, grassy site with mature trees. From A515 (Asbourne–Buxton) road turn left onto B5054, then left again for Alstonfield and Beresford Dale.
5acres 50pitches 20♥ 30▲ (awnings)
2♨☉ 5wc 1cdp ☉ calor gas

HARTSOP
Cumbria
Map 12 NY41

▶▶▶ ❸❶⚠
Skyeside Camping Site *(NY408132)*
Signposted ☎Glenridding (08532) 239 Mar–17 Nov must book Last arrival 22.00hrs Last departure 14.00hrs no caravans or motorvans
A level grassy site surrounded by mountains. Off A592, 3m S of Patterdale.
5acres 80pitches SA 80▲ awnings
2♨☉ late arrivals enclosure 16wc lit all night 2cdp washbasins hc central hot water (🛁hc) ☉ (wash) spin (dry) iron cold storage calor gas camping gaz paraffin toilet fluid ☎ off licence 🏪
↦ stables 🏂 ✦ launderette pub

HARVINGTON
Hereford and Worcester
Map 4 SP04

▶▶▶ ②❶⚠
Small Moors Holiday Park *(SP061488)*
Anchor Ln Signposted ☎Evesham (0386) 870446 15 Mar–Oct booking advisable peak periods Last arrival mdnt no tents no cars by caravans
A level, grassy site with mature trees and bushes, near the river and set among hilly woodland country. On A439 4m N of Evesham.
7acres 130pitches 100 static SA 130♥ or 130♥ (awnings) ltr
4♨ Individual pitches late arrivals enclosure 22wc lit all night 3cdp washbasins hc central hot water (🛁hc) ☉ supervised games room cold storage childrens playground calor gas camping gaz toilet fluid ☎ ⊞ 🏪
↦ ✦
see advertisement on page 133

HARWOOD, GREAT
Lancashire
Map 7 SD73

▶ ① ❶ ⚠
Harwood Bar Caravan Park
(SD751328) Mill Ln Signposted
☎(0254) 884853 Mar–Oct booking
advisable peak periods Last arrival
21.30hrs Last departure noon no
unaccompanied under 18s

*Quiet site overlooking Calder Valley and
Pendle Hill on the fringe of the Ribble
Valley. Off A680.*

2acres 25pitches 90static 15🚐£3.50
5🚐£3.50 5▲£3.50 (awnings) ltr

11🚐⊘ 15wc lit all night 1cdp 🚱
(washbasins hc) (🔥hc⊙) supervised
(dry iron) cold storage childrens
playground calor gas camping gaz toilet
fluid ☎ 🛒
↔ stables golf cinema ♪ launderette
pub

HASGUARD CROSS
Dyfed
Map 2 SM80

▶▶▶ ② ❷ ⚠
Hasguard Cross Caravan Park
(SM850108) Signposted ☎Broad
Haven (043783) 443 All year must book
Last arrival 23.59hrs Last departure
noon no tents

---

*This site, pleasantly situated in
Pembrokeshire National Park, is
screened by trees and shrubs with views
of surrounding hills. 1½m from sea and
beach at Little Haven. Approach on
B4327 from Haverfordwest to Dale, after
7m turn right at crossroads and site is
first entrance on right.*

2acres 25pitches 35static 25🚐£3.50 or
25🚐£3.50 awnings

5🚐 Individual pitches late arrivals
enclosure wc lit all night 1cdp
washbasins hc (🔥hc⊙) spin iron
licensed club/bar childrens playground
calor gas camping gaz paraffin ☎ 🛒
↔ stables golf ♣ ♪ pub

Redlands Touring Caravan Site
(SM851109) ☎Broad Haven (043783)
301 Etr–Sep must book peak periods
Last departure noon no tents

*This level grass site, situated in
Pembrokeshire National Park, is 1½m
from sea and beach at Little Haven. 7m
W of Haverfordwest on B4327 Dale
Road.*

5acres 60pitches 60🚐£3.50 or
60🚐£3.50 awnings

4🚐 Individual pitches late arrivals
enclosure 12wc lit all night 1cdp 🚱
washbasins hc (🔥hc) ⊙ spin (dry) iron
cold storage ☎ 🛒
↔ stables ♣ ♪ pub

HASTINGS & ST LEONARDS
E Sussex
Map 5 TQ80
See also Three Oaks

▶▶▶ ② ❷ ⚠
Shearbarn Holiday Park *(TQ842112)*
Barley Ln Signposted ☎(0424) 423583
Apr–Oct booking advisable public hols
& Jul–Sep Last arrival 22.00hrs Last
departure noon no unaccompanied
under 18's no single sex groups

*Situated on the outskirts of Hastings,
close to sea and beach.*

19acres 400pitches 250static
130🚐£5.50 20🚐£5.50 250▲£5.50
awnings

11🚐 Individual pitches for caravans ⊘
late arrivals enclosure 48wc lit all night
3cdp 🚱 washbasins hc 🔥hc ⊙
supervised (wash dry iron) cold storage
licensed club/bar childrens playground
calor gas camping gaz toilet fluid cafe
☎ (hairdryers) 🛒
↔ stables golf ♣ cinema ♪
launderette pub

Sykeside Camping Site
Brotherswater, Patterdale, Cumbria, CA11 0NZ.

AA ▶▶▶

Sykeside is a small family camping site set in the
heart of the mountains. Ideally situated for walking,
climbing and touring. Modern facilities: flush
toilets, showers, laundry, shop. Cycle hire and boat
hire. Adjacent to the site (250 yards) is a Country Inn
which provides licensed bar and restaurant.

It is advisable to book in advance.

SAE or telephone Glenridding 239.

HATFIELD
South Yorkshire
Map 8 SE60

▶▶▶ 🄬 ❷ ⚠

Hatfield Marina Caravan & Camp Site
(SE668101) Signposted ☎Doncaster
(0302) 841572 Mar–Oct Last arrival
18.00hrs Last departure noon

*A local council site with specialised
facilities for water sports. 400yds from
A18 and adjacent to marina.*

10acres 60pitches SA 60🚐£1.80 or
60🚐£1.80 or 60🛆£1–£1.80 awnings

4🅰 late arrivals enclosure wc lit all night
2cdp washbasins hc central hot water
🛁hc ☺ cafe 🎣 canoeing, rowing,
sailing, fishing, windsurfing

↔ stables 🏇 🎿 launderette pub 🍴

HAVERTHWAITE
Cumbria
Map 7 SD38
See Cark-in-Cartmel sketch map

▶▶▶ 🄬 ❶ ⚠

Bigland Hall Caravan Park *(SD344833)*
Signposted ☎Newby Bridge (0448)
31702 Mar–Oct booking advisable
public hols Last arrival 23.30hrs Last
departure 13.00hrs no tents

*A well-wooded site in part of the Bigland
Estate within the Lake District National
Park. 3m from the southern end of Lake
Windermere and near the Haverthwaite
Steam Railway.*

10acres 86pitches 49static 86🚐£3.50
or 86🚐£3.50 (awnings)

4🅰 Individual pitches late arrivals
enclosure wc lit all night 3cdp
washbasins hc (🛁hc) ☺ supervised
(wash dry iron) CTV cold storage calor
gas off licence 🍴

↔ stables 🎿 launderette pub

HAWES
North Yorkshire
Map 7 SD88

▶▶ 🄬 ❶ ⚠

**Bainbridge Ings Caravan & Camping
Site** *(SD879895)* Signposted ☎ (09697)
354 Apr–Oct must book Last arrival
21.00hrs Last departure 14.00hrs no
groups of motorcyclists

*A family run site in open countryside –
close to Hawes in the heart of Upper
Wensleydale. Off A684.*

4acres 55pitches 15static 8🚐£3.20
10🚐£2.70 40🛆£2.70 (awnings)

3🅰 Individual pitches ◎ 15wc lit all
night 1cdp washbasins hc (central hot
water) (🛁hc) ☺ supervised (spin) calor
gas camping gaz paraffin

↔ stables 🎿 pub 🍴

HAWICK
Borders *Roxburghshire*
Map 12 NT51

▶▶▶ 🄬 ❷ ⚠

Riverside Caravan Park *(NT537169)*
Signposted ☎(0450) 73785 Apr–Oct

Last arrival 20.30hrs Last departure
noon

*A part level, part sloping grassy site
situated on banks of River Teviot. Near
A698 Hawick–Kelso road 2½m E of
Hawick.*

2acres 50pitches 35static 36🚐£3.25–
£4 48 🚐£3.25–£4 66🛆£3.25–£4
(awnings) ltr

7🅰 Individual pitches ◎ 17wc lit all
night 1cdp washbasins hc (🛁hc) ☺
supervised wash spin (cold storage)
childrens playground calor gas camping
gaz toilet fluid cafe ☎ 🍴

↔ stables golf cinema 🎿 launderette
pub

HAWKCHURCH
Devon
Map 3 ST30

▶ 🄬 ❷ ⚠

Scouse Farm Caravan Park
(SY345988) Scouse Farm ☎(02977)
402 end May–14 Nov rs 15 Mar–end
May must book

*Level grassy site partially sheltered by
small woodland; good views. On B3165
between Hunters Lodge crossroads and
Marshwood.*

8acres 170pitches 170🚐£3.50 or
170 🚐£3.25 70🛆£3.50 (awnings)

17🅰 34wc lit all night 1cdp (3washbasin
hc 3central hot water) (🛁hc) ☺
supervised (spin dry iron) games room
CTV (cold storage) licensed club/bar
childrens playground calor gas camping
gaz ☎ restaurant 🍴

↔ stables cinema fishing launderette
pub

HAYFIELD
Derbyshire
Map 7 SK08

▶▶ 🄬 ❷ ⚠

Hayfield Campsite *(SK049868)* Kinder
Rd Signposted ☎New Mills (0663)
45394 Apr–Oct booking advisable
public hols & Jul–Aug Last arrival &
departure 21.00hrs no caravans

*Pleasant site near the River Sett and
bordered by mature trees. It is near the
Peak District National Park and off A624.*

7acres 90pitches 90 🚐 fr£3.60 or 90 🛆
fr£3.60 awnings

5🅰 Individual pitches 12wc lit all night
1cdp washbasins hc 🛁hc ☺ supervised
camping gaz ☎ hair dryer 🍴

↔ stables 🎿 launderette pub

HAYLE
Cornwall
Map 2 SW53
See sketch map on page 148

▶ 🄬 ❶ ⚠

St Ives Bay Chalet & Caravan Park
(SW577398) The Holiday Centre, Upton

Towans ☎(0736) 752274 May–Sep no
bookings 14 Jul–25 Aug Last departure
09.00hrs

*The site is set amidst undulating
grassland and sand dunes adjoining the
beach. 1m N of Hayle off B3301.*

12acres 200pitches 150static
200🚐£6.90 or 200 🚐£6.90 or
200🛆£6.90 (awnings)

30🅰 90wc lit all night 6cdp (🛁hc)
supervised (wash spin dry iron) CTV
licensed club/bar childrens playground
private beach calor gas camping gaz
paraffin cafe ☎ crazy golf, putting
green, table tennis 🍴

↔ stables golf 🏇 cinema 🎿
launderette pub

HAYLING ISLAND
Hampshire
Map SZ79

▶▶ 🄬 ❶ ⚠

Fleet Farm Caravan & Camping Site
(SU724018) Yew Tree Rd Signposted
☎(07016) 3684 Mar–Oct booking
advisable public hols & Jul–Aug no
motorcycles

*A level, grassy and partly sheltered site
with trees and hedges. Off A3023.*

3½acres 75pitches 160static 25🚐
50 🚐 or 50🛆 awnings

4🅰 Individual pitches for caravans ◎
14wc lit all night 1cdp washbasins hc
(🛁hc) ☺ licensed club/bar childrens
playground calor gas camping gaz toilet
fluid boating, putting, skittles 🍴

↔ stables golf 🏇 cinema 🎿
launderette pub

HAY-ON-WYE
Powys
Map 3 SO24

▶ 🄬 ❶

Hollybush Inn *(SO205406)* Signposted
☎Glasbury (04974) 371 Good Fri–Oct
booking advisable public hols Last
arrival mdnt Last departure noon

*A small, level grass site in pleasant
surroundings 2m from Hay-on-Wye. Off
B4350.*

1¾acres 17pitches 5 static 17🚐£4 or
17 🚐£3 or 17🛆£3 awnings ltr

4🅰 4wc lit all night 1cdp (🛁hc) ☺
supervised licensed club/bar childrens
playground calor gas camping gaz bar
food available

↔ stables 🏇 🎿 pub

HEATHFIELD
East Sussex
Map 5 TQ52

▶▶▶ 🄬 ❷ ⚠

Greenview Caravan Fields *(TQ605223)*
Broad Oak ☎(04352) 3531 14 Mar–Oct
must book Last departure 10.30hrs 🏕

*Small, attractive site adjoining main
A265 in village of Broad Oak 1m E of
Heathfield.*
→

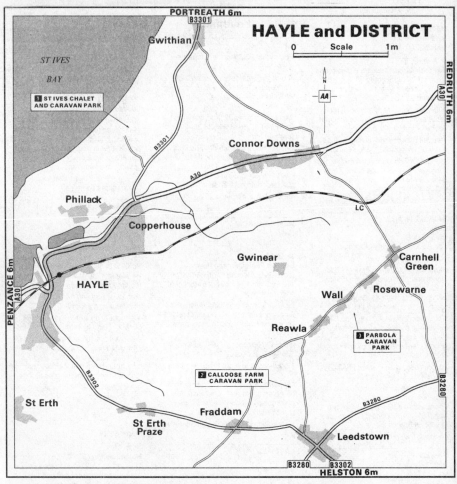

HAYLE and DISTRICT

Sites listed under: **1** Hayle **2** Leedstown **3** Wall

148

1½acres 9pitches 51static SA 9🚐 £3.80 or 9🚐 £3.80 or 9▲£2–£3.80 (awnings)

4🚃7wc lit all night 1cdp washbasins hc 🚿hc 🛁hc ☺supervised (wash iron) games room TV (licensed club/bar) calor gas camping gaz toilet fluid ☎ 🧺 ↔ launderette pub

HEDGE END
Hampshire
Map 4 SU41

▶▶🄝🄞⚠

Grange Caravan Park (SU492144)
Shamblehurst Ln Signposted ☎Botley (04892) 3895 All year no tents

A level grassy site, 6m E of Southampton off B3035.

⅔acre 26pitches 154static 26🚐 £2.50 or 26🚐 £2.50 awnings

1🚃 Individual pitches 2wc lit all night 1cdp 4washbasins hc central hot water (4🛁hc) 1☺calor gas camping gaz ☎ 🧺 ↔ golf ⛳ launderette pub

HELMSLEY
North Yorkshire
Map 8 SE68
See Harome and Nawton

HELSTON
Cornwall
Map 2 SW62

▶▶▶🄝🄞⚠

Glenhaven Touring Park (SW665274)
Clodgey Ln Signposted ☎(03265) 2734

Etr–Oct booking advisable Jul & Aug Last arrival mdnt Last departure 13.00hrs

This is a flat, well laid-out touring site adjacent to outskirts of Helston. Situated S of town on A3083 Helston–Lizard road.

4½acres 70pitches 76static 70🚐 £3.90 or 70🚐 £3.60 or 70▲£3.90 (awnings) ltr

11🚃 Individual pitches 12wc 1cdp 🚽 washbasins hc (🛁hc) ☺supervised (wash dry) iron cold storage childrens playground calor gas camping gaz toilet fluid ☎ hair dryers 🧺 ↔ stables golf ⛏ cinema ⛳ launderette pub

▶▶▶🄝🄞⚠

Trelowarren Chateau Camping
(SW721238) Trelowarren, Mawgan (3m S off B3293 to St Keverne) ☎Mawgan (032622) 224 & 637 18 Apr–Sep must →

book peak periods Last arrival 20.00hrs
Last departure noon

14acres 225pitches 225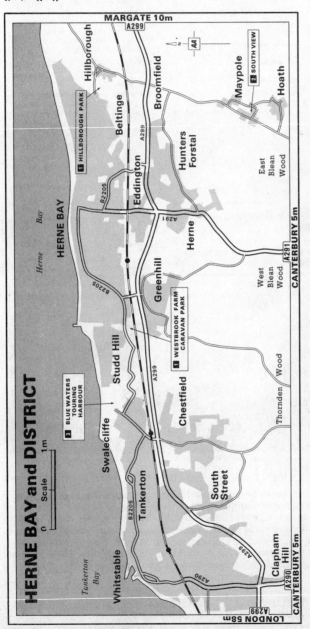£6.04 or
225 £6.04 or 225▲£6.04 awnings

20 Individual pitches late arrivals
enclosure 28wc lit all night 3cdp
31washbasins hc ⇔hc 16 hc 12☺
supervised (wash spin iron) games room
TV (cold storage licensed club/bar)
childrens playground calor gas camping
gaz paraffin toilet fluid cafe restaurant
☎ 🏔

⊖ 🍴 launderette pub

HEMINGFORD ABBOTS
Cambridgeshire
Map 4 TL27

▶▶▶ 1 ❶ ⚠
Quiet Waters Caravan Park *(TL283712)*
Signposted ☎St Ives (0480) 63405
Apr–Oct rs Nov–Mar no bookings Last
arrival 22.00hrs Last departure noon

Level grassy site in a picturesque village
on the River Ouse. Set in meadowland
adjacent to A604.

½acre 20pitches 40static 20 £3.50 or
20 £3 or 20▲£4 (awnings)

2 Individual pitches 11wc lit all night
1cdp (washbasins hc hc) ☺
supervised iron calor gas camping
gaz boating, fishing 🏔

⊖ stables golf ⛷ cinema 🍴
launderette pub

HERNE BAY
Kent
Map 5 TR16
See sketch map

▶ 2 ❶ ⚠
Hillborough Park *(TR209679)* Reculver
Rd ☎(02273) 4618 Apr–16 Oct must
book Last arrival & departure 22.00hrs
🚫 no tents

Set on high ground, amidst well-kept
lawns, the site is situated a few minutes
from the sea and shopping centre.

1acre 20pitches 398static 20 or 20
(awnings)

1 16wc lit all night 1cdp (central
hot water) hc ☺ supervised (wash dry
iron) games room (licensed club/bar)
childrens playground calor gas camping
gaz toilet fluid ☎ 🏔

⊖ stables golf ⛷ cinema 🍴
launderette pub

▶ 1 ❶ ⚠
Westbrook Farm Caravan Park
(TR158673) Sea St ☎(02273) 5586
Jun–16 Oct rs Apr–May bookings
advisable public hols Last arrival
21.00hrs

Small site within easy reach of the
Thanet Way (A299) and Herne Bay. The
Club house is in an attractive 17th-
century farmhouse surrounded by fields.

5acres 66static £3.50 £3.50
▲£3.50 (awnings)

6 Individual pitches 15wc lit all night
3cdp (central hot water hc) ☺

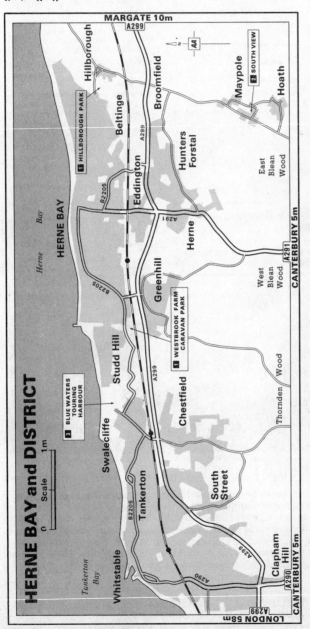

Sites listed under:
1 Herne Bay
2 Hoath
3 Whitstable

MARGATE 10m
A299

Hillborough

Broomfield

Maypole

2 SOUTH VIEW

Hoath

Beltinge

1 HILLBOROUGH PARK

Hunters
Forstal

East
Blean
Wood

Eddington

Herne Bay

B2205

A299

A291

HERNE BAY

Herne
Bay

Herne

CANTERBURY 5m
A291

Greenhill

West
Blean
Wood

B2205

1 WESTBROOK FARM
CARAVAN PARK

Studd Hill

A299

Chestfield

Thorden Wood

HERNE BAY and DISTRICT

3 BLUE WATERS
TOURING
HARBOUR

Scale 1m

0

Swalecliffe

South
Street

Tankerton

Clapham
Hill

Tankerton
Bay

Whitstable

B2205

A290
A299

A299

CANTERBURY 5m
A290

LONDON 58m
A299

supervised (licensed club/bar) childrens playground calor gas camping gaz toilet fluid ☎ 🏪
⟷ stables 🪃 cinema 🎵 launderette pub

HEWAS WATER
Cornwall
Map 2 SW94
See St Austell sketch map

▶▶▶ 🗲 ❷ ⚠

Trencreek Farm Caravan Park
(SW966485) Signposted ☎St Austell (0726) 882540 Etr–Sep rs Oct must book Jul & Aug Last arrival 22.00hrs Last departure 11.00hrs

Part level, part sloping grass site with mature trees and bushes close to river and lake. Off B3287, 1m from junction with A390.

10acres 130pitches 37static SA 130🚐 fr £3.28 or 130 🚐 fr £3.28 or 130🛖fr £3.28 (awnings)

10🏕 Individual pitches 19wc lit all night 🛢washbasins hc (central hot water 🚿hc) ☺ supervised (wash spin dry iron) 🎱 games room CTV childrens playground calor gas camping gaz ☎ coarse & trout fishing take-away meals badminton 🏪

⟷ stables golf launderette pub

HEXHAM
Northumberland
Map 12 NY96
See sketch map

▶▶▶ 🗲 ❷ ⚠

Causey Hill Caravan Park *(NY925625)* Benson's Fell Farm ☎(0434) 602834 Mar–Oct must book public hols Last arrival 20.00hrs Last departure noon

On sloping ground attractively screened by trees.

2½acres 50pitches 105static 50🚐 or 50 🚐 (awnings) ltr

5🏕 24wc lit all night 4cdp 14washbasins hc 6central hot water 12🚿hc 2☺ supervised (wash dry) childrens playground calor gas ☎ 🏪

⟷ stables golf 🎵 launderette pub

▶▶▶ 🗲 ❷ ⚠

Lowgate Caravan Site *(NY903642)* Signposted ☎(0434) 602827 21 Mar–Oct booking advisable public hols & Aug Last arrival 21.00hrs no tents

Level, grass site with mature trees and bushes set in hilly wooded and moorland country. 2m SW from Hexham on B6305 and turn immediate right at telephone box.

½acre 10pitches 65static 10🚐£3 or 10 🚐£3 (awnings) ltr

2🏕 Individual pitches 16wc 1cdp 14 washbasins hc 8🚿hc 5☺ supervised calor gas ☎

⟷ stables golf 🪃 cinema 🎵 pub 🏪

HIGH BENTHAM
North Yorkshire
Map 7 SD66

▶▶ 🗲 ❷ ⚠

Riverside Caravan Park *(SD665688)* Wenning Av Signposted ☎Bentham (0468) 61272 Mar–Oct must book Last arrival 21.00hrs Last departure 13.00hrs

This site is set on the banks of the River Wenning, in delightful countryside and screened by trees. Off B6480.

30pitches 30🚐£2.85 or 30 🚐£2.85 or 30🛖£2.85 (awnings) ltr

3🏕 7wc lit all night 1cdp 🛢washbasins hc (🚿hc) ☺ (dry) games room TV childrens playground calor gas ☎ 🏪

⟷ golf 🎵 launderette pub

HIGHBRIDGE
Somerset
Map 3 ST34

▶▶▶ 🗖 ❶ ⚠

Edithmead Dairy Trailer Park *(ST337459)* Signposted ☎Burnham-on-Sea (0278) 783475 Mar–Oct must book

→

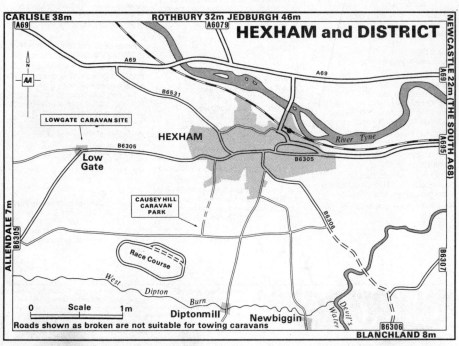

Roads shown as broken are not suitable for towing caravans

All sites listed under Hexham

Last arrival 00.30hrs Last departure noon

Level, compact site adjacent to M5.

5acres 30pitches 86static SA 30🚐£3 or 30🚐£3 or 30▲£3 awnings

8🛁🌀 late arrivals enclosure 14wc lit all night 1cdp 🔌 washbasins hc central hot water (🚿hc) ☺ supervised (wash spin dry iron) games room cold storage childrens playground calor gas camping gaz toilet fluid cafe ☎ 🎲 🛒

↔ stables golf ⛳ cinema ♪ pub

HILLBERRY (*Near Douglas*)
Isle of Man
Map 6 SC37

▶▶ 🔟 0 ▲

Glen Dhoo International Farm Camping Site (*SC383796*) Signposted ☎Douglas (0624) 21254 May– Sep rs Apr–May & Oct Last arrival 23.00hrs Last departure noon no unaccompanied under 18's

A simple camping site, situated in a sheltered wooded valley 2½m from Douglas. Entrance to site is 100yds from Hillberry Corner on the mountain road and TT course.

12acres 120pitches 40 🚐£4.70 80▲£4.70 awnings

4🛁 Individual pitches ⌀ 10wc lit all night 1cdp (10 washbasins hc) (6🚿hc) 2☺ supervised (wash dry iron) games room (cold storage) calor gas camping gaz ☎ 🛒 video films

↔ golf ⛳ cinema ♪ launderette pub

HOATH
Kent
Map 5 TR26
See Herne Bay sketch map

▶▶ 🔟 0 ▲

South View (*TR205648*) Maypole Ln Signposted ☎Chislet (022786) 280 Mar–Oct booking advisable public hols & Jul–Aug Last arrival 23.00hrs Last departure 22.00hrs 🕊 no ball games

A small rural site, level and well secluded. Off A299 or A28.

2acres 30pitches 15🚐 or 15 🚐 15▲ (awnings)

1🛁🌀 8wc lit all night 1cdp 6washbasins hc (🚿hc) ☺ cold storage calor gas camping gaz

↔ stables ♪ launderette pub 🛒

HODDESDON
Hertfordshire
Map 5 TL30

▶▶ 🔟 0 ▲

Dobbs Weir Caravan Park (*TL383082*) Essex Rd Signposted ☎(0992) 462090 15 Apr–Oct must book public hols Last arrival 21.30hrs Last departure 18.00hrs no tents

8acres 100pitches 100static 100🚐£5 or 100🚐£5 awnings

4🛁 19wc lit all night 1cdp washbasins hc central hot water 🚿hc ☺ supervised calor gas ☎ fishing 🛒

↔ cinema launderette pub

HOLLYBUSH
Strathclyde *Ayrshire*
Map 10 NS31

▶▶ 🔟 0 ▲

Skeldon Caravans (*NS389144*) Signposted ☎Dalrymple (029256) 202 Apr–Sep must book Jul & Aug Last arrival 19.00hrs Last departure 10.30hrs

A level, sheltered grass site on banks of River Doon. 2m from Dalrymple on B7034.

3acres 20pitches 10static SA 20🚐£3 or 20🚐£3 or 20▲£3 (awnings) ltr

5🛁 7wc lit all night washbasins hc central hot water (🚿hc) ☺ supervised childrens playground calor gas camping gaz ☎ fishing 🛒

↔ stables golf ♪ pub

HOLMROOK
Cumbria
Map 6 SD09

▶▶▶ 🔟 0 ▲

Seven Acres Caravan Park (*NY074025*) Seven Acres (1m S of Gosforth, on A595) Signposted ☎Gosforth (09405) 480 Mar–14 Nov must book May–Sep & public hols Last departure noon

A level, well kept site with good backdrop of Lakeland fells.

3acres 45pitches 58static SA 45🚐£3.50 or 45🚐£3 or 45▲£3.50 (awnings) ltr

4🛁 11wc lit all night 2cdp washbasins hc (🚿hc) ☺ supervised (wash spin) (iron) (licensed club/bar) childrens playground calor gas camping gaz toilet fluid ☎ 🛒

↔ golf ♪ launderette pub

HOLMSLEY
Hampshire
Map 4 SZ29
See Christchurch sketch map

▶▶▶ 🔟 0 ▲

Holmsey Camp Site (*SZ218992*) Holmsley Old Aerodrome, Hinton Signposted ☎Lyndhurst (042128) 3141 (Forestry Commission Office) & 3771 (from early 1984) 13 Apr–Sep booking advisable Spring Bank Hol Last departure noon

A large Forestry Commission site, set in rural surroundings on the fringe of the New Forest. See under Forestry Commission for further information.

89acres 700pitches 700🚐 ✳£3.20–£4.20 or 700▲£3.20–£4.20 awnings

12🛁 74wc lit all night 6cdp washbasins hc 🚿hc ☺ supervised calor gas camping gaz cafe ☎ facilities for disabled 🛒

↔ stables golf pub

HOLTON HEATH
Dorset
Map 3 SY99

▶▶▶▶ 🔟 0 ▲

Sandford Park Caravans (*SY938906*) Signposted ☎Bournemouth (0202) 622513 3 Apr–Oct no bookings Last arrival mdnt Last departure 11.00hrs 🕊 (21 May–Aug) no groups of unaccompanied teenagers

Level, grassy and gravel site with mature trees set in wooded meadowland with direct access to A351 Poole–Wareham road.

12acres 250pitches 260static 250🚐 or 250🚐 or 250▲ (awnings)

35🛁 Individual pitches ⌀ late arrivals enclosure 120wc lit all night washbasins hc central hot water (➰hc 🚿hc) ☺ supervised (wash spin dry iron) ▭ CTV licensed club/bar childrens playground calor gas camping gaz toilet fluid cafe restaurant ☎ 🛒

↔ stables golf ⛳ cinema ♪

HOLYWELL BAY
Cornwall
Map 2 SW75
See Newquay sketch map

▶▶▶ 🔟 0 ▲

Trevornick Caravan & Camping Park (*SW776586*) Signposted ☎Crantock (0637) 830531 21 May–10 Sep rs 11–30 Sep must book Jul & Aug Last arrival 22.00hrs Last departure noon no single sex groups

Holmrock, Cumbria
Telephone: (094 05) 480

Privately owned caravan park nestling in the western boundary of the Lake District National Park, three miles from the Wasdale Valley. The park is only three miles from the sand dunes of Drigg and Seascale beaches combined with an eighteen hole golf course open to non-members. Plus excellent fishing on local rivers for salmon and trout. The site shop is well stocked with most items for the caravanner and camper plus use of a public telephone. Licensed bar and recreation room. Fully tiled throughout, clean and spacious toilet, shower and washbasin facilities. Launderette with washing machines and tumble dryers plus a dish washing room with stainless steel suites. **Proprietors: Mr & Mrs W and E Temple**

Ideal family site. Off A3075.
20acres 450pitches 100🚐£6 100🚐 or
150▲ (awnings)
14🏕 Individual pitches 40wc lit all night
3cdp washbasins hc (🚿hc) ☺
supervised (wash) spin (dry) iron 🏊
(games room) CTV (cold storage)
licensed club/bar childrens playground
calor gas camping gaz toilet fluid cafe
restaurant ☎ 🎱 golf pony trekking
fishing sauna solarium 🦺
↩ stables golf 🎣 cinema 🎵
launderette pub
see advertisement on page 193

HONEYBOURNE
Hereford and Worcester
Map 4 SP14

▶▶▶ 🄂 ❶ ⚠
Ranch Caravan Park *(SP113444)*
Signposted ☎Evesham (0386) 830 744
25 Mar–Oct must book public hols &
Jul–Aug Last arrival 20.00hrs Last
departure 15.00hrs no tents no single
sex groups
*Level grassy site with trees and bushes
set in farmland in the Vale of Evesham,
2m from B4035.*
12acres 100pitches 180static SA
100🚐£4 or 100🚐£4 (awnings) ltr
21🏕 32wc lit all night 1cdp ⬛
34washbasins hc (central hot water)
(11🚿hc) 7☺ supervised (wash) spin

(dry) iron (🏊) games room (cold
storage
licensed club/bar) childrens playground
calor gas camping gaz toilet fluid ☎ Bar
meals 🦺
↩ stables golf 🎣 🎵 launderette pub

HONITON
Devon
Map ST10

▶ 🄂 ❶ ⚠
Otter Valley Park *(ST175014)* Northcote
Signposted ☎(0404) 2917 mid Mar–
mid Nov Last arrival 20.00hrs Last
departure noon no motorcycles, no
single sex groups
*A mainly level, grassy site with some
trees, saplings and bushes. Situated in
the urban area with direct access to
main road (A30).*
10acres 140pitches 96static
100🚐£3.50 20🚐£3.50 20▲£3.50
(awnings) ltr
8🏕 16wc 1cdp 16washbasins hc
(16🚿hc) ☺ supervised (wash spin dry
iron) childrens playground calor gas
camping gaz ☎ 🦺
↩ stables golf cinema 🎵 launderette
pub

HOPE
Derbyshire
Map 7 SK18

▶▶ 🄂 ❶ ⚠
Laneside Caravan Park *(SK178832)*
Laneside Farm Signposted ☎Hope
Valley (0433) 20214 Apr–Oct must book
public hols & Jul–Aug Last departure
14.00hrs no motorcycles, no
unaccompanied groups of teenagers
*A pleasantly situated rural site on east
side of Hope Village. Surrounded by
wooded hills.*
4acres 52pitches 22static 52🚐£3 or
52🚐£2 or 40▲£3 (awnings) ltr
8🏕☺ 17wc lit all night 2cdp ⬛
washbasins hc (🚿hc) ☺ (spin dry) (cold
storage) calor gas camping gaz toilet
fluid 🦺
↩ stables golf 🎵 pub

HORNS CROSS
Devon
Map 2 SS32

▶▶▶ 🄂 ❷ ⚠
Steart Farm *(SS356228)* Signposted
☎Clovelly (02373) 239 Etr–Oct rs Nov–
Mar must book mid Jul–Aug Last
arrival mdnt Last departure 11.00hrs
*Undulating grass and gravel site with
mature trees, set in meadowland in rural
area with access to A39 to Bideford and
Barnstaple Bay.* →

4acres 60pitches 9static 20🚐 10 🚃
30▲ (awnings)
6🏕⊘ 12wc lit all night 1cdp
12washbasins hc (4🚿hc) 9☺ (spin)
(cold storage) childrens playground
calor gas camping gaz
⊖ stables ✔ pub 🍴

HOUGHTON
Cambridgeshire
Map 4 TL27

▶▶ ② ❶ ⚠
**Houghton Mill Caravan & Camping
Park** (TL284709) Mill St Signposted
🕾St Ives (0480) 62413 Etr–3 Oct must
book peak periods Last arrival 22.00hrs
Last departure noon no single sex
groups

5acres 50pitches SA 25🚐£4.50 or
25 🚃£4.50 25▲£4.50 (awnings) ltr

2🏕⊘ late arrivals enclosure 6wc 1cdp
washbasins hc 🚿hc ☺ calor gas
camping gaz toilet fluid 🕾 launching
facilities for small boats 🍴
⊖ stables golf 🏌 cinema ✔
launderette pub

HOWEY
Powys
Map 3 SO05

▶ ② ❶ ⚠
Dalmore Camping Site (SO045568)
Signposted 🕾Llandrindod Wells (0597)
2483 Feb–Nov must book Jul & Aug Last
arrival 21.00hrs Last departure 10.00hrs

Small touring site; on A483 but screened
from road and traffic noise by hedgerow.
1½m S of village.

½acre 6pitches 6static SA 6🚐£2 or
6 🚃£2 or 6▲£2 (awnings) ltr

3🏕⊘ 4wc lit all night 2cdp (🚿hc) ☺
supervised cold storage calor gas
camping gaz
⊖ stables golf 🏌 ✔ launderette pub 🍴

HUBBERT'S BRIDGE
Lincolnshire
Map 8 TF24

▶▶▶ ② ❷ ⚠
Orchards Caravan Park (TF273433)
Signposted 🕾(020579) 328 Apr–Oct
Last arrival 20.00hrs Last departure
noon no tents

A level, grassy site with mature trees and
bushes, not far from the canal. 3½m W
of Boston on B1192.

2acres 30pitches 120static 30🚐 or
30 🚃 (awnings)

10🏕 29wc lit all night 1cdp washbasins
hc 🚿hc ☺ supervised cold storage
childrens playground toilet fluid 🕾 🍴
⊖ ✔pub

HUGHLEY
Shropshire
Map 7 SO59

▶▶▶ ② ❷ ⚠
Mill Farm Caravan Site (SO564979)

Signposted 🕾Brockton (074 636) 208
Mar–Oct must book Last arrival 20.00hrs
Last departure noon no motorcycles or
single sex groups

Level grass and gravel site with mature
trees and bushes, set in meadowland
adjacent to river.

12acres 22 pitches 50static SA 22🚐£3
or 22 🚃£3 or 22▲£3 (awnings)

12🏕 Individual pitches ⊘ late arrivals
enclosure 12wc lit all night 3cdp 🚻
(washbasins hc central hot water 🚿hc)
☺ supervised (wash spin dry iron cold
storage) calor gas camping gaz cafe 🍴
⊖ stables

HULME END
Staffordshire
Map 7 SK15

▽ ②
Endon Cottage (SK109587)
🕾Hartington (029884) 617

Level paddock on high ground in Peak
District; isolated surroundings with wide
country views.

15pitches 5🚐✳£1 or 5 🚃£1 10▲fr50p
🏕 cdp

HUNSTANTON
Norfolk
Map 9 TF64

▶▶▶ ② ❷ ⚠
Searles Camping Ground (TF671400)
South Beach Signposted 🕾(04853)
2342 Apr–Sep booking advisable Jul &
Aug Last arrival 18.00hrs Last departure
noon no single sex groups

A level, grassy site with bushes,
adjacent to sea and beach. On B1161, in
South Hunstanton, off A149 King's Lynn
road.

5acres 150pitches 400static SA
75🚐 fr£4 10 🚃 fr£4 75▲fr£3.50
(awnings) ltr

10🏕⊘ late arrivals enclosure 15wc lit
all night cdp 🚻 washbasins hc central
hot water 🚿hc ☺ supervised (wash spin
iron (🍳) (games room) (licensed club/
bar) childrens playground calor gas
camping gaz toilet fluid cafe restaurant
🕾 hairdressing sauna Jacuzzi 🍴
⊖ stables golf 🏌 ✔ launderette pub

HUNTINGDON
Cambridgeshire
Map 4 TL27

▶▶ ③ ❶ ⚠
**Anchor Cottage Riverside Caravan &
Camping Site** (TL253725) Church Ln,
Hartford Signposted 🕾(0480) 55642
Mar–Oct rs Nov–Feb booking advisable
Jul & Aug Last arrival 22.00hrs Last
departure noon nc16yrs

A level grassy site with mature trees and
bushes set in woodland with river

---

nearby. 1m NE of Huntingdon on A141.

1½acres 29pitches 15static 29🚐 or
29 🚃 or 29▲ (awnings)

2🏕 Individual pitches 5wc 1cdp
(washbasins hc 🚿hc) ☺ supervised
⊖ stables golf 🏌 cinema ✔
launderette pub 🍴 ·

HURN
Dorset
Map 4 SZ19

▶▶▶ ③ ❸ ⚠
Tall Trees (SZ128999) Matcham Ln
Signposted 🕾Christchurch (0202)
477144 Mar–Dec must book Jul & Aug
Last arrival 22.30hrs Last departure
11.00hrs no tents no motorcycles

From Hurn village follow signs Sopley
then Matchams for 1½ miles. From A31
(west of Ringwood) follow signs
Verwood B3081 then beneath A31 turn
into Hurn Lane, unclass. Proceed for 3
miles towards Hurn passing through
Matchams.
Set in secluded woodland setting within
easy reach of Bournemouth and the New
Forest.

1½acres 20pitches 21static
20🚐£3.50–£5.50 or 20 🚃£3.50–£5.50
awnings

10🏕 Individual pitches 12wc lit all night
2cdp 🚻 washbasins hc 🚿hc ☺
supervised (wash dry) iron (games
room) (cold storage) childrens
playground calor gas camping gaz 🕾
off licence crazy golf 🍴
⊖ stables golf ✔ pub

ILFRACOMBE
Devon
Map 2 SS54
See Ilfracombe sketch map

▶ ② ❶ ⚠
Big Meadow Camping Site (SS546484)
Lydford Farm Signposted 🕾(0271)
62282 May–Sep 🎯 no groups of males
no caravans no motorcycles

Level, grassy site with a variety of trees
and shrubs set in wooded meadowland
with access to sea, beach, river and
A399. Opposite Watermouth Castle.

9acres 225pitches SA 225 🚃 £2.70 or
225▲£2.70 awnings

6🏕 17wc lit all night washbasins hc
(🚿hc) ☺ supervised cold storage
childrens playground calor gas camping
gaz paraffin toilet fluid 🕾 🍴
⊖ stables golf 🏌 cinema ✔
launderette pub

INCHTURE
Tayside Perthshire
Map 11 NO22

▶ ② ❷ ⚠
Inchmartine Caravan Park & Nurseries
(NO263277) Dundee Rd 🕾Rait (08217)
212 Apr–Oct Last arrival 20.00hrs Last
departure noon no tents

A level and grassy site with mature trees
and bushes, set amidst hills, mountains,
moorland, woodland and downs. →

154

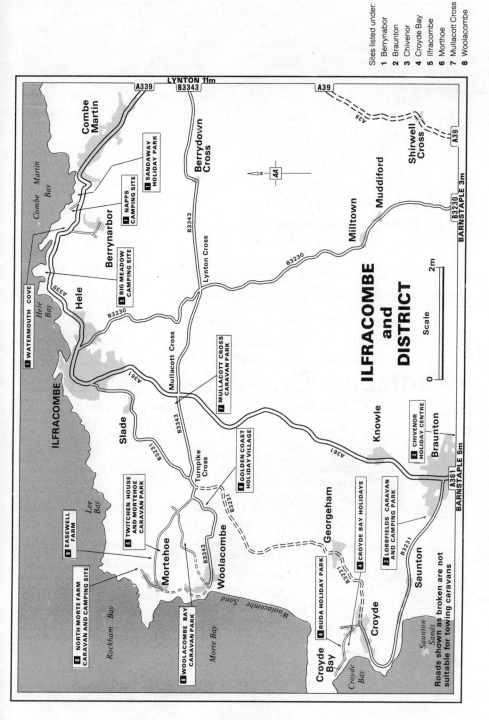

ILFRACOMBE and DISTRICT

Sites listed under:
1 Berrynabor
2 Braunton
3 Chivenor
4 Croyde Bay
5 Ilfracombe
6 Morthoe
7 Mullacott Cross
8 Woolacombe

LYNTON 11m
A339
B3343
A39
A39
Combe Martin
Shirwell Cross
Berrydown Cross
3 SANDAWAY HOLIDAY PARK
1 NAPS CAMPING SITE
Berrynarbor
B3343
Lynton Cross
Muddiford
Milltown
B3230
Hele
Combe Martin Bay
Hele Bay
Watermouth Cove
1 WATERMOUTH COVE
5 BIG MEADOW CAMPING SITE
B3230
Mullacott Cross
B3230
BARNSTAPLE 3m
ILFRACOMBE
Slade
A361
7 MULLACOTT CROSS CARAVAN PARK
Knowle
Scale
0   2m

Lee Bay
B3231
Turnpike Cross
B3343
8 GOLDEN COAST HOLIDAY VILLAGE
3 CHIVENOR HOLIDAY CENTRE
Braunton
A361
BARNSTAPLE 5m

6 EASEWELL FARM
6 TWITCHEN HOUSE AND MORTEHOE CARAVAN PARK
Mortehoe
B3343
B3231
Woolacombe
Georgeham
A361
Saunton

Rockham Bay
6 NORTH MORTE FARM CARAVAN AND CAMPING SITE
8 WOOLACOMBE BAY CARAVAN PARK
Morte Bay
Woolacombe Sand
4 RUDA HOLIDAY PARK
4 CROYDE BAY HOLIDAYS
2 LOBBFIELDS CARAVAN AND CAMPING PARK
B3231
Saunton Sands

Croyde Bay
Croyde Bay
Croyde
Saunton Sands

Roads shown as broken are not suitable for towing caravans

155

Near to A85 Perth–Dundee road.
8acres 45pitches 45🚐£3 or 45🚐£3
awnings
3🏕 8wc lit all night 12washbasins hc
(🚿hc) ☺ supervised
⊖ launderette pub 🍺

INKBERROW
Hereford & Worcester
Map 4 SP05

▽ ①
Broad Close Farm *(SP004573)* Stonepit
Ln 🕾(0386) 792266 All year must book
Last arrival 18.00hrs no single sex
groups

Gently sloping farm meadowland on
outskirts of village.
5acres 50pitches 50🚐£2 or 50🚐£2 or
50▲£2 awnings
1🏕 2wc lit all night 2cdp riding stables
⊖ pub

INSTOW
Devon
Map 2 SS43

▶ ① ❶ ⚠
Lagoon Holiday Park *(SS491316)*
Signposted 🕾(0271) 860423 Whit–1st
wk Oct rs Etr–Whit must book Last
arrival 23.00hrs Last departure 10.00hrs
🌂

This quiet site, situated in rolling
parkland overlooking the Taw Estuary, is
an ideal base for touring North Devon.
On the A39.
8acres 139pitches 66static 94🚐£3.50–
£6 or 94🚐£3–£5.50 45▲£3–£5.50
awnings
🏕 late arrivals enclosure 33wc lit all
night 1cdp 2🚿 16washbasins hc central

hot water 12⌂ hc 5☉ supervised (wash spin dry) iron games room CTV cold storage licensed club childrens playground calor gas camping gaz ☎ 🛅

↔ stables ⅃ cinema ♪ pub

INVERARAY
Strathclyde *Argyllshire*
Map 10 NN00

▶ ▶ ▶ ② ❷ ⚠

Battlefield Caravan Park *(NN075055)*
Signposted ☎(0499) 2285 Apr–Oct

Attractive site set in wooded area on shores of Loch Fyne. 2½m S from Inveraray on A83.

52acres 210pitches 200static 60🚐£3.50 150🚐£3.25 or 150▲£3 (awnings) ltr

12🚐 Individual pitches for caravans ⊘ late arrivals enclosure 48wc lit all night 5cdp washbasins hc ⌂ hc ☉ supervised (wash dry iron) games room CTV (licensed club/bar) childrens playground private beach calor gas camping gaz toilet fluid cafe restaurant ☎ fishing 🛅

↔ stables ⅃ ♪ launderette

INVERCHAPEL
Strathclyde *Argyllshire*
Map 10 NS18

▶ ▶ ▶ ② ❷ ⚠

Stratheck International Caravan Park
(NS144865) Signposted ☎Kilmun (036984) 472 Apr–Oct must book peak periods Last arrival 21.00hrs Last departure noon

Level grass site with all-weather pitches amidst mature trees and bushes, set in mountainous woodland country of Argyll Forest Park. It is close to river, loch and main road. 7m N of Dunoon on A815.

8acres 50pitches 50static SA 50🚐£3.50 or 50🚐£3.50 or 50▲£3.50 (awnings) ltr

6🚐 ⊘ late arrivals enclosure 18wc lit all night 1cdp 🚽 washbasins hc ⇥hc ⌂ hc ☉ supervised (wash spin dry iron) games room (cold storage) childrens playground private beach calor gas camping gaz toilet fluid ☎ ⊞ off licence boat launching facilities football pitch batterys charged fishing bicycle hire putting green 🛅

↔ stables golf ⅃ ♪ launderette pub

INVERGARRY
Highland *Inverness-shire*
Map 14 NH30

▶ ② ❸ ⚠

Faichem Park *(NH285023)* Ardgarry, Faichem Signposted ☎(08093) 226 Mar–Oct booking advisable Jul & Aug Last arrival 21.00hrs Last departure noon

Small quiet touring site in elevated position with good clean facilities and countryside views. From the A82 at Invergarry take the A87 for one mile, turn right at 'Faichem' signpost, site is on the right.

3½acres 30pitches 15🚐£4.25 15🚐£4.25 or 15▲£4.25 awnings ltr

3🚐☉ 6wc lit all night washbasins hc (central hot water) ⌂ hc ☉ supervised cold storage calor gas camping gaz hair dryer pony rides 🛅

↔ stables ⅃ ♪ pub

INVERMORISTON
Highland *Inverness-shire*
Map 14 NH41

▶ ▶ ② ❷ ⚠

Loch Ness Caravan & Camping Park
(NH424150) Easter Port Clair Signposted ☎Glenmoriston (0320) 51207 15 Mar–15 Oct Last arrival 22.00hrs Last departure noon

Part level, part sloping, grass and gravel site amid mountains and wooded hill country, with access to Loch Ness. 4½m N of Fort Augustus.

8acres 91pitches 6static SA 50🚐£5 10🚐£5 31▲£5 (awnings)

10🚐 13wc lit all night 3cdp washbashins hc ⌂ hc ☉ supervised (wash spin dry

---

iron games room) childrens playground private beach ☎

↔ stables golf ⅃ ♪ launderette pub 🛅

INVERNESS
Highland *Inverness-shire*
Map 14 NH64
See sketch map

▶ ▶ ▶ ① ❷ ⚠

Bught Caravan & Camping Site
(NH658438) Apply to: Inverness District Council, Parks Superintendent, Town House, Inverness IV1 1JJ Signposted ☎Inverness (0463) 236920 Etr–mid Oct no bookings Last arrival 22.00hrs Last departure noon

Large municipal touring site close to some of the town's other leisure amenities. 1m W of Inverness on A82.

245pitches SA 245🚐£3.50 or 245🚐£3.50 or 245▲£3.50 (awnings)

6🚐 Individual pitches 48wc lit all night 6cdp washbasins hc central hot water ⌂ hc ☉ dry childrens playground calor gas camping gaz cafe restaurant ☎ 🛅

↔ golf ⅃ cinema ♪ launderette pub

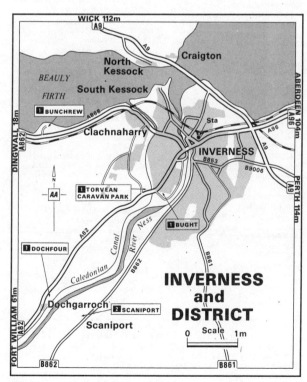

Sites listed under: **1** Inverness   **2** Scaniport

▶▶▶ ② ❷ ⚠

Bunchrew Caravan Park *(NH618460)*
Bunchrew ☎(0463) 237802 Apr–Sep
booking advisable Jul & Aug Last arrival
21.00hrs Last departure noon

A well laid out and carefully maintained site with touring pitches separate from the residential area. 3m W of Inverness on road to Beauly and Dingwall (A862).

7acres 100pitches 61static 50☗ or 50☗ 50▲£3 (awnings) ltr

11☭⏱ 18wc lit all night 1cdp ☗(washbasins hc) central hot water (🛁hc)☺(wash) (dry) iron childrens playground private beach calor gas camping gaz ☎ ⚓

↝ golf ⚓ cinema ⚓ launderette

▶▶▶ ① ❷ ⚠

Torvean Caravan Park *(NH654438)*
Glenurquhart Rd Signposted ☎(0463) 220582 25 Mar–Oct must book Jul & Aug Last arrival 21.00hrs Last departure noon no motorcycles no tents no traders no all male groups

Small, neatly maintained site behind caravan sales complex, adjacent to canal and golf course. 1m W on A82 Fort William road.

50pitches 11static 50☗£4 or 50☗£4 (awnings)

9☭ Individual pitches 12wc lit all night 1cdp 10☗ washbasins hc 🛁hc☺ supervised (wash dry iron) (licensed club/bar) childrens playground calor gas camping gaz toilet fluid ☎ cruises on canal ⚓

↝ stables golf ⚓ cinema ⚓ launderette pub

▶▶ ① ❶ ⚠

Dochfour Site *(NH616404)*
Dochgarroch ☎Dochgarroch (046386) 218 May–Sep no bookings Last arrival 20.00hrs Last departure 11.00hrs

Level, grassy site adjacent to Caledonian Canal. 4½m SW of Inverness on A82.

5acres 190pitches 90☗ fr£3.50 or 90☗ fr£3.50 100▲ fr£3.50 awnings

7☭⏱ 36wc lit all night 1cdp washbasins hc 🛁hc☺ calor gas camping gaz ⚓

↝ golf ⚓ ⚓

INVERUGLAS
Strathclyde *Dunbartonshire*
Map 10NN30

▶▶ ② ❶ ⚠

Loch Lomond Holiday Park
(NN320092) ☎(03014) 224 Apr–Oct

---

booking advisable Jul & Aug Last arrival 22.00hrs Last departure 22.00hrs no tents

Level site with mature trees and bushes, on A82 between Inverbeg and Ardlui.

3acres 10pitches 50static 7☗ 3☗ (awnings) ltr

2☭ 10wc lit all night 1cdp washbasins hc central hot water (🛁hc)☺ supervised private beach calor gas camping gaz toilet fluid

↝ ⚓ ⚓ pub ⚓

ISLE OF MAN
Map 6
See under Hillberry and Laxey

ISLE OF WHITHORN
Dumfries & Galloway *Wigtownshire*
Map 11 NX43

▶▶▶▶ ② ❷ ⚠

Burrow Head Holiday Farm
(NX450346) Signposted ☎Whithorn
(09885) 252 Etr–Sep rs Mar–Etr & Oct
no bookings Last departure 14.00hrs

Part level, part sloping grass site with bushes set in hilly moorland country on cliff edge with access to sea for fishing only. 2m W of Isle of Whithorn.

40acres 260pitches 300static 260☗£3.50 or 260☗£3.50 or 260▲£3.50 awnings ltr

☭ 53wc lit all night 1cdp washbasins hc (🛁hc)☺ (wash dry iron) ⚓ (games room) CTV (cold storage) licensed club/bar childrens playground calor gas toilet fluid cafe ☎ sea fishing pony trekking ⚓

↝ stables ⚓ ⚓ pub

ISLE OF WIGHT
Places with AA-classified caravan and campsites are indicated on the location map on page 4 of the atlas section. Full details of these will be found under individual placenames within the gazetteer section.

ISLES OF SCILLY
(No map)
No sites on the islands hold AA classification. See page 78.

JEDBURGH
Borders *Roxburghshire*
Map 12 NT62

▶▶▶▶ ② ❸ ⚠

Lilliardsedge Park *(NT620267)* Ancrum
☎Ancrum (08353) 271 Etr–Whit & end

Jun–Aug booking advisable peak periods Last arrival 23.00hrs Last departure noon no firearms

Well managed site offering choice of parkland or forest areas. On A68 6m NW of Jedburgh.

25acres 190pitches 30static 100☗ 10☗ 80▲£3–£4 (awnings) ltr

18☭ late arrivals enclosure 49wc lit all night 4cdp ☗ washbasins hc central hot water (🛁hc)☺ supervised (wash spin dry iron) (cold storage) licensed bar childrens playground calor gas camping gaz paraffin toilet fluid ☎ take-away food, bar meals, roller skating ⚓

↝ golf ⚓ launderette

▶▶▶ ① ❸ ⚠

Elliot Park *(NT658218)* Edinburgh Rd
Signposted ☎(0835) 63393 Apr–Sep
Last arrival 22.00hrs Last departure noon

A touring site on northern edge of town, nestling at foot of cliffs close to Jed Water. Off A68.

2¾acres 45pitches 45☗ or 45☗ or 45▲ awnings

7☭⏱ 9wc lit all night 1cdp washbasins hc 🛁hc☺ supervised (iron) ☎ mobile shop

↝ stables golf ⚓ pub ⚓

JERSEY
Channel Islands
Map 16
See St Brelade, St Martin, St Ouen

JOHN O'GROATS
Highland *Caithness*
Map 15 ND37

▶▶ ② ❷ ⚠

John O'Groats Caravan Site
(ND382733) Signposted
☎(095581) 250 or 329 Apr–Sep Last
arrival 23.00hrs Last departure noon

Situated in open position right above the seashore looking out towards the Orkney Islands, at the end of A9.

2acres 45pitches SA 45☗£2.50 or 45☗£2.50 or 45▲£2.50 (awnings) ltr

8☭ 10wc lit all night 1cdp 12washbasins hc (4🛁hc) 2☺ cold storage calor gas camping gaz ⚓

↝ ⚓

▶ ① ❶ ⚠

Stroma View Site *(NO362730)* Huna
Signposted ☎(095581) 313 Apr–Oct
booking advisable Jul Last arrival
23.00hrs Last departure 11.00hrs

Slightly sloping, grass site set in downland with cliff scenery and access to sea and beach. 1½m W of John O'Groats on A836.

¾acre 15pitches SA 15🚐 £2.20 or 15 🚐 £2 or 10🛆£2 (awnings) ltr

3🐾 Individual pitches ☾ 3wc lit all night 1cdp 🔌 washbasins hc (central hot water) (🛁hc) ☺ cold storage camping gaz cafe ☎ mobile shop

↔ golf 🎣 launderette 🧺

KEITH
Grampian *Banffshire*
Map 15 NJ45

▶▶ ① ❸ ⚠
Keith Caravan Site *(NJ435501)*
Signposted ☎Elgin (0343) 45121 Etr–20 Sep booking advisable peak periods Last arrival 20.00hrs Last departure noon

A compact, newly developed site, located on the southern edge of town off the A6. Adjacent to housing estate.

3½acres 24pitches 20static 23🚐 £3.19 or 23 🚐 £3.19 or 10🛆£2.53–£3.19 (awnings) ltr

3🐾 Individual pitches ☾ 12wc lit all night 1cdp washbasins hc central hot water (🛁hc) ☺ (wash spin) iron childrens playground

↔ golf 🎣 pub 🧺

KELSO
Borders *Roxburghshire*
Map 12 NT73

▶▶▶ ❸ ❷ ⚠
Springwood Caravan Park *(NT720334)*
Signposted ☎(0573) 24596 Apr–Sep must book Jul & Aug Last departure 14.00hrs no tents

The site is located in a secluded position close to the tree-lined River Teviot about 1m W of the town.

5acres 25pitches 230static 30🚐 £3 or 30 🚐 £3 (awnings) ltr

3🐾 wc lit all night 1cdp 🔌 washbasins hc 🛁hc ☺ (wash) iron games room (cold storage) childrens playground calor gas ☎ skittles table tennis 🟁

↔ golf cinema 🎣

KEMPSEY
Hereford & Worcester
Map 3 SO84

▶ ① ❸ ⚠
Court Meadow Caravan Park
(SO848492) Signposted ☎Worcester (0905) 820295 All year no tents

---

Mainly level, grass site amidst a variety of trees and bushes. Set in meadowland adjacent to main road and River Severn. Situated 2m S of Worcester off A38 in Kempsey village.

2acres 20pitches 20🚐 £3.50 or 20 🚐 £3.50 (awnings) ltr

6🐾 20wc lit all night washbasins hc (🛁hc) ☺ (wash spin dry) calor gas boats for hire slipway

↔ stables golf 🪝 cinema 🎣 launderette pub 🧺

KENDAL
Cumbria
Map 7 SD59

▶▶ ❷ ① ⚠
Millcrest Caravan Park *(SD525949)*
Signposted ☎(0539) 21075 Apr–Oct booking advisable public hols & Jul–Aug Last arrival 21.00hrs Last departure 13.00hrs

Sloping grass site, set in hilly woodland and meadowland. Situated on the A6, 1½m N of Kendal.

2acres 36pitches 36🚐 £2.80 (awnings) ltr

🐾 Individual pitches wc lit all night 1cdp washbasins hc (🛁hc) ☺ supervised spin (dry iron) childrens playground calor gas camping gaz ☎

↔ stables golf cinema 🎣 launderette 🧺

KENMORE
Tayside *Perthshire*
Map 11NN74

▶▶▶ ❷ ❷ ⚠
Kenmore Caravan & Camping Park
(NN772458)
Signposted ☎(08873) 226 Etr–mid Oct rs late Mar–Etr booking advisable mid Jul–mid Aug Last arrival 22.00hrs Last departure noon single sex groups only by arrangement

Part level, part sloping, grass site with trees, set in mountains, woods and meadowland, adjacent to River Tay, W of Aberfeldy on A827.

7acres 160pitches 60static 60🚐 £3.30 10 🚐 £2.70 90🛆£2.50 awnings

10🐾 Individual pitches for caravans ☾ 35wc lit all night 2cdp washbasins hc 🛁hc ☺ supervised spin dry iron cold storage childrens playground calor gas camping gaz toilet fluid ☎ ⊞ 🧺

↔ stables golf 🪝 🎣 launderette pub

KENNACK SANDS
Cornwall
Map 2 SW71
See Mullion sketch map

▶▶▶ ❸ ❷ ⚠
Chy Carne Caravan Site *(SW737167)*
Signposted ☎The Lizard (0326) 290541 30 Mar–Oct must book Jul & Aug Last arrival 22.00hrs Last departure noon 🛪 no motorcycles no single sex groups

Small personally run site with lovely country views, set above a gentle valley with well kept grounds.

6acres 12pitches 12static 12🚐 £3–£4 or 12 🚐 £3–£4 or 12🛆£3–£4 awnings

8🐾 Individual pitches 6wc lit all night 4cdp 🔌 washbasins hc (central hot water) (🛁hc) ☺ (wash spin dry) games room cold storage childrens playground calor gas camping gaz toilet fluid ☎ ⊞ 🧺

↔ stables 🎣 launderette pub

▶▶▶ ❷ ❷ ⚠
Sea Acres Caravan Park *(SW728162)*
Signposted
☎The Lizard (0326) 290665 Etr–Sep booking advisable Jul–Aug Last arrival 23.00hrs Last departure 10.00hrs no single sex groups

Mainly level site with some bushes, set in meadowland and adjacent to sea and beach; 10m SE of Helston.

10acres 50pitches 100 static SA 50🚐 £2–£4.50 or 50 🚐 £2–£4.50 or 50🛆£2–£4.50 (awnings) ltr

10🐾 late arrivals enclosure 27wc lit all night (washbasins hc) (🛁hc ☺) supervised (wash spin iron) CTV (licensed club) calor gas camping gaz toilet fluid ☎ ⊞ 🧺

↔ stables golf 🪝 🎣 launderette pub

▶▶ ❷ ① ⚠
Silver Sands Holiday Park *(SW727166)*
Signposted ☎The Lizard (0326) 290631 Apr–Oct must book Jul–Aug

Level, grass site with young trees and bushes, set in moorland and meadowland with access to sea and beach at Kennack Sands.

1acre 20pitches 24static 20🚐 £3.90 or 20 🚐 £3.90 or 20🛆£3.90 (awnings)

4🐾 10wc lit all night 1cdp 🔌 (washbasins hc 🛁hc) ☺ supervised (spin dry iron) cold storage childrens playground calor gas camping gaz cafe restaurant ☎ 🧺

↔ stables pub

KENNFORD
Devon
Map 3 SX98

▶▶▶▶ ⓩ ❸ ⚠
Kennford International Caravan Park
(SX912857) Signposted ☎Exeter
(0392) 833046 15 Mar–15 Jan booking
advisable public hols & Jul–Aug Last
departure noon

*Situated to the S of Exeter in a central
position for touring South Devon.*

8acres 150pitches 150🚐fr£4 or
150🚐fr£4 or 150▲fr£4 (awnings) ltr

16🚙 Individual pitches late arrivals
enclosure 39wc lit all night 4cdp 🚿

washbasins hc (🚿hc🛁hc) ☺
supervised (wash spin dry iron) (cold
storage) childrens playground calor gas
camping gaz paraffin toilet fluid ☎ 🎲 🛒

↔ stables golf 🏌 launderette pub

KENTISBEARE
Devon
Map 3ST00

▶▶▶ ⓩ ❷ ⚠
Forest Glade Holiday Park *(ST100075)*
Signposted ☎Broadhembury (040484)
381 15 Mar–14 Nov must book peak

periods Last arrival 22.00hrs no
caravans

*Site situated on top of Black Down with
signposting off the A373 linking M5
(Cullompton) and A30 (Honiton). There
is no need to enter Kentisbeare Village
from either direction.*

6acres 85pitches 41static 85 🚐 £6.10 or
85▲£6.10 awnings ltr

6🚙☽ late arrivals enclosure 12wc lit all
night 1cdp 🚿 washbasins hc (🛁hc) ☺
supervised (wash spin dry iron) ⊇ 🎾
CTV (cold storage) childrens playground
calor gas camping gaz toilet fluid ☎ 🎲
take-away food, facilities for disabled, 🛒

↔ stables 🏌 launderette pub

Caravan & Camping Park

A small country estate surrounded by forest with deer
LARGE, FLAT, SHELTERED CAMPING PITCHES
Modern toilet block with showers, launderette and washing-up facilities
DELUXE 2/4/6 BERTH FULL SERVICE CARAVANS ALSO FOR HIRE
AND SELF-CONTAINED FLAT FOR 2 PERSONS

Shop, Heated Swimming Pool, Adventure Play Area, Electric Hook-up Points,
Forest walks, Riding, gliding and fishing nearby. Freedom for the children, peace
for the adults. Central for touring S.W. Easy access coast, moors and motorway.
Motor caravans welcome – *Facilities for the Disabled.*
S.A.E. for free colour brochure.

FOREST GLADE HOLIDAY PARK
KENTISBEARE, CULLOMPTON, DEVON EX15 2DT
Tel. (040484) 381 (Evenings also)

*Enjoy a delightful holiday
at this high quality touring
Caravan & Camping Park
in the heart of
Glorious rural Devon*

**Exeter's 4 Pennant Park with individually-hedged pitches, mains electric
hook-ups, many picnic tables and a Children's Adventure Playground.
Situated just beyond the end of the M5 on the A38 four miles south of Exeter.
The ideal touring centre for Dartmoor, Torbay and the South West.
The deluxe pine-panelled toilet facilities which include many individual
cabins for complete privacy and two Bath Rooms have been praised as 'the
Best in the Country'.
There is no on-site entertainment at KENNFORD INTERNATIONAL
ensuring a quiet and relaxing stay but there are a variety of Pubs and
Restaurants only a short walk away in the villages of Kennford and the
13th Century thatched hamlet of Kenn.**

KENNFORD INTERNATIONAL CARAVAN PARK, EXETER, GLORIOUS DEVON. (0392) 833046.

KESSINGLAND
Suffolk
Map 5 TM58

▶▶ ① ❷ ⚠

Denes Holiday Village (TM535852)
☎Lowestoft (0502) 740636 Jul–Aug rs
Apr–Jun & Sep must book Last arrival
23.00hrs Last departure 10.00hrs

*Level, grass and gravel site set in
meadowland with direct access to sea
and beach.*

7acres 90pitches 175static SA 90🚐£5
or 90🚐£5 or 90▲£5 awnings

7🚐 Individual pitches Ⓥ late arrivals
enclosure 4wc lit all night 1cdp 🔌
14washbasins hc 🚿hc ☺ supervised
(wash spin dry) iron ⟿ ⚲ games room
(cold storage) licensed club/bar
childrens playground calor gas camping
gaz toilet fluid cafe restaurant ☎ 🛒

↺ stables golf ⚑ cinema ♪
launderette pub

▶▶ ③ ❷ ⚠

Heathland Caravan Park (TM533877)
London Rd Signposted ☎Lowestoft
(0502) 740337 Apr–Oct must book Last
arrival 22.00hrs Last departure noon 🍴

*Level, grass site with mature trees and
bushes set in meadowland with direct
access to sea, beach and A12,
Lowestoft road via B1437.*

4acres 40pitches 200static SA 40🚐£4
or 40🚐£4 or 40 ▲£4 (awnings)

3🚐 Ⓥ 17wc lit all night 1cdp 🔌
washbasins hc
🚿hc ☺ supervised (wash dry iron) (cold
storage) childrens playground private
beach calor gas camping gaz toilet fluid
☎ fishing 🛒

↺ stables golf ⚑ cinema ♪
launderette pub

KIELDER
Northumberland
Map 12 NY69

▶▶ ② ❷ ⚠

Kielder Camp Site (NY626938)
Signposted ☎Bellingham (0660) 50209
29 Mar–Sep no bookings Last departure
11.00hrs

*Set in riverside fields with Kielder Water
a few minutes drive away. Proceed north*

from Kielder village towards the Scottish
Border for approx 500yds, the site is on
the right-hand side (east) of the road.

10acres 70pitches 70🚐 or 70🚐 or
70▲ awnings

2🚐 10wc 1cdp washbasins hc calor gas
camping gaz

↺ stables ♪ 🛒

KILBERRY
Strathclyde Argyllshire
Map 10 NR76

▶▶ ① ❶ ⚠

Port Ban Park (NR710655)
☎Ormsary (08803) 224 Apr–Oct
rsNov–Mar booking advisable Etr & Jul–
Aug

*Beautiful, secluded sea-front site with
uninterrupted views of Islay and Jura.*

2acres 30pitches 45static 15🚐 or 15🚐
15▲ (awnings) ltr

3🚐 Individual pitches 12wc 1cdp
17washbasins hc 4🚿hc (spin) (⚲)
games room private beach calor gas
camping gaz toilet fluid ☎ putting, crazy
golf & boats for hire

↺ ⚑ ♪ 🛒

KILKHAMPTON
Cornwall
Map 2 SS21

▶▶▶ ② ❷ ⚠

Easthorne Caravan & Camping Park
(SS260110) Signposted ☎(028882)
235 Apr–Oct rsNov–Mar must book Jul
& Aug Last arrival 21.30hrs Last
departure noon

*Small rural campsite situated adjacent to
non-working farm, ideally positioned for
touring Devon and Cornwall. In village
centre follow B3254 Launceston road for
approx ¾m.*

10acres 30pitches 1static SA 30🚐 or
30🚐 or 30▲ (awnings)

4🚐 late arrivals enclosure 5wc lit all
night 1cdp (washbasins hc central hot
water 🚿hc) ☺ supervised dry games
room (cold storage) childrens
playground calor gas camping gaz toilet
fluid take-away meals 🛒

↺ stables golf ⚑ cinema ♪
launderette pub

KILLIN
Central Perthshire
Map 11NN53

▶▶ ② ❷ ⚠

High Creagan (NN594352) Morenish
(3m NE A827) ☎(05672) 449 Apr–Oct
must book Last arrival 21.00hrs Last
departure noon no tents

*Level, grass and gravel site with trees,
set in mountainous moorland country
adjacent to river and loch.*

1acre 15pitches 15static 15🚐 or 15🚐
awnings

4🚐 Individual pitches late arrivals
enclosure 8wc lit all night 1cdp
9washbasins hc 🚿hc ☺ supervised cold
storage calor gas toilet fluid 🛒

↺ golf ⚑ ♪ pub

KILMARNOCK
Strathclyde Ayrshire
Map 10 NS43

▶ ① ❶ ⚠

**Cunningham Head Estate Caravan
Park** (NS370418) Cunningham Head
Signposted ☎Torranyard (029485) 238
Jul–Aug rs Apr–Jun & Sep no bookings
Last arrival 22.00hrs Last depature
14.00hrs

*Compact site within the grounds of a
farmland estate, 3½ NE of Irvine on
B769.*

2acres 100pitches 100static 40🚐£3.50
20 🚐£3.50 40▲£3.50 (awnings)

5🚐 Ⓥ late arrivals enclosure 22wc lit all
night washbasins hc (central hot water)
(🚿hc) (wash spin dry) (games room
cold storage) (licensed club/bar)
childrens playground camping gaz toilet
fluid ☎ 🛒

↺ stables golf cinema ♪ launderette

KILNINVER
Strathclyde Argyllshire
Map 10 NM82

▶▶▶ ② ❷ ⚠

Glen Gallain Caravan Park
(NM843196) Signposted ☎(08526) 200
Whit–5 Nov rs 25 Mar–Whit no bookings

→

Last arrival 22.00hrs Last departure 11.30hrs

Part level, part sloping grass and gravel site with young trees, set in mountainous wooded hill country adjacent to River Euchar and 10m S of Oban.

4acres 65pitches SA 30🏕£3.40–£3.80 or 30🏕£3.20–£3.60 35▲£3–£3.40 (awnings) ltr

2🚐 Individual pitches for caravans 6wc lit all night 1cdp washbasins hc (central hot water ⇋🛁hc) ☺ (dry iron cold storage) childrens playground calor gas camping gaz paraffin toilet fluid fishing 🛒

↪ ⚓ ⚲ ✦

KILTARLITY
Highland *Inverness-shire*
Map 14 NH54

▶ 🔟 ❷ ⚠

Glaichbea Caravan & Camping Site
(NH516400) The Filling Station, Glaichbea ☎(046374) 496 Mar–Oct

7pitches 7🏕£2.50–£3.50 or 7🏕£2.50–£3.50 or 7▲£2–£3 awnings

2🚐 4wc washbasins hc central hot water 🛁hc ☺ cold storage calor gas

↪ ✦ 🛒

KINGHORN
Fife
Map 11 NT28

▶▶▶▶ ❷ ❶ ⚠

Pettycur Bay Caravan Park
(NT259865) Signposted ☎(0592) 890321 24 Mar–Sep must book mid Jul–Aug Last arrival 22.00hrs Last departure noon no motorcycles, no single sex groups

This sloping, hillside, terraced site has splendid views of Edinburgh across the River Forth.

4acres 39pitches 350static SA 25🏕 25🏕 14▲ (awnings) ltr

14🚐 ☺ late arrivals enclosure 56wc lit all night 5cdp 25washbasins hc (6⇋hc 12🛁hc) 4☺ (wash spin dry) iron CTV childrens playground calor gas toilet fluid cafe ☎ ⊞ 🛒

↪ golf ✦ launderette pub

KINGSBRIDGE
Devon
Map 3 SX74

▶ ❷ ❶ ⚠

Island Lodge Farm *(SX742469)* Slade Cross, Ledstone (1½m N off A381) ☎(0548) 2956 All year booking advisable Jun–Aug Last arrival 23.00hrs Last departure 16.00hrs no single sex groups

2acres 30pitches 5🏕£2.50 25🏕£2 or 25▲£2 (awnings)

2🚐 4wc lit all night 1cdp washbasins hc (🛁hc) ☺ supervised cold storage childrens playground calor gas ☎ mobile shop

---

↪ stables ⚲ cinema ✦ launderette pub 🛒

▶ ❷ ❶ ⚠

Parkland *(SX727464)* Sorley Green Cross ☎(0548) 2723 Etr–mid Oct must book Last arrival 21.30hrs Last departure 11.00hrs no dogs

Level grassy site situated 1m N of Kingsbridge on B3194.

3acres 40pitches 15🏕✳£3 or 15🏕✳£2 25▲✳£2 (awnings)

4🚐 ☺ 5wc lit all night 1cdp central hot water (🛁hc) ☺ supervised (cold storage) childrens playground cafe

↪ stables ⚲ cinema ✦ launderette pub 🛒

▽ ❷

Beachcroft *(SX707458)* Churchstow (2m NW A379) ☎(0548) 2003 Etr–Oct must book

Level hedged paddock ½m W of Churchstow Church.

½acre 8pitches 3🏕 ▲£1.75 (awnings)

1🚐 1wc 🛒

↪ stables golf ⚲ ✦ launderette pub

KINGSBURY
Warwickshire
Map 4 SP29

▽ 🔟

Tame View *(SP209979)* Cliff (1m N A51) ☎Tamworth (0827) 873853 All year

Enclosed level small meadow on high bank overlooking River Tame.

5acres 5pitches 5🏕fr£1 or 5🏕fr£1 ▲fr50p awnings

1🚐 late arrivals enclosure 1wc 2cdp river fishing

↪ golf ⚲ ✦ launderette pub 🛒

KINGS CAPLE
Hereford & Worcester
Map 3 SO52

▽ ❷

Lower Ruxton Farm *(SO548292)* ☎Carey (043270) 223 mid Jul–Aug must book Last arrival 21.00hrs Last departure 19.00hrs no motorcycles no caravans or motor caravans

Secluded level meadowland on the left bank of the Wye.

16acres 15pitches 15▲£2

4🚐 1cdp

KINGSNORTH
Kent
Map 5 TR03

▶▶▶ 🔟 ❶ ⚠

Broad Hembury Farm *(TR009387)* Steeds Ln Signposted ☎Ashford (0233) 20859 Mar–Oct must book Jul & Aug Last arrivals mdnt Last departure 18.00hrs

---

This is a small farm site surrounded by sheep grazing land and high hedges. It is well secluded from the B2070 and approx. 4m from centre of Ashford.

3acres 55pitches 25static 55🏕£4.50 or 55🏕£4.50 or 55▲£4.50 awnings ltr

8🚐 Individual pitches ☺ 16wc lit all night 1cdp 🔌 8washbasins hc 6🛁hc 2☺ supervised (wash spin dry) iron games room CTV (cold storage) childrens playground calor gas camping gaz ☎ 🛒

↪ stables golf cinema ✦ launderette pub

KINNERLEY
Shropshire
Map 7 SJ32

▶▶▶ ❷ ❸ ⚠

Cranberry Moss Caravan & Camping Park *(SJ361214)* Signposted Apr–Sep rs Oct no bookings

Part level, part sloping site, with a variety of trees. Direct access to A5 Shrewsbury–Llangollen road.

4acres 60pitches 60🏕£2.60 or 60🏕£2.60 or 60▲£2.10 awnings ltr

3🚐 late arrivals enclosure 6wc lit all night 1cdp 🔌 (5washbasins hc) (20🛁hc) ☺ spin iron cold storage childrens playground calor gas camping gaz paraffin toilet fluid ☎ 🛒

↪ ✦ pub

KINROSS
Tayside *Kinross-shire*
Map 11 NO10

▶▶▶ ❷ ❶ ⚠

Loch Leven Caravan Site *(NO123019)* Sandport Signposted ☎(0577) 63560 Apr–Sep must book Jul & Aug Last arrival 23.00hrs Last departure noon

This level, grassy site is situated behind the town and on the shores of Loch Leven with good views. Location is relatively secluded being off the main road.

2acres 30pitches 44static SA 30🏕£3.50 or 30🏕£3 or 30▲£3.50 (awnings)

5🚐 15wc lit all night 1cdp 🔌 washbasins hc (🛁hc) ☺ supervised (wash dry iron) games room CTV (cold storage) calor gas camping gaz ☎ 🛒

↪ golf ⚲ ✦ launderette

▶ 🔟 ❶ ⚠

Milk Bar *(NT129985)* Hatchbank Signposted ☎(0577) 63506 Apr–Oct rsNov–Mar

Level, grassy site in hilly country near lake, 2m S of Kinross and ½m N of junction 5 at M90.

2acres 30pitches 6static 15🏕 or 15🏕 15▲ (awnings) ltr

1🚐 10wc lit all night 1cdp washbasins hc 🛁hc ☺ wash licensed club/bar childrens playground calor gas camping gaz cafe ☎ 🛒

↪ stables golf cinema ✦ launderette pub

KIPPFORD
Dumfries & Galloway *Kirkcudbrightshire*
Map 11 NX85

▶▶▶ ② ❷ ⚠

Kippford Caravan Site *(NX844564)*
Signposted ☎(055662) 636 Mar–Oct
no bookings Last arrival & departure
22.00hrs

*Part level, part sloping grass site with
bushes, set in hilly country adjacent to
Urr Water estuary, main road and stony
beach.*

5acres 45pitches 85static 45🚐£3.50 or
45🚐£3.50 or 45▲£3.50 (awnings)

5🏕 Individual pitches 12wc lit all night
1cdp washbasins hc central hot water
🛁hc ☺ supervised spin iron childrens
playground calor gas ☎ 🍴

↔ stables golf ♪ pub

KIRKBY-IN-FURNESS
Cumbria
Map 7 SD28

▶▶▶ ① ❶ ⚠

Longlands Caravan Park *(SD239836)*
Signposted ☎(022989) 342 Mar–Oct
booking advisable public hols Last
arrival 22.30hrs Last departure noon

*Part level, part sloping site with bushes,
overlooking Duddon Sands; 1m NE of
village off A595.*

1½acres 30pitches 120static SA
30🚐£3.50 or 30🚐 10▲£3.50 awnings

2🏕 6wc lit all night 1cdp washbasins hc
🛁hc ☺ childrens playground calor gas
camping gaz ☎ 🍴

↔ stables golf cinema ♪ launderette
pub

KIRKBY THORE
Cumbria
Map 12 NY62

▶ ① ❶ ⚠

Low Moor Caravan Site *(NY624259)*
☎(0930) 61231 Apr–Oct Last arrival
23.00hrs

*Part level, part sloping grass site 7m SE
of Penrith on A66.*

1½acres 25pitches 25static 12🚐£2
12🚐£2 or 25▲£2 (awnings)

3🏕☺ 8wc lit all night 1cdp washbasins
hc central hot water (🛁hc) ☺ supervised
cold storage childrens playground calor
gas camping gaz ☎ 🍴

↔ pub

KIRKCALDY
Fife
Map 11 NT29

▶▶▶ ② ❸ ⚠

Dunnikier Caravan Site *(NT285942)*
Dunnikier Rd Signposted ☎(0592)
267563 or 261395 Apr–Sep must book
Jul & Aug Last arrival 20.00hrs Last
departure noon

*Level grass site with trees and bushes,
within the urban area on B926.*

2acres 72pitches 72🚐 ✳£3 or 72🚐 £3
25▲£1.80 (awnings) ltr

10🏕 Individual pitches ☺ late arrivals
enclosure 19wc lit all night 6🚐
washbasins hc central hot water 🛁hc ☺
(wash spin dry iron) (cold storage)
(childrens playground) calor gas ☎ 🍴

↔ stables golf cinema ♪ launderette
pub

KIRKCUDBRIGHT
Dumfries & Galloway *Kirkcudbrightshire*
Map 11 NX65
See Gatehouse of Fleet sketch map

▶▶▶ ② ❸ ⚠

Seaward Caravan Park *(NX665494)*
Dhoon Bay (2m SW off B727 Borgue
Road) ☎Borgue (05577) 267 Mar–Oct
must book Spring Bank Hol & Jul–Aug
Last arrival 21.30hrs Last departure
11.30hrs

*Site is in an elevated position
overlooking the Dee estuary.*

3acres 26pitches 30static 20🚐fr£4 or
20🚐fr£4 6▲fr£4 (awnings) ltr

10🏕 Individual pitches ☺ late arrivals
enclosure 6wc lit all night 1cdp 🚐
washbasins hc 🛁hc ☺ supervised
(wash spin dry iron) ⚟ (games room)
CTV (cold storage) childrens playground
calor gas camping gaz paraffin toilet
fluid ☎ ⊞ sauna sunbed TV aerial hook-
up 🍴

↔ stables golf ⚡ ♪ pub

▶▶ ① ❷ ⚠

Silvercraigs Caravan & Camping Site
(NX686508) Silvercraigs Rd Apply to:
Stewartry District Council, Director of
Administration, Council Offices,
Kirkcudbright DG6 4PJ ☎(0557) 30291
16 Apr–Sep no bookings Last departure
noon

*Purpose built site with good sanitary
facilities and a range of recreational
activities. Set in elevated position
overlooking the Dee estuary.*

6¼acres 50pitches 37🚐fr£2.75 or
37🚐fr£2.75 13▲fr£2.75 awnings ltr

5🏕 Individual pitches ☺ 6wc lit all night
1cdp washbasins hc 🛁hc ☺ wash iron
childrens playground ☎ 🍴

↔ stables golf ⚡ ♪

KIRKFIELDBANK
Strathclyde *Lanarkshire*
Map 11 NS84

▶▶ ② ❷ ⚠

Clyde Valley Caravan Park *(NS868441)*
Signposted ☎Lanark (0555) 3951 Mar–
Oct no bookings Last arrival 22.00hrs
Last departure 22.00hrs 🚫 no
motorcycles

*Level, grass site with trees and bushes
set in mountains and hilly country with
access to river.*

5acres 50pitches 50🚐 or 50🚐 or 50▲
(awnings) ltr

5🏕☺ 16wc washbasins hc (🛁hc) ☺
supervised (wash) spin (dry) calor gas
camping gaz 🍴

↔ stables golf ⚡ cinema ♪
launderette pub

KIRKGUNZEON
Dumfries & Galloway *Dumfrieshire*
Map 11 NX86

▶▶▶ ① ❶ ⚠

Mossband Caravan Park *(NX873664)*
Signposted ☎(038776) 280 Etr–Oct
booking advisable mid Jul–mid Aug
Last arrival 22.00hrs Last departure
13.00hrs

*Level park on site of old railway station in
hilly country with trees and bushes;
adjacent to A711 road to Dalbeattie.*

3½acres 37pitches 3static 37🚐£3.30
or 37🚐£3.30 or 37▲£3.30 (awnings) ltr

6🏕 late arrivals enclosure 8wc lit all
night 1cdp 🚐 washbasins hc 🛁hc ☺
supervised (spin) ⚟ 🅿 cold storage
childrens playground calor gas camping
gaz toilet fluid cafe restaurant 🍴

↔ golf cinema ♪ pub

KIRKHAM
Lancashire
Map 7 SD43

▶▶▶▶ ② ❷ ⚠

Ribby Hall Park *(SD409319)* The
Leisure Village, Wrea Green (1½m W of
Kirkham B5259) Signposted ☎(0772)
685356) Mar–Oct must book Last
departure 14.00hrs nc1yr

*Set in open countryside and part of a
leisure village. An array of leisure
facilities available including squash and
badminton.*

102acres 350pitches 350🚐£4 or
350🚐£4 or 350▲£3

100🏕☺ late arrivals enclosure 60wc lit
all night 3cdp 🚐 washbasins hc
(🛒hc🛁hc) ☺ supervised (wash spin)
dry (iron) (🅿) games room TV cold
storage (licensed club/bar) childrens
playground calor gas camping gaz
paraffin toilet fluid cafe restaurant ☎ ⊞
sports centre craft village 🍴

↔ ♪ launderette pub

KIRKPATRICK FLEMING
Dumfries & Galloway *Dumfriesshire*
Map 11 NY27

▶▶ ① ❶ ⚠

Bruce's Cave & Caravan Site
(NY266705) Signposted ☎(04618) 285
Apr–Oct rsNov–Mar Last arrival
23.00hrs Last departure 16.00hrs

*Part level, part sloping grass, gravel,
and sand site with trees and bushes, set
in 80 acres of wood and meadowland
country with direct access to the river.
Off A74 at Kirkpatrick.*

80acres 40pitches 20 static SA 20🚐£2
5🚐£2 15▲£2 (awnings)

1cdp 🚐 washbasins hc (🛒hc🛁hc) ☺

→

163

supervised (cold storage) childrens playground calor gas camping gaz cafe restaurant ☎ 🏬

↤ stables golf 🎿 🗡 launderette pub

KIRRIEMUIR
Tayside *Angus*
Map 15 NO35

▶ ▶ ▶ ② ❸ ⚠

Drumshademuir Caravan Park
(NO381509) Roundyhill Signposted ☎(0575) 73284 Apr–Oct must book Jul & Aug Last arrival 23.00hrs Last departure 18.00hrs no unaccompanied under 18s

Mainly level, part sloping, grass site with saplings and bushes. Set in a valley in hilly country 2¼m S of Kirriemuir on A928.

5acres 76pitches 34static 76🚗£3 or 76🚐£3 or 76🛆£3 (awnings) ltr

5🏕 14wc lit all night 2cdp 🏪 washbasins hc (🛁hc) ☺ supervised (wash spin dry iron) cold storage calor gas camping gaz toilet fluid ☎ 🏬

↤ golf 🗡 pub

KNOCK
Cumbria
Map 12 NY62

▶ ② ❶ ⚠

Silver Band Caravan Park *(NY681269)*
Signposted ☎Kirkby Thore (09306) 218 Mar–Oct rs wknds Nov–Feb must book Last arrival 20.00hrs Last departure 10.00hrs no tents

Small, unspoilt site beneath Cross Fell, overlooking Eden Valley. Site is situated 5m N of Appleby off A66 Appleby–Penrith road, near Kirkby Thore.

½acre 2pitches 2🚗 or 2🚐 (awnings)

1🏕 Individual pitches 2wc lit all night 1cdp (🛁hc) ☺ supervised calor gas paraffin toilet fluid garage, petrol, post office 🏬

LACOCK
Wiltshire
Map 3 ST96

▶ ▶ ② ❶ ⚠

Piccadilly Caravan Site *(ST913683)*
Folly Ln Signposted ☎(024973) 260 Apr–Oct booking advisable Last arrival 21.00hrs Last departure noon

This site is ½m from Lacock village off the A350 Chippenham/Melksham road signposted to Gastard.

1¾acres 22pitches 22🚗£3 or 22🚐£3 or 22🛆£3 awnings ltr

Kirkpatrick Fleming
―
Landrake

2🏕 6wc lit all night 1cdp washbasins hc 🛁hc ☺ supervised calor gas camping gaz

↤ stables golf cinema 🗡 launderette pub 🏬

LADRAM BAY
Devon
Map 3 SY08

▶ ② ❶ ⚠

Ladram Bay Caravan Site *(SY096853)*
Signposted ☎Colaton Raleigh (0395) 68398 Spring Bank Hol–Aug rsApr–Sep must book peak periods for caravans Last arrival 20.00hrs Last departure 10.00hrs

A large caravan site with many static vans and a separate camping area which is on terraced ground in wooded surroundings. Overlooks rocky, shingle beach.

14acres 315pitches 435static SA 75🚗 or 75🚐 240🛆 (awnings)

🏕 Individual pitches for caravans ⚪ 43wc (washbasins hc) ☺ (wash spin dry iron) licensed bar private beach calor gas camping gaz cafe ☎ 🏬

↤ 🎿 🗡 launderette pub

LAIRG
Highland *Sutherland*
Map 14 NC50

▶ ❶ ❶ ⚠

Woodend Caravan & Camping Site
(NC551127) Signposted ☎(0549) 2248 Apr–Sep Last arrival 23.00hrs Last departure noon

Part level, part sloping, grass site set in hilly moorland and woodland country with access to sea, beach, river and Loch Shin, off A836 to Tongue.

4acres 52pitches 8static 52🚗£2.50 or 52🚐£2.50 or 52🛆£2.50 awnings

3🏕 11wc lit all night 1cdp washbasins hc (central hot water) (🛁hc) ☺ supervised (wash spin dry) cold storage childrens playground ☎ (hair dryer) 🏬

↤ 🎿 🗡

LALEHAM
Surrey
Map 4 TQ06

▶ ▶ ② ❶ ⚠

Laleham Park Camping Site
(TQ052684) Thameside ☎Chertsey (09328) 64149 Apr–Sep must book Jul &

Aug for tents Last arrival & departure 21.00hrs no cars by caravans/tents

Site set in a field among trees beside a peaceful stretch of the River Thames.

3acres 60pitches 8🚗£3.30 or 8🚐£3.30 52🛆£2.70

awnings 5🏕 15wc lit all night 1cdp washbasins hc central hot water 🛁hc ☺ supervised childrens playground ☎

↤ 🎿 cinema 🗡 launderette pub 🏬

LAMORNA
Cornwall
Map 2 SW42
See St Buryan sketch map

▶ ❶ ❶ ⚠

Boleigh Farm Camp Site *(SW435249)*
☎St Buryan (073672) 305 Mar–Oct must book Jul & Aug Last arrival 20.00hrs Last departure 10.00hrs

5m S of Penzance on B3315. Small site with views of countryside.

1½acres 30pitches SA 15🚗£3.25 15🚐£3 or 15🛆£3 (awnings)

3🏕 3wc lit all night washbasins hc (central hot water) (🛁hc) ☺ calor gas camping gaz mobile shop

↤ 🗡

LAMPLUGH
Cumbria
Map 11 NY02

▶ ▶ ▶ ❸ ❶ ⚠

Inglenook Caravan Park *(NY086207)*
Fitzbridge Signposted ☎(094686) 240 Mar–13 Nov must book peak periods no groups of motorcyclists

Situated just off the A5086 in beautiful surroundings and an ideal touring centre.

3acres 42pitches 15static 36🚗£4.50 or 36🚐£4.50 6🛆£4.50 awnings

2🏕 Individual pitches ⚪ late arrivals enclosure 8wc lit all night 1cdp (washbasins hc) (central hot water) (🛁hc) ☺ supervised spin childrens playground calor gas camping gaz ☎ 🏬

↤ stables golf 🎿 🗡 launderette pub

LANDRAKE
Cornwall
Map 2 SX36

▶ ▶ ▶ ② ❶ ⚠

Dolbeare Caravan Park *(SX358618)* St Ive Rd Signposted ☎(075538) 332 Apr–Oct booking advisable Jul & Aug

---

A mainly level grass site with trees and bushes set in meadowland. Situated ¾m N of Landrake off A38.

9acres 60pitches 60 £4–£5 or 60 £4–£5 or 60▲£4–£5 (awnings)

7 late arrivals enclosure 6wc 1cdp washbasins hc (hc) ⊙ supervised (wash dry iron) games room CTV childrens playground calor gas camping gaz toilet fluid ☎ hair dryers

stables golf pub

LANDSHIPPING
Dyfed
Map 2 SN01
See Tenby sketch map

►►► 1 ❶ ▲

New Park Caravan Site *(SN026111)*
☎Martletwy (083485) 284 Spring Bank Hol–Sep must book peak periods Last arrival 20.00hrs Last departure noon

Sloping grass site with trees. 7m W of Narberth.

2acres 15pitches 30static 5 or 5 10▲ awnings

1 10wc lit all night 1cdp 8washbasins hc 1central hot water (6 hc) 2⊙ supervised (wash) (dry) (cold storage) paraffin toilet fluid cafe post office

launderette pub

LANIVET
Cornwall
Map 2 SW06

►► 1 ❶ 1

Reperry Manor Touring Park
(SX046634) Reperry Manor Signposted ☎(020883) 863 or Bodmin (0208) 4061 Apr–Oct booking advisable Jul & Aug Last departure noon

Caravan site ideal for touring North and South Cornish coastlines.

2¼acres 44pitches 44 £3.70–£4.20 or 44 £3.70–£4.20 or 44▲£3.70–£4.20 (awnings)

4 8wc lit all night 1cdp washbasins hc hc ⊙ (spin)

stables pub

LANLIVERY
Cornwall
Map 2 SX05

►►► 2 ❷ ▲

Powderham Castle Caravan & Tourist Park *(SX083593)* Signposted
☎Bodmin (0208) 872277 Apr–Oct booking advisable peak periods Last arrival 22.00hrs Last departure noon

Set amongst woodland in hilly country, this level and grassy site has mature trees and bushes. 1½m SW of Lostwithiel.

10acres 76pitches 30static SA 40 fr£3.10 12 fr£2.85 24▲fr£3.10 awnings

15 Individual pitches late arrivals enclosure 15wc lit all night 1cdp washbasins hc (central hot water) (hc) ⊙ supervised (wash spin dry iron) games room TV cold storage childrens playground calor gas camping gaz ☎

stables golf launderette pub

LAUDER
Borders *Berwickshire*
Map 12 NT54

►► 2 ❷ ▲

Thirlestane Castle Caravan Site
(NT536473) Thirlestane Castle Signposted ☎(05782) 542 Etr–Sep booking advisable Jul & Aug

Mainly level grass site set in the grounds of the impressive Thirlestane Castle. The site is situated off the A697.

4acres 60pitches 60 £4 or 60 £4 or 60▲£4 (awnings) ltr

4 10wc lit all night 1cdp washbasins hc central hot water hc ⊙ ☎

stables golf launderette pub

LAUGHARNE
Dyfed
Map 2 SN31

►►► 2 ❷ ▲

Ants Hill Caravan Park *(SN299118)*
Signposted ☎(099421) 293 Mar–Oct booking advisable public hols Last arrival 23.00hrs Last departure 11.00hrs

A small touring site on sloping grassy ground, located near the village, on the Taff estuary.

4acres 60pitches 60static 20 £3 or 20 £3 or 20▲£3 (awnings) ltr

3 Individual pitches 20wc lit all night 1cdp washbasins hc central hot water (hc) ⊙ supervised (wash dry) (games room) TV (cold storage) licensed club/bar childrens playground calor gas camping gaz toilet fluid bar snacks

stables launderette pub

LAUNCESTON
Cornwall
Map 2 SX38

► 2 ❷ ▲

Travadlock Hall Holiday Park
(SX261792) Signposted ☎Coads Green (056682) 392 Apr–Oct Last arrival mdnt Last departure noon no single sex groups

A mainly level grassy site with trees situated amidst woodland and meadowland. 6m SW on A30 then B3257 and unclassified road.

2acres 12pitches 43static 4 £5 4 £5 4▲£5 (awnings)

2 3wc lit all night 1cdp washbasins hc central hot water (hc) ⊙ supervised (wash spin iron) licensed club/bar childrens playground calor gas camping gaz toilet fluid cafe ☎

stables golf cinema launderette

LAXEY
Isle of Man
Map 6 SC48

► 1 ❶ ▲

Laxey Commissioners Campsite
(SC438841) Signposted ☎(0624) 781764 Apr–Sep must book no caravans

Level grassy site set in hilly country with access to sea, beach and hills.

1½acres 40pitches 40 £2.30 or 40▲£2.30 awnings

3 5wc lit all night (central hot water) (hc) ⊙

pub

LEBBERSTON
North Yorkshire
Map 8 TA08
See Scarborough sketch map

►►► 2 ❷ ▲

Flower of May Caravan Park
(TA096830) Signposted
☎Scarborough (0723) 584311 Good Fri–Sep must book Last arrival 22.00hrs Last departure 13.00hrs no motorcycles or scooters no groups of young persons

Situated on level, sloping ground overlooking the Wolds within 400yds of cliffs with beach access.

13acres 320pitches 103static 150 fr£3 10 fr£3 160▲fr£3 (awnings) ltr

32 Individual pitches for caravans late arrivals enclosure 49wc lit all night 3cdp washbasins hc central hot water (hc) ⊙ supervised (wash spin dry) iron () games room TV (cold →

storage) licensed bar childrens playground calor gas camping gaz toilet fluid ☎ ⊞ 🛍

↤ stables golf ⅄ cinema ⌐ launderette pub

see advertisement on page 228

▶▶▶ ② ❷ △
Lebberston Caravan Park *(TA080821)*
Signposted ☎Scarborough (0723) 582254 28 Apr–Sep must book peak periods Last arrival 21.00hrs Last departure noon no tents

A part level and part sloping grass site with saplings and bushes set in meadowland. Off A165 Filey–Scarborough road.

7½acres 125pitches 125🔌£2 or 125🚐 £2 (awnings)

8🚿 Individual pitches 24wc lit all night 2cdp 🔌 washbasins hc 🛁hc ☉ childrens playground calor gas camping gaz mobile shop

↤ launderette pub

LEEDSTOWN *(near Hayle)*
Cornwall
Map 2 SW63
See Hayle sketch map

▶▶▶ ② ❶ △
Calloose Farm Caravan Park
(SW597352) Signposted ☎(0736) 850431 May–Oct rs Apr must book Jul & Aug ⅋ Last arrival 22.30hrs Last departure 11.00hrs no single sex groups

A level and grassy site with bushes, set in hilly country, not far from Hayle. Follow B3302 from 'Duke of Leeds' public house in Leedstown centre for approx ½m.

5acres 108pitches 12static 108🚐£4.40 or 108 🚐£4.40 or 108▲£4.40 (awnings)

7🚿 Individual pitches 14wc 4cdp washbasins hc (🛁hc) ☉ supervised (wash dry) iron cold storage childrens playground calor gas camping gaz ☎ take away food service 🛍

↤ stables ⌐ pub

LEISTON
Suffolk
Map 5 TM46

▶▶▶ ③ ❷ △
Cakes & Ale *(TM432637)* Abbey Ln Signposted ☎(0728) 831655 Apr–Oct must book school and public hols

Level, well maintained site, offering extensive hard standing. Ideal base for touring. From A12 at Saxmundham turn E onto B1119 for 3 miles. Then follow by-road over level crossing and signs to caravan park.

10acres 100pitches 200static 100🚐£4.60–£6.90 or 100 🚐£4.60–£6.90 or 100▲£4.60–£6.90 awnings ltr

5🚿 20wc lit all night 1cdp 🔌 washbasins hc central hot water 🛁hc ☉ supervised (wash dry) iron ⅋ childrens

---

playground calor gas camping gaz ☎ 🛍

↤ stables cinema ⌐ launderette pub

LELANT DOWNS
Cornwall
Map 2 SW53
See St Ives sketch map

▶▶ ② ❷ △
Sunny Meadow Caravan Park
(SW528359) ☎Hayle (0736) 752243 Apr–Oct must book Jul & Aug Last arrival 20.00hrs Last departure 11.00hrs no single sex groups

Level, grass site with varied trees and bushes, set in wood and meadowland. 1½m from nearest beach, adjacent to river and near A3074 St. Ives road.

¼acre 6pitches 6static 6🚐£4 or 6 🚐£4 or 6▲£4 (awnings)

1🚿 Individual pitches 4wc lit all night 1cdp 🔌 washbasins hc (🛁hc) ☉ supervised (wash) (dry iron) cold storage calor gas 🛍

↤ stables golf ⅄ cinema ⌐ launderette pub

LETHAM FEUS
Fife
Map 11 NO30

▶▶▶ ② ❷ △
Letham Feus Caravan Park
(NO369084) Signposted ☎Kennoway (0333) 350323 Apr–Sep must book Jul & Aug Last arrival 22.00hrs Last departure 12.00hrs no tents

Set on high ground amidst farming land and sheltered by woodland to rear. Fine views across distant Firth of Forth. On A916 2m NE of Kennoway.

1acre 11pitches 100static 11🚐 or 11 🚐 awnings ltr

5🚿 late arrivals enclosure 14wc lit all night 1cdp 🔌 16washbasins hc 6🛁hc 4☉ (wash) (dry iron) (games room) CTV cold storage childrens playground calor gas camping gaz paraffin toilet fluid ☎ 🛍

↤ golf ⅄ cinema ⌐ launderette pub

LEVENS
Cumbria
Map 7 SD48

▶▶ ① ❶ △
Sampool Caravan Site *(SD478843)*
☎Witherslack (044852) 265 15 Mar–Oct booking advisable peak periods Last arrival 23.00hrs Last departure noon no tents

Level and open site located off A590, ½m from its junction with the A6.

2acres 30pitches 185static SA 30🚐 £3.50 or 30 🚐£3.50 awnings ltr

2🚿 9wc lit all night 1cdp washbasins hc 🛁hc ☉ supervised (wash spin dry)

---

childrens playground calor gas ☎ 🛍

↤ ⌐ launderette pub

LEWIS, ISLE OF
Western Isles *Ross and Cromarty*
Map 13 NB
See Coll Sands

LITTLE HAVEN
Dyfed
Map 2 SM81
For details of sites see Hasguard Cross

LITTLE TORRINGTON
Devon
Map 2 SS41

▶▶▶ ② ❶ △
Smytham Caravan & Camp Site
(SS493168) Signposted ☎Torrington (08052) 2110 15 Mar–Oct must book Jul & Aug

A small site situated in a secluded wooded area in the grounds of an old manor house adjacent to A386. Access is by a good approach road with ramps.

2acres 40pitches 40static 15🚐£2.50 or 15 🚐£2.50 25▲£2.50 (awnings)

8🚿☉ 9wc lit all night 1cdp 8washbasins hc (🛁hc) ☉ (wash spin) iron ▭ games room (cold storage) childrens playground calor gas camping gaz paraffin ☎ 🛍

↤ stables golf cinema ⌐ launderette pub

LLANBEDROG
Gwynedd
Map 6 SH33

▶▶ ① ❶ △
Crugan Caravan Site *(SH335323)*
Signposted ☎Abersoch (075881) 2045 Mar–Oct must book Last arrival 18.00hrs Last departure 10.00hrs no tents or motorvans no dogs no motorcycles

Mainly level grass site with slight gradient, trees and bushes. Set in meadowland in urban area overlooking Llanbedrog Bay. Off N side of the A499 ¼m E of town.

20pitches 20🚐 fr£4.50 awnings

2🚿 Individual pitches 14wc lit all night 1cdp washbasins hc central hot water (🛁hc) ☉ supervised (wash spin dry) (cold storage) ☎ mobile shop

↤ stables golf ⅄ ⌐ launderette pub 🛍

LLANDRE
Dyfed
Map 6 SN68

▶▶▶ ① ❶
Riverside Park *(SN631872)* Signposted Mar–Oct must book

Level, grass site with trees and bushes set in woodland and meadowland with access to River Leri. On A487, 4m from Aberystwyth, take B4353 and turn right at second turning.

4acres 30pitches 76static SA 10🚐 £3 20▲£1.50 (awnings) ltr

3♠⊘ 8wc lit all night 1cdp washbasins
hc (⋔hc ⊙) supervised (wash spin dry)
iron childrens playground calor gas toilet
fluid ☎ ⅃
↔ stables golf ⅄ cinema ♪
launderette pub

LLANDRILLO
Clwyd
Map 6 SJ03

▶▶ ② ❶
Hendwr Farm Site *(SJ035386)*
Signposted ☎(049084) 210 or 252
Apr–Oct rs Nov–Mar must book public
& school hols Last arrival 22.00hrs Last
departure 16.00hrs

*Level grass site with mature trees near
river, hills, woodland and moorland. 4m
SW of Corwen on A5, then left onto
B4401.*

4acres 40pitches 80static SA 20♣£4 or
20♣£4 20🅰£3.50 (awnings)

6♠⊘ 14wc lit all night 2cdp 🔌
washbasins hc ⋔hc ⊙ supervised
(wash spin dry) iron (cold storage) calor
gas camping gaz toilet fluid ☎ ⊞ ⅃
↔ ♪ launderette pub

LLANGADOG
Dyfed
Map 3 SN72

▶▶ ② ❸
Abermarlais Caravan Park *(SN695298)*
Signposted ☎(05503) 868 Mar–Dec
booking advisable Jul & Aug Last arrival
23.00hrs Last departure noon

*Part level, part sloping grass site
situated in a wooded valley on edge of
Brecon Beacons National Park. It is by
the River Marlais and off A40 Llandeilo–
Llandovery road.*

8acres 88pitches SA 60♣£4 or
60♣£3.45 28🅰£4 (awnings) ltr

4♠ Individual pitches⊘ late arrivals
enclosure 14wc lit all night 1cdp
washbasins hc central hot water ⋔hc ⊙
supervised cold storage childrens
playground calor gas camping gaz toilet
fluid ☎ ⊞ ⅃
↔ ♪ pub

LLANGOLLEN
Clwyd
Map 7 SJ24

▶▶▶ ③ ❷ ⚠
Ty-Ucha Farm *(SJ232415)* Maesmawr
Rd Signposted ☎(0978) 860677 Etr–
Oct booking advisable peak periods
Last arrival 22.00hrs Last departure
14.00hrs no tents

*Small, neat touring site in quiet position
yet conveniently placed close to A5.
Ideal for country and mountain walking,
with small stream traversing its south
boundary.*

4½acres 40pitches 30♣£3.50
10♣£3.25 (awnings)

4♠ Individual pitches late arrivals
enclosure 6wc lit all night 1cdp 🔌

---

washbasins hc (⋔hc) ⊙ supervised
games room (cold storage) calor gas
camping gaz toilet fluid ☎ ⅃
↔ stables ♪ launderette pub

LLANGRANOG
Dyfed
Map 2 SN35

▶▶▶ ① ❶ ⚠
Gilfach Farm Caravan Park
(SN342547) ☎(023978) 250 Etr–Oct
must book peak periods Last arrival
mdnt Last departure 12.00hrs

*A static and touring site set in open
countryside within 2m of the sea.*

4acres 110pitches 180static SA 30♣
20♣ 60🅰 (awnings)

8♠⊘ 20wc lit all night 1cdp
13washbasins hc (8⋔hc) 4⊙ (wash)
(games room) cold storage licensed
club/bar calor gas camping gaz ☎ ⅃
↔ stables ♪ launderette pub

LLANGYNIEW
Powys
Map 6 SJ10

▶▶▶ ③ ❷ ⚠
Henllan Caravan Park *(SJ136088)*
Signposted ☎Llanfair Caereinion
(0938) 810343 Mar–Oct must book peak
periods Last arrival 22.00hrs Last
departure noon

*Level, grassy site near river, good centre
for exploring the Border Counties.*

1acre 10pitches 57static SA 10♣ or
10♣ or 10🅰 (awnings)

6♠ Individual pitches 4wc lit all night
2cdp 🔌 washbasins hc central hot
water (⋔hc) ⊙ supervised wash (dry)
iron games room TV cold storage
(licensed club/bar) childrens
playground calor gas camping gaz ☎
basket meals ⅃
↔ stables golf ♪ launderette pub

LLANIDLOES
Powys
Map 6 SN98

▶ ② ❶ ⚠
Dol-Llys-Site *(SN962856)* Dol-Llys-
Farm Signposted ☎(05512) 2694 Etr–
Oct must book public hols

*This site is situated on the banks of the
River Severn ¾m from the small market
town of Llanidloes. Ideal for touring mid
Wales.*

2acres 25pitches 20♣ or 20♣ 5🅰
awnings

2♠⊘ late arrivals enclosure 4wc lit all
night 1cdp (washbasins hc) (central hot
water) (⋔hc) ⊙ supervised cold storage
calor gas camping gaz
↔ golf ⅄ ♪ launderette pub ⅃

LLANON
Dyfed
Map 6 SN56

▶▶▶ ② ❷ ⚠
Woodlands Caravan Park *(SN511668)*
Signposted ☎(09748) 342 Apr–Oct
rsMar (no electricity) must book peak
periods Last arrival 23.00hrs Last
departure 12.00hrs

*Level grass site with trees and bushes,
set in hilly wood and meadowland,
adjacent to sea, beach and river. 11m
from Aberystwyth on A487.*

4acres 90pitches 60static SA 40♣ or
40♣ 50🅰 (awnings) ltr

3♠ Individual pitches ⊘ wc lit all night
1cdp 🔌 (washbasins hc) (⋔hc) ⊙
supervised (dry) (cold storage)
childrens playground calor gas camping
gaz paraffin toilet fluid ☎ ⅃
↔ stables pub

LLANRHYSTUD
Dyfed
Map 6 SN56

▶▶▶ ② ❶ ⚠
Pengarreg Caravan Park *(SN539697)*
Signposted ☎Llanon (09748) 247 Mar–
Oct must book

*Level, stony and grass site near sea and
river. On A487, Aberystwyth 9m,
Aberaeron 7m.*

5acres 75pitches 150static 25♣ 25♣
25🅰 (awnings)

20♠⊘ late arrivals enclosure 48wc lit
all night 6cdp (27washbasins hc)
(central hot water) (⋔hc) ⊙ supervised
childrens playground calor gas camping
gaz toilet fluid ☎ ⊞ laundry room ⅃
↔ stables ♪

LLANRUG
Gwynedd
Map 6 SH56
See Caernarfon sketch map

▶▶ ① ❶
Tyn-Y-Coed Camping Site *(SH543624)*
Signposted ☎Caernarfon (0286) 3565
May–Sep must book Last arrival
21.00hrs Last departure noon

*Part sloping, part level site set in hilly
country.*

1½acres 40pitches 50static 10♣£2.40
10♣£2.40 20🅰£2.40 awnings

3♠ 12wc lit all night 1cdp washbasins
hc ♨hc ⋔hc ⊙ calor gas camping gaz
↔ stables golf ⅄ cinema ♪
launderette pub ⅃

▶ ② ❶ ⚠
Bryn Teg Caravan Park *(SH524636)*
Signposted ☎Llanberis (0286) 871374
Mar–Oct booking advisable peak
season Last arrival 21.00hrs Last
departure noon no motorcycles

*Level grass site with mature trees, set in
mountainous wooded meadowland
country adjacent to lake. 3m from
Llanberis on A4086.* →

168pitches 68 ⚏ £2.40–£4.50 or
68 ⚏ £2.40–£4.50 100▲£2–£4
(awnings)

10🏕⚡ 25wc lit all night 2cdp ⚙
12 washbasins hc central hot water
(12🚿 hc)☺ supervised 🖀 games room
CTV cold storage licensed club/bar
childrens playground calor gas camping
gaz ☎ 🛒
↔ stables ✦ launderette pub

LLANRWST
Gwynedd
Map 6 SH86

▶ ▶ 🛂 ❷
Bodnant Caravan Site *(SH805609)*
Nebo Rd Signposted ☎(0492) 640248
Mar–Oct must book Last arrival 22.00hrs
Last departure 11.00hrs no tents

*Small, well maintained level touring site. S
of village off A470.*

3acres 30pitches 25⚏ fr£3.10 5 ⚏ fr£3
(awnings)

Individual pitches 9wc lit all night 1cdp
(washbasins hc central hot water 🚿 hc)☺
supervised (cold storage) childrens
playground calor gas camping gaz hair
dryer 🛒
↔ stables golf ✦ pub

▶ 🛂 ❶
Kerry's Orchard Camping Site
(SH802615) School Bank Rd Signposted
☎(0492) 640248 or 640683 Etr–Oct must
book Last arrival 22.00hrs Last departure
11.00hrs no tents

*Grass and gravel site, level pitches
adjacent to River Conwy on outskirts of
town. Turn right at first crossroads on
entering Llanrwst from A5 and A470.*

1acre 29pitches 2static 5 ⚏ fr£2.80 24▲
fr£2.80 (awnings)

2🏕 7wc lit all night (washbasins hc 🚿 hc)
☺ calor gas camping gaz 🛒
↔ stables golf ✦ pub

LLANTWIT MAJOR
South Glamorgan
Map 3 SS96

▶ ▶ 🛂 ❷ ⚠
Rosedew Farm Camping Site
(SS973678) ☎(04465) 3331 or 2227
Apr–Oct booking advisable public hols &
Jul–Aug Last arrival 22.00hrs Last
departure 15.00hrs

*A quiet country site on meadowland. From
Llantwit Major follow B4265 south.*

4½acres 105pitches SA 45⚏ fr£4
60 ⚏ fr£4 or 60▲fr£4 awnings ltr

3🏕 19wc lit all night 1cdp (19washbasins
hc)(8🚿 hc)☺ supervised (wash spin dry
iron) calor gas camping gaz 🛒
↔ stables golf ✦ pub

LLANWRDA
Dyfed
Map 3 SN73

▶ 🛂 ❶
Feathers Inn Petrol Station *(SN712320)*

Lampeter Rd Signposted ☎ Llangadog
(05503) 491 Apr–Oct rs Mar & Nov

*Level, grass site with bushes, near river
and mountains. W of Llandovery on A482.*

2acres 28pitches ⚏ ⚏ (awnings) ltr

1🏕 4wc 1cdp ☺ supervised calor gas
camping gaz toilet fluid ☎ ⊞ 🛒

LLWYNGWRIL
Gwynedd
Map 6 SH50

▶ ▶ 🏕 ❶ ⚠
Gwril Caravan Site *(SN592099)*
☎Fairbourne (0341) 250431 Good Fri–
Sep booking advisable public hols Last
departure noon no single sex groups no
tents

*Grass and gravel site near to roadside and
facing the sea.*

3acres 25pitches 280static 25⚏ £3.45 or
25 ⚏ £3.45 awnings ltr

10🏕 56wc lit all night 1cdp washbasins hc
🚿 hc☺ iron calor gas camping gaz ☎
take away food 🛒
↔ ✦ pub

LOCHGILPHEAD
Strathclyde *Argyllshire*
Map 10 NR88

▶ ▶ 🏕 ❶ ⚠
Lochgilphead Caravan Site *(NR859881)*
Signposted ☎(0546) 2003 Apr–Oct Last
arrival mdnt Last departure noon

*Mainly level grassy site set in the most
beautiful mountain and loch scenery in
Argyll. Fishing and sailing available on the
loch. From A83 in Lochgilphead follow
signs to Campbeltown.*

4acres 40pitches 20static 40⚏ £3 or
40 ⚏ £3 or 40▲£3 (awnings) ltr

5🏕⚡ 15wc lit all night 1cdp washbasins
hc 🚿 hc☺ supervised calor gas camping
gaz toilet fluid 🛒
↔ golf cinema ✦ pub

LOCHMABEN
Dumfries & Galloway *Dumfriesshire*
Map 11 NY08

▶ ▶ 🏕 ❸ ⚠
Halleaths Caravan Site *(NY098818)*
Signposted ☎(038781) 321 Apr–Oct
Last arrival 22.00hrs

*Level, grassy site with hard standing.
Situated within an estate in a sheltered
position with a wood on one side and a
high hedge on the other. From Lockerbie
on A74 take A709 to Lochmaben– ½m on
right after crossing River Annan.*

3acres 80pitches 40⚏ 20 ⚏ 20▲
(awnings)

5🏕 Individual pitches ⊘ late arrivals
enclosure 12wc lit all night 1cdp ⚙
(washbasins hc) central hot water (🚿 hc)

(☺) childrens playground
↔ golf cinema ✦ 🛒

▶ ▶ 🛂 ❷ ⚠
Kirkloch Brae Caravan Site *(NY082825)*
Signposted Etr–Oct no power boats on
the Loch

*Mainly level, grass site with mature trees
set in meadowland, adjacent to Loch and
main road.*

30pitches 30⚏ £2.55 or 30 ⚏ £2.55
(awnings) ltr

1🏕 Individual pitches 8wc lit all night
1cdp washbasins hc 🚿 hc☺ spin
childrens playground private beach 🛒
↔ golf ✦ pub

LOCHNAW
Dumfries & Galloway *Wigtownshire*
Map 10 NW96

▶ ▶ ▶ 🛂 ❷ ⚠
Drumlochart Caravan Park *(NW997634)*
Signposted ☎Leswalt (077687) 232
Mar–Oct Last arrival 23.00hrs Last
departure noon

*Part level, part sloping, grass site with
trees and bushes set in hilly woodland–
adjacent to Loch Ryan and Luce Bay. 5m
NW of Stranraer on B7043.*

4acres 24pitches 96static 24⚏ £4.50 or
24 ⚏ £4.50 or 24▲£4.50 (awnings) ltr

6🏕⚡ late arrivals enclosure 14wc lit all
night 1cdp ⚙ washbasins hc 🚿 hc☺
supervised (wash dry iron) ➡ games
room (cold storage) licensed club/bar
childrens playground calor gas camping
gaz toilet fluid ☎ boating, fishing 🛒
↔ stables golf ⚓ ✦ pub

LOCKERBIE
Dumfries & Galloway *Dumfriesshire*
Map 11 NY18

▶ ▶ 🏕 ❶ ⚠
Glasgow Road Caravan Site Apply to:
Annandale & Eskdale District Council,
Council Chambers, Annan, Dumfriesshire
(NY133823) Signposted Etr–Oct no
bookings

*Level, grass site set in an urban area,
close to A74 on outskirts of town.*

55pitches 10static 35⚏ £2.55 or
35 ⚏ £2.55 20▲£1.55 (awnings) ltr

2🏕 12wc lit all night 2cdp washbasins hc
🚿 hc☺
↔ stables golf cinema ✦ pub 🛒

LONDON (GREATER)
Details of sites within the London postal
area are listed below.
*For details of other sites in the vicinity of
London, see also Hoddesdon (23m),
Laleham (19m), West Drayton (15m).*

ABBEY WOOD
SE2
Map 5 TQ47

▶ ▶ ▶ 🛂 ❶ ⚠
*Co-operative Woods Camping &
Caravan Site* *(TQ473784)* Federation Rd

Signposted ☎01-3102233 All year must book peak periods (except tents) no unaccompanied under 18's

Well secluded and pleasantly wooded site, situated in quiet residential area on the outskirts of London. Easy access to central London from the British Rail (Southern Region) Station at Abbey Wood.

9acres 330pitches 330🚐 or 330🚙 or 330▲ (awnings)

7♻⊙ late arrivals enclosure 46wc lit all night 3cdp 🚿 washbasins hc 🛉 hc⊙ supervised iron calor gas camping gaz toilet fluid ☎ off licence 🛒

↔ stables golf cinema launderette pub

CHINGFORD
E4
Map 5 TQ39

▶▶▶ 🅸 ❷ ⚠

Sewardstone Caravan Park *(TQ381970)*
Sewardstone Rd Signposted ☎01-529 5689 All year booking advisable peak periods Last arrival 22.00hrs Last departure noon

A new campsite overlooking King George's reservoir.

12acres 242pitches 242🚐 £5 or 242🚙 £5 or 242▲ £4 awnings

6♻ late arrivals enclosure 86wc lit all night 3cdp 🚿 46washbasins hc 3central hot water 44🛉 hc 6⊙ supervised (wash spin

dry iron) calor gas camping gaz ☎ 🛒

↔ stables golf ◢ launderette

EDMONTON
N9
Map 4 TQ39

▶▶▶ 🅸 ❸ ⚠

Picketts Lock Centre *(TQ360945)*
Signposted ☎01-803 4756 All year booking advisable peak periods Last arrival 22.00hrs Last departure noon

Level grass site with trees set in meadowland with direct access to River Lee and main road.

4acres 200pitches 125🚐 £5 or 125🚙 £5 75▲ £4 awnings

4♻ 19wc lit all night 28washbasins hc (7🛉 hc) 3⊙ supervised (wash) (❄heated ☌) (games room) licensed club/bar childrens playground calor gas camping gaz cafe restaurant ☎ ⊞ sports hall sauna solarium roller skating squash courts 🛒

↔ golf cinema ◢ launderette pub

LONG DOWNS
Cornwall
Map 2 SW73
See Falmouth sketch map

▶ 🅸 ❶ ⚠

Calamankey Farm *(SW745342)*
Signposted ☎Stithians (0209) 860314 Etr–Oct Last arrivals 22.00hrs Last departure noon no caravans

This farm site is situated on A394. Falmouth and Helston are in close proximity and the whole of the Land's End Peninsula can be explored from here.

3acres 60pitches 4static SA 15 🚙 £3 45▲ £3 awnings

7♻ 13wc lit all night (🛉 hc)⊙ supervised cold storage calor gas 🛒

↔ stables ◢ pub

LONGRIDGE
Lancashire
Map 7 SD63

▶▶▶ 🅸 ❷ ⚠

Beacon Fell View Caravan Park
(SD618382) 110 Higher Rd Signposted ☎(077478) 5434 Mar–Oct booking advisable public hols & mid summer wknds

7acres 100pitches 343static 100🚐 £4 or 100 🚙 £4 or 100▲ £4 (awnings) ltr

10♻ Individual pitches 25wc lit all night 4cdp 🚿 14washbasins hc (10🛉 hc) 5⊙ supervised ☌ games room licensed club/bar childrens playground calor gas camping gaz toilet fluid ☎ 🛒

↔ stables golf cinema ◢ pub

LOOE

Cornwall
Map 2 SX25
See sketch map

▶▶▶▶▶ ③❷⚠
'Treble B' Holiday Centre *(SX228533)*
Polperro Rd Signposted ☎ (05036) 2425
Whit–Sep rs May–Whit must book Last
departure noon no single sex groups
exceeding three

*A site situated on undulating high ground
with pleasant country views. Comprises
three fields on mainly level ground and
has tarmac internal roads.*

20 acres 558 pitches 30 static
558🚐 £3.80–£5.50 or 558 🚙 £3.80–
£5.50 or 558▲£3.80–£5.50 (awnings)

50🏕late arrivals enclosure 100wc lit all
night 4cdp 🚿 washbasins hc (🛁hc)☉
supervised (wash spin dry) iron 🛎 games
room CTV cold storage licensed club/bar
childrens playground calor gas camping
gaz toilet fluid cafe restaurant ☎ ⊞ take
away food 🛒

↔ stables golf ⚓ ⛵ launderette pub

▶▶▶ ③❷⚠
Polborder House *(SX283557)*
☎ Widegates (05034) 265 Etr–mid Oct
booking advisable Jul & Aug Last arrival
22.00hrs Last departure 11.00hrs

*Mainly level, grass site with mixed trees
and bushes set in meadowland, 2½m E of
Looe.*

TREGOAD
CARAVAN
& CAMPING PARK
St. Martin, Looe
Tel: (05036) 2718

Approximately 1½ miles
from Looe, 200yds. off the
B3253 Plymouth–Looe road,
with fine sea and rural views.
Terraced sites, electric hook-
ups, toilets, showers,
launderette, shop, licensed
club and beer garden.
Golf, water sports, pony
trekking, boat trips and
sandy beaches nearby. Trout
and course fishing on site.

3acres 36pitches 3static 36🚐 £3.70–£5
or 36 🚙 £3.70–£5 or 36▲£3.70–£5
(awnings)

3🏕 Individual pitches 14wc lit all night
1cdp 12washbasins hc (1central hot
water) (8🛁hc) 4☉supervised (wash dry
iron) (cold storage) calor gas camping
gaz 🛒

↔ stables golf ⚓ ⛵ launderette pub

▶▶▶ ②❷⚠
Tencreek Caravan & Camping Park
(SX233525) Signposted ☎ Looe (05036)
2447 Etr–Sep must book peak periods
Last departure noon

*Gently sloping grass site set in
meadowland adjacent to sea, sandy
beach and A387.*

14acres 244pitches 42static SA
244🚐 £3.50–£6 or 244 🚙 £3.50–£6 or
244▲£3.50–£6 awnings ltr

13🏕 Individual pitches 29wc lit all night
2cdp central hot water washbasins hc
🛁hc☉ supervised (wash spin) iron 🛎
games room (cold storage) licensed club/
bar childrens playground calor gas
camping gaz toilet fluid cafe crazy golf ☎ 🛒

↔ stables golf ⚓ ⛵ launderette pub

▶▶▶ ②❷⚠
Tregoad Caravan & Camping Park
(SX273559) St Martin Signposted
☎ (05036) 2718 Spring Bank hol–Oct rs
Apr no bookings Last departure
10.30hrs →

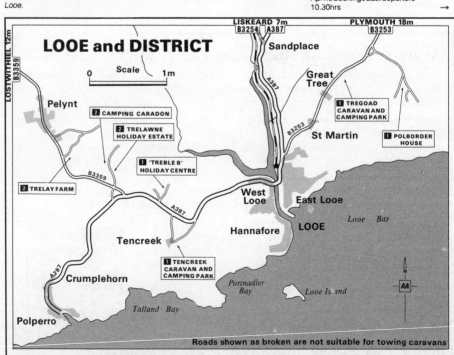

LOOE and DISTRICT

LOSTWITHIEL 12m
B3359

LISKEARD 7m
B3254 A387

PLYMOUTH 18m
B3253

Sandplace

Scale 0 — 1m

Great Tree

Pelynt

② CAMPING CARADON

② TRELAWNE HOLIDAY ESTATE

A387

B3253

① TREGOAD CARAVAN AND CAMPING PARK

St Martin

① POLBORDER HOUSE

① 'TREBLE B' HOLIDAY CENTRE

B3359

A387

② TRELAY FARM

West Looe

East Looe

Hannafore

LOOE

Looe Bay

Tencreek

A387

① TENCREEK CARAVAN AND CAMPING PARK

Portnadler Bay

Looe Island

Crumplehorn

N
AA

Talland Bay

Polperro

Roads shown as broken are not suitable for towing caravans

Sites listed under: **1** Looe   **2** Pelynt

Holiday Centre Ltd Looe Cornwall

For all self-catering holidays. Camping, Caravanning, Flats and Chalets. Write or 'phone for free brochure. Tel. LOOE (05036) 2425
Set in lovely countryside on the main A387, midway between Looe and Polperro. Ideally situated either as a touring centre for the South West, or for spending your holiday on the site.
We have all the facilities your family requires for real holiday enjoyment.

☆☆☆☆☆   **FIVE STAR FREE FACILITIES FOR EVERYONE**   ☆☆☆☆☆

☆ FREE heated swimming and paddling pools, deck chairs and sun loungers.
☆ FREE membership of the TREBLE B Club; live groups in the Ballroom and the BEE HIVE Disco.
☆ FREE entry to three colour television lounges.
☆ FREE use of barbeque pit and tables, childrens' play areas and large field for games.
☆ FREE hot water at sinks and washbasins.

☆ PLUS ☆
All these other facilities are available ON SITE:–
☆ Late closing self-service store and off licence ☆ Ladies and Gents' hairdressing salon ☆ Games Room with Amusement Arcade and Table Tennis ☆
☆ Restaurant and Take-Away ☆ Launderette and Dryers—Open 24 hours a day ☆ Battery charging and ice pack service ☆ Public Telephones ☆
☆ Tarmac roads with street lighting ☆ Separate dog exercise areas ☆ Electric Hook-Ups for Tourers ☆

TRY AN EARLY OR LATE HOLIDAY (MAY, JUNE OR SEPTEMBER). IT'S MUCH CHEAPER AND QUIETER EVERYWHERE.
☆ REMEMBER ☆ THE TREBLE B HOLIDAY CENTRE IS SOUTH EAST CORNWALL'S ONLY A.A RATED 5 PENNANT SITE.
Rallies are always welcome.
Please contact us for particulars regarding our very attractive rates. Enquiries to DEPT. 03

Camping in Cornwall

On a peaceful and beautifully kept, 'family-sized' site for tents and tourers. In a delightful country setting, close to the sea, on Cornwall's spectacular South Coast, between Looe and Polperro.

Top class facilities include:
Licensed Club, (entertainment and meals), Shop, Laundry Room and Childrens' Play Areas.

Brochure with pleasure from -   Mr A Gurney,
Camping Caradon, Trelawne Gardens, Trelawne, Looe,
Cornwall   PL13 2NA   Telephone Polperro 72388

Excellent access and level pitches for 85 units

the **Caradon** way

TENCREEK CARAVAN PARK   AA
LOOE, CORNWALL   Tel: (050-36) 2447
Res Prop: C. R. & J. E. Wright

Tencreek, situated between Looe and Polperro, is a family site. Ideal for touring and walking this beautiful countryside of Cornwall. It has a wonderful family atmosphere and scenic coastal views.
Clean, well equipped holiday vans to hire. All main services. Touring caravans, tents, motor homes welcome.
Amenities: Shop, swim/pool, games room, licensed bar, live entertainment, launderette, hot showers, childrens play ground. Telephone on site. Dogs on lead. SAE.

171

The site has fine sea and rural views and is a good base for touring Cornwall. 1m NE of Looe on B3253.

7acres 150pitches 2static 65🚐 10 🚐 75▲ awnings

15🚐⊘ 20wc lit all night 1cdp 10washbasins hc (2 central hot water) (5🛁hc) 3⊙ (1wash 1spin 1dry 2iron) games room (cold storage) (licensed club/bar) childrens playground calor gas camping gaz ☎ ⊞ 🖪

⊖ stables golf ✈ ♪ launderette pub

LOSSIEMOUTH
Grampian *Morayshire*
Map 15 NJ08

▶▶▶ 2 ❷ ⚠

Silver Sands Leisure Park *(NJ205710)*
Covesea, West Beach (2m W B9040)
Signposted ☎ (034381) 3262 Apr–Oct must book Jul & Aug Last arrival 22.30hrs Last departure noon

A grass and sandy site with direct access to beach. From Lossiemouth follow B9040 to site.

7½acres 150pitches 140static 150🚐£2.60–£4.50 or 150 🚐£2.60–£4.50 or 150▲£2.60–£4.50 (awnings) ltr

16🚐34wc lit all night 3cdp 🚾 39washbasins hc 14🛁hc 4⊙supervised (wash dry iron) games room CTV licensed club/bar childrens playground private beach calor gas camping gaz cafe restaurant ☎ 🖪

⊖ stables golf ♪ launderette pub

LOSTWITHIEL
Cornwall
Map 2 SX15

▶ 2 ❶ ⚠

Downend Camp Site *(SX117598)*
Signposted ☎ Bodmin (0208) 872363 Apr–Oct booking advisable school hols Last arrival 23.00hrs Last departure 11.00hrs

Level, grass site with trees and bushes, set in hilly meadowland, adjacent to A390.

15pitches 3static SA 15🚐£2 or 15 🚐£2 or 15▲£2 (awnings) 3🚐6wc lit all night 1cdp (6washbasins hc) (2🛁hc) 1⊙ supervised cold storage calor gas camping gaz toilet fluid 🖪

⊖ stables

LOTHERSDALE
North Yorkshire
Map 7 SD94

▶▶ 1 ❷ ⚠

Springs Caravan Park *(SD944451)*
Springs Farm Signposted ☎ Cross Hills (0535) 32533 Etr–Oct must book always for motorvans & peak periods for caravans & tents Last arrival 20.00hrs Last departure 15.00hrs

Set on rising ground in rural setting overlooking a small trout lake on edge of Yorkshire Dales and moors. Well signposted from A6068 at Cross Hills.

3½acres 30pitches 7static 25🚐 £2.75 1 🚐£2.75 4▲£2.75 (awnings)

2🚐5wc 1cdp washbasins hc central hot water 🛁hc ⊙supervised (cold storage) calor gas

⊖ stables golf pub 🖪

LOWESTOFT
Suffolk
Map 5 TM59

▶ 1 ❶ ⚠

North Denes Caravan Site *(TM553946)*
North Denes Signposted ☎ (0502) 3197 Apr–17 Oct must book for caravans

A level, sandy and grassy site near the sea. Approach is from the A12 Lowestoft–Great Yarmouth road via The Ravine in North Lowestoft or from the South via Whapload Road.

30acres 775pitches 250static 25🚐 750 🚐 or 750▲ (awnings) ltr

22🚐⊘ late arrivals enclosure wc lit all night 4cdp washbasins hc central hot water 🛁hc ⊙ (wash spin dry) iron (🌡) licensed bar (childrens playground) private beach calor gas camping gaz cafe restaurant ☎ ⊞ 🖪

⊖ stables golf ✈ cinema ♪ launderette pub

LUDCHURCH
Dyfed
Map 2 SN11
See Tenby sketch map

▶▶▶ 3 ❷ ⚠

Little Kings Caravan Site *(SN145092)*
☎ Llanteg (083483) 330 mid May–Oct rs Etr–mid May must book peak periods Last departure 10.00hrs no single sex groups

Level, hedged site in rolling downland. 2m N of the beach at Amroth.

4acres 55pitches 20static SA 35🚐£4 or 35 🚐£4 20▲£4 (awnings)

5🚐⊘ late arrivals enclosure 9wc lit all night 1cdp 🚾 washbasins hc central hot water (🛁hc) ⊙supervised (wash spin) dry iron 🚿 games room cold storage licensed club/bar childrens playground calor gas camping gaz ☎ mobile shop

⊖ stables ✈ ♪ launderette pub 🖪

LUNDIN LINKS
Fife
Map 12 NO40

▶▶ 2 ❸ ⚠

Woodland Gardens *(NO418031)*
Blindwell Rd Signposted ☎ Upper Largo (03336) 319 Mar–Oct no bookings Last arrival 22.00hrs Last departure noon

A predominantly touring site situated in hilly country at the foot of Largo Law and about ½m from Lundin Links. It has level grass areas and is bordered by well-established trees and shrubs which give seclusion and shelter.

½acre 20pitches 5static 20🚐£3.15 or 20 🚐£3.15 or 20▲£3.15 (awnings)

2🚐late arrivals enclosure 7wc lit all night 1cdp washbasins hc 🛁hc ⊙supervised (iron) CTV (cold storage) childrens playground calor gas camping gaz ☎ 🖪

⊖ golf ♪ pub

LUSS
Strathclyde *Dunbartonshire*
Map 10 NS39

▶▶ 2 ❶ ⚠

Luss Camping Ground *(NS360936)*
Signposted ☎ (043686) 658 Apr–Sep bookings advisable peak periods Last arrival 22.30hrs Last departure noon no caravans or motorvans

Grassy site on west shore of Loch Lomond. ¼m N of Luss village on A82 Glasgow–Fort William road.

19½acres 90pitches 90▲ awnings

5🚐late arrivals enclosure 12wc lit all night 1cdp 🛁hc supervised childrens playground private beach camping gaz ☎ 🖪

⊖ ✈ ♪

LYDFORD
Devon
Map 2 SX58

▶▶ 2 ❸ ⚠

Pulborough Farm Caravan & Camping Park *(SX512853)* The Croft Signposted ☎ (082282) 275 Etr–mid Sep booking advisable public hols & Jul–Aug Last arrival 21.00hrs Last departure noon

Site on mainly level ground looking towards the western slopes of Dartmoor at the edge of the village.

4acres 70pitches 70🚐£4.50 or 70 🚐£4.50 or 70▲£4.50 awnings

9🚐Individual pitches 18wc lit all night 1cdp 🚾 12washbasins hc 8🛁hc 2⊙spin iron calor gas camping gaz paraffin

⊖ stables ♪ pub 🖪

LYNDHURST
Hampshire
Map 4 SU30

▽ 2

Denny Wood Camp Site *(SU335067)* (2m E off B3056) Signposted ☎ (042128) 3771 (from early 1984) or 3141 (Forestry Commission Office) 13 Apr–Sep booking advisable Spring Bank Hol Last departure noon 🏕

Quiet site in pleasant surroundings of mixed woodland, grass and gravel surface.

170pitches 170▲ ✱£2–£2.20 awnings

2🚐2cdp calor gas camping gaz mobile shop

⊖ stables golf pub 🖪

▽ 2

Holidays Hill Camp Site *(SU274070)* (2m SW off A35) Signposted ☎ (042128) 3771 (from early 1984) or 3141 (Forestry Commission Office 13 Apr–Sep booking advisable Spring Bank Hol Last departure noon 🏕

Pleasant woodland site.

100 pitches 100🚐 ✳£2–£2.20 or
100▲£2–£2.20 awnings
2🏕 Individual pitches 2 cdp supervised
calor gas camping gaz mobile shop
⊕→ golf pub🛒

▽②
Matley Wood Camp Site *(SU332075)*
(2m E off B3056) Signposted ☎(042128)
3771 (from early 1984) or 3141 (Forestry
Commission Office) 13 Apr–Sep booking
advisable Spring Bank Hol Last departure
noon

*Clearings in pleasant partially wooded
area.*

70 pitches 70🚐 ✳£2–£2.20 or 70▲£2–
£2.20 awnings

1🏕 1 cdp mobile shop
⊕→ stables golf pub🛒

LYNEAL *(near Ellesmere)*
Shropshire
Map 7 SJ43

▶▶▶ ②❷⚠
Fernwood Caravan Park *(SJ445346)*
Signposted ☎ Bettisfield (094875) 221
Apr–Oct booking advisable public hols
Last arrival 22.00hrs no unaccompanied
teenagers no tents

*Set in wooded country, this mainly level
grassy site is not far from Canal, 4m SE of
Ellesmere off B5063.*

8 acres 50 pitches 150 static 50🚐 £3.15 or
50🚐 £3.15 (awnings) ltr

15🏕 27 wc lit all night 1 cdp 🚐
washbasins hc (📷 hc)☺ supervised
(wash) spin (dry iron) childrens
playground calor gas toilet fluid ☎🛒
⊕→ 🎵 pub

LYNTON
Devon
Map 3 SS74
See sketch map →

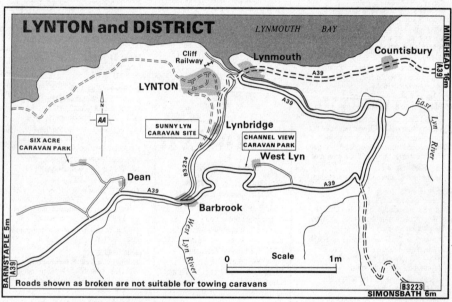

All sites listed under Lynton

▶▶▶ 2 ⓵ ⚠

Channel View Caravan Park *(SS724482)*
Manor Farm Signposted ☎ (05985) 3349
Whit–Oct rs Etr–Whit must book Jul & Aug
Last arrival 23.00hrs Last departure noon

The site is situated on the A39 and has panoramic views over Lynton and the Channel.

6acres 76pitches 36static SA 76🚐 or 76🚐 or 76▲ (awnings)
14🚏 28wc lit all night 1cdp washbasins hc
🛁 hc ☺ supervised (wash) (dry iron) games room TV licensed club/bar calor gas camping gaz toilet fluid ☎ 🏪
↔ stables 🍴 launderette pub

see advert on page 173

▶▶▶ 2 ⓶ ⚠

Sunny Lyn Caravan Site *(SS719486)*
Lynbridge Signposted ☎ (05985) 3384
20 Jul–Aug rs Etr, Spring Bank Hol–19 Jul & Sep–Oct Last arrival 20.00hrs Last departure noon no groups of motorcyclists

Part level, part sloping site, bordering trout stream, in a wooded combe; sea within 1 mile. On B3234.

1acre 37pitches 31static 7🚐 £4.50 or 7🚐 £4.07 30▲£4.83 (awnings)

3🚏🌳 12wc lit all night 1cdp 🚻
washbasins hc 🛁 hc ☺ (wash spin dry iron) games room CTV (cold storage) licenced club/bar calor gas camping gaz paraffin cafe restaurant ☎ 🎬 disco, trout fishing 🏪
↔ stables ⚓ cinema 🍴 launderette pub

▶▶ 2 ⓶ ⚠

Six Acre Caravan Park *(SS701483)* Six Acre Farm Signposted ☎ (05985) 3224
15 Mar–15 Nov must book 15 Jul–10 Sep
Last departure noon

A level grassy site, with bushes, set below hill, with well-wooded countryside around. 2m SW of Lynton off A39 Barnstaple–Minehead road.

4acres 105pitches SA 105🚐 £3.60 or 105🚐 £3.60 or 105▲£3.60 awnings

7🚏 Individual pitches ⊘ 21wc lit all night 1cdp washbasins hc (central hot water) (🛁 hc) ☺ supervised (dry iron) (cold storage) calor gas camping gaz ☎ 🏪
↔ stables ⚓ cinema 🍴 launderette pub

LYTCHETT MINSTER
Dorset
Map 3 SY99

▶▶▶ 2 ⓵ ⚠

South Lytchett Manor Caravan Park
(SY954926) ☎ (0202) 622577 Apr–15
Oct must book Whit & Jul–Aug Last arrival 22.00hrs Last departure 11.00hrs

A mainly level site with mature trees set in meadowland. On B3067 off A35, 200yds on right.

10acres 150pitches 68🚐 £4.80–£6 or 68🚐 £4.80–£6 80▲£4.80–£6 (awnings) ltr

30🚏 Individual pitches ⊘ 16wc lit all night 1cdp 🚻 washbasins hc 🛁 hc ☺ (wash dry iron) CTV (cold storage) childrens playground calor gas camping gaz cafe ☎ 🏪
↔ stables 🍴 launderette pub

LYTHAM ST ANNES
Lancashire
Map 7 SD32

▶▶▶▶ 2 ⓶ ⚠

Eastham Hall Caravan Site *(SD379291)*
Saltcotes Rd Signposted ☎ Lytham
(0253) 737907 Mar–Oct must book public hols Last arrival 22.00hrs Last departure 15.00hrs no tents

A level secluded site with trees and hedgerows, in rural surroundings. From Preston on A584, turn right onto B5259 to site in ¾m.

12acres 160pitches 240static
140🚐 £4.50 20 🚐 £4.50 (awnings) ltr

20🚏 Individual pitches late arrivals enclosure 32wc lit all night 10cdp 🚻 washbasins hc (🛁 hc) ☺ supervised (wash spin dry) games room cold storage childrens playground calor gas camping gaz toilet fluid ☎ 🏪
↔ stables golf 🍴 launderette pub

MABLETHORPE
Lincolnshire
Map 9 TF58

▶▶▶▶ 2 ⓶ ⚠

Golden Sands Estates *(TF501861)*
Quebec Rd ☎ (05213) 2671 26 May–Sep
rs Etr–25 May no bookings no tents

A level, grassy site near the sea and beach. 1m W of town off A1031 Cleethorpes road.

20acres 400pitches 1400static SA
350🚐 £4.50 🚐 £4 (awnings) ltr

10🚏 80wc 4cdp 80washbasins hc
40🛁 hc 12 ☺ supervised (wash) (dry iron) 🚻 games room CTV licensed club/bar childrens playground calor gas camping gaz toilet fluid cafe restaurant ☎ 🎬 🏪
↔ stables golf ⚓ cinema 🍴 launderette pub

▶▶ ⓵ ⓵ ⚠

Mermaid Caravan & Tenting Site
(TF505843) Seaholme Rd Signposted
☎ (05213) 3273 15 Mar–20 Oct
no bookings

A level and grassy site, ½m SW of Mablethorpe.

8acres 240pitches 300static 32🚐 £3.90 or 32🚐 £2.60 200▲£3.40 (awnings)

3late arrivals enclosure 36wc lit all night washbasins hc hc games room licensed club/bar childrens playground calor gas camping gaz cafe

stables golf cinema launderette pub

▶🔟🅰⚠

Highfield Camping & Caravan Club Site
(TF497846) 120 Church Ln ☎(0521) 72374 Apr–Sep booking advisable public hols Last arrival 21.00hrs Last departure noon

Level, mainly grassy site situated off main road about 1m from sea.

5acres 110pitches 110 or 110
110 awnings

4 late arrivals enclosure 12wc lit all night 1cdp washbasins hc (hc) supervised calor gas camping gaz toilet fluid

stables golf cinema launderette pub

MACDUFF
Grampian *Banffshire*
Map 15 NJ76

▶▶▶🔟🔞⚠

Myrus Caravan Site (NJ710634)
Signposted ☎Banff (02612) 2845 Jun–early Oct rs Apr–May & Sep booking advisable Jul & Aug Last departure noon

Part level, part sloping, grass site with trees and bushes, set in meadowland. On main A947.

1½acres 38pitches 30static 30 £2.50 or 30 £2.50 £2.50 (awnings) ltr

8 21wc lit all night 1cdp washbasins hc (hc) supervised (wash spin dry iron) (cold storage) childrens playground calor gas camping gaz toilet fluid ☎ cycles for hire

golf launderette pub

MAIDENS
Strathclyde *Ayrshire*
Map 10 NS20

▶▶🔟🔟⚠

Sandy Beach Caravan Park (NS215082)
☎Turnberry (06553) 456 or Ayr (0292) 262408 Apr–14 Oct must book Jun–Aug Last arrival 19.00hrs Last departure 11.00hrs no tents

This is a mainly level grass site near to the sea and beach. At Turnberry follow B7023 signposted off A77 Glasgow–Stranraer road.

5pitches 37static SA 5 £3 or 5 £2.50 ltr

2 Individual pitches late arrivals enclosure 9wc lit all night washbasins

---

hc hc (wash spin) games room (cold storage) childrens playground private beach calor gas toilet fluid ☎

stables golf launderette pub

MAN, ISLE OF
Map 6
See under Hillberry and Laxey

MANSTON
Kent
Map 7 ST36

▶🔟❶⚠

Manston Caravan & Camping Park
(TR348662) 2 Manston Court Cottages, Manston Court Rd Signposted ☎(084389) 442 Etr–Oct booking advisable public hols & Jul–Aug Last arrival mdnt Last departure noon no unaccompanied children under 18yrs

A level grassy site with mature trees situated near Manston Airport and convenient for the seaside resorts on the Isle of Thanet.

6acres 100pitches 30static 100 £3.50 or 100 £3.50 or 100 £3.50 (awnings)

2 13wc lit all night 1cdp washbasins hc (central hot water) (hc) (wash dry iron) childrens playground calor gas camping gaz ☎ hair dryer

stables golf cinema launderette pub

MARTIN MILL
Kent
Map 5 TR34

▶▶🔟❷⚠

Hawthorn Caravan & Camping Site
(TR342464) Signposted ☎Dover (0304) 852658 Mar–Oct no alsatian dogs

This pleasant rural site is screened by young trees and hedgerows. Its grounds include a rose garden and woods.

20acres 180pitches 155static SA 103 ✳£4.60 or 103 £4.60 77 £4.60 awnings ltr

50 36wc lit all night 2cdp washbasins hc hc supervised (wash spin) (cold storage) calor gas camping gaz toilet fluid ☎

stables golf pub

MARYCULTER
Grampian Aberdeenshire
Map 15 NO89

▶🔟❶⚠

Lower Deeside Caravan Park

(NJ855001) Signposted ☎Aberdeen (0224) 733860 Apr–Oct Last arrival 20.00hrs Last departure noon

A level and grassy site with mature trees, near river. 5m SW of Aberdeen.

3acres 30pitches 85static 30 £3.75 or 30 £3.75 or 30 £3.75 (awnings) ltr

3 6wc lit all night washbasins hc central hot water hc supervised (wash dry) iron games room CTV childrens playground calor gas ☎

pub

MATLOCK
Derbyshire
Map 8 SK36

▶▶🔟❷⚠

Packhorse Farm (SK323617) Matlock Moor ☎(0629) 2781 Mar–Oct must book public hols

A level, grassy site set amidst hills and moorland. 2m NE of Matlock off A632 at the Tansley signpost.

2acres 30pitches SA 15 or 15 15 awnings

2 Individual pitches 4wc lit all night 1cdp washbasins hc (hc)

stables golf cinema launderette pub

▽🔟

Canada Farm (SK345585) High Ln, Tansley (2m E off A615) ☎Dethick (062984) 385 booking advisable

Level orchard type paddock on high ground with wide country views.

20pitches 5 ✳£1.50 or 5 £1.50 15 fr50p (awnings)

cdp

MAWGAN PORTH
Cornwall
Map 2 SW86
See Padstow sketch map

▶▶▶🔟❷⚠

Gluvian Caravan & Camping Site
(SW861669) Signposted ☎St Mawgan (06374) 373 Etr–Oct booking advisable Jul & Aug Last arrival 22.00hrs Last departure noon

Part level, part sloping, sheltered grass site with mature trees and stream in Vale of Lanherne. It is ¾m from sea and fine sandy beach.

5acres 96 pitches 36static 28 £6.10 or 38 £6.10 58 £6.10 awnings

9 Individual pitches 21wc lit all night 4cdp washbasins hc central hot water →

---

hc⊙supervised (wash spin dry iron)
(cold storage) childrens playground calor
gas camping gaz toilet fluid ☎ 🦺
↔ stables golf 🏌 launderette pub

▶▶▶ ☑ ❷ ⚠
Trevarrian Holiday Park (SW852666)
Signposted ☎ St Mawgan (06374) 381
Etr–Oct must book Jun–Aug Last arrival
22.00hrs Last departure 11.00hrs

Level, grassy site set amongst Cornish
Downland. Adjacent to sea and river.

5acres 125pitches SA 125🚐 or 125🚐 or
125🛆 (awnings)

8🏕⚘ late arrivals enclosure 26wc lit all
night 1cdp (washbasins hc) (central hot
water) (➡hc) (🚿hc)⊙supervised (wash
spin dry iron)🎱 games room TV (cold
storage) childrens playground calor gas
camping gaz toilet fluid ☎ 🦺
↔ stables golf 🎿 cinema 🏌 launderette
pub

see advertisement on page 191

MEALSGATE
Cumbria
Map 11 NY24

▶▶▶ ☑ ❷ ⚠
Larches Caravan Park (NY205415)
Signposted ☎ Low Ireby (09657) 379
Mar–Oct booking advisable Spring Bank
Hol & Jul–Aug Last arrival 23.00hrs Last
departure noon no single sex groups

Set in wooded rural surroundings on the
fringe of the Lake District National Park.
Situated on A595 Carlisle–Cockermouth
road.

4acres 73pitches 177static 73🚐 £3.75 or
73🚐 £3.50 or 73🛆 £3.50 (awnings)

7🏕⚘ late arrivals enclosure 21wc lit all
night 1cdp 🚽 20washbasins hc (8🚿 hc)
4⊙supervised (wash dry iron)🎱 (games
room) (cold storage) licensed club/bar
childrens playground calor gas camping
gaz toilet fluid ☎ 🦺
↔ golf 🏌 launderette pub

Gluvian

**Chalet, Caravan and
Camping Park**

A quiet family-run holiday park
nestling in the beautiful and unspoilt
Vale of Lanherne with a level walk,
¾ mile, to an excellent sandy beach.
Detached chalets and superior
caravans for hire. Tents and tourers
accommodated in a sheltered, level
and well drained meadow. No club
or bar.
Brochure from:
**Gluvian Caravan Park,
Mawgan Porth,
Near Newquay, Cornwall.
Telephone: St Mawgan (063 74) 373**
▶▶▶

Mawgan Porth — Middleton

MELROSE
Borders Roxburghshire
Map 12 NT53

▶▶ ☐ ❷ ⚠
Gibson Park Caravan Site (NT545341)
Apply to: Ettrick & Lauderdale District
Council, Parks Superintendent, Paton St,
Galashiels TD13AS Signposted
☎ Galashiels (0896) 4751 ext 47 Apr–Oct
must book Etr & Jul–Aug Last arrival
21.00hrs Last departure noon no single
sex groups

A secluded, sloping grass site partially
screened by mature trees, with views of
Eildon Hills. The site adjoins a recreation
park and is situated a short distance from
the small border town shopping centre.

3acres 80pitches 50🚐 or 50🚐 30🛆
awnings ltr

1🏕 Individual pitches⊘ late arrivals
enclosure 8wc lit all night 1cdp
washbasins hc🚿 hc⊙ (🅿) games room
childrens playground putting green
mobile shop 🦺
↔ stables golf 🏌 launderette pub

MEMUS
Grampian Angus
Map 15 NO45

▶▶ ☑ ❷ ⚠
Glens Caravan Site (NO426592)
☎ Foreside (030786) 258 Apr–Oct must
book Aug Last arrival 22.00hrs

Level, grass site with trees and bushes set
in mountainous meadowland. 5m off A94.

1acre 9pitches 12static SA 9🚐 £2.40 or
9🚐 £2.40 or 9🛆 £2.40 (awnings)

1🏕 Individual pitches 5wc lit all night
washbasins hc🚿 hc⊙supervised calor
gas camping gaz paraffin toilet fluid ☎ 🦺
↔ stables golf 🏌 pub

MERSHAM
Kent
Map 5 TR03

▽ ☑
Broad Oak Farm (TR042382)
☎ Aldington (023372) 344

In remote open farmland site.

5acres 🚐 ✳fr60p or 🚐 fr60p 🛆 fr60p
🏕cdp

MERTHYR MAWR
Mid Glamorgan
Map 3 SS87

▶▶ ☑ ❷ ⚠
Candleston Camp Site (SS873772)
Signposted ☎ Bridgend (0656) 2038 Etr–
Sep rs Mar–Etr must book late May Bank
Hol & Aug Last departure 14.00hrs no
caravans no unaccompanied under 18's

Attractive undulating site with level
pitches among mature conifers, woods
and dunes. Convenient for touring South

---

and West Wales. It is situated 6m from M4
(exit 35) 2½m from Bridgend. Follow
signs from Ogmore Road, Ewenny or A48
Bridgend bypass.

5acres 70pitches 70🚐 £3.80 or
70🛆 £3.80 ltr

10🏕 Individual pitches 12wc lit all night
washbasins hc🚿 hc supervised calor gas
camping gaz barbecue 🦺
↔ cinema 🏌 launderette pub

MIDDLETON (Near Morecambe)
Lancashire
Map 7 SD45
See Morecambe sketch map

▶▶▶ ☑ ❶ ⚠
Hawthorn Camping Site (SD415575)
Carr Ln ☎ Heysham (0524) 52074 Etr–
Oct must book public hols

Level grass site with trees and bushes set
in woodland. Access to sea and beach at
Middleton Sands.

6acres 70pitches SA 10🚐 £3 10 🚐 £2
50🛆 £3 (awnings)

3🏕⚘ 11wc lit all night 1cdp washbasins
hc central hot water🚿 hc⊙supervised
spin (iron) games room (cold storage)
childrens playground calor gas camping
gaz toilet fluid cafe 🦺
↔ stables golf 🏌 launderette pub

▶▶▶ ☑ ❶ ⚠
Melbreak Camp Site (SD415584) Carr Ln
☎ Heysham (0524) 52430 Apr–Sep Last
arrival 21.30hrs Last departure noon

Small, simple site set in open countryside
to the south of Morecambe.

1½acres 50pitches SA 30🚐 £2.75
20 🚐 £2.10 or 20🛆 £2.30 (awnings)

2🏕 7wc lit all night 1cdp (washbasins hc)
(🚿 hc)⊙supervised (wash dry) calor gas
camping gaz toilet fluid 🦺
↔ golf 🏌 launderette pub

GIBSON PARK
CARAVAN SITE ▶▶
Melrose, Scotland

Set in the Border heartland
overlooked by the Eildon Hills,
the Gibson Park offers an
excellent grassed site with full
facilities. The town of Melrose,
while boasting a 12th Century
Abbey, also offers ample
opportunity to sample the town
and country life of the area.
For bookings, contact the
**Parks Department,
Department (AA), Ettrick &
Lauderdale District
Council, Paton St,
Galashiels TD1 3AS
Tel: Galashiels 4751**

MIDDLETOWN
Powys
Map 7 SJ31

▶▶ 🔲②🅞🛆
Bank Farm Caravan Park (SJ293123)
Signposted ☎Trewern (093874) 260
May–Oct Last arrival 20.00hrs families
only

Part level, part sloping grass site near hills, mountains and woodland.

2acres 20pitches 36static 20🚐 or 20🚙
10🅰awnings

6🏕10wc lit all night 1cdp (washbasins hc) 🍴hc⊙ spin (iron) calor gas

↦ 🍴 pub

MIDDLEWICH
Cheshire
Map 7 SJ76

▽②
Briar Pool Farm (SJ724653) Cledford Ln,
Kinderton (2m SE on unclass rd off A533)
☎(060684) 2134 All year Last arrival
mdnt

Level meadow in open farmland.

4acres 30pitches 20🚐 £1.50 10🚙 £1.50
or 10🅰£1.50

🏕late arrivals enclosure lit all night 1cdp
central hot water (⊙) calor gas fishing 🎣

↦ pub

MILLBROOK
Cornwall
Map 2 SX45

▶▶▶ ②🅞🛆
Whitsand Bay Holiday Camp
(SX415513) Signposted ☎Plymouth
(0752) 822597 Apr–Oct must book public
hols Last departure 10.00hrs 🍴no single
sex groups

8acres 100pitches 33🚐£1.72–£4.60 or
33🚙£1.72–£4.60 67🅰£1.72–£4.60
awnings

14🏕 Individual pitches⊙ late arrivals
enclosure wc lit all night 1cdp
(washbasins hc central hot water 🍴hc)⊙
supervised (wash spin dry iron) 🔁 games
room TV (cold storage) (licensed club/
bar) childrens playground calor gas
camping gaz ☎ take-away food 🎣

↦ stables golf ⚓ launderette pub

MINSTER (Thanet)
Kent
Map 5 TR36

▶▶ 🔲③🅞🛆
Wayside Caravan Park (TR319651) Way
Hill ☎Thanet (0843) 821272 Mar–Oct
booking advisable public hols Last arrival
dusk Last departure noon 🍴nc12

*Small secluded site overlooking open
farmland. Situated ½m from Minster and
3½m from Sally line at Ramsgate
Harbour.*

¼acre 10pitches 54static 10🚐£3.25 or
10🚙£3.25 or 10🅰£3.25 (awnings)

4🏕⊙ 7wc lit all night 🔁 6washbasins hc
(3🍴hc) 1⊙supervised (iron) calor gas
camping gaz

↦ stables golf cinema ⚓ launderette pub
🎣

MINTLAW
Grampian *Aberdeenshire*
Map 15 NK04

▶▶ ②🅞🛆
Aden Country Park Caravan Park

(NJ995484) Signposted ☎Macduff
(0261) 32861 May–Sep must book Last
arrival 21.00hrs Last departure 09.00hrs

*Pleasant grassy site, partially screened
by trees, set at entrance of country park.
1m W of Mintlaw on A950 Peterhead–
Banff road.*

4¾acres 55pitches 5static 51🚐 or 51🚙
4🅰(awnings)

🏕13wc lit all night 1cdp 12washbasins hc
6🍴hc 6⊙supervised (wash spin dry)
childrens playground ☎

↦ stables golf ⚓ launderette pub🎣

MITCHEL TROY
Gwent
Map 3 SO41

▶▶ 🔲②🅞🛆
Glen Trothy Caravan & Camping Site
(SO495106) Signposted ☎Monmouth
(0600) 2295 Apr–Oct booking advisable
public hols & Jul–Aug Last arrival
22.00hrs Last departure noon

*Level, grass site with trees, set in
meadowland amid hills on banks of River
Trothy. 2m SW of Monmouth on old Raglan
road.*

7acres 88pitches 38static 38🚐 £4.95
10🚙 £4.50 40🅰£4.50 awnings ltr

5🏕⊙ late arrivals enclosure 10wc lit all
night 1cdp 🔁 washbasins hc (🍴hc)⊙
supervised (wash spin iron) (cold
storage) childrens playground calor gas
camping gaz toilet fluid fishing 🎣

↦ stables golf ⚓ ⚓ launderette pub

MODBURY
Devon
Map 3 SX65
See sketch map   →

▶▶▶ 2️⃣ 3️⃣ ⚠️

Broad Park Caravan Site *(SX690523)*
Higher East Leigh Farm Signposted
☎(0548) 830256 18 May–2 Oct booking
advisable Spring Bank Hol & Jul–Aug
Last arrival 22.00hrs Last departure
11.00hrs

*This site is in the heart of the South Hams in
a rural setting, within striking distance of
Salcombe, Thurlescombe and Bigbury
Bay, on B3207.*

5acres 75pitches SA 75🚐 £3.20–£3.80
or 75🚐 £3.20–£3.80 30▲£3.20–£3.80
(awnings)

12🏕️Individual pitches⊘ late arrivals
enclosure 20wc lit all night 1cdp 🚽
washbasins hc (🛁hc)☺(spin dry iron)
(cold storage) childrens playground calor
gas camping gaz toilet fluid ☎ ⊞
badminton court mobile shop 🛒

↪ stables cinema 🎿 pub

▶▶▶ 2️⃣ 2️⃣ ⚠️

Camping & Caravanning Club
(SX705530) California Cross ☎Gara
Bridge (054882) 297 Apr–26 Sep must
book Whit wk & Jul–Aug Last arrival
21.00hrs Last departure 11.00hrs no all
male groups

*This site slopes gently eastwards and is
protected by high hedges around
perimeter.*

5acres 89pitches 89🚐 or 89 🚐 or 89▲
awnings

12🏕️18wc lit all night 2cdp 🚽
washbasins hc central hot water 🛁hc☺
supervised calor gas camping gaz ☎
mobile shop 🛒

↪ stables

▶▶▶ 2️⃣ 0️⃣ ⚠️

Pennymoor Camping & Caravan Park
(SX685516) Signposted ☎(0548)
830269 or 83054 2 15 Mar–14 Nov
booking advisable Jul & Aug Last arrival
22.00hrs Last departure noon

*A grassy site with some bushes and
hedges situated in hilly woodland, with
moorland nearby. 10m SE of Plymouth off
A379.*

6acres 155pitches 70static SA 120🚐 £2–
£3.50 35🚐 £1.80–£3 or 35▲£2–£3.50
(awnings)

12🏕️☉ late arrivals enclosure 40wc lit all
night 2cdp 🚽 washbasins hc (🛁hc)☺
supervised (wash) spin (dry iron) (cold
storage) childrens playground calor gas
camping gaz ☎ 🛒

↪ stables golf 🎿 launderette pub

see advertisement on page 177

▶▶▶ 2️⃣ 0️⃣ ⚠️

South Leigh Caravan Park *(SX682515)*
☎(0548) 830346 20 May–19 May booking advisable for caravans
Spring Bank Hol & Jul–Aug Last arrival
23.00hrs Last departure noon

*Situated in the heart of the South Hams in
rural surroundings. This site offers
seclusion and protection provided by
high hedges around perimeter.*

4acres 80pitches 86static SA 15🚐 £2–
£4.20 or 15 🚐 £1.40–£2.40 65▲£1.80–
£2.80 (awnings) ltr

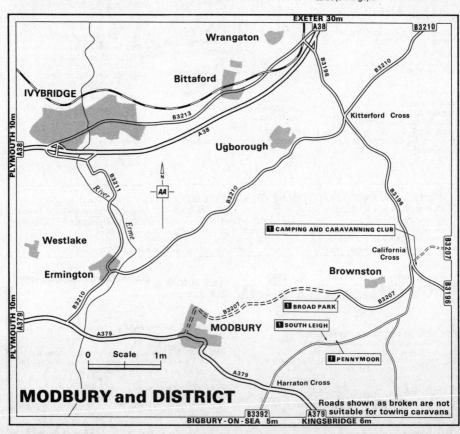

MODBURY and DISTRICT

EXETER 30m
A38
Wrangaton
B3210
B3196
B3210
Bittaford
IVYBRIDGE
B3213
Kitterford Cross
A38
Ugborough
PLYMOUTH 10m
A38
B3211
River Erme
N
AA
B3210
B3196
B3207
■1 CAMPING AND CARAVANNING CLUB
Westlake
California Cross
B3196
Ermington
Brownston
B3210
B3207
■1 BROAD PARK
B3207
■1 SOUTH LEIGH
MODBURY
A379
■1 PENNYMOOR
Scale 0 ... 1m
A379
Harraton Cross
B3392
A379
BIGBURY-ON-SEA 5m
KINGSBRIDGE 6m

Roads shown as broken are not
suitable for towing caravans

All sites listed under Modbury

&⊘ wc lit all night 3cdp 🔌 (washbasins hc central hot water) (🚿hc) ⊙ supervised (wash spin dry iron) cold storage licensed club/bar childrens playground calor gas camping gaz toilet fluid restaurant ☎ 🅱
↩ stables golf pub

MOFFAT
Dumfries & Galloway *Dumfriesshire*
Map 11 NT00

▶▶▶ ②❷⚠
Camping Club Site *(NT080051)*
Hammerland's Farm ☎ (0683) 20436
Apr–Sep Last arrival 21.00hrs Last departure noon
Well maintained level grass touring site.
7½ acres 200 pitches 200🔌 or 200🔌 or 200🔺 awnings

4& late arrivals enclosure 23wc lit all night 1cdp 12🔌 washbasins hc central hot water 🚿 hc ⊙ supervised (wash spin dry iron) cold storage calor gas camping gaz 🅱
↩ golf ⅄ launderette pub

MOLLAND
Devon
Map 3 SS82

▶▶▶ ②❷⚠
Molland Caravan Park *(SS787264)*
Black Cock Hotel Signposted ☎ Bishop's Nympton (07697) 297 15 Mar–14 Nov must book Jul & Aug Last departure noon
Mainly level site in hilly countryside within sight of Exmoor, ¾ m N of A361 Taunton–Barnstaple road at Coombsland New Cross.
7 acres 75 pitches SA 55🔌 £4.50 10 🔌 £4 10🔺 £4.50 (awnings)

4& late arrivals enclosure 15wc lit all night 1cdp 11 washbasins hc 1 central hot water 🚿 hc ⊙ supervised (wash spin dry) iron (▭) games room (cold storage) licensed club/bar childrens playground calor gas camping gaz toilet fluid cafe restaurant ☎ sauna 🅱
↩ stables ∫ launderette pub

MONIFIETH
Tayside *Angus*
Map 12 NO43

▶▶▶ ①②⚠
Riverview Caravan Park *(NO502322)*
Apply to: General Manager of Parks, Parks Dept, 353 Clepington Rd, Dundee DD3 8PL Signposted ☎ Dundee (0382) 23141 ext 413 Apr–Oct must book Jul & Aug Last arrival 21.00hrs Last departure 12.30hrs
A level, grassy site near sea and beach, 400yds S of A930. Situated approx 7m E from Dundee town centre.
10 acres 180 pitches SA 180🔌 or 180 🔌 or 180🔺 awnings
7& Individual pitches 35wc lit all night 4cdp washbasins hc (🚿 hc) ⊙ (Ⓟ) TV childrens playground ☎ ⊞ 🅱
↩ stables golf ⅄ cinema ∫ launderette

MONTROSE
Tayside *Angus*
Map 15 NO75

▶▶ ②❷⚠
South Links Site *(NO725575)* Traill Dr
Apply to: Director of Parks & Cemeteries, Angus District Council, Town House,

---

Montrose, Angus DD10 8QW Signposted ☎ (0674) 2044 Apr–20 Oct must book Jul & Aug Last arrival 21.00hrs Last departure noon
A grassy, sloping site near the sea and beach.
6 acres 160 pitches 160🔌 ✳£3–£3.70 or 160 🔌 £3–£3.70 12🔺 £1.85–£2.35 (awnings)
18& Individual pitches ⊘ 34wc lit all night 4cdp washbasins hc central hot water 🚿 hc ⊙ (wash spin) dry iron childrens playground ☎ 🅱
↩ stables golf ∫ launderette pub

MORECAMBE
Lancashire
Map 7 SD46
See sketch map

▶▶▶ ①②⚠
Regent Caravan Park *(SD431629)*
Westgate ☎ (0524) 413940 mid Mar–Oct must book Last arrival 22.00hrs Last departure noon 🎯 no tents no single sex groups
A level, grass site with mature trees, set in urban area with direct access to main road. From A589 follow signs to Heysham and Morecambe.
30 pitches 300 static 28🔌 £4.50–£6.50 2 🔌 £4.50–£6.50
6& Individual pitches 30wc lit all night 3cdp washbasins hc 🚿 hc ⊙ supervised (wash spin dry) iron ⊐ (licensed club/bar) childrens playground calor gas camping gaz cafe restaurant ☎ amusement arcade shower room & WC for disabled 🅱
↩ stables golf ⅄ cinema ∫ launderette
see advertisement on page 181

▶▶▶▶ ①❶⚠
Venture Caravan Park *(SD436633)*
Westgate Signposted ☎ (0524) 412986
→

RIVERVIEW CARAVAN PARK, MONIFIETH

Modern caravan facilities (180 pitches) situated approximately 7/8 miles east from Dundee town centre, on Monifieth foreshore adjacent to a safe sandy beach and Riverview Park which offers leisure and recreation facilities.

Booking facilities available on site and further details of charges etc, or prior booking can be obtained from the General Manager of Parks, 353 Clepington Road. Phone Dundee 23141 Ext 413.

Molland Caravan Park
Black Cock Hotel, Molland, N. Devon
Tel: Bishops Nympton 297

🔌 A Member Of: N.F.S.O.
🔺   English Tourist Board
🔌   A.A. ▶ ▶ ▶

Open: 15th March–15th November

A quiet Touring Caravan Park, with modern toilet block, hot showers, shaving points, hairdryers, washing and ironing facilities and telephone. There is also a pleasant bar with live entertainment each weekend and meals are available at the bar or take away.
There is a childrens play area, also available – Pony Trekking and riding, with or without instruction.
South Molton is just 4½ miles away (on the A361) with a very good shopping and gift centre.
Indoor heated swimming pool 50p per day. Sauna – £2 per Session up to 4 persons.
The park is within sight of Exmoor and is an ideal base from which to explore the North Devon coast and the many places of interest.
Dogs are allowed, but must be kept on a lead at all times.

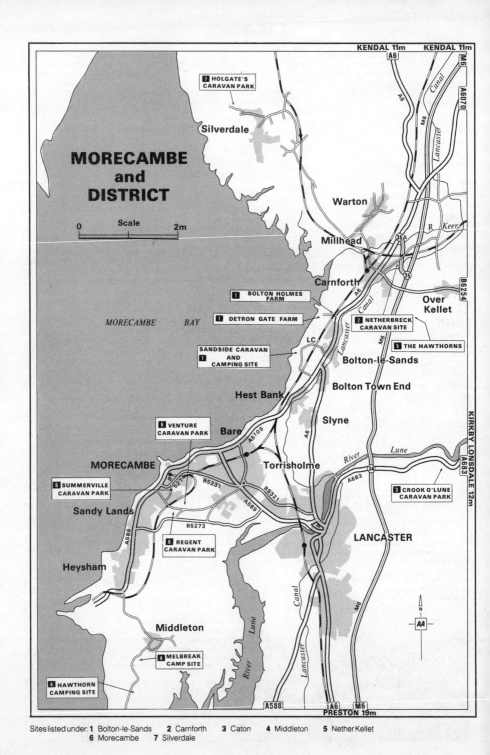

MORECAMBE and DISTRICT

Scale
0 ————— 2m

7 HOLGATE'S CARAVAN PARK

Silverdale

KENDAL 11m

KENDAL 11m

Warton

Millhead

Carnforth

Over Kellet

1 BOLTON HOLMES FARM

1 DETRON GATE FARM

2 NETHERBRECK CARAVAN SITE

5 THE HAWTHORNS

MORECAMBE BAY

1 SANDSIDE CARAVAN AND CAMPING SITE

Bolton-le-Sands

Bolton Town End

Hest Bank

Slyne

6 VENTURE CARAVAN PARK

Bare

MORECAMBE

Torrisholme

Lune

River

6 SUMMERVILLE CARAVAN PARK

3 CROOK O'LUNE CARAVAN PARK

Sandy Lands

LANCASTER

6 REGENT CARAVAN PARK

Heysham

Middleton

6 MELBREAK CAMP SITE

4 HAWTHORN CAMPING SITE

PRESTON 19m

KIRKBY LONSDALE 12m

AA

Sites listed under: **1** Bolton-le-Sands **2** Carnforth **3** Caton **4** Middleton **5** Nether Kellet **6** Morecambe **7** Silverdale

180

Mar–Oct booking advisable Whit & Jul–Aug Last arrival 22.30hrs Last departure 14.00hrs no tents

This level grassy site is situated in the urban area off the A589.

3½acres 56pitches 304static 56 £3–£4 or 56 £3–£4 (awnings)

23 Individual pitches 48wc lit all night 2cdp washbasins hc hc (wash dry iron) childrens playground calor gas camping gaz toilet fluid

stables golf cinema pub

▶ 1

Summerville Caravan Park *(SD432636)* 82 Acre Moss Ln (0524) 414249 Mar–Oct must book Last arrival 20.30hrs Last departure 10.00hrs no tents, no single sex groups no awnings

Small site located on the west side of the town.

1acre 16pitches 12static 12 £2.50–£3.50 4 £2.50–£3.50 ltr

Individual pitches 9wc lit all night 2cdp washbasins hc central hot water (hc) supervised (wash spin) cold storage calor gas batteries charged

stables golf cinema launderette pub

MORFA BYCHAN
Gwynedd
Map 6 SH53
See Criccieth sketch map

▶▶▶ 1

Cardigan View Caravan Park *(SH543371)* Signposted Porthmadog (0766) 2032 Etr–Oct rs Mar–Etr must book Jul & Aug Last departure noon no motorcycles no dogs no tents

Level grassy site, well maintained; shale and concrete standings for tourers. 2½m SW of Porthmadog.

2acres 35pitches 192static 35 fr£3.50 or 35 fr£3.50 (awnings)

6 Individual pitches 12wc lit all night washbasins hc central hot water hc supevised (wash spin dry iron) games room childrens playground private beach calor gas

golf cinema launderette pub

▶▶▶ 2

Greenacres Caravan Site *(SH540374)* Hemel Hempstead (0442) 48661 Mar–Oct must book peak periods Last arrival 21.00hrs Last departure 10.00hrs (Jul & Aug) no tents no motorcycles no single sex groups

Level grassy site with trees, set in mountainous country on the south side of main road and near to beach.

70pitches 700static 70 or 70 awnings

Individual pitches late arrivals enclosure wc lit all night supervised (wash spin dry) (games room) cold storage (licensed club/bar) childrens playground camping gaz fish & chip shop

golf launderette pub

MORTEHOE
Devon
Map 2 SS44
See Ilfracombe sketch map

▶▶▶ 2

Easewell Farm *(SS465455)* Signposted Woolacombe (0271) 870225 20 May–Sep rs Apr–19 May booking advisable 21 Jul & Aug Last arrival 22.00hrs Last departure noon no single sex groups

A level, grassy site set in hilly country, adjacent to sea and shingle rocky beach and viewpoint.

250pitches 5 £5 25 £4 220 £4 awnings ltr

6 60wc lit all night 1cdp washbasins hc (hc) supervised (wash spin dry) iron games room TV (cold storage) (licensed club/bar) childrens playground calor gas camping gaz cafe restaurant

stables golf cinema launderette pub

▶▶▶ 2

Twitchen House & Mortehoe Caravan Park *(SS465448)* Signposted Woolacombe (0271) 870476 May–Sep rs Etr–May & Oct must book Jul & Aug Last arrival 23.00hrs Last departure 10.00hrs no single sex groups

Part level, part sloping grass site with trees and bushes. Set in downland and wooded meadowland.

131pitches 295static SA 51 80 or 80 awnings

Individual pitches for caravans late arrivals enclosure 53wc lit all night 1cdp 32washbasins hc 20 hc 7 (wash spin dry) iron (games room) CTV (cold storage) licensed club/bar calor gas camping gaz toilet fluid cafe restaurant

stables cinema launderette pub

▶ 2

North Morte Farm Caravan & Camping Site *(SS461457)* North Morte Signposted Woolacombe (0271) 870381 Etr–Oct must book for caravans Last arrivals 22.00hrs no single sex groups →

MORECAMBE **FOR YOUR HOLIDAYS BY THE SEA.**

★ **Tourers.** Our touring park is situated amongst grass, trees and rose borders. White shaled hard standings, tarmac roads and a grass reservation for sun bathing. Our park is 30 mins drive to the Lake District.
★ **For Hire.** Modern caravans with H&C water, toilet, shower, TV and fridge.
★ **For sale.** A nice selection of new and used caravans sited on our park.

Park Amenities. Licensed Club with Dancing and Cabaret. Heated Swimming Pool and Childrens Play Pool. Amusement Arcade, Cafe, Supermarket, Launderette, Kiddies Playground and Rose Gardens.

Write or Phone for a brochure to

REGENT CARAVAN PARK
Westgate, Morecambe. Tel. 0524–413940

Venture Caravan Park
Westgate, Morecambe Telephone: Morecambe (0524) 412986

Situated near Morecambe town centre about 1 mile from the promenade and shore. Excellent facilities include washbasins, hot showers, toilets, laundrette, shop, telephone and a children's playground. Both trailer caravans and motor caravans are accommodated on hard level standing. Cars park alongside their vans. Awnings and dogs, however, are not permitted.

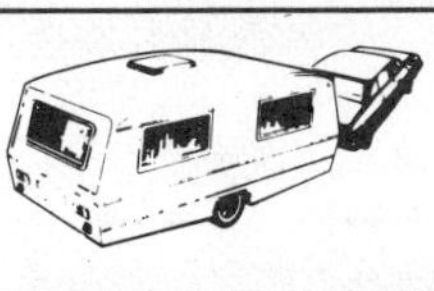

Set amid moorland and downs, this level and grassy site is near the sea and beach. Off B3343. Turn right at Post Office, site on left opposite Rockham Bay hotel.

210 pitches 62 static SA 10🚐 ✻£3.14 or 10 🚐£2.75 200▲£2.75 awnings ltr

🕐 19wc lit all night 1cdp (washbasins hc) (🛁hc)☺ supervised (wash spin dry iron) (cold storage) calor gas camping gaz 🛒

↔ stables cinema ⚓ launderette pub

MORTON-ON-SWALE
North Yorkshire
Map 8 SE39

▽②

Fairholm (SE325896) ☎ Northallerton (0609) 2741 from Apr must book Last arrival 20.00hrs Last departure noon

Level grass field in open country close to the River Swale. Just before Moreton-on-Swale; after crossing bridge turn S on private road.

3acres 5pitches 1static 5🚐

2🌣🕐 1wc lit all night 1cdp

↔ stables pub

MOUSWALD
Dumfries & Galloway Dumfriesshire
Map 11 NY07

▶▶②🅰

Mouswald Caravan Park (NY060740) Signposted ☎ (038783) 226 Etr–Oct must book Jul & Aug Last arrival 22.30hrs

Level, grass site with mature trees and bushes. Off A75 Dumfries–Annan road.

4acres 50pitches 15static 35🚐£3 or 35🚐£37▲£3 (awnings)

3🌣🕐 10wc lit all night 1cdp 🚐 washbasins hc central hot water (🛁hc)☺ supervised (wash spin) iron (cold storage) calor gas toilet fluid restaurant ☎

↔ stables launderette pub 🛒

MUCH WENLOCK
Shropshire
Map 7 SO69

▽①

Bourton Westwood Farm (SO613987) Signposted ☎ Telford (0952) 727393

10 Mar–Oct bookings advisable public hols Last arrival 22.30hrs

Mainly level enclosed field close to farm overlooking Wenlock and The Wrekin. On the B4378 from Much Wenlock to Ludlow; approx 1m from junc of B4378 & A458 on N side of road.

1½acres 25pitches 5🚐£1 or 5🚐£1 20▲£1 awnings ltr

1🏕1cdp

↔ pub 🛒

MULLACOTT CROSS
Devon
Map 2 SS54
See Ilfracombe sketch map

▶▶▶▶②🅰

Mullacott Cross Caravan Park (SS511446) Signposted ☎ Ilfracombe (0271) 62212 Etr–Oct must book Last arrival 20.00hrs Last departure 10.30hrs no groups of motorcyclists

This meadowland site is set on gentle grass slopes with views over the Atlantic coastline. It is 2m S of Ilfracombe and 3m E of the sandy beach at Woolacombe. Located adjacent to A361 Braunton–Ilfracombe road.

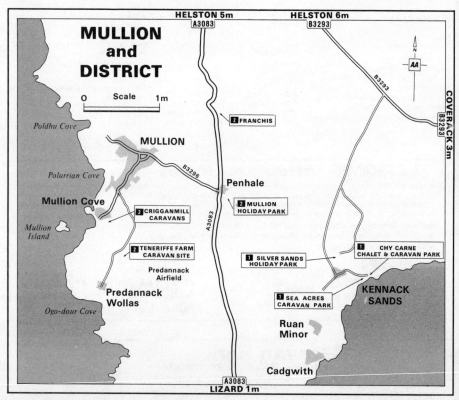

MULLION and DISTRICT

HELSTON 5m A3083 HELSTON 6m B3293

B3293

COVERACK 3m · B3293

N AA

Scale 0 — 1m

Poldhu Cove

MULLION

② FRANCHIS

B3296

Polurrian Cove

Penhale

Mullion Cove

② CRIGGANMILL CARAVANS

② MULLION HOLIDAY PARK

A3083

Mullion Island

② TENERIFFE FARM CARAVAN SITE

① SILVER SANDS HOLIDAY PARK

① CHY CARNE CHALET & CARAVAN PARK

Predannack Airfield

Predannack Wollas

Ogo-dour Cove

① SEA ACRES CARAVAN PARK

KENNACK SANDS

Ruan Minor

Cadgwith

A3083 LIZARD 1m

Sites listed under: **1** Kennack Sands **2** Mullion

8acres 125pitches 145static 65🚐 £3.50–
£4.75 60 🚐 £3.50–£4.75 or 60▲£2.75–
£4 (awnings) ltr

14🏕Individual pitches for caravans⊘
late arrivals enclosure 49wc lit all night
1cdp 🔌 (washbasins hc central hot
water) (🚿hc) (☺) (wash spin iron) CTV
cold storage licensed club/bar childrens
playground calor gas camping gaz toilet
fluid cafe restaurant ☎ take-away food
amusement arcade pony trap rides 🏠

↔ stables ⅄ cinema 🎿 launderette pub
see advertisement on page 156

MULLION
Cornwall
Map 2 SW61
See sketch map

▶▶▶ 🄲🄾⚠
Franchis *(SW698203)* Cury Cross Lanes
Signposted ☎ (0326) 240301 Etr–Oct
must book end Jul & Aug Last arrival
22.30hrs Last departure noon

*This site is surrounded by hedges and
coppice, situated on the A3083 between
Helston and The Lizard, an ideal position
for exploring the Peninsula.*

4acres 70pitches 7static 33🚐 £4 37 🚐 £4
or 37▲£4 (awnings)

10🏕 11wc lit all night 1cdp washbasins hc
(🚿hc) ☺ supervised cold storage calor
gas camping gaz toilet fluid 🏠

↔ stables golf 🎿 launderette pub

▶▶▶▶ 🄲🄾⚠
Mullion Holiday Park *(SW699182)*
Penhale Cross Signposted ☎ (0326)
240428 Etr–Sep must book peak periods
Last arrival 20.00hrs Last departure noon

*A level, grass site with bushes set in
rugged moorland on the Lizard peninsula,
adjacent to A3083 Helston road.*

7½acres 150pitches 320static 150🚐 or
150 🚐 or 150▲ awnings ltr

2🏕 late arrivals enclosure 15wc lit all night
1cdp 🔌 washbasins hc central hot water
(🚿hc) ☺ (wash) spin (dry iron) 🏊 (🏂)
games room (cold storage) licensed club/
bar childrens playground calor gas
camping gaz toilet fluid cafe restaurant ☎
⊞🏠

↔ stables golf ⅄ 🎿 launderette pub

Mullacott Cross
—
Nairn

▶▶ 🄲🄾⚠
Criggan Mill Caravans *(SW670179)*
Mullion Cove ☎ (0326) 240496 Apr–Oct
must book Jul & Aug Last arrival 23.00hrs
🎿

*A secluded site with level pitches set in a
combe near to Mullion Cove. From the
A3083 Helston road take B3296 to
Mullion.*

1acre 10pitches 22static 10🚐 £4–£5 or
10 🚐 £4–£5 or 10▲£4–£5 awnings ltr

2🏕 Individual pitches⊘ 6wc lit all night
1cdp 🔌 (washbasins hc) (🚿hc) (🚿hc) ☺
supervised (wash dry iron) (cold storage)
calor gas ☎ mobile shop

↔ stables golf ⅄ 🎿 launderette pub 🏠

▶ 🄰🄾⚠
Teneriffe Farm Caravan Site
(SW674166) Signposted ☎ (0326)
240293 19 Apr–Oct must book Jul & Aug
no motorcycles

*Part level, part sloping grass site set in
meadowland adjacent to sandy beach
and rocky scenery.*

3acres 15pitches 5static SA 15🚐 £2.75 or
15 🚐 £2.75 or 15▲£2.75 (awnings)

7🏕 5wc lit all night 1cdp 🔌 washbasins
hc (central hot water) (🚿hc) ☺ supervised
calor gas camping gaz ☎

↔ stables golf ⅄ 🎿 launderette pub 🏠

MUSSELBURGH
Lothian *Midlothian*
Map 11 NT37

▶▶▶▶ 🄲🄾⚠
Drum Mohr Caravan Park *(NT373734)*
Levenhall Signposted ☎ 031-665 6867
Mar–Oct Last arrival 22.00hrs Last
departure noon

*A fine site not far from the A1; 2m E of
Musselburgh between A198 and B1348.*

9acres 120pitches 90🚐 £3.30–£4.50 or
90 🚐 £3.30–£4.50 30▲£3.30–£4.50
(awnings)

9🏕 Individual pitches late arrivals
enclosure 26wc lit all night 2cdp 🔌
washbasins hc 🚿 hc ☺ supervised (wash)
(dry iron) cold storage childrens

---

playground calor gas camping gaz toilet
fluid ☎ toilet facilities for disabled 🏠

↔ stables golf launderette pub

NACTON
Suffolk
Map 5 TM23

▶▶ 🄸🄾⚠
Priory Park *(TM198409)* ☎ Ipswich
(0473) 77393 late May–late Sep rs late
Sep–late May booking advisable public &
school hols no single sex groups

*Well screened south facing site with
panoramic views overlooking Orwell.
Conveniently situated for new Ipswich
southern bypass and Felixstowe car ferry.*

15acres 150pitches 250static SA
150🚐 £4.50–£8.05 or 150 🚐 £4.50–
£8.05 or 150▲£4.50–£8.05 awnings ltr

6🏕 late arrivals enclosure 13wc lit all night
2cdp 🔌 washbasins hc central hot water
🚿 hc ☺ supervised (wash spin dry iron)
(Smugglers Beach only) 🛥 games room
TV licensed club/bar childrens
playground private beach calor gas
camping gaz cafe restaurant ☎ water
skiing fishing boat launching windsurfing
🏠

↔ stables golf ⅄ cinema 🎿 launderette
pub

NAIRN
Highland *Nairnshire*
Map 14 NH85

▶▶▶ 🄸🄰⚠
Delnies Woods Caravan Park
(NH846552) Signposted ☎ (0667) 52561
Apr–Oct booking advisable Jul & Aug

*An attractive site set amongst pine trees.
Situated about 3m W of Nairn on the A96.*

4acres 50pitches 30static 50🚐 or 50 🚐
30▲ awnings

10🏕 Individual pitches⊘ late arrivals
enclosure 8wc lit all night 2cdp 🔌
washbasins hc central hot water (🚿hc) ☺
supervised calor gas camping gaz
paraffin toilet fluid ☎ hair dryers mobile
shop

↔ stables golf ⅄ cinema 🎿 launderette
pub 🏠

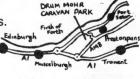

▶▶▶ ① ❷ ⚠

East Beach Caravan Park *(NH895574)*
East Beach Signposted ☎ (0667) 53764
15 Mar–Oct booking advisable peak
periods Last arrival 21.00hrs Last
departure 10.00hrs

*A level site bordered by the beach, the
River Nairn and golf course.*

2¾acres 100pitches 280static 50🛠
20🛠 30▲ (awnings)

6🔄 Individual pitches ⊘ late arrivals
enclosure 15wc lit all night 2cdp
19washbasins hc 3central hot water
6🔥 hc 6☉ supervised (wash spin dry iron)
childrens playground private beach calor
gas camping gaz toilet fluid ☎ ⊞ 🛒

↔ stables golf ⚘ cinema ⚙ launderette
pub

NARBERTH
Dyfed
Map 2 SN11
See Tenby sketch map

▶▶▶▶ ② ❷ ⚠

Redford Caravan Park *(SN135134)*
Princes Gate ☎ (0834) 860251 Apr–7
Oct booking advisable 28 Jul–8 Aug Last
arrival 23.55hrs Last departure 11.55hrs

*Sloping grass site with mature trees, just
off A40 on B4314.*

10acres 50pitches 55static 50🛠 £1.50–
£4.50 or 50🛠 £1.50–£4.50 or
50▲ £1.50–£4.50 (awnings) ltr

5🔄 Individual pitches late arrivals
enclosure 18wc lit all night 2cdp 🔧
(12washbasins hc) (5🔥 hc) 4☉
supervised (wash spin dry iron) ⊇ games
room (cold storage) licensed club/bar
childrens playground calor gas camping
gaz toilet fluid restaurant ☎ ⊞ 🛒

↔ stables ⚙ launderette pub

▶ ① ❶ ⚠

Noble Court Caravan Site *(SN111158)*
Redstone Rd Signposted ☎ (0834)
860213 Mar–Oct must book Jul & Aug
Last departure noon no single sex groups

*A small, well-maintained site on sloping
ground, with fine open country views,
situated 7m from coastal resorts. Situated
on B4313, ½m S of A40 and ½m N of
Narberth.*

2acres 40pitches 60static 40🛠 £2.50–
£3.50 or 40🛠 £2.50–£3.50 or
40▲ £2.50–£3.50 (awnings) ltr

8🔄 late arrivals enclosure 12wc lit all night
(🔥 hc) ☉ supervised licensed club/bar
childrens playground calor gas camping
gaz ☎ 🛒

↔ stables ⚙ launderette pub

NARBOROUGH
Norfolk
Map 9 TF71

▶▶▶ ③ ❸ ⚠

Pentney Park *(TF742141)* Gayton Rd
Signposted ☎ (0760) 337479 Mar–Oct
must book Spring Bank Hol & Jul–Aug
Last arrival 22.00hrs Last departure noon

*Level, grass site with mature trees and
bushes. Set in woodland and
meadowland adjacent to A47 Swaffham–
King's Lynn Road.*

16acres 201pitches 201🛠 £4 or
201🛠 £4 or 201▲ £4 (awnings)

7🔄 late arrivals enclosure 38wc lit all night
3cdp 🔧 34washbasins hc 14🔥 hc ☉
supervised (wash spin dry iron) games
room (cold storage) childrens playground
calor gas camping gaz toilet fluid ☎ ⊞ 🛒

↔ stables ⚙ pub

NAWTON
North Yorkshire
Map 8 SE68

▶▶ ② ❶ ⚠

Wrens of Ryedale Caravan Site
(SE656839) Signposted ☎ Helmsley
(0439) 71260 Apr–Sep must book public
hols & Jul–Aug Last arrival 22.30hrs

*A level, grassy site with mature trees and
bushes set in the Rye Valley. ½m S of
Beadlam village off A170.*

3½acres 45pitches 20static
20🛠 ✳£2.60 or 20🛠 £2.60 25▲ £2.60
(awnings) ltr

3🔄 Individual pitches ⊘ 10wc lit all night
1cdp washbasins hc (🔥 hc) ☉ supervised
cold storage calor gas camping gaz
restaurant 🛒

↔ stables golf pub

NETHER KELLET
Lancashire
Map 7 SD56

▶▶▶ ② ❷ ⚠

The Hawthorns *(SD514686)*
☎ Carnforth (052473) 2079 Mar–Oct
must book

*A very well kept and planned site in a rural
setting on the edge of the village. Some
good recreational facilities and various
animals for children.*

7acres 10pitches SA 10🛠 ✳fr£3.45 or
10🛠 fr£3.45 or 10▲ £3.45 (awnings)

5🔄 Individual pitches ⊘ 9wc lit all night
1cdp 🔧 washbasins hc central hot water
(🔥 hc) ☉ (wash dry iron) games room cold
storage childrens playground calor gas
pitch & putt & putting 🛒

↔ stables ⚘ ⚙ launderette pub

NEWBRIDGE
Isle of Wight
Map 4 SZ48

▶▶▶▶ ② ❸ ⚠

Orchards Holiday Caravan Park
(SZ441879) Signposted ☎ Calbourne
(098378) 331 Etr–Sep must book Spring &
Aug Bank Hols Last arrival 22.00hrs Last
departure 11.00hrs

*Gently sloping grass site with mature trees
and bushes, set in downland and
meadowland adjacent to B3401 and near
the sea.*

8acres 175pitches 60static 175🛠 £4–£7
or 175🛠 £4–£7 or 175▲ £4–£7 awnings

10🔄 Individual pitches 34wc lit all night
34🔧 30washbasins hc (3↪hc) (10🔥 hc)
12☉ supervised (wash) spin (dry) iron ⊇
CTV cold storage childrens playground
calor gas camping gaz toilet fluid ☎
battery charger 🛒

↔ pub

see advertisement on page 186

NEWCASTLE EMLYN
Dyfed
Map 2 SN34

▶▶▶ ② ❸ ⚠

Afon Reifi Caravan & Camping Site
(SN338405) Pentre Farm, Pentrecagal
(2m E A484) Signposted ☎ Velindre
(0559) 370532 Apr–Oct booking
advisable peak period Last arrival
22.00hrs Last departure 18.00hrs

*Very attractive and well managed site in
secluded valley.*

6acres 75pitches 50🛠 fr£3 20🛠 fr£2.80
5▲ fr£2.80 (awnings)

10🔄 ⊘ late arrivals enclosure 15wc lit all
night 1cdp 🔧 washbasins hc (🔥 hc) ☉
supervised (wash spin dry) (cold storage)
childrens playground calor gas camping
gaz ⊞ 🛒

↔ stables ⚙ pub

▶▶ ③ ❶ ⚠

Dolbryn Farm *(SN298382)* Capel Ifan Rd
Signposted ☎ (0239) 710683 Jun–Sep
Last arrival 20.00hrs Last departure noon

*A simple farm site in an area of great
natural beauty. 1½m along Capel Ifan
road.*

2½acres 25pitches 2static SA 25🛠 £3 or
25🛠 £3 or 25▲ £3 awnings

5🔄 6wc lit all night 1cdp 🔧 washbasins
hc (🔥 hc) ☉ supervised spin dry ⅌ (cold
storage) (licensed club/bar) childrens
playground calor gas camping gaz
badminton, barbeque 🛒

↔ stables ⚙ launderette pub

NEWCHURCH
Isle of Wight
Map 4 SZ58

▶▶▶ ② ❸ ⚠

Southland Camping Park *(SZ557847)*
Signposted ☎ Arreton (098377) 385
Mar–Oct booking advisable Last arrival
22.00hrs

*Attractive site secluded by trees situated
in Arreton Valley. Off A3056.*

5acres 100pitches 100🛠 ✳£3.40 or
100🛠 £3.40 or 100▲ £3.40 awnings

7🔄 Individual pitches late arrivals
enclosure 12wc lit all night 1cdp 🔧
washbasins hc (🔥 hc) ☉ (wash spin dry
iron) (cold storage) calor gas camping
gaz toilet fluid ☎ hair dryers 🛒

↔ stables golf ⚘ cinema ⚙ launderette
pub

see advertisement on page 187

Pentney Park

Caravan & Camping Site

Pentney, Kings Lynn, Norfolk
Telephone: Narborough (0760) 337479
Proprietor: Bryan & Hilary Webster

Very Good
excellent site
Heated swimming pool
e.vana awning
£6.50 1986
august.

The Site

The park is family run with the proprietors in permanent residence – ensuring that constant high standards in all facilities are maintained. Particular attention is given to the placement and spacing of guests caravans and tents. The site covers nearly 17 acres of mature woodland clearing and grassland on level well maintained and drained ground. This picturesque area of outstanding beauty enjoys a high annual sunshine record and equally important, low rainfall!

Ideally situated for many places of interest and sporting/recreational facilities – you'll find the entrance to the site is situated on the B1153 Gayton Road, at its junction with the A47.

Facilities

Three well-sited toilet blocks with hot water, showers, razor points and WC's. ★ Hair dryers ★ Two laundry rooms ★ Shop with fresh milk and bread daily and an off licence facility ★ Barbeque area ★ Childrens play area ★ Public telephone ★ Well equipped games room ★ Caravan and camping accessory shop, with new and used caravan sales ★ Late arrivals area.

There are numerous attractions including the historic town of Kings Lynn, Caley Mill Lavender fields, the Wolferton Royal Station Museum and Sandringham. For the sportsman – sailing, golf, bowling, tennis, speedway, hiking, wildfowling and much more.

Open March to October

BEST PLACED FOR BEAUTIFUL NORFOLK!

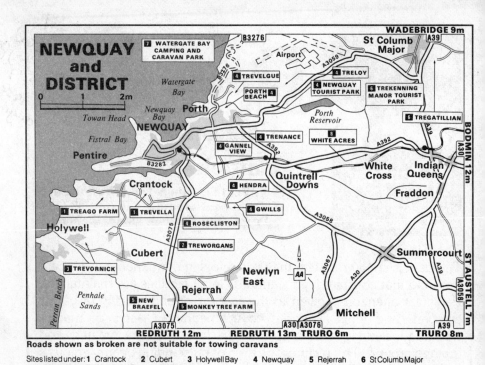

NEWQUAY and DISTRICT

WADEBRIDGE 9m

Roads shown as broken are not suitable for towing caravans

Sites listed under: **1** Crantock **2** Cubert **3** Holywell Bay **4** Newquay **5** Rejerrah **6** St Columb Major **7** Watergate Bay **8** Whitecross

NEW FOREST The New Forest covers 144 square miles and is composed of broadleaf and coniferous woodland, open common land and heath. This unique area was originally a royal hunting forest and there are long-established rights of access. It is not a 'Forest Park' but similar facilities for visitors are maintained by the Forestry Commission; these include caravan and camp sites, picnic sites, car parks, way-marked walks and ornamental drives.

The forest is always popular but advance booking at caravan sites is not possible except for the Spring Bank Holiday period, when access to Forestry Commission sites is strictly limited to holders of campsite access tickets. Details of this scheme may be found in a leaflet, published by the Forestry Commission, this also lists sites in the New Forest and explains the regulations which control camping and caravanning in this protected area. It is available from the Deputy Surveyor of the New Forest, Forestry Commission, Southampton Road, Lyndhurst, Hants SO4 7NH Tel Lyndhurst (042128) 2801.

See Ashurst, Brockenhurst and Holmsley for AA pennant classified sites.

AA 'Venture' sites are listed under the following locations: Brockenhurst, Lyndhurst, Nomansland (Wiltshire) and Sway.

NEWGALE
Dyfed
Map 2 SM82

▶ ▶ ② ⓪ △
Chapel Farm Caravan Park & Touring Site (SM856209) ☎ St Davids (0437) 721786 Apr–Sep booking advisable Jul & Aug last departure 11.00hrs (Jul–Aug) no groups of motorcyclists no tents

A level grassy site adjacent to southern end of Newgale Sands.

5½ acres 50 pitches 25 static 50 🚐 £3.45 or 50 🚐 £3.45 (awnings)
5 ⛺ Individual pitches late arrivals

enclosure 22 wc lit all night 1 cdp (washbasins hc) (🛁 hc) ☺ supervised (dry) ᛩ cold storage childrens playground calor gas cafe
⊖ stables 🛠 ⌘ pub 🍺

NEWHAVEN
Derbyshire
Map 7 SK16

▶ ▶ ② ⓪ △
Newhaven Holiday Camping & Caravan Park (SK167602) Signposted ☎ Hartington (029884) 300 Mar–Oct must book public hols

A pleasantly situated site within the Peak District National Park, between Ashbourne–Buxton on A515 at junction with A5012.

5 acres 95 pitches 45 static 95 🚐 £3–£3.50 or 95 🚐 £3–£3.50 or 95 △ £3–£3.50 (awnings) ltr
8 ⛺ Individual pitches ⓐ late arrivals enclosure 18 wc lit all night 1 cdp washbasins hc 🛁 hc ☺ supervised (wash dry iron) games room cold storage childrens playground calor gas camping gaz toilet fluid ⊞ 🍺
⊖ launderette pub

NEW MILTON
Hampshire
Map 4 SZ29
See Christchurch sketch map

▶ ▶ ▶ ▶ ③ ❸ △
Bashley Park (SZ252968) Sway Rd Signposted ☎ (0425) 612340 Mar–Oct must book peak periods no single sex groups no tents

This site is located in reasonably flat open fields with hard gravel standings, and is bordered by woodland and shrubbery.

25 acres 420 pitches 380 static 420 🚐 or 420 🚐 (awnings) ltr
70 ⛺ Individual pitches late arrivals enclosure wc lit all night 4 cdp 🚐 washbasins hc central hot water ➔ hc 🛁 hc ☺ (wash spin dry iron) ⊿ (ᛩ) games room (licensed club/bar) childrens

playground calor gas camping gaz toilet fluid cafe restaurant ☎ 🍺
⊖ stables golf ⌘ launderette pub

NEWQUAY
Cornwall
Map 2 SW86
See sketch map

▶ ▶ ▶ ▶ ▶ ② ❷ △
Hendra Tourist Park (SW833601) Lane (2m SE) Signposted ☎ (06373) 5778 27 Jun–1 Sep rs Apr–26 Jun & 2–30 Sep must book Jul & Aug Last arrival dusk Last departure noon (10.00hrs Sat)

A partly level and sloping site with mature trees and bushes set in downland; 2m SE of Newquay, off Lane–Quintrel Down road.

31 acres 1004 pitches 504 🚐 £2.60–£5.90 or 504 🚐 £2.60–£5.90 500 △ £2.60–£5.90 (awnings)
52 ⛺/○ late arrivals enclosure wc lit all night 4 cdp 🚐 washbasins hc (🛁 hc) ☺ supervised (wash spin dry iron) ⊿ games room CTV (cold storage) (licensed club) (childrens playground) calor gas camping gaz toilet fluid cafe ☎ hairdresser fish bar sauna cycle hire trampolines 🍺
⊖ stables golf 🛠 cinema ⌘ launderette pub

▶ ▶ ▶ ▶ ② ❷ △
Newquay Tourist Park (SW853626) St Columb Minor (3m E off A3059) Signposted ☎ (06373) 71111 19 May–14 Sep booking advisable Jul & Aug Last departure 10.00hrs no single sex groups

A pleasant informal touring and holiday site situated on rising ground affording country views.

14 acres 312 pitches 34 static SA 312 🚐 fr £2.60 or 312 🚐 fr £2.60 or 312 △ fr £2.60 awnings
18 ⛺ Individual pitches late arrivals enclosure 54 wc lit all night 2 cdp 🚐 washbasins hc 🛁 hc ☺ supervised wash spin iron ⊿ TV licensed club/bar childrens playground calor gas camping gaz paraffin toilet fluid cafe ☎ crazy golf, pitch & putt 🍺
⊖ stables golf 🛠 cinema ⌘ launderette pub

see advertisement on page 188

EVERYTHING A HOLIDAY SHOULD HAVE

Newquay

TOURIST PARK

NOW AWARDED AA 5 PENNANTS

▶▶▶▶▶

▶ **Superb scenery**
▶ **Free entertainment**
▶ **Free Pools.**

● New 3-pool complex and sun terraces.
● FREE nightly entertainment in the fabulous FIESTA club. Children welcome.
● FREE hot showers.
● Purpose built amenity complex. Every modern facility for campers and touring caravanners.
● Individual pitches in a landscaped parkland setting.

Newquay tourist park AA ▣

Dial-A-Brochure 06373-71111

NEWQUAY CORNWALL

▶▶▶▶ ②❷⚠

Rosecliston Touring Park Trevemper (2m S on A3075) Signposted ☎ Crantock (0637) 830326 May–Oct rs Apr must book peak periods Last arrival 22.00hrs Last departure 22.00hrs ✝

Small, well organised and managed site with attractively arranged and well positioned pitches.

6acres 117pitches 117🚗 or 117🚐 or 117▲ awnings

10🅗 Individual pitches ⊘ late arrivals enclosure 14wc lit all night 2cdp 🔌 22washbasins hc (11🚿 hc) 4☉ supervised (wash) (dry) iron ⊇ games room CTV cold storage licensed club/bar childrens playground calor gas camping gaz toilet fluid cafe restaurant ☎ ⊞ 🛍

⊖ stables golf ⚒ cinema ⬛ launderette pub

▶▶▶▶ ②❷⚠

Trevelgue Caravan Park (SW839633) Signposted ☎ (06373) 3475 or 5905 Apr–Oct booking advisable mid Jul–mid Aug Last departure noon ✝

Level grass site set in meadowland with direct access to Porth and Whipsiderry beaches. Off B3276 Porth-Padstow road.

12acres 267pitches 142static 267🚗 £6.40 or 267🚐 £6.40 or 267▲ £6.40 (awnings)

18🅗 Individual pitches late arrivals enclosure 32wc lit all night 2cdp 🔌 washbasins hc (🚿 hc) ☉ supervised (wash spin dry) iron ⊇ games room TV (cold storage licensed club/bar) childrens playground calor gas camping gaz ☎ Jacuzzi 🛍

⊖ stables golf ⚒ cinema ⬛ launderette pub

see advertisement on page 192

▶▶▶ ②❷⚠

Gannel View Caravan Park (SW828606) Lane (2m SE) Signposted ☎ (06373) 4634 Jun–Sep rs May must book mid Jul–mid Aug Last arrival 19.00hrs Last departure 14.00hrs ✝ no single sex groups

Gently sloping and level grass-surfaced site close to A392.

28pitches 46static SA 28🚗 £4.50 or 28🚐 £4.50 or 28▲ £4.50 awnings

---

6🅗 24wc lit all night 1cdp washbasins hc central hot water ✲ hc (🚿 hc) ☉ supervised (wash spin) dry (iron) ⊇ (games room) CTV (cold storage) licensed club/bar childrens playground calor gas camping gaz toilet fluid ☎ ⊞ 🛍

⊖ stables golf ⚒ cinema ⬛ launderette pub

▶▶▶ ②❸⚠

Gwills Caravan Park (SW830592) Lane (2m SE) Signposted ☎ (06373) 3617 Etr–Oct must book Jul & Aug Last departure noon no all male groups

This part level and part sloping site situated near the river has clumps of trees. From A30 turn right at Indian Queens to A392 then follow unclass road between Lane and Newlyn East.

10acres 150pitches 36static SA 40🚗 £2.50–£4.25 10🚐 £2.50–£4.25 100▲ £2.50–£4.25 (awnings)

7🅗 Individual pitches ⊘ late arrivals enclosure 13wc lit all night 2cdp 🔌 15washbasins hc 7🚿 hc ☉ supervised (wash spin dry iron) games room (cold storage) childrens playground calor gas camping gaz ☎ fishing 🛍

⊖ stables golf ⚒ cinema ⬛ launderette pub

▶▶▶ ③❸⚠

Porth Beach Tourist Park (SW838632) Porth (1m NE) ☎ (06373) 6531 Apr–Oct must book Jul & Aug Last departure noon no single sex groups

Mainly level, grass site with saplings and bushes set in meadowland adjacent to sea and beach. Off B3276.

6acres 201pitches 201🚗 £2.30–£9.72 or 201🚐 £2.30–£9.72 or 201▲ £2.30–£9.72 (awnings)

8🅗 Individual pitches late arrivals enclosure 24wc lit all night 1cdp 🔌 washbasins hc (🚿 hc) ☉ supervised (spin) dry (iron) childrens playground calor gas camping gaz cafe restaurant 🛍

⊖ stables golf cinema ⬛ launderette pub

▶▶▶ ①❷⚠

Treloy Tourist Park (SW853625) Signposted ☎ (06373) 2063 May–Sep must book mid Jul–mid Aug Last arrival 23.00hrs Last departure noon

3m E of Newquay on A3059.

11¼acres 100pitches SA 100🚗 £3.57–£5.75 or 100🚐 £3.57–£5.75 or 100▲ £3.57–£5.75 awnings

6🅗 ⊘ late arrivals enclosure 24wc lit all night 1cdp 🔌 20washbasins hc (8🚿 hc) 2☉ supervised (spin dry iron) ⊇ games room CTV (cold storage) licensed bar childrens playground calor gas camping gaz toilet fluid ☎ ⊞ take-away food hair dryers 🛍

⊖ stables golf ⚒ cinema ⬛ launderette pub

▶▶▶ ①❶⚠

Trenance Caravan & Chalet Park (SW818612) Edgcumbe Av ☎ (06373) 3447 May–Sep rs Apr must book Last arrival 23.00hrs Last departure 10.00hrs ✝ no single sex groups, no tents

A partly level and sloping grassy site 1m S of Newquay on A3075.

1½acres 80pitches 80🚗 £6 or 80🚐 £6 (awnings)

6🅗 Individual pitches late arrivals enclosure 52wc lit all night 2cdp washbasins hc (🚿 hc) ☉ (wash spin iron) (games room) (cold storage) calor gas camping gaz ☎ hairdressing salon 🛍

⊖ stables golf ⚒ cinema ⬛ launderette pub

NEWTON ABBOT
Devon
Map 3 SX87

▶▶▶ ②❸⚠

Stover International Caravan Park (SX832738) Lower Staple Hill (3m N off A38) Signposted ☎ (0626) 82446 16 May–Sep rs 15 Mar–15 May & Oct–15 Dec must book Jun–Aug (minimum 5 nights stay Jul & Aug) Last arrival 23.00hrs Last departure noon No all male groups No groups of motorcyclists

Excellent site for touring Dartmoor and Torbay. Coarse, salmon and trout fishing →

nearby.

13½ acres 246 pitches 246 ⬚ £3.60–£5.10 or 246 ⬚ £3.60–£5.10 or 246▲£3.60–£5.10 (awnings) ltr

15 late arrivals enclosure 59 wc lit all night 3 cdp ⬚ washbasins hc (⬚ hc ⬚ hc) ⊙ supervised (wash spin) dry (iron) (games room) (cold storage) licensed bar childrens playground calor gas camping gaz toilet fluid cafe ☎ (hair dryers) facilities for disabled

⟿ stables cinema ♪

see advertisement on page 245

▶▶ ① ❶ ⚠

Country Touring Caravan Centre
(SX846679) Two Mile Oak ☎ Ipplepen

(0803) 812628 May–Oct Last arrival 23.00 hrs Last departure noon no all male groups no tents

Site with hard standings and views towards Dartmoor National Park. Situated 2m S of Newton Abbot on A381.

½ acre 18 pitches 12 ⬚ £2.50 6 ⬚ £2.50 (awnings) ltr

2 Individual pitches 3 wc lit all night 1 cdp ⬚ (washbasins hc) central hot water (⬚ hc ⊙) supervised (spin dry) iron cold storage calor gas toilet fluid

⟿ stables cinema ♪ launderette pub

NEWTONMORE
Highland *Inverness-shire*
Map 14 NN79

▶▶ ③ ❷ ⚠
Invernahaven Caravan Park
(NN685955) Glentruim Signposted ☎ (05403) 534 & 221 Apr–Oct Last arrival 23.00 hrs Last departure noon

This site is on level ground close to River Truim, surrounded by woodlands and mountain scenery. Situated S of Newtonmore off A9.

12½ acres 150 pitches SA 50 ⬚ £3.25–£4 50 ⬚ £3.25–£4 50▲£2–£2.25 (awnings) ltr

8 Individual pitches ⊘ late arrivals →

TREVORNICK HOLIDAY PARK

the Holiday Park by the sea ··

Trevornick Holiday Park is only ½ mile across our fields to the beach. Our amenities are superb ··· where else can you get all this on one Holiday Park?

- Heated swimming & paddling pools
- 2 Licensed bars
- Children's bars
- Quick food cafeteria
- Self service shop
- Discotheque
- Video shows
- Amusement arcade
- Sauna baths
- Solarium
- Launderette
- Unisex hairdressing
- Coarse fishing
- 2 Golf courses
- Roller skating
- Skateboarding
- Go karts
- Bumperboats
- Aqua bikes
- Mini-motorbikes
- Crazy golf
- Dogs allowed

DIAL A BROCHURE CRANTOCK **0637 830 531**

CHILDREN FREE May June & Sept

TREVORNICK Holiday Park
Holywell Bay Newquay
Cornwall TR8 5PW

FOR CAMPERS & TOURERS ONLY

enclosure 36wc lit all night 3cdp washbasins hc central hot water (🛁 hc)☺ supervised (wash dry) iron cold storage calor gas camping gaz fishing pony trekking ☎ 🛠

↪ stables golf 🥾 launderette pub

NEWTON STEWART
Dumfries & Galloway *Wigtownshire*
Map 10 NX46

▶▶▶ 🚽 1️⃣ 🔵 △
Creebridge Caravan Park *(NX415656)*
☎(0671)2324 Apr–Oct no bookings

Level, grass and gravel site with trees set in urban area. ¼m E of Newton Stewart on A75.

¼acre 36pitches 50static 22🚐 6 🚐 8▲ (awnings)

6🏕☺24wc 1cdp washbasins hc 🛁 hc☺ supervised (wash spin) (iron) games room childrens playground calor gas camping gaz toilet fluid ☎ 🛠

↪ stables golf cinema 🥾 launderette pub

▽🚽 2️⃣
Talnotry Caravan Park *(NX492719)*
Palnure (7mNE off A712) For bookings: Chief Forester, Kirroughtree Forest Office, Daltamie, Newton Stewart, Wigtownshire ☎(0671)2170 Signposted Apr–Sep Last departure noon

Fine open grassy site by bank of small stream set amidst the rugged grandeur of Galloway Forest Park; site is close to A712.

10acres 100pitches 100🚐£1.70–£2.50 or 100 🚐£1.70–£2.50 or 100▲fr£1.50 awnings

7🏕 late arrivals enclosure 2cdp calor gas toilet fluid ☎ 🛠

↪ 🥾

NOMANSLAND
Wiltshire
Map 4 SU21

▽🚽 1️⃣
Pipers Wait *(SU251166)* (1m SW towards B3078) ☎Lyndhurst (042128) 2269 (10am–6pm) Southampton (0703) 812888 (other times) nc

Secluded site amidst mixed woodland in old gravel pit.

40pitches 40🚐 or 40 🚐 or 40▲
🏕cdp

NORTH BERWICK
Lothian *East Lothian*
Map 12 NT58

▶▶▶ 🚽 2️⃣ 🔵 △
Rhodes Caravan Site *(NT566850)*
Signposted end Mar–Sep no bookings Last departure 10.30hrs

Level grass site in meadowland in urban area with direct access to sea and beach. Located off A198 Dunbar road.

10acres 350pitches SA 350🚐 ✳£3.50–£4 or 350 🚐£3.50–£4 or 350▲£3.50–£4 (awnings) ltr

17🏕 Individual pitches ☺ late arrivals enclosure 68wc lit all night 8cdp 54washbasins hc 24🛁 hc☺ (wash spin) childrens playground calor gas camping gaz ☎ 🛠

↪ stables golf cinema 🥾 pub

NORTH KILWORTH
Leicestershire
Map 4 SP68

▶🚽 1️⃣ 🔵 △
Kilworth Caravan Park *((SP605838)*
☎Market Harborough (0858) 880385 or 880597 Apr–Oct rs Nov–Mar no bookings Last arrival 20.00hrs Last departure noon no tents no motorcycles

Gently sloping, grass and gravel site with mixed vegetation. Set in hilly woodland and meadowland with access to A427 Market Harborough road, and near canal.

4acres 50pitches 100static 40🚐£2.20 10 🚐£2.20 (awnings)

2🏕6wc lit all night 1cdp (🛁 hc)☺ supervised childrens playground calor gas camping gaz

↪ stables golf 🛠 launderette 🛠

NORTH SOMERCOTES
Lincolnshire
Map 9 TF49

▶▶▶▶ 🚽 2️⃣ 🔵 △
Lakeside Holiday Park *(TF436955)*
Signposted ☎(050785) 315 Spring Bank Hol–mid Sep rs Etr–Spring Bank Hol & mid Sep–Oct must book peak periods

Last departure noon no single sex groups

A large coastal site surrounded by a Forestry Commission plantation. Situated on the A1031 Cleethorpes–Skegness road just south of the village.

15acres 150pitches 220static 150🚐 or 150 🚐 or 150▲ awnings

8🏕23wc lit all night 2cdp 🚐 26washbasins hc (10🛁 hc) 10☺ supervised (wash dry iron) 🛁 games room CTV (cold storage) licensed club/bar childrens playground calor gas camping gaz toilet fluid cafe ☎ fishing, skateboard track 🛠

↪ stables 🌲 cinema launderette

NORTH STAINLEY
North Yorkshire
Map 8 SE27

▶▶▶ 🚽 2️⃣ 🔵 △
Sleningford Water Mill *(SE280783)*
☎Ripon (0765) 85201 Apr–Oct booking advisable Last arrival 21.00hrs Last departure noon no unaccompanied youths

Level, grassy site with mature trees set in wood and meadowland adjacent to River Ure and A6108.

14acres 80pitches 50🚐£4 30 🚐£4 or 30▲£4 (awnings)

24🏕 Individual pitches for caravans ☺ late arrivals enclosure 18wc lit all night 6cdp washbasins hc 🛁 hc☺ supervised (wash spin dry) iron (games room) childrens playground calor gas camping gaz toilet fluid cafe ☎ facilities for disabled 🛠

↪ golf 🥾 pub

NOSTELL
West Yorkshire
Map 8 SE41

▶▶ 🚽 2️⃣ 🔵 △
Nostell Priory Holiday Homes
(SE402185) Top Park Wood Signposted ☎Wakefield (0924) 863938 Apr–Sep must book public hols Last arrival 22.00hrs Last departure noon

From the Wakefield–Doncaster road (A638) turn north along B6428 near the hamlet of Wragby (Wakefield 6m; Doncaster 14m). Site is then 7m on left.

3½acres 60pitches 80static 60🚐 or
60🚐 or 60🛆 (awnings) ltr

4🚐12wc lit all night 1cdp 16washbasins
hc 8🛁 hc 4☉ supervised (wash spin dry
iron) childrens playground calor gas
camping gaz toilet fluid ☎ mobile shop

⊖→ 🗲 launderette pub 🏪

NOTTER BRIDGE
Cornwall
Map 2 SX36

▶ ▶ ▶ ③ ❸ ⚠

Notter Bridge Caravan & Camping Park
(SX384608) ☎ Saltash (07555) 2318
Apr–Oct must book public hols & Jul–Aug
Last arrival 23.15hrs Last departure
11.00hrs 🕏

*Level, grass site with mature trees and
bushes set in hilly wooded meadowland,
adjacent to river and A38, 3m W of Saltash.*

2½acres 55pitches 24static 55🚐 £3.45–
£4.50 or 55🚐£3.45–£4.50 or
55🛆£3.45–£4.50 (awnings)

4🚐 late arrivals enclosure 11wc lit all night
2cdp 🚐 washbasins hc (🛁 hc)☉
supervised (wash spin dry iron) 🍴 cold
storage childrens playground calor gas
camping gaz ☎ ⊞ salmon & trout fishing

⊖→ stables golf 🗲 launderette pub

OKEHAMPTON
Devon
Map 2 SX59

▶ ▶ ▶ ② ❸ ⚠

Okehampton Motel Caravan Harbour
(SX684927) Signposted ☎ (0837) 2879
Etr–Sep booking advisable Last arrival
22.30hrs Last departure noon

*Small site with hedges that offer seclusion
and protection from prevailing winds, with
good views of Dartmoor. 1m E of
Okehampton on A30.*

2acres 25pitches 25🚐 or 25 🚐 or 25🛆
awnings

3🚐 Individual pitches ⊘ 9wc lit all night
1cdp 12washbasins hc 2central hot water
(1🖐hc) 4🛁 hc 5☉ supervised spin iron 🍴
(cold storage) licensed bar childrens
playground cafe restaurant ☎ ⊞

⊖→ stables golf cinema 🗲 launderette pub
🏪

OLD CLIPSTONE
Nottinghamshire
Map 8 SK66

▶ ▶ ▶ ③ ❷ ⚠

Sherwood Forest Caravan Park
(SK590651) Signposted ☎ Mansfield
(0623) 823132 Apr–Sep must book public

Nostell
—
Orleton

hols Last arrival 20.30hrs Last departure
18.00hrs no unaccompanied under 18's

*Level, grass site with mature trees,
saplings and bushes, set in meadowland,
adjacent to River Maun and lake. 2m SW of
Edwinstowe off B6030.*

14acres 100pitches 10static SA 100🚐 £5
or 100 🚐 £5 or 100🛆£5 awnings ltr

12🚐 Individual pitches late arrivals
enclosure 20wc lit all night 4cdp
🚐 washbasins hc (🛁 hc)☉ supervised
(wash spin) dry (iron) (cold storage)
childrens playground calor gas camping
gaz toilet fluid ☎ 🏪

⊖→ stables golf 🗲 launderette

OLNEY
Buckinghamshire
Map 4 SP85

▶ ▶ ▶ ② ❶ ⚠

Emberton Park (SP886500) Signposted
☎ Bedford (0234) 711575 Apr–Oct rs
Nov–Mar must book peak periods no
caravans Nov–Mar

*This site is situated 1m outside Olney and
set in pleasant surroundings in the Ouse
Valley adjacent to the river. There are four
main areas of water for sailing.*

56pitches 114static 56🚐 or 56 🚐 or 56🛆

10🚐 Individual pitches 3wc lit all night
3cdp washbasins hc 🛁 hc☉ calor gas
camping gaz cafe ⊞

⊖→ stables pub 🏪

ORGANFORD
Dorset
Map 3 SY99

▶ ▶ ▶ ② ❷ ⚠

Pear Tree Farm Caravans & Camping
(SY938922) Etr–15 Oct no bookings Last
arrival 23.00hrs Last departure noon no
single sex groups

*Level, grass site with mature trees and
bushes set in wooded meadowland. 6m W
of Poole off A351 at Holton Heath.*

7½acres 105pitches 60 🚐 fr£4.50 or
60 🚐 fr£4.50 45🛆 fr£4.50 (awnings)

7🚐 Individual pitches ⊘ 21wc lit all night
2cdp 🚐 washbasins hc (🛁 hc)☉
supervised (spin dry iron) (cold storage)
calor gas camping gaz 🏪

⊖→ stables golf ⚓ cinema 🗲 launderette
pub

▶ ② ❶ ⚠

Organford Manor (SY943926)
☎ Lytchett Minster (0202) 622 202
15 Mar–Oct no bookings during peak
periods

*A quiet secluded site in the grounds of the
manor house. Level grassy areas with
trees and shrubs. Take the first turning on
left off A35 after the Lytchett roundabout at
the junc of A35/A351, site entrance is a
short distance on the right.*

3acres 75pitches 45static SA 43🚐 £4
10 🚐 £3.50 22🛆£4 (awnings)

15🚐 wc lit all night 2cdp washbasins hc
central hot water (🛁 hc)☉ supervised
(iron) (cold storage) childrens playground
calor gas camping gaz paraffin 🏪

⊖→ stables 🗲 launderette pub

ORLETON
Hereford & Worcester
Map 7 SO46

▶ ▶ ② ❷ ⚠

Orleton Rise Caravan Park (SO477680)
Green Ln Signposted ☎ Richards Castle
(058474) 617 16 Mar–23 Oct must book
Etr & public hols no tents

*Site set amid scenic National Trust
countryside on borders of Herefordshire
and Shropshire. Off B4361.*

½acre 20pitches 20🚐 fr£2.50 or
20 🚐 fr£2.50 (awnings)

9🚐 12wc lit all night 2cdp washbasins hc
central hot water (🛁 hc)☉ supervised iron
cold storage calor gas ☎

⊖→ 🗲 pub 🏪

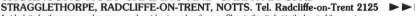

ORMSKIRK
Lancashire
Map 7 SD40

▶▶▷ ② ❷ △
Abbey Farm Caravan Site *(SD434098)*
Blyth Ln ☎ (0695) 72686 All year must
book public hols & Jul–Aug Last arrival
22.00hrs Last departure 13.00hrs

*Screened by trees and bushes, this site is
in grounds of Burscough Abbey. Off A59.*

1acre 35pitches SA 10🚐 £4 25🚐 £4 or
25▲£3 (awnings)

7🔌 Individual pitches ⊘ 12wc lit all night
1cdp 🔲 washbasins hc (🚿 hc 🌡️ hc) ☉
supervised (wash spin dry) iron calor gas
camping gaz ☎ 🔋
↪ launderette pub

OSMINGTON MILLS
Dorset
Map 3 SY78

▶▶ ② ❶ △
Osmington Mills Holidays *(SY736823)*
Signposted ☎ Weymouth (0305) 832311
Whit–Sep rs Etr–Whit & Oct must book
May–Sep

*Undulating, grass site with mature trees,
saplings and bushes–set in hilly
woodland and meadowland with direct
access to sea, beach, lake and main road.
The area is classed as one of outstanding
natural beauty. 4m E of Weymouth off
A353.*

13acres 175pitches 100static
25🚐 £2.50–£6 150▲£2–£6

10🔌⊘ wc lit all night washbasins hc 🌡️ hc
☉ (wash spin dry iron) games room (cold
storage) licensed club/bar childrens
playground calor gas camping gaz cafe
restaurant ☎ 🔋
↪ stables ✈ launderette pub

OSMOTHERLEY
North Yorkshire
Map 8 SE49

▶ ① ❶ △
Cote Ghyll Caravan Park *(SE461983)*
Signposted ☎ (060983) 425 Apr–Oct
must book public hols Last arrival
21.00hrs Last departure 12.30hrs

*Quiet site in pleasant valley on edge of
moors. Situated off A19.*

8acres 77pitches 57🚐 or 57🚐 20▲
(awnings)

12🔌⊘ 9wc lit all night 1cdp washbasins
hc (🌡️ hc) ☉ supervised calor gas
↪ ✈ pub 🔋

OWER
Hampshire
Map 4 SU31

▶ ② ❶ △
Green Pastures Farm *(SU321158)*
Signposted ☎ Southampton (0703)
814 444 15 Mar–Oct must book peak
periods no tents

*Open level grassy site on farm in rural
surroundings. Situated on edge of New
Forest. Off A31.*

4acres 45pitches 45🚐 or 45🚐 (awnings)
7🔌 Individual pitches 7wc lit all night
1cdp 7washbasins hc (central hot water)
(4🌡️ hc) 2☉ supervised (cold storage)
calor gas camping gaz ☎ 🔋
↪ stables ✈ launderette pub

OWERMOIGNE
Dorset
Map 3 SY78

▶▶▷ ② ❷ △
Sandy Holme Caravan Park *(SY768863)*
Moreton Rd Signposted ☎ Warmwell
(0305) 852677 Apr–mid Oct must book
public hols & Jul–Aug Last arrival
21.30hrs Last departure noon

*Level, grass site with trees and bushes set
in woodland and near coast at Lulworth
Cove. 1m N of A352.*

15acres 270pitches 35static SA 70🚐 or
70🚐 200▲ (awnings)

10🔌 Individual pitches for caravans ⊘
late arrivals enclosure 24wc lit all night 🔲
washbasins hc (central hot water) (🌡️ hc)
☉ supervised (wash spin dry iron) (games
room) (cold storage) (licensed club/bar)
childrens playground calor gas camping
gaz toilet fluid cafe restaurant ☎ 🎫
bicycles for hire 🔋
↪ stables golf ✈ launderette pub

OXFORD
Oxfordshire
Map 4 SP50

▶▶ ① ❸ △
Oxford Camping International
(SP518041) 426 Abingdon Rd
Signposted ☎ (0865) 246551 All year no
bookings Jul & Aug Last arrival 22.00hrs
Last departure noon

*Situated on the south side of Oxford, take
A4144 to city centre from the Ring road,
site is ¼m on left at rear of Texaco filling
station.*

5acres 105pitches 105🚐 £4.45 or
105🚐 £4.45 or 105▲£4.45 awnings

5🔌 Individual pitches ⊘ late arrivals
enclosure 21wc lit all night 1cdp 🔲
22washbasins hc 10🌡️ hc 11☉
supervised (wash spin dry iron) childrens
playground calor gas camping gaz toilet
fluid ☎ (hair dryer) 🔋
↪ stables ✈ cinema ✈ launderette pub

PADSTOW
Cornwall
Map 2 SW97
See sketch map

▶ ② ❷ △
Dennis Cove Camping Park
(SW918743) Signposted ☎ (0841)
532349 Jun–12 Sep rs 21 May–Jun & 13–
30 Sep booking advisable Jul–Aug Last
arrival 19.00hrs Last departure noon no
caravans

*Level and slightly sloping site with grass
and mature trees set in meadowland with*

*access to River Camel estuary and
Padstow Bay beach. Approach Padstow
on A389 and turn right into Sarah's Lane.*

3acres 75pitches SA 15🚐 fr £2.50 60▲ fr
£2.50 awnings

3🔌⊘ wc lit all night 1cdp (central hot
water) 🌡️ hc ☉ supervised (spin) (△)
childrens playground private beach calor
gas camping gaz toilet fluid cafe boating
pool slipway windsurfing tuition 🔋
↪ stables ✈ cinema ✈ launderette pub

PAIGNTON
Devon
Map 3 SX86
See sketch map on page 198

▶▶▶▷ ② ❷ △
**Beverley Parks Caravan & Camping
Site** *(SX886582)* Goodrington Rd
Signposted ☎ Churston (0803) 843887
19 May–29 Sep rs Apr–20 May & 30 Sep–
Oct must book Jun–Aug except for tents
Last arrival 22.00hrs Last departure
10.00hrs ✖

*A large commercial site on raised ground
adjacent to residential area south of the
town; with pleasant sea views.*

12acres 266pitches 40static 80🚐 £3–
£6.50 or 80🚐 £3–£6.50 186▲£2.50–
£5.50 (awnings)

14🔌⊘ late arrivals enclosure 60wc lit all
night 1cdp 🔲 washbasins central hot
water (🚿 hc) 🌡️ hc ☉ supervised (wash
spin dry iron) △ games room TV (cold
storage) licensed club/bar childrens
playground calor gas camping gaz toilet
fluid cafe restaurant ☎ 🎫 🔋
↪ stables golf ✈ cinema ✈ launderette
pub

see advertisement on page 200

▶▶▶▷ ② ❷ △
Blagdon Park Camping Site *(SX853601)*
☎ (0803) 521684 Whit–Sep rs Etr–Whit
must book Last arrival 22.00hrs Last
departure 10.00hrs no caravans no single
sex groups

*Gently sloping grass site with mixed
vegetation, set in meadowland within
urban area. 2m from river and Paignton
beach. Situated on A385 between Totnes
and Paignton.*

13acres 250pitches SA 50🚐 200▲
awnings ltr

16🔌 Individual pitches late arrivals
enclosure 50wc lit all night 3cdp
50washbasins hc 16🌡️ hc 10☉
supervised (wash) (dry) iron △ (games
room) CTV (cold storage) licensed club/
bar childrens playground calor gas
camping gaz toilet fluid cafe restaurant ☎
🎫 🔋
↪ stables golf ✈ cinema ✈ launderette
pub

see advertisement on page 199

▶▶▶▷ ② ❸ △
Grange Court Holiday Centre
(SX888588) Grange Rd ☎ (0803) 558010
or 550141 Etr–Sep rs Mar–Etr & Oct must
book Last arrival 21.00hrs Last departure
10.00hrs ✖ no tents, no teenage groups

→

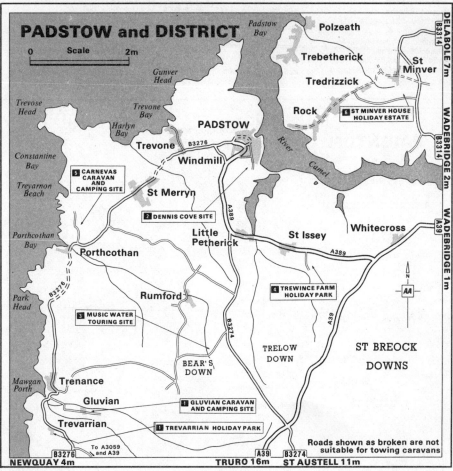

PADSTOW and DISTRICT

Sites listed under: **1** Mawgan Porth   **2** Padstow   **3** Rumford   **4** St Issey   **5** St Merryn   **6** St Minver

Large grassy site situated amidst woodland near to sea. 1½m from Paignton on Brixham road.

10 acres 157 pitches 512 static
157 ⊞ £3.50–£8.50 or 157 ⊞ £3.50–£8.50 awnings ltr
15 ⊞ Individual pitches late arrivals enclosure 36 wc lit all night 3 cdp
⊞ washbasins hc ⊞ hc ⊙ supervised (wash dry iron) ⊞ (✗) (games room)

licensed club/bar childrens playground calor gas camping gaz café ☎ putting green ⊞
⊖ stables golf ⊁ cinema ♫ launderette pub
▶ ▶ ▶ ② ⊘ ⚠
Holly Gruit Camp *(SX875588)* Brixham Rd Signposted ☎ (0803) 550 763 Spring

Bank Hol–Sep rs Etr–mid May must book Jul & Aug Last arrival 23.00 hrs Last departure 10.30 hrs no caravans or motorvans

A grass site with mixed trees and bushes, set in hilly meadowland, within the urban area. Off A3022 Brixham road.

3 acres 70 pitches 70 ▲ fr £3.50
2 ⊞ 11 wc lit all night washbasins hc 2 central hot water ⊞ hc 2 ⊙ supervised (iron) (games room) TV (cold storage)

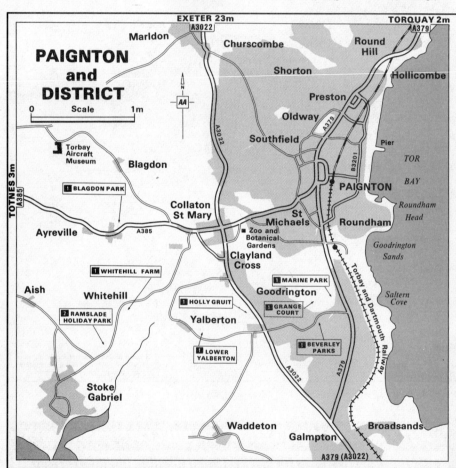

PAIGNTON and DISTRICT

Scale 0 — 1m

Sites listed under: **1** Paignton   **2** Stoke Gabriel

licensed club/bar childrens playground calor gas camping gaz bar snacks 🛒

⊖→ stables golf 🏌 cinema 🎦 launderette pub

▶▶▶ 🔟❷🅰

Lower Yalberton Caravan Park & Camping Site (SX869584) Long Rd Signposted ☎(0803) 558127 Jun–Sep rs Etr–May must book Jul & Aug Last departure 11.00hrs no single sex groups

A partly level and sloping grassy site with mature trees. Off Paignton Ring Road.

25acres 545pitches 8static SA 242♦ 80♥ 223♦ (awnings)

14♦♨ 100wc 3cdp washbasins central hot water ✒hc ⛊hc☉(wash spin dry iron) (❄)CTV(cold storage) licensed club/bar childrens playground calor gas camping gaz toilet fluid ☎ snack bar🛒

⊖→ stables golf 🏌 cinema 🎦 laundrette pub

▶▶▶ 🔟❷🅰

Marine Park Holiday Centre (SX886587) Grange Rd Signposted ☎Churston

(0803) 843887 19 May–29 Sep must book Jul & Aug Last arrival 22.00hrs Last departure 10.00hrs ✝

2m S of Paignton on A3022 ring road, turn left into Goodrington road, then left into Grange road.

1½acres 40pitches 66static SA 40♥£4– £5.50 or 40♥£4–£5.50 ♦£4 (awnings)

4♨ Individual pitches late arrivals enclosure 18wc lit all night 1 cdp⊖ washbasins hc central hot water (✒hc) ⛊hc☉ supervised (wash spin dry iron) (cold storage) childrens playground calor gas camping gaz toilet fluid ☎ 🛒

⊖→ stables golf 🏌 cinema 🎦 launderette pub

Beverley Park

FOR YOUR SUNSHINE HOLIDAY

Looking for a Holiday Centre that will suit the whole family?
Look no more — your search is over.
Beverley Park is one of Devon's finest Caravan Parks and has every ingredient for the perfect holiday.

- Located in Paignton, the Park overlooks beautiful Torbay.
- There is a delightful site for Touring Caravans and Tents, with immaculate toilet buildings, providing flush sanitation and free hot and cold water to hand basins. Showers, baths and a laundry are also on site.
- Paignton's wonderful sandy beaches are close by and on site you will find heated swimming pools, children's playground and a fully licensed club and shops.
- Evenings won't be dull either with dancing in our luxurious club and Cabaret.
- Also on site are luxury static caravans, all with own private bath (shower), toilet and colour television and every modern amenity.

Send now for free colour brochure.

An English Tourist Board
Rose Award Park

Please send details of Beverley Park

Name ....

Address ....

AA
5 PENNANTS   Beverley Park (Dept.C.C.H.), Goodrington Road,
Paignton Devon. Tel: Churston (0803) 843887

TORBAY
WHITEHILL FARM
CAMPING AND TOURING CARAVAN PARK
CARAVANS FOR HIRE

This lovely park is beautifully situated amongst the rolling green Devonshire hills, yet within easy reach of the sea.

Amenities:
Self Service Shop – Children's Playground – Colour Television
Laundrette – Free Showers – Games Room – Bus stop at entrance
2 Telephones – Free Hot Water – Families and Couples only – No dogs
Licensed Bar – Heated Swimming Pool – Take-away food
Family Room

How to get there; Turn off Paignton–Totnes Road (A385) at "Parkers Arms", ½ mile from Paignton Zoo. Signpost to Stoke Gabriel. Camping Park 1 mile.

Send S.A.E. for 1984 Prices and Colour Brochure to:
WHITEHILL FARM HOLIDAY ESTATE
STOKE ROAD, PAIGNTON, DEVON TQ4 7PF
Tel: Stoke Gabriel 338 (STD 080 428)

▶▶▶ 2 0 ⚠

Whitehill Farm Caravan & Camping Site
(SX857588) Stoke Gabriel Rd Signposted
☎ Stoke Gabriel (080 428) 338 Spring
Bank Hol–Sep rs 1 May–Spring Bank Hol
must book for caravans & advisable for
tents Jul–Aug Last arrival 22.00hrs Last
departure noon ✻

*This site is situated in rural surroundings
approx. 1m from Paignton and within
striking distance of the Dartmoor National
Park and Torquay. Ideal for those who like
the seaside and country.*

30acres 411pitches 66static SA 50 🚐
361 ⛟ or 361 ▲ awnings

10 ⌖ Individual pitches for caravans ⊘
55wc lit all night 1cdp ⌁ washbasins hc
central hot water �📷 hc ☉ (wash spin dry)
iron ⊒ heated games room CTV (cold
storage) licensed bar childrens
playground calor gas camping gaz toilet
fluid cafe ☎ ⛟

↪ stables golf ⅄ cinema ♪

PAR
Cornwall
Map 2 SX05
See St Austell sketch map

▶▶▶ 2 0 ⚠

Mount Holiday Park *(SX070529)* The
Mount ☎ (072 681) 2616 Apr–Oct
booking advisable Jul & Aug Last arrival
20.00hrs Last departure noon no
caravans

*Gently sloping grass site with mature trees
and bushes set in hilly, meadowland
country adjacent to sea, beach and lake.*

3acres 20pitches 55static 20 ⛟ £4.50 or
20▲£4.50

6 ⌖ Individual pitches ⊘ 9wc lit all night
1cdp ⌁ washbasins central hot water
➤ hc �📷 hc ☉ supervised (wash dry) iron
TV licensed club/bar childrens
playground calor gas camping gaz toilet
fluid cafe restaurant ☎ ⛟

↪ stables golf ⅄ cinema ♪ launderette
pub

▶ ☐ 0 ⚠

Par Beach Caravan & Camp Park
(SX083533) Signposted ☎ (072 681)
2868 Apr–Sep no bookings Last
departure 10.30hrs

*Level, grass and sand site with various
trees and bushes. Situated on coast on
A3082, Fowey–St Austell road, close to
river, lake, beach and sea.*

6acres 175pitches 210static 175 ⛟ £2–
£4.50 or 175 ⛟ £2–£4.50 or 175 ▲ £2–
£4.50 awnings ltr

13 ⌖ 70wc lit all night 1cdp washbasins hc
central hot water �📷 hc ☉ supervised wash
spin dry iron ⅌ games room childrens
playground private beach calor gas cafe
restaurant ☎ facilities for disabled ⛟

↪ stables golf ⅄ cinema ♪ launderette
pub

PARTON
Dumfries & Galloway *Kirkcudbrightshire*
Map 11 NX67

▶▶▶ 2 3 ⚠

Loch Ken Holiday Centre *(NX687702)*
Signposted ☎ (06447) 282 late Mar–
early Nov booking advisable public hols &
late Jul–Aug

*A compact touring site on eastern shores
of Loch Ken. Off A713.*

5acres 80pitches 26static SA 32 ⛟ £3.75
or 32 ⛟ £3.75 48 ▲ £3.75 (awnings) ltr

10 ⌖ Individual pitches ⊘ 8wc lit all night
1cdp ⌁ washbasins hc (�📷 hc ☉) (wash
spin dry iron) (cold storage) childrens
playground camping gaz toilet fluid ☎ ⊞
boating sailing fishing canoeing cycling
barbecue ⛟

↪ stables ⅄ fishing launderette pub

PATHFINDER VILLAGE
Devon
Map 3 SX89

▶▶▶▶ 3 3 ⚠

Pathfinder Touring Caravan Park
(SX845934) Signposted ☎ Tedburn St
Mary (06476) 239 or 710 All year Last
departure noon no tents

*A partly level and sloping grass and gravel
site set in meadowland. 5m W of Exeter off
A30.*

2acres 25pitches 25 ⛟ £4.25 or
25 ⛟ £4.25 (awnings)

3 ⌖ Individual pitches late arrivals
enclosure 6wc lit all night 1cdp ⌁
6washbasins hc (1central hot water) �📷 hc
☉ (wash spin) dry licensed club/bar
childrens playground calor gas camping
gaz toilet fluid restaurant ☎ take-away
meals hairdressers ⛟

↪ stables launderette pub

PATRICK BROMPTON
North Yorkshire
Map 8 SE29

▶▶▶ 2 0 ⚠

Akebar Park *(SE193905)* Signposted
☎ Bedale (0677) 50201 Etr–Oct rs Mar
must book peak periods Last departure
18.00hrs

*Part level, part sloping grass site with
some trees. A golf course is directly
adjacent to the site. Off A684 2m W of
village.*

23acres 110pitches 80static 60 ⛟ or
60 ⛟ 50▲ (awnings)

9 ⌖ ⊘ late arrivals enclosure 32wc lit all
night 4cdp washbasins hc (�📷 hc) ☉
surpvised (wash spin dry) iron ▱ ⅌ (cold
storage) childrens playground calor gas
camping gaz toilet fluid ☎ ⊞ fishing
sauna & solarium ⛟

↪ stables golf

PEEBLES
Borders *Peeblesshire*
Map 11 NT24

▶▶▶▶ 2 0 ⚠

Rosetta Caravan & Camping Park
(NT245415) Signposted ☎ (0721) 20770
Apr–Oct rs Nov & Feb–Mar booking
advisable public hols & Jul–Aug no single
sex groups no groups of motorcyclists
under 25yrs

*Part level, part sloping, grass site with
mature trees and bushes, set in hilly
woodland country. ½m from town centre
off A72.*

22acres 160pitches 29static SA
120 ⛟ £3–£3.50 40 ⛟ £3–£3.50 or
40▲£3–£3.50 (awnings) ltr

5 ⌖ Individual pitches ⊘ 31wc lit all night
2cdp washbasins ⌁ hc ☉ supervised
(wash) spin (dry) iron games room CTV
cold storage licensed club/bar childrens
playground calor gas camping gaz cafe
restaurant ☎ horse riding ⛟

↪ stables golf ⅄ ♪ launderette pub

▶▶▶ 2 0 ⚠

Crossburn Caravan Park *(NT248417)*
Edinburgh Rd ☎ (0721) 20501 Apr–14
Oct booking advisable peak periods Last
arrival 23.00hrs Last departure noon

*A gently sloping, grassy site in a peaceful
and relatively quiet location, despite the
proximity of the main road which partly
borders the site as does the Eddleston
Water.*

2acres 25pitches 95static SA 25 ⛟ £3.50
or 25 ⛟ £3.50 or 25▲£3.50 (awnings)

11 ⌖ Individual pitches 17wc lit all night
2cdp ⛟ washbasins hc (�📷 hc ☉) (wash
spin dry) iron children's playground calor
gas camping gaz toilet fluid ⛟

↪ stables golf ⅄ ♪ launderette pub

PEEL
Isle of Man
Map 6 SC28   →

▶ ① ❶ ⚠
Peel Camping Park *(SC252839)* Derby Rd Signposted ☎ (062484) 2341 May–Sep booking advisable for TT Races no caravans

Level site surrounded by hedges. On A20 ¼m from Peel.

4 acres 100 pitches 100 ⏣ £3.75 or 100 ▲ £3.75 awnings

6 ⏢ 12wc lit all night washbasins hc �🛁 hc ☺ (wash dry) ▨

⇸ stables golf ⚓ ⚊ launderette pub

PELYNT
Cornwall
Map 2 SX25
See Looe sketch map

▶▶▶ ② ❷ ⚠
Camping Caradon *(SX218539)* Trelawne Signposted ☎ Polperro (0503) 72388 26 May–15 Sep rs 10 Apr–25 May & 16–30 Sep must book Jul & Aug Last arrival 22.00hrs Last departure 11.00hrs no single sex groups no motorcycles

Level, grassy site with trees and bushes set in meadowland and woodland. Off B3359.

3½ acres 85 pitches 40 static 85 ⏣ fr£3.50 or 85 ⏣ fr£3.50 or 85 ▲ fr£3.50 awnings

3 ⏢ Individual pitches 10wc lit all night 1 cdp washbasins hc ⟨ 🛁 hc ⟩ ☺ (wash dry iron) TV licensed club/bar childrens playground calor gas camping gaz cafe ☎

⇸ stables ⚓ ⚊ launderette pub ▨

see advertisement on page 171

▶▶▶ ② ❷ ⚠
Trelawne Holiday Estate *(SX219538)* Signposted ☎ Polperro (0503) 72151 Etr wk & 5 May–28 Sep Last departure 10.00hrs 🏃 no single sex groups no tents

This site is situated in a wooded area off B3359, midway between Looe and Pelynt offering good seclusion on level touring pitches.

1¼ acres 30 pitches 253 static 30 ⏣ £3–£7.50 or 30 ⏣ £3–£7.50 awnings ltr

2 ⏢ Individual pitches 15wc lit all night 1 cdp washbasins hc ⟨ 🛁 hc ⟩ ☺ (wash spin dry) iron ⚊ games room licensed club childrens playground cafe restaurant ☎ ballroom ▨

⇸ stables golf ⚓ ⚊ launderette pub

▶ ① ❶ ⚠
Trelay Farm *(SX209543)* Signposted ☎ Lanreath (0503) 2025624 May–Sep rs Apr–23 May must book Jul & Aug Last arrival 20.00hrs Last departure noon

A sloping, grass site with bushes, ½m from Pelynt village off B3359. 3m from Looe & Polperro.

3 acres 30 pitches 20 static 10 ⏣ £3.40 5 ⏣ £3.10 15 ▲ £3.10 (awnings) ltr

6 ⏢ 8wc 1 cdp (washbasins hc) ⟨ 🛁 hc ⟩ ☺ calor gas

⇸ stables golf ⚓ ⚊ laundrette pub ▨

PENRHYNDEUDRAETH
Gwynedd
Map 6 SH63
See Criccieth sketch map

▶ ① ❶
Bwlch Bryn Caravan Park *(SH600392)* Signposted ☎ (0766) 770365 Mar–Oct must book Jun–Sep Last departure noon no tents

A sloping stony and grass site set in hills close to Festiniog Railway. Off A487.

2½ acres 10 pitches 40 static SA 10 ⏣ or 10 ⏣

7 ⏢ late arrivals enclosure 12wc lit all night 1 cdp ⟨ 🛁 hc ⟩ ☺ supervised iron cold storage calor gas toilet fluid

⇸ stables golf cinema ⚊ launderette ▨

PENRITH
Cumbria
Map 12 NY53

▶▶▶ ① ❷ ⚠
Thacka Lea Caravan Site *(NY509310)* Thacka Ln Signposted ☎ (0768) 63319 Mar–Oct booking advisable public hols Last arrival mdnt Last departure noon

A mainly level, grassy site in urban area at northern end of town.

2 acres 25 pitches 25 ⏣ £2.70 or 25 ⏣ £2.70 (awnings)

4 ⏢ Individual pitches late arrivals enclosure 7wc lit all night 1 cdp washbasins hc ⟨ 🛁 hc ⟩ ☺ supervised cold storage calor gas ▨

⇸ stables golf cinema ⚊ launderette pub

PENRUDDOCK
Cumbria
Map 12 NY42

▶▶▶ ① ❶ ⚠
Beckses Caravan Site *(NY419278)* Signposted ☎ Greystoke (08533) 224 Etr–Oct must book

A small site on sloping ground with some bushes and trees on edge of National Park. Views of distant fells. From A66 towards Keswick turn right onto B5288.

3 acres 21 pitches 16 static 16 ⏣ £3.50 or 16 ⏣ £3.50 5 ▲ £3 (awnings)

3 ⏢ Individual pitches 11wc lit all night 1 cdp ⚡ washbasins hc central hot water 🛁 hc ☺ spin (cold storge) childrens playground calor gas camping gaz toilet fluid ▨

⇸ stables pub

PENTEWAN
Cornwall
Map 2 SX04
See St Austell sketch map

▶▶▶▶ ② ❷ ⚠
Sun Valley Caravan Park *(SX005486)* Nansladron House Signposted ☎ Mevagissey (0726) 843266 Apr–Oct must book Jul–Sep Last arrival 23.00hrs Last departure 10.30hrs no single sex groups

---

Mainly level, grass site with mature trees and bushes set in wood and meadowland. It is 1m from sea, beach and river and situated on B3273 St Austell–Mevagissey road.

3 acres 30 pitches 60 static SA 30 ⏣ £3–£6 or 30 ⏣ £3–£6 or 30 ▲ £3–£6 (awnings)

9 ⏢ ☺ late arrivals enclosure 26wc lit all night 1 cdp ⚡ 18 washbasins hc (2 central hot water) (10 🛁 hc) 4 ☺ supervised (wash spin dry) iron ⚊ games room CTV (cold storage) licensed club/bar childrens playground calor gas camping gaz toilet fluid cafe restaurant ☎ ⊞ ▨

⇸ stables golf ⚓ cinema ⚊ launderette pub

▶▶▶ ① ❶ ⚠
Penhaven Tourist Park *(SX008481)* Signposted ☎ Mevagissey (0726) 843687 Apr–Oct must book Jul & Aug Last arrival 20.00hrs Last departure noon

Level, landscaped site in wooded valley, with river running by. 1m from sandy beach at Pentewan. Situated on B3273 St Austell–Mevagissey road.

6¼ acres 105 pitches SA 105 ⏣ £3–£5.50 or 105 ⏣ £3–£5.50 or £105 ▲ £3–£5.50 awnings

7 ⏢ Individual pitches late arrivals enclosure 12wc lit all night 1 cdp ⚡ washbasins hc (🛁 hc) ☺ supervised (wash dry iron) (cold storage) childrens playground calor gas camping gaz toilet fluid ☎ take away food ▨

⇸ stables ⚓ cinema ⚊ launderette pub

▶▶▶ ② ❶ ⚠
Pentewan Sands Holiday Park *(SX018468)* ☎ Mevagissey (0726) 843485 19 May–15 Sep rs Apr–18 May & 16 Sep–Oct must book Jul & Aug Last departure 10.30hrs no dogs

Located adjacent to the beach, this site has well-spaced grass pitches. 4m S of St Austell on B3273.

23 acres 550 pitches 50 static 550 ⏣ £2.80–£8 or 550 ⏣ £2.80–£8 or 550 ▲ £2.80–£8 awnings

27 ⏢ Individual pitches late arrivals enclosure 77wc lit all night 2 cdp ⚡ 72 washbasins hc 28 🛁 hc 19 ☺ (wash spin dry iron) ⚊ games room CTV (cold storage) licensed club/bar childrens playground private beach calor gas camping gaz toilet fluid ☎ take away snack bar battery charging ▨

⇸ ⚓ ⚊ landerette pub

PENTRAETH
Gwynedd
Map 6 SH57

▶ ① ❶ ⚠
Rhos Caravan Park *(SH517794)* Signposted ☎ (024870) 214 Mar–Sep booking advisable public hols & Aug Last departure noon

Site on level, grassy ground situated off main road to Amlwch.

18acres 106pitches 66static SA
52🚐 £2.80 4 🚐 £2.50 50▲£2.50
(awnings) ltr
11🏕⊘ 24wc lit all night 2cdp
(washbasins hc)(central hot water)(🛁hc)
⊙supervised (iron) cold storage calor
gas camping gaz toilet fluid ☎ 🛒
↔ stables 🎣 cinema 🎵 launderette pub

PENTREBEIRDD
Powys
Map 7 SJ11

▶▶▶ 🗓⊙⚠
Valley View Caravan Park *(SJ192144)*
Signposted ☎Meifod (093884) 265 Mar–
Oct no bookings
*Elevated terraced site overlooking
countryside east of Meifod Valley. 5m out
of Welshpool on A490 Llanfyllin road.*
25pitches 50static 25🚐 or 25 🚐 ▲
(awnings)
1🏕⊘ 2wc lit all night 1cdp washbasins hc
central hot water (🛁hc)⊙games room
licensed club/bar calor gas camping gaz
☎
↔ golf cinema 🎵 launderette pub 🛒

PENYBONTFAWR
Powys
Map 6 SJ02

▶▶ 🗓❷
Parc Farm *(SJ092245)* Signposted
☎Pennant (069174) 204 Etr–Oct must
book peak periods Last arrival 22.00hrs
Last departure 16.00hrs no tents
*Quiet site in beautiful surroundings
beside river on B4391.*
1acre 15pitches 65static 15🚐 £2.50 or
15 🚐 £2.50 awnings
2🏕12wc lit all night 1cdp washbasins hc .
(central hot water)(🛁hc)⊙supervised
(wash) childrens playground calor gas
camping gaz ☎ 🛒
↔ stables 🎵

PENYCWM
Dyfed
Map 2 SM82

▶▶ 🗓⓪⚠
Park Hall Caravan Park *(SM841244)*

Pentraeth
—
Perth

Maerdy Farm Signposted ☎St Davids
(067485) 721282 Apr–Oct booking
advisable Last arrival 22.00hrs Last
departure noon
*The site is situated on a 300-acre working
farm on St David's Peninsula. Off A487,
2m NW of Penycwm on unclass road.*
5acres 70pitches 20static 40🚐 10 🚐
20▲ (awnings)
4🏕late arrivals enclosure 8wc lit all night
1cdp 🚿(12washbasins hc)(4🛁hc)3⊙
calor gas fishing
↔ stables golf 🎣 🎵 pub 🛒

PERRANARWORTHAL
Cornwall
Map 2 SW73

▶▶▶ 🗓⓪⚠
Cosawes Caravan Park *(SW768376)*
Signposted ☎Truro (0872) 863724 All
year booking advisable mid Jul–mid Aug
Last arrival 23.00hrs Last departure
14.00hrs
*Level site with a slight gradient on grass
and gravel with mixed vegetation. Set in
hilly woodland country and meadowland;
close to sea. 6m W of Truro on A39.*
2acres 40pitches 85static 15🚐 £4.50
5 🚐 £4.25 20▲£4–£5 (awnings)
4🏕⊘ 6wc lit all night 1cdp 🚿
washbasins hc 🛁hc⊙spin calor gas
camping gaz ☎ squash court 🛒
↔ stables 🎣 🎵 launderette

PERRANPORTH
Cornwall
Map 2 SW75
See sketch map on page 204

▶▶▶▶ 🗓⓪⚠
Perranporth Camping & Touring Site
(SW768542) Budnick Rd Signposted
☎(087257) 2174 Whit–13 Sep rs Etr–
Whit & 14–30 Sep booking advisable Jul &
Aug Last arrival 23.00hrs Last departure
noon

---

*Part level, part sloping grass site with
bushes, set in meadowland with direct
access to sandy beach and sea. ½m E off
B3285.*
10acres 180pitches 8static SA 35🚐 or
35 🚐 145▲ (awnings)
12🏕late arrivals enclosure 29wc lit all
night 1cdp 🚿 washbasins hc (central hot
water ➡hc)🛁hc⊙supervised (wash
spin dry) iron 🚿 games room CTV (cold
storage) licensed club/bar childrens
playground calor gas camping gaz toilet
fluid ☎ 🖽 hair dryers 🛒
↔ stables golf 🎣 🎵 launderette pub

PERROTT'S BROOK
Gloucestershire
Map 4 SP00

▶▶ 🗓❶
Mayfield Park *(SP020055)* Mayfield
☎North Cerney (028583) 301 Etr–Sep
must book public hols & Jun–Aug Last
arrival dusk Last departure 10.30hrs no
tents
*Part level, part sloping grass site, set in
hilly meadowland in the Cotswolds, an
area of outstanding natural beauty.
Situated off A435, 2m from Cirencester,
12m from Cheltenham.*
1½acres 20pitches 24static 20🚐 £4 or
20 🚐 £4 (awnings)
1🏕5wc lit all night (central hot water)
(🛁hc)⊙supervised
↔ golf cinema launderette pub 🛒

PERTH
Tayside *Perthshire*
Map 11 NO12

▶▶ 🗓⊙⚠
Windsor Caravan Park *(NO110225)*
Windsor Ter Signposted ☎(0738) 23721
Apr–Sep Last departure noon no tents
*A small, sloping, grass site situated within
residential area of the city but with a
pleasant rural atmosphere owing to the
effective screening by bushes and mature
trees. An attractive feature is the waterfall
tumbling over a natural rocky outcrop at
one end of the park.*
7pitches 16static 7🚐 or 7 🚐 ltr
1🏕Individual pitches 6wc lit all night →

1cdp 7washbasins hc (2🛁hc) 2⊙calor gas 🎵

⊖→ stables golf cinema 🌙 launderette

PETERCHURCH
Hereford and Worcester
Map 3 SO33

▶▶ 2 ❶ ⚠

Poston Caravan & Camping Park
(SO355373) ☎(09816) 225 Etr–Oct rs
Mar–Etr booking advisable public hols &
16 Jul–Aug Last arrival 21.00hrs Last
departure noon no single sex groups

A level, grassy site with mature trees in hilly country near River Dore, 11m W of Hereford on B4348.

5acres 64pitches 22static SA 30🚐£4 or 30 🚐£3.65 34▲£3.65 (awnings) ltr

🌳Individual pitches ⊘ wc lit all night 1cdp washbasins hc (🛁hc)⊙supervised (wash spin iron) (⊒) games room (cold storage) calor gas camping gaz ☎ ⊞ off licence 🎵

⊖→ stables 🌙 pub

PEVENSEY BAY
East Sussex
Map 5 TQ60

▶▶▶▶ 2 ❸ ⚠

Castle View Caravan Site (TQ647033)
Eastbourne Rd ☎ Eastbourne (0323)
763038 Apr–Oct rs Nov–Mar must book
Last arrival 22.00hrs Last departure noon

Situated ½m from the beach this is a particularly well-kept site, although close to the main road, fencing and bushes ensure privacy.

12acres 75pitches 32static SA 75🚐£6 or 75 🚐£5.50 ▲£5.50 (awnings) ltr

20🌂⊘ late arrivals enclosure 25wc lit all night 2cdp 🚿washbasins hc ➔hc 🛁 hc ⊙ supervised in season (wash dry iron) (cold storage) childrens playground calor gas gamping gaz toilet fluid cafe ☎ 🎵

⊖→ stables 🎣 cinema 🌙 launderette pub

PITLOCHRY
Tayside *Perthshire*
Map 14 NN95
See sketch map

▶▶▶ 2 ❷ ⚠

Faskally Home Farm (NN916603)
Signposted ☎(0796) 2007 15 Mar–Oct
booking advisable Jul & Aug

This site is situated outside the town and on the banks of the River Gay, which is bordered on one side by the main road. It is on gently sloping grassland dotted with trees and with splendid views. Turn off A9 Pitlochry by-pass ½m N of town then proceed 1m N on A924.

23acres 400pitches 60static 250🚐£3.80 or 250 🚐£3.70 150▲£3.30 (awnings)

22🌂⊘ 104wc lit all night 1cdp 🚿 104washbasins hc (central hot water) 18🛁hc 24⊙(wash dry iron) (games room) cold storage childrens playground calor gas camping gaz toilet fluid ☎ 🎵

⊖→ stables golf 🎣 cinema 🌙 launderette pub

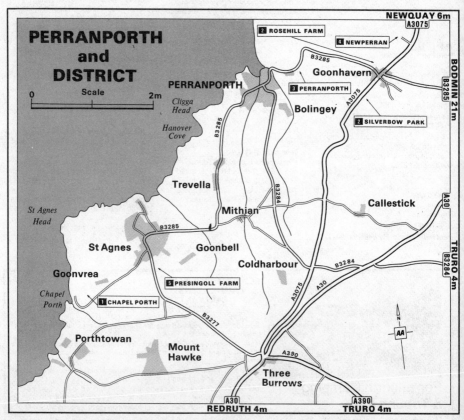

PERRANPORTH and DISTRICT

Scale
0 ——————— 2m

NEWQUAY 6m
A3075

2 ROSEHILL FARM
4 NEWPERRAN
B3285
Goonhavern
3 PERRANPORTH
A3075
PERRANPORTH
Cligga Head
Bolingey
Hanover Cove
2 SILVERBOW PARK
B3285
B3284
St Agnes Head
Trevella
Callestick
A30
Mithian
B3285
BODMIN 21m B3285
St Agnes
Goonbell
Coldharbour
B3284
TRURO 4m B3284
Goonvrea
5 PRESINGOLL FARM
A3075 A30
Chapel Porth
1 CHAPEL PORTH
B3277
Porthtowan
Mount Hawke
A390
Three Burrows
A30 A390
N
AA
REDRUTH 4m A30 TRURO 4m A390

Sites listed under: **1** Chapel Porth **2** Goonhavern **3** Perranporth **4** Rejerrah **5** St Agnes

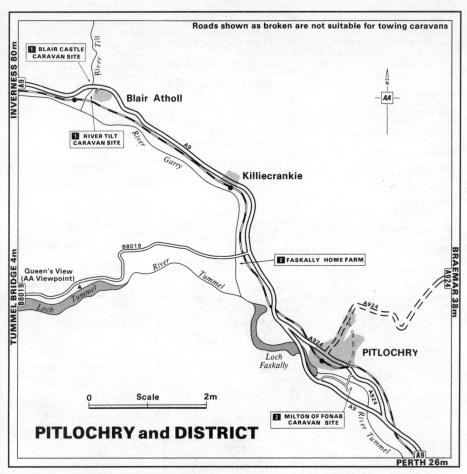

Roads shown as broken are not suitable for towing caravans

INVERNESS 80m (A9)

1 BLAIR CASTLE CARAVAN SITE

River Tilt

Blair Atholl

1 RIVER TILT CARAVAN SITE

River Garry

A9

Killiecrankie

N AA

TUMMEL BRIDGE 4m (B8019)

B8019

Queen's View (AA Viewpoint)

River Tummel

Loch Tummel

2 FASKALLY HOME FARM

BRAEMAR 38m (A924)

A924

A924

Loch Faskally

PITLOCHRY

0   Scale   2m

2 MILTON OF FONAB CARAVAN SITE

A9 A924

River Tummel

PITLOCHRY and DISTRICT

A9 PERTH 26m

Sites listed under: **1** Blair Atholl   **2** Pitlochry

MILTON OF FONAB CARAVAN SITE

PITLOCHRY, PERTHSHIRE

Ideally situated on the banks of River Tummel ½ mile south of Pitlochry.
All modern amenities – flush sanitation, hot baths and showers, hot and cold in wash basins, electric shaving points, laundry facilities, shop.

This site is renowned for the high standard of cleanliness and the peace and quietness maintained, through strict observance of commonsense rules.

Separate sections for touring caravans, motor caravans, tents with cars. Fully equipped modern caravans for hire. We regret no all male groups, no advance bookings of tents, campers must arrive by car, no hitch-hikers or motor cyclists and no generators. SAE for reply.

Tel: Pitlochry 2882.

▶▶▶ ②③⚠

Milton of Fonab Caravan Site
(NN945573) Signposted ☎ (0796) 2882
26 Mar–16 Oct no bookings for tents Last
arrival 21.00hrs Last departure 13.00hrs
no single sex groups, no motorcycles

Level, grass site with mature trees on
banks of River Tummel, ½m S of town.

13 acres 160 pitches 36 static 100🚐 £3.75
20🚐 £3.30 40⚠£3.75 (awnings) ltr

15⚏ Individual pitches for caravans ⊘
late arrivals enclosure 45 wc lit all night
1 cdp washbasins hc (☗hc☖hc)☺
supervised (wash) spin (dry) iron
(childrens playground) calor gas
camping gaz toilet fluid ☎ 🎣

↩ stables golf ⚲ cinema ♪ launderette
pub
see advert on page 205

PITTENWEEM
Fife
Map 12 NO50

▶▶▶ ②②⚠

Grangemuir Caravan Site (NO538042)
(1m NW unclass) Signposted
☎ Anstruther (0333) 311213 Etr–Oct no
bookings Last arrival 23.00hrs Last
departure 10.00hrs

Site covers 7 acres within the 70 acre
estate of Grange Muir House which also
includes self catering log cabins. A level
grass site with mature trees sheltered and
secluded, one mile inland from the fishing
village of Pittenweem.

5 acres 45 pitches 45🚐 £4 or 45 🚐 £4 or
45⚠£4 (awnings Jul & Aug)

2⚏⊘ late arrivals enclosure 10 wc lit all
night 2 cdp 2 washbasins hc 2 central hot
water 4☗hc 2☺ supervised (wash spin
dry) iron games room CTV (cold storage)
(licensed club/bar) childrens playground
toilet fluid ☎ ⊞ 🎣

↩ golf ⚲ ♪ launderette pub

PLUMPTON
Cumbria
Map 12 NY43

▶▶▶ ②①⚠

Greenacres Caravan Park (NY501371)
Signposted ☎ (076884) 206 Etr–Sep rs
Oct must book public hols Last arrival
21.00hrs Last departure noon

A small, level grassy site, situated 200yds
E of A6. Approach via B6413 from village
centre.

¼ acre 16 pitches 34 static 8🚐 £3 4 🚐 £3
4⚠£3 (awnings)

4⚏ Individual pitches wc 1 cdp 🚐
washbasins hc ☗hc☺ (cold storage)
licensed club/bar calor gas cafe 🎣

PLYMOUTH
Devon
Map 2 SX45

▶▶▶ ②③⚠

Riverside Caravan Park (SX515575)
Longbridge Rd, Marsh Mills, Plympton
(3m E off A38) Signposted ☎ (0752)
334122 All year booking advisable Jul &

Aug Last arrival mdnt Last departure noon

Level site with central tarmac road
bordered on one side by the River Plym
and the other by woods. Approach by way
of Longbridge road, which is E of Marsh
Mills roundabout.

12½ acres 260 pitches 200🚐 or 200 🚐
60⚠ (awnings)

12⚏ late arrivals enclosure 50 wc lit all
night 2 cdp 🚐 washbasins hc ☗hc☺
supervised wash spin dry iron ⌂ games
room CTV cold storage childrens
playground calor gas camping gaz toilet
fluid ☎ ⊞ take-away food 🎣

↩ stables golf ⚲ cinema ♪ launderette
pub

PONTLYFNI
Gwynedd
Map 6 SH45

▶ ②①⚠

Llyn-y-Gele Farm & Caravan Park
(SH432523) Signposted ☎ Clynnogfawr
(028686) 283 Etr–Oct booking advisable
Jul & Aug Last arrival 22.00hrs Last
departure noon

Quiet farm site within 5 minutes walking
distance of the beach. Centrally situated
for touring the Lleyn Peninsula, Anglesey
and Snowdonia, off A499.

4 acres 30 pitches SA 6🚐 £3 4 🚐 £2
20⚠£2.60 (awnings)

5⚏⊘ 7 wc lit all night 1 cdp washbasins hc
(☗hc)☺ supervised (spin iron) games
room private beach calor gas 🎣

↩ stables ♪

PONT-RUG
Gwynedd
Map 6 SH56

See Caernarfon sketch map

▶▶▶

▶ ②❶

Riverside Camping (SH505630) Caer
Glyddyn ☎ Caernarfon (0286) 2524 Etr–
Oct booking advisable public hols & Jul–
Aug Last departure 19.00hrs

Level grassy site bordered by a salmon
river, 2m E of Caernarfon on A4086.

4 acres 60 pitches 20🚐 £2.80 or
20 🚐 £2.50 40⚠£2.50 (awnings)

2⚏ 6 wc lit all night 1 cdp washbasins hc
central hot water (☗hc)☺ supervised
cold storage camping gaz paraffin

↩ stables golf ⚲ cinema ♪ launderette
pub 🎣

POOLEWE
Highland Ross and Cromarty
Map 14 NG88

▶▶▶ ②③⚠

Inverewe Stage House (NG861811)
Signposted ☎ (044586) 249 Apr–Sep no
bookings for tents Last arrival 20.00hrs
Last departure noon

Formerly the site of a military camp, this
small touring park lies on Loch Ewe Bay
not far from the famous Inverewe
Gardens.

4 acres 45 pitches 35🚐 or 35 🚐 10⚠
(awnings)

4⚏ Individual pitches 10 wc lit all night
1 cdp 10 washbasins hc (4☗hc) 2☺ (wash
spin) calor gas camping gaz toilet fluid
mobile shop 🎣

↩ ♪ pub

POOLEY BRIDGE
Cumbria
Map 12 NY42

▶ ❶①⚠

Hillcroft Caravan & Camping Site
(NY478241) Signposted ☎ (08536) 363
Mar–Oct must book peak periods for
caravans Last departure noon

The site stands on a hillside overlooking a
valley close to Ullswater, but offers only a
glimpse of the lake.

8 acres 125 pitches 200 static 25🚐 10 🚐
90⚠ (awnings)

10⚏⊘ 45 wc lit all night 1 cdp
28 washbasins hc 20☗hc 4☺ supervised
(wash dry) (cold storage) calor gas
camping gaz 🎣

↩ stables ⚲ ♪ launderette pub

PORLOCK
Somerset
Map 3 SS84

▶▶▶ ②②⚠

Porlock Caravan Park (SS882469)
Signposted ☎ (0643) 862269 Mar–Oct
booking advisable Etr & Whit Last arrival
23.59hrs Last departure noon no tents

A well-planned site, in valley with shrubs
and trees.

3 acres 65 pitches 56 static 40🚐 £3.50–£4
25 🚐 £3–£3.50 (awnings)

10⚏ 25 wc lit all night 3 cdp 🚐
washbasins hc (☗hc)☺ supervised

(wash spin dry iron) childrens playground calor gas camping gaz toilet fluid ☎ 🏋
⇔ stables ✐ pub

PORTHCAWL
Mid Glamorgan
Map 3 SS87

▶ 🗓 ❶

Broadawell Campsite *(SS817790)* Moor Ln Signposted ☎ (065671) 3231 Apr–Oct must book Last departure noon no single sex groups

A level, grassy touring and camping site positioned in quiet surroundings within 1½m of the seaside resort.

4 acres 75 pitches 10💶 £3.40 5 💶 £3.40 60▲£3.40 (awnings) ltr

4🅿 10wc lit all night 1 cdp (central hot water 🏠 hc) ☺ supervised iron (games room) CTV (cold storage) childrens playground calor gas camping gaz 🏋
⇔ stables golf 🏌 cinema ✐ launderette pub

PORTKNOCKIE
Grampian *Banffshire*
Map 15 NJ46

▶ 🗓 ❷ ⚠

Macleod Park Camping Site *(NJ494684)* Signposted ☎ Cullen (0542) 40270 9 Apr–Sep

A level, grassy site near to the sea and beach.

30 pitches 5 static 20💶 or 20 💶 10▲ ltr

🅿 Individual pitches ⚡ 6wc lit all night washbasins hc (🏠 hc) ☺ (wash dry) ⊞ 🏋
⇔ golf 🏌 ✐ launderette pub

PORTPATRICK
Dumfries & Galloway *Wigtownshire*
Map 10 NX05

▶ ▶ ▶ 🗓 ❷ ⚠

Galloway Point Holiday Park *(NX005537)* Portree Farm Signposted ☎ (077681) 561 Etr–Sep no bookings Last arrival 22.30hrs

A sprawling site on gorse clad downland facing the North Sea 1m S of town.

18 acres 90 pitches 70 static SA 40💶 £3–£4 10 💶 £3–£4 40▲£3–£4 awnings ltr

🕐 late arrivals enclosure 20wc lit all night 1 cdp 💶 washbasins hc central hot water (🏠 hc) ☺ supervised (wash spin dry iron) cold storage childrens playground calor gas camping gaz toilet fluid hair driers 🏋
⇔ stables golf 🏌 ✐ launderette pub

PORTSOY
Grampian *Banffshire*
Map 15 NJ56

▶ 🗓 ❷

Portsoy Links Site *(NJ592662)* Apply to: Director of Leisure & Recreation, Banff & Buchan District Council, 1 Church St, Macduff, Banffshire AB41 1UF Signposted ☎ Macduff (0261) 32861 Apr–Sep must book Last arrival 21.00hrs Last departure 09.00hrs

Local authority run site, in pleasant position on sea-front giving unrestricted views over Moray Firth, 8m NW of Banff. In Portsoy turn north off A98 into Church Street then in 100 yards turn right into Institute Street.

2½ acres 45 pitches 37 static 35💶 or 35 💶 10▲ (awnings)

2🅿 20wc lit all night 1 cdp (26 washbasins hc) 🏠 hc ☺ (wash spin dry) childrens playground calor gas camping gaz paraffin toilet fluid ☎ 🏋
⇔ stables 🏌 ✐ pub

POTTERNE
Wiltshire
Map 3 ST95

▶ ▶ ▶ 🗓 ❸ ⚠

Potterne Wick Touring Caravan Park *(SU000579)* Potterne Wick Signposted ☎ Devizes (0380) 3277 Apr–Oct booking advisable public hols & Jul–Aug Last arrival 22.00hrs Last departure noon

Part level, part sloping, grass site with mature trees and bushes. ½m S of Potterne on A360 Devizes–Salisbury road, near the Kennet and Avon Canal.

1½ acres 30 pitches 30💶 ✳£2.90–£3.50 or 30 💶 £2.90–£3.50 or 30▲£2.90–£3.50 (awnings)

1🅿 6wc lit all night 1 cdp washbasins hc 🏠 hc ☺ wash spin dry iron calor gas camping gaz ☎ 🏋
⇔ stables cinema ✐ pub

see advertisement on page 208

POUNDSTOCK
Cornwall
Map 2 SX29

▶ ▶ 🗓 ❶ ⚠

Cornish Coasts Caravan & Camping Site Middle Penlean *(SX201979)* Signposted ☎ Widemouth Bay (028885) 380 Etr–Oct must book Last departure noon

Part level, part sloping, grass site with trees and bushes, situated in hilly downland 5m S of Bude on A39.

3½ acres 78 pitches 3 static 78💶 £1.15–£3.50 or 78 💶 £1.15–£3.50 or 78 ▲£1.15–£3.50 (awnings) ltr

5🅿 13wc lit all night 1 cdp (12 washbasins hc) (1 central hot water) (4🏠 hc) 2 ☺ supervised (spin dry) cold storage childrens playground calor gas camping gaz cafe 🏋
⇔ stables ✐ launderette pub

POWFOOT
Dumfries & Galloway *Dumfriesshire*
Map 11 NY16

▶▶▶ ② ❷ △
Queensberry Bay Caravan Park
(NY140654) Signposted
☎ Cummertrees (04617) 205 Apr–Oct
must book Jul & Aug

*Touring and static site in quiet location
beside the Solway Firth adjacent to beach
and golf course.*

7 acres 50 pitches 70 static SA
60☎ £3.50–£4.50 or 50 ☎ £3.50–£4.50
or 50▲£3.50–£4.50 awnings

3☎ 13 wc lit all night 1 cdp ☻ washbasins
hc ᵐ hc ☺ supervised spin iron calor gas
camping gaz toilet fluid ☎ ⮞

↔ stables golf cinema ⫽ launderette pub

PRAA SANDS
Cornwall
Map 2 SW52
See sketch map

▶▶▶ ① ❷ △
Pengersick Caravan & Camping Site
(SW580284) ☎ Germoe (073676) 2201
All year no bookings Last arrival 20.00hrs
Last departure 10.00hrs.

*Part level, part sloping, grass site set in
meadowland, adjacent to sea and beach
at the Hoe Point and Rinsey Head. Off
A394 Helston–Penzance road.*

10 acres 200 pitches 86 static 50☎ or
50 ☎ 150▲ (awnings)

22 ☙ ⊘ 28 wc lit all night 3 cdp washbasins
hc (central hot water) (⮮ ᵐ hc) ☺
supervised (wash spin dry iron) (cold
storage) childrens playground calor gas
camping gaz ⮞

↔ golf ⫽ pub

▶▶▶ ② ❶ △
Praa Sands Caravan Park (SW580288)
Signposted ☎ St Austell (0726) 65551
Spring Bank Hol–16 Sep rs Etr–Spring
Bank Hol must book Last arrival 22.00hrs
Last departure 10.00hrs no pets

*Partly level, partly sloping, grass site with
bushes, set in meadowland with access to
beach and sea at Praa Sands. 4m SE of
Marazion on the A394 Helston road.*

12 acres 72 pitches 107 static 24☎ 18 ☎
30▲ awnings ltr

5 ☙ Individual pitches 36 wc lit all night
2 cdp washbasins hc central hot water
ᵐ hc ☺ supervised (wash spin iron) ⇒
games room licensed club/bar childrens
playground calor gas camping gaz ☎ bar
snacks ⮞

↔ golf ⫽ launderette pub

PRESTATYN
Clwyd
Map 6 SJ08

▶▶▶ ② ❶ △
Presthaven Sands Caravan Park
(SJ052829) Signposted ☎ St Austell
(0726) 67071 Good Fri–Sep rs Mar–Good
Fri booking advisable public hols Last
departure noon no motorcycles, no
single, sex groups, no tents

*A large, level commercial holiday site
situated behind sand dunes on beach and
near railway. Hillside country views form a
pleasant background.*

97 pitches 97☎ or 97 ☎ awnings

10 ☙ late arrivals enclosure 26 wc lit all
night 2 cdp 20 washbasins hc 8 ᵐ hc ☺
supervised (wash spin dry iron) ⇒ (⚲)
games room (cold storage) licensed club/
bar childrens playground private beach
calor gas camping gaz cafe restaurant ☎
⊞ ⮞

↔ stables golf ⚼ cinema ⫽ launderette
pub

PRESTEIGNE
Powys
Map 3 SO36

▶▶ ② ❷ △
Rock Bridge Caravan & Camping Park
(SO292654) ☎ Whitton (05476) 300 Apr–
Oct booking advisable public hols Last
arrival 23.00hrs Last departure noon

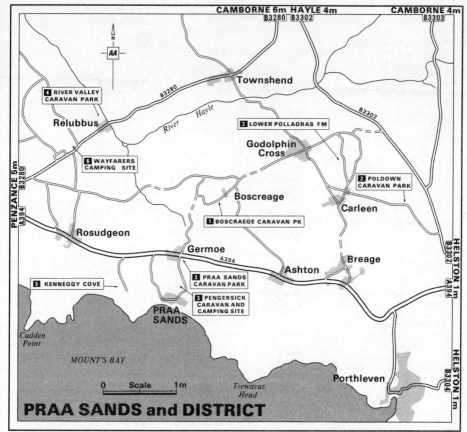

PRAA SANDS and DISTRICT

Roads shown as broken are not suitable for towing caravans

Sites listed under: **1** Ashton **2** Carleen **3** Praa Sands **4** Relubbus **5** Rosudgeon **6** St Hilary

---

Part level, part sloping grass site with trees and bushes, set in hilly wood and meadowland country with access to River Luga. 1m W of Presteigne off B4356.

4½ acres 35 pitches 20 static SA 10♥ £3 15♥ £3 10▲ £3 (awnings) ltr

3♣ 4wc lit all night 2cdp 4washbasins hc (2⋔hc)☺supervised cold storage calor gas camping gaz

↔ stables golf ✦ launderette pub ♨

PRESTON PATRICK
Cumbria
Map 7 SD58

▶▶ ① ❶ ⚠
Milness Hill Camping Site *(SD533838)*
Signposted ☎Crooklands (04487) 306
Mar–Sep booking advisable Jul & Aug

This level and stony site is surrounded by hedges, bushes and trees. Located ½ m from exit 36 on M6, an excellent position for touring the Lake District and Yorkshire

Dales National Park.

2acres 24pitches SA 14♥ £2.60 or 14♥ £2.20 10▲ £2 (awnings) ltr

3♣☀ late arrivals enclosure 6wc lit all night 1cdp washbasins hc central hot water ⋔hc☺cold storage

↔ stables ✦ ♨

PRIDDY
Somerset
Map 3 ST55
See Cheddar sketch map

▶▶ ② ❶ ⚠
Mendip Heights Caravan & Camping Park *(ST524518)* Townsend Signposted
☎(074987) 241 Mar–Oct booking advisable public hols & Jul–Aug Last arrival 21.00hrs Last departure noon no motorcycles, no groups

Situated in an open field in an elevated position overlooking the Mendip Hills, signposted from A39 at Green Ore.

4acres 90pitches 15♥ 75♥ or 75▲ (awnings) ltr

3♣ Individual pitches for caravans ⊘ 10wc lit all night 1cdp washbasins hc (⋔hc)☺supervised (spin dry) (cold storage) childrens playground calor gas camping gaz cafe restaurant take-away food ♨

↔ stables pub

PWLLHELI
Gwynedd
Map 6 SH33

▶▶▶ ② ❶ ⚠
Gimblet Rock Caravan Park
(SH387343) South Beach Signposted
☎Abersoch (075881) 2045 Mar–Oct
must book Last arrival 18.00hrs Last departure 10.00hrs ✖ no motorcycles, no single sex groups, no tents

Level, grass, gravel and sand site with direct access to sea, beach and harbour. A497 to Pwllheli, ¾m from Station Square.

→

2acres26pitches 111static 26🏕 awnings

7🚐Individual pitches 11wc lit all night 1cdp 5washbasins hc 5central hot water (4🛁hc) 2☉supervised (wash dry) (licensed club/bar) calor gas camping gaz toilet fluid ☎🛒

↦stables golf⛳cinema🚶launderette pub

QUATT (near Bridgnorth)
Shropshire
Map 7 SO78

▽③

Coton Hall (SO774864)Coton (2m SE off A442)☎(0746) 780227 booking advisable

Rolling parkland adjacent to ancestral home of Robert E Lee's family. A pleasant location overlooking Severn Vale.

15pitches 15🏕 or 15🚐 or 15▲

🚐

RADFORD
Hereford & Worcester
Map 4 SP05

▽①

Wheelbarrow Castle (SP012549)
☎Inkberrow (0386) 792207 All year

Level enclosed paddock in Vale of Evesham, situated at rear of country inn.

3acres 15pitches 5🏕£1.50 or 5🚐£1.50 10▲75p awnings

2🚐☉ 3wc 1cdp washbasins hc☉ supervised games room licensed club/bar childrens playground

RATTERY
Devon
Map 3 SX76

▶▶②❶⚠

Edeswell Caravan & Camping Park (SX731606)Edeswell Farm Signposted ☎South Brent (03647) 2177 15 Mar–Oct booking advisable Aug

Gently sloping, grass site with mature trees, in hilly country and near river, off A385.

2acres 40pitches 22static SA 30🏕£2.30–£3.50 or 30🚐£2.30–£3.50 10▲£2.30–£3.50 (awnings) ltr

10🚐Individual pitches☉ late arrivals enclosure 15wc lit all night 1cdp🚐 washbasins hc central hot water hc☉ supervised (wash dry iron) games room CTV cold storage licensed club/bar childrens playground calor gas camping gaz cafe☎ fishing table tennis badminton🛒

↦stables golf🚶

RAVENGLASS
Cumbria
Map 6 SD09

▶▶②❷⚠

Walls Caravan Park (SD103966)
Signposted ☎(06577) 250 Etr–Sep must book Last arrival 20.00hrs Last departure

noon no motor cycles no single sex groups

This site is set in a woodland park and is part level and part sloping, with hard standing pitches, off A595.

5acres 50pitches 50🏕£4.50 or 50🚐£4.50 awnings

5🚐Individual pitches late arrivals enclosure 8wc lit all night 1cdp washbasins hc (🛁hc)☉supervised calor gas

↦🚶pub🛒

RAVENSTRUTHER
Strathclyde *Lanarkshire*
Map 11 NS94

▶▶②❷⚠

Newhouse Farm (NS926456)
Signposted ☎Carstairs (055587) 228 All year

Level grass and gravel site, with young trees and bushes, situated on A70 Ayr–Edinburgh road, 3m E of Lanark.

20pitches SA 10🏕£2.25 5🚐£2.25 or 5▲£2.25 awnings

2🚐5wc lit all night 1cdp🚐 washbasins hc (🛁hc)☉cold storage childrens playground calor gas camping gaz

↦stables golf🚶🚶launderette pub🛒

REAY
Highland *Caithness*
Map 14 NC96

▶①❶⚠

Dunvegan Euro Camp Site (NC960644)
Signposted ☎(084781) 405 Jun–Sep Last arrival 22.00hrs Last departure noon

Level and grassy site with slight gradients, trees and bushes. The site is adjacent to the A836 in the centre of the village.

1acre 25pitches 10🏕£3.5 🚐£3 10▲£3 (awnings) ltr

1🚐4wc lit all night (washbasins hc) (🛁hc)☉supervised private beach ☎🛒

↦stables golf🚶🚶

REDHILL
Avon
Map 3 ST46

▶①❶⚠

Brook Lodge Caravan Park (ST485620)
Signposted ☎Wrington (0934) 862311 Mar–Oct must book Jun–Aug Last arrival 23.00hrs Last departure 13.00hrs

This farm site is in slightly sloping meadowland with a small orchard and walled garden. Off A38.

2acres 29pitches SA 29🏕 or 29🚐 or 29▲ (awnings)

5🚐☉ late arrivals enclosure 8wc lit all night 1cdp🚐 washbasins hc central hot water (🛁hc)☉supervised (wash spin iron) (cold storage) childrens playground calor gas camping gaz toilet fluid ☎

↦stables🚶launderette pub🛒

REDRUTH
Cornwall
Map 2 SW64
See sketch map

▶▶▶②❷⚠

Cambrose Farm Camp Site (SW684453)
Portreath Rd Signposted ☎Porthtowan (0209) 890747 Etr–Oct must book Jul–Aug Last arrival 23.00hrs Last departure 10.00hrs

A level, grassy site with mature trees and bushes. 2m from Redruth off B3300 (signposted 'Porthtowan and Portreath' from A30).

3acres 50pitches SA 50🏕£3.20 or 50🚐£2.80 50▲£3.20 (awnings)

4🚐Individual pitches 12wc lit all night 1cdp washbasins hc central hot water 🛁hc☉supervised (wash spin dry iron) ⚓ cold storage childrens playground calor gas camping gaz toilet fluid ☎ take-away food & off-licence 🛒

↦stables golf cinema🚶launderette pub

▶▶▶②❷⚠

Lanyon Farm Caravan Park (SW685389)Four Lanes Signposted ☎(0209) 216447 Whit–Sep rs Etr–Whit

Part level, part sloping, grass site with young trees and bushes. Situated in meadowland within the urban area. 2m S of Redruth off B3297.

1½acres 26pitches 49static 26🏕 or 26🚐 or 26▲ awnings ltr

3🚐7wc lit all night 1cdp washbasins hc 🛁hc☉supervised (wash dry iron) cold storage childrens playground calor gas golf course🛒

↦stables cinema🚶launderette pub

▶▶▶②❷⚠

Tehidy Caravan Park (SW682432)Harris Mill, Illogan (2m NW off B3300 on N side of A30) Signposted ☎(0209) 216489 Apr–Oct booking advisable Jul & Aug Last arrival 22.00hrs Last departure 11.00hrs 🏹no single sex groups

A well kept site with landscaped static sites and a most carefully arranged and maintained small area for campers and tourers.

1acre 18pitches 32static 18▲£3–£4 (awnings)

4🚐Individual pitches☉ 3wc lit all night washbasins hc (🛁hc)☉supervised (wash spin dry iron) (games room) (cold storage) childrens playground calor gas camping gaz☎🛒

↦golf cinema🚶launderette pub

REJERRAH
Cornwall
Map 2 SW85

▶▶▶▶②❷⚠

Newperran Tourist Site (SW796551)
Hendra Croft Signposted ☎Perranporth (087257) 2407 or Crantock (0637) 830308

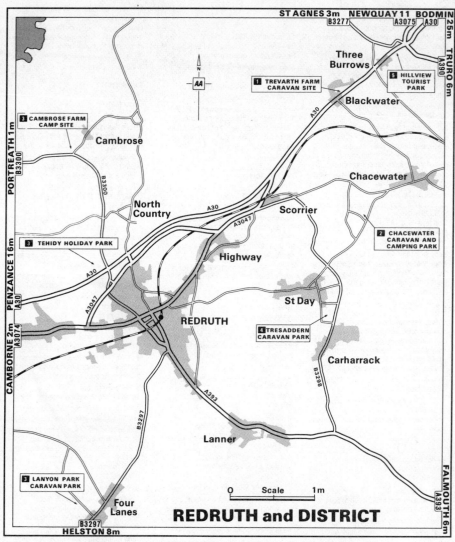

REDRUTH and DISTRICT

Sites listed under: **1** Blackwater **2** Chacewater **3** Redruth **4** St Day **5** Three Burrows

mid May–mid Sep must book Jul & Aug

A level, grassy site with well-dispersed bushes. 4m SE of Newquay and 1m S of Rejerrah on A3075.

25acres 350pitches 350⊞ or 350⊞ or 350▲ awnings

25⊕ Individual pitches late arrivals enclosure 47wc lit all night 2cdp ⊟ washbasins hc central hot water (⋔ hc) ☉ supervised (wash) spin (dry) iron ⥮ games room TV cold storage childrens playground calor gas camping gaz toilet

fluid cafe restaurant ☎ ⊞ crazy golf ⅁
↦ stables golf ⅄ cinema ✈ launderette pub
See Newquay and Perranporth sketch maps

▶ ▶ ▶ ▶ ② ❷ ⚠

Monkey Tree Farm Tourist Park
(SW803554) Signposted ☏ Perranporth (087257) 2032 May–Sep rs Etr must book Jul & Aug Last arrival 22.00hrs Last departure 13.00hrs

Situated amidst downland and meadowland. Access from Rejerrah–Zelah road off A3075.

12acres 185pitches 185⊞ or 185⊞ or 185▲ awnings

12⊕ Individual pitches late arrivals enclosure 32wc lit all night 1cdp ⊟ washbasins hc (⋔ hc) ☉ supervised (wash) spin (dry) iron games room TV cold storage childrens playground calor gas camping gaz toilet fluid cafe ☎ ⊞ ⅁
↦ stables golf ⅄ cinema ✈ pub

see advertisement on page 190

▶▶▶ ② ❷ ⚠

New Braefel Tourist Park *(SW792546)*
Signposted ☎Perranporth (087257)
2561 Whit—Sep rs Etr—Whit & Oct must
book school hols

*Level, grass site with young trees and
bushes, set in meadowland, with access
to the sea, Holywell beach and A3075
Newquay road. W of Rejerrah village off
unclassified road.*

6acres 135pitches 2static 135🚐 or
135🚐 or 135▲ awnings ltr

7⚡Individual pitches⚦ late arrivals
enclosure 22wc lit all night 1cdp 🚽
washbasins hc central hot water (🛁hc)⊙
supervised (wash spin dry) iron⚒ games
room TV cold storage licensed club/bar
childrens playground calor gas camping
gaz toilet fluid ☎ ⊞ 🛒

↔ stables🏇🎣🎿 pub

RELUBBUS
Cornwall
Map 2 SW53
See Praa Sands sketch map

▶▶▶ ③ ❸ ⚠

River Valley Caravan Park *(SW565320)*
Signposted ☎Germoe (073676) 3398
Mar—Oct booking advisable peak periods
Last arrival 21.00hrs Last departure noon

*Level, grass and gravel site with mature
trees and bushes, set in woodland and
meadowland with direct access to
shallow trout stream. Situated in a
picturesque valley 4m from N and S coast
sandy beaches. Site is partly wooded,
well-drained and sheltered by gently
sloping hills. 3m from Marazion on B3280.*

18acres 90pitches 70🚐 fr £4.02 10🚐 fr
£4.02 10▲fr £4.25 (awnings)

17⚡⚦ 31wc lit all night 1cdp washbasins
hc central hot water 🛁hc⊙ supervised
calor gas camping gaz toilet fluid ☎ trout
fishing 🛒

↔ golf🎣 pub

RESIPOL (Loch Sunart)
Highland *Argyllshire*
Map 13 NM76

▶▶ ② ❷ ⚠

Resipole Farm *(NM725639)*☎Salen
(096785) 235 Apr—Sep

*A spacious and grassy site in isolated
roadside position overlooking Loch
Sunart.*

8acres 45pitches SA 20🚐 £2.70
5🚐 £2.70 20▲£2.70 awnings

5⚡⚦ 11wc lit all night 1cdp washbasins
hc (🛁hc)⊙supervised (wash spin dry)
calor gas camping gaz toilet fluid hair
dryer🛒

↔ stables🎿🎣 launderette pub

REYNALTON
Dyfed
Map 2 SN00
See Tenby sketch map

▶▶▶ ② ❷ ⚠

Croft Caravan Park *(SN092094)*

☎Narberth (0834) 860315 Whit—Oct rs
Etr—Whit & Oct must book last wk Jul & 1st
2wks Aug Last departure noon

*Set in meadowland, this site has level
grassy pitches.*

5acres 85pitches 60static 65🚐 £4 or
65🚐 £4 20▲£4 awnings

4⚡Individual pitches 20wc lit all night
1cdp washbasins hc central hot water
(🛁hc)⊙supervised iron licensed club/
bar childrens playground calor gas
camping gaz paraffin🛒

↔ stables pub

RHOSGOCH
Powys
Map 3 SO14

▶ ② ❷ ⚠

Rhosgoch Holiday Park *(SO189467)*
☎Painscastle (04975) 253 Mar—Oct
must book public hols Last arrival
23.00hrs Last departure 14.00hrs no
motorcycles

*Level, sheltered site in peaceful valley
surrounded by Radnor Hills, 5½m from
Hay-on-Wye.*

1½acres 15pitches 15static 10🚐 £4 or
10🚐 £3.25 5▲£4 awnings ltr

2⚡⚦ late arrivals enclosure 3wc lit all
night 1cdp washbasins hc 🛁hc⊙
supervised (wash spin) dry iron (cold
storage) calor gas camping gaz pony
trekking fishing boating golf🛒

↔ stables golf🎿🎣 pub

RHOSNEIGR
Gwynedd
Map 6 SH37

▶ ① ①

Bodfan Farm *(SH324737)*☎ (0407)
810563 May—Sep rs Mar—Apr must book
Jul & Aug no motorcycles

*A farm site on gentle sloping ground with
sea and country views. Within walking
distance of sea.*

25acres SA 6🚐 25🚐 60▲ (awnings)

6⚡⚦ 16wc 1cdp washbasins hc (central
hot water) (🛁hc)⊙supervised spin dry
cold storage calor gas camping gaz🛒

↔ stables golf🎿🎣 launderette pub

RHYDCYMERAU
Dyfed
Map 2 SN53

▶▶ ② ❶ ⚠

Rhydcymerau Camping & Caravan Site
(SN577839)☎Talley (05583) 409 Apr—
Aug

*A pleasant, secluded grassy site, slightly
sloping at rear, set amidst wooded
surroundings on the edge of Brechfa
Forest. A small river runs through the
centre of the park.*

11acres 20pitches 5static 10🚐 10🚐 ▲
(awnings)

3⚡Individual pitches⚦ 6wc lit all night
1cdp washbasins hc central hot water
🛁hc⊙supervised (wash spin dry iron)
cold storage childrens playground calor
gas camping gaz paraffin toilet fluid cafe
☎ 🛒

↔ stables🎣 launderette

RICHMOND
North Yorkshire
Map 7 NZ10

▶▶ ① ① ⚠

Swale View Caravan Site *(NZ134013)*
Reeth Rd ☎ (0748) 3106 Mar—Oct must
book peak periods Last arrival 22.00hrs

*A level, grassy site shaded by trees, lying
on the banks of the River Swale in
picturesque Swaledale country.*

2acres 50pitches 100static SA
25🚐 £3.40 10🚐 £3.10 15▲£3.40
(awnings) ltr

10⚡⚦ late arrivals enclosure 22wc lit all
night 1cdp washbasins hc (central hot
water) 🛁hc⊙supervised (wash spin dry)
iron (cold storage) childrens playground
calor gas camping gaz toilet fluid ☎ 🛒

↔ golf🎣 launderette pub

RINGWOOD
Hampshire
Map 4 SU10

▶▶ ② ❷ ⚠

Copper Kettle *(SU152039)*266
Christchurch Rd ☎ (04254) 3904 Mar—
Oct must book peak periods

*A small, secluded level grassy site, with
hedges and fields to rear, situated ½m
from Ringwood.*

2½acres 54pitches 18🚐 £5 or
18🚐 £4.72 or 36▲£5 (awnings)

2⚡Individual pitches 9wc lit all night
1cdp washbasins hc (🛁hc⊙) supervised
calor gas camping gaz ☎ 🛒

↔ stables golf🎣 launderette pub

RIPON
North Yorkshire
Map 8 SE37

▶▶▶ ② ❶ ⚠

Ure Bank Tourist Caravan Site
(SE317726) Ure Bank Signposted
☎ (0765) 2964 Mar—Oct must book
public hols Last arrival 21.30hrs

*Near the town centre, this pleasant and
well maintained site stands on high
ground overlooking the River Ure.*

8acres 199pitches 175🚐 or 175🚐 24▲
(awnings)

11⚡Individual pitches for caravans⚦
65wc lit all night 5cdp washbasins hc 🛁hc
⊙supervised games room childrens
playground calor gas camping gaz toilet
fluid ☎ 🛒

↔ golf cinema🎣 launderette pub

▽ ①

North Sutton Farm *(SE283741)*Sutton
Grange (3m NW unclass road) ☎
(0765) 4037 All year booking advisable

212

Last arrival 22.00hrs Last departure 18.00hrs

Fenced off area of larger field at rear of farm barns, in isolated rural area.

½acre 5pitches 1static 5🚐 £2 or 5 🚙 £2 or 5▲£2 awnings ltr

1🏕1cdp

⊖→ 🍴 launderette 🍴

RIXTON
Cheshire
Map 7 SJ69

▶▶ 1 0 ⚠

Holly Bank Caravan Park *(SJ693904)*
Warburton Bridge Rd Signposted ☎061–775 2842 All year must book public hols Last arrival 22.00hrs Last departure noon

Set in rural surroundings, just off A57 close to Manchester Ship Canal. Convenient to M6 and 12m from Manchester.

6acres 70pitches SA 60🚐 £2.65 or 60 🚙 £2.65 10▲£2.65 (awnings) ltr

3🏕 Individual pitches ⚲ late arrivals enclosure 6wc lit all night 🚽 washbasins hc central hot water (🛁hc) ☺ supervised (wash spin) iron games room (cold storage) childrens playground calor gas camping gaz paraffin toilet fluid ☎ 🍴

⊖→ stables golf 🏹 🍴 launderette pub

ROBESTON WATHEN
Dyfed
Map 2 SN01

▶ 1 0 ⚠

Dyrham Caravan Site *(SN085157)*
Signposted ☎ Narberth (0834) 860367 Etr–Oct must book Jul & Aug

A small site in an elevated position offering open views, set close to the A40, but sheltered from traffic noise. Located at rear of service station in village.

2½acres 20pitches 15static 20🚐 or 20 🚙 or 20▲ (awnings)

3🏕 Individual pitches ⚲ late arrivals enclosure 4wc lit all night 1cdp🛁hc☺ supervised cold storage childrens playground calor gas camping gaz toilet fluid ☎ ⊞ 🍴

⊖→ stables 🍴 launderette pub

ROCHESTER
Kent
Map 5 TQ76

▶ 2 0 ⚠

Woolmans Wood Caravan Park
(TQ746638) Bridgewood Signposted ☎Medway (0634) 67685 All year booking advisable Jun–Aug no unaccompanied persons under 16yrs 🌂

Small site alongside the city airport and close to the London/Dover road. 3¼m S of Rochester. from M2 motorway leave at junction 3, then via A229 and B2097, ¾m from junction 3.

4acres 60pitches 50🚐 £2.50 or 50 🚙 £2.50 10▲£2.50 (awnings)

6🏕 Individual pitches ⚲ late arrivals enclosure 7wc lit all night 1cdp🚐 (central

---

hot water 🛁hc) ☺ (spin iron) cold storage childrens playground calor gas camping gaz toilet fluid ☎ mobile shop

⊖→ stables golf cinema 🍴 launderette pub 🍴

ROCKBEARE
Devon
Map 3 SY09

▶▶▶ 2 0 ⚠

Bidgood Arms Caravan Site
(SY025955) Signposted ☎Whimple (0404) 822262 16 Mar–Oct booking advisable Jul & Aug Last arrival mdnt

This site is on level ground with grass pitches. It is a convenient night stop, 7m E of Exeter on A30.

2acres 30pitches 20🚐 or 20 🚙 10▲ awnings

2🏕 9wc lit all night 1cdp washbasins hc central hot water (🛁hc) ☺ supervised games room cold storage licensed club/bar childrens playground calor gas camping gaz cafe restaurant ☎ mobile shop

⊖→ stables 🍴 pub

RODBOROUGH (Near Stroud),
Gloucestershire
Map 3 SO80

▶▶▶ 2 0 ⚠

Rodborough Fort Holiday Camping & Caravanning Centre *(SO849041)*
Signposted ☎Stroud (04536) 3478 Apr–Sep must book

Level, sloping grass site with saplings and bushes, set in hilly country, ¾m E of Stroud from A46.

5acres 60pitches 21static 40🚐 or 40 🚙 20▲ (awnings)

4🏕 Individual pitches ⚲ late arrivals enclosure 11wc 1cdp 🚐 10washbasins hc central hot water 6🛁hc 3☺ supervised

(wash) spin iron calor gas camping gaz 🍴

⊖→ stables golf launderette pub

RODNEY STOKE
Somerset
Map 3 ST44
See Cheddar sketch map

▶▶▶ 3 0 ⚠

Bucklegrove Caravan & Camping Park
(ST487502) Signposted ☎Priddy (074987) 261 Mar–Oct booking advisable peak periods Last arrival 22.00hrs Last departure 13.00hrs (in peak times) 🌂

A well sheltered site situated on the southern slopes of the Mendip Hills and an ideal touring base. Off A371.

5acres 98pitches 25static 78🚐 £4 or 78 🚙 £4 20▲£4 (awnings)

12🏕☀ late arrivals enclosure 22wc lit all night 1cdp 🚐 washbasins hc (➕hc 🛁hc) ☺supervised (wash spin dry iron ▢) (cold storage) licensed club/bar childrens playground calor gas camping gaz toilet fluid ☎ ⊞ 🍴

⊖→ stables cinema 🍴 launderette pub

see advertisement on page 113

ROLLESTON
Nottinghamshire
Map 8 SK75

▶▶ 2 0 ⚠

Trax Campsite *(SK7355526)* Southwell Racecourse Signposted ☎Newark (0636) 812081 19 Apr–16 Sep no bookings Last arrival 22.30hrs Last departure noon

Mainly level, grass site set in meadowland. Approach is via Southwell on A612.

4acres 60pitches 60🚐 *£3–£3.70 or 60 🚙 £3–£3.70 or 60▲£3–£3.70 awnings

3🏕 15wc lit all night 1cdp 10washbasins hc 2🛁hc 2☺ (wash spin) TV childrens playground calor gas camping gaz ☎

⊖→ stables 🏹 cinema launderette 🍴

ROSEHEARTY
Grampian *Aberdeenshire*
Map 15 NJ96

▶▶ 1 0 ⚠

Rosehearty Caravan Site *(NJ935675)*
Apply to: Director of Leisure & Recreation, Banff & Buchan District Council, 1 Church St, Macduff, Banffshire AB4 7UF Signposted ☎Macduff (0261) 32861 May–Sep must book Last arrival 21.00hrs Last departure 09.00hrs

A level, grass site near the sea and beach. 3½m W of Fraserburgh on B9031.

1acre 30pitches 10static 20🚐 or 20 🚙 10▲ (awnings)

2🏕 9wc lit all night 1cdp 12washbasins hc 6🛁hc 4☺ (wash spin dry) childrens playground calor gas camping gaz paraffin toilet fluid 🍴

⊖→ golf 🍴 pub

ROSS-ON-WYE
Hereford and Worcester
Map 3 SO52

▶▶▶ 🔟 ❶ ⚠

Cottage Caravan Park (SO603252)
Ledbury Rd Signposted ☎(0989) 62362
mid Mar–Oct must book school & public
hols Last arrival 21.30hrs Last departure
noon no single sex groups

*Partly level and sloping grass site with
mature trees and bushes, set in downland
and meadowland within the urban area;
views overlooking Chase Hill woods. ¼m
NE of Ross-on-Wye.*

2acres 47pitches 32static 27🚐 £4.50 or
27 🚐 £4 20▲£4.50 (awnings)

4🏕 Individual pitches ⊘ 6wc lit all night
1cdp 🚽 6washbasins hc (🛁 hc) 2☺
supervised spin (iron) calor gas camping
gaz ☎

↔ stables golf cinema ✈ launderette pub
🛒

ROSUDGEON
Cornwall
Map 2 SW52
See Praa Sands sketch map

▶▶ 🔟 ❶ ⚠

Kenneggy Cove Holiday Park
(SW562287) Higher Kenneggy
Signposted ☎Germoe (073676) 3453
Apr–Oct booking advisable peak periods
Last arrival 23.00hrs

*A level, grassy site with bushes, near the
sea and beach. Set in hilly woodland
country near moorland and downs. 6m W
of Helston off A394, overlooking Mounts
Bay.*

3acres 60pitches 9static 30🚐 fr£1.90
30 🚐 fr£1.90 or 30▲fr£1.90 (awnings)

7🏕 12wc lit all night 1cdp 🚽 washbasins
hc (central hot water) (🛁 hc) ☺ supervised
spin (dry iron) cold storage childrens
playground calor gas camping gaz ☎

↔ stables golf ✈ launderette pub 🛒

ROTHBURY
Northumberland
Map 12 NU00

▶▶ 🔟 ❷ ⚠

Coquetdale Caravan Park (NU055007)
Whitton Signposted ☎(0669) 20549
Apr–Oct booking advisable school hols
no groups of youths

*Partly level and sloping grass site with
mixed vegetation set in hilly country
adjacent to River Coquet. It is overlooked
by Simonside Hills and moorland; ½m SW
of Rothbury on Newtown road.*

2acres 50pitches 154static SA 50🚐 £3 or
50 🚐 £3 or 50▲£3 awnings

11🏕 15wc 2cdp washbasins hc (6🛁 hc)
☺ supervised (iron) (cold storage)
childrens playground calor gas camping
gaz 🛒

↔ stables golf ✈ pub

ROUSDON
Devon
Map 3 SY29

▶▶▶ 🔟 ❷ ⚠

West Hayes Caravan Park (SY298913)
Sidmouth Rd ☎Seaton (0297) 23456
May–Sep rs Oct–Apr booking advisable
peak periods Last arrival 23.00hrs Last
departure 11.00hrs no tents

*Level, grass site set in downland
overlooking the Axe Valley. On A3052
between Sidmouth and Lyme Regis.*

7acres 150pitches 150🚐 £3–£5.50 or
150 🚐 £3–£5.50 (awnings) ltr

6🏕 Individual pitches late arrivals
enclosure 15wc lit all night 1cdp 🚽
(washbasins hc 🛁 hc) ☺ supervised wash
(dry) iron ⬛ games room (cold storage)
licensed bar childrens playground calor
gas camping gaz toilet fluid restaurant ☎
⊞ 🛒

↔ stables golf ⚓ cinema ✈ launderette
pub

▶▶ 🔟 ❷ ⚠

Shrubbery Caravan Park (SY286918)
Signposted ☎Lyme Regis (02974) 2227
15 Mar–14 Nov must book peak periods
Last arrival 21.00hrs Last departure noon

*Mainly level, grass site adjacent to main
road.*

10½acres 87pitches 87🚐 £4.50 or
87 🚐 £4 10▲£4.50 (awnings)

28🏕 late arrivals enclosure 30wc lit all
night 1cdp 🚽 washbasins hc (🛁 hc) ☺
(wash spin) iron cold storage childrens
playground calor gas camping gaz
paraffin toilet fluid ☎ 🛒

↔ stables golf ⚓ cinema ✈ launderette
pub

ROWLANDS GILL
Tyne & Wear
Map 12 NZ15

▶▶ 🔟 ❶ ⚠

Derwent Park Caravan Site (NZ168586)
Signposted ☎(02074) 3383 Apr–Sep
booking advisable Public hols & Jul–Aug
Last arrival 22.00hrs Last departure noon

3 acres 60pitches 25static 60🚐 or 60 🚐
or 60▲ (awnings) ltr

3🏕 Individual pitches ⊘ late arrivals
enclosure 11wc lit all night 1cdp 🚽
washbasins hc (🛁 hc ☺ supervised (wash)
(dry iron) (✗) cold storage childrens
playground calor gas camping gaz toilet
fluid ☎ ⊞ fishing crazy golf bowling
green 🛒

↔ stables golf ✈ launderette pub

ROY BRIDGE
Highland *Inverness-shire*
Map 14 NN28

▶ 🔟 ❷ ⚠

Bunroy Caravan Park (NN273806)
Signposted ☎Spean Bridge (039781)
332 Apr–Sep Last arrival 22.00hrs Last
departure noon

*Level, grass site sheltered by mature trees
and bordered by River Spean, set in
mountainous country. 300yds off A86.*

2acres 30pitches 1static SA 30🚐 £3.50 or
30 🚐 £3 or 30▲£3–£3.50 (awnings)

3🏕 8wc lit all night (washbasins hc) (🛁 hc)
☺ supervised (cold storage)

↔ golf ⚓ ✈ pub 🛒

▶ 🔟 ❶ ⚠

Stronreigh (NN258812) ☎Spean
Bridge (039781) 275 Mar–Oct

*Part level, part sloping, grass and gravel
site with trees and bushes, set in
meadowland adjacent to River Spean. On
A86 9m N of Fort William.*

¾acre 13pitches 15static 5🚐 £1 or
5 🚐 £1 8▲£1 awnings ltr

3🏕 5wc lit all night (3washbasins hc
central hot water) (1🛁 hc) 2☺ spin cold
storage childrens playground calor gas
☎

↔ golf ✈ 🛒

RUABON
Clwyd
Map 7 SJ34

▶▶ 🔟 ❷ ⚠

James Farm (SJ300434) Signposted
☎(0978) 820148 Mar–Oct rs Nov–Feb
Last arrival 23.00hrs Last departure
10.00hrs

*Small secluded site in the heart of the
Welsh countryside. Within easy walking
distance of leisure centre in nearby
village.*

4acres 40pitches 20🚐 10 🚐 10▲
(awnings)

4🏕 late arrivals enclosure 4wc lit all night
1cdp washbasins hc central hot water
(🛁 hc) ☺ supervised 🛒

↔ stables golf launderette pub

RUDSTON
Humberside
Map 8 TA06

▶▶▶ 3 ❸ 🅰

Thorpe Hall Caravan & Camping Site
(TA108677) Thorpe Hall Signposted
☎ Kilham (026282) 393 last wknd Mar–
Oct must book public hols & Jul–Aug Last
departure noon no motorcycles

The site is contained within what used to
be the walled kitchen garden of Thorpe
Hall. A rural situation in a central wold
position about 4m W of Bridlington
adjacent to B1253 road.

4½ acres 90 pitches 90 ⊕ £3.20–£5.40 or
90 ⊕ £3.20–£5.40 or 90 ▲ £3.20–£5.40
(awnings)

9 ⇄ Individual pitches late arrivals
enclosure 18wc lit all night 2cdp ⊕
13 washbasins hc 2 central hot water
2 ⇚ hc 6 🚿 hc 4 ☺ supervised (wash spin
dry iron) games room (cold storage) calor
gas camping gaz toilet fluid ☎ facilities
for disabled 🛒

⊖ stables launderette pub

RUGELEY
Staffordshire
Map 7 SK01

▶ ② ❶ 🅰

Silver Trees Caravan & Chalet Park
Penkridge Bank (SK014173) ☎ (08894)
2185 Apr–Oct booking advisable public
hols Last arrival 23.00hrs Last departure
noon no tents

Situated on rising ground on Cannock
Chase amidst attractive woodland. Off
Penkridge–Rugeley road, 2m from
Rugeley.

12 pitches 57 static SA 12 ⊕ £2.75 or
12 ⊕ £2.75 (awnings) ltr

7 ⇄ Individual pitches late arrivals

---

enclosure 15wc lit all night 3cdp (central
hot water) (🚿 hc) ☺ supervised (wash spin
dry iron) ⇚ ℗ games room CTV cold
storage chidrens playground calor gas
☎ 🛒

⊖ stables golf cinema ♪ launderette pub

RUMFORD
Cornwall
Map 2 SW87
See Padstow sketch map

▶▶▶▶ 3 ❷ 🅰

Music Water Touring Park (SW905686)
Signposted ☎ (08414) 257 Apr–Oct
booking advisable mid Jul–Aug Last
departure 10.00hrs (Jul–Aug)

Quiet park in rural surroundings near
sandy beaches. Slightly sloping, level
grass and gravel site in moorland and
meadowland, 4m S of Padstow on B3274.

7½ acres 140 pitches 3 static
140 ⊕ frf3.15 or 140 ⊕ frf3.15 or
140 ▲ frf3.15 (awnings)

10 ⇄ ☺ late arrivals enclosure 21wc lit all
night 2cdp ⊕ washbasins hc (🚿 hc) ☺
supervised wash spin iron (cold storage)
licensed club/bar childrens playground
calor gas camping gaz toilet fluid ☎ ⊞ 🛒

⊖ stables golf ⚓ cinema ♪ launderette
pub

RUTHERNBRIDGE
Cornwall
Map 2 SX06

▶▶▶ 3 ❷ 🅰

Ruthern Valley Holidays (SX014665)
Signposted ☎ Bodmin (0208) 831395
Apr–Oct booking advisable Jul & Aug
Last arrival 22.00hrs Last departure
11.00hrs

Gently sloping, grass site with mature
trees, set in hilly woodland country,
adjacent to River Ruthern. 2m SW of
Bodmin off A30. Follow signs.

2 acres 30 pitches 6 static 30 ⊕ £4.10–
£4.90 or 30 ⊕ £3.60–£4.20 or
30 ▲ £4.10–£4.90 (awnings)

2 ⇄ Individual pitches 4wc lit all night
1cdp washbasins hc 🚿 hc ☺ supervised
(cold storage) childrens playground calor
gas camping gaz 🛒

⊖ stables ♪ pub

ST AGNES
Cornwall
Map 2 SW75
See Perranporth sketch map

▶▶ ❶ ❶ 🅰

Presingoll Farm (SW720498)
☎ (087255) 2333 Apr–Oct must book Jul
& Aug

Level, grassy site set in meadowland
within the urban area, with cliff scenery
close to sand/shingle beach. 3m off A30
on B3277.

3½ acres 90 pitches 2 static 90 ⊕ £2.40 or
90 ⊕ £2.40 or 90 ▲ £2.40 awnings

5 ⇄ 8wc lit all night 1cdp (washbasins hc)
(🚿 hc) ☺ supervised (spin iron) (cold
storage) childrens playground ☎

⊖ stables golf ♪ launderette pub 🛒

ST ANDREWS
Fife
Map 12 NO51

▶▶▶▶ 3 ❸ 🅰

Craigtoun Meadows Holiday Park
(NO482150) Mount Melville Signposted
☎ (0334) 75959 Mar–Oct booking
advisable Jul & Aug Last arrival 21.00hrs
Last departure noon

Set in downland with mixed woodland and
pasture, 2m from sea and sandy beaches.
→

2m from St Andrews on the Craigtoun road.

8acres 108pitches 146static
108🚐 fr£3.50 or 108 🚐 fr£3.50 or
108▲fr£3 (awnings)
40🚐Individual pitches⊘ late arrivals
enclosure 21wc lit all night 2cdp 🔌
washbasins hc 🚿hc⊖supervised (wash
spin dry) iron games room CTV cold
storage childrens playground calor gas
camping gaz toilet fluid cafe restaurant ☎
⊞ bicycles & golf clubs for hire 🏌
⊕ stables golf 🏌 cinema 🎬 launderette
pub

▶▶▶ 🆔 ❷ ⚠
Kinkell Braes Caravan Site *(NO522156)*
Apply to: North East Fife District Council,
Department of Recreation, County
Buildings, Cupar, Fife ☎ (0334) 53722 or
74250 late Mar–early Oct must book Last
arrival & departure 20.00hrs

A large, predominantly static site in open
position high above the town with fine
panoramic views across St Andrews and

St Andrews — St Brelade

*Firth of Tay. Lovely sandy beaches
nearby.*

2acres 60pitches 613static 69🚐£3.20 or
69🚐£3.20 or 69▲£1.70–£3.20
(awnings)

17🚐Individual pitches late arrivals
enclosure 116wc lit all night 1cdp
146washbasins hc 20🚿hc 31⊖
supervised (wash dry) childrens
playground calor gas camping gaz ☎ 🏌
⊕ golf 🏌 cinema 🎬 launderette pub

ST AUSTELL
Cornwall
Map 2 SX05
See sketch map on page 217
▶▶▶ 🆔 ❷ ⚠
Trewhiddle Caravan & Camping Park
(SX006511) Signposted ☎ (0726) 2659
Apr–Sep must book peak periods Last
arrival 23.00hrs Last departure 11.00hrs

---

*Secluded wooded site with well-kept
gardens, lawns and flower beds.*

7acres 142pitches 84static 142🚐 or
142 🚐 or 142▲ (awnings)
8🚐37wc 2cdp washbasins hc (central
hot water) (🚿hc)⊖supervised (wash dry
iron) games room (cold storage) licensed
club/bar childrens playground calor gas
camping gaz paraffin ☎ 🏌
⊕ stables golf 🏌 cinema 🎬 launderette
pub

see advertisement on page 218

ST BRELADE
Jersey, Channel Islands
Map 16

▶▶▶ 🆔 ❶ ⚠
Quennevais Camping Site Les Ormes
Farm Signposted ☎ Jersey (0534) 42436
Jul–Aug rs Apr–Jun & Sep must book
Jun–Aug Last arrival 22.00hrs Last
departure noon 🚶 no caravans or
motorvans

Partly level, partly sloping grass and sand
site with trees and bushes set in hilly →

216

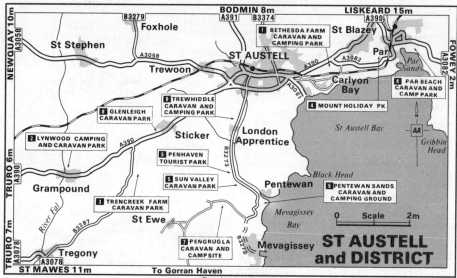

ST AUSTELL and DISTRICT

Roads shown as broken are not suitable for towing caravans

Sites listed under: **1** Carlyon Bay **2** Grampound **3** Hewas Water **4** Par **5** Pentewan **6** St Austell **7** St Ewe **8** Sticker

---

THE SEA VIEW INTERNATIONAL
16, Boswinger, Gorran Haven, St Austell, Cornwall
Telephone 0726 843425 3½ miles S.W. of Mevagissey Harbour
Six beautiful sandy beaches within a radius of 2 miles, nearest ½ mile.

First outright winner in Britain of AA Trail "Site of the Year" Award 1979

1983 English Tourist Board Rose Award for excellence

Large, level, pitches, 70 with electrical hook-up facility, many with own waste water and waste gulley. Also electric power for tents with our revolutionary "International Tent Powerpac".
Separate meadow with quality caravans for hire, with full mains services and colour TV.
Free use of two **heated swimming pools**, ½ acre of sun decks overlooking the bay, plus 7 acres of well equipped recreational space for the children.

★★★★★
FREEDOM AND RELAXATION
(NO NOISY CLUBHOUSE)

Our AA quality gradings
Environment – excellent
Sanitary installations – excellent
General facilities – excellent

The Michell family will be delighted to send you the fully illustrated site brochure. SAE please.

woodland country. Near airport on B43 road.

15acres200pitches200▲awnings

6♨Late arrivals enclosure33wc lit all night washbasins hc central hot water ⋔hc☉supervised(wash spin dry iron games room)CTV(cold storage) childrens playground calor gas camping gaz paraffin toilet fluid cafe restaurant ☎⊞♨

↤ stables golf ⤬ ◢ launderette pub

▶▶❶❶⚠
Rose Farm Route des Genets Signposted ☎Jersey(0534)41231 May–Sep must book Jun–Aug 🍴(Jul&Aug)no caravans or motorvans

Sloping grassy site consisting of four separate fields and well sheltered by trees. 1m W of St Aubin's village on A13. Last arrival and departure time as soon as possible after car ferry docks.

5acres150pitches150▲awnings

7♨20wc lit all night washbasins hc ⋔hc ☉supervised(spin dry)iron games room CTV childrens playground calor gas camping gaz paraffin cafe ☎ ▮

↤ stables golf ⤬ ◢ launderette pub

ST BURYAN
Cornwall
Map 2 SW42
See sketch map

▶▶▶❷❸⚠
Treverven Camping & Touring Site (SW410237)Treverven Farm Signposted ☎(073672)221 Etr–Oct must book end Jul & Aug Last departure noon

A well-maintained campsite with panoramic views. Off B3315.

6acres115pitches115♥ fr£3.50 or 115♥ fr£3.50 or 115▲fr£3.50 awnings

9♨Individual pitches10wc lit all night 1cdp washbasins central hot water ⋔hc ☉supervised(wash spin dry iron)cold storage camping gaz ☎ mobile shop

↤ ◢

▶▶❷❶⚠
Lower Treave Caravan Park (SW388272)Crows-an-Wra Signposted ☎(073672)559 Apr–Oct booking

see page 216 for entry

---

advisable Jul & Aug Last arrival 22.30hrs Last departure noon

Terraced, grass site with trees and bushes, set in meadowland, 4m NE of Land's End off A30.

4½acres80pitches5static30♥£4 15♥£4 or 35▲£4(awnings)

18♨Individual pitches☉ late arrivals enclosure 12wc lit all night 1cdp washbasins hc(⋔hc)☉supervised (wash spin dry iron)cold storage calor gas camping gaz toilet fluid ☎ hair dryers ▮

↤ stables ◢ pub

▶▶❷❸⚠
Tower Farm Caravan & Camping Park (SW406263)Signposted ☎(073672)286 Mar–Oct rs Nov–Feb Last departure noon

This is a farm site situated near Land's End and 4m from Sennen Cove and Porthcurno. Off A30 and B3283.

6acres102pitches6static SA 102♥£3.40–£3.90 or 102 ♥£3.40–£3.90 or 102▲£3.40–£3.90(awnings)

13♨☉22wc lit all night 2cdp🚽 18washbasins hc(10⋔hc)6☉ supervised(wash spin dry iron)CTV(cold storage)childrens playground calor gas camping gaz ☎

↤ ✈ ◢ launderette pub ▮

ST CLETHER
Cornwall
Map 2 SX28

▶▶▶❷❶⚠
Ta-Mill(SX187848)☎Otterham Station (08406)381 Mar–Oct no booking

Small site situated on a non working farm, only a short distance from the coast. Off A395.

3acres20pitches11static20♥£2.50 or 20♥£2.50 or 20▲£2.50(awnings)

3♨☉2wc lit all night 1cdp washbasins hc (⋔hc)☉supervised(wash spin dry)iron cold storage(licensed club/bar) childrens playground ☎ trout fishing ▮

↤ stables golf ⤬ ◢ pub

ST COLUMB MAJOR
Cornwall
Map 2 SW96
See Newquay sketch map

▶▶▶❸❶⚠
Tregatillian Caravan Park(SW923630) Tregatillian Signposted ☎St Columb (0637)88048226 May–14 Sep rs 12–25 May & 15–30 Sep must book school hols Last departure noon no single sex groups

A level site set slightly inland from the North Cornish Coast 1½m E of town. Approach from town is only via by-pass.

8acres17pitches84static SA 17♥£2–£5 or 17♥£2–£5 or 17▲£2–£5(awnings)

18♨☉17wc lit all night 2cdp🚽 washbasins hc⋔hc☉supervised(wash spin dry iron)games room CTV licensed bar childrens playground calor gas camping gaz toilet fluid ☎ ▮

↤ stables fishing launderette pub

▶▶▶❷❶⚠
Trekenning Manor Tourist Park (SW911622)Trekenning Signposted ☎(0637)880462 Apr–Oct booking advisable Jul & Aug Last arrival mdnt Last

---

departure noon

2 acres 50 pitches SA 50🚐 £3.35–£5.75 or 50🚐 £3–£5.50 or 50▲£3.35–£5.75 (awnings)

4🏕8wc lit all night 1cdp 🚐 8washbasins hc (4🚿hc) 2☉supervised (wash) iron〰 games room CTV cold storage licensed club/bar childrens playground calor gas camping gaz ☎ bar snacks & meals available 🍴

↔ stables 🧺 launderette pub

see advertisement on page 194

ST DAVID'S
Dyfed
Map 2 SM72

▶▶🅟🅞❶△
Caerfai Bay Caravan & Camping Park
(SM759244)☎(0437) 720274 20 May–Sep rs 14 Apr–19 May booking advisable school hols for caravans Last arrival 20.00hrs Last departure noon no single sex groups

---

Grassy site with bushes set in meadowland, with magnificent coastal scenery – bathing beach 300yds from park entrance. Off A487, end of unclass road to Caerfai Bay.

9 acres 80 pitches 30 static 30🚐 10🚐 40▲ (awnings) ltr

13🏕 Individual pitches caravans only ⊘ 16wc lit all night 2cdp (washbasins hc) (central hot water) (🚿hc) ☉ (wash dry) (cold storage) calor gas camping gaz ☎

↔ stables golf 🏌 🧺 pub 🍴

▶▶🅟🅞❶△
Dwr Cwmwdig Caravan Park
(SM805305) Berea Signposted ☎Croesgoch (03483) 376 4 Apr–10 Oct must book Last arrival mdnt Last departure 11.59hrs

---

Small grassy site in open country near the Pembrokeshire coastal path. Situated at the junction of two unclass roads 1½m W of Croesgoch on the A487 St Davids–Fishguard road.

1 acre 40 pitches 10 static SA 20🚐 £3.25 or 20🚐 £2.50 20▲£2.50 (awnings) ltr

4🏕 Individual pitches for caravans ⊘ 7wc lit all night 1cdp washbasins (central hot water) (🚿hc) ☉ supervised cold storage childrens playground calor gas hair dryer boat hire mobile shop

↔ stables 🏌 🧺 pub 🍴

▶▶🅟🅞❶△
Hendre Eynon Site (SM773280)
Signposted ☎(0437) 720474 Apr–Sep must book Jul & Aug Last arrival mdnt

Mainly level grassy site in farmland. 2m NE of St Davids on unclassified road.

7 acres 80 pitches 5 static 45🚐 £1.60–£3.20 or 45🚐 £1.60–£2 30▲£1.60–£3 awnings →

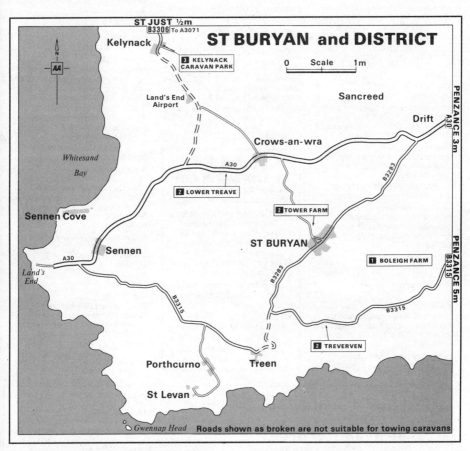

ST JUST ½m | B3306 To A3071

Kelynack

ST BURYAN and DISTRICT

3 KELYNACK CARAVAN PARK

0 Scale 1m

Land's End Airport

Sancreed

Drift

Crows-an-wra

Whitesand Bay

A30

2 LOWER TREAVE

2 TOWER FARM

PENZANCE 3m A30

Sennen Cove

ST BURYAN

1 BOLEIGH FARM B3315

Sennen

A30

B3283

B3283

PENZANCE 5m B3315

Land's End

B3315

B3315

2 TREVERVEN

Porthcurno

Treen

St Levan

Gwennap Head **Roads shown as broken are not suitable for towing caravans**

Sites listed under: **1** Lamorna **2** St Buryan **3** St Just

12⚏ Individual pitches ⊘ late arrivals enclosure 12wc lit all night 1 cdp 🔌 washbasins hc central hot water 🚿hc☉ supervised (wash) dry iron (cold storage) childrens playground calor gas camping gaz paraffin toilet fluid ☎ horse riding
↔ stables golf ⚒ ⚓ launderette pub 🍺

ST DAY
Cornwall
Map 2 SW74
See Redruth sketch map

▶▶▶ 🖭 ❷ ⚠
Tresaddern Caravan Park *(SW733422)*
Signposted ☎ (0209) 820459 Etr–Oct must book last wk Jul–1st 2wks Aug Last arrival 22.00hrs Last departure noon

Sloping, grass site with trees and bushes set in meadowland and downland, 2m NE of Redruth on B3298.

2acres 25pitches 12static SA 25🚐 £2.70–£3.30 or 25 🚐 £2.70–£3.30 or 25▲£2.70–£3.30 awnings

3⚏ Individual pitches 7wc lit all night 1 cdp 🔌 washbasins hc (🚿hc☉ supervised iron (cold storage) calor gas camping gaz ☎ battery charging 🍺
↔ stables cinema launderette pub

ST EWE
Cornwall
Map 2 SW94
See St Austell sketch map

▶▶ 🖾 ❶ ⚠
Pengrugla Caravan & Campsite
(SX001469) Signposted ☎ Mevagissey (0726) 843485 19 May–Sep must book Jul & Aug Last departure 10.30hrs

Part level, part sloping, grassy site with trees and bushes situated amidst woodland and meadowland near main road, off B3273.

7acres 120pitches 60🚐 £2–£5 60 🚐 £2–£5 or 60▲£2–£5 awnings

7⚏ Individual pitches late arrivals enclosure 12wc lit all night 1 cdp 🔌 16washbasins hc (6🚿hc) 4☉(wash spin dry iron) (cold storage) calor gas camping gaz toilet fluid ☎ 🍺
↔ golf ⚓ launderette pub

ST FILLANS
Tayside *Perthshire*
Map 11 NN72

▶▶▶ 🖭 ❷ ⚠
Lochearn Caravan Park (NN680239)
South Shore Rd ☎ (076485) 270 Apr–24 Oct Last arrival 20.00hrs Last departure noon no tents

Part level, part sloping gravel site with trees and bushes, set in mountainous

---

country adjacent to lake. 6m W of Comrie on A85.

5acres 40pitches 200static 40🚐 or 40 🚐 (awnings)

10⚏28wc lit all night 1 cdp washbasins hc (central hot water) (🚿hc)☉ supervised (wash dry iron) games room (cold storage) private beach calor gas toilet fluid ☎ ⊞ 🍺
↔ golf ⚒ ⚓ launderette pub

ST FLORENCE
Dyfed
Map 2 SN10

▶▶▶ 🖭 ❷ ⚠
New Minerton Caravan Park
(SN093027) Devonshire Dr ☎ Carew (06467) 461 mid May–Sep rs Apr–mid May booking advisable peak periods Last arrival 19.00hrs Last departure noon no single sex groups

Level grass site with bushes and trees W of village on B4318.

12acres 140pitches 120static 40🚐 £5 or 40 🚐 £5 100▲£4 (awnings)

12⚏ individual pitches for caravans ⊘ wc lit all night 1 cdp washbasins hc (central hot water) (🚿hc)☉ (wash spin dry iron) games room CTV (cold storage) (licensed club/bar) childrens playground calor gas camping gaz toilet fluid ☎ 🍺
↔ stables golf ⚒ cinema ⚓ pub

ST HELENS
Isle of Wight
Map 4 SZ68
See Shanklin sketch map

▶▶▶ 🖭 ❷ ⚠
Nodes Point Holiday Village
(SZ637899) Nodes Rd Signposted ☎ Bembridge (098387) 2401 19 May–22 Sep no telephone bookings Last arrival mdnt Last departure noon 🗡 no single sex groups

Part of large holiday complex. Site on slight gradient with grass surface and near beach. The campsite entrance is off Duver Road.

25acres 275pitches 30🚐 £5.75 or 30 🚐 £4.60 245▲£3.45 (awnings)

12⚏26wc lit all night washbasins hc central hot water 🚿hc☉ supervised (wash spin dry iron) 🍴 games room cold storage licensed club/bar childrens playground calor gas camping gaz toilet cafe restaurant ☎ ⊞ 🍺
↔ stables ⚲ cinema ⚓ launderette pub

ST HILARY
Cornwall
Map 2 SW53
See Praa Sands sketch map

▶▶▶ 🖭 ❷ ⚠
Wayfarers Camping Site *(SW556315)*
Signposted ☎ Germoe (073676) 3326 All year booking advisable Jul & Aug Last arrival 22.00hrs Last departure noon Jul & Aug

A level, grass site with trees, saplings and bushes adjacent to B3280. 1m past Relubbus village, on right.

4acres 60pitches 6static 60🚐 fr£3.15 or 60 🚐 fr£2.80 or 60▲fr£3.15 (awnings)

5⚏ late arrivals enclosure 11wc lit all night 1 cdp washbasins hc (central hot water) (🚿hc)☉ supervised (wash spin dry iron) (cold storage) childrens playground calor gas camping gaz paraffin toilet fluid ☎ hair dryer battery charging TV & equipment hire 🍺
↔ stables golf ⚒ ⚓ launderette pub

ST ISSEY
Cornwall
Map 2 SW97
See Padstow sketch map

▶▶▶ 🖭 ❷ ⚠
Trewince Farm Holiday Park
(SW937714) Signposted ☎ Wadebridge (020881) 2830 Etr–Oct must book peak periods Last arrival 23.00hrs Last departure 10.30hrs

---

A rural wooded site situated near to the Camel Estuary. 4m from Wadebridge, 4m from Padstow.

5acres 90pitches 25static 30 🏠 fr£3 or 30 🏠 60▲fr£3 awnings ltr

12🅿Individual pitches ⊘ late arrivals enclosure 5wc lit all night 1cdp 🌀 washbasins hc central hot water (🛁hc)☺ wash (spin dry iron) (games room cold storage) childrens playground calor gas camping gaz toilet fluid ☎ 🎏 🎿

⟺ stables golf 🦯 cinema ⌦ launderette pub

see advertisement on page 198

ST IVES
Cornwall
Map 2 SW54
See sketch map on page 223

▶▶▶ 🅿 ⊘ ⚠
Ayr Holiday Park (SW509408)
Signposted ☎ Penzance (0736) 795855
Apr–Oct must book Jul & Aug Last arrival 20.00hrs Last departure 10.00hrs no single sex groups

Part level, part sloping, grass site set in

meadowland, adjacent to sea and sandy beach. ½m W of B3306.

2acres 40pitches 43static SA 40 🏠 £4.50–£7.50 or 40 🏠 £4–£6.20 or 40▲£4.50–£7.50 (awnings)

2🅿11wc lit all night 1cdp 🌀 washbasins hc central hot water 🛁hc☺supervised (wash spin dry iron) (cold storage) calor gas camping gaz ☎ battery charging 🎏

⟺ stables golf 🦯 cinema ⌦ launderette pub

New Minerton Leisure Park
DEVONSHIRE DRIVE, ST FLORENCE
Nr. TENBY, Dyfed. Telephone CAREW 461 (06467)

* Luxury 4 & 6 berth caravans with full services, colour TV and fridge.
* Licensed Club and Children's Room.
* Heated Swimming Pool & Recreation Area.
* Self Service Shop.
* Tents & Tourers — 10 acre level paddock with 1st class amenities.

Under the personal supervision of
ALAN & EILEEN HIGGS
Colour Brochure Available
Stamp only appreciated

NODES POINT CAMPING AND TOURING PARK

A fun-packed camping holiday on England's "Treasure Island"

Our well-kept Holiday Park lies on the east side of the Isle of Wight, overlooking lovely Bembridge Bay. There's fun for all the family with our excellent facilities and entertainment. And you can bring your own tent or hire one of our fabulous 6-berth Supertents.

● **Lovely location overlooking Bembridge Bay, Isle of Wight**
● **First-class amenities**
● **Heated swimming pool**

● Excellent facilities including:
Supermarket, Launderette, Hairdresser
● Live entertainment nightly
● Children's Starcruiser Club
● Indoor games and amusements

WRITE OR TELEPHONE FOR FURTHER DETAILS AND BOOKINGS

To: Dept. AA01 **Nodes Point Holiday Village**, St Helens, Ryde, Isle of Wight PO33 1YA
Tel: Ryde (098 387) 2401

221

▶▶②❷⚠
Polmanter Farm Campsite *(SW510388)*
Halsetown Signposted ☎ Penzance
(0736) 795640 Whit–Sep rs Apr–Whit
must book Jul & Aug Last arrival 22.00hrs
Last departure 10.00hrs no motorcycles

*Level grass site set in meadowland with
access to sea, beach, hills and St Ives
Bay. On B3311.*

8acres 200pitches SA 60 ➈ £4.15 or
140 ➈ £4 or 140 ⚊£4 (awnings)
16 ➪ ⊘ 23wc lit all night 1cdp ⊡
washbasins hc (⌂ hc) ☉ supervised
(wash spin dry iron) (𝒫) (cold storage)
childrens playground calor gas camping
gaz toilet fluid ☎ ⚎
↪ stables golf ⚴ cinema ✔ launderette
pub

▶ 🛈 ❶ ⚠
Higher Penderleith Site *(SW497375)*
Towednack Signposted ☎ Penzance
(0736) 796576 Apr–Oct Last departure
11.00hrs no open fires

*A level and sloping grass site 1m SW of
Halsetown on B3311.*

4acres 75pitches SA 20 ➈ 55 ➈ or 55⚊
(awnings)
5 ➪ ⊘ 10wc lit all night 1cdp (⌂ hc) ☉
supervised
↪ stables golf ⚴ cinema ✔ launderette
pub ⚎

ST JUST
Cornwall
Map 2 SW33
See St Buryan sketch map

▶▶▶②❷⚠
Trevaylor Caravan Park *(SW368322)*
Truthwall Signposted ☎ Penzance
(0736) 787016 Etr–Oct booking
advisable Jul & Aug Last departure
14.00hrs

On the B3306 St Ives–St Just road.

3½acres 65pitches SA 45 ➈ £3.60 or
45 ➈ £3.60 20⚊£3.60 awnings
12 ➪ ⊘ 9wc lit all night 1cdp ⊡
8washbasins hc 2central hot water ⌂ hc
☉ supervised (wash dry iron) cold storage
childrens playground calor gas camping
gaz paraffin toilet fluid ☎ hair dryers
↪ stables golf ✔ launderette pub

▶▶②❶⚠
Kelynack Caravan Park *(SW374301)*
☎ St Buryan (073672) 465 Apr–Oct must
book Jul & Aug Last departure 14.00hrs

*Level, grass and gravel site with mature
trees and bushes set in moorland and
meadowland close to sea, ¾m S of St Just
on B3306.*

½acre 10pitches 10static SA 10 ➈ £3.75
or 10 ➈ £3.75 or 10⚊£3.75 awnings
6 ➪ individual pitches 6wc lit all night
1cdp ⊡ (washbasins hc) (⌂ hc) ☉ (iron)
childrens playground calor gas camping
gaz ☎
↪ stables ✔ launderette pub ⚎

ST JUST-IN-ROSELAND
Cornwall
Map 2 SW83

▶▶▶②❷⚠
Trethem Mill Caravan Site *(SW860365)*
Signposted ☎ Portscatho (087 258) 504
or St Maws (0326) 270427 Jun–Oct rs Apr,
May & Oct must book Jul & Aug Last
departure 11.00hrs

*Part level, part sloping, grass site with
young trees and bushes. Set in hilly
meadowland country close to sea and
main road.*

3acres 84pitches 84 ➈ £4.40–£6.20 or
84 ➈ £4.40–£6.20 or 84⚊£4.40–£6.20
awnings
5 ➪ Individual pitches 16wc lit all night
1cdp 12washbasins hc (⌂ hc) ☉ (wash
spin) iron cold storage licensed club/bar
childrens playground calor gas camping
gaz paraffin toilet fluid ☎ ⚎
↪ stables ⚴ ✔ launderette pub

ST LAWRENCE
Isle of Wight
Map 4 SZ57

▽🛈
The Orchard *(SZ513769)* ☎ Isle of Wight
(0983) 730381 Etr–Oct rs winter Last
arrival dusk Last departure 16.00hrs no
caravans & no motorcycles or barbecues

*A series of three sheltered terraced
clearings in the undercliff. Whole site is on
south slope well sheltered from the north
and east.*

5acres 50pitches 50 ➈ £2.30 or
50⚊£2.30 awnings
3 ➪ ⊘ 1cdp supervised private beach
↪ stables ✔ pub ⚎

ST LEONARDS
Dorset
Map 4 SU00

▶▶▶②❷⚠
Camping International *(SU104024)*
Athol Lodge Signposted ☎ Ferndown
(0202) 872817 Apr–Oct must book Jun–
Aug Last arrival 23.30hrs Last departure
10.30hrs no single sex groups

---

*Small, well-equipped, level camping site
surrounded by trees adjacent to main
A31.*

3acres 60pitches 15 ➈ £4–£5.50 or
5 ➈ £4–£5.50 or 40⚊£4–£5.50 awnings
9 ➪ Individual pitches ⊘ late arrivals
enclosure 16wc lit all night 1cdp
12washbasins hc 8⌂ hc 6☉ supervised
(spin dry warm iron) games room CTV
(cold storage) (licensed bar) childrens
playground calor gas camping gaz toilet
fluid cafe restuarant ☎ ⊞ battery
charging ⚎
↪ stables golf ✔ launderette pub

▶▶▶②❸⚠
Shamba Holiday Park *(SU105029)*
Signposted ☎ Ferndown (0202) 873302
Apr–Sep rs Oct–Mar must book public
hols & Jul–Aug Last arrival mdnt Last
departure noon ✟ Whit & Jul–Aug

*Level grassy site with mixed vegetation,
set in hilly wooded country. 3m W of
Ringwood off A31.*

7acres 150pitches 23 ➈ £4.50 or
150 ➈ £4.50 or 150⚊£4.50 awnings
3 ➪ Individual pitches late arrivals
enclosure 20wc lit all night 1cdp
washbasins hc central hot water (⌂ hc) ☉
supervised wash spin iron games room TV
licensed club/bar childrens playground
calor gas camping gaz toilet fluid cafe
restaurant ☎ amusement arcade ⚎
↪ stables ✔ launderette pub
see advert on page 224

▶▶▶②❷⚠
Village Holidays *(SU095014)*
Signposted ☎ Ferndown (0202) 875422
Mar–Oct Last arrival 22.00hrs Last
departure noon no single sex groups no
motorcycles

*Level, grass site set in commonland. 3m W
of Ringwood on A31.*

40acres 523pitches 200static SA
374 ➈ £7 or 374 ➈ £7 149⚊£7 awnings
➪ individual pitches ⊘ 84wc lit all night
3cdp ⊡ washbasins hc central hot water
⌂ hc ☉ supervised (wash dry iron) ⚎
games room licensed club/bar calor gas
camping gaz toilet fluid cafe ☎ riding
stables bicycles ⚎
↪ stables ✔ launderette

ST MABYN
Cornwall
Map 2 SX07

▶▶▶②❶⚠
St Mabyn Holiday Park *(SX053733)*
Signposted ☎ (020884) 236 21 May–18
Sep rs Apr–20 May & 19 Sep–Oct must
book Jul & Aug Last departure noon no →

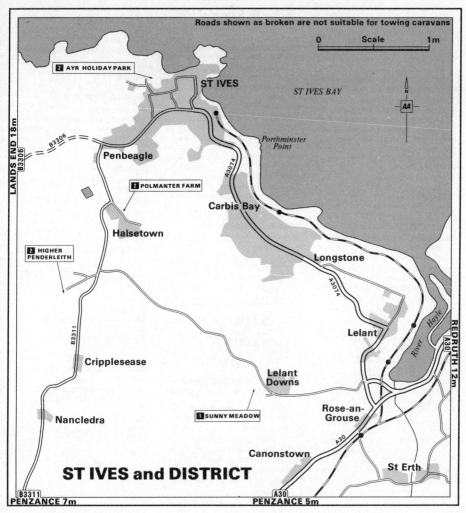

Roads shown as broken are not suitable for towing caravans

0   Scale   1m

2 AYR HOLIDAY PARK

ST IVES

ST IVES BAY

Porthminster Point

B3306

LANDS END 18m

Penbeagle

A3074

2 POLMANTER FARM

Carbis Bay

Halsetown

2 HIGHER PENDERLEITH

Longstone

A3074

River Hayle

B3311

Lelant

REDRUTH 12m

A30

Cripplesease

Lelant Downs

Nancledra

1 SUNNY MEADOW

Rose-an-Grouse

A30

Canonstown

ST IVES and DISTRICT

St Erth

B3311
PENZANCE 7m

A30
PENZANCE 5m

Sites listed under: **1** Lelant Downs   **2** St Ives

single sex groups

Site divided into three enclosures on level and well drained land. Situated in delightful rural area between moors and sea. Off B3266.

12acres 150pitches 22static 150⊞£3.45–£4.80 or 150 ⊞£3.45–£4.80 or 150▲£3.45–£4.80 awnings ltr

9⚲ Individual pitches☺ late arrivals enclosure 24wc lit all night 2cdp☺ 22washbasins hc 2central hot water (10⋔hc) 4☺supervised (wash spin dry iron)⊟ games room CTV (cold storage) licensed club/bar childrens playground calor gas camping gaz toilet fluid cafe restaurant ☎ ⊞ 🏊

↔ stables cinema ▰ pub

ST MARTIN
Jersey, Channel Islands
Map 16

▶▶▶②◐⚠
Beuvelande Camping Site Signposted ☎ Jersey (0534) 53575 Apr–Oct must book no caravans or motorvans

Level grass site with mature trees and bushes, set in rural area 1m from beach. Take A6 from St Helier and then B28 to site.

3acres 80pitches 80▲✳£4.75–£8.75

3⚲ 10wc lit all night 24washbasins hc (10⋔hc) 4☺supervised (wash spin dry iron)⊟ games room CTV (cold storage) childrens playground calor gas camping gaz paraffin toilet fluid ☎ 🏊

↔ golf ▰ launderette pub

▶▶▶②◑⚠
Rozel Camping Park Summerville Farm ☎ Jersey (0534) 51989 Apr–Sep must book 🎯 no all male groups (from 12 Jun–8 Sep) no caravans or motorvans

Level grass site surrounded by tall trees. From St Helier follow Bagatelle Road (A6) or St Saviour's Road (A7) then B38. Last arrival and departure time as soon as possible after car ferry docks.

▲fr£1.70 awnings

2⚲9wc lit all night washbasins hc ⋔hc☺ supervised (wash) spin (dry) iron games room CTV cold storage childrens

---

St Mabyn
—
St Monans

playground calor gas camping gaz paraffin cafe restaurant ☎ bikes for hire 🏊

↔ stables golf ▰ launderette pub

ST MERRYN (near Padstow)
Cornwall
Map 2 SW87
See Padstow sketch map

▶②❷⚠
Carnevas Caravan & Camping Site
(SW862728) Carnevas Farm Signposted ☎ Padstow (0841) 520230 Jun–mid Sep rs Apr–May & mid Sept–Oct must book end Jul & Aug

Level, grass site set in meadowland. Off B3276 Padstow–Newquay road 2m SW of village.

8acres 188pitches 14static SA 188⊞£3 or 188 ⊞£2.40 or 188▲£3 (awnings)

⚲21wc lit all night 1cdp washbasins hc

Shamba Holiday Park

230 Ringwood Road,
St. Leonards, Hampshire

Quiet AA 4 pennant, family run site for touring caravans and tents, with easy reach to the South Coast Beaches and the New Forest. A home from home with bar, shop, showers, laundry, immaculate toilets and babies washroom. Booking advisable.

Tel: Ferndown (0202) 873302

(central hot water) (⋔hc)☺ (wash spin) dry (iron) (cold storage) calor gas camping gaz toilet fluid ☎ 🏊

↔ stables golf ✖ ▰ launderette pub

ST MINVER
Cornwall
Map 2 SW97
See Padstow sketch map

▶▶▶②◐⚠
St Minver House Holiday Estate
Signposted ☎ Trebetherick (020 886) 2305 mid May–mid Sep rs Etr–mid May must book peak periods Last arrival 18.00hrs Last departure 10.00hrs 🎯

A level site amongst sylvan surroundings.

15acres 233pitches 130static 83⊞ 150⊞ ltr

⚲◑ wc lit all night washbasins hc central hot water (⋔hc)☺ (wash spin iron)⊟ games room CTV licensed club/bar children playground calor gas camping gaz ☎ ⊞ crazy golf 🏊

↔ stables golf ✖ cinema ▰ launderette pub

ST MONANS
Fife
Map 12 NO50

▶①❷⚠
St Monans Caravan Site *(NO529019)*
☎ (03337) 778 or Cupar (0334) 53722 late Mar–early Oct must book Last arrival & departure 20.00hrs

Mainly static site on fringe of coastal village adjacent to main road and public park.

¼acre 12pitches 123static 12⊞£3.20 or 12⊞£3.20 or 12▲£1.70–£3.20 (awnings)

7⚲ Individual pitches 19wc lit all night 1cdp 13washbasins hc 4⋔hc 4☺ (wash dry) ☎ 🏊

↔ golf ✖ ▰

FUN AND FREEDOM HOLIDAYS FOR <u>ALL</u> THE FAMILY

Whatever your age or interests, there's a whole world of action and relaxation in a Village Holiday, with facilities that include:-
- Children's Adventure Playground and entertainments.
- Licensed Clubhouse, Teen's Disco.
- 2 heated pools, indoor and outdoor.
- Solarium, sauna, gym.
- Launderette, General Store and Barbecue, Cafeteria and Takeaway.
- Horse riding, Pony Trekking, stables, bike hire, plus fishing nearby.

(Some facilities available only at peak times).

The ideal, all-weather, all-year-round holiday for mum, dad and the kids! The Village comprises a 50 acre, well equipped caravan/camping site in beautiful forest surroundings only 8 miles from Bournemouth.
- Pre-bookable pitches.
- 'Super Plots' with plug-in mains electricity and water.
- 6 berth luxury caravans for hire.
- Fully equipped Rent-a-Tent.
- Static holiday homes for sale.

FANTASTIC OFF-PEAK BARGAINS Ask for details!

Village Holidays

I enclose S.A.E. for full details ☐
'Off-Peak' Bargains' ☐   Please Tick

Name _____

Address _____

_____

Village Holidays at Oakdene Holiday Park, Dept.   St. Leonards, Ringwood, Hants. 24 hr Tele-brochure service: 0202 875422.

nr. Bournemouth

Approved by AA
Camping Club of Gt. Britain.
▶▶▶

STNICHOLASATWADE
Kent
Map 5 TR26

▶ 🗓 ❶ △
St Nicholas-at-Wade Camping Site
(TR254672) Court Rd Signposted
☎ Thanet (0843) 81245 Etr–Oct must
book Jul–Aug Last arrival 22.00hrs Last
departure 16.00hrs no caravans

*A small site near an attractive farmhouse
and well secluded by tall hedges. It is
situated in a pleasant country village, off
A299 and A28.*

3acres 75pitches SA 5 🚐 £2.70
70 ▲ £3.20 (awnings) ltr

3🚐 8wc lit all night washbasins hc 🚿 hc ⊙
supervised cold storage childrens
playground calor gas camping gaz 🛢
↩ stables golf ⚓ launderette pub

ST OSYTH
Essex
Map 5 TM11

▶ ▶ 🗓 ❶ △
Hutleys Caravan Park (TM128128) St
Osyth Beach Signposted ☎ Clacton-on-
Sea (0255) 820712 Apr–Sep rs Mar must
book school hols 🏕 no tents

*Situated on St Osyth Marshes, a flat area
overlooking the sea. It has a seashore car
park and picnic area and is on B1027.*

4acres 25pitches 475static 25🚐 or 25 🚐
awnings

90🚐 Individual pitches wc lit all night cdp
🚐 20washbasins hc 🚿 hc ⊙ (wash spin
dry iron) games room TV (cold storage)
licensed bar childrens playground private
beach calor gas cafe restaurant 🛢
↩ stables ⚓ launderette pub

ST OUEN
Jersey, Channel Islands
Map 16

▶ ▶ 🗓 ❸ △
Summer Lodge Camp Site Leoville
Signposted ☎ Jersey (0534) 81921 mid
Apri–20 Sep booking advisable Jun–Aug
Last arrival 21.00hrs Last departure
10.30hrs 🏕 no caravans or motorvans no
single sex groups

Off B55.

5½acres 55pitches 55▲ awnings

3🚐 ⊙ 7wc lit all night washbasins hc
central hot water (🚿 hc) ⊙ supervised
(wash spin dry iron) ➔ (games room) CTV
(cold storage) calor gas camping gaz
toilet fluid cafe restaurant ☎ ⊞
↩ stables golf ⚓ ⚓ launderette pub 🛢

SALCOMBE
Devon
Map 3 SX73

▶ ▶ ▶ 🗓 ❶ △
**Alston Farm Camping & Caravanning
Site** *(SX729409)* Malborough,
Kingsbridge (1½m W of town off A381
towards Malborough) Signposted
☎ Galmpton (0548) 561260 Etr–Sep rs
Oct Last departure noon 🏕

13½acres 270pitches 40static SA
75🚐 fr£3.50 5 🚐 fr£2.50 190 ▲ fr£2.50
(awnings) ltr

18🚐 Individual pitches for caravans ⊙
33wc lit all night 1 cdp washbasins hc
(🚿 hc) ⊙ (iron) calor gas camping gaz
toilet fluid ☎ 🛢
↩ stables golf ⚓ cinema ♦ launderette
pub

SALCOMBE REGIS
Devon
Map 3 SY18

▶ ▶ ▶ 🗓 ❶ △
**Kings Down Tail Caravan & Camping
Site** *(SY173907)* Kings Down Tail Farm
Signposted ☎ Branscombe (029785)
313 15 Mar–15 Nov must book peak
periods Last arrival 22.00hrs Last
departure noon

*Situated on level ground on east side of
Sid Valley in tree-sheltered position.
Opposite Branscombe water tower on
A3052. 3m NE of Sidmouth and 1m W of
junction A3052/B3174.*

5acres 100pitches 2static SA
100 frf4.25 or 100 frf3.75 or
100Afrf4.25 (awnings)

14 late arrivals enclosure 13wc lit all
night 2cdp washbasins hc hc
supervised (spin dry) (games room) (cold
storage) calor gas camping gaz hair
dryers

stables cinema launderette pub

► ► 2 ⊘ ⚠
**Salcombe Regis Caravan & Camping
Site** Signposted Sidmouth (0395)
4303 Etr–Sep must book Last arrival
20.00hrs Last departure 10.00hrs

Pleasant hilltop site bordered by
hedgerows; situated approx 2m from
Sidmouth.

100pitches 10static 40 or 40 60A
(awnings)

9 Individual pitches lit all night 1cdp
washbasins (central hot water) (hc)
(iron) calor gas camping gaz

stables golf cinema launderette
pub

SALISBURY
Wiltshire
Map 4 SU12

► ► ► 2 ⊘ ⚠
Coombe Nurseries Touring Park
(SU108283) Race Plain, Netherhampton
(2m SW off A3094) Signposted (0722)
28451 All year must book public hols &
Jul–Aug Last arrival 23.00hrs Last
departure noon no tents no motorcycles

A level, grass hill-top site adjacent to
racecourse with views over the valley.

3acres 50pitches 50 £4 or 50 £4
(awnings)

4 Individual pitches late arrivals
enclosure 12wc lit all night 2cdp
12washbasins hc 2central hot water 1
(6 hc) 3 supervised (wash spin dry
iron) cold storage childrens playground
calor gas camping gaz toilet fluid
battery charging

stables golf pub

SAMPFORD COURTENAY
Devon
Map 2 SS60

► ► ► 2 ⊘ ⚠
Culverhayes Campsite (SS631019)
Signposted North Tawton (083782)
431 15 Mar–Oct booking advisable Jun–
Aug

Part level, part sloping, grass site set in
meadowland and off A3072.

3½acres 75pitches 75 or 75 or 75A
awnings

8 14wc lit all night 1cdp washbasins
hc central hot water (hc) supervised
(wash dry iron) games room childrens
playground calor gas camping gaz

stables pub

► ► ► 1 ⊘ ⚠
Moorcroft Caravan Park (SX627986)
Belstone Corner, Crediton Rd Signposted
North Tawton (083782) 293 15 Mar–14
Nov booking advisable Jul & Aug Last
arrival mdnt

Pleasant level touring site with grass on
gravel surface, close to Dartmoor and
within easy reach of both coasts. 3½m
from Okehampton on the B3215.

1acre 20pitches 40static 20 £3.50 or
20 £2.50 or 20A£2.50 awnings

3 Individual pitches 5wc lit all night
1cdp washbasins hc (hc)
supervised (wash dry iron) games
room CTV cold storage licensed club/bar
childrens playground calor gas camping
gaz cafe

stables cinema launderette pub

SANDFORD-ON-THAMES
Oxfordshire
Map 4 SP50

► ► 2 ⊘ ⚠
Temple Farm Country Club (SP533018)
Henley Rd Signposted Oxford (0865)
779359 Mar–Oct must book Last
departure noon

2acres 20pitches 12static 20 £3 or
20 £3 or 20A£3 (awnings)

6 late arrivals enclosure 8wc lit all
night 1cdp washbasins hc hc
games room cold storage licensed club/
bar

stables golf cinema launderette
pub

SANQUHAR
Dumfries & Galloway Dumfriesshire
Map 11 NS70

► ► 1 ⊘ ⚠
Castle View Caravan Park (NS786095)
Signposted (06592) 291 Mar–Oct no
bookings Last arrival 22.00hrs Last
departure noon

Small site set behind filling station and
general store on edge of village in Upper
Nithsdale.

2acres 30pitches 15static SA 30 or
30 or 30A (awnings)

2 4wc lit all night 1cdp
washbasins hc (hc) supervised (wash
spin) cold storage calor gas camping gaz
paraffin mobile shop

golf pub

SARACEN'S HEAD (nr Holbeach)
Lincolnshire
Map 8 TF32

► ► ► 2 ⊘ ⚠
Whaplode Manor Caravan Park
(TF341278) Whaplode Manor Signposted
Holbeach (0406) 22837 or 24848 Apr–
Oct

1acre 20pitches SA 20 £3 or 20 £3 or
20A£3 (awnings)

3 4wc lit all night 1cdp washbasins hc
(central hot water) (hc) supervised
games room cold storage childrens
playground calor gas camping gaz

launderette pub

SARNAU
Dyfed
Map 2 SN35

► 2 ⊘ ⚠
Brynawelon Caravan Park (SN319508)
Llangranog (023978) 584 Apr–Oct
booking advisable peak periods Last
arrival 23.00hrs Last departure noon

A level, grassy site within 2m of beach and
400yds from A487 along unclassified
road opposite Sarnau Chapel.

1½acres 20pitches SA 20 £1.75–
£2.50 or 20 £1.75–£2.50 or
20A£1.75–£2.50 awnings

4 Individual pitches late arrivals
enclosure 7wc lit all night 1cdp (central
hot water) (hc) supervised spin cold
storage childrens playground calor gas

SAUNDERSFOOT
Dyfed
Map 2 SN10
See Tenby sketch map

► ► ► 2 ⊘ ⚠
Saundersvale Caravan Park
(SN118055) Valley Rd Mar–Oct must
book Last arrival mdnt Last departure
15.00hrs no caravans

Part level, part sloping grass site with
bushes, set in meadowland. 4m from
Tenby.

    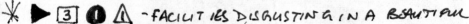 — FACILITIES DISGUSTING IN A BEAUTIFUL SETTING.

4acres 100pitches 61static SA20 🚐 £4 80▲£4ltr

2🚐⊘ wc lit all night 1cdp 4washbasins hc 1central hot water ⚬hc 4🚿hc 2☺ (wash spin dry) iron (games room) cold storage licensed club/bar childrens playground calor gas camping gaz toilet fluid cafe restuarant ☎ 🛒

↔ stables golf ⛳ ☞ launderette pub

SAWLEY
North Yorkshire
Map 8 SE27
▽[2]
Hallgates Farm (SE256671)☎(076586) 275 Apr–Oct booking advisable peak periods

Mainly level field on south side of road out of Sawley towards Fountains Abbey.

1acre 25pitches 5🚐£1 or 5🚐£1 20▲£1 (awnings)
1🚐⊘ 1cdp
↔ stables pub🛒

SCANIPORT
Highland *Inverness-shire*
Map 14 NH63
See Inverness sketch map
▶[1]❶△
Scaniport Caravan Park (NH628398)
May–Sep no bookings Last arrival 20.00hrs Last departure 11.00hrs

A level and grassy site with some trees, set in hills, woodland, moorland and near canal. On B862 Inverness-Foyers road about 5m S of Inverness. Entrance to site is opposite Scaniport Post Office.

2acres 30pitches 15🚐 fr£2.50 or 15🚐 fr£2.50 15▲fr£2.50 awnings
1🚐⊘ 6wc lit all night washbasins hc 🚿hc☺ calor gas camping gaz ☎ 🛒
↔ pub

SCARBOROUGH
North Yorkshire
Map 8 TA08
see also Burniston
See sketch map
▶▶▶[2]❶△
Scalby Manor Caravan & Camping Site (TA025912) Apply to: Department of Tourism & Amenities, Londesborough Lodge, The Crescent, Scarborough YO11 2PW Signposted ☎(0723) 66212
25 Mar–Oct bookings advisable peak periods Last arrival 19.00hrs (21.00hrs Fri & Sat) Last departure noon no unaccompanied under 18's

Level, grass site with mature trees, within walking distance of the cliff top and beach. On A165 Whitby coast road.

20acres 345pitches 270🚐 or 270🚐 75▲ (awnings)

5🚐52wc lit all night 1cdp 40washbasins hc (18🚿hc) 20☺ supervised (wash dry) childrens playground calor gas camping gaz toilet fluid ☎ bicycle hire fish & chip shop🛒
↔ golf ⛳ cinema ☞ launderette pub

▶▶▶[2]❶△
Burniston Road Caravan Site (TA008934) Apply to: Department of Tourism & Amenities, Londesborough Lodge, The Crescent, Scarborough YO11 2PW Signposted ☎(0723) 66212
25 Mar–Sep booking advisable peak periods Last arrival 19.00hrs (21.00hrs Fri & Sat) Last departure noon no unaccompanied under 18's, no tents
4acres 85pitches 85🚐 or 85🚐 (awnings)
3🚐15wc lit all night 1cdp 16washbasins hc (8🚿hc) 4☺ supervised (wash dry) childrens playground calor gas camping gaz toilet fluid ☎ bicycle hire mobile shop
↔ golf ⛳ cinema ☞ launderette pub🛒

SCOLE
Norfolk
Map 5 TM17

▶▶▶ 2 ❷ ⚠
Willows Camping & Caravan Park
(TM139790) Signposted ☎ Diss (0379)
740271 Apr–Sep booking advisable
public & school hols Last arrival 23.00hrs
Last departure 18.00hrs

Level, peaceful site on the banks of the
River Waveney, bordered by willow trees.
Take A143 from Scole to Diss, site 400yds
on left after Scole crossroads.

4acres 45pitches 45 ⊟ £3.75 or
45 ⊟ £3.75 or 45 ▲ £3.75 (awnings)

2 ⚲ Individual pitches late arrivals
enclosure 7wc lit all night 1cdp
washbasins hc central hot water ⌁ hc ☉

supervised spin iron cold storage
childrens playground calor gas camping
gaz paraffin toilet fluid

⟷ stables golf ⟋ launderette pub ⬛

SCILLY, ISLES (No map)
No sites on the islands hold AA
classification. See preface notes at
commencement of this Guide, page 78

SCONE
Tayside *Perthshire*
Map 11 NO12

▶▶▶ 2 ❸ ⚠
Camping Club Site *(NO106273)* Scone
Racecourse Signposted ☎ (0738) 52323

Apr–Sep Mar booking advisable Jul & 14
Aug Last arrival 22.00hrs Last departure
noon

A well sheltered site near to the River Tay
and 2½m north of Perth off A93.

14acres 150pitches 20static 150 ⊟
150 ⊟ 150 ▲ awnings

9 ⚲ ☉ late arrivals enclosure 29wc lit all
night 2cdp washbasins hc ⌁ hc ☉
supervised (wash spin iron) (cold
storage) licensed club/bar childrens
playground calor gas camping gaz toilet
fluid ☎ ⬛

⟷ stables golf ⟋ cinema ⟋ launderette
pub

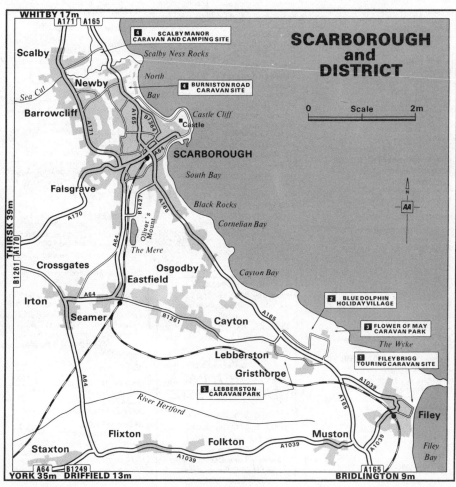

Sites listed under: **1** Filey **2** Gristhorpe Bay **3** Lebberston **4** Scarborough

SCORTON
Lancashire
Map 7 SD54

▶▶▶ 🅘 🕦 △
Six Arches Caravan Site *(SD495494)*
☎Forton (0524) 791683 Jun–Oct rs Mar–
May must book public hols & Jul–Aug
Last arrival 21.00hrs Last departure noon
no tents

*A modern site on mainly level ground with
mature trees and bushes. It gains its name
from the six railway arches at the entrance
crossing the River Wyre.*

1½ acres 30 pitches 280 static 30 🚐 £3.50
or 30 🚐 £3.50 awnings

🏕 Individual pitches wc lit all night 1 cdp
washbasins hc (🚿 hc)☺ (wash spin dry)
iron 🍴 games room CTV (licensed club/
bar) childrens playground calor gas cafe
☎ river fishing 🛒
↔ stables ⛳ launderette pub

SCOTCH CORNER
North Yorkshire
Map 8 NZ20

▶▶▶ 🅘 🕄 △
Scotch Corner Caravan Park
(SD210054) Signposted ☎Richmond
(0748) 2530 & 4424 Etr–mid Oct booking
advisable public hols Last arrival 22.30hrs
Last departure 14.00hrs no
unaccompanied groups of young people

*A level grassy site off A6108 Richmond
road.*

7 acres 60 pitches SA 60 🚐 £4.55 or
60 🚐 £4.05 or 60 🅰 £4.55 (awnings) ltr

9 🏕 Individual pitches 14 wc lit all night
1 cdp 🍴 washbasins hc 🚿 hc ☺
supervised (wash dry iron) cold storage
licensed bar childrens playground calor
gas camping gaz toilet fluid cafe
restaurant ☎ 🛒
↔ stables golf cinema ⛳ launderette pub

SCOURIE
Highland *Sutherland*
Map 14 NC14

▶▶ 🅘 🕄 △
Scourie Caravan & Camping Site
(NC153446) Signposted ☎ (0971) 2217
Apr–Oct Last arrival 22.00hrs Last
departure noon

*Mainly level site adjacent to beach and
sea. In centre of village off the Kylesku–
Laxford road A894.*

4 acres 80 pitches 25 🚐 £3 20 🚐 £3
35 🅰 £3 (awnings) ltr

2 🏕 Individual pitches 10 wc lit all night
1 cdp 16 washbasins hc (4 🚿 hc) 2 ☺
supervised (wash) spin (dry) iron cold
storage cafe restaurant 🛒
↔ 🦮 ⛳ pub

SCRATBY
Norfolk
Map 9 TG51
See Yarmouth (Great) sketch map

▶▶▶ 🄝 🄞 △
Scratby Hall Caravan Park *(TG501155)*
Signposted ☎Great Yarmouth (0493)
730283 Whit–mid Sep rs 21 Mar–Whit &
mid Sep–Oct must book Whit wk & Jul–
Aug Last departure noon no motorcycles
no single sex groups

*This is a quiet, level grass site surrounded
by trees, close to beach and the Norfolk
Broads.*

4½ acres 108 pitches 108 🚐 £1.25–£3.80
or 108 🚐 £1.25–£3.80 or 108 🅰 £1.25–
£3.80 (awnings)

20 🏕 Individual pitches 18 wc lit all night
1 cdp 🍴 14 washbasins hc 10 🚿 hc 3☺
(wash dry iron) games room (cold
storage) calor gas camping gaz toilet fluid
hairdressing salon 🛒
↔ stables golf ⛳ launderette pub

SEDBERGH
Cumbria
Map 7 SD69

▶▶▶ 🄝 🄞 △
Pinfold Caravan Park *(NY665921)*
Signposted ☎ (0587) 20576 Mar–Oct
booking advisable public hols Last arrival
23.00hrs Last departure 10.00hrs

*A mature site set amongst beautiful
scenery on a river bank; at edge of village
on the Hawes road.*

4½ acres 54 pitches 56 static 28 🚐 £3.70
or 28 🚐 £3.70 26 🅰 £3.70 (awnings) ltr

4 🏕 late arrivals enclosure 11 wc lit all
night cdp 🍴 washbasins hc central hot
water (🚿 hc) ☺ supervised (wash dry iron)
(cold storage) calor gas camping gaz 🛒
↔ ⛳ launderette pub

Riverside location.
Facilities for all the family
including indoor swimming
pool.
Plus all the magic of the
Scottish Borders within easy
access.

SELKIRK –
VICTORIA PARK
CARAVAN SITE

... **your holiday centre
in the Scottish Borders**

For details, write:
Dept AA,
Victoria Park Caravan Site,
PO Box 4, Paton Street,
Galashiels, TD1 3AS

SELKIRK
Borders *Selkirkshire*
Map 12 NT42

▶▶ 🄝 🄞 △
Victoria Park Caravan Park *(NT465287)*
Buccleuch Rd Apply to: Ettrick and
Lauderdale District Council, Park
Superintendant, Paton St, Galashiels,
Selkirkshire Apr–Oct

*Site forms part of public park and
swimming pool complex close to river
Ettrick.*

50 pitches 50 🚐 ✳ £2.50–£3 or
50 🅰 £2.50–£3 awnings ltr

4 🏕 10 wc lit all night washbasins hc
central hot water 🚿 hc ☺ (wash spin iron)
games room cold storage childrens
playground
↔ stables golf 🦮 ⛳ pub 🛒

SEVERN BEACH
Avon
Map 3 ST58

▶ 🄝 🄞 △
Villa Caravan Park ☎Pilning (04545)
2540 Mar–Oct booking advisable peak
periods Last arrival 22.00hrs

*A level, grassy site set within 5m of
motorways, with the cities of Bristol and
Bath to the E and the Severn Road Bridge
to the NW. Exit 21 (M4) from NE and Wales,
Exit 18 (M5) from SW.*

2½ acres 25 pitches 75 static 10 🚐 £2.75
5 🚐 £2.50 10 🅰 £2.75 (awnings)

🏕 late arrivals enclosure 17 wc 1 cdp
(washbasins hc central hot water) (🚿 hc)
☺ (wash) childrens playground calor gas
camping gaz 🛒
▶ pub

▶ 🄝 🄞 △
Salthouse Farm Caravan Site
(ST543854) Signposted ☎Pilning
(04545) 2274 Apr–Sep Last arrival
22.00hrs Last departure 14.00hrs

*Level, grass site with trees and bushes set
in meadowland close to beach, river and
Severn estuary at Avonmouth, close to
B4054.*

½ acre 10 pitches 80 static SA 10 🚐 £2.75
or 10 🚐 £2.75 or 10 🅰 £2.75 awnings ltr

6 🏕 Individual pitches 14 wc 1 cdp
12 washbasins hc 2 central hot water
4 🚿 hc 3☺ (cold storage) childrens
playground calor gas camping gaz
paraffin ☎ 🛒
↔ stables pub

SHANKLIN
Isle of Wight
Map 4 SZ58
See sketch map on page 233

▶▶▶▶ 🄝 🄞 △
Lower Hyde Leisure Park *(SZ575819)*
Lower Hyde Rd Signposted ☎ (0983)
866131 20 Mar–Oct booking advisable
Jul & Aug Last arrival mdnt Last departure
noon no pets no single sex groups

*Part of a holiday complex, site is on a
sloping area with some level ground.*

10acres120pitches122static40♨£7.30
40♥£7.3040▲£7.30awnings
13♫⊘latearrivalsenclosure26wclitall
night2cdpwashbasinshccentralhot
water♨hc☺supervised(wash)(dry)iron
⌸(♪gamesroom)TVcoldstorage
licensedclub/barchildrensplayground
calorgascampinggaztoiletfluidcafe☎
pitch&puttentertainmentnightly🍴
↔stablesgolfcinema✈launderettepub
▶▶①❶⚠
NinhamCamping & CaravanningPark
*(SZ578824)*Signposted☎(0983)
864243or86204926May–6SeprsApr–
25May&7–15Sepbookingadvisable25

Jul–7AugLastarrival22.00hrsLast
departure18.00hrsnopets
Level, grass site with young trees and
bushes set in downland and
meadowland, near to sea, beach and
lake. Signed from A3056 via White Cross
Lane.
18acres130pitches130♨£4.50
130♥£4.50130▲£4.50awnings
24♫latearrivalsenclosure22wclitall
night1cdp♨washbasinshc(♨hc)☺
supervised(washspindry)ironTV(cold

storage)childrensplaygroundcalorgas
campinggaztoiletfluid☎grassskiing
coarsefishingvideostudio🍴
↔stablesgolf✈cinema✈launderette
pub

SHELFORD,GREAT
Cambridgeshire
Map5TL45

▶▶▶②❸⚠
CampingClubSite*(TL455539)*torearof
212CambridgeRdSignposted
☎Cambridge(0223)841185Apr–Sep
bookingadvisableSpringBankHol&Jul–
AugLastarrival21.00hrsLastdeparture
16.00hrs   →

12acres 100pitches 100⊞✳£5.90 or
100⊞£5.90 or 100▲£5.90

5⅋late arrivals enclosure 17wc lit all night
2cdp⊞ washbasins hc🛁hc☉
supervised (wash dry iron) cal or gas
camping gaz☎🛒
↩stables golf✚cinema♪launderette
pub

SHEPTON MALLET
Somerset
Map 3 ST64

▶①❶⚠
Manleaze Caravan Park *(ST625423)*
Cannards Grave ☎(0749) 2404 All year
booking advisable Jun–Aug

A level, grass site 1m S of Shepton Mallet
on A371.

¾acre 25pitches 6static 25⊞£2.70 or
25⊞£2.70 or 25▲£2.70 (awnings)
3⅋4wc lit all night 1cdp (🛁hc)☉
supervised cold storage cal or gas
camping gaz toilet fluid cafe ☎🛒
↩stables golf launderette pub

SHIEL BRIDGE
Highland *Ross and Cromarty*
Map 14 NG91

▶①❶⚠
Shiel Bridge Caravan Site *(NG938185)*
Dochgarroch ☎Glenshiel (059981) 221
May–Sep no bookings Last arrival
20.00hrs Last departure 11.00hrs

Shelford (Great)
_
Sidcot

Level grass and gravel site, set in
mountainous country with access to sea,
beach and river estuary. 15m from Kyle of
Lochalsh.

2½acres 65pitches 40⊞fr£3.50 or
40⊞fr£3.50 25▲fr£3.50 awnings
4⅋8wc lit all night 1cdp washbasins hc
🛁hc☉cal or gas camping gaz cafe🛒
↩♪pub

SHOTTISHAM
Suffolk
Map 5 TM34

▶②❷
St Margaret's Guest House *(TM323447)*
Signposted ☎(0394) 411247 Apr–Oct
must book public & school hols Last arrival
22.30hrs Last departure noon

Level, grass and sand site with trees and
bushes set in wood, moor and
meadowland, adjacent to River Deben
estuary with sea and beach to east. Turn
south on to B1083 at roundabout junction
A1152/B1083 near Wilford Bridge.

1½acres 25pitches 15⊞£2 10⊞£2
10▲£2–£2.20 (awnings)
2⅋Individual pitches ☉4wc lit all night
1cdp washbasins hc (🛁hc)☉supervised
cold storage childrens playground cal or

---

gas camping gaz🛒
↩golf♪pub

SHRAWLEY
Hereford & Worcester
Map 3 SO86

▶▶②❷⚠
Lenchford Caravan Park *(SO812638)*
☎Worcester (0905) 620246 Mar–Oct rs
Nov–Feb must book public hols Last
arrival 22.30hrs Last departure noon no
motorcycles no single sex groups

Level, grass site with trees and bushes,
set in meadowland close to River Severn;
7m N of Worcester on B4196 Stourport
road and 1m S of Shrawley.

2acres 15pitches 60static 15⊞£4 or
15⊞£4 or 15▲£4 (awnings) ltr
4⅋9wc 1cdp washbasins hc central hot
water 🛁hc☉supervised (wash dry iron)
games room TV childrens playground
restaurant ☎
↩stables✚♪pub🛒

SIDCOT
Avon
Map 3 ST45
See Cheddar sketch map

▶②❶⚠
**Netherdale Caravan & Camping
Ground** *(ST428574)* Bridgwater Rd
Signposted ☎Winscombe (093 484)

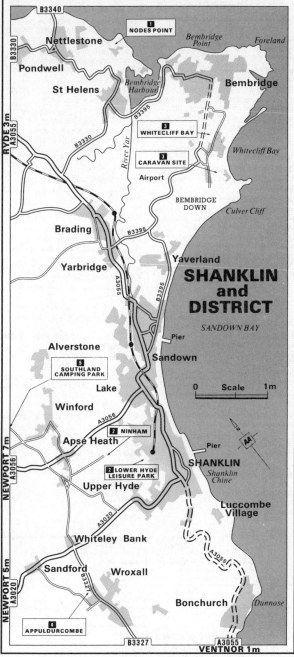

Roads shown as broken are not suitable for towing caravans

Sites listed under: **1** St Helens **2** Shanklin **3** Whitecliff Bay
4 Wroxall **5** Newchurch

3481 Mar–Oct booking advisable public hols Last arrival 22.00hrs Last departure noon

An elevated and wooded site alongside main road (A38).

2acres 30pitches 36static 30 £3.35 or 30 £3.35 or 30 £3.35 (awnings) ltr

8 12wc lit all night 1cdp (central hot water) (hc) supervised (spin) cold storage childrens playground calor gas camping gaz

stables launderette pub

SILECROFT
Cumbria
Map 6 SD18

Silecroft Caravan Site *(SD124811)*
Millom (0657) 2659 Mar–Oct must book public hols & Jul–Aug Last arrival 22.00hrs Last departure noon no dogs

A quietly situated site close to the shore, near the small village of Silecroft, 4N of Millom.

5acres 60pitches 120static 45 £3.40 or 45 £2.80 15 £2.80 awnings ltr

10 Individual pitches 36wc lit all night 1cdp washbasins hc hc supervised

stables golf cinema launderette pub

SILLOTH
Cumbria
Map 11 NY15

Stanwix Park Holiday Centre
(NY097526)(1m SW on B5300)
Signposted (0965) 31671 Etr–Oct booking advisable 14 Jul–12 Aug Last arrival 22.30hrs Last departure 11.00hrs

Family camp site within easy reach of the Lake District National Park and beaches.

4acres 107pitches 186static
107 fr£3.50 or 107 fr£3.50 or 107 fr£3.50 (awnings)

38 Individual pitches late arrivals enclosure 19wc lit all night 2cdp washbasins hc (hc hc) supervised (wash spin dry iron) games room TV (cold storage) licensed club/bar childrens playground calor gas camping gaz toilet fluid cafe restaurant

stables golf launderette

Tanglewood Caravan Park *(NY131534)*
Causewayhead Signposted (0965) 31253 Etr–Oct booking advisable public hols & last wk Jul–first wk Aug Last arrival 23.00hrs Last departure noon

Mainly level, grass site sheltered by a variety of trees and bushes; set in meadowland adjacent to B5302 Wigton–Silloth road.

2acres 31pitches 41static 21 £4 or 21 £4 10 £4 (awnings) ltr

5 12wc 2cdp washbasins hc (central hot water) (hc) supervised (wash dry) iron games room TV (cold storage) →

licensed club/bar childrens playground calor gas camping gaz ☎ battery charging 🛢
↔ stables golf ⚑ launderette pub

SILSDEN
West Yorkshire
Map 7 SE04

▶ 🗓 ❶ Ⓐ
Dales Bank Holiday Park *(SE036483)*
Low Lane (1m NW on unclass rd)
Signposted ☎ Steeton (0535) 53321
Good Fri–Oct booking advisable Jun–Aug Last departure 16.00hrs

Simple site set in open countryside of typical Dales scenery.

5½acres 72pitches 52 🛏 £3 or 52 🚐 £3 20▲£3 (awnings) ltr

7🏕 Individual pitches ◔ late arrivals enclosure 11wc lit all night 1cdp washbasins hc central hot water 🗋 hc ☺ supervised games room licensed club/bar childrens playground calor gas cafe restaurant
↔ golf ⚒ ⚑ launderette pub 🛢

SILVERDALE
Lancashire
Map 7 SD47
See Morecambe sketch map

▶ ▶ ▶ 🗓 ❷ Ⓐ
Holgate's Caravan Park *(SD455762)*
Cove Rd Signposted ☎ (0524) 701508
Mar–6 Nov must book school & public hols Last arrival 22.30hrs Last departure 16.00hrs no single sex groups

Partly level, partly sloping, grass and gravel site with mature trees and bushes. Set in woodland country overlooking Morecambe Bay, adjacent to sea and beach. 5m NW of Carnforth on A6.

7acres 70pitches 350static 50 🛏 £3.25–£5.75 or 50 🚐 £3.25–£5.75 20▲£3.25–£5.75 (awnings) Ltr

7🏕 Individual pitches late arrivals enclosure 76wc lit all night 4cdp 🟦 76washbasins hc (24🗋 hc) 4☺ supervised (wash dry iron) ⏛ (games room) (cold storage) children's playground calor gas camping gaz toilet fluid cafe ☎ 🖼 🛢
↔ stables golf ⚑ launderette pub

Silloth
—
Slapton

SKEGNESS
Lincolnshire
Map 9 TF56

▶ ▶ ▶ 🗓 ❷ Ⓐ
Richmond Drive Carapark *(TF559625)*
Signposted ☎ (0754) 2097 Spring Bank Hol–mid Sep rs 15 Mar–Spring Bank Hol & mid Sep–Oct booking advisable public hols & mid Jul–Aug Last arrival 23.00hrs Last departure 18.00hrs no tents

Level, grass site with young trees, set in meadowland, near to sandy beach and dunes, off A52.

12acres 200pitches 700static 200 🛏 £2.50–£3.20 or 200 🚐 £2.50–£3.20 (awnings)

23🏕 Individual pitches 121wc lit all night 3cdp (🟦) 45 washbasins hc (3central hot water 13🗋 hc) 6☺ (wash dry iron) licensed club/bar childrens playground calor gas camping gaz toilet fluid cafe ☎ paddling pool childrens room entertainment & dancing nightly end May–mid Sep 🛢 launderette
↔ stables golf ⚒ cinema ⚑

SKELWITH BRIDGE (near Ambleside)
Cumbria
Map 7 NY30
See Windermere sketch map

▶ ▶ ▶ 🗓 ❶ Ⓐ
Neaum Crag Camping & Caravan Site *(NY342039)* Signposted ☎ Ambleside (09663) 3221 Mar–16 Nov must book Last arrival 22.00hrs Last departure 11.00hrs no animals

An extensive site of enclosed fell and woodland.

8acres 80pitches 33static 38 🛏 or 38 🚐 40▲ awnings ltr

6🏕 Individual pitches for caravans 4wc lit all night 4cdp 12washbasins hc 6central hot water 7🗋 hc 7☺ supervised cold storage calor gas camping gaz ☎ 🖼 🛢
↔ stables ⚒ cinema ⚑ launderette pub

SKIPSEA
Humberside
Map 8 TA15

▶ ▶ ▶ 🗓 ❷ Ⓐ
Low Skirlington Caravan Site
(TA188528) Signposted ☎ (026 286) 213 Mar–Oct must book

Part level, part sloping, grass site with young trees and bushes, set in meadowland adjacent to sea and beach 3m N of Hornsea on B1242.

15acres 285pitches 400static SA 285 🛏 or 285 🚐 or 285▲ (awnings) ltr

🏕 Individual pitches ◔ wc lit all night 2cdp 🟦 washbasins hc ↔hc 🗋 hc ☺ supervised (wash spin dry iron) games room TV (cold storage) licensed club/bar childrens playground private beach calor gas camping gaz toilet fluid cafe restaurant ☎ 🛢
↔ stables golf ⚒ ⚑ launderette pub

SKIPTON
North Yorkshire
Map 7 SD95

▶ ▶ ▶ 🗓 ❶ Ⓐ
Overdale Trailer Park (SD997526)
Harrogate Rd Signposted ☎ (0756) 3480 Feb–Dec booking advisable peak periods Last arrival 22.00hrs Last departure noon no tents →

Mainly level grassy site surrounded by trees and bushes situated ½m from the centre of Skipton on the A59 Harrogate road. Caravans are parked on a tarmac area.

3acres 20pitches 172static 20 🛏 or 20 🚐 (awnings) ltr

13🏕 Individual pitches late arrivals enclosure 45wc lit all night 3cdp 🟦 washbasins hc (↔hc 🗋 hc) ☺ supervised (wash spin dry iron) games room CTV cold storage childrens playground calor gas toilet fluid ☎ 🛢
↔ stables golf ⚒ cinema ⚑ launderette pub

SKYE, ISLE OF
Highland *Inverness-shire*
Map 13 NG
See Camustianavaig, Dunvegan, Edinbane and Staffin

SLAPTON
Devon
Map 3 SX84

▶▶ ③ ❶ ⚠
Camping Club Site *(SX826447)* Middle
Grounds ☎ Kingsbridge (0548) 580538
Apr–Oct must book Etr, Whit & Jul–Aug
Last arrival 20.00hrs Last departure noon

*The site overlooks Start Bay within a few
minutes walk of the beach.*

5½ acres 140 pitches 8♥ 132♥ or 132▲
awnings

4 🌤 Individual pitches 12 wc lit all night
1 cdp washbasins hc 🔥 hc ☺ supervised
(spin) childrens playground calor gas
camping gaz ☎ (hair dryer) 🍴
↻ stables ⚒ ✦ ⚒ pub

SLIMBRIDGE
Gloucestershire
Map 3 SO70

▶▶▶ ① ❶ ⚠
Tudor Arms Caravan Site *(SO728040)*
Shepherds Patch Signposted
☎ Cambridge (045 389) 483 All year
booking advisable public & school hols
Last arrival 23.00hrs Last departure
13.00hrs no groups of young people

*Level, grass and gravel site with trees and
bushes, set in meadowland, adjacent to
canal, off A38. Nearby is the Wildlife Trust.*

7½ acres 75 pitches SA 35♥ or
35♥ £4.55 50▲ £4.30 (awnings) ltr

6 🌤 12 wc lit all night 1 cdp ♥ (washbasins
hc) (🔥 hc) ☺ supervised iron (cold
storage) licensed club/bar calor gas
camping gaz toilet fluid cafe restaurant 🍴
↻ ✦ launderette pub

SLINGSBY
North Yorkshire
Map 8 SE67

▶ ② ❶ ⚠
Camping Club Site Railway Street
(SE699755) ☎ Hovingham (065382) 355

Slapton
—
Snape

end Mar–Sep booking advisable public
hols & Jul–Aug Last arrival 18.00hrs Last
departure noon

3 acres 70 pitches 70♥ £4.90 or
70♥ £4.90 or 70▲ £4.20 awnings

7 🌤 Individual pitches late arrivals
enclosure 7 wc lit all night 1 cdp ♥
washbasins hc 🔥 hc ☺ supervised calor
gas camping gaz toilet fluid ☎
↻ stables ✦ pub

▶▶ ② ❶ ⚠
**Green Dyke Camping Site & Robin
Hood Caravan Park** *(SE701748)* Green
Dyke Ln ☎ Hovingham (065382) 391
Apr–Oct booking advisable Whit & Jul–
Aug Last arrival 22.30hrs Last departure
15.00hrs

*A small quiet site on the edge of the village,
developed from a shallow, disused, well
grassed quarry/gravel pit.*

2 acres 30 pitches 2 static 10♥ £3.50–£4
20♥ £3.50–£4 or 20▲ £3.50–£4
(awnings) ltr

4 🌤 5 wc lit all night 2 cdp (5 washbasins
hc) (2🔥 hc) (2☺) supervised iron (cold
storage) childrens playground calor gas
camping gaz 🍴
↻ stables ✦ pub

SMITHALEIGH
Devon
Map 2 SX55

▶▶▶ ② ❶ ⚠
Smithaleigh Caravan & Camping Park
(SX585554) Signposted ☎ Ivybridge
(07554) 3194 & Plymouth (0752) 332000
15 Mar–15 Nov booking advisable public
hols & Jul–Aug

6 acres 50 pitches 30♥ £3.50 or

30♥ £3.50 20▲ £3.50 (awnings)

6 🌤 late arrivals enclosure 9 wc lit all night
1 cdp ♥ washbasins hc (🔥 hc) ☺
supervised (wash spin dry iron) (cold
storage) childrens playground calor gas
camping gaz ☎ 🍴
↻ stables launderette pub

see advertisement on page 206

SNAINTON
North Yorkshire
Map 8 SE98

▶▶ ② ❶ ⚠
Jasmin Site *(SE928813)* Low Rd
Signposted ☎ Scarborough (0723)
85240 Mar–Oct must book public hols &
Jul–Aug Last arrival 21.00hrs Last
departure noon no motorcycles

*Level, grass site with trees and hedges in
rural setting. 1m off A170 Pickering–
Scarborough road; turn off opposite
school into Barker Lane.*

5 acres 70 pitches SA 50♥ or 50♥ 20▲
(awnings) ltr

6 🌤 Individual pitches ☺ late arrivals
enclosure 14 wc lit all night 1 cdp
(washbasins hc) central hot water (🔥 hc)
☺ supervised (spin) cold storage calor
gas
↻ stables pub 🍴

SNAPE
North Yorkshire
Map 8 SE28

▽ ①
Castle Arms *(SE267845)* ☎ Bedale
(0677) 70270 All year booking advisable
during club meetings

Level paddock at rear of village inn.

1 acre 5 pitches 5♥ £1 or 5♥ £1 or 5▲ £1
awnings

1 🌤 licensed club/bar childrens
playground ☎ 🍴
→

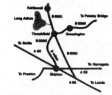

↩ stables golf ⚟ launderette pub

SOURTON DOWN
Devon
Map 2 SX59

▶▶▶ ① ❷ ⚠
Griggs Prewley Caravan Site
(SX546916) Signposted ☎ Bridestowe
(083786) 349 15 Mar–15 Nov booking
advisable Jul–Sep

*Adjacent to junction A30/A386. This site is
on the border of the Dartmoor National
Park having fine views.*

4 acres 52 pitches 43🚐 or 43 🚐 or 52 🛆
(awnings)
4♨⊘ late arrivals enclosure 15 wc lit all
night 1 cdp 🚰 (washbasins hc central hot
water 🛁 hc) ⊙ (wash spin) iron ⊟ cold
storage childrens playground calor gas
camping gaz off license ▤
↩ stables golf cinema ⚟ pub

SOUTH BRENT
Devon
Map 3 SX66

▶▶▶ ③ ❷ ⚠
Great Palstone Caravan Park
(SX717603) Signposted ☎ (03647) 2227
mid Mar–mid Nov booking advisable Last
arrival 20.00 hrs Last departure noon no
groups of young persons

*Site is situated 1 m from South Brent in
open countryside on the edge of Dartmoor
National Park.*

5½ acres 50 pitches 50🚐 £3–£4 or
50 🚐 £3–£4 or 50🛆 £3–£4 (awnings) ltr
2♨⊘ late arrivals enclosure 12 wc lit all
night 1 cdp washbasins hc 🛁 hc ⊙
supervised (wash dry iron games room
cold storage) calor gas camping gaz ▤
↩ stables golf ⚟ launderette pub

SOUTH CAVE
Humberside
Map 8 SE93

▶ ② ❷ ⚠
Waudby's Caravan Site (SE928301)
Brough Rd Signposted ☎ North Cave
(04302) 2523 Apr–Oct booking advisable
public hols

*Previously part of a productive farm with
adjoining outbuilding now converted to
camping, adjacent to A63.*

2 acres 15 pitches 15🚐 £2–£2.50 or
15 🚐 £2–£2.50 🛆 £2–£2.50 awnings ltr
4♨ Individual pitches 5 wc lit all night
1 cdp 🚰 washbasins hc central hot water
🛁 hc ⊙ supervised childrens playground
calor gas camping gaz paraffin toilet fluid
☎ fishing ▤
↩ stables golf ⚟ pub

SOUTH CERNEY
Gloucestershire
Map 4 SU09

▶▶▶▶ ② ❷ ⚠
Cotswold Caravan Park (SU055958)
Broadway Ln Signposted ☎ Cirencester
(0285) 860216 mid May–Sep rsEtr–mid

May must book Last arrival 19.00 hrs Last
departure 10.00 hrs no single sex groups

*A large holiday centre on flat grassy
ground and adjoining the Cotswold Water
Park.*

304 pitches 60 static 304🚐 or 304 🚐 or
304 🛆 awnings ltr
♨ Individual pitches late arrivals
enclosure wc lit all night 6 cdp 🚰
washbasins hc central hot water (🛁 hc) ⊙
supervised (wash) (dry iron) ⊟ & ⊿ (🌣)
games room CTV licensed club/bar
childrens playground calor gas camping
gaz cafe restaurant ☎ crazy golf ▤
↩ stables ⚒ cinema ⚟ launderette pub

SOUTHERNESS
Dumfries & Galloway *Dumfriesshire*
Map 11 NX95

▶▶▶ ② ❷ ⚠
Southerness Holiday Village
(NX976545) Signposted ☎ Kirkbean
(038788) 281, 278 & 256 Mar–Oct

*A large campsite situated in close
proximity to sandy beach.*

8 acres 250 pitches 400 static
150🚐 £2.75–£3.75 50 🚐 £2.75–£3.75
50🛆 £2.75–£3.75 (awnings) ltr
11♨ Individual pitches ⊘ late arrivals
enclosure 44 wc lit all night 🚰 washbasins
hc 🛁 hc ⊙ (wash spin dry iron) (games
room) cold storage childrens playground
private beach calor gas camping gaz
toilet fluid cafe restaurant ☎ ▤
↩ golf ⚟ launderette pub

SOUTH SHIELDS
Tyne and Wear
Map 12 NZ36

▶ ① ❶ ⚠
Lizard Lane Caravan & Camping Site
(NZ401647) Apply to: South Tyneside

Griggs Prewley
CARAVAN and CAMPING PARK
At junction of A30/A386
Mr. D. Wilson & Mr. M. Taylor
SOURTON CROSS,
OKEHAMPTON, DEVON
Bridestowe 349

1 Picturesque Secluded Park
2 Flush Toilets
3 H&C Showers
4 H&C Washbasins
5 Swimming Pool
6 Laundry Room
7 Site Shop
8 Pony Trekking Arranged
9 Dartmoor Walks
10 Fishing Nearby
11 Inns within walking distance
12 South and north coasts within 40 minutes drive
13 Electrical hook-up points available

Borough Council, Cultural & Leisure
Activities, Central Library Building,
Catherine St, South Shields, Tyne & Wear
☎ 553405 (nightly bookings) & (0632)
557411 (for wkly bookings) Etr–Oct Last
arrival 19.00 hrs Last departure 10.00 hrs

*Sloping, grass site near sea and beach,
2 m S of town centre on A183 Sunderland
road.*

3 acres 45 pitches 10 static 45🚐 or 45 🚐
or 45🛆 (awnings) ltr
15♨ 14 wc 1 cdp washbasins hc central
hot water 🛁 hc ⊙ supervised dry calor gas
camping gaz toilet fluid ☎ ▤
↩ stables golf cinema ⚟ launderette pub

STAFFIN
Isle of Skye, Highland *Inverness-shire*
Map 13 NG46

▶▶ ② ❶ ⚠
Staffin Caravan & Camping Site
(NG496668) Signposted ☎ (047 062)
213 Apr–Sep rs Oct booking advisable Jul
& Aug Last arrival 22.00 hrs Last departure
11.00 hrs

*Level and gently sloping, gravel, grass
and sand site with young trees and
bushes, set in hilly downland and
meadowland, adjacent to sea, beach and
river. 15 m N of Portree on A855.*

83 pitches 6 static SA 20🚐 £2.50
20 🚐 £2.50 43🛆 £2.50 (awnings) ltr
5♨ Individual pitches ⊘ late arrivals
enclosure 8 wc lit all night 1 cdp
washbasins hc 🛁 hc ⊙ supervised cold
storage childrens playground private
beach calor gas camping gaz cafe
restaurant mobile shop ▤
↩ ⚒ ⚟

STAINFORTH
North Yorkshire
Map 7 SD86

▶▶▶ ② ❷ ⚠
*Knight Stainforth Hall Caravan & Camp
Site* (SD816672) Signposted ☎ Settle
(07292) 2200 Mar–Oct booking
advisable public hols & Jul–Aug Last
arrival 22.00 hrs Last departure noon no
persons under 18 unless accompanied
by an adult

*Site is located in the Yorkshire Dales
National Park in a rural setting adjacent to
river.*

6 acres 100 pitches 60 static 35🚐 £3 or
35 🚐 £2.75 65🛆 £3 (awnings) ltr
11♨ 24 wc lit all night 2 cdp 13 washbasins
hc (8🛁 hc) ⊙ supervised (wash dry) iron
(games room) CTV cold storage childrens
playground calor gas camping gaz toilet
fluid ☎ ▤
↩ stables golf ⚟ pub

STAMFORD BRIDGE
Humberside
Map 8 SE75

▶▶▶ ② ❷ ⚠
Weir Caravan Park (SE713557)
☎ (0759) 71377 Apr–Oct Last arrival

22.30hrs Last departure noon no unaccompanied youths

Slightly sloping grass site near urban area and River Derwent. 50yds off A166 on entering village from York.

2acres 60pitches 108static 60⚑ ✳£4.30 or 60⚑ £4.30 or 60▲£4.30 awnings

🐾wc lit all night ⊞ washbasins hc (🕳hc 🔥hc)☉ (wash spin iron) games room childrens playground calor gas camping gaz toilet fluid ☎ boats for hire fishing 🎣 ↔ 🍴 launderette pub

STANDLAKE
Oxfordshire
Map 4 SP30

▶▶ 🗓 ❶
Standlake Caravans *(SP395028)* Lincoln Farm, High St Signposted ☎(086 731) 239 Apr–Oct booking advisable public hols & Jul–Aug Last arrival 22.00hrs Last departure noon

This level grass site is situated in a quiet Oxfordshire village on the A415.

4acres 80pitches 40⚑ £2.75 30 ⚑ £2.75 10▲£2.75 (awnings)

3🐾 late arrivals enclosure 10wc lit all night 1cdp ⊞ washbasins hc central hot water 🔥hc☉ (/∅) cold storage childrens playground calor gas camping gaz toilet fluid 🔥 private lake for fishing and swimming 🎣 ↔ stables 🎣 launderette pub

STANLEY
Co Durham
Map 12 NZ15

▶ 🗓 ❷ 🔺
Harperley Country Caravan Park *(NZ176532)* Harperley, Tanfield Lea (2m NW B6173) Signposted ☎(0207) 34168 Apr–Oct Last arrival 23.00

A small neat site adjoining an attractive Country Park situated 2m NW of the town in the village of Tanfield Lea.

½acre 70pitches 20static 20⚑ £4 or 20 ⚑ £4 50▲£2.80–£3.50 (awnings) ltr

4🐾∅ 7wc lit all night washbasins hc☉ supervised (wash) childrens playground calor gas camping gaz ☎ ↔ golf pub

STARCROSS
Devon
Map 3 SX98

▶▶▶ 🗓 🔺
Cofton Farm Caravan Park *(SX967801)* Signposted ☎(0626) 890358 15 Mar–Oct must book Jul & Aug Last arrival 20.00hrs

---

Partly level and sloping grass site 1m S of Starcross on A379.

16acres 355pitches 60static 355⚑ ✳£3.40–£4.40 or 355 ⚑ £3.40–£4.20 or 355▲£3.40–£4.20 (awnings)

14🐾 Individual pitches ⊘ late arrivals enclosure 72wc lit all night 1cdp ⊞ washbasins hc central hot water 10🔥hc ☉ (wash spin dry iron) (games room) cold storage childrens playground calor gas camping gaz toilet fluid ☎ 🎣 ↔ golf 🎣 pub

see advertisement on page 125

STAVELEY
Cumbria
Map 7 SD49

▶▶▶▶ 🗓 ❷ 🔺
Ashes Lane Caravan & Camping Park *(NY478962)* Ashes Ln Signposted ☎(0539) 821119 Etr–13 Nov rs Mar–Etr booking advisable public hols & late Jun–early Sep Last departure noon

Large site set in natural lakeland scenery.

17acres 300pitches 50static 100⚑ £5.10 or 100 ⚑ £4.30 200▲£5 (awnings) ltr

10🐾∅ late arrivals enclosure 60wc lit all night 2cdp 60 washbasins hc central hot water 🕳hc 🔥hc☉ supervised (wash spin) (iron) (games room) CTV (cold storage licensed club/bar) childrens playground calor gas camping gaz toilet fluid cafe restaurant ☎ ⊞ 🎣 ↔ stables golf 🎣 cinema 🎣 launderette pub

see advertisement on page 261

STICKER
Cornwall
Map 2 SW95
See St Austell sketch map

▶▶ 🗓 ❶ 🔺
Glenleigh Caravan Park *(SW975501)* Grampound Rd Signposted ☎ St Austell (0726) 65633 Apr–Oct rs Nov–Mar must book Jul–Sep Last departure 10.00hrs

Level grass site with mature trees and bushes, on A390, 3m W of St Austell.

3½acres 40pitches 40static SA 40⚑ £2– £3.85 or 40 ⚑ £2–£3.85 or 40▲£2–£3.85 (awnings)

7🐾 12wc lit all night 1cdp washbasins hc (🔥hc)☉ supervised iron (cold storage) childrens playground calor gas camping gaz ☎ 🎣 ↔ stables golf 🎣 cinema 🎣 launderette pub

---

STICKLEPATH
Devon
Map 2 SX69

▶▶▶ 🗓 ❷ 🔺
Coombe Head Farm *(SX626951)* Signposted ☎(083 784) 323 15 Mar–Oct booking advisable Jul & Aug

Level grass site with bushes set in moorland and meadowland, 2m from Okehampton on A30.

6½acres 40pitches 20static 40⚑ ✳£4 or 40 ⚑ £4 or 40▲£4 awnings ltr

5🐾 late arrivals enclosure 7wc lit all night 1cdp washbasins hc (🔥hc)☉ supervised (wash dry iron)⊠ (games room) TV (cold storage) licensed club/bar childrens playground calor gas camping gaz toilet fluid restaurant ☎ 🎣 ↔ stables golf cinema 🎣 launderette pub

▶▶ 🗓 ❶ 🔺
Olditch Farm Caravan Park Olditch Caravan Park Signposted ☎(083 784) 734
14 Mar–14 Nov booking advisable Jul & Aug

Partly level and partly sloping site with trees and bushes set in Dartmoor National Park. ½m E of village on A30; 3m from Okehampton.

2¾acres 45pitches 7static 45⚑ £4 or 45 ⚑ £3.75 or 45▲£3.50 (awnings) ltr

🐾 late arrivals enclosure 12wc lit all night 1cdp ⊞ washbasins hc 🔥hc☉ supervised (dry iron) games room CTV (cold storage) licensed bar childrens playground calor gas camping gaz cafe restaurant 🎣 ↔ stables 🎣 pub

STIRLING
Central *Stirlingshire*
Map 11 NS79

▶▶ 🗓 ❶ 🔺
Cornton Caravan Park *(NS786952)* Signposted ☎(0786) 4503 Apr–Oct rs Nov–Mar Last arrival 21.30hrs Last departure noon

This is a level, grass site situated on the outskirts of the town and near to the main road. Some nearby housing development is apparent but splendid views are obtained of both Stirling and the Wallace Monument.

1½acres 40pitches 17static 16⚑ £3.80 or 16 ⚑ £3.60 24▲£3.80 (awnings)

3🐾∅ 13wc lit all night 1cdp ⊞ washbasins hc 🔥hc☉ supervised (wash spin dry iron) (cold storage) childrens playground calor gas camping gaz toilet fluid ☎ 🎣 ↔ stables golf cinema 🎣 launderette pub

---

STOKE FLEMING
Devon
Map 3 SX84

▶▶▶ ② ❷ ⚠

Deer Park Holiday Estate *(SX864493)*
Signposted ☎ (080427) 253 15 May–Oct
must book peak periods Last arrival
20.00hrs Last departure noon

*Level, grass and gravel site with young
trees, set in hilly meadowland, near to sea,
beach, river and Start Bay.*

6acres 140pitches 30static 20🚐 £5
20🚐 £4.50 or 120▲£4.50 (awnings)

5♿ Individual pitches 17wc lit all night
2cdp washbasins hc (🛁 hc)☉ (wash dry
iron) games room (cold storage) licensed
club/bar childrens playground calor gas
camping gaz cafe restaurant ☎ 🛒
↔ stables 🛒 cinema ♪ launderette pub
see advertisement on page 125

STOKE GABRIEL
Devon
Map 3 SX85
See Paignton sketch map

▶▶▶ ② ❷ ⚠

Ramslade Holiday Park *(SX861592)*
Stoke Rd Signposted ☎ (080428) 575
15 Mar–15 Nov booking advisable peak
season 🏃 in peak season no single sex
groups

*This site is situated in the South Devon
countryside, between Paignton and the
picturesque village of Stoke Gabriel on the
River Dart. 1½m from A385 Paignton–
Totnes road, ¾m from Stoke Gabriel.*

5acres 135pitches 40🚐 £4.40 or
40🚐 £3.90 or 95▲£4.40 (awnings)

5♿☉ 16wc lit all night 1cdp 🚽
washbasins hc 🛁 hc☉ supervised (spin
iron) CTV (cold storage) childrens
playground calor gas camping gaz toilet
fluid ☎ 🛒
↔ stables golf 🛒 cinema ♪ launderette
pub

STONEHAVEN
Grampian *Kincardineshire*
Map 15 NO88

▶▶▶ ① ❷ ⚠

Queen Elizabeth Caravan Site
(NO875866) Apply to: Kincardine &
Deeside District Council, Leisure &
Recreation Dept, View Mount,
Stonehaven, Kincardineshire.
Signposted ☎ (0569) 62001 Apr–Oct
must book Jun–Aug min 1wk booking
Last arrival 20.00hrs Last departure noon
no tents, motor caravans or awnings

A gently sloping grass site offering a good

*range of recreational facilities, situated
between a main road and seafront
adjoining a public park.*

5acres 40pitches 80static 40🚐 ltr

Individual pitches late arrivals enclosure
24wc lit all night 4cdp washbasins hc
(🛁 hc)☉ (wash dry iron 👕) childrens
playground
↔ stables golf 🛒 ♪ launderette pub 🛒

STOWBRIDGE
Norfolk
Map 5 TF60

▶▶▶ ③ ❸ ⚠

Woodlakes Caravan & Camping Park
(TF615075) Holme Rd Signposted
☎ King's Lynn (0553) 810414 Apr–Oct
must book peak periods

*Set in wood and grassland by a 12 acre
lake in an ideal position for touring East
Anglia. From King's Lynn take the A10 for
about 8m then turn right at sign for
Woodlakes. Site is approx 1½m further
on.*

26acres 90pitches 60🚐 £4.70 or
60🚐 £4.70 30▲£4.70 (awnings) ltr

11♿☉ late arrivals enclosure wc lit all
night 2cdp washbasins hc central hot
water 🛁 hc☉ games room cold storage
childrens playground calor gas camping
gaz paraffin toilet fluid ☎ coarse & trout
fishing rowing boat hire 🛒
↔ 🛒 ♪ launderette pub

STRACHAN
Grampian *Kincardineshire*
Map 15 NO69

▶▶ ② ❷ ⚠

Feughside Caravan Site *(NO642926)*
☎ Feughside (033045) 669 Apr–mid Oct
no tents

*Level, grass site with young trees and
bushes, set in hilly moorland and
woodland country, adjacent to Water of
Feugh. 5m W of Banchory and 9m E of
Aboyne, just off B976. Situated beside the
Feughside Inn, 2m W of Strachan.*

¾acre 10pitches 40static 10🚐 or 10🚐
(awnings)

♿ Individual pitches wc lit all night 1cdp
washbasins hc central hot water 🛁 hc☉
(wash spin dry) iron games room cold
storage childrens playground calor gas
camping gaz
↔ stables ♪ pub

STRACHUR
Strathclyde *Argyllshire*
Map 10 NN00

▶▶ ② ❷ ⚠

Strathlachlan Caravan Park
(NN013953) Signposted ☎ (036986) 300
Apr–Oct Last arrival 22.00hrs Last
departure noon no tents

*Mainly level grass site screened by
mature trees on edge of river. Views of
Loch Fyne. From Strachur follow the A886
for 3m then turn right onto B8000 (Kilfinan)
road; site in approx 3m.*

1acre 12pitches 95static 12🚐 £3.50 or
12🚐 £3.50 awnings ltr

6♿ Individual pitches 9wc lit all night
washbasins hc 🛁 hc☉ supervised (wash
spin dry) calor gas camping gaz toilet fluid
🛒
↔ ♪

STRAGGLETHORPE
Nottinghamshire
Map 8 SK63

▶▶▶ ② ❷ ⚠

Thornton's Holt Camping Site
(SK638377) Signposted ☎ Radcliffe-on-
Trent (06073) 2125 Apr–Oct Last arrival
23.00hrs Last departure 18.00hrs

*A level grass site with young trees and
bushes, set in meadowland ½m S of A52
and 2m N of A46. Nearby (2m) is the
National Water Sports Centre at Holme
Pierrepoint.*

4acres 70pitches 70🚐 £2.95 or
70🚐 £2.95 or 70▲£2.95 (awnings)

6♿ Individual pitches late arrivals
enclosure 9wc lit all night 1cdp
washbasins hc (🛁 hc☉) supervised (iron)
(cold storage) childrens playground calor
gas camping gaz ☎ 🛒
↔ stables golf 🛒 ♪ launderette pub
see advertisement on page 195

STRANRAER
Dumfries & Galloway *Wigtownshire*
Map 10 NX06

▶▶▶ ② ① ⚠

Aird Donald Caravan Park *(NX075605)*
Signposted ☎ (0776) 2025 All year must
book Last arrival 22.00hrs Last departure
14.00hrs

*Level, grass and sand site with trees,
bushes and tarmac hard standings. Set in
woodland and meadowland within the
urban area. Off A75.*

12½acres 100pitches 20static 50🚐 or
50🚐 50▲ (awnings) ltr

8♿☉ 28wc lit all night 3cdp washbasins

hc central hot water (🛁 hc) ☺ supervised (wash spin iron) childrens playground calor gas camping gaz ☎ 🛍

↔ stables golf ⛳ ✦ launderette pub

▶▶▶ ☑️❷⚠️
Wig Bay Holiday Park *(NX034655)*Loch Ryan Signposted ☎Kirkcolm (077685) 233 May–Sep rsMar–Apr & Oct must book Jul Open 24hrs

Site set in sheltered position on western shores of Loch Ryan. 3m NW of Stranraer off A718.

2acres 26pitches 100static SA 26🚐£3.50 or 26🚎£3.50 or 26🛖£3.50 (awnings)

3⛺⏀ late arrivals enclosure 18wc lit all night 1cdp washbasins hc 8🛁 hc 5☺ supervised (wash dry iron) games room cold storage licensed club/bar childrens playground calor gas camping gaz toilet fluid 🛍 paddling pool mobile shop 🛍

↔ stables golf ⛳ ✦ launderette pub

STRATFORD-UPON-AVON
Warwickshire
Map 4 SP25

▶▶ ☑️❷⚠️
Elms Camp *(SP213558)* (access from south side of Avon Bridge, Stratford) ☎(0789) 292312 Apr–Oct must book Last departure noon

Level grass site with mature trees and bushes, 1m from Stratford on B4086. Own slipway on River Avon.

4acres 165pitches (awnings)

10⛺⏀ wc lit all night 1cdp washbasins hc central hot water🛁 hc☺ iron childrens playground calor gas camping gaz toilet fluid 🛍

↔ stables golf ⛳ cinema ✦ launderette pub

STRATHAVEN
Strathclyde *Lanarkshire*
Map 11 NS74

▶▶ ①❸⚠️
Gallowhill Caravan Park *(NS708440)* Lesmahagow Rd Signposted ☎(0357) 21267 Apr–Sep Last arrival 23.00hrs Last departure 13.00hrs

Level grass site with young trees, set in meadowland, adjacent to river. On A726 ½m S of Strathaven.

2acres 30pitches 30🚐£3 or 30🚎£3 or 30🛖£3 (awnings)

3⛺6wc lit all night 1cdp washbasins hc (🛁hc)☺ (wash spin dry) calor gas camping gaz toilet fluid

↔ stables ✦ 🛍

STUSTON (Near Diss)
Suffolk
Map 5 TM35

▶▶▶ ①❷⚠️
Osiers Caravan & Camping Park *(TM145788)* The Osiers, Old Bury Rd Signposted ☎Scole (037978) 335 Mar–Sep rs Oct–Feb

6acres 32pitches SA 32🚐£3 or 32🚎£3 or 32🛖£3 awnings

2⛺ late arrivals enclosure 6wc lit all night 1cdp washbasins hc 🛁hc☺supervised (iron) cold storage childrens playground calor gas camping gaz toilet fluid ☎ canoe hire battery charging 🛍

↔ stables golf ⛳ ✦ launderette pub

SUNDERLAND
Cumbria
Map 11 NY13

▶▶ ①❶⚠️
Skiddaw View Caravan Park *(NY179368)* Signposted ☎Aspatria (0965) 20404 Apr–Nov must book Last arrival 20.00hrs Last departure noon

Level site near hills, moors and mountains of the Lake District. Approach by way of a A591 road 1½m S of Bothel.

3acres 55pitches 72static SA 35🚐 or 35🚎 20🛖 (awnings) ltr

6⛺17wc lit all night 2cdp (washbasins hc) (🛁hc) calor gas camping gaz toilet fluid

↔ stables golf ⛳ ✦ pub 🛍

SUTTON
Kent
Map 5 TR34

▶▶▶ ☑️❷⚠️
Sutton Vale Caravan Park *(TR339498)* ☎Deal (03045) 4155 (due to change to Deal (0304) 374155 Mar–Oct Last arrival 19.00hrs Last departure noon no tents No motorcycles no single sex groups

Small and well-sited park offering well-equipped caravans for hire with limited space for tourers.

14pitches 100static 14🚐£4 or 14🚎£4 (awnings) ltr

10⛺20wc lit all night 1cdp 🚽 central hot water (🛁hc)☺supervised (wash spin dry iron) ⤳ (𝒫 games room) TV licensed bar childrens playground calor gas toilet fluid cafe restaurant ☎ 🛍

↔ stables golf ⛳ cinema ✦ launderette pub

SUTTON COLDFIELD
West Midlands
Map 7 SP19

▽☑️
Uppaland *(SP154979)* London Rd ☎021-378 1470

Mainly level enclosed paddock off the W side of A446.

15pitches 15🚐 ✳£1 or 15🚎£1 or 15🛖£1 ⛺cdp

SWAINBY
North Yorkshire
Map 8 NZ40

▶①❶⚠️
Blacksmith's Arms *(NZ475023)* ☎Stokesley (0642) 700303 Apr–Sep

Level grass site near river, hills, moorland and woodland, off A172.

12pitches 12🚐£3 or 12🚎£3 or 12🛖£3 awnings

3⛺3wc lit all night 1cdp☺supervised cold storage licensed club/bar childrens playground calor gas camping gaz cafe restaurant ☎ 🛍

↔ stables ✦ launderette pub

SWANAGE
Dorset
Map 4 SZ07

▶▶▶ ☑️❷⚠️
Ulwell Cottage Caravan Park *(SZ019809)* Ulwell Cottage, Ulwell (1½m N on Studland Rd) ☎(0929) 422823 Spring Bank Hol–mid Sep rs Apr–Spring Bank Hol & mid Sep–Oct booking advisable public hols & mid Jul–Aug Last arrival 22.00hrs Last departure noon no tents Jul & Aug

Nestling under the Purbeck Hills surrounded by scenic walks and only 2 miles away from the beach.

3acres 70pitches 140static 70🚐£3–£6 or 70🚎£2–£5 or 70🛖£3–£6 (awnings)

5⛺16wc lit all night 3cdp 🚽 17washbasins hc 7central hot water 6🛁hc 6☺supervised (wash spin dry) iron licensed club/bar calor gas camping gaz toilet fluid ☎ 🛍

↔ stables golf ⛳ cinema ✦ launderette pub

see advert on page 240

SWAY
Hampshire
Map 4 SZ29

▽☑️
Setthorns *(SU263004)* (2m NW towards Burley) ☎Lyndhurst (042128) 2269 (10am–6pm) or Southampton (0703) 812888 All year

Pleasant level site in woodland.

270pitches 270🚐 or 270🚎 or 270🛖 5⛺cdp

TAIN
Highland *Ross & Cromarty*
Map 14 NH78

▶▶▶ ①❷⚠️
Meikle Ferry Caravan & Camping Park *(NH748844)* Signposted ☎(0862) 2292 All year Booking advisable Jul & Aug Last arrival mdnt Last departure noon

Roadside site on A9.

3acres 65pitches 12static 65🚐£3.50 or 65🚎£3.50 or 65🛖£3.50 awnings

12⛺Individual pitches late arrivals enclosure 9wc lit all night 1cdp 🚽 14washbasins hc (central hot water) (4🛁hc) 5☺supervised wash spin (dry iron) 𝒫 (games room) CTV cold storage licensed club/bar childrens playground private beach calor gas camping gaz toilet fluid restaurant ☎ 🏓 pool/snooker trampolenes bicycles swing balls 🛍

↔ stables golf ⛳ ✦ launderette pub

TALGARTH
Powys
Map 3 SO 13

▶▶▶▶ ③❸⚠

Riverside International Caravan & Camping Park *(SO148346)* Signposted ☎(0874) 711320 Etr–Oct booking advisable peak periods Last arrival 21.30hrs Last departure noon 🌂

Well-appointed touring site with pitches available on riverside. Elevated position with magnificent views of the Black Mountains. Off A479.

10 acres 85 pitches 6 static SA 85🚐 or 85🚐 or 85🛆 awnings

15🚞 Individual pitches⊘ late arrivals enclosure 14wc lit all night 1cdp🚽 washbasins hc (✦hc🛁hc)☺ supervised (wash spin dry) iron⟰ games room CTV (cold storage) licensed bar childrens playground calor gas camping gaz toilet fluid cafe restaurant ☎ ⊞ 🍴

⟷ stables golf 🏌 🚣 launderette pub

TAL-Y-BONT (Near Barmouth)
Gwynedd
Map 6 SH 52

▶▶▶ ①❶⚠

Islaw R'ffordd Caravan Site *(SH583213)* Signposted ☎ Dyffryn (03417) 269 Etr–Oct rs Feb & Mar Last arrival 22.00hrs Last departure noon no bonfires

Level grass site set in meadowland

See previous page for entry

---

adjacent to sea and beach, amid Snowdonia National Park scenery. 4m N of Barmouth.

12 acres 225 pitches 200 static SA 25🚐 or 25🚐 200🛆 awnings

10🚞⊘ 30wc lit all night 1cdp washbasins hc (🛁hc)☺ wash dry iron (cold storage) licensed club/bar private beach calor gas camping gaz paraffin toilet fluid ☎ 🍴

⟷ stables 🏌 🚣 launderette

TARLAND
Grampian *Aberdeenshire*
Map 15 NJ 40

▶▶▶ ②❸⚠

Drummie Hill Caravan Park *(NJ478045)* Signposted ☎(033981) 388 Apr–mid Oct booking advisable Jul & Aug Last arrival 23.00hrs Last departure noon

Landscaped site set on edge of village amidst hill and farmland. Enter Tarland on B9119, bear left before bridge and continue for 600yds. Site is on left.

2 acres 30 pitches 30 static SA 30🚐 or 30🚐 or 30🛆 (awnings)

6🚞 Individual pitches for caravans⊘ late arrivals enclosure 12wc lit all night 1cdp washbasins hc🛁hc☺ supervised (spin dry iron) (cold storage) childrens playground calor gas camping gaz ☎ 🍴

⟷ stables golf 🚣 pub

TAUNTON
Somerset
Map 3 ST 22

▶▶▶ ②❸⚠

St Quintin Hotel Caravan & Camping Park Bridgwater Rd, Bathpool Signposted ☎(0823) 73016 All year booking advisable peak periods Last arrival 23.00hrs Last departure noon

Level and grassy site set in meadowland adjacent to the Taunton–Bridgwater Canal. 1m from exit 25 of M5, on A38 behind the Bathpool Inn.

5½ acres 125 pitches 24 static 125🚐 £5.70 or 125 🚐 £5.70 or 125🛆 £5.77 (awnings) ltr

6🚞 late arrivals enclosure 18wc 1cdp🚽 25 washbasins hc 12🛁hc 1☺ (wash spin dry) iron CTV childrens playground calor gas camping gaz toilet fluid cafe restaurant ☎ bicycle & boat hire fishing 🍴

⟷ stables golf 🏌 cinema 🚣 launderette pub

TAVISTOCK
Devon
Map 2 SX 47

▶▶▶ ②❷⚠

Harford Bridge Park *(SX504768)* Signposted ☎ Mary Tavy (082281) 349 Apr–Oct booking advisable Jul & Aug Last departure noon

---

Ulwell Cottage Caravan Park
Isle of Purbeck

Nestling under lovely Purbeck Hills and near safe sandy beaches of Swanage and Studland. Golf and riding nearby. Bournemouth approximately 9 miles via Sandbanks Ferry. Corfe Castle 5 miles.

Vans to let and touring spaces (weekly bookings accepted). Site has showers, laundry room, shop, licensed bar, with quiet beer garden and children's room. Grassy site with sheltered corners and superb views of Swanage Bay and Purbeck countryside.

Mrs. J. M. Scadden **Tel: Swanage 0929 422823**
Brochure available

Level, grassy site with mature trees, set in Dartmoor National Park, near river. 2m N of Tavistock on A386.

30 acres 100 pitches 80 static SA 100🚐 or 100🚐 or 100▲ (awnings) ltr

12🚐 Individual pitches late arrivals enclosure 15 wc lit all night 1 cdp 🚐 washbasins hc (central hot water) (🛁 hc) ⊙ supervised spin iron (👗) cold storage childrens playground calor gas camping gaz toilet fluid ☎ 🛍

⟿ stables golf ⚓ launderette pub

▶▶▶ 2 0 ⚠
Higher Longford Farm Caravan Site
(SX520747) Signposted ☎ (0822) 3360 All year booking advisable Jul & Aug Last arrival mdnt Last departure noon

Site is adjacent to B3357 between Ashburton and Tavistock in the Dartmoor National Park.

2½ acres 52 pitches 24 static 52🚐 £4 or 52🚐 £4 or 52▲ £4 awnings ltr

3🚐 Individual pitches ⦵ 8 wc lit all night 2 cdp washbasins hc (🛁 hc) ⊙ (wash spin dry iron) (games room) cold storage licensed club/bar childrens playground calor gas camping gaz toilet fluid cafe ☎ bicycle hire barbecues 🛍

⟿ stables golf ⚓ launderette pub

▶ 2 0 ⚠
Langstone Manor Country Club & Caravan Park Moortown Signposted
☎ (0822) 3371 Apr–Oct must book Last departure 11.00 hrs no cars by tents

Part Level, part sloping, grass site with mature trees and bushes set in hilly moorland. Off B3357 in Dartmoor National Park.

12 pitches 26 static 12▲ £4 (awnings)

4🚐 8 wc lit all night 1 cdp (central hot water 🛁 hc) ⊙ supervised licensed club/bar childrens playground camping gaz ☎ 🛍

⟿ stables launderette pub

TAYINLOAN
Strathclyde *Argyllshire*
Map 10 NR74

▶▶▶ 2 0 ⚠
Point Sands Caravan Park (NR698484)
Point Sands Signposted ☎ (05834) 263 Apr–Oct must book

Attractive level site situated by lovely safe sandy beach on western shore of Kintyre peninsula with views towards islands of Gigha, Jura and Islay.

9 acres 135 pitches 58 static 100🚐 £4–£4.50 or 100🚐 £4–£4.50 35▲ £3.50–£4 awnings

12🚐⦵ 35 wc lit all night 2 cdp washbasins hc (central hot water) 🛁 hc ⊙ supervised (wash) (dry iron) (cold storage) childrens playground private beach calor gas camping gaz toilet fluid ☎ 🛍

⟿ ⚓ launderette pub

TAYPORT
Fife
Map 12 NO42

▶▶ 1 3 ⚠
East Common Site (NO465283) Apply
to: North East Fife District Council, Dept of Recreation, County Buildings, Cupar, Fife Signposted ☎ Cupar (0334) 53722 late Mar–Oct must book Last arrival 20.00 hrs Last departure 20.00 hrs

A links site situated on reclaimed land with outlook across Tay Estuary.

1 acre 20 pitches 20 static 20🚐 £3.20 or 20🚐 £3.20 or 20▲ £1.70–£3.20 (awnings)

Individual pitches 13 wc lit all night 1 cdp 16 washbasins hc (🛁 hc) ⊙ (wash spin) iron games room TV ☎

⟿ golf ⚓ launderette pub 🛍

TEBAY
Cumbria
Map 12 NY60

▶▶▶ 2 0 ⚠
Tebay Caravan Park (NY609060) Orton
Signposted ☎ Orton (05874) 351 or 482 Mar–Oct booking advisable public hols Last arrival mdnt Last departure noon no tents

Basically a transit site tucked away in a hollow, adjacent to the Tebay Service

Area. Access from M6 – ¾m north of exit 38 for Northbound traffic. For Southbound traffic join Northbound at exit 38 and follow same route.

3½ acres 70 pitches 70🚐 £4 or 70🚐 £4 (awnings) ltr

6🚐 Individual pitches late arrivals enclosure 11 wc lit all night 1 cdp 🚐 washbasins hc central hot water 🛁 hc ⊙ supervised licensed club/bar calor gas camping gaz paraffin toilet fluid cafe restaurant ☎ 🛍

⟿ stables ⚓ pub

TEDBURN ST MARY
Devon
Map 3 SX89

▶▶▶ 1 0 ⚠
Woodlands Park (SX831936)
Signposted ☎ (06476) 609 Apr–Oct must book peak periods Last departure noon

Well situated site for Exeter and Dartmoor, E of Tedburn St. Mary on old A30.

½ acre 12 pitches 20 static 12🚐 or 12🚐 or 12▲ (awnings) ltr

4🚐 late arrivals enclosure 6 wc lit all night 1 cdp 10 washbasins hc central hot water 4 🛁 hc 6 ⊙ supervised iron mobile shop

⟿ stables launderette pub 🛍

TENBY
Dyfed
Map 2 NSN10
See sketch map

▶▶▶▶ 2 0 ⚠
Kiln Park Caravan Park (SN119002) Kiln
Park ☎ (0834) 4121 mid May–Sep rs Etr–mid May must book Last arrival 21.00 hrs Last departure 10.00 hrs 🍴 (mid Jun–Aug)

A large, commercial touring, camping and static holiday site, situated on level ground on the town's outskirts. A short walk through sand dunes leads to the sandy south beach with Caldey Island in the background. On A4139.

20 acres 240 pitches 550 static SA 60🚐 £18–£38 (wkly charge) or 60🚐 £16–£30 (wkly charge) 180▲ £16–£30 (wkly charge) awnings →

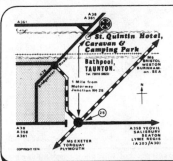

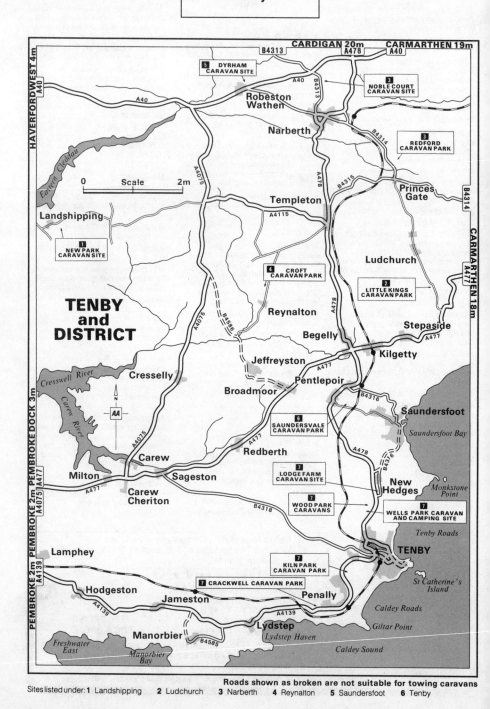

Roads shown as broken are not suitable for towing caravans

Sites listed under: **1** Landshipping **2** Ludchurch **3** Narberth **4** Reynalton **5** Saundersfoot **6** Tenby

47☠☺ late arrivals enclosure 120wc lit all night 2cdp ⚑ washbasins hc central hot water (➍hc⋔hc)☺ supervised (wash spin dry) iron ⇨ games room TV cold storage (licensed club/bar) childrens playground private beach calor gas camping gaz toilet fluid cafe restaurant ☎ ⊞ amusement arcade hairdressing ▨
↔ stables golf ⌇ cinema ✦ launderette pub

▶▶▶ ❷❶⚠
Crackwell Caravan Park *(SN107987)*
Penally (2m SW A4139) ☎(0834) 2688 mid Apr–mid Oct rs Etr must book peak periods Last departure noon

Pleasant well organised site in secluded position convenient for beaches and touring. Good range of family recreational facilities.

9acres 110pitches 53static SA 25☠ £4 or 25 ☠£4 ▲£3.50 (awnings) ltr
6☠ Individual pitches☺ late arrivals enclosure 20wc lit all night 4cdp ⚑ washbasins hc central hot water ⋔hc☺ supervised (wash spin) dry iron games room CTV TV (cold storage) licensed club/bar childrens playground calor gas camping gaz toilet fluid cafe ☎ ▨
↔ stables golf ⌇ cinema ✦ launderette pub

▶▶▶ ❶❶⚠
Well Park Caravan Camping Site
(SN125020) New Hedges Signposted ☎(0834) 2179 Spring Bank Hol–mid Sep

rs Apr–Spring Bank Hol & Mid Sep–Oct must book peak periods Last arrival 23.00hrs Last departure noon no single sex groups

Slightly sloping and level grass site with trees and bushes. 1½m N of Tenby off A478 New Hedges bypass.

4½acres 90pitches 42static 10☠ fr£2 10☠ fr£1.50 70▲fr£1.50 awnings
7☠ Individual pitches for caravans☺ 17wc lit all night 1cdp (washbasins hc central hot water ⋔hc)☺ supervised (spin dry iron) (games room) CTV (cold storage) childrens playground calor gas camping gaz ☎ ▨
↔ stables golf ⌇ cinema ✦ launderette pub

▶▶▶ ❷❶⚠
Wood Park Caravans *(SN126026)* New Hedges Signposted ☎(0834) 3414 Spring Bank Hol–mid Sep rs Etr–Spring Bank Hol must book Spring Bank Hol & Jul–Aug Last arrival 23.00hrs Last departure 10.00hrs ✶ last wk Jul–Aug no single sex groups

Slightly sloping and level, grass site with trees and bushes. 1½m N of Tenby off A478 New Hedges bypass.

2½acres 60pitches 90static 20☠ 40 ☠ or 40▲ (awnings)

5☠ Individual pitches for caravans 25wc lit all night 1cdp (washbasins hc ⋔hc)☺ (wash spin dry iron) games room (cold storage licensed club/bar) childrens playground calor gas camping gaz ☎ ▨
↔ stables golf ⌇ cinema ✦ launderette pub

▶☐❶
Lodge Farm Caravan Site *(SN131029)* New Hedges Signposted ☎(0834) 2468 Mar–Aug must book for caravans Last departure noon

This site is set in level grassy ground 1½m from Tenby.

20acres 60pitches 40static SA 10☠ or 10☠ 50▲ awnings
4☠ Individual pitches 26wc lit all night 1cdp (washbasins hc) (⋔hc)☺ calor gas mobile shop ▨
↔ stables golf ⌇ cinema ✦ launderette pub

THORNESS BAY
Isle of Wight
Map 4 SZ49

▶▶▶ ❷❶⚠
Thorness Bay Holiday Village
(SZ448928) ☎Newport (0983) 523109 21 May–17 Sep rs 7–20 May & 18–24 Sep must book Jul & Aug Last departure 10.00hrs no motorcycle groups no single sex groups →

Situated in the centre of a holiday complex of chalets and static caravans on level grassy ground. 5m W of Cowes on rising ground with views of Thorness Bay and the Solent.

200pitches 360static 200🚐 £6 or 200 🚐 £6 or 200▲£6 awnings

wc lit all night 🚿 washbasins hc 🛁 hc ☺ (wash spin dry) iron ⌣ games room CTV licensed club/bar childrens playground private beach calor gas camping gaz cafe ☎ ⊞ mini gym riding stables sauna 🛍

↔ golf ⚓ 🧺 launderette pub

THORNTON CLEVELEYS
Lancashire
Map 7 SD34

▶▶▶ ① ❷ ⚠

Kneps Farm *(SD353429)* River Rd
☎ Cleveleys (0253) 823632 Mar–Oct must book Last departure noon no tents

A level, stony and grassy site with mature trees near a river. 5m N of Blackpool on A587 Thornton Cleveleys road.

3acres 65pitches 100static 65🚐 £4.60 or 65 🚐 frf4.02 (awnings)

8🏕 Individual pitches late arrivals enclosure 33wc lit all night 2cdp 🚿 washbasins hc 16🛁hc 8☺supervised (wash) (games room) cold storage childrens playground calor gas camping gaz toilet fluid cafe ☎ ⊞ off licence 🛍

↔ stables golf ⚓ 🧺 launderette pub

THORPE CULVERT
Lincolnshire
Map 9 TF46

▶▶▶ ❷ ❷ ⚠

Swan Lake Leisure Caravan Park
(TF464606) Culvert Rd ☎ Skegness (0754) 880469 30 Mar–3 Oct Last departure noon

6acres 40pitches 15static SA 25🚐 £2.50 or 25 🚐 £2.50 or 25▲£2.50 (awnings)

3🏕 Individual pitches ☂ 4wc lit all night 1cdp washbasins hc central hot water (🛁 hc) ☺supervised (wash spin) iron (cold storage) childrens playground calor gas camping gaz ☎ ⊞ mobile shop

↔ stables 🧺 launderette pub 🛍

THRAPSTON
Northamptonshire
Map 4 SP97

▶ ❷ ❶ ⚠

Mill Marina Caravan & Boat Park
(SP994781) Signposted ☎ (08012) 2850 Apr–Oct booking advisable public hols Last arrival 22.00hrs Last departure 20.00hrs no single sex groups

Level grass site with mature trees, saplings and bushes, set in urban area with access to River Nene. ½m S of town on A605.

7acres 30pitches 5static SA 30🚐 £2.75 £2.25 or 30 🚐 £2.75 20▲£2.75 (awnings) ltr

3🏕 Individual pitches ☂ late arrivals enclosure 8wc lit all night 1cdp washbasins hc 2central hot water (🛁 hc)

☺supervised (⌂) licensed club/bar childrens playground calor gas camping gaz cafe 🛍

↔ 🧺 launderette pub

THREE BURROWS
Cornwall
Map 2 SW74
See Redruth sketch map

▶▶▶ ❷ ❸ ⚠

Hillview Tourist Park *(SW746468)*
Signposted ☎ Truro (0872) 560315 Apr–Oct booking advisable Jul & Aug

The site is conveniently positioned for touring Cornwall and offers extensive views.

4acres 93pitches 93🚐 £3.50 or 93 🚐 £3.50 or 93▲£3.50 awnings

4🏕 6wc lit all night 1cdp washbasins hc (🛁hc) ☺supervised cold storage calor gas camping gaz 🛍

↔ stables ⚓ launderette pub

THREE OAKS
East Sussex
Map 5 TQ81

▶▶▶ ❷ ❸ ⚠

Old Coghurst Farm Caravan & Camping Park *(TQ832138)* Rock Ln Signposted ☎ Hastings (0424) 753622 20 Mar–Oct rs 1–19 Mar must book peak periods Last arrival 22.00hrs Last departure noon

Part level, part sloping, grassy site with trees and bushes. Set in hilly country amidst woodland and meadowland. Off unclassified road – between A259 and A28 – 4m NE of Hastings.

4acres 60pitches 60🚐 £4.10 or 60 🚐 £4 or 60▲£3.80 (awnings) ltr

3🏕 Individual pitches late arrivals enclosure 10wc lit all night 1cdp 🚿 washbasins hc central hot water 🛁 hc ☺ supervised (wash dry iron) (✍) (cold storage) calor gas camping gaz toilet fluid ☎ 🛍

↔ stables golf ⚓ cinema 🧺 launderette pub

see advertisement on page 147

THRESHFIELD
North Yorkshire
Map 7 SD96

▶▶▶ ❷ ❷ ⚠

Long Ashes Caravan Park *(SD984645)*
Signposted ☎ Grassington (0756) 752261 15 Mar–Oct must book public hols Last arrival 21.00hrs Last departure 18.00hrs no tents no singles under 21 no motorcycles

Level grass site with trees and bushes set in wooded hills and meadowland adjacent to River Wharfe. 1m from Grassington town centre on Skipton road.

110acres 70pitches 350static 70🚐 £3–£4.50 or 70 🚐 £3–£4.50 (awnings) ltr

---

60🏕 Individual pitches late arrivals enclosure 60wc lit all night 3cdp washbasins hc central hot water 🛁 hc ☺ wash spin dry iron (⌂) games room CTV licensed club/bar childrens playground calor gas cafe restaurant ☎ gym jacuzzi sauna solarium squash 🛍

↔ stables 🧺 launderette pub

see advertisement on page 235

THURSO
Highland *Caithness*
Map 15 ND16

▶▶ ❷ ⚠

Thurso Burgh Caravan Site *(ND111688)*
Scrabster Rd Signposted May–Sep no bookings Last arrival 22.00hrs Last departure noon

A level and grassy site near the sea and beach, ½m from Post Office on A882.

4½acres 130pitches 10static 80🚐 £2.50–£3 or 80 🚐 £2.50–£3 50▲£2.50–£3 (awnings)

8🏕 Individual pitches ☂ late arrivals enclosure 23wc lit all night 1cdp washbasins hc central hot water (🛁hc) ☺ wash spin dry iron TV cafe restaurant ☎ disabled facilities 🛍

↔ stables golf ⚓ cinema 🧺 launderette pub

TILSHEAD
Wiltshire
Map 4 SU04

▶▶ ❷ ❷ ⚠

Brades Acre *(SU035477)* The Bungalow Signposted ☎ Shrewton (0980) 620402 Apr–Oct booking advisable Jul & Aug Last arrival 19.00hrs Last departure 10.00hrs

Small level site surrounded by shrubs and trees on the Salisbury side of village with pleasant rural aspects.

1½acres 25pitches 25🚐 £3 or 25 🚐 £3 or 25▲£2.50 awnings ltr

2🏕 ☂ late arrivals enclosure 4wc lit all night 1cdp washbasins hc central hot water 🛁hc ☺ supervised cold storage calor gas camping gaz 🛍

↔ stables pub

TINTAGEL
Cornwall
Map 2 SX08

▶▶▶ ❷ ❷ ⚠

Ocean Cove Caravan Park *(SX065888)*
☎ (08404) 325 17 May–18 Sep rs Apr–16 May no bookings Last arrival 23.00hrs no tents

Partly level, partly sloping, grass site in meadowland, adjacent to sea, beach and downs. 18m W of Launceston on B3263.

¾acre 12pitches 159static 12🚐 or 12 🚐 (awnings)

10🏕 Individual pitches 31wc lit all night 1cdp 28washbasins hc central hot water (6🛁hc) ☺ (wash dry iron) licensed bar childrens playground calor gas 🛍

↔ stables ⚓ 🧺 launderette pub

► ② ❶ △
Headland Caravan & Camping Site
(SX056888) ☎ Camelford (0840) 770239
Apr–Sep Last arrival 22.00hrs Last
departure noon
Undulating grass site set in meadowland
adjacent to sea and sandy beach.
4acres 85pitches 25static 85 ⊞ or 85 ⊞
or 85▲ (awnings)
6ⅆ late arrivals enclosure 13wc lit all night
2cdp washbasins hc (⋔ hc) ☺ supervised
calor gas camping gaz
↔ stables ⅃ ♪ launderette pub ⤓

TIPTREE
Essex
Map 5 TL81

▽ ②
Villa Farm *(TL881155)* West End Rd
☎ Maldon (0621) 815217
Grassland site on fruit farm quiet, except
mid June to mid July which is picking
season.
5acres 5pitches 5 ⊞ or 5 ⊞ or 5▲
ⅆ cdp

TORRINGTON (GREAT)
Devon
Map 2 SS41

► ► ► ① ❷ △
Greenways Valley Holiday Park
(SS511192) Signposted ☎ (08025) 2153

Tintagel
—
Trentham

Apr–Oct rs last wk Mar booking advisable
Jul Last arrival 20.00hrs Last departure
noon no tents
Level, grassed site with trees and bushes
set in hilly woodland. 2m SE of town off
B3227 South Molton road.
1acre 4pitches 19static 4 ⊞ fr£3 or
4 ⊞ fr£3 (awnings)
4ⅆ 5wc lit all night ♨ washbasins hc ⋔ hc
☺ supervised iron ⌷ cold storage
childrens playground calor gas camping
gaz take-away food ⤓
↔ stables golf cinema ♪ launderette pub

TOWYN (Near Abergele)
Clwyd
Map 6 SH97

► ► ► ① ❷ △
Ty Mawr Holiday Park *(SH965792)*
Towyn Rd, Abergele Signposted
☎ Abergele (0745) 822079 Apr–Oct
booking advisable public hols & summer
mths Last arrival 22.00hrs Last departure
15.00hrs no single sex groups no
motorcycles
This North Wales Coast site is on the A548,
¼m west of Towyn village.
15acres 218pitches 355static SA
218 ⊞ fr£3.70 or 218 ⊞ fr£3.70 or ▲£3.15
(awnings)

7ⅆ ☾ late arrivals enclosure wc lit all night
♨ washbasins hc (➔ hc ⋔ hc) ☺
supervised (wash spin dry iron) ⌷ games
room CTV (cold storage) licensed club/
bar childrens playground calor gas
camping gaz cafe restaurant ☎ ⊞
hairdressers sauna solarium ⤓
↔ stables golf ⅃ cinema ♪ launderette
pub

TREFRIW
Gwynedd
Map 6 SH76

► ► ③ ❷
Plas Meirion Caravan Park *(SH783630)*
Gower Rd ☎ Llanrwst (0492) 640247 Etr–
Sep booking advisable school hols Last
arrival 21.30hrs Last departure 10.30hrs
❄ no tents
A level site with mature trees set in the
Conwy Valley and Snowdonia National
Park. Off B5106 Conwy–Betws-y-Coed
road.
15pitches 15static 15 ⊞ £3.50 or
15 ⊞ £3.50 ltr
7ⅆ Individual pitches 6wc lit all night
1cdp ♨ (washbasins hc central hot water
➔ hc ⋔ hc) ☺ (dry) iron cold storage
childrens playground calor gas ⤓
↔ stables golf ⅃ ♪ pub

TRENTHAM
Staffordshire
Map 7 SJ84   →

▶▶▶▶ ② ❷ ⚠

Trentham Gardens Caravan Park
(SJ864419) Trentham Estate Signposted
☎Stoke-on-Trent (0782) 657341 Apr–
Oct Last departure 22.00hrs

Level woodland, grass and meadowland site adjacent to River Trent and Trentham Lakes. Access to A34 and exit 15 of M6.

50acres 200pitches SA 200🚐 £6 or 200🚗 £6 or 200▲£6 awnings

15🚐60wc lit all night 5cdp (washbasins hc) ☺ supervised (dry) games room licensed club/bar childrens playground calor gas camping gaz toilet fluid cafe restaurant ☎ ⊞ 🍴
↪ stables golf ⚲ launderette pub

TRESAITH
Dyfed
Map 2 SN25

▶▶ ② ❸

Gwalia Falls Caravan Park *(SN279517)*
☎Aberporth (0239) 810361 Apr–Oct booking advisable peak periods Last arrival 22.00hrs Last departure 10.00hrs no tents

Well-situated in its own valley and within easy reach of beach. 1m N of Aberporth.

¾acre 18pitches 58static 18🚐 or 18🚗

5🚐 late arrivals enclosure 9wc lit all night 1cdp (washbasins hc central hot water) (🍴hc) ☺ supervised (spin) iron childrens

playground calor gas camping gaz mobile shop 🍴
↪ stables ⚲ launderette pub

TRIMINGHAM
Norfolk
Map 9 TG23

▶▶▶ ③ ❸ ⚠

Woodlands Caravan Park *(TG284388)*
☎Southrepps (026379) 301 Apr–Sep booking advisable peak periods Last arrival 23.00hrs Last departure noon no tents

Level grass site with mature trees, set in woodland and meadowland, adjacent to cliffs overlooking North Sea. 4m SE on coast road, B1154.

20acres 146pitches 154static 146🚐 £3.10–£3.90 or 146 🚗 £3.10–£3.90 awnings

7🚐 Individual pitches 31wc lit all night 2cdp washbasins hc (🍴hc ☺ childrens playground calor gas ☎ 🍴
↪ golf ⚲ cinema ⚲ launderette pub

TROUTBECK (near Penrith)
Cumbria
Map 11 NY32

▶ ① ❶ ⚠

Hutton Moor End *(NY365269)*
Signposted ☎Threlkeld (059683) 615 Etr–Oct booking advisable public hols Last arrival 22.00hrs Last departure noon no dogs

Level and slightly sloping grass site with bushes and mature trees, set in hilly wooded countryside. Ideal position for touring Lake District. 7m E of Keswick and 4m W of Penrith on A66.

4acres 35pitches 15static 20🚐 £3.50 or 20 🚗 £3.50 15▲£3.50 awnings

🚐 Individual pitches ⊙ 11wc lit all night 1cdp washbasins hc central hot water (🍴hc) ☺ iron calor gas camping gaz
↪ stables golf ⚲ pub 🍴

TRURO
Cornwall
Map 2 SW84

▶▶▶▶ ② ❸ ⚠

Leverton Place *(SW774453)*
Greenbottom, Chacewater Signposted ☎(0872) 560462 Etr–Sep rs Oct–mid Apr must book peak periods Last arrival 22.00hrs Last departure 10.00hrs

This attractive site is situated close to Truro yet in a pleasant rural area 3½m W of city, off A390 at Greenbottom.

9acres 125pitches 15static 125🚐 fr£4 or 125 🚗 fr£4 or 125▲fr£4 awnings

13🚐 Individual pitches late arrivals

enclosure 36wc lit all night 3cdp 🔌
washbasins hc 🚿 hc ⊙ supervised (wash
spin dry iron) ⚲ games room CTV cold
storage licensed bar childrens
playground calor gas camping gaz cafe
restaurant ☎ ⊞ 🛒
⟷ stables golf cinema ♪ launderette pub

TURRIFF
Grampian *Aberdeenshire*
Map 15 NJ75

▶ 1️⃣ ❷
Kinnaird House *(NJ733506)* Banff Rd
Signposted ☎ (0888) 62550 Apr–Sep
booking advisable Jul & Aug Last arrival
22.00hrs Last departure noon
Mainly level grass site with mature trees→

CHACEWATER CAMPING AND CARAVAN PARK

Cox Hill, Chacewater, Truro, Cornwall.
Tel: St Day (0209) 820762

You'll find us half a mile west of Chacewater village off a quiet country lane surrounded by farmland. There's a friendly atmosphere centred around our special residents lounge with its wood burning stove. Resident proprietors Pauline and Colin Flood make sure that the site and toilet block are well kept and clean. Brochure on request.

For full facilities please see entry under Chacewater.

LEVERTON PLACE, TRURO, CORNWALL

 ▶▶▶▶

Campsite of the Year National Finalist 1979,
West of England Winner 1980

Ideally central for seeing all of Cornwall yet only a few miles from the beautiful beaches of Perranporth. Large site facilities with small site seclusion, cleanliness and friendliness. Modern caravans and chalets. Good camping and caravanning with electric hook ups. Heated swimming pool.

Write to Pete and Barbara Vallance, Leverton Place, Truro, Cornwall TR4 8QW.
Telephone: 0872 560462

WOODLAND CARAVAN PARK

Trimingham, Norfolk. Telephone Southrepps (026 379) 301

This is a pleasantly undulating site surrounded by mature woodland where the caravans are so sited as to allow plenty of open space for recreational purposes, at the same time within reasonable distances of all toilet facilities. A site manager is on hand to give assistance and information where required; a small shop carrying essential goods is also available. Calor-gas is obtained at all reasonable times. Dogs are allowed on the park provided they are kept strictly under control. Woodland Park is essentially a quiet and peaceful site, and this is the way we want it to stay. Please contact Mrs J. Harrison at the above telephone number for terms and any other details.

and bushes, set in woodland adjacent to the A947.

¼acre 6pitches 2static 6🚐 £2.50 or 6🚐 £2.50 or 6🛆 £2.50 (awnings) ltr

1🏕Individual pitches 2wc lit all night 🔌 washbasins hc central hot water 🚿 hc☉ supervised (wash spin) iron cold storage childrens playground calor gas

⟷ golf ⚓ 🎣 pub 🍴

▶ 🔟 🛈 🛆
Turriff Caravan Site *(NJ725494)*
Signposted ☎Macduff (0261) 32861
May–Sep must book Last arrival 21.00hrs
Last departure 09.00hrs

A level roadside site situated in a redeveloped railway yard, bordering large park. Access off the A947.

1¾acres 30pitches 10static 25🚐 or 25🚐 5🛆 (awnings)

4🏕10wc lit all night 1cdp 12washbasins hc 6🚿hc 4☉ (wash spin) childrens playground crazy golf boating pond 🍴

⟷ golf ⚓ 🎣 launderette pub

TUSHIELAW
Borders *Selkirkshire*
Map 11 NT31

▶ 2️⃣ 🛈 🛆
Honey Cottage Caravan Site
(NT295164) Ettrick Valley Signposted
☎Ettrick Valley (07506) 246 Apr–Oct no bookings

Pleasantly situated near River Ettrick.

6acres 15pitches 44static 15🚐 or 15🚐 or 15🛆 (awnings)

8🏕☉ 16wc washbasins hc 🚿hc☉ games room TV cold storage childrens playground calor gas camping gaz paraffin toilet fluid ☎ 🍴

⟷ stables 🎣 pub

TUXFORD
Nottinghamshire
Map 8 SK77

▶ ▶ 🔟 🛈 🛆
Greenacres *(SK751719)* Lincoln Rd
Signposted ☎(0777) 870264 Apr–Oct
must book public hols Last arrival
23.30hrs Last departure 17.00hrs

Level and slightly sloping grass site with trees, set in rural area outside Tuxford, ¾m E of A1 on A6075 near railway line.

3acres 60pitches 20static 60🚐 £2.75–£3.50 or 60 🚐 £2.75–£3.50 or 60🛆£2.75–£3.50 (awnings) ltr

3🏕☉ 9wc lit all night 1cdp washbasins hc (central hot water) (🚿hc) 2☉ supervised (wash dry iron) cold storage calor gas camping gaz toilet fluid disabled wc shower & WHB

⟷ pub 🍴

TYWYN
Gwynedd
Map 6 SH50

▶ ▶ 🔟 🛈 🛆
Ynysymaengwyn Caravan Park
(SH599024) Apply to: Meirionnydd
District Council Offices, Neptune Rd,
Tywyn, Gwynedd LL36 9EB ☎(0654)
710684 Apr–Oct booking advisable Aug
Last arrival 21.00hrs Last departure noon

A level grass site with mature trees, situated on the A493 Dolgellau road 1½m N of town centre. The Talyllyn narrow gauge railway runs near the site.

5acres 80pitches 115static 20🚐 or 20 🚐 60🛆 (awnings) ltr

4🏕☉ 10wc lit all night 1cdp (washbasins hc central hot water) (🚿hc ☉) supervised (iron) calor gas ☎

⟷ stables cinema 🎣 launderette pub 🍴

▶ ▶ 2️⃣ 🛈 🛆
Ysguboriau Caravan Site *(SH604023)*
☎(0654) 710321 wk before Etr–Oct must
book public hols

Mainly level site 1m inland from Tywyn on A493 Dolgellau road. The Talyllyn narrow gauge railway runs near the site.

3½acres 35pitches 140static 35🚐 or 35 🚐 (awnings)

8🏕33wc 2cdp (8washbasins hc) (8🚿hc) 2☉free river fishing

⟷ stables cinema 🎣 launderette 🍴

UGTHORPE
North Yorkshire
Map 8 NZ71

▶ ▶ 2️⃣ 🛈 🛆
Burnt House Caravan Park *(NZ784112)*
Signposted ☎Whitby (0947) 840448
Apr–Oct must book public hols Last
arrival 22.00hrs Last departure 11.00hrs
no motorcycles no single sex groups

Level grass site with trees and bushes set in moorland. 4½m from sea and beach and 9m W of Whitby off A171 Teesside road.

6acres 120pitches 20static 90🚐 £3 10 🚐 £3 20🛆 £3 (awnings)

7🏕 late arrivals enclosure 20wc lit all night 1cdp 12washbasins hc (6central hot water) (12🚿hc) 6☉ supervised (cold storage) childrens playground calor gas camping gaz toilet fluid ☎ battery charging 🍴

⟷ stables golf ⚓ 🎣 pub

ULLESKELF
North Yorkshire
Map 8 SE54

▶ ▶ 2️⃣ 🛈 🛆
White Cote Caravan Park *(SE525397)*
Ryther Rd ☎Tadcaster (0937) 835231
Mar–Oct must book peak periods Last
arrival 22.00hrs Last departure noon 🎯

On small-holding, well screened from the road and surrounded by an agricultural area. From the A162, follow the B1223 through the village for the site on right, opposite nurseries.

1acre 14pitches 4static 14🚐 £3.50 or 14 🚐 £3.50 or 14🛆 £3.50 (awnings)

3🏕Individual pitches 4wc 1cdp washbasins hc (🚿hc) ☉ supervised cold storage childrens playground

⟷ 🎣 pub 🍴

UMBERLEIGH
Devon
Map 2 SS62

▶ ▶ 2️⃣ ☉ 🛆
Overweir Caravan & Camping Park
(SS603239) Overweir Signposted
☎High Bickington (0769) 60387 15 Mar–
15 Nov booking advisable Jul & Aug Last
arrival mdnt

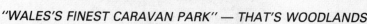

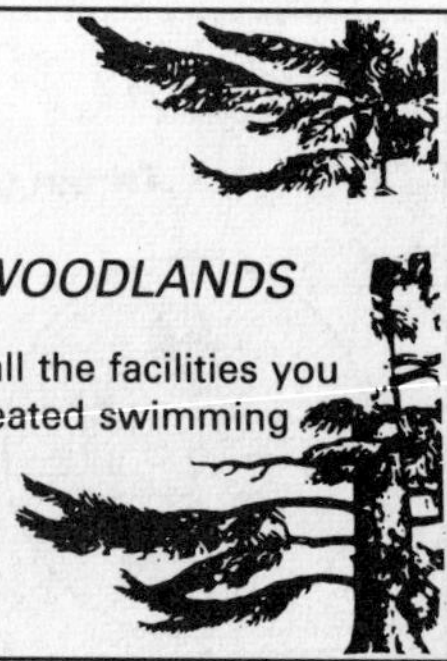

A gently sloping site adjacent to wooded area and offering panoramic views. Approached by metalled road and has wide entrance. Situated on the B3227, 200yds from the A377 at Umberleigh.

3acres 60pitches SA 40🚐£2.50 or 40🚐£2.50 20▲£2.50 (awnings)

2☆Individual pitches⊙ 11wc lit all night 1cdp washbasins hc🔥hc⊙supervised (wash spin dry iron)♪ games room CTV (cold storage) childrens playground calor gas camping gaz toilet fluid ☎🛒
↝ stables ♪ pub

UPLYME
Devon
Map 3 SY39

▶▶▶ �2 🔾 ⚠
Hook Farm Camping & Caravan Park
(SS324930) Signposted ☎ Lyme Regis (02974) 2801 Etr–Nov rs Dec–Etr booking advisable public hols & 19 Jul–1 Sep Last arrival 22.30hrs Last departure noon no caravans

This sloping and level site is situated adjacent to the village of Uplyme in a wooded valley. 1½m NW of Lyme Regis.

5acres 100pitches 18static 100🚐£3.68–£4.50 or 100▲£3.65–£4.50 awnings

10☆⊙ 29wc 2cdp 16washbasins hc (5🔥hc) 6⊙supervised (wash spin dry) (cold storage) calor gas camping gaz🛒
↝ stables golf🏌cinema ♪ launderette pub

UPPER ELKSTONE
Staffordshire
Map 7 SK05

▽ 2
Mount Pleasant Farm *(SK057590)*
☎Blackshaw (Q53834) 380 All year booking advisable public hols Last arrival 20.00hrs

Isolated farm site in Peak District part level, part sloping.

½acre 5pitches 5🚐£2.50 or 5🚐£2.50 or 5▲£2.50 awnings ltr

1☆1wc lit all night washbasins⊙

Umberleigh — Wallingford

VERYAN
Cornwall
Map 2 SW93

▶▶▶ �2 🔾 ⚠
Tretheake Manor Tourist Site
(SW935415) Signposted ☎ Truro (0872) 501213 Etr–Sep must book Jul & Aug Last arrival 20.00hrs Last departure noon

A quiet site situated on slightly undulating land with pleasant country views.

9acres 175pitches 175🚐£4.60 or 175🚐£4.60 or 175▲£4.60 awnings ltr

7☆Individual pitches 20wc lit all night 1cdp 🖥 washbasins hc🔥hc⊙(wash spin dry iron) games room TV (cold storage) childrens playground calor gas camping gaz toilet fluid ☎ coarse fishing 🛒
↝ stables ♪ launderette pub

see advertisement on page 226

WADEBRIDGE
Cornwall
Map 2 SW97

▶ �2 🔾 ⚠
Little Bodieve Holiday Park *(SW995734)*
Signposted ☎(020881) 2323 Mar–Oct must book Jul & Aug Last arrival noon no motorcycles

Level grassy site 1m from centre of Wadebridge in quiet rural area.

11acres 225pitches 45static 225🚐 or 225🚐 or 225▲ (awnings)

4☆late arrivals enclosure 29wc lit all night 1cdp 🖥 washbasins hc (🔥hc)⊙supervised (wash spin) iron (games room) (cold storge) childrens playground calor gas camping gaz toilet fluid ☎ ⊞ 🛒
↝ stables cinema ♪ launderette pub

WALDRINGFIELD
Suffolk
Map 5 TM24

▶▶▶ �3 🔾 ⚠
Moon & Sixpence *(TM263454)*
Signposted ☎(047336) 650 Apr–Oct rs low season must book Last arrival 21.00hrs Last departure noon

Level sand and grass site with bushes and mature trees set in sylvan surroundings. 8m E of Ipswich turn south off A12 near Martlesham. Camp site is geared to cater for people using Felixstowe car ferries.

5acres 90pitches 160static 90🚐£5.18–£8.57 or 90🚐£5.18–£8.57 or 90▲£5.18–£8.57 awnings ltr

15☆late arrivals enclosure 24wc 1cdp 🖥 washbasins hc central hot water ♨hc 🔥hc⊙supervised (wash dry) iron TV (licensed club/bar) childrens playground private beach calor gas camping gaz toilet fluid restaurant ☎🛒
↝ stables golf🏌cinema ♪ launderette pub

WALL
Cornwall
Map 2 SW63
See Hayle sketch map

▶▶▶ �2 🔾 ⚠
Parbola Caravan Park *(SW612366)*
☎Praze (0209) 831503 Etr–Oct must book Jul & Aug Last departure 10.00hrs no single sex groups

A level grassy site in Cornish downland.

2acres 10pitches 18static SA 10🚐£5.50 or 10🚐£3 £3 awnings

7☆⊙ 10wc lit all night 1cdp 🖥 washbasins hc central hot water (🔥hc)⊙supervised iron (games room) TV (cold storage) childrens playground calor gas camping gaz paraffin ☎ take-away food🛒
↝ stables golf🏌cinema ♪ launderette pub

WALLINGFORD
Oxfordshire
Map 4 SU68

▶▶ 1 🔾
Riverside Caravan & Camping Site
(SP609895) Apply to: South Oxfordshire District Council, PO Box 21, Council Offices, Crowmarsh, Wallingford, Oxon OX10 8HQ Signposted ☎(0491) 35351 mid May–mid Sep booking advisable Last arrival 21.30hrs Last departure 21.30 🚶no cars by caravans/tents

Level grassy meadow site surrounded by trees and next to the River Thames. For →

LITTLE BODIEVE HOLIDAY PARK

Ideal touring centre for all parts of Cornwall. Mobile bungalows and caravans for hire complete with all main services, colour TV and fridges. First class accommodation in delightful surroundings and within easy reach of beautiful beaches excellent facilities for tourers and campers, on two large level well mown fields. An added attraction this year is our newly built heated swimming pool.
Under the personal supervision of Dennis and Carol Hopkins, resident proprietors.
Your enjoyment is our first consideration. Details with pleasure from:
**Little Bodieve Holiday Park
Wadebridge, Cornwall PL27 6EG
Telephone: 020 881 2323**

caravans approach from the east via Henley and A423.

1 acre 25 pitches ✳25 ⊞ £4 or 25 ⊞ £4 or 25▲£4 awnings

2⚲Individual pitches 8wc lit all night washbasins hc⌂hc☉(⊇)☎🎇

↔ stables golf ⤞ ⤵ launderette pub

WARDEN POINT
Kent
Map 5 TR07

▶ ⊞❶⚠

Warden Spring Caravan Park
(TR017726)☎Eastchurch (079588) 216
Jun–Oct rs Mar–May Last arrival mdnt

The site is in country surroundings on a well wooded private estate in a valley overlooking sea. Take A249 to Sheerness and turn right at roundabout onto B2231 Eastchurch road. Turn left at Eastchurch church and take first right to Warden Point.

30 pitches 250 static SA 30 ⊞ or 30 ⊞ ▲ (awnings) ltr

30⚲30wc lit all night 1cdp washbasins hc central hot water⌂hc☉supervised (wash spin dry) iron TV licensed club/bar childrens playground private beach calor gas camping gaz restaurant ☎ 🎇

↔ stables ⤞ ⤵ launderette pub

WAREHAM
Dorset
Map 3 SY98

▶ ▶ ▶ ❶❶⚠

Hunter's Moon Caravan & Camping Site (SY898902) Cold Harbour Signposted ☎Wareham (09295) 6605 Etr–Oct rs 16 Mar–19 Apr booking advisable peak periods Last arrival 22.00hrs Last departure noon

This site is 2½m W of Wareham along the Bere Regis road.

5 acres 90 pitches 90 ⊞ fr £2.75 or 90 ⊞ fr £2.75 or 90▲fr £2.75 (awnings)

8⚲19wc lit all night 1cdp washbasins hc central hot water (⌂hc)☉supervised (wash dry) iron (cold storage) calor gas camping gaz wc for disabled 🎇

↔ golf ⤞ cinema ⤵ launderette pub

Wallingford
–
Warsill

▶ ▶ ⊞❸⚠

Manor Farm Caravan Park (SY872866)
Manor Farm Cottage, East Stoke
☎Bindon Abbey (0929) 462870 Apr–mid Oct booking advisable school hols Last departure 11.30hrs
no motorcycles no single sex groups

From Wareham follow Dorchester road for 2m then turn left onto B3070, at first crossroads turn right, then next crossroads turn right; site is on the left. From Wool take B3071 and follow Bindon Lane unclass, in 1¾ turn left.

2½ acres 40 pitches 40 ⊞ £3.20 or 40 ⊞ £3.20 or 40▲£3.20 (awnings)

4⚲6wc lit all night 1cdp washbasins hc (⌂hc)☉supervised cold storage calor gas camping gaz toilet fluid hair dryer 🎇

↔ stables golf ⤞ cinema ⤵ launderette pub

WARSASH
Hampshire
Map 4 SU40

Warden Point, Eastchurch, Isle-of-Sheppey, Kent ME12 4HF.
Telephone: Eastchurch (079588) 216

EASTCHURCH (2½ m N). A Spurrier, B2231. Sea own foreshore. BR Sheerness 6 m. Bus 300 yds. Gas. Seasonal pitches £300/£350 per annum. Touring pitches £3.50 per night. Dogs. Cars park by vans, Shop, Club, Showers, Laundry, Winter storage, Caravan Sales, SAE brochure.

▶ ▶ ⊞❸⚠

Dibles Park (SU505060) Dibles Rd Apply to: Fareham Borough Council Civic Offices, PO Box 18, High Street, Fareham, Hants PO16 7PS Signposted ☎Locks Heath (04895) 5232 2 Apr–Oct must book peak periods Last arrival 20.30hrs Last departure 13.00hrs no tents

Level, grass site with young trees and bushes, set in wood and meadowland. Near River Hamble and the Solent. At Park Gate on A27 turn opposite Lloyds Bank into Locks Road then Fleet End Road.

1 acre 22 pitches 41 static 22 ⊞ £3.75–£4 or 22 ⊞ £3.75–£4 (awnings)

1⚲Individual pitches late arrivals enclosure 7wc lit all night 1cdp 8 washbasins hc (4⌂hc) 4☉supervised calor gas 🎇

↔ stables ⤵ launderette pub

▶ ⊞❶⚠

Solent Breezes Holiday Estate (SU504041) Signposted ☎Locks Heath (04895) 2084 Mar–Oct must book Last arrival 23.00hrs Last departure 11.30hrs

Situated in a secluded rural area overlooking Southampton Water.

3 acres 60 pitches 218 static 40 ⊞ or 40 ⊞ 20▲(awnings)

6⚲Individual pitches 10wc lit all night 1cdp 3 washbasins hc 10central hot water 2➔hc⌂hc 1☉supervised (wash spin dry) ♪ licensed club/bar childrens playground private beach calor gas toilet fluid cafe ☎ 🎇

↔ stables golf ⤞ ⤵ launderette pub

WARSILL
North Yorkshire
Map 8 SE26

▶ ▶ ⊞❷⚠

Warren House Caravan Site (SE225653)
☎Sawley (076586) 683 Apr–Oct booking advisable public hols

Part level, part sloping grass site with trees and bushes set amongst hills, moor and woodland.

3 acres 70 pitches 70 static 30 ⊞ £2.88 or 30 ⊞ fr £2.02 or 10▲fr £1.75 awnings ltr

5⚲Individual pitches ◑ late arrivals enclosure 18wc lit all night 2cdp ⊞

(washbasins central hot water ⋔ hc) ☺
supervised (dry) cold storage childrens
playground calor gas camping gaz toilet
fluid ☎ ⚍

WATCHET
Somerset
Map 3 ST04
See sketch map

▶▶▶▶ ② ❸ △
Doniford Holiday Village (ST095433)
Signposted ☎ Williton (0984) 32423 mid
May–mid Sep rs Etr–mid May & end Sep
booking advisable Last arrival 20.00hrs
Last departure 10.00hrs no pets

*A level site with some hardstanding
pitches for caravans and surfaced
internal roadways. E of Watchet off A39
and overlooking the sea (Minehead Bay).*

11 acres 120 pitches 240 static 100 ⚌ or
100 ⚍ 20 ▲ awnings ltr

20 ⚏ Individual pitches ⊘ late arrivals
enclosure 22 wc lit all night 2 cdp
12 washbasins hc central hot water 8 ⋔ hc
☺ supervised (3 wash 2 spin) 1 dry (iron)
⫘ ℘ games room (cold storage)
(licensed club) childrens playground
calor gas camping gaz toilet fluid cafe
restaurant ☎ ⊞ TV hire ⚍

↤ stables ⚲ cinema ⚙ launderette pub

▶▶▶ ① ❶ △
Warren Bay Caravan Park (SP052433)
Signposted ☎ (0984) 31460 Etr–Oct rs
Mar–19 Apr no bookings Last departure
noon

*Undulating grass site with mixed trees
and bushes, set in hilly downland and
wooded country. Adjacent to sea and
beach with rocky foreshore and sandy
bays. 1m W of town on B3191.*

7 acres 155 pitches 155 static 75 ⚌ fr £3 or
75 ⚍ fr £3 80 ▲ fr £3 awnings charged
peak periods

38 wc lit all night 2 cdp washbasins hc
(central hot water ⟞hc ⋔ hc) ☺
supervised (wash spin dry iron) cold
storage private beach calor gas camping
gaz ☎ ⊞ ⚍

↤ stables ⚲ ⚙ launderette pub

▶ ② ❶ △
Sunny Bank Caravan Park (SP093429)
Doniford Signposted ☎ Williton (0984)
32237
Mar–Nov rs Feb–20 May & Oct–Nov
booking advisable school hols Last arrival
20.00hrs Last departure 11.00hrs

*Coastal site in elevated position
developed to accommodate holiday
caravans with a good area set aside for
tourers. 1¾m E of town on the Doniford
road.*

1 acre 16 pitches 30 static 16 ⚌ £3
16 ⚍ £3 16 ▲ £3 (awnings)

6 ⚏ Individual pitches 4 wc lit all night
1 cdp ⚌ washbasins hc (central hot
water) (⋔ hc) ☺ supervised (wash spin
iron) ⫘ (games room) calor gas camping
gaz ☎ off licence ⚍

↤ stables ⚲ ⚙ launderette pub

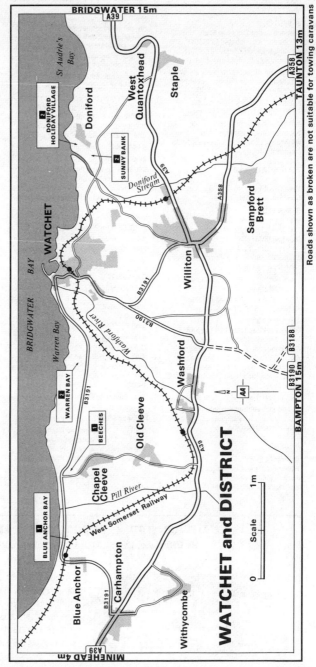

BRIDGWATER 15m A39

St Audrie's Bay

Doniford

② DONIFORD HOLIDAY VILLAGE

② SUNNY BANK

West Quantoxhead

Staple

Doniford Stream

A39

A358

Sampford Brett

WATCHET

BRIDGWATER BAY

Williton

B3191

B3180

A358

B3188

B3190 | B3191

BAMPTON 15m

TAUNTON 13m

Roads shown as broken are not suitable for towing caravans

Warren Bay

② WARREN BAY

Washford River

Washford

Old Cleeve

① BEECHES

N ⊕ AA

Chapel Cleeve

Pill River

West Somerset Railway

① BLUE ANCHOR BAY

Blue Anchor

B3191

Carhampton

Withycombe

MINEHEAD 4m A39

WATCHET and DISTRICT

0 Scale 1m

Sites listed under: **1** Blue Anchor   **2** Watchet

251

WATERBECK
Dumfries & Galloway *Dumfriesshire*
Map 11 NY27

▶▶▶ 🖿②🅰
Fallford Lodge Caravan Site
(NY268807) Signposted ☎(04616) 275
Etr–Sep booking advisable public hols
Last arrival 22.00hrs Last departure noon

*A quiet, country site picturesquely
situated in a fold of the hills beside the
Kirtle Water. Off B722.*

1½acres 10pitches 10🚐 fr£3.50 or
10🚙 fr£3.50 10🛆 fr£3.50 awnings ltr

4🅰Individual pitches late arrivals
enclosure 4wc lit all night 1 cdp
washbasins hc 🖿 hc ☉ supervised cold
storage calor gas

WATERGATE BAY
Cornwall
Map 2 SW86
See Newquay sketch map

▶▶▶ 🖿②🅰
Watergate Bay Holiday Park
(SW850653) Tregurrian Signposted ☎St
Mawgan (06374) 387 Spring Bank Hol–
mid Sep rsEtr–Spring Bank Hol booking
advisable Jul & Aug Last arrival 23.00hrs
Last departure noon

*Level site with hard core roads, ½m from
Watergate beach. Off the B3276.*

8acres 171pitches 171🚐 £3–£6 or
171🚙 £3–£6 or 171🛆 £3–£6 awnings

9🅰Individual pitches late arrivals
enclosure 25wc lit all night 1 cdp
washbasins hc (central hot water 🖿 hc)☉
supervised (wash dry iron) 🍽 games
room CTV (cold storage) licensed club/
bar childrens playground calor gas
camping gaz toilet fluid cafe restaurant ☎
⊞🍴

↦ stables cinema 🍴 launderette pub

see advertisement on page 191

WATERLOO CROSS
Devon
Map 3 ST01

▶▶▶ 🖿②🅰
**Waterloo Cross Camping & Caravan
Park** *(ST054139)* Signposted
☎Craddock (0884) 40317 15 Mar–15

Nov booking advisable Jul & Aug Last
arrival mdnt Last departure 12.00hrs
*A level grassy site with bushes and mature
trees. Leave M5 at junction 27; follow A38
towards Waterloo Cross, the site is just
before the latter.*

4½acres 50pitches 50🚐 fr£3 or
50🚙 fr£3 or 50🛆 fr£3 (awnings) ltr

7🅰Individual pitches☉ late arrivals
enclosure 7wc lit all night 1 cdp 🔌
13 washbasins (🖿 hc)☉ supervised
licensed bar childrens playground calor
gas camping gaz cafe restaurant ☎ 🍴

↦ stables golf 🍴 launderette pub

▶▶ 🖿②🅰
Old Well Caravan Park *(ST053138)* Old
Well Roadhouse (junc A38/B3181 ½m E
of M5 junc 27) ☎Craddock (0884) 40873
15 Mar–14 Nov booking advisable public
hols & Aug

2acres 20pitches 20🚙 £2.50 or
20🚙 £2.50 or 20🛆 £2.50 (awnings) ltr

2🅰late arrivals enclosure 4wc lit all night
1 cdp 🔌 6 washbasins hc (2🖿 hc) 3☉
supervised cold storage childrens
playground calor gas camping gaz toilet
fluid cafe ☎ 🍴

↦ stables golf 🍴 pub

WATERMILLOCK
Cumbria
Map 12 NY42

▶▶▶ 🖿②🅰
Quiet Site *(NY431236)* Signposted
☎Pooley Bridge (08536) 337 Mar–Oct
booking advisable public hols & Jul–Aug
Last arrival 22.00hrs Last departure
14.00hrs

Tranquil site 1½m N of A591 set in the fells.

6acres 60pitches 22static 10🚐 £4 or
10🚙 £4 50🛆 £3.50 (awnings)

6🅰☉ late arrivals enclosure 15wc lit all
night 1 cdp 6🔌 washbasins hc 🖿 hc☉
supervised (wash spin dry iron) games
room CTV (cold storage) licensed club/
bar childrens playground calor gas
camping gaz toilet fluid ☎ 🍴

↦ stables ⚓🍴

▶▶▶ 🖿②🅰
Ullswater Caravan & Camping Park
(NY437231) Signposted ☎Pooley
Bridge (08536) 666 Mar–14 Nov booking
advisable public hols Last arrival 22.00hrs
Last departure noon no motorcycles

*Level site surrounded by trees next to
farm, 4m SW of Penrith off A592
Ambleside Road.*

9acres 155pitches 55static SA
40🚐 £4.70 115🚙 £4.70 or 115🛆 £4.70
(awnings)

10🅰☉ 31wc lit all night 1 cdp 🔌
washbasins hc 🖿 hc☉ supervised (wash
spin) dry (cold storage) licensed club/bar
childrens playground calor gas camping
gaz paraffin toilet fluid cafe ☎ 🍴

↦ stables ⚓ 🍴 launderette pub

WEELEY
Essex
Map 5 TM12

▶▶▶ 🖿②🅰
Weeley Bridge Caravan Park
(TM145218) Signposted ☎(0255)
830403 Etr–mid Oct booking advisable
Whit & Aug Bank Hol
no single sex groups or unaccompanied
young people

*Level grass site in two adjacent sections
beside Weeley Station and a busy freight
depot.*

9acres 90pitches 250static 90🚐 £4–£5
or 90🚙 £4–£5 or 90🛆 £4–£5 awnings ltr

3🅰10wc lit all night 1 cdp 13washbasins
hc (4🖿 hc) 5☉ supervised cold storage
licensed club/bar childrens play area
calor gas camping gaz toilet fluid ☎ 🍴

↦ launderette pub

WEETON
Lancashire
Map 7 SD33

▶ 🖿①🅰
High Moor Farm Caravan Park
(SD388365) Signposted ☎(039 136) 273
Mar–Oct booking advisable Jul–Sep Last
arrival 23.00hrs Last departure 14.00hrs

*A small site set in open farmland about 6m
from Blackpool. Situated N of M55 (exit 3)
off A585 Fleetwood road on B5260.*

4acres 60pitches SA 60🚐 £2.50 or
60 🚐 £2.50 or 60▲£2.50 (awnings)
2♫ Individual pitches ◔ late arrivals
enclosure 12wc lit all night washbasins hc
central hot water � hc 🛁 hc☉ (wash spin)
(cold storage) childrens playground calor
gas ☎ 🛍
↩ launderette pub

WELLS
Somerset
Map 3 ST54
See Wookey Hole

WEM
Shropshire
Map 7 SJ52

▶▶▶ 2 ❶ ⚠
Lower Lacon Caravan Park (SJ534304)
Signposted ☎(0939) 32376 Apr–Oct
Last departure 19.00hrs

Level grass site, set in meadowland. 1½m
E of town centre on B5065.

31acres 100pitches 20static SA
80🚐 £3.50 or 80 🚐 £3.50 20▲£3.50
(awnings) ltr

14♫◔ 12wc lit all night 2cdp 🚐
washbasins hc (central hot water 🛁 hc)☉
supervised (wash spin dry iron) games
room (cold storage) childrens playground
calor gas camping gaz toilet fluid ☎ take-
away food fishing off licence hair dryers 🛍
↩ stables ♦ launderette pub

WENTNOR
Shropshire
Map 7 SO39

▶▶ 🔲 ❶ ⚠
Green Camping & Caravanning Site
(SO379928) The Green Signposted
☎ Linley (058 861) 605 Etr–Oct no
bookings

Level grass site set in meadowland. 15m
SW of Shrewsbury and N of A489 Craven
Arms–Newtown road.

8acres 125pitches 15static SA 75🚐 or
75 🚐 50▲ awnings

8♫ 12wc lit all night 2cdp washbasins hc
(🛁 hc)☉ supervised (cold storage) calor
gas camping gaz 🛍
↩ ♦ pub

Weeton
—
Weston

WEST BRIDGFORD
Nottinghamshire
Map 8 SK53

▶ ▶ 🔲 ❸ ⚠
Green Acres (SK605385) ☎ Nottingham
(0602) 821615 All year Last arrival
23.00hrs Last departure 17.30hrs no tents

Partly level and gently sloping grass and
gravel site with trees and bushes, near
River Trent in wooded part of urban area.
Turn N from A52 at signpost, site ½m on
right.

2½m 8pitches 85static SA 8🚐 or 8 🚐 ltr
1♫ 3wc lit all night 1cdp washbasins hc
(central hot water 🛁 hc)☉ supervised dry
calor gas ☎
↩ stables ♦♦ launderette pub

WEST COKER
Somerset
Map 3 ST51

▶ ▶ 🔲 ❷ ⚠
Partway Lane Caravan Park (ST505134)
Signposted ☎(093 586) 2871 Mar–Oct
Last arrival 20.00hrs Last departure noon

Well-run and well-maintained site with
good views over surrounding
countryside. 2m S off A30, travelling S turn
right at Coker Bridge, travelling N turn
right at East Chinnock. Site is in village of
Hartington Mandeville.

20pitches 11static 10🚐 £35 🚐 £2.50 or
5▲£3 (awnings)
3♫ Individual pitches 5wc lit all night
1cdp 🚐 6washbasins hc (1central hot
water 4🛁 hc) 1☉ (spin) (🌂) (cold storage)
calor gas camping gaz 🛍
↩ stables golf cinema ♦ launderette pub

WEST DRAYTON
Gt London
Map 4 TQ07

▶ 🔲 ❶ ⚠
Riverside Caravans (TQ052791)
Thorney Mill Rd Signposted ☎(08954)
46520 All year must book Last arrival
18.00hrs Last departure 11.00hrs no tents

Level site with sand and gravel surface;
bushes are in abundance. Set adjacent to
river in the urban area. Access from M4
(exit 4) then via A408 to West Drayton.

2acres 33pitches SA 33🚐 £5 or 33 🚐 £5
5♫ Individual pitches 9wc lit all night
3cdp washbasins hc (🛁 hc)☉ dry (games
room) calor gas camping gaz toilet fluid 🛍
↩ stables golf ♦ launderette pub

WESTHAM
East Sussex
Map 5 TQ60

▶▶▶ 🔲 ❸ ⚠
**Fairfields Farm Caravan & Camping
Site** (TQ639039) Eastbourne
Signposted ☎ Eastbourne (0323)
763165 Etr–Oct booking advisable peak
periods

A pleasant quiet country touring site on the
B2191, signposted from the east side of
Eastbourne and off A27.

3acres 60pitches SA 60🚐 £4.30 or
60 🚐 £4 or 60▲£4.30 (awnings)
5♫◔ 12wc lit all night 1cdp washbasins
hc central hot water 🛁 hc☉ supervised
cold storage calor gas camping gaz
fishing riding & clay pigeon shooting 🛍
↩ stables golf cinema ♦ launderette
pub

WESTON
Devon
Map 3 SY18

▶▶▶ 🔲 ❷ ⚠
Oakdown Touring Caravan Park
(SY168901) Signposted ☎ Sidmouth →

(03955) 3731 15 May–15 Sep rs Apr–15
May & 15 Sep–15 Oct booking advisable
Jul & Aug Last arrival 22.00hrs Last
departure 11.00hrs

*This is a level site with short approach road
from A3052 between Seaton–Sidmouth.*

4acres 52pitches 46🚐 fr£4.50 or
46 🚐 fr£4.50 6▲fr£4.50 (awnings)

6🏕Individual pitches⊘ 8wc lit all night
1cdp 🔌 washbasins hc🚿hc☉
supervised (wash dry) iron (cold storage)
childrens playground calor gas camping
gaz ☎ 🛁

↦ stables golf 🎣 cinema 🎬 launderette
pub

WESTON-SUPER-MARE
Avon
Map 3 ST36
See sketch map on page 256

▶ ▶ ▶ 🄩 🄰 △
Country View Caravan Park *(ST335647)*
Sand Rd, Sand Bay Signposted ☎(0934)
27595 Etr–Oct must book school hols Last
arrival 21.00hrs no single sex groups

7acres 150pitches 36static SA
50🚐 fr£3.50 50 🚐 fr£3 50▲fr£3.50
(awnings)

10🏕Individual pitches⊘ late arrivals
enclosure wc lit all night 🔌 washbasins
(🚿hc)☉(wash spin dry iron) childrens
playground calor gas camping gaz toilet
fluid ☎ 🛁

↦ stables golf 🎣 cinema 🎬 launderette
pub

▶ ▶ ▶ 🄩 🄰 △
Oak Tree & West End Caravan Park
*(ST354600)*Locking (3m E off A371)
Signposted ☎Banwell (0934) 822529
Mar–Oct booking advisable peak periods
Last arrival 22.00hrs Last departure noon
no single sex groups

*Secluded site with views of Weston-
super-Mare and surrounding
countryside.*

8acres 75pitches SA 75🚐 or 75 🚐 or
75▲(awnings)

8🏕Individual pitches⊘ 15wc lit all night
1cdp washbasins hc (🚿hc)☉supervised
(wash dry iron) (cold storage) childrens
playground calor gas camping gas toilet
fluid ☎ hair dryers battery charging 🛁

↦ stables golf 🎣 cinema 🎬 launderette
pub

▶ ▶ ▶ � 🄾 🄰 △
Weston Gateway Caravan Site
*(ST370631)*West Wick Signposted
☎(0934) 33201 May–Sep rsOct–Apr
Last departure 14.00hrs no single sex
groups

*A mainly level grassy site with trees and
bushes, near main road. 3m E of A370,
close to M5, junction 21.*

15acres 375pitches 375🚐 or 375 🚐 or
375▲(awnings)

30🏕⊘ 65wc lit all night 1cdp 🔌
40washbasins hc 3central hot water
(18🚿 hc) 4☉supervised (wash spin) dry
(iron) TV (cold storage) licensed club/bar

---

childrens playground calor gas camping
gaz toilet fluid restaurant ☎ 🛁

↦ stables golf cinema 🎬 launderette pub

see advertisement on page 256

▶ ▶ 🄩 🄾 🄰 △
Manor Farm Caravan Park *(ST325583)*
Grange Rd, Uphill Signposted ☎(0934)
29731 Etr–Sep Last arrival 10.00hrs Last
departure noon no tents

*Farm site with separate touring field in
open country, near Uphill Woods. Turn off
A370 into Grange Road for site on left.*

2acres 35pitches 40static 35🚐 6 🚐 ltr

9🏕16wc lit all night 1cdp (washbasins hc
central hot water) (🚿 hc)☉calor gas
camping gaz 🛁

↦ stables golf 🎣 cinema 🎬 launderette
pub

▶ ▶ � 🄾 🄰 △
Purn Farm Caravan Park *(ST335571)*
Bleadon (3m SE on A370) Signposted
☎Bleadon (0934) 812203 Mar–Oct must
book

*Purpose-built site situated on flat, open
land alongside main road.*

8acres 150pitches 80static SA 100🚐 or
100 🚐 50▲(awnings)

14🏕⊘ 52wc lit all night 1cdp
34washbasins hc (6🚿 hc)☉supervised
(wash spin iron) (cold storage) childrens
playground calor gas camping gaz ☎ 🛁

↦ stables golf 🎣 cinema 🎬 launderette
pub

▶ 🄾 🄰 △
Ardnave Caravan & Chalet Park
*(ST332632)*Crooks Ln, Kewstoke
☎(0934) 22319 Mar–Nov must book Jul
& Aug Last departure 10.00hrs no tents

*A level grassy site with mature trees set in
the country close to Sand Bay beach.*

¾acre 12pitches 105static 12🚐 £3–£4
or 12 🚐 £3–£4 (awnings)

2🏕late arrivals enclosure 22wc lit all night
1cdp washbasins hc 🚿 hc☉dry iron
childrens playground calor gas 🛁

↦ stables golf 🎣 cinema 🎬 launderette
pub

WESTWARD
Cumbria
Map 11 NY24

▶ ▶ ▶ 🄩 🄾 🄰 △
Clea Hall Holiday Park *(NY279425)*
Signposted ☎Wigton (09654) 2880 Mar–
13 Nov Late arrivals 22.00hrs

*Level grassy site with bushes and mature
trees in hilly country, with surrounding
woodland, moorland and mountains,
3½m S of A595.*

5acres 50pitches 90static 35🚐 £3.50–£4
5 🚐 £3.50–£4 10▲£3.50–£4 (awnings)

4🏕wc lit all night 1cdp 🔌 washbasins hc
(♨hc)🚿hc☉supervised (wash spin) 🍽

---

games room licensed club/bar childrens
playground calor gas cafe ☎ 🛁

WEST WITTERING
West Sussex
Map 4 SZ79

▶ ▶ 🄾 🄰 △
Wicks Farm Caravan Park *(SU797996)*
Redlands Ln Signposted ☎(024 366)
3116 14 Mar–Oct booking advisable
peak periods Last arrival 22.00hrs Last
departure noon

3acres 40pitches 60static 40 🚐 £2.75–
£3.50 or 40▲£2.75–£3.50 awnings

5🏕Individual pitches⊘ 9wc lit all night
1cdp 🔌 washbasins hc (🚿 hc)☉
supervised (dry) iron (𝒫) (cold storage)
childrens playground calor gas camping
gaz toilet fluid ☎

↦ stables ▲ 🎣 launderette pub 🛁

WEYBOURNE
Norfolk
Map 9 TG14

▶ 🄩 🄾
Kelling Heath Caravan & Camping Site
*(TG117418)*Signposted ☎(026 370) 224
Spring Bank Hol–Oct rsEtr–Spring Bank
Hol must book 24 Jul–Aug

*Level grassy site set amid pine trees and
sandy, open spaces. Follow
'Kellingheath' sign from village centre on
A149 Cromer road.*

16acres 250pitches 400static 100🚐 or
100 🚐 150▲awnings ltr

10🏕Individual pitches for caravans⊘
50wc lit all night 5cdp washbasins hc 🚿 hc
☉supervised wash dry iron games room
CTV (cold storage) licensed bar childrens
playground calor gas camping gaz toilet
fluid cafe ☎ 🎏 🛁

↦ stables golf 🎬 launderette pub

WEYMOUTH
Dorset
Map 3 SY67
*See also Fleet, Dorset and Chickerell for
details of other sites in the vicinity.*

▶ ▶ ▶ � 🄾 🄰 △
Littlesea Holiday Park *(SY654783)*
Lynch Ln ☎Hemel Hempstead (0442)
51163 mid May–Sep rs Apr–mid May Last
arrival 19.00hrs Last departure 10.00hrs
no single sex groups no motorcycles

*Level, grass site set in meadowland
adjacent to sea. 1½m W of Weymouth on
B3157 Chickerell road.*

20acres 265pitches 680static 140🚐 or
140 🚐 125▲awnings ltr

30🏕⊘ 130wc lit all night 1cdp
washbasins hc 🚿 hc☉(wash dry iron) 🍽
(licensed club/bar) childrens playground
calor gas camping gaz toilet fluid cafe ☎
🛁

↦ stables golf 🎣 cinema 🎬 launderette
pub

255

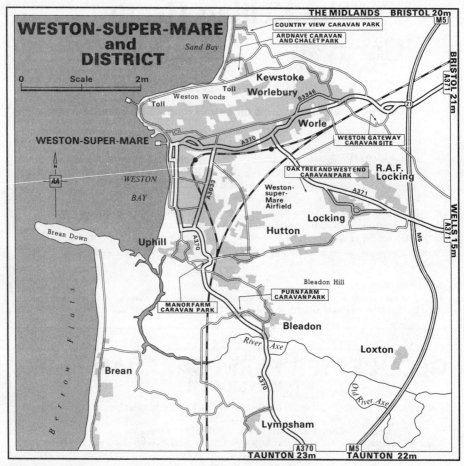

WESTON-SUPER-MARE and DISTRICT

THE MIDLANDS   BRISTOL 20m   M5

COUNTRY VIEW CARAVAN PARK

ARDNAVE CARAVAN AND CHALET PARK

Sand Bay

Scale   0   2m

Kewstoke

Toll   Weston Woods   Toll   Worlebury   B3346

Toll

Weston Woods

Worle

WESTON-SUPER-MARE

WESTON GATEWAY CARAVAN SITE

A370

OAK TREE AND WEST END CARAVAN PARK

R.A.F. Locking

WESTON BAY

Weston-super-Mare Airfield

A371

A3033

Locking

Brean Down

Uphill   A370   Hutton

Bleadon Hill

PURN FARM CARAVAN PARK

MANOR FARM CARAVAN PARK

Bleadon

River Axe

Loxton

Berrow Flats

Brean

A370

Old River Axe

Lympsham

A370   M5

TAUNTON 23m   TAUNTON 22m

BRISTOL 21m   A371

WELLS 15m   A371

All sites listed under Weston-super-Mare

Weston Gateway Tourist Caravan Park

WEST WICK, Nr WESTON-SUPER-MARE, AVON.
TELEPHONE 33201

Ideally situated for caravanners and campers using the M5 motorway. Within reach locally are many beauty spots. – Cheddar Caves, Wookey Hole etc. Also locally – horse riding, fishing and golf. Weston-Super-Mare – 3 miles.
On site we have a licensed club, children's arcade, shop, launderette, children's play area, flush toilets and showers. Dogs taken – but must be kept under strict control.

256

WHALEY BRIDGE
Derbyshire
Map 7 SK08

► 🚻 ❶ ❶ ⚠
Happy Vans Caravan Site (SK025802)
Tunstead Milton ☎ 061-483 8888 or 061-432 2995 All year booking advisable public hols Last arrival 22.00hrs no tents

Grass and gravel site with trees and bushes set in meadowland near River Goyt. On A6, between Chapel-en-le-Frith and Whaley Bridge. Site entrance opposite Rose & Crown public house.

¼acre 6pitches 14static 6 ⊕ £2.40 or 6 ⊕ £2.40 (awnings)
2 ⊕ 4wc lit all night 1cdp ⊕ (4 washbasins hc) (2 ⋔ hc) 2 ☺ (wash spin) calor gas camping gaz 🛒
↩ stables golf 🏌 🎣 launderette pub

► 🚻 ❶ ⚠
Ringstones Caravan Park (SK005824)
Yeardsley Ln ☎ (06633) 2152 Mar–Oct no bookings

A secluded site on sloping ground surrounded by hills, with trees and bushes. 1m W of A6 at Furness Vale.

2acres 40pitches 36static SA 10 ⊕ or 10 ⊕ 40 ▲ (awnings) ltr
5 ⊕ ⊘ 8wc 1cdp (⋔ hc) supervised calor gas
↩ stables golf cinema 🎣 launderette pub 🛒

WHATSTANDWELL
Derbyshire
Map 8 SK35

► ► ► 🚻 ❶ ⚠
Haytop Farm Caravanseral (SK330538)
Signposted ☎ Ambergate (077 385) 2063 Apr–Oct rsNov–Mar booking advisable public hols no unaccompanied youths under 18

A sloping, stony and grassy site with mature trees set in sylvan surroundings. Off A6 between Belper and Matlock.

60pitches SA 30 ⊕ £4.50 10 ⊕ £3.50 20 ▲ fr £3.50 (awnings) ltr
6 ⊕ ⊘ late arrivals enclosure 9wc lit all night 1cdp ⊕ washbasins hc (⋔ hc) ☺ (spin dry iron) cold storage calor gas

camping gaz paraffin ☎ fishing
↩ stables 🏌 cinema pub 🛒

► 🚻 ❶ ⚠
Mere Brook Caravan & Camping Park (SK333545) Signposted ☎ Ambergate (077 385) 3100 & 2154 Apr–Oct rsNov–Mar booking advisable peak periods Last arrival 23.30hrs Last departure noon

A partly level and sloping, grass site in hilly woodland and moorland country with river and canal nearby. 5m S of Matlock on A6.

1½acres 75pitches 116static SA 75 ⊕ or 75 ⊕ or 75 ▲ (awnings) ltr
6 ⊕ ⊘ 22wc lit all night 2cdp washbasins hc (central hot water ⋔ hc) ☺ supervised (spin) (cold storage) calor gas camping gaz mobile shop 🛒
↩ stables golf 🏌 🎣 launderette pub

WHITBY
North Yorkshire
Map 8 NZ81

► ► ► 🚻 ❶ ⚠
Whitby Holiday Village (NZ909109)
Saltwick Bay Signposted ☎ (0947) 602664 mid May–Sep booking advisable Jul, Aug & public hols Last arrival 22.00hrs Last departure noon 🎀 no motorcycles no single sex groups

Part of a large holiday village complex of self-catering chalets and caravans positioned on the clifftop, 2m east of Whitby harbour and Abbey.

4½acres 135pitches 116static 15 ⊕ fr £3.50 120 ⊕ fr £3.50 or 120 ▲ fr £3.15 awnings
5 ⊕ Individual pitches ⊘ late arrivals enclosure 15wc lit all night 1cdp washbasins hc (⋔ hc ☺) supervised (wash) spin (dry iron) games room cold storage licensed club/bar childrens playground private beach calor gas camping gaz cafe ☎ 🛒
↩ stables golf 🏌 cinema 🎣

WHITECLIFFE BAY
Isle of Wight
Map 4 SZ68
See Shanklin sketch map

► ► ► ► 🚻 ❷ ⚠
Whitecliffe Bay Holiday Park
(SZ636865) Signposted ☎ Bembridge (098 387) 2671 (due to change to Isle of Wight (0983) 872671) Etr–Sep must book Jun–Aug 🎀 no single sex groups

A partly level and sloping site with mature trees and bushes; situated 20 minutes walk from the sea. The caravan site is situated in the main Holiday Park with the camping area the other side of the road, overlooking Bembridge Airport.

18acres 505pitches 240static SA ✳ 200 ⊕ £3.80–£6 or 200 ⊕ £3.80–£6 305 ▲ £3.80–£6 awnings

26 ⊕ ⊘ 63wc lit all night 17cdp ⊕ washbasins hc central hot water ⚡hc (⋔ hc) ☺ supervised (wash spin dry) iron ⨼ games room CTV licensed club/bar childrens playground private beach calor gas camping gaz toilet fluid cafe restaurant ☎ ⊞ (crazy golf) 🛒
↩ stables golf 🏌 cinema 🎣 launderette pub

► ► ► 🚻 ❷ ⚠
Caravan Site (SZ638861) Signposted ☎ Bembridge (098 387) 3051 or 2715 15 May–26 Sep must book no pets no motorvans or tents

Part level, part sloping site overlooking bay with path down to shingle and sand beach. Along B3395 turn right at airfield.

2acres 30pitches 300static SA 30 ⊕ (awnings)
12 ⊕ 66wc lit all night 1cdp washbasins hc (⋔ hc) ☺ supervised (wash dry) childrens playground private beach calor gas camping gaz ☎ ⊞ off licence 🛒
↩ stables 🎣 launderette pub

WHITECROSS
Cornwall
Map 2 SW86
See Newquay sketch map

► ► ► 🚻 ❶ ⚠
White Acres Holiday Park (SW890598)
Signposted ☎ St Austell (0726) 860220 Spring Bank Hol–Sep rs beginning of May booking advisable Jul & Aug Last arrival 23.00hrs Last departure noon no groups of young people →

Part level, part sloping grass site with mixed trees and bushes set in typical Cornish downland scenery. 2m off A30 on A392 Newquay road.

10acres 268pitches 80static 150🚐 £2.35–£5.75 or 150 🚐 £2.35–£5.75 118▲£2.35–£5.75 awnings

24🏕late arrivals enclosure 30wc lit all night 2cdp washbasins hc (🛢hc)☉ supervised (wash spin dry iron) 🍴 games room CTV (cold storage) licensed club/bar childrens playground calor gas camping gaz paraffin toilet fluid cafe ☎ 🛍

↦ stables ✒

see advertisement on page 192

WHITSTABLE
Kent
Map 5 TR16
See Herne Bay sketch map

▶▶▶ ②❶△
Blue Waters Touring Harbour
(TR145675) St John's Rd Signposted Apr–16 Oct no bookings Last arrival 22.00hrs Last departure 22.00hrs 🚫 no tents no motorcycles

Level, grass site with trees and bushes near to sand/shingle beach, 3m from town on A299.

12acres 20pitches 452static SA 20🚐 £3.25 or 20 🚐 £3.25 (awnings)

4🏕 Individual pitches 11wc lit all night 2cdp (central hot water) (🛢hc)☉ (wash dry) cold storage childrens playground private beach calor gas camping gaz toilet fluid ☎ take-away food 🛍

↦ stables golf cinema ✒ launderette pub

WHITSTONE
Cornwall
Map 2 SX29

▶▶▶ ②❶△
Keywood Caravan Park Signposted ☎ Week St. Mary (028 884) 338 Etr–Oct must book Jul & Aug Last departure 10.00hrs Last arrival 10.00hrs

Level and slightly sloping site on B3254, Launceston–Bude road.

1acre 25pitches 50static 25🚐 £2 or 25 🚐 £2 or 25▲£2 awnings

4🏕 12wc lit all night 1cdp washbasins hc central hot water (🛢hc)☉ supervised (wash spin) iron cold storage licensed club/bar childrens playground calor gas camping gaz ☎ ⊞ 🛍

↦ stables golf cinema launderette pub

WIGHT, ISLE OF
Places with AA-classified caravan and campsites are indicated on the location map on page 4 of the atlas section. Full details of these will be found under individual placenames within the gazetteer section.

WILLINGHAM
Cambridgeshire
Map 5 TL47

▶ ②❷△
Allwyn Camping & Caravan Site
(TL396701) Over Rd ☎ (0954) 60977 Mar–Oct booking advisable public hols

Level grass site set in pastureland.

4acres 80pitches 80🚐 £2.30 or 80 🚐 £2.30 or 80▲£2.30

4🏕 11wc lit all night 2cdp 🚽 11washbasins hc 3central hot water 6🛢hc 1☉ supervised wash spin iron cold storage childrens playground calor gas camping gaz toilet fluid ☎

↦ ✒ launderette pub 🛍

WIMBORNE MINSTER
Dorset
Map 4 SZ09

▶▶▶ ②❸△
Wilksworth Farm Caravan Park
(SU004018) Cranborne Rd Signposted ☎ Wimborne (0202) 883769 Mar–Oct must book Spring Bank Hol & Jul–Aug Last arrival 22.30hrs Last departure noon

Level, grass and gravel site, set in farmland, 1m N on B3078.

8acres 85pitches 60static ✱60🚐 £3.50–£4.50 or 60 🚐 £3.50–£4.50 25▲£3.50–4.50 awnings

8🏕☉ 15wc lit all night 1cdp 🚽 washbasins hc central hot water 🛢hc☉ supervised (wash spin dry iron) (🏠) games room cold storage childrens playground calor gas camping gaz toilet fluid ☎ 🛍

↦ stables golf ✒ launderette pub

WINCHESTER
Hampshire
Map 4 SU42

▶▶ ③❷
Mornhill Caravan Site *(SU523295)*
Mornhill Signposted ☎ (0962) 69877 Apr–Oct booking advisable peak periods Last arrival 20.00hrs Last departure noon

A well laid out site in secluded spot surrounded by trees. 2¼m E of city centre off Alton road (A31) near New Inn.

9acres 150pitches 132🚐 £5.60 or 132 🚐 £5.60 18▲£5.40 (awnings)

6🏕 Individual pitches ☉ late arrivals enclosure wc lit all night 3cdp 🚽 washbasins hc 🛢hc☉ supervised (spin) calor gas camping gaz toilet fluid ☎

↦ golf cinema ✒ launderette pub 🛍

▶ ❶❶△
Winchester Recreation Centre
(SU486299) Gordon Rd Signposted ☎ (0962) 69525 May–Oct must book Last arrival 22.30hrs Last departure noon no caravans or motorvans

Mainly level, grassy site with trees and bushes, near main road. Campsite fee includes free entry to Winchester

---

Recreation Centre during normal opening hours.

50pitches 50▲£6

2🏕 Individual pitches 6wc lit all night washbasins hc 🛢hc☉ (🏠) (♇) licensed bar childrens playground camping gaz cafe ☎ 🛍

↦ golf cinema ✒ launderette pub

WINDERMERE
Cumbria
Map 7 SD49
See sketch map

▶▶▶ ②❶△
White Cross Bay Caravan Park
(NY397004) Troutbeck Bridge ☎ (09662) 3937 Etr–5 Nov rs Mar–Etr booking advisable peak periods Last arrival 23.00hrs Last departure noon no tents

A vast mature wooded site which rambles onto the Lake shore conveniently situated on the A591 between Windermere and Ambleside.

5acres 125pitches 353static 125🚐 or 125 🚐 (awnings)

25🏕 Individual pitches late arrivals enclosure 36wc lit all night 4cdp 🚽 18washbasins hc 10🛢hc 6☉ (wash dry iron) games room CTV licensed club/bar childrens playground private beach calor gas toilet fluid cafe restaurant ☎ fishing slipway 🛍

↦ stables golf ⚓ cinema pub

see advertisement on page 260

▶▶▶ ❶❶△
Park Cliffe Farm Caravan & Camping Site *(SD391912)* Tower Wood Signposted ☎ Newby Bridge (0448) 31344 Mar–Oct booking advisable Jul & Aug Last arrival 23.00hrs Last departure noon no groups of motorcyclists

A hillside site on level and sloping ground with trees, bushes, rocks and mountain stream. 4m S of Windermere off A592.

25acres 250pitches 50static 5🚐 £3.50–£5 20 🚐 £3.50–£5 or 225▲£3.50–£5 (awnings) ltr

8🏕☉ 37wc lit all night 2cdp central hot water 🛢hc☉ supervised (wash spin) dry iron calor gas camping gaz ☎ 🛍

↦ stables ✒ launderette pub

▶▶ ❶❷△
Braithwaite Fold Touring Caravan Park
(SD400961) Glebe Rd. Apply to: South Lakeland District Council, Tourism & Recreation Dept, Ashleigh, Windermere, Cumbria LA23 2AG Signposted no tents

Level, grass site with trees and bushes set in urban area adjacent to lake and ferry. It is situated ½m S of town of Bowness.

4acre 60pitches 60🚐 fr £4.50 or 60 🚐 fr £4.50 awnings

3🏕 Individual pitches 12wc lit all night 1cdp washbasins hc central hot water 🛢hc☉ supervised calor gas camping gaz toilet fluid ☎ 🛍

↦ stables golf ⚓ cinema ✒ launderette pub

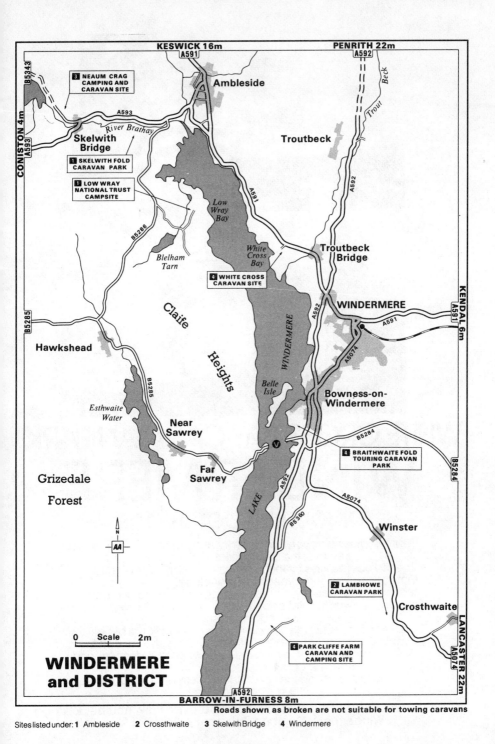

KESWICK 16m
A591
PENRITH 22m
A592

3 NEAUM CRAG CAMPING AND CARAVAN SITE

CONISTON 4m
B5343
A593

Ambleside

Troutbeck

A593
River Brathay

Skelwith Bridge

1 SKELWITH FOLD CARAVAN PARK

1 LOW WRAY NATIONAL TRUST CAMPSITE

A591

B5286

Low Wray Bay

White Cross Bay

Troutbeck Bridge

A592

4 WHITE CROSS CARAVAN SITE

Blelham Tarn

B5285

Claife

KENDAL 6m
A591

WINDERMERE
A591

Hawkshead

Heights

WINDERMERE

A5074

Esthwaite Water

B5285

Belle Isle

Bowness-on-Windermere

Near Sawrey

Far Sawrey

V

B5284

4 BRAITHWAITE FOLD TOURING CARAVAN PARK

B5284

Grizedale

Forest

LAKE

A592

A5074

B5360

Winster

N
AA

2 LAMBHOWE CARAVAN PARK

Crosthwaite

LANCASTER 22m
A5074

0   Scale   2m

WINDERMERE and DISTRICT

4 PARK CLIFFE FARM CARAVAN AND CAMPING SITE

A592
BARROW-IN-FURNESS 8m

Roads shown as broken are not suitable for towing caravans

Sites listed under: **1** Ambleside   **2** Crossthwaite   **3** Skelwith Bridge   **4** Windermere

259

WHITE CROSS BAY CARAVAN PARK
WINDERMERE
for touring caravans

This prestigious caravan park is set in landscaped grounds at the centre of the Lake District National Park.

The site has facilities for touring caravans from Easter through to October, with superb amenities that include – a well-appointed marine and chandlery, hard standings, well maintained access roads, mains water, toilet and shower blocks, launderette, bar and well equipped shop.

Direct access to Lake Windermere is an additional benefit. White Cross Bay lies on the north-east shore of the Lake on the A591, 2 miles north of the major tourist towns of Windermere and Bowness and 4 miles south of Ambleside..

For the tourist visiting the Lake District, there is no better centre than White Cross Bay.

Full details available from **White Cross Bay Caravan Park, Troutbeck Bridge, Windermere, Cumbria. Telephone: 096 62 3937.**

WINKFIELD
Berkshire
Map 4 SU97

▶ ① ❶ △

Sunnybend Farm Caravan Park
(SU899724) Parkers Ln, Maidens Gdns
Signposted ☎ Winkfield Row (0344)
882846 Apr–Oct rs Nov–Mar booking
advisable public hols Last arrival 20.00hrs
Last departure noon

*A very quiet, level grass site, set in rural
countryside. Ideal for trips to Windsor
Safari Park, off Windsor–Bracknell road,
B3022.*

6acres 120pitches 7static 120⊞ £4.50 or
120⊞ £4 or 120▲£4.50 (awnings)

5⚲⊙ 24wc 1cdp (washbasins hc central
hot water (ⓜhc) ⊙ supervised TV licensed
club/bar calor gas camping gaz cafe
restaurant ☎ ⓛ

↔ stables golf ⚑ cinema ✔ launderette
pub

WINKSLEY
North Yorkshire
Map 8 SE27

▶ ▶ ▶ ② ❷ △

**Woodhouse Farm Caravan & Camping
Park** *(SE241715)* Signposted ☎ Kirkby
Malzeard (076583) 309 Etr–Oct booking
advisable public hols Last arrival 23.00hrs
no unaccompanied children

*Situated in well-wooded area amongst
pleasant agricultural surroundings. 6m W
of Ripon off B6265 Pateley Bridge road,
2½m from Fountains Abbey.*

15acres 95pitches 15static SA
40⊞ £3.15 5 ⊞ £3.15 50▲£3.15
(awnings)

9⚲⊙ late arrivals enclosure 17wc lit all
night 1cdp washbasins hc (central hot
water (ⓜhc) ⊙ (wash dry) iron games room
CTV (cold storage) childrens playground
calor gas camping gaz paraffin toilet fluid

---

cafe ☎ battery charging freezer pack
service ⓛ

↔ ✔ launderette pub

WINSTON
Co Durham
Map 12 NZ11

▶ ② ❶ △

Winston Caravan Park *(NZ140167)*
Signposted ☎ Darlington (0325) 730228
Mar–Oct must book Last arrival 21.00hrs
no unaccompanied under 18's

*A quiet secluded site, ideal base for
touring the Teesdale area.*

1acre 10pitches 12static SA 10⊞ £3 or
10 ⊞ £3 10▲£3 (awnings) ltr

3⚲⊙ 5wc lit all night ❷ washbasins hc
central hot water (ⓜhc) ⊙ supervised
cold storage calor gas camping gaz
restaurant ☎ off licence ⓛ

↔ stables golf ✔ pub

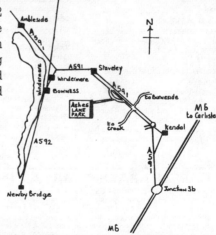

WOLVEY
Warwickshire
Map 4 SP48

▶▶▶ 🅿②🅰

Wolvey Villa Farm Caravan & Camping Site (SP428869) ☎ Hinckley (0455)
220493 All year booking advisable Jul & Aug Last arrival 23.15hrs Last departure noon
no unaccompanied under 18's

Level, grass site with mature trees and bushes set in meadowland. About 1m S of Wolvey.

6acres 120pitches 120🚐 £2.30 or 120 🚍 £2.30 or 120▲£2.20 (awnings)

5🏳 late arrivals enclosure 14wc lit all night 2cdp 🚿 washbasins hc 🛁 hc central hot water (☉) supervised (wash spin dry) iron TV (cold storage) calor gas camping gaz toilet fluid ☎ fishing putting green 🎣

↔ stables 🌶 launderette pub

WOODBURY
Devon
Map 3 SY08

▶▶▶ 🅿②🅰

Castle Brake Caravan Park (SY029878)
☎ (0395) 32431 21 May–6 Oct rs Etr booking advisable school hols Last arrival 22.00hrs Last departure 10.00hrs

Situated in a picturesque part of East Devon, the site lies on the edge of Woodbury Common in a secluded position.

1 acre 46pitches 2static SA 12🚐 £4.50 12 🚍 £4 15▲£4 (awnings)

5🏳 Individual pitches ⊘ 5wc lit all night 1cdp 🚿 washbasins hc (🛁 hc)☉ supervised (spin iron) games room TV (cold storage) licensed club/bar childrens playground calor gas camping gaz toilet fluid cafe restaurant ☎ ⊞ 🎣

↔ stables golf 🌶 🌶 launderette pub

WOODHALL SPA
Lincolnshire
Map 8 TF16

▶▶▶▶ 🅿③🅰

Bainland Park (TF215640) Horncastle Rd ☎ (0526) 52903 Apr–Oct must book wknds Last arrival 23.00hrs
no tents

4½acres 30pitches 30🚐 £4 or 30 🚍 £4 (awnings) ltr

3🏳 Individual pitches late arrivals enclosure 5wc lit all night 1cdp 🚿 washbasins hc central hot water 🛁 hc☉ supervised (wash spin) iron (☎ 🅿) (games room) cold storage (licensed bar) childrens playground calor gas toilet fluid

---

cafe restaurant ☎ ⊞ croquet boules sauna solarium jacuzzi golf 🎣
↔ stables golf 🌶 cinema 🌶 launderette

WOOKEY HOLE
Somerset
Map 3 ST54
See Cheddar sketch map

▶▶▶ 🅿①🅰

Homestead Caravan & Camping Park (ST532474) Signposted ☎ Wells (0749) 73022 Etr–Oct no bookings Last arrival 22.00 Last departure noon

Grass site with mature trees, set in hilly woodland and meadowland, with access to river and Wookey Hole. 1½m off A371 Wells–Cheddar road.

2acres 55pitches 30static 55🚐 £5.40 or 55 🚍 £5.10 or 55▲£5.60 (awnings)

3🏳 13wc lit all night 1cdp 🚿 washbasins hc (➡hc 🛁 hc)☉ supervised (wash dry) iron (☎ 🅿) cold storage (licensed club/bar) calor gas camping gaz toilet fluid cafe ☎ crazy golf 🎣

↔ stables golf cinema pub

WOOL
Dorset
Map 3 SY88

▶▶▶ 🅿③🅰

Whitemead Caravan Park (SY841869)
East Burton Rd Signposted ☎ Bindon Abbey (0929) 462241 Apr–Sep booking advisable peak periods Last departure noon

Well laid out level site in valley of River Frome, 300yds W off A352.

5½acres 90pitches 90🚐 £4.03–£4.66 or 90 🚍 £4.03–£4.66 or 90▲£4.03–£4.66 (awnings)

11🏳 Individual pitches late arrivals enclosure 13wc lit all night 1cdp 🚿 washbasins hc 🛁 hc☉ (wash spin dry iron) cold storage childrens playground calor gas camping gaz toilet fluid 🎣

↔ stables golf cinema launderette pub

WOOLACOMBE
Devon
Map 2 SS44
See Ilfracombe sketch map

▶▶▶▶ 🅿③🅰

Golden Coast Holiday Village (SS482436) Station Rd Signposted ☎ (0271) 870343 & 870418 Jun–Oct rs Apr–May booking advisable Jun–Aug Last arrival mdnt Last departure 10.00hrs no pets no single sex groups

---

This holiday village includes villas and static caravans as well as the camping site. Woolacombe is surrounded by National Trust land.

9½acres 330pitches SA 230🚐 or 230 🚍 100▲ awnings

26🏳 Individual pitches ⊘ late arrivals enclosure 61wc lit all night 2cdp 🚿 washbasins hc central hot water 🛁 hc☉ (wash) spin (dry) iron ➡ games room TV licensed club/bar childrens playground calor gas camping gaz toilet fluid cafe restaurant ☎ ⊞ squash court sauna solarium 🎣

↔ stables golf 🌶 cinema 🌶 launderette pub

▶ 🅿②🅰

Woolacombe Bay Caravan Park (SS468442) Signposted ☎ (0271) 87022 121 May–Sep rs Apr–20 May & Oct must book peak periods Last arrival 21.00hrs Last departure 10.00hrs no single sex groups no groups of unaccompanied teenagers

Sloping, grass site in meadowland overlooking sea and sands.

8acres 190pitches 30🚐 160 🚍 or 160▲ awnings

5🏳 Individual pitches for caravans ⊘ wc lit all night 1cdp (washbasins hc) (🛁 hc)☉ supervised (wash dry iron) (➡) games room licensed club/bar childrens playground calor gas camping gaz cafe ☎ nightly entertainment 🎣

↔ stables pub

WOOLER
Northumberland
Map 12 NT92

▶▶▶ 🅿①🅰

Bridge End Caravan Site (NT998277)
Bridge End Signposted ☎ (0668) 81447 Mar–Oct booking advisable public hols & Jul–Aug

A level, grassy site with trees and bushes set in woodland and moorland near river, ¼m S of Wooler on A697.

55pitches 130static 25🚐 £4 or 25 🚍 £3.40 30▲£3.20 (awnings) ltr

🏳 Individual pitches ⊘ 5wc lit all night 2cdp 🚿 washbasins hc (central hot water) (🛁 hc)☉ supervised (wash spin dry) 🅿 games room (cold storage) childrens playground calor gas camping gaz toilet fluid cafe ☎ pony trekking fishing 🎣

↔ stables golf 🌶 launderette pub

WORKINGTON
Cumbria
Map 11 NX92

▶ ▶ ▶ ☑ ❷ △

Oldside Caravan Club Site (NX996299)
Signposted ☎ (0900) 2125 Mar–2 Nov
Last arrival 20.00hrs Last departure noon

*This quiet site is situated on land
reclaimed from the sea, on the Cumbrian
coast, just north of Workington and an
ideal touring base.*

80 pitches 60 ⊕ or 60 ⊕ 20 ▲ (awnings)

5 ⚏ Individual pitches ⌀ late arrivals
enclosure 8 wc lit all night 2 cdp
washbasins hc ⋔ hc ⊙ (wash) childrens
playground calor gas camping gaz
↔ stables golf ⚷ cinema ⫦ launderette
pub ⚲

WORSBROUGH
South Yorkshire
Map 8 SE30

▶ ☑ ❶ △

Greensprings Holiday Park (SE330020)
Rockley Ln Signposted ☎ Barnsley
(0226) 88298 Apr–Oct
no bookings

*Part level, part sloping, grass site with
young trees and bushes, set in wood and
meadowland with access to river. From
exit 36 off M1 turn along A61 to Barnsley,
then signposted.*

4 acres 73 pitches SA 73 ⊕ £3 or 73 ⊕ £3
or 73 ▲ £3 (awnings) ltr

8 ⚏ 12 wc lit all night 2 cdp washbasins hc
(⋔ hc) ⊙ calor gas camping gaz
↔ stables golf cinema ⫦ launderette pub
⚲

WORTHAM
Suffolk
Map 5 TM07

▶ ▶ ☐ ❶ △

Honeypot Caravan & Camp Park
(TL086771) Honeypot Farm Signposted
☎ Mellis (037983) 312 Apr–Oct booking
advisable public hols Last arrival 23.00hrs
Last departure noon

1½ acres 32 pitches SA 12 ⊕ £3.85 or
12 ⊕ £3.65 20 ▲ £3.65 (awnings) ltr

2 ⚏ ⚪ 3 wc lit all night 1 cdp washbasins hc
central hot water ⋔ hc ⊙ supervised (cold
storage) childrens playground calor gas
camping gaz ☎ ⚲
↔ golf ⫦ launderette pub

WORTWELL
Norfolk
Map 5 TM28

▶ ☐ ❷ △

Little Lakeland Caravan Park
(TM287857) Signposted ☎ Homersfield
(098 686) 646 & Harleston (0379) 852423
(out of season) 20 Mar–Oct booking
advisable public hols Last departure
16.00hrs no ball games

*Level grass site with bushes and trees set
in meadowland with direct access to river
and lake, 2m from Harleston town centre.*

4½ acres 30 pitches 30 ⊕ £4 or 30 ⊕ £4
awnings

14 ⚏ Individual pitches 4 wc 1 cdp ⋔ hc ⊙

**OLDSIDE
CARAVAN SITE,
WORKINGTON,
CUMBRIA**

Quiet modern local authority
site close to sea. Ideal base
for touring Lakes and Solway
Coast. Pitches for 60 touring
caravans and tents with up to
date facilities. Caravan Club
administered; open to non
members.

Open April 1st–November
1st.

games room childrens playground calor
gas camping gaz fishing ⚲
↔ stables ⫦ pub

▶ ☐ ❷ △

Lone Pine Camping Site *(TM274843)*
Low Rd Signposted ☎ Homersfield
(098 686) 646 & Harleston (0379) 852423
May–Sep booking advisable public hols
no caravans no open fires

*A mainly level, grassy site with saplings
and bushes set in downland and
meadowland.*

2 acres 27 pitches 27 ⊕ £3 or 27 ▲ £3
awnings

2 ⚏ Individual pitches ⌀ 4 wc (⋔ hc) ⊙
calor gas camping gaz ⚲
↔ stables ⫦ pub

WOTTON-UNDER-EDGE
Gloucestershire
Map 3 ST79

▶ ▶ ▶ ☐ ❷ △

Cotswold Gate Caravan Park
Signposted ☎ Dursley (0453) 843128
Mar–Oct booking advisable public hols &
Jun–Aug Last arrival 21.00hrs Last
departure noon

*Level, grassy site with mature trees and
bushes, 1m NW of town. 4m E of exit 14
(M5) by B4509.*

6 acres 60 pitches ✳ 25 ⊕ £5.18 or
35 ⊕ £5.18 35 ▲ £5.18 (awnings)

8 ⚏ late arrivals enclosure 6 wc lit all night
4 cdp ⚪ washbasins hc (central hot
water) ⋔ hc ⊙ supervised iron (cold
storage) licensed bar childrens
playground calor gas camping gaz ⊞ ⚲
↔ golf ⫦ launderette pub

WROXALL
Isle of Wight
Map 4 SZ57
See Shanklin sketch map

▶ ▶ ▶ ☐ ❷ △

*Appuldurcombe Gardens Caravan &
Camping Park* (SZ542805)
Appuldurcombe Rd ☎ Ventnor (0983)
852597 May–Sep rs Mar & Apr, Oct & Nov
must book peak periods Last arrival
23.00hrs Last departure 23.00hrs →

WYCLIFFE (near Barnard Castle)
Co Durham
Map 12 NZ11

▶ ▶ ② ❶ ⚠

Thorpe Hall (NZ105141) (off unclass road between Whorlton and A66 (Greta Bridge) Signposted ☎ Teesdale (0833) 27230 Apr–Sep rs Mar & Oct booking advisable public hols & Aug Last arrival 21.00hrs Last departure noon no single sex groups no motorcycles no tents (except by arrangement)

Site lies S of River Tees and 5 miles from Barnard Castle.

2 acres 12 pitches 16 static 12 ☜ £3.50 or 12 ☜ £3.50 (awnings) ltr

3 ☜ Individual pitches 6wc lit all night 1 cdp washbasins hc 🚿 hc ☉ supervised calor gas ☎

↔ ♪ pub ⬛

WYKEHAM
North Yorkshire
Map 8 SE98

▶ ▶ ▶ ② ❸ ⚠

St Helens Caravan Park (SE967836)
Signposted ☎ Scarborough (0723) 862771 Mar–Oct booking advisable peak periods Last departure noon

Part level, part sloping, grass site with young trees and bushes in the Rye Valley, on the north side of A170 E of village.

25 acres 250 pitches 250 ☜ £5.80 or 250 ☜ £5.80 or 250 ▲ £5.80 (awnings)

20 ☜ Individual pitches late arrivals enclosure 48wc lit all night 4cdp 🔌 washbasins hc 🚿 hc ☉ (wash spin dry iron) (cold storage) (licensed club/bar) childrens playground calor gas camping gaz toilet fluid restaurant ☎ ⊞ ⬛

↔ stables ♪ launderette pub

YARMOUTH (GREAT)
Norfolk
Map 5 TG50
See sketch map

▶ ▶ ▶ ▶ ② ❸ ⚠

Vauxhall Holiday Park (TG520083)
Signposted ☎ (0493) 50621 19 May–1 Oct rs Etr must book Last arrival 22.00hrs Last departure 11.00hrs no single sex groups

Level grass site with trees and bushes, set in urban area with access to sea, beach, river, estuary, lake and main A47.

15 acres 315 pitches 630 static 193 ☜ £4.50–£7.50 20 ☜ £4.50–7.50 102 ▲ £4.50–£7.50 awnings

16 ☜ Individual pitches ⊕ late arrivals enclosure wc lit all night 2cdp 🔌 washbasins hc 🚿 hc ☉ supervised (wash spin dry) iron ⬛ games room CTV cold storage licensed club/bar childrens playground calor gas camping gaz toilet fluid cafe restaurant ☎ ⊞ boat hire nightly entertainment ⬛

↔ stables golf ⚓ cinema ♪ launderette pub

YETHOLM
Borders Roxburghshire
Map 12 NT82

▶ ▶ ③ ❷ ⚠

Kirkfield Caravan & Camping Site
(NT821281) Signposted ☎ (057382) 346 Apr–Oct booking advisable public hols & Jul–Aug Last arrival 20.00hrs Last departure noon →

GREAT YARMOUTH and DISTRICT

Map labels: B1159, Hemsby Hole, ⑤ SCRATBY HALL, Scratby, Ormesby St Margaret, California, Ormesby St Michael, A149, B1159, A149, Filby, A1064, A1064, Thrigby, Caister-on-Sea, West Caister, ④ GRASMERE, West End, ④ THE OLD HALL CARAVAN PARK, A149, Race Course, River Bure, ⑥ VAUXHALL HOLIDAY PARK, Newtown, North Beach, A47, Acle Marshes, Runham, B1138, Scale 0 1m, Water, N WALSHAM 17m, A149, ACLE 5m, A1064, NORWICH 17m, A47, ROADS, YARMOUTH, Fishers Marshes, Southtown, GT YARMOUTH, Breydon, B1143, Burgh Castle Marshes, ② BLUE SKY, South Beach, Burgh Castle, South Denes, ③ CHERRY FARM, A143, Bradwell, A12, B1370, B1192, Gorleston-on-Sea, Belton, ❶ WILD DUCK CARAVAN AND CHALET PARK, A143 BECCLES 14m, A12 LOWESTOFT 8m

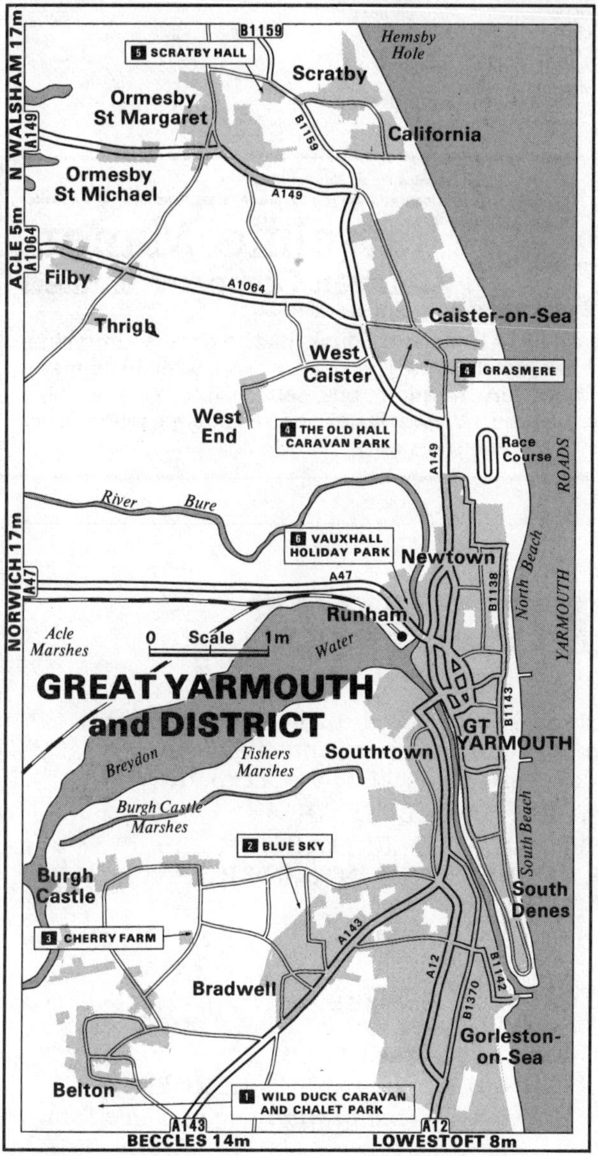

Sites listed under: **1** Bradwell **2** Burgh Castle **3** Caister-on-Sea **4** Scratby **5** Yarmouth (Great)

Part level, part sloping, grass site with trees and bushes, set in hilly moorland country adjacent to river. 7m S of Kelso on B6352.

1acre 34 pitches 15 static 34 ⟐ £3.50 or 34 ⟐ £3.50 or 34 ▲£3.50 (awnings)
3⟐⊘ 12wc lit all night washbasins ⋔ hc ⊙ supervised cold storage calor gas camping gaz paraffin ▨
⟿ stables ✔ pub

YORK
North Yorkshire
Map 8 SE65

▶ ▶ ▶ ② ❷ △
Rawcliffe Manor Caravan Site
(SE583553) Manor Ln, Shipton Rd
Signposted ☎ (0904) 24422 Mar–Oct
booking advisable peak periods Last arrival time 20.00hrs Last departure noon

Situated on an ex-RAF bomber airfield, the site makes use of the concrete 'aprons', dispersal bays and the grassy areas between. Many young trees have been planted on this level site with the distant views of the Minster.

5½ acres 155 pitches 105 ⟐ £4.20–£5.10 or 105 ⟐ £4–£4.80 50▲£4–£5 (awnings)
5⟐ Individual pitches ⊘ late arrivals enclosure 28wc lit all night 2 cdp ⊟
washbasins hc central hot water (⋔ hc) ⊙ supervised (wash spin dry iron) ♀ games room (cold storage) licensed club/bar childrens playground calor gas camping gaz toilet fluid cafe ☎ ⊞ ▨
⟿ stables ⚓ cinema ✔ launderette pub

AA SUPERGUIDES

A Guide for every occasion at home or abroad — holidays in the sun, quiet weekends in the country, wining and dining out, fascinating places for day trips—all backed by AA expertise.

HOTELS AND RESTAURANTS IN BRITAIN
CAMPING AND CARAVANNING IN BRITAIN
GUESTHOUSES, FARMHOUSES AND INNS IN BRITAIN
SELF CATERING IN BRITAIN
STATELY HOMES, MUSEUMS, CASTLES AND GARDENS IN BRITAIN
EAT OUT IN BRITAIN FOR AROUND £5
TRAVELLERS' GUIDE TO EUROPE
CAMPING AND CARAVANNING IN EUROPE
GUESTHOUSES, FARMHOUSES AND INNS IN EUROPE
All these Guides and many more AA publications are available from AA shops and major booksellers.

Sites listed in counties

Places appearing in the gazetteer are here arranged in County order (Regional order in Scotland). Look for the County in which you wish to stay to find the names of places where AA recommended sites are situated, these places names appear alphabetically within the gazetteer.

England

AVON
Bath
Redhill
Severn Beach
Sidcot
Weston-super-Mare

BEDFORDSHIRE
Dunstable

BERKSHIRE
Winkfield

BUCKINGHAMSHIRE
Dorney Reach
Olney

CAMBRIDGESHIRE
Chittering
Comberton
Ely
Grafham
Hemingford Abbots
Houghton
Huntingdon
Shelford, Great

CHESHIRE
Acton Bridge
Chester
Middlewich
Rixton

CLEVELAND
Boosbeck
Guisborough

CORNWALL
Ashton
Blackwater
Bodinnick
Bodmin
Bolventor
Boswinger
Bude
Camborne
Camelford
Carleen
Carlyon Bay
Carnon Downs
Chacewater
Chapel Porth
Chapmans Well
Crackington Haven
Crantock
Cubert
Delabole
Dobwalls
Edgcumbe
Falmouth
Fowey
Goonhavern
Gorran
Grampound
Hayle
Helston
Hewas Water
Holywell Bay
Kennack Sands
Kilkhampton
Lamorna
Landrake
Lanlivery
Lanlivet
Launceston
Leedstown
Lelant Downs
Long Downs
Looe
Lostwithiel
Mawgan Porth
Mullion
Newquay
Notter Bridge
Padstow
Par
Pelynt
Pentewan
Perranarworthal
Perranporth
Poundstock
Praa Sands
Redruth
Rejerrah
Relubbus
Rosudgeon
Rumford
Ruthernbridge
St Agnes
St Austell
St Buryan
St Clether
St Columb Major
St Day
St Ewe
St Hilary
St Issey
St Ives
St Just
St Just-in-Roseland
St Mabyn
St Merryn
St Minver
Sticker
Three Burrows
Tintagel
Truro
Veryan
Wadebridge
Wall
Watergate Bay
Whitecross
Whitstone

CUMBRIA
Ambleside
Appleby
Ayside
Barrow-in-Furness
Beckfoot
Bewaldeth
Blackford
Bouth
Braithwaite
Brampton
Cark-in-Cartmel
Carlisle
Cockermouth
Crosthwaite
Cumwhitton
Dalston
Eamont Bridge
Gilcrux
Hale
Hartsop
Haverthwaite
Holmrook
Kendal
Kirkby-in-Furness
Kirkby Thore
Knock
Lamplugh
Levens
Mealsgate
Penrith
Penruddock
Plumpton
Pooley Bridge
Preston Patrick
Ravenglass
Sedbergh
Silecroft
Silloth
Skelwith Bridge
Staveley
Sunderland
Troutbeck
Watermillock
Westward
Windermere
Workington

DERBYSHIRE
Ashbourne
Ashford in the Water
Bakewell
Buxton
Derby
Doveridge
Edale
Elvaston
Fenny Bentley
Hartington
Hayfield
Hope
Matlock
Newhaven

Whaley Bridge
Whatstandwell

DEVON
Ashburton
Barnstaple
Berrynarbor
Bickington
Braunton
Bridestowe
Bridgerule
Brixham
Brixton
Buckfastleigh
Chillington
Chivenor
Chudleigh Knighton
Clifford Bridge
Cove
Croyde Bay
Dalwood
Dartmouth
Dawlish
Dittisham
Dunkeswell
East Allington
East Anstey
East Worlington
Gulworthy
Haldon Racecourse
Hawkchurch
Honiton
Horns Cross
Ilfracombe
Instow
Kennford
Kentisbeare
Kingsbridge
Ladram Bay
Little Torrington
Lydford
Lynton
Millbrook
Modbury
Molland
Mortehoe
Mullacott Cross
Newton Abbot
Okehampton
Paignton
Pathfinder Village
Plymouth
Rattery
Rockbeare
Rousdon
Salcombe
Salcombe Regis
Sampford Courtenay
Slapton
Smithaleigh
Sourton Down
South Brent
Starcross

Sticklepath
Stoke Fleming
Stoke Gabriel
Tavistock
Tedburn St Mary
Torrington (Great)
Umberleigh
Uplyme
Waterloo Cross
Weston
Woodbury
Woolacombe

DORSET
Bournemouth
Bridport
Cerne Abbas
Charmouth
Chideock
Christchurch
Corfe Castle
Crossways
Evershot
Eype
Fleet
Holton Heath
Hurn
Lytchett Minster
Organford
Osmington Mills
Owermoigne
St Leonards
Swanage
Wareham
Weymouth
Wimborne Minster
Wool

CO DURHAM
Castleside
Sedgefield
Stanley
Winston
Wycliffe

ESSEX
Bardfield, Great
Bradfield
Braintree
Colchester
St Osyth
Tiptree

GLOUCESTERSHIRE
Alvington
Cheltenham
Perrott's Brook
Rodborough
Slimbridge
South Cerney
Wootton under Edge

HAMPSHIRE
Alton
Andover
Ashurst
Bransgore
Brockenhurst
Hayling Island
Hedge End
Holmsley
Lyndhurst
New Milton
Nomansland
Ower
Sway

Warsash
Winchester

HERTFORDSHIRE
Hoddesdon

HEREF & WORCS
Bromsgrove
Bromyard
Comberton, Great
Drayton
Grafton Flyford
Harvington
Hereford
Honeybourne
Inkberrow
Kempsey
Kings Caple
Peterchurch
Radford
Ross-on-Wye
Shrawley

HUMBERSIDE
Bridlington
Broughton
Rudston
Skipsea
South Cove
Stamford Bridge

ISLE OF WIGHT
Cowes
Newbridge
St Helens
St Lawrence
Shanklin
Thorness Bay
Whitecliffe Bay
Wroxhall

KENT
Biddenden
Birchington
Canterbury
Densole
Folkestone
Herne Bay
Hoath
Kingsnorth
Manston
Martin Hill
Mersham
Minster (Thanet)
Rochester
St Nicholas at Walde
Sutton
Warden Point
Whitstable

LANCASHIRE
Blackpool
Bolton-le-Sands
Carnforth
Caton
Croston
Eccleston (Great)
Fleetwood
Gisburn
Harwood (Great)
Kirkham
Lytham St Anne's
Middleton
Morecambe
Nether Kellet
Ormskirk

Scorton
Silverdale
Thornton Cleveleys
Weeton

LEICESTERSHIRE
Casterton (Great)
North Kilworth

LINCOLNSHIRE
Chapel Hill
Coningsby
Hubberts Bridge
Mablethorpe
Market Rasen
North Somercotes
Skegness
Thorpe Culvert
Woodhall Spa

LONDON (GREATER)
Abbey Wood (SE2)
Chingford E4
Edmonton (N9)
West Drayton

MIDLANDS, WEST
Sutton Coldfield

NORFOLK
Bacton
Belton
Bradwell
Burgh Castle
Caister-on-Sea
Cawston
Clippesby
Dereham
East Runton
Fakenham
Hunstanton
Narborough
Scole
Scratby
Stowbridge
Trimingham
Weybourne
Wortwell
Yarmouth (Great)

NORTHANTS
Hargrave
Thrapston

NORTHUMBERLAND
Bamburgh
Beadnell
Belford
Berwick-upon-Tweed
Haltwhistle
Hexham
Kielder
Rothbury
Wooler

NOTTINGHAMSHIRE
Nottingham
Old Clipstone
Rolleston
Stragglethorpe
Tuxford
West Bridgford

OXFORDSHIRE
Banbury
Cassington

Sandford-on-Thames
Standlake
Wallingford

SHROPSHIRE
Diddlebury
Hughley
Kinnerley
Lyneal
Much Wenlock
Orleton
Quatt
Wem
Wentor

SOMERSET
Blue Anchor
Burnham-on-Sea
Cheddar
Exford
Highbridge
Porlock
Priddy
Rodney Stoke
Shepton Mallet
Taunton
Watchet
Wells
West Coker
Wincanton

STAFFORDSHIRE
Cheadle
Drayton Bassett
Fazeley
Hulme End
Rugeley
Trentham
Upper Elkstone
Uttoxeter

SUFFOLK
Bungay
Butley
East Bergholt
Gisleham
Kessingland
Lowestoft
Newmarket
Shottisham
Stanton
Stuston
Waldringfield
Wortham

SURREY
Churt
Laleham

EAST SUSSEX
Bodiam
Catsfield
Crowhurst
Ewhurst Green
Hastings & St Leonards
Heathfield
Pevensey Bay
Plumpton Racecourse
Three Oaks
Westham

WEST SUSSEX
Aldingbourne
Billingshurst

Bolney
Chichester
Fontwell
Gatwick Airport
Goodwood

TYNE & WEAR
Newcastle upon Tyne
Rowlands Gill
South Shields

WARWICKSHIRE
Alcester
Aston Cantlow
Kingsbury
Stratford-upon-Avon
Warwick
Wolvey

WILTSHIRE
Devizes
Nomansland
Potterne
Tilshead

WORCESTERSHIRE
Evesham
Far Forest

NORTH YORKSHIRE
Acaster Malbis
Acaster Selby
Allerton Park
Bishop Monkton
Brompton-on-Swale
Burniston
Coneysthorpe
Constable Burton
Crockley Hill
Cropton
Eavestone
Elvington
Filey
Fylingdales
Grewelthorpe
Gristhorpe Bay
Harome
Harrogate
High Bentham
Lebberston
Lothersdale
Moreton on Swale
Nawton
North Stainley
Osmotherly
Patrick Brompton
Richmond
Ripon
Sawley
Scarborough
Scotch Corner
Skipton
Snainton
Snape
Stainforth
Swainby
Thirsk
Threshfield
Ugthorpe
Warsill
Whitby
Winksley
Wykeham
York

SOUTH YORKSHIRE
Doncaster
Hatfield
Worsbrough

WEST YORKSHIRE
Nostell
Silsden
Wetherby

CHANNEL ISLANDS
Guernsey:
Câtel (Fauxquets Valley)
Jersey:
St Brelade
St Martin

ISLE OF WIGHT
Hilberry
Laxey
Peel

Wales

CLWYD
Eyton
Glan-yr-Afon
Glyn Ceiriog
Llandrillo
Llangollen
Prestatyn
Ruabon

DYFED
Aberystwyth
Bettws Evan
Broad Haven
Cenarth
Clynderwen
Croesgoch
Dinas Cross
Fishguard
Hasguard Cross
Landshipping
Laugharne
Llandre
Llanon
Llanrhystud
Llanwrda
Ludchurch
Narberth
Newcastle Emlyn
Penycwm
Reynalton
Rhydcymerau
Robeston Wathen
St David's
St Florence
Sarnau
Saundersfoot
Tenby
Tresaith

MID GLAMORGAN
Merthyr Mawr
Porthcawl

WEST GLAMORGAN
Fairwood

GWENT
Chepstow
Dingstow
Mitchel Troy

GWYNEDD
Abersoch
Bala
Barmouth
Beaumaris
Beddgelert
Bethesda
Betws Garmon
Bryncrug
Brynsiencyn
Brynteg
Caernarfon
Cerrigceinwen
Conwy
Criccieth
Dinas Dinlle
Dulas
Llanbedrog
Llanrug
Llanrwst
Llwyngwril
Morfa Bychan
Penrhyndeudraeth
Pentraeth
Pontllyfni
Pont-Rug
Pwllheli
Rhosneigr
Tal-y-Bont
Trefriw
Tywyn

POWYS
Abercrave
Abermule
Bronllys
Church Stoke
Crossgates
Hay-on-Wye
Howey
Llangyniew
Llanidloes
Middletown
Pentrebeirdd
Penybontfawr
Presteigne
Rhosgoch
Talgarth

SOUTH GLAMORGAN
Llantwit Major

Scotland

BORDERS
Cockburnspath
Hawick
Jedburgh
Kelso
Lauder
Melrose
Peebles
Selkirk
Tushielaw
Yetholm

CENTRAL
Auchenbowie
Balmaha
Blairlogie
Bridge of Allan
Callander
Gartmore

Killin
Luib
Stirling

DUMFRIES & GALLOWAY
Amisfield
Annan
Auchenmaig
Balminnoch
Brighouse Bay
Cairn Ryan
Castle Douglas
Creetown
Crocketford
Dalbeattie
Dumfries
Eastriggs
Ecclefechan
Gatehouse of Fleet
Glenluce
Glen Trool
Gretna
Gretna Green
Isle of Whithorn
Kippford
Kirkcudbright
Kirkgunzeon
Kirkpatrick Fleming
Lochmaben
Lochnaw
Lockerbie
Moffat
Mouswald
Newton Stewart
Parton
Portpatrick
Powfoot
Sanquhar
Southerness
Stranraer
Waterbeck

FIFE
Crail
Guardbridge
Kinghorn
Kirkcaldy
Letham Feus
Lundin Links
Piltenweem
St Andrews
Tayport

GRAMPIAN
Aberchirder
Aberdeen
Aberlour
Aboyne
Alford
Alves
Ballater
Banff
Brodie
Buckie
Cullen
Cuminestown
Elgin
Findhorn
Findochty
Fochabers
Fraserburgh
Keith
Lossiemouth
Macduff
Maryculter

Memus
Mintlaw
Portknockie
Portsoy
Rosehearty
Stonehaven
Strachan
Tarland
Turriff

HIGHLAND
Applecross
Ardmair
Aviemore
Balmacara
Beauly
Boat of Garten
Brora
Camustianavaig
 (Isle of Skye)
Corpach
Cromarty
Daviot
Dingwall
Dornoch
Dunbeath
Dunnet
Dunvegan (Isle of Skye)
Durness
Fortrose

Fort William
Gairloch
Gairlochy
Glencoe
Grantown-on-Spey
Halkirk
Invergarry
Invermoriston
Inverness
John O'Groats
Kiltarlity
Lairg
Nairn
Poolewe
Reay
Resipol
Rosemarkie
Roy Bridge
Scaniport
Scourie
Shiel Bridge
Staffin (Isle of Skye)
Thurso

LOTHIAN
Dunbar
Edinburgh
Haddington
Musselburgh
North Berwick

STRATHCLYDE
Ardgartan
Ardvaine
Ayr
Balloch
Barcaldine
Benderloch
Blairmore
Bothwell
Carradale
Castle Sween
Connel
Coylton
Dalmellington
Dalrymple
Dunoon
Glendaruel
Hollybush
Inveraray
Inverchapel
Inveruglas
Kilberry
Kilmarnock
Kilninver
Kirkfieldbank
Lochgilphead
Luss
Maidens
Ravenstruther

Strachur
Strathaven
Tayinloan

TAYSIDE
Aberfeldy
Birnam
Blair Atholl
Bridge of Cally
Cargill
Carnoustie
Comrie
Crieff
Dundee
Dunkeld
Forfar
Inchture
Kenmore
Kinross
Kirriemuir
Monifieth
Montrose
Perth
Pitlochry
St Fillans
Scone

WESTERN ISLES
Coll Sands (Lewis)
Drinnishadder (Harris)

Sites open all year

The following sites are open all year (some with restricted services) according to information supplied by the proprietors before going to press (July 1983). It is advisable to check with your chosen site in advance to ascertain the current conditions, especially during the winter months.

England

AVON
Bath Newbridge Caravan Park
Bath Newton Mill Touring Centre

BERKSHIRE
Winkfield Sunnybend Farm Caravan Park (rs Nov–Mar)

CAMBRIDGESHIRE
Huntingdon Anchor Cottage Riverside Caravan & Camping Site (rs Nov–Feb)

CHESHIRE
Middlewich Briar Pool Farm
Rixton Holly Bank Caravan Park

CORNWALL
Perranarworthal Cosawes Caravan Park
St Buryan Tower Farm Caravan & Camping Park (rs Nov–Feb)
St Hilary Wayfarers Camping Site
Sticker Glenleigh Caravan Park
Truro Leverton Place (rs Oct–mid Apr)

CUMBRIA
Appleby Wild Rose Park
Carlisle Orton Grange Caravan Park
Hale Fell End Caravan Park (rs 17 Nov–Feb)

DERBYSHIRE
Derby Alvaston Mobile Home Park
Doveridge Cavendish Garage
Edale Coopers Caravan Site
Whaley Bridge Happy Vans Caravan Site
Whatstandwell Haytop Farm Caravanserai (rs Nov–Mar)

DEVON
Ashburton Ashburton Caravan Park
Buckfastleigh Beara Farm
Kingsbridge Island Lodge Farm
Pathfinder Village Pathfinder Touring Caravan Site
Plymouth Riverside Caravan Park
Rousdon West Hayes Caravan Park (rs Oct–Apr)
Tavistock Higher Longford Farm Caravan Site

DORSET
Christchurch Hoburne Farm Caravan Park (rs Nov–Feb)
St Leonards Shamba Holiday Park (rs Oct–Mar)
Uplyme Hook Farm Camping & Caravan Park (rs Dec–mid Apr)

GLOUCESTERSHIRE
Alvington Clanna Caravan and Camping Park
Slimbridge Tudor Arms Caravan Site

HAMPSHIRE
Andover Wyke Down Touring Caravan & Camping Park
Hedge End Grange Caravan Park

HEREFORD & WORCESTER
Broadway Leedon's Park
Inkberrow Broad Close Farm
Kempsey Court Meadow Caravan Park
Radford Wheelbarrow Castle
Shrawley Lenchford Caravan Park (rs Nov–Feb)

HUMBERSIDE
Bridlington Poplars Caravan Site
Broughton Briggate Lodge Caravan & Picnic Site

KENT
Densole Black Horse Farm (rs Nov–Mar)
Rochester Woolman's Wood Caravan Park

LANCASHIRE
Cabus Robinsons Caravans
Ormskirk Abbey Farm Caravan Site

LEICESTERSHIRE
North Kilworth Kilworth Caravan Park (rs Nov–Mar)

LONDON, GREATER
Chingford, E4 Sewardstone Caravan Park
Edmonton, N9 Picketts Lock Centre
West Drayton Riverside Caravans

OXFORDSHIRE
Oxford Oxford Camping International

SOMERSET
Burnham-on-Sea Home Farm Touring Park (rs Nov–Mar)
Shepton Mallet Manleaze Caravan Park
Taunton St Quintin Hotel Caravan & Camping Park

STAFFORDSHIRE
Cheadle Hales Hall Caravan & Camping Park
Drayton Bassett Ashdene Farm
Upper Elkstone Mount Pleasant Farm

SUFFOLK
Bungay Outney Meadow Caravan Park
East Bergholt Grange Caravan Park
Nacton Priory Park (rs late Sep–late May)
Stuston Osiers Caravan Park (rs Oct–Feb)

SUSSEX, EAST
Pevensey Bay Castle View Caravan Site (rs Nov–Mar)

WARWICKSHIRE
Alcester Hoo Mill (rs Dec–Feb)
Kingsbury Tame View
Wolvey Wolvey Villa Farm Caravan & Camping Site

WILTSHIRE
Salisbury Coombe Nurseries Touring Park

YORKSHIRE, NORTH
Ripon North Sutton Farm
Snape Castle Arms

Wales

CLWYD
Llandrillo Hendwr Farm Site (rs Nov–Mar)

DYFED
Aberystwyth 'U' Tow Caravans Aberystwyth Holiday Village
Hasguard Cross Hasguard Cross Caravan Park

POWYS
Bronllys Anchorage Caravan Park (rs Nov–Etr)

Scotland

CENTRAL
Stirling Cornton Caravan Park (rs Nov–Mar)

DUMFRIES & GALLOWAY
Gretna Braids Caravan Site (rs Oct–Apr)
Kirkpatrick Fleming Bruce's Cave & Caravan Site (rs Nov–Mar)

HIGHLAND
Aviemore Dalraddy Caravan Park
Aviemore Glen More
Dornoch Grannie's Heilan Home
Dunbeath Inver Caravan Park (rs winter months)
Tain Meikle Ferry Caravan and Camping Park

LOTHIAN
Haddington Monksmuir Caravan Park (rs Oct–Mar)

STRATHCLYDE
Ayr Crofthead Caravan Park
Bothwell Strathclyde Park Caravan Site
Coylton Sundrum Castle Holiday Park (rs Oct–Mar)
Dunoon Cowal Caravan Park
Ravenstruther Newhouse Farm

TAYSIDE
Blair Atholl River Tilt Caravan Park

Caravan Club/Trax Racecourse Campsites

1984 Availability Dates and Charges

The peak period is from 13 July–1 September inclusive.

All charges include 15% VAT and are for 2 persons and 1 motor vehicle.

Separate charges (Extras) apply to all extra persons aged 18 or over and to the first, third etc extra person under 18. Also to any additional small tent or motor vehicle.

There are no charges for awnings or for hot water, including showers.

►►► ①❷△
AYR
Off-peak £2.60; Extras 60p   **Peak £3.40; Extras 60p**
Open 19–24 April and 25 May–15 September.
Free access to racing on 25 & 26 May; 22 & 23 June; 14, 16, 17, 20 & 21 July; 7 & 8 August.

►► ②❷△
CHELTENHAM   *NO TENTS*
Off-peak £2.60; Extras 60p   **Peak £3.40; Extras 60p**
Open 19 April–6 October, except 9 & 10 May.

►►► ②❶△
CHEPSTOW
Off-peak £2.60; Extras 60p   **Peak £3.40; Extras 60p**
Open 19 April–29 September.
Free access to racing on 23 & 24 April; 28 & 29 May; 30 June; 10 July; 27 & 28 August; 15 September

---

►► ②❶△
DONCASTER
Off-peak £2.40; Extras 60p   **Peak £2.80; Extras 60p**
Open 25 May–8 September.
Free access to racing on 26 & 28 May; 29 & 30 June; 1 & 2 August

---

►►► ①❸△
EXETER (HALDEN RACECOURSE)
Off-peak £3.00; Extras 60p   **Peak £4.00; Extras 60p**
Open from 19 April–22 September.
Free access to racing on 7 & 28 May; 9, 22 & 23 August; 4 September when movement in and out of site only before 1200 & after 1800 hours.

►► ②❶△
FAKENHAM
Off-peak £2.60; Extras 60p   **Peak £3.70; Extras 60p**
Open from 19 April–30 September.
Free access to racing on 23 April; 28 May; 28 September
Peak charges also apply from 25–28 May.

►► ①❶△
FONTWELL PARK
Off-peak £2.60; Extras 60p   **Peak £3.40; Extras 60p**
Open from 1 June–3 September, except 14 & 15 August

►►►②❷⚠
GOODWOOD
Off-peak £2.60; Extras 60p　　　　　　　　　　　　**Peak £3.70; Extras 60p**
Open from 12 April–29 September, except 21–24 May; 29 July–6 August; 23–25 August; 13–17 September

►►①❷⚠
HEREFORD
Off-peak £2.60; Extras 60p　　　　　　　　　　　　**Peak £3.40; Extras 60p**
Open from 19 April–22 September.
Free access to racing on 23 April; 3, 12 & 28 May; 25 August; 1 & 7 September

►►②❶⚠
HEXHAM
Off-peak £2.40; Extras 60p　　　　　　　　　　　　**Peak £2.80; Extras 60p**
Open from 18 May–8 September.

►►②❷⚠
MARKET RASEN
Off-peak £2.40; Extras 60p　　　　　　　　　　　　**Peak £2.80; Extras 60p**
Open from 18 May–22 September, except 4–6 August
Free access to racing on 2 June when movement in and out of site only before 1200 hours; also on 18 & 25 August when movement in and out of site only before 1100 and after 1800 hours.

►►►①❶⚠
NEWCASTLE UPON TYNE
Off-peak £2.40; Extras 60p　　　　　　　　　　　　**Peak £3.40; Extras 60p**
Open from 18 May–15 September.

►►►②❸⚠
NEWMARKET　　*NO DOGS*
Off-peak £2.60; Extras 60p　　　　　　　　　　　　**Peak £3.40; Extras 60p**
Open from 25–31 May and 5pm 2 June–15 September.

►►②❶⚠
PLUMPTON　　*NO TRAILER CARAVANS*
Off-peak £2.40; Extras 60p　　　　　　　　　　　　**Peak £2.80; Extras 60p**
Open from 25 May–8 September, except 16, 17, 26 & 27 August.

►►①❶⚠
SEDGEFIELD
Off-peak £2.40; Extras 60p　　　　　　　　　　　　**Peak £2.80; Extras 60p**
Open from 7pm 25 May–8 September.

►►②❷⚠
THIRSK
Off-peak £2.60; Extras 60p　　　　　　　　　　　　**Peak £3.40; Extras 60p**
Open from 18 May–6 September, except 31 May–2 June; 18 & 19 June (re-opening 7pm 19 June); 19 & 20 July (re-opening 7pm 20 July); 2 & 4 August.

►►①❷⚠
UTTOXETER
Off-peak £2.40; Extras 60p　　　　　　　　　　　　**Peak £2.80; Extras 60p**
Open from 1 June–15 September.

►►►①❷⚠
WARWICK　　*NO TENTS*
Off-peak £2.60; Extras 60p　　　　　　　　　　　　**Peak £3.40; Extras 60p**
Open from 4 May–29 September.
Free access to racing on 7, 19 & 26 May; 9 & 23 June; 5, 11 & 28 July; 27 August; 22 September.

►►①❷⚠
WETHERBY
Off-peak £2.60; Extras 60p　　　　　　　　　　　　**Peak £3.40; Extras 60p**
Open from 1 June–15 September.

►►①❶⚠
WINCANTON
Off-peak £2.60; Extras 60p　　　　　　　　　　　　**Peak £3.40; Extras 60p**
Open from 4 May–10 September.

A–Z of Legal and Technical Hints

A synopsis of some of the more important provisions applicable in Great Britain which affect the ordinary car user when towing a caravan or trailer, together with some handy hints on looking after your car and caravan and keeping them within the law. The contents are believed correct as at 1st April 1983 but members may check the position through their AA Regional Offices.

The measurements quoted have been extracted from the relevant authorities and this accounts for the fact that some are metric and others imperial.

Automatic gearboxes

The fluid in an automatic gearbox becomes hotter and thinner when it has to cope with the extra weight of a caravan, so there is more slip and more heat generated in the gearbox. The oil temperature should not rise above 120°C and many manufacturers recommend the fitting of a gearbox oil cooler. Check with the manufacturer what is suitable for your car.

Cars which incorporate the 1, 2 and D gear shift positions offer advantages over models which do not. These gear positions should be used to reduce the work required of the torque convertor. It is beneficial also to downshift (D–2) when descending a long or steep hill, thus reducing the work required of the car braking system.

Brakes

Generally, every trailer exceeding 750kg maximum gross weight must have an efficient braking system, whose requirements vary according to the date of the trailer's manufacture. A trailers' maximum gross weight is the weight which it is designed not to exceed when laden and travelling on a road. The weight must be clearly and conspicuously marked on the outside of all unbraked trailers on the nearside and may not be exceeded when the trailer is being used on the road. Unbraked trailers whose unladen weight is 102kg or less, and which were manufactured before 1st October 1982, have until 1st October 1986 to comply with the above requirements. Trailers required to have brakes must have parking and running brakes. The latter must be capable of being applied by the driver (or in some cases by an attendant) although automatic overrun brakes provide an exception to this requirement.

Every part of the braking system and its means of operation must, at all times while the trailer is used on a road, be maintained to prescribed standards, be in good and efficient working order and be properly adjusted. Check especially the fluid level in the brake reservoir and the thickness of the brake lining material. It is of the utmost importance for the brake fluid to be completely changed in accordance with the manufacturer's instructions or at intervals of not more than 18000 miles. It is good advice to change the brake fluid regardless prior to departing on a Continental holiday, particularly if the journey includes a hilly or mountainous area. Ensure that the caravan braking mechanism is adjusted to suit the car brakes. If a breakaway safety mechanism is used, the cable between the car and the caravan must be firmly anchored so that the trailer brakes are pulled on immediately if the two part. Most modern caravans incorporate an auto-reverse braking system. If your caravan/trailer does not possess this luxury, these brakes must be put out of action before reversing. If you stop on a down slope and the safety latch is difficult to engage, chock the caravan wheels, and ease the car forward. Alternatively an electrically controlled system, which cancels the brake automatically as soon as reverse gear is selected, may be added as an accessory fitment.

Finally, please note that any person in charge of a motor vehicle or trailer drawn thereby must ensure that when the trailer is detached from the towing vehicle at least one of its wheels is prevented from turning by the setting of the brake or the use of a chain.

Clutch and Cooling system

Both will be under more strain, particularly in hilly country, and should be well serviced: the clutch adjustment checked; the cooling system examined for blockage, leaks, faulty thermostat and worn fanbelt; the radiator cap checked for damage. Get any clutch slip (ie when the engine speed increases but the car speed does not) rectified immediately, as continued driving will burn out the linings.

Dimensions

The maximum permitted overall length for a trailer is 7 metres excluding the drawbar fittings. If the trailer has at least four wheels and the distance between the front and rear wheels on the same side is not less than ⅗ths of its overall length and the drawing vehicle weighs more than 2030kg, the maximum length of the trailer allowed is 12 metres. The maximum permitted width is generally 2.3 metres, but may be 2.5 metres if prescribed conditions are met.

Direction indicators

All trailers (other than 'excepted trailers') manufactured after 1 July 1955 and before 1 January 1974 must be fitted either with semaphore arm or flashing light type direction indicators or direction indicators of the flashing amber light type optically separate from other lamps. Trailers drawn by vehicles fitted with this type of direction indicator must be fitted with similar direction indicators. All trailers (other than 'excepted trailers') manufactured on or after 1 January 1974 must be fitted with amber-coloured flashing indicators optically separate from any other lights on the vehicle. They must be marked with the prescribed E approval mark and a specified number. The indicators may be of single or dual intensity but it is worth checking up on the wiring conditions which apply to the latter. 'Excepted trailers' include trailers whose dimensions are such that when they are squarely behind a towing vehicle, both rear or both side direction indicators on the towing vehicle are visible from a point 6 metres behind the rear of the trailer whether it is loaded or not. Any trailer may meet the alternative requirements introduced in 1977 which cover technical and positional matters.

All six direction indicators must be working at between 60 and 120 flashes per minute and a special heavy duty unit or a relay device warning light should be fitted.

Fire extinguishers

There is no legal requirement for a fire extinguisher to be carried in a private saloon car, or trailer towed by such a car.

Insurance

Any trailer drawn by a vehicle on a road must be covered by effective road traffic insurance, generally by an extension of the towing vehicle's policy cover. There is no legal requirement for a trailer to be separately covered, but it is recommended that it be insured against loss or damage, and legal liability, even when it is not being towed. Also check with your insurers that your policy covers the use of vehicles on private camp sites.

Lay-bys

Lay-bys may not be used for overnight stops except where provided for by authorised traffic signs. See Obstruction and Parking.

Lights

If the distance between drawing vehicle and trailer is more than 5ft both must be lit as if they were separate vehicles. The distance is that between the nearest point of the two vehicles disregarding the drawbar or any fitting or attachment. A trailer, not exceeding 1600mm in width, is exempt from the requirement for showing lights to the front, but must carry two front-facing white reflectors meeting specified requirements. If any load carried on a trailer projects sideways by more than 12ins, additional front lamps must be carried in order to indicate the limit of the projection.

Headlamps

The vertical positioning of the car headlamps is raised when the caravan is attached so the lamps should be reset when car and caravan are fully laden.

Parking lights

Although certain vehicles may park on a road during the hours of darkness without lights, a vehicle with trailer attached must display lights.

Rear lamps

A trailer must be fitted with two rear lamps in prescribed positions. On a trailer manufactured on or after 1 August 1973, and first used on or after 1 January 1974, the lamps must be marked with a prescribed E approval mark and specified number. If the load projects more than 3ft 6in beyond the vehicle's tail lights, there must be an additional red rear lamp attached to within 3ft 6in of the rear of the load. If the load overhangs laterally by more than 12in an additional rear lamp is required to be hung, at most, 12in from the load's outer edge, on the same side as the overhang.

Rear fog lamps

All trailers, subject to specified exceptions, manufactured on or after 1 October 1979 and first used on or after 1 April 1980, must be equipped with not more than two rear fog lamps meeting prescribed requirements. Any rear fog lamp fitted to a trailer must be at least 100mm away from a stop lamp and must not be lit by applying the brakes. The regulations provide that such lamps may only be used if visibility conditions are poor.

Rear reflectors

Generally speaking, during the hours of darkness a trailer must carry two red reflectors marked either with an 'E' approval mark and number or a BS specification number and certain other markings.

Stop lamps

Normally, all trailers manufactured before 1 January 1971 must be fitted with one rear red stop lamp on or to the right of the centre line. Trailers manufactured on or after that date must have two red stop lamps meeting specified requirements and in the prescribed position. They must also be marked with an E approval mark and a specified number. They can be of single or dual intensity as long as the particular wiring conditions are observed in the latter type.

Mirrors

Regulations provide that, subject to exceptions, every motor vehicle must be equipped either internally or externally with a mirror so constructed and fitted to the motor vehicle as to assist the driver, if he so desires, to become aware of traffic to the rear of the vehicle. The majority of motor vehicles (including motor cars, dual-purpose vehicles and goods vehicles) made after November 1977 and first used after May 1978 must be equipped with both an interior rear view mirror and an exterior rear view mirror fitted to the off-side of the vehicle. If the interior mirror does not provide an adequate view of the road to the rear of the vehicle an additional exterior mirror must be fitted on the near-side of the vehicle. When the vehicle is drawing a trailer, the mirrors must assist the driver to become aware of the traffic to the rear of the trailer. In addition it should be noted that there are regulations governing the type of mirror fitted, its specifications and its position. The lack of adequate rear vision may help to substantiate a charge of negligence in a claim for damages, or a charge of driving without due care and attention.

The accessories available to assist visibility when towing include extensions that clip on existing wing mirrors, arms to extend wing mirrors, long-arm or door mirrors, and periscopes which are fitted on the car roof and reflect the rear view through the caravan window. A periscope and wing mirrors used together should eliminate all blind spots. The longer the mirror arm is, the more rigid its mounting has to be. Some mirrors have supporting legs or extra brackets to minimise vibration. A mirror mounted on the door pillar gives a wider field of vision because it is close to the driver. However, it has the disadvantage that it is at a greater angle to his forward line of sight. Convex mirrors give an even wider field of vision, but practice is needed before distance can be judged accurately, due to the diminished image.

Motorways

A vehicle drawing a trailer must not use the right outside lane of a three-lane carriageway when all three lanes are open for use by traffic going in the same direction, unless passing a vehicle of such exceptional width that it can only be passed by using the outside lane. This also applies to any length of motorway carriageway with four traffic lanes.

Number plates

A duplicate number plate must be fitted to the rear of the trailer and illuminated at night. Reflecting number plates are compulsory on cars registered on or after 1 January 1973, but not on trailers, where they are merely discretionary.

Obstruction

It is an offence to cause unnecessary obstruction on the highway. Vehicles must not be left for an unreasonable or unnecessary time, or in a dangerous position. The Police can remove vehicles that are causing obstruction or parked contrary to waiting restrictions and charge for that removal and subsequent storage. With few exceptions, the roadside verge is part of the highway. A build-up of traffic behind a vehicle towing a caravan may constitute the basis of an offence.

Parking

Drivers have no automatic right to park on a public highway except at an authorised parking place. Parking at picnic sites and rest areas is subject to local by-laws. Generally speaking, the use of common land, town or village greens is limited to rights of access and recreation purposes only. By-laws generally prohibit the parking of caravans on such land and the Local Authority concerned should be consulted before doing so. It is an offence to drive any vehicle on all other land subject to statutory control, or to camp, or to light a fire. It is not an offence to park a vehicle on open land within 15 yards of the road (subject to local by-laws). See Trespassing, Obstruction.

Passengers

It is an offence to use a caravan for the carriage of passengers.

Radio and television

A radio (other than a CB radio) fitted in a car or

caravan does not require a licence. A separate television licence is needed if the set is fitted permanently in a motor vehicle. A television screen must not be visible to the driver either wholly, partly or by reflection.

Road tax
No additional excise duty is payable when a trailer is towed by a privately licenced vehicle.

Speed limits
General purpose roads:
The maximum speed limit at which a trailer may be drawn on such roads is 50mph, subject to specified conditions being observed. If these are not complied with, the limit is reduced to 40mph. The conditions referred to above are:

1 The kerbside weight of the drawing vehicle must be marked on the outside of the vehicle on its nearside, or inside the vehicle.

2 The maximum gross weight of a living-van trailer or non-goods trailer must be marked on its nearside.

3 The weights in 1 and 2 may be expressed in either imperial or metric units but the same units should be used for both.

4 A '50" plate of prescribed form must be fitted to the rear of a trailer.

5 The following weight ratios must be observed:

   a The maximum gross weight of a living-van trailer, the laden weight of a braked goods trailer and the maximum gross weight of any other kind of braked trailer must not exceed the kerbside weight of the drawing vehicle.

   b The laden weight of an unbraked goods trailer and the maximum gross weight of any other unbraked trailer (not being a living-van) must not exceed 60% of the kerbside weight of the drawing vehicle.

Motorways
Trailers with less than four wheels, or close-coupled four-wheeled trailers, are restricted to a maximum speed of 50mph when drawn on a motorway. ('Close-coupled' means that the wheels on the same side of the trailer are so fitted that at all times while it is in motion they remain parallel to the longitudinal axis of the trailer, and that the distance between the centres of the respective areas of contact with the road surface does not exceed 33in). This is reduced to 40mph when the drawing vehicle has an unladen weight not exceeding 30cwt and the trailer is two-wheeled or a close-coupled four-wheeled trailer,

in circumstances where the speed limit for the vehicle on ordinary roads is 40mph or less.

Springs
All trailers must be equipped with suitable springs between each wheel and the frame of the vehicle.

Storing
Before storing the caravan at home, check whether doing so would contravene local by-laws or any clauses in the title documents relating to the property. As long as the use of the caravan is incidental to the enjoyment of the house, and it is parked behind the building line, there should be no contravention of the Town and Country Planning Acts.

Trespassing
Anyone camping other than on a licenced site must be sure that they are not either breaking the law or trespassing.

In England and Wales a member of the public should not enter land unless

   a he is given permission to do so by the owner or

   b he is authorised by Act of Parliament or

   c he is using a right of way

A trespasser can be sued by the owner or occupier of the land even if no damage has been caused and can be ordered to leave or be ejected from the land by the shortest possible route. A trespasser cannot be prosecuted unless he has committed or attempts to commit a crime. In Scotland, camping without permission on private land, or lighting a fire on or near a private road or cultivated land constitutes a criminal offence. Only if actual damage occurs can compensation be obtained, but a Court Order to prevent repetition may be sought. Trespassing in pursuit of game animals or fish is illegal and is usually dealt with as poaching.

Tyres
The minimum legal tread depth is 1mm, but in addition to this the regulations prohibit the use of tyres with cuts, bumps, bulges, exposed ply cords and worn down tread patterns. All tyres fitted must be suitable, given the type of use to which a trailer is being put, and in particular it is an offence to fit tyres of different methods of construction to the same axle. Similarly it is an offence for radial ply tyres to be fitted to the front axle and cross ply tyres on the rear axle of the drawing vehicle. Each faulty tyre can constitute a separate offence. It is an endorsable offence to drive a car, or for a car to tow a trailer, with

defective tyres. Apart from this a person convicted of a tyre offence might invalidate his insurance policy. Subjecting tyres to loads above their recommended maximum can be dangerous and would certainly be classified as an offence; the caravan or tyre manufacturers should be consulted before any change is made to the size or type of tyre used. Find out the recommended tyre pressures suitable for the extra load from the manufacturer. They will vary according to the type, size and ply rating of the tyres. If a lot of high speed driving is to be done, check that the ply rating is adequate. The rear tyre pressures, for example, may have to be increased by 2–3lb per square inch. Pressures can only be checked accurately when the tyres are cold. See also Caring for your Caravan for tips on storing.

Warning triangles

These are used voluntarily, and at your own risk, in the UK to warn traffic that a vehicle has stopped or broken down ahead. The triangle should be placed at least 50 yards away from the obstruction (150 yards on the hard shoulder of motorways) and in such a position that it will warn traffic approaching on the same side of the carriageway. It must be of reflective material and conform to prescribed conditions.

Weight and weight distribution

Generally, the total weight transmitted to the road surface by any two wheels of a trailer in line transversely must not exceed 9150kg. The total laden weight of a trailer with less than 6 wheels (not forming part of an articulated vehicle) must not exceed 1423kg. The total laden weight of a trailer manufactured before 27 February 1977 which has no other brake than a parking brake and brakes which automatically come into operation on the overrun of the trailer, must not exceed 3560kg. The total laden weight of a trailer manufactured on or after 27th February 1977 and fitted with brakes which automatically come into operation on the overrun of the trailer, whether or not any other brake is fitted, must not exceed 3500kg. Generally speaking, the total laden weight of a trailer plus that of the drawing vehicle must not exceed 22360kg. Caravan literature usually refers to weights as Ex-works or Delivered but they can be misleading due to the fact that it normally is based on a standard model and need not necessarily take into account any extras fitted. If the weight is referred to as above and the manufacturer cannot be contacted it is recommended that the as-delivered weight be obtained by having it weighed at the nearest Public Weighbridge. This weight subtracted from the manufacturer's recommended maximum gross weight will give you the weight that can be utilised for personal effects and equipment. The kerbside weight of the tow car is defined as the weight of the vehicle (inclusive of any towing bracket with which it is normally equipped) when it carries no person, a full supply of fuel, a supply of other liquids incidental to its propulsion, eg water, oil, brake fluid etc, and no load other than the loose tools and equipment with which the vehicle is normally equipped.

The caravan should be level, or very slightly nose down when linked to the car and fully laden. A nose-up attitude can be corrected by a hitch height adjuster, available in various heights from caravan manufacturers and dealers. An adaptor plate can be used to lower the tow ball mounting, but it does put extra bending stresses on the bracket.

Generally stability will be improved by keeping as much weight as possible near the trailer axle. Heavier equipment should be stored on or near the caravan floor, to cut down the possibility of pitching. The front of the trailer should be heavier than the rear by about 25–50kg (approx 60–100lb), depending on the manufacturer's recommendations. Check the nose weight when the caravan is laden, using bathroom scales or a spring balance. A twin axle trailer must be weighed when the coupling is at the exact towing height. Too much weight can result in excessive pitching, too little can lead to instability.

Wings

Unless adequate protection is afforded by the body of the trailer, the rear wheels of every trailer and both wheels of a two-wheeled trailer must be fitted with mud wings or similar fittings.

Don't Drink & Drive

Caring for Your Caravan

Compared to the car, a caravan is a relatively simple structure which is, for the greater part of its life, stationary. Nevertheless, for your own comfort and safety, it is imperative that it is thoroughly examined twice a year in addition to the routine checks you normally carry out while the van is in regular use.

In the Spring

During the winter your van will have been stored on its corner legs – tips on winter storage can be found on page 280. While the van is still chocked up, inspect the chassis and underside thoroughly for rust. A certain amount will be inevitable, but to detect a more serious problem, try tapping all the way along with a small hammer (¼ to ½lb) or similar object. If the hammer bounces off the metal with a sharp, clear knock the corrosion is not too serious. If, however, the hammer does not bounce back and the sound is a dull thud you have a problem which should be referred to your local dealer, car body repairer or garage. Incidentally, don't lie immediately underneath the area you are tapping or you are likely to get an eye-full of dirt or rust!

While you are underneath, check all the visible wiring for signs of deterioration or nibbling by mice. Gas pipes should also be carefully checked for perished areas or fractures and if any water pipes run beneath the floor, these too can be inspected. Remember that any loose wires or pipes will be less likely to wear if they are firmly secured to prevent rubbing and flexing. Finally, before emerging from underneath your caravan, take a look at the wooden beams which link the chassis to the caravan body.

Wheels and Tyres

Whether they have been removed and stored, or kept on the caravan during the winter, the tyres must be carefully examined before being put to use. They should be inflated to the correct pressure and valve caps checked. The minimum tread depth should be 1mm, but 2mm would be far preferable. Because the caravan spends much of its time standing, cracking of the tyre walls can occur and these too should be thoroughly inspected.

Parking brake

Apply the parking brake and ensure that it holds on the ratchet. Then check each brake drum in turn to see that you are unable to turn either drum. If one drum can be turned while the other cannot

there is a braking fault which must be investigated before the caravan is used. Having carried out this check, release the parking brake and again check the drums. On this occasion they should turn quite freely. If all is well the brakes can be adjusted in accordance with the manufacturer's instructions shown in the handbook.

Wheel bearings

If you don't feel confident enough to dismantle, clean, inspect and lubricate your wheel bearings you should go to your local caravan dealer or garage, but checking their adjustment is a simpler matter. Hold the wheel (or, if removed, the brake drum) at the top and bottom and rock the drum. Barely perceptible movement should be felt – no movement or free movement indicates that adjustment is necessary. Before making the adjustment spin the drum. If it does not revolve easily and quietly either or both the bearings in that hub require attention.

Suspension

While the wheels are off it is a good time to examine springs for collapse or broken coils. Check also that no oil is seeping down the main body of the shock absorbers and that the rubber mountings top and bottom are intact. Also check the main axle beam or arms, mountings and pivots.

Corner legs

Oil or grease the threads and pivot points and ensure that they operate freely when you let the caravan down. Also check that the main components have not become distorted.

Exterior

You will naturally want to wash and polish the caravan before it re-emerges for another season – some blemishes do appear during winter storage. While you are doing this, check all the seams and gutters to see if the sealer is still intact.

Interior

A good spring-clean is the order of the day, paying special attention to the panels around doors and windows where damp may be discovered. Other danger spots are in corners, under carpets and inside lockers. Ventilation is very important so check that all ventilators are free and unobstructed. If any extra gas-burning equipment has been added since you bought the caravan it is possible that the ventilation is now inadequate – which could prove extremely dangerous.

Coupling

Clean all grease from the ball and socket and connect the caravan to the car, checking for movement between the two. Although there is no legal dimensional tolerance for the ball, it is considered that no more than 1mm of wear is acceptable. Don't forget to lubricate with new grease.

Lights

Finally, switch on the ignition, couple the 7-pin connector(s) and check that all the lights are fully operational, not forgetting the rear number plate lamp and fog light (if fitted). The law requires the indicators on the front and rear of the car to illuminate as well as those on the rear of the caravan. This checking will, of course, be easier if you have some assistance, otherwise you will need to keep the brake pedal depressed with a piece of wood or a brick while it is checked.

Now you are ready to go and, unless you plan to do an enormous mileage, all that will be needed is a periodic check on obligatory lamps, tyre pressure and condition.

In the Winter

For winter storage it is always better to find somewhere under cover for your caravan, but whether or not this is possible, the following procedures will help to preserve its condition.

Interior

Empty and thoroughly clean the interior of the caravan, including all cupboards and lockers. Old paper and material makes ideal nesting material for mice and insects! Open the cupboard and locker doors to allow maximum circulation of air and, if the caravan is under cover, slightly open the roof ventilator. If it is not possible to store cushions and mattresses in the house (enclose them in polythene bags) stand them where air can circulate freely around them. If possible remove water pipes and clean them thoroughly, clean sink waste pipe with washing soda and hot water and install the sink plug. It is also a good idea to tie up the outside end and blank it off with a cork.

Exterior

Thoroughly clean the paintwork and apply a good coating of wax polish. Look out for any dents which may need to be repaired or damaged paintwork. Small chips and scratches can be touched up using a small brush, but larger areas should be treated in the same way as a car and sprayed. Brush painting could reduce the resale value of the caravan. If gas bottles are stored in a lockable locker, they may be left, but check that they are properly turned off. Otherwise, remove and store them in a shed or garage in a well-ventilated position.

Coil the 7-pin plugs and cables spray with a protective agent and allow to hang in a downward facing position (and put in a plastic bag off the ground). Grease the brake actuating shaft, using the nipples provided, and the inside of the coupling. This, too, can be sprayed with a protective compound and enclosed in a plastic bag. Oil the coupling release lever. Oil or grease the threads of the jacking-type jockey wheels and smear grease on the outer sleeve. Oil the locking screw threads.

Chassis and Underside

By far the most unpleasant task of all, but none of these points should be overlooked if the life and safety of your caravan is to be preserved.

First of all jack up the caravan, one side at a time, and place axle stands beneath the chassis members as close to the wheels as possible. The corner legs should be lowered merely to steady the caravan. Gently shake the van to ensure that it is safe.

Now check the chassis and underside for damage and corrosion, using the method already described. Remove any surface rust and dirt with a wire brush then treat the surface, either by painting (use a good zinc-based primer first) or by using a proprietary underbody protective material. Applying a liberal coating of waste engine oil is an excellent and cheap preservative but do not allow oil to come into contact with rubber components. The same can be used on the corner legs. Also oil the brake rods and attachments.

Remove the wheel, inflate the tyres 5–10lbs/in^2 over recommendation and, while they are off, examine the axle and main suspension components for damage or worn parts. Protect, with whichever method decided upon, those parts of the understructure which are exposed. The wheels can then be replaced or preferably stored elsewhere under cover. Note: Exposure to sunlight accelerates degradation of tyres, so if at all possible protect by covering. Make sure the parking brake is left off.

Bridges, tunnels and ferries in Great Britain

The map reference given in the text refers to the atlas section at the end of this book. No details of prices are given, but when a free service operates it is stated.

More detailed information is given in the booklets: 'Bridges, tunnels and ferries in Great Britain' (HR54) and 'Scottish Islands', (HR98); available free of charge to members on request from any AA office.

Principal bridges and tunnels in Great Britain

Special regulations apply to the Erskine, Forth (No breakdown charges), Severn, Tamar (driver responsible for obtaining assistance), and Tay toll bridges and to the Clyde, Dartford, Mersey, and Tyne Tunnels. Brief details are given below.

Stopping is not allowed. In some cases, parking facilities are provided at one end of the bridge. Toll booths are situated at one end only. The correct money should be held ready – in some cases there are automatic collection facilities. Charges normally cover driver and passengers.

In the event of a breakdown (*including wheel changes*) the driver and passengers should remain with the vehicle, which will be removed by the bridge or tunnel authority breakdown service. In some cases traffic is observed by the control room or patrol car and in others breakdown telephones are provided along the carriageway. A charge is made for the removal of any vehicle; there is no standard rate but charges range between a basic minimum of £1.80/£12.50 to £20/£50.

In tunnels, overtaking is prohibited and maximum and minimum speeds are specified. Stopping is not permitted unless directed. Vehicles carrying goods of a dangerous nature, such as inflammable or corrosive substances, are subject to certain restrictions. Vehicles carrying no more than two cylinders of hydrocarbon gas (e.g. butane, Calor Gas) for leisure purposes are usually permitted without escort, but the Authority have the right to impose restrictions, or require an inspection, at any time. It is prohibited to refuel a vehicle in the tunnel. *It should be especially noted that if the towing vehicle is using liquid petroleum gas for propulsion the total amount of fuel carried by the whole outfit could exceed the permitted limits and this is especially applicable if using Dartford, Mersey or Tyne toll tunnels; or Blackwall, Rotherhithe and Clyde (toll free) tunnels.*

PRINCIPAL BRIDGES

(Toll or limited by service conditions)

Batheaston *Map 3ST76*
Near Bath, off A4
Limit weight 4 tons

Cleddau *Map 2SM90*
A477 Pembroke–Haverfordwest
Limit Restrictions on high vehicles when wind speed exceeds 45mph

Clifton *Map 3ST57*
Bristol B3124 W of city
Limit weight 4 tons width 8ft 2½in
Mechanical system of toll collection

Dunham *Map 8SK87*
A57 Lincoln–Worksop 12m W of Lincoln

Erskine *Map 11NS47*
10m NW of Glasgow ☎041-812 2022

Forth *Map 11NT17*
10m W of Edinburgh ☎031-331 1699

Humber *Map 8TA02*
Approximately 5m upstream from Hull ☎0482-647161

Itchen *Map 4SU41*
A3025 Woolston–Southampton
(Mon–Fri 06.00–09.30 & 16.00–18.30 car toll is increased 50%)

Middlesbrough (Cleveland Transit) *Map 8NZ42*
Transporter Bridge A178 N of town
Service frequent 05.00–22.50 (14.00–22.50 Sun)
Limit weight 3 tons, length 44ft ☎0642-248211

Newport Gwent *Map 3ST38*
Transporter Bridge, B4327 across R Usk conveys up to 6 cars. Free
Service frequent subject to weather conditions 05.30–22.52 (Tue, Wed 22.30) (Sun 05.30–08.00 then 13.00–22.52) (22.15 winter) ☎Cwmbran 06333-64580

Penrhyndeudraeth (Briwet Bridge) *Map 6SH63*
Unclassified road between A496 and A487 3½m E of Porthmadog (saves 6½m on road to Barmouth)
Limit weight 2 tons
Caravans not permitted

Porthmadog *Map 6SH53*
A487 E of town

Selby *Map 8SE63*
A19 NE of town ☎0757-703126

Severn *Map 3ST59*
M4 3m SE of Chepstow between A38 and A48 ☎04545-2436

Shard *Map 7SD34*
A588 Blackpool–Lancaster
Limit weight 12 tons ☎0253-883328

Swinford *Map 4SP40*
B4044 Oxford–Witney 5½m W of Oxford ☎0865-881325

Tamar *Map 2SX45*
A38 Plymouth–Liskeard ☎0752-361577
Toll payable one direction only, from Cornwall into Devon

Tay *Map 12NO42*
Newport–Dundee ☎0382-21881/2

Warburton Map 7SJ68
B51596m E of Warrington across Manchester Ship Canal
Limit weight 5 tons width 8ft
Whitchurch Map 4SU67
B471 Pangbourne–Whitchurch
Limit weight 10 tons (weight limit in village 3 tons)
Whitney Map 3SO24
B4350 Hereford–Hay-on-Wye ☎04973-555

PRINCIPAL TUNNELS
see also general notes page 281
(Toll, or limited by service conditions)

Blackwall Map 5TQ37
River Thames 3m E of Tower Bridge. Twin tunnels. Free.
Open always. Limit height: northbound 13ft 4in, southbound 15ft 6in, width 8ft 2in.
The carriage of explosives and inflammable materials is prohibited but this is usually waived for domestic caravans provided no more than 2 cylinders of gas each of 10lb (4.5kg) capacity is carried. For further details contact the Petrol Inspectorate (GLC) ☎*01-633 4632 (also applicable to Rotherhithe Tunnel (below)).*
Clyde Map 11NS56
River Clyde W side of Glasgow at Whiteinch. No toll charge. Breakdown service charges payable. Open always. Caravans restricted to carrying 3 cylinders of compressed or liquified gas. ☎041-339 2236.
Dartford Map 5TQ57
River Thames 15m E of Tower Bridge. Open always.
☎0322-21222
Conveyance of gas cylinders restricted to 2 containers each of 16kgs (36lb) capacity, or 50kg (110lb) in cylinders not exceeding 5kgs (11lbs)
Mersey Map 7SJ39
River Mersey between Liverpool and Birkenhead and Liverpool and Wallasey. Open always.
Queensway tunnel ☎051-647 8814 Limit height 13ft 6ins
Kingsway tunnel ☎051-638 9441 Limit height 16ft 6ins
Conveyance of gas cylinders for leisure purposes restricted to 32kgs (72lbs) in cylinders not exceeding 16kgs (36lbs) or 50kgs (100lbs) in cylinders not exceeding 5kgs (11lbs). All gas taps must be in the 'OFF' position when passing through the tunnel. Escort arrangements are required under the dangerous goods regulations if these amounts are exceeded.
Rotherhithe Map 5TH38
River Thames 1m E of Tower Bridge. Free. Open always.
Conveyance of gas cylinders, see as for Blackwall Tunnel, above.
Limit height 14ft 9in width 7ft 6in.
Tyne Map 12NZ36
River Tyne 5m E of Newcastle
Open always.
Conveyance of gas cylinders restricted to 2 × 36lb (16kg each) cylinders ☎Wallsend 624451

FERRIES

Ferries are listed below in alphabetical order; England, mainland Ferries (including Isle of Wight) shown first, followed by Scotland, mainland ferries (including islands where site facilities are available). More detailed information is given in the booklets 'Bridges, tunnels and Ferries in Great Britain' HR54 and 'Scottish Islands' HR98,

available free of charge to members on request from any AA Office. The information following gives: name and map reference, vehicle carrying capacity, frequency of service and daily period of operation, and telephone number. Services are described as frequent if they operate every 30 minutes or less. Services may be altered at Christmas and Bank Holidays, and are operated subject to tide, weather, and other conditions. Journeys are undertaken at the vehicle owner's risk. On ferries where passengers are allowed to remain in their vehicles, enough room must be left between to allow doors to be opened in an emergency.

Gas Cylinders
The carriage or shipment of inflammable materials is subject to regulations, but the interpretation or implementation is a matter for the company concerned. In practice, providing no more than two cylinders of hydrocarbon gas (e.g. butane, Calor Gas) are carried, there is usually no formality, but the operating company has the right to impose restrictions, or require an inspection, at any time. Pierced cartridges or cylinders cannot be carried abroad under any circumstances.

England Mainland Ferries
Bodinnick–Fowey Map 3SX15
6–8 cars limit weight 3 tons. Service according to demand. 07.00 (08.00 Sun)–20.45 (or dusk whichever is earliest) Not Christmas, Boxing Day, New Years' Day (Bank Holidays as Sun)
☎072687-232
Approaches are narrow and steep. Not advised for caravans.
Dartmouth Higher Map 4SX85
18 cars, Service frequent 06.30 (09.00 Sun)–22.50 (Christmas Day 09.00–12.00 then 15.00–18.00)
Closed for annual overhaul approximately last week in Feb and first week in March.
☎08043-3351
Dartmouth Lower Map 4SX85
8 cars, service freqeunt 07.00 (08.00 Sun)–22.45
Christmas Day no service. Boxing Day restricted service limited hours. Other Bank Holidays, normal service
☎080425-342
King Harry–Philliegh Map 2SW83
28 cars
Service F Summer: 08.00–20.00 mid May–early Jul (21.00 early Jul–end of Aug; 20.00 Sep–early Oct) (Sun 10.00; then mid Apr–early May 18.00; mid May–early Jul 20.00; mid Jul–early Sep 21.00; Sep–early Oct 20.00).
Winter 08.00–18.00 Oct–mid May (Sun no service Oct–early Apr). No service Christmas Day, Boxing Day and New Years' Day. Other Bank Holidays as Sun.
☎Devoran (0872) 2463
Limit weight 10 tons, height 11ft 6ins.
Reedham Map 5TG40
4 cars.
Service according to demand 08.00 (09.00 Sun)–22.00. No service Christmas Day and Boxing Day.
☎0493-700429
Limit 7 tons length 30ft. Approach road not advised for caravans.

Isle of Wight

From the Mainland
Service from the mainland operate between the following places.
On these services it is advisable to make advance reservations for all sailings, and essential for travel at summer weekends and at Easter and Christmas. For travel on Fri, Sat and Sun end May – early Sep arrangements must be made at least six weeks before date of travel. (Advance reservations are not accepted for solo motor cycles or scooters as they are conveyed as space permits). Full details and booking forms are available from the AA, or the operating company.

Portsmouth–Fishbourne *Map 4SZ59*
Operator: Sealink Car-Ferry Services Bookings: Sealink Isle of Wight Services, PO Box 59, Portsmouth, Hants PO1 2XB
☎0705-27744
Lymington–Yarmouth *Map 4SZ38*
Operator: Sealink Car-Ferry Services, for travel on Fri, Sat or Sun between May and early Sep see Portsmouth address above; on other days throughout the year: Sealink Car-Ferry Booking Office, Lymington Pier, Lymington, Hants SO4 8ZE
☎0590-73301
Southampton (Dock Gate no. 7) – Cowes (East & West) *Map 4SZ49/59*
Operator: Red Funnel Services, 12 Bugle Street, Southampton SO9 4LJ
☎0703-26211 or Cowes (IoW) (0983) 292101
Written applications for booking at summer weekends.

On the Island
Cowes–East Cowes (chain ferry) Isle of Wight *Map 4SZ49*
16 cars
Service frequent 05.30 (Sun 07.00) – 23.15 (late service every night at midnight)
☎Cowes (IoW) (0983) 293041

Sandbanks–Shell Bay *Map 4SZ08*
28 cars
Service frequent Summer: (1st Mon May–1st Sun Oct): 07.00–23.00
Winter: (1st Mon Oct–1st Sun May) 07.00 (08.00 Sun) – 21.00 Restricted service Christmas Day and New Year's Day).
☎092944-203
Torpoint–Devonport *Map 2SX45*
32 cars
Service frequent day and night (hourly 01.00–05.00)
☎0752-812233
Alternative route via Tamar (*toll*) bridge always open.
Windermere *Map 7SD39*
10 cars
Service according to demand Easter–Sep 06.50 (Sun 09.10) – 21.50 Mid Sep–Sun before Easter 06.50 (Sun 09.50) – 20.50 Not Christmas or Boxing Days. New Year's Day 10.10–17.30 Some delay during summer peak; advisory signs displayed.
Woolwich–North Woolwich *Map 5TQ47*
45 cars all vehicles free
Service frequent 06.00–22.15 (Sun 07.40–21.45)
Alternative routes via Blackwall Tunnel (free) or Dartford (toll) Tunnel.
☎01-854 3488

Scotland
Ferries and services to selected islands

Mainland
Corran–Ardgour (Loch Linnhe) *Map 14NN06*
20 cars
Service frequent Easter to 30 Sep 07.40 (Sun 09.00) – 21.00 or dusk if earlier. Remainder of year 07.45 (Sun 10.00) – 18.30
No service 25, 26 Dec and 1,2 Jan. Normal service other Bank Holidays.
☎08555-243 slight delays at low tide.
Dunoon–Gourock *Map 10NS17*
40 cars
Service frequent 06.45–20.05 (08.45–19.45 Sun)
Winter 06.45–19.45; Sun 08.45–19.45. Reduced service, Christmas Day, Boxing Day and 1 and 2 Jan, apply to operator for details.
Operator Caledonian-MacBrayne Ltd
☎0475-33755
Dunoon (Hunters Quay) – **Gourock** (McInroy's Point) *Map 10NS17*
18–26 cars
Service frequent/hourly throughout year 07.00 (Sun 08.00) – 22.00 (Fri, Sat & Sun 23.30) reduced service 25, 26 Dec and 1, 2, 3, Jan.
☎041-332 9766.
Kylesku (Kylesku Narrows) *Map 14NC23*
16 cars.
Service frequent 09.00–21.00 or dawn (if later)/dusk (if earlier)
No service Christmas Day, Boxing Day and 1 and 2 Jan signs erected at Laxford Bridge and Skiag Bridge giving warning if ferry is inoperative for any lengthy period.
☎Kylestrome (097-183)
Renfrew-Yoker *Map 13NS56*
15 cars.
Service continuous day and night
☎041-221 8733

Islands
This is not a comprehensive list of services to all the Scottish islands; only those islands where site facilities are available are included.
Harris: Uig (Skye) – Tarbert (and via Lochmaddy, North Uist) *Map 13NB10*
1–2 services daily. Winter: 3 sailings weekly: Tue, Thu, Sat. Spring and Autumn: 1 service daily 1 extra Tues (Spring) via Lochmaddy) No Sun service. Advance reservations: Caledonian MacBrayne Ltd, Ferry Terminal, Gourock, Renfrewshire PA19 1QP
☎0475-33755 (general enquiries).
Lewis: Ullapool–Stornoway *Map 13NB43*
2 sailings daily. Late May–Mid Oct (1 winter: 2 sailings Tue, Thu,) No Sun service. Advance reservations: details as for Harris, Uig.
Skye: Kyle of Lochalsh–Kyleakin *Map 13NG72*
Frequent daily service, Sun-frequent service (hourly winter) commencing 10.15. Operator as for Harris, Uig.
Skye: Mallaig–Armadale *Map 13NG60*
Service 3–5 sailing daily. No Winter Service (for vehicles) or Sun service.
Operator as for Harris.

Tall, Dark and Handsome...

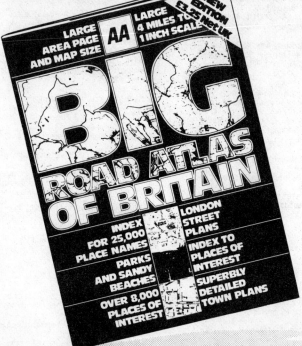

don't be without one.

Size: 15⅛ x 11¼. Map scale 4 miles to 1". Contains London Street Plans, detailed town plans. Index for 25,000 place-names and to 8,000 places of interest.

Please visit your local AA Centre...

Confidential report form   1984

The purpose of this form is for readers to voice their complaints – if they feel that a campsite they have visited does not come up to standard. The form should be completed in conjunction with the list on page 255.

Please send to:
The Automobile Association
Hotel and Information Services Department
Fanum House
Basingstoke Hants RG21 2EA

BLOCK CAPITALS PLEASE

Name of site

Address of site

Arrival date

Length of stay

I do/do not agree to my name being used in the event of any correspondence with the site concerned.

Your name

Your address

Membership No.

Do you agree with the classification?   Yes ☐ No ☐

What is your qualitative assessment if different from that given? (For details see page   ).

Did you speak to the site warden about any complaint?   Yes ☐ No ☐

Comments

Comments (cont)

_____
_____
_____
_____
_____
_____
_____
_____
_____
_____
_____
_____
_____
_____
_____
_____
_____
_____
_____
_____
_____
_____
_____
_____
_____
_____
_____
_____

Please complete questionnaire opposite

For office use only

Head office action

Regional office action

Acknowledged

Recorded

Action   Date

Campers' Check List

- [ ] AA Camping & Caravanning in Britain
- [ ] AA Stately Homes, Museums, Castles and Gardens in Britain
- [ ] Air mattresses and pump
- [ ] All purpose knife
- [ ] Barbecue
- [ ] Bath towels, hand towels
- [ ] Blankets
- [ ] Bucket
- [ ] Buckets and spades
- [ ] Camera and films
- [ ] Can opener
- [ ] Cards, games, books
- [ ] Clothes, including swimwear
- [ ] Cooker and fuel
- [ ] Corkscrew/bottle opener
- [ ] Dish cloth
- [ ] First Aid Kit
- [ ] Fish slice
- [ ] Folding table and chairs
- [ ] Food
- [ ] Food containers
- [ ] Hair brush and comb
- [ ] Hot water bottles
- [ ] Icebox
- [ ] Insect repellant
- [ ] Kettle
- [ ] Kite
- [ ] Knives, forks and spoons
- [ ] Lantern
- [ ] Mallet
- [ ] Matches
- [ ] Measuring jug
- [ ] Mirror
- [ ] Paper towels
- [ ] Pillows
- [ ] Plates, dishes and cups
- [ ] Polythene bags
- [ ] Pressure cooker
- [ ] Radio
- [ ] Rope, clothesline and pegs
- [ ] Rubbish sacks
- [ ] Saucepans and frying pan
- [ ] Sewing repairs kit
- [ ] Shoe cleaning materials
- [ ] Sleeping bags
- [ ] Soap, toothpaste etc
- [ ] Spare groundsheet
- [ ] String
- [ ] Suntan cream
- [ ] Teapot
- [ ] Tea strainer
- [ ] Tea towels
- [ ] Tent, poles and pegs
- [ ] Tissues
- [ ] Torch and spare batteries
- [ ] Vegetable knife and peeler
- [ ] Washing powder
- [ ] Washing-up bowl and drainer
- [ ] Washing-up liquid
- [ ] Water containers
- [ ] Waterproofs and Wellies
- [ ] Windshield

If you have a dog, remember its food, feeding bowls, bed, collar and lead. A dog tether is also a useful extra.

The National Grid

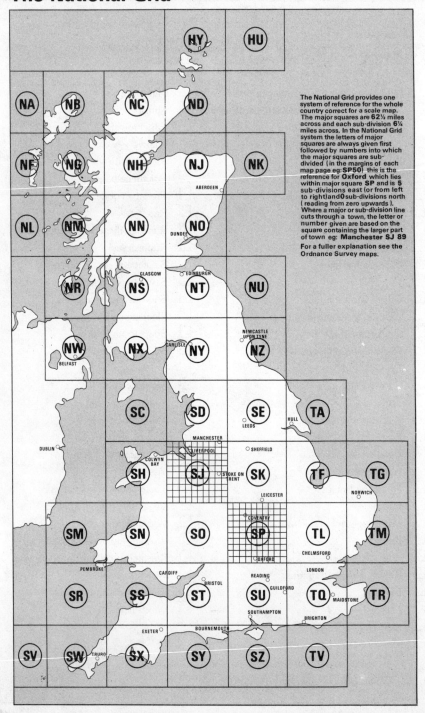

The National Grid provides one system of reference for the whole country correct for a scale map. The major squares are 62½ miles across and each sub-division 6¼ miles across. In the National Grid system the letters of major squares are always given first followed by numbers into which the major squares are sub-divided (in the margins of each map page eg: **SP50**) this is the reference for **Oxford** which lies within major square **SP** and is **5** sub-divisions east (or from left to right) and **0** sub-divisions north (reading from zero upwards). Where a major or sub-division line cuts through a town, the letter or number given are based on the square containing the larger part of town eg: **Manchester SJ 89**

For a fuller explanation see the Ordnance Survey maps.

Key to Atlas

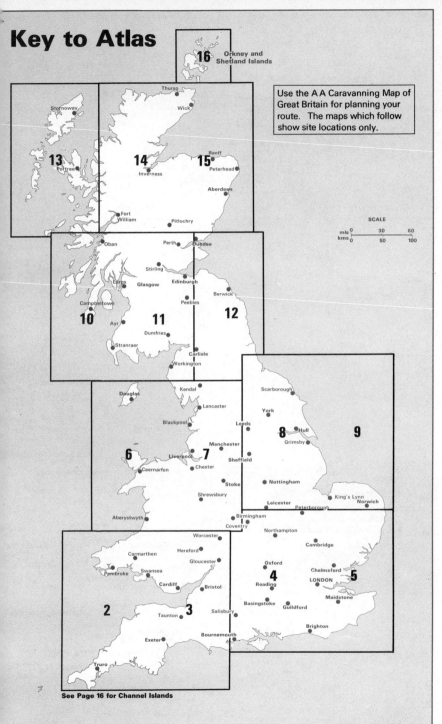

16 Orkney and Shetland Islands

Use the A A Caravanning Map of Great Britain for planning your route. The maps which follow show site locations only.

Stornoway

Thurso
Wick

13 Portree

14 Inverness

15 Banff
Peterhead

Aberdeen

Fort William

Pitlochry

Oban

Perth
Dundee

Stirling

Largs
Glasgow
Edinburgh

Campbeltown

Peebles
Berwick

10

Ayr

11 Dumfries

12

Stranraer

Carlisle
Workington

SCALE

mls 0   30   60
kms 0   50   100

Douglas

Kendal

Scarborough

Lancaster

York

Blackpool

Leeds

8 Hull

Grimsby

Manchester

9

Liverpool

7

Sheffield

6

Caernarfon

Chester

Stoke

Nottingham

Shrewsbury

Leicester

King's Lynn
Norwich

Aberystwyth

Birmingham
Coventry

Peterborough

Worcester

Northampton

Carmarthen

Hereford

Cambridge

Pembroke

Swansea

Gloucester

Oxford

Chelmsford

Cardiff

Bristol

4 Reading

LONDON

5

Maidstone

2

3 Salisbury

Basingstoke
Guildford

Taunton

Bournemouth

Brighton

Exeter

Truro

See Page 16 for Channel Islands

Maps produced by
The AA Cartographic Department
(Publications Division), Fanum House,
Basingstoke, Hampshire RG21 2EA

This atlas is for location purposes Only: see Member's Handbook for current road and AA road services information

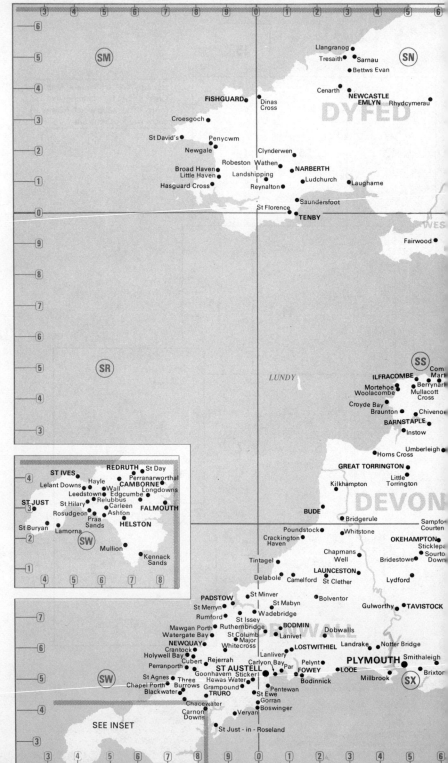

SM

SN

Llangranog
Tresaith • Sarnau
• Bettws Evan

Cenarth •
NEWCASTLE
EMLYN • Rhydcymerau

DYFED

FISHGUARD • Dinas
Cross

Croesgoch •

St David's • Penycwm
Newgale • Clynderwen •

Robeston Wathen •
Broad Haven • Landshipping NARBERTH •
Little Haven • Ludchurch •
Hasguard Cross • Reynalton • Laugharne •

St Florence • Saundersfoot •
TENBY • IVES

Fairwood •

SR

LUNDY

SS Com
Mar

ILFRACOMBE • Berrynar
Mortehoe • Mullacott
Woolacombe • Cross
Croyde Bay • Chiveno
Braunton •
BARNSTAPLE •
• Instow

Umberleigh •
Horns Cross •

GREAT TORRINGTON •
Little
Kilkhampton • Torrington

DEVON

BUDE •
• Bridgerule Sampfo
Poundstock • Courten
Crackington • Whitstone •
Haven OKEHAMPTON •
Chapmans Sticklepa
Well • Sourto
Tintagel • Bridestowe • Down

LAUNCESTON •
Delabole • Camelford • St Clether • Lydford •

PADSTOW • St Minver • Bolventor •
St Merryn • St Mabyn • Gulworthy • TAVISTOCK •
Rumford • Wadebridge •
St Issey •
Mawgan Porth • Ruthernbridge • BODMIN • Dobwalls •
Watergate Bay • St Columb Lanivet • Landrake • Notter Bridge •
NEWQUAY • Major • LOSTWITHIEL •
Crantock • Whitecross •
Holywell Bay • Cubert • Lanlivery • PLYMOUTH Smithaleigh •
Perranporth • Rejerrah • Carlyon Bay • Pelynt •
St Agnes • ST AUSTELL • Par • FOWEY • LOOE • Brixtor
Three Goonhavern Sticker • Bodinnick • Millbrook • SX
Chapel Porth • Burrows Hewas Water •
Blackwater • Grampound • Pentewan •
Chacewater • TRURO • St Ewe •
Carnon Gorran •
Downs Boswinger •
SEE INSET Veryan •
St Just - in - Roseland •

REDRUTH St Day •
ST IVES • Perranarworthal •
Hayle • CAMBORNE •
Lelant Downs • Wall • Longdowns •
Leedstown • Edgcumbe •
ST JUST St Hilary • Relubbus Carleen • FALMOUTH •
Rosudgeon • Ashton •
St Buryan • Praa HELSTON
Lamorna • Sands
SW
Mullion •
Kennack
Sands

2

For continuation pages refer to numbered arrows

ENGLISH CHANNEL

3

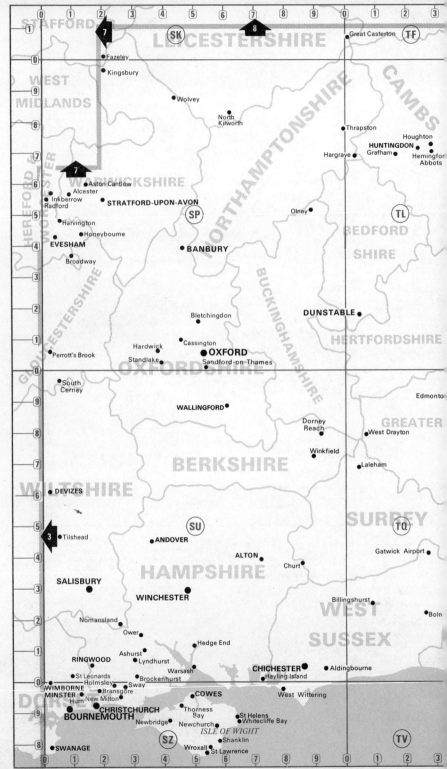

For continuation pages refer to numbered arrows

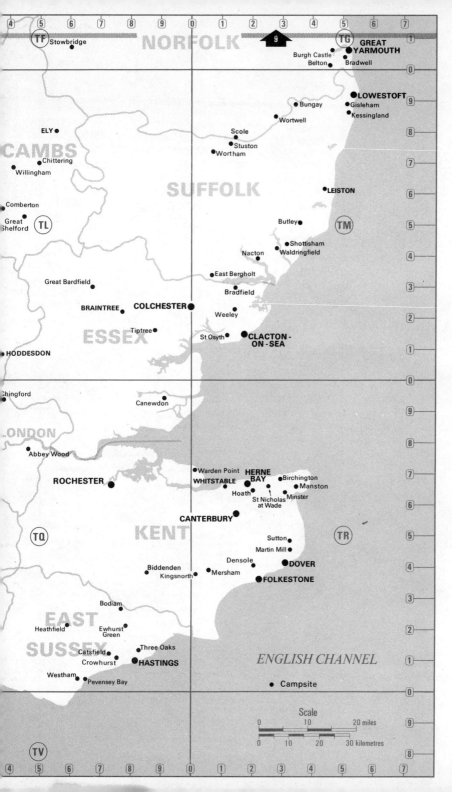

9

TF Stowbridge

TG GREAT YARMOUTH

Burgh Castle
Belton • Bradwell

●LOWESTOFT

● Bungay •Gisleham
Wortwell •Kessingland

Scole
•Stuston
•Wortham

ELY ●

CAMBS
•Chittering
• Willingham

SUFFOLK

●LEISTON

• Comberton
Great
Shelford **TL**

Butley ●

TM

•Shottisham
Nacton • Waldringfield
• East Bergholt
Bradfield

Great Bardfield •

BRAINTREE • COLCHESTER ●
Weeley
Tiptree • St Osyth • ●CLACTON-ON-SEA

ESSEX

●HODDESDON

Chingford

Canewdon

ONDON

• Abbey Wood

ROCHESTER ●

Warden Point • **HERNE BAY**
WHITSTABLE ● •Birchington
Hoath • •Manston
St Nicholas Minster
at Wade

CANTERBURY ●

KENT

TQ

TR

Sutton •
Martin Mill •
Densole •
Biddenden • •DOVER
Kingsnorth • Mersham • ●FOLKESTONE

Bodiam •

EAST
Heathfield • Ewhurst
Green
SUSSEX
Catsfield • •Three Oaks
Crowhurst ●HASTINGS
Westham • •Pevensey Bay

ENGLISH CHANNEL

• Campsite

Scale

0   10   20 miles

0   10   20   30 kilometres

TV

5

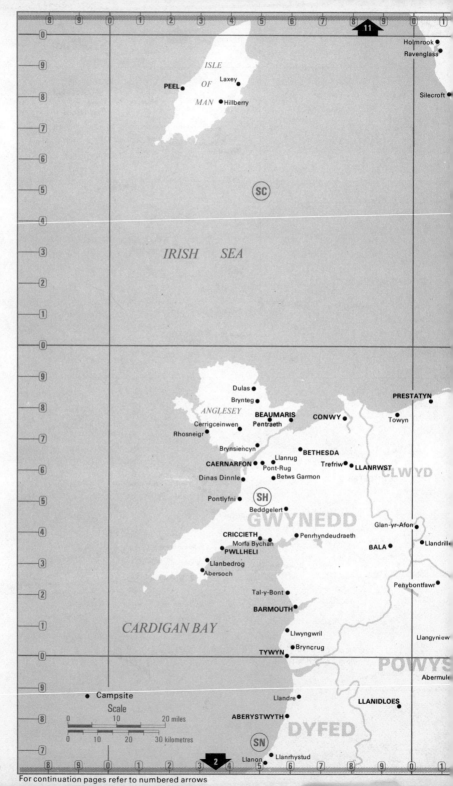

Holmrook
Ravenglass

Silecroft

ISLE
OF   Laxey
PEEL
MAN   Hillberry

SC

IRISH   SEA

Dulas
Brynteg
ANGLESEY   BEAUMARIS   CONWY   PRESTATYN
Cerrigceinwen   Pentraeth   Towyn
Rhosneigr
Brynsiencyn   BETHESDA
CAERNARFON   Llanrug   Trefriw   LLANRWST
Pont-Rug
Dinas Dinlle   Betws Garmon   CLWYD
Pontlyfni   SH
Beddgelert
GWYNEDD
CRICCIETH   Penrhyndeudraeth   Glan-yr-Afon
Morfa Bychan   BALA   Llandrille
PWLLHELI
Llanbedrog   Penybontfawr
Abersoch

Tal-y-Bont
BARMOUTH

CARDIGAN BAY   Llwyngwril   Llangyniew

Bryncrug
TYWYN   POWYS
Abermule

● Campsite   Llandre
Scale   LLANIDLOES
0   10   20 miles   ABERYSTWYTH   DYFED
0   10   20   30 kilometres
SN
Llanon   Llanrhystud

2

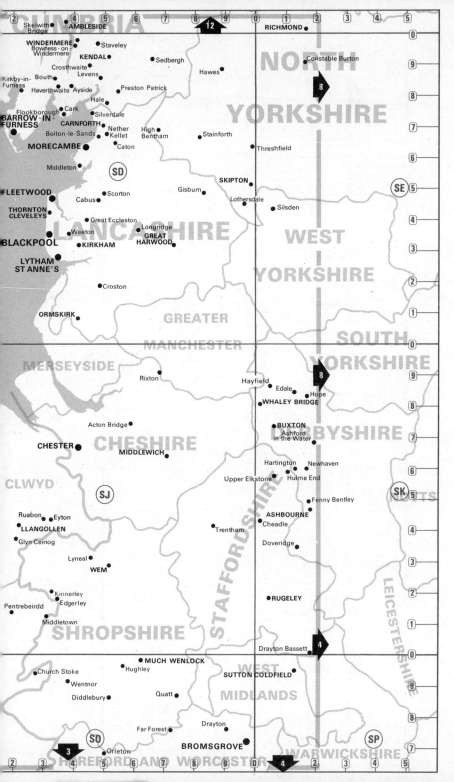

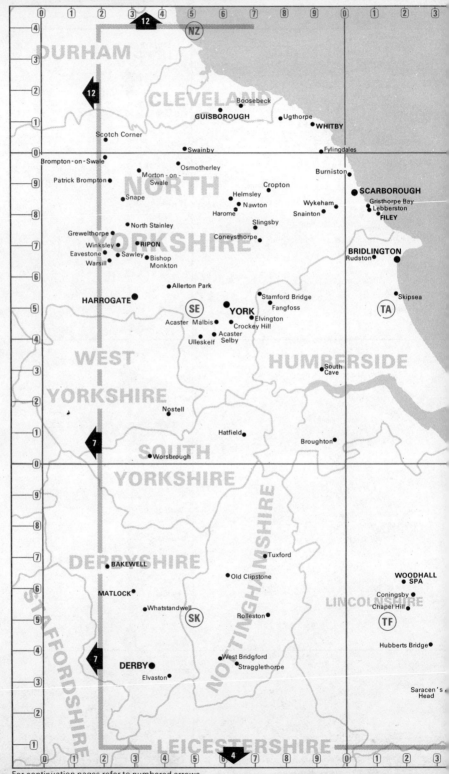

8

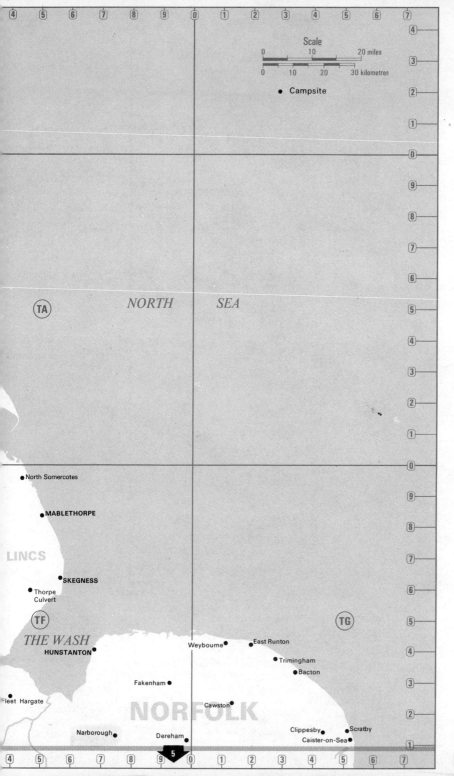

Scale

0   10   20 miles

0   10   20   30 kilometres

● Campsite

NORTH   *SEA*

(TA)

● North Somercotes

● **MABLETHORPE**

LINCS

● **SKEGNESS**

● Thorpe
Culvert

(TF)   (TG)

THE WASH   Weybourne ●   ● East Runton

HUNSTANTON ●

● Trimingham

● Bacton

Fakenham ●

Fleet Hargate ●   Cawston ●

NORFOLK

Narborough ●   Dereham ●   Clippesby ● ● Scratby

Caister-on-Sea ●

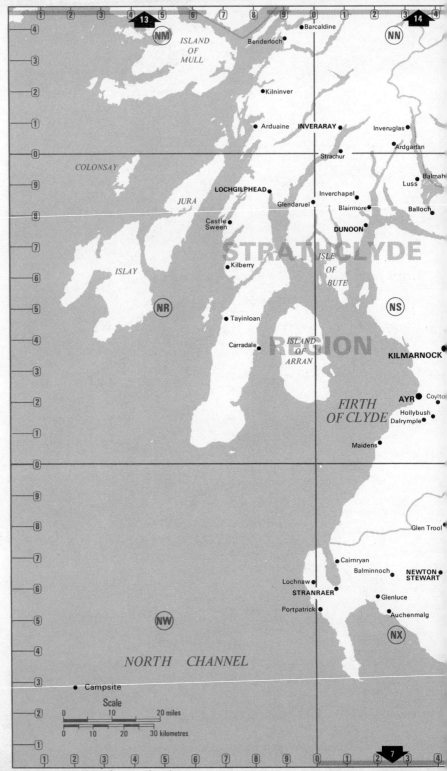

ISLAND OF MULL

NM

NN

Barcaldine
Benderloch

Kilninver

Arduaine INVERARAY

Inveruglas
Ardgartan
Strachur

COLONSAY

JURA

LOCHGILPHEAD

Luss
Balmah

Inverchapel
Glendaruel
Blairmore
Balloch

Castle Sween

DUNOON

STRATHCLYDE

ISLE OF BUTE

ISLAY

Kilberry

NR

NS

Tayinloan

ISLAND OF ARRAN

REGION

KILMARNOCK

Carradale

FIRTH OF CLYDE

AYR   Coylto
Hollybush
Dalrymple

Maidens

Glen Trool

Cairnryan
Balminnoch
NEWTON STEWART

Lochnaw

STRANRAER

NW

Portpatrick

Glenluce

Auchenmalg

NX

NORTH CHANNEL

Campsite

Scale

0   10   20 miles

0   10   20   30 kilometres

10

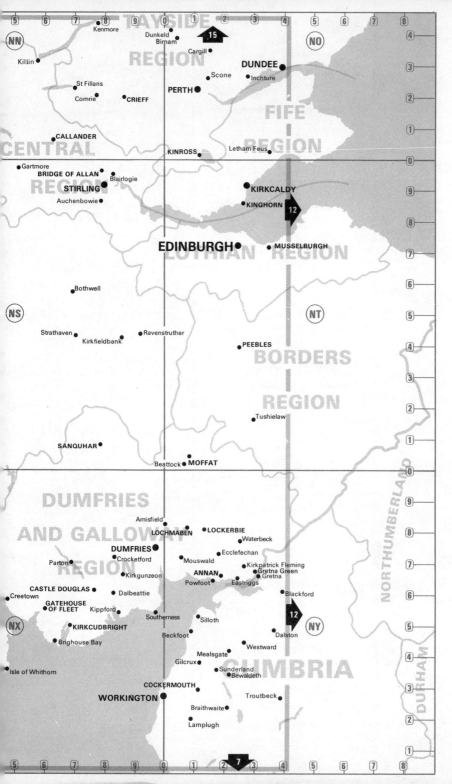

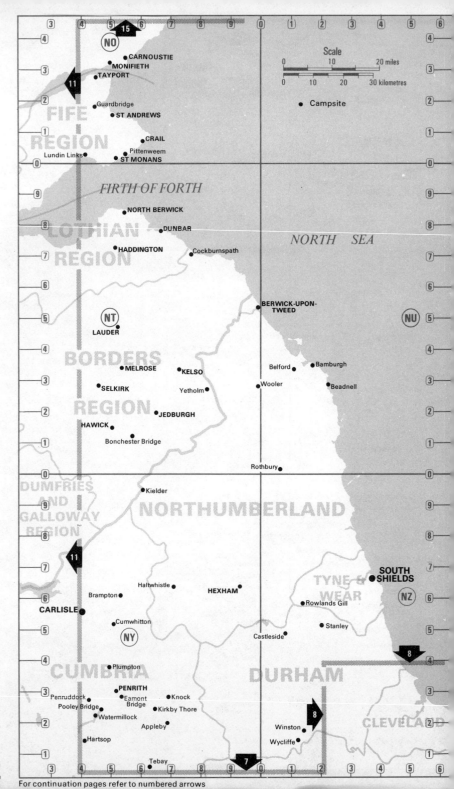

Scale

0   10   20 miles

0   10   20   30 kilometres

● Campsite

NO

15

11

● CARNOUSTIE
● MONIFIETH
● TAYPORT
● Guardbridge
● ST ANDREWS

FIFE REGION

● CRAIL
Lundin Links ●
● Pittenweem
● ST MONANS

FIRTH OF FORTH

NORTH SEA

● NORTH BERWICK
● DUNBAR
● HADDINGTON
● Cockburnspath

LOTHIAN REGION

NT
LAUDER

BERWICK-UPON-TWEED

NU

BORDERS REGION

● MELROSE
● SELKIRK
● KELSO
● Yetholm
● JEDBURGH
HAWICK ●
● Bonchester Bridge

Belford ●
● Bamburgh
Wooler ●
● Beadnell

● Rothbury

DUMFRIES AND GALLOWAY REGION

● Kielder

NORTHUMBERLAND

11

● Haltwhistle
Brampton ●
HEXHAM ●
CARLISLE ●
● Cumwhitton

NY

SOUTH SHIELDS
● Rowlands Gill
● Stanley
Castleside ●

TYNE & WEAR

NZ

8

● Plumpton

CUMBRIA

PENRITH
● Eamont Bridge
● Knock
Penruddock ●
Pooley Bridge ●
● Kirkby Thore
● Watermillock
Appleby ●
Hartsop ●

DURHAM

8
Winston ●
Wycliffe ●

CLEVELAND

Tebay ●

7

12

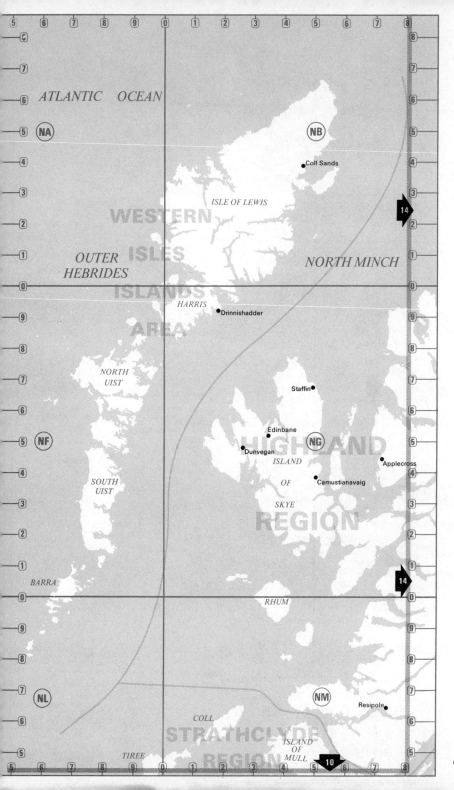

ATLANTIC OCEAN

NA

NB

Coll Sands

ISLE OF LEWIS

WESTERN

OUTER ISLES

HEBRIDES

ISLANDS

AREA

NORTH MINCH

HARRIS

Drinnishadder

NORTH UIST

Staffin

NF

Edinbane

Dunvegan

HIGHLAND

NG

ISLAND

Applecross

OF

Camustianavaig

SOUTH UIST

SKYE

REGION

BARRA

RHUM

NL

NM

Resipole

COLL

STRATHCLYDE

TIREE

ISLAND OF MULL

REGION

14

14

10

13

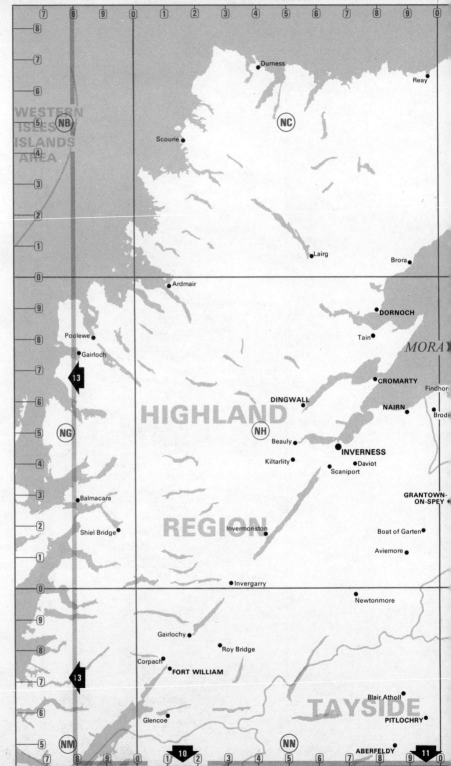

WESTERN
ISLES
ISLANDS
AREA

NB

NC

Durness

Reay

Scourie

Lairg

Brora

Ardmair

DORNOCH

Poolewe

Tain

MORAY

Gairloch

13

CROMARTY

Findhorn

NG

HIGHLAND

DINGWALL

NAIRN

Brodie

NH

Beauly

INVERNESS

Balmacara

Kiltarlity

Daviot

Scaniport

**GRANTOWN-
ON-SPEY**

Shiel Bridge

REGION

Invermoriston

Boat of Garten

Aviemore

Invergarry

Newtonmore

Gairlochy

Roy Bridge

Corpach

13

FORT WILLIAM

Blair Atholl

TAYSIDE

PITLOCHRY

Glencoe

NM

NN

ABERFELDY

11

10

14

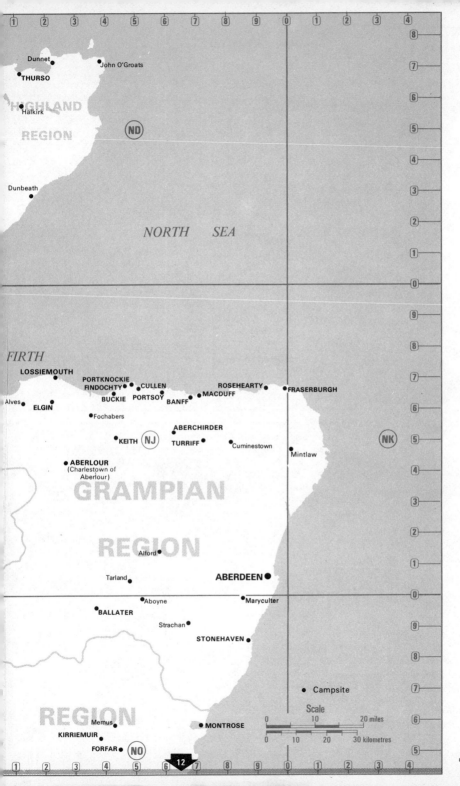

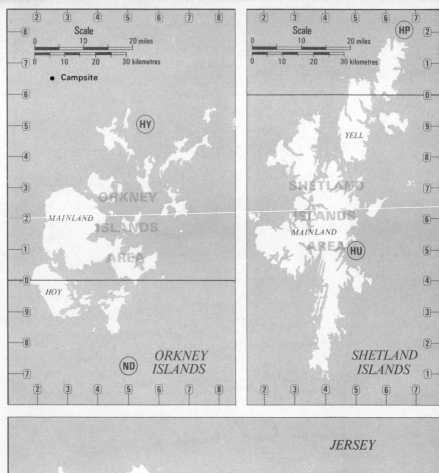

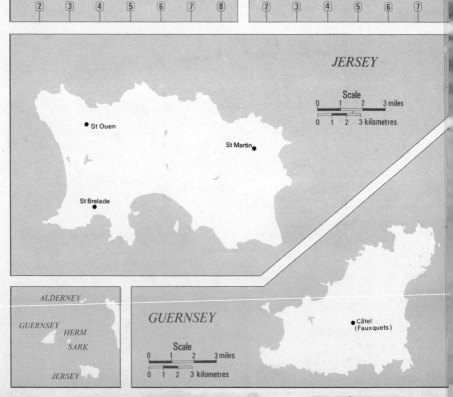

ORKNEY ISLANDS

Scale
0   10   20 miles
0   10   20   30 kilometres

● Campsite

HY

ORKNEY
ISLANDS
AREA

MAINLAND

HOY

ND

SHETLAND ISLANDS

Scale
0   10   20 miles
0   10   20   30 kilometres

HP

YELL

SHETLAND
ISLANDS
AREA

MAINLAND

HU

JERSEY

Scale
0   1   2   3 miles
0   1   2   3 kilometres

● St Ouen

St Martin ●

St Brelade ●

ALDERNEY

GUERNSEY   HERM

SARK

JERSEY

GUERNSEY

Scale
0   1   2   3 miles
0   1   2   3 kilometres

● Câtel
(Fauxquets)